Prentice Hall 3/14/72

ANALYSIS
FOR
FINANCIAL
MANAGEMENT

ANALYSIS
FOR
FINANCIAL
MANAGEMENT

LOUIS K. BRANDT

University of Southern Mississippi

PRENTICE-HALL, INC.

ENGLEWOOD CLIFFS, NEW JERSEY

© 1972   Prentice-Hall, Inc., Englewood Cliffs, New Jersey.

Printed in the United States of America

ISBN: 0-13-033142-2

Library of Congress Catalog Card Number: 70-160251

10 9 8 7 6 5 4 3 2 1

PRENTICE-HALL INTERNATIONAL, INC., *London*
PRENTICE-HALL OF AUSTRALIA, PTY. LTD., *Sydney*
PRENTICE-HALL OF CANADA, LTD., *Toronto*
PRENTICE-HALL OF INDIA PRIVATE LIMITED, *New Delhi*
PRENTICE-HALL OF JAPAN, INC., *Tokyo*

Dedicated
to
the Memory of

Henry G. Lee

and to

Walter A. Morton

Contents

PART VII

CAPITAL BUDGETING:
THE FINANCING DECISION

PART VIII

SPECIAL MANAGEMENT
PROBLEMS

Preface

The writer would like to believe that in this book he has made a contribution, however slight, to more effective teaching and to a better understanding of the essential issues in *financial management*.

The teaching method employed is to establish basic goals and to apply over and over the tools and techniques of analysis to these goals at various levels of financial management, so that by the time the student has completed the book, certain analytic and decision-making skills will have become a permanent part of his total educational experience.

The book differs from others in the field in several important respects, not the least of which is the method of *interlocking the capital management decision with the current operating decision.* The term *capital constraint* is employed in the early chapters to place the capital management decision in its proper perspective to the optimizing problems of current operations. Optimization is applied to income, cost, profit, inventory, receivables, and cash management. The common goal is to maximize the value of the company's shares; and to realize this goal, communication media must be developed that are understandable in the securities market and that reflect the success and failure of internal financial management decisions.

The three chapters of Part II are designed to give the student an overview of regular arithmetic, algebra, and finite mathematics for financial analysis. These chapters contain a sufficient amount of elementary mathematics so that when the tools are applied in later chapters, the student will have the knowledge of basic quantitative concepts that is required for building up confidence for decision making. Statistical analysis is fed into the total framework so that, even without a formal course in statistics, the reader will understand the tools and their place in financial analysis.

Capital budgeting in this book is primarily a means of relaxing the capital constraint so that future current operations can be expanded and share values increased; it is a means to an end rather than an end in itself.

In discussing capital budgeting techniques, the positive rather than the negative approach is used when applying the *internal rate of return and the present value* methods of analysis. Instead of stressing the inconsistencies in the two techniques for decision making, it is shown that, by allowing us to make realistic assumptions about the cost of capital as the cutoff rate for investment, the two methods may be valuable complements to each other. The credit for developing the underlying analysis of capital budgeting is placed where it rightfully belongs in economic theory. Recognizing as we do its economic foundations, the theory of capital budgeting should take on more meaning and be easier for the student to understand.

The book will supply the needs of a one-semester or one-quarter undergraduate course in corporation finance, business finance, or financial management, whatever the catalog designation for the course happens to be. After completing the course, the student should be adequately grounded for continuing to more advanced work; or, if this is the only course that he will take, it should prepare him for going out into the business world and making practical financial decisions.

It is difficult to single out individuals for acknowledgment when I am indebted to so many of my colleagues in the field, but I should like to express my special indebtedness to William Beranek, whose work, particularly his methodology, has influenced me greatly over recent years. I should like to express my appreciation also to Robert E. Stewart, for his review and suggestions in the early stages of writing, along with my colleagues here at the University of Southern Mississippi, particularly in the Departments of Economics and Finance. Special mention is due a graduate student, William B. Singley, who saved the writer many hours of labor in the later stages of the writing with his assistance in table construction in the text and problems. Thanks is extended also to Joseph A. Greene, Jr., Dean of the School of Business Administration at the University of Southern Mississippi, and to the University administration for the encouragement and for numerous tangible aids that greatly facilitated my work. A special note of thanks to my three typists, Roberta S. Levens, Mary Jean Tanksley, and Leslie M. Webb, whose good natures withstood the severest tests during the several months of typing and retyping. Finally, I should like to express my personal thanks to Mrs. Ann Marie McCarthy in the Editorial-Production Department of Prentice-Hall, Inc. for her personal interest and direction in bringing this project to a close.

LOUIS K. BRANDT
University of Southern Mississippi

**ANALYSIS
FOR
FINANCIAL
MANAGEMENT**

PART I

GOALS
AND
SUBSTANCE
OF
FINANCIAL
MANAGEMENT

1

Guidelines
to
Decision
Making

In approaching any new subject the student needs guidelines so that he can place the subject in its proper perspective to other subjects in training for a career in business. The guidelines presented here will identify business finance as an independent analytical and decision-making subject that trains business managers to take action specifically for financial goal attainment. Three general guidelines to decision making are set up in this chapter. First is the establishment of a goal that is common to this subject. Second is the identification of value functions that are related to this common goal in a cause and effect relationship. And third is the identification of a methodology for the analysis of financial issues for decision making that leads to goal attainment.

THE COMMON GOAL

The common goal in making financial decisions is to maximize the present value of the owner's share of the business. The owner's share in a business, whether it is a single proprietorship, a partnership, or a corporate form of enterprise, is the cash sale value of the equity or net worth of the business. The market value of a firm's equity or net worth is a collective concept when the business is owned by more than one person as it is in the partnership and corporate forms; in some cases this is called the *worth* of the business, signifying its worth to the owners. But as a cautionary note, the student is reminded that this sales value concept of ownership is not to be confused with the book value or the balance sheet value of a firm's equity or net worth. The book value of a company's net worth plays an important part, as will be seen later, in borrowing funds for short and long run operations which may affect indirectly the present value of the owner's share of the business. But net worth on the balance sheet is the business entity's own value and is not affected by the market value of the *owners' claims* to the worth of the business. Another way of looking at this goal is to think of the financial managers seeking to make decisions that would enable the owners of a business to liquidate their collective present interests in the business at a maximum value.

Thus far we have been speaking of ownership of a business in a collective sense as the total market value of a firm's worth. This was done to broaden the share concept to include ownership of the proprietorship form of business owned by one person and the partnership which may be owned by as few as two persons as well as the corporate form which is typically owned by many persons. But because the corporation is the model form of business for financial analysis, we wish to give a somewhat more limited but more practical interpretation to ownership as a single marketable unit called *the* share or *a* share of ownership. It is a more realistic approach from the financial manager's point of view to direct his decision making to maximizing the value of a company's individual shares rather than to the composite value of these shares evidenced by the total worth of a business to its owners. For the most part in this book the term *shares* will be used to mean shares of *common stock*, the primary evidences of ownership in the corporate form of business, and the term *shareholder* will be used to mean the holder of common shares of *corporate stock*. Restating the goal of financial management then: it is to maximize the sales or market value of the corporation's shares of common stock.

Now let us explore briefly the risk-taking implications of being a common shareholder. Shareholders are the prime risktakers in a business venture; in the proprietorship as in the general partnership form, they risk their personal assets if the business fails. In incorporated businesses they run the risk of losing their total investment in the shares in case of a business failure but not their personal assets as in the other two forms. In all three forms, nevertheless, they subject their funds to the highest risk of loss of all classes of investors. Later on in the book we will see that risk taking is a matter of degree; certain perferred shareholders take less risk than common shareholders, and all shareholders, preferred as well as common, take more risk than another important class of investors called *creditors*. For the present we are concerned only with the primary risk takers: the common shareholders who take the maximum risk among the owners but who also expect in return for taking this risk a chance of maximizing the value to their share of ownership in the business. What do the shareholders risk exactly? They risk great loss in the market value of their shares if financial managers make too many wrong decisions, and they stand to gain great appreciation in the market value of their shares if financial managers make correct decisions. One final point about the maximizing goal: readers may label this as an antisocial objective, but this is not the case at all. Social and community services are an important function of the business entity, and as financial managers we have the right to assume that our decisions are being made in a framework of a socially responsible institution.

Now that the external aspect of the share-maximizing goal has been described, let us look more closely at its implications to internal financial management. The goal of financial management, to become effective, must pervade all levels of the nonfinancial as well as the financial organization. But to attain this objective requires a carefully planned financial communication and educational system that will bridge the gap between goal-attainment standards set finally in the external securities markets and goal-attainment standards set by limited segments of the internal financial and nonfinancial organizations of the business. Today, with the extensive specialization and interdependence that exist within the total management organization, financial-goal needs have to be communicated on a broad scale to nonfinancial groups in production and sales as well as to lower levels of the financial organization if favorable results are to be realized finally in the financial indicators that affect share values. Production and sales have their own "subgoals" to attain which are mainly to increase volume of output and sales respectively during a given time interval; but, the subgoals in these important nonfinancial areas of management may have adverse effects on the financial indicators that affect share values unless the decision makers in these segments of the business understand the financial implications of their actions. More specifically, on the production side management needs to be aware of financial costs and the way that they vary with volume of physical output to affect finally the financial condition of a business, and on the sales side management needs to be aware of the impediment to share values of a large volume of sales that may be returned or that later cannot be collected. In conclusion, we need to take a final look at the concept of share value maximization. Whether or not maximizing the value of a company's shares is ever actually attained, the fact that a maximization goal guides the actions of management is vitally important in shaping a positive approach to financial management issues. In seeking this goal the term *present value* will appear often in the book. Present management is concerned with making the kind of decisions that will maximize the present value of the shares. Financial managers cannot rest on the laurels of decisions made in the past, for their effect on share values is past. In the following section we will consider the general areas of financial management that are communicable to the securities markets and that will bring about a definite pattern of response to a company's shares.

FOUR VALUE FUNCTIONS

Financial managers of business are guided by the fundamental premise that, given the state of the economy, correct decisions in managing the company's resources will render the shares more valuable while incorrect decisions will render them less valuable. Ruling out the effect of general changes in the level of economic activity on the total securities market, the present value of outstanding shares is purposively related to four internally controllable segments of a company's financial condition. We use the term *value functions* to mean that the value of a company's shares is related purposively to the four financial conditions that are described below. To emphasize the binding nature of the relationship between present share value and these four conditions, the relationships will be graphed.

The present value of a company's shares is related directly to the amount of the after-tax net profit per share *expected* for a given time in the future. This is not just an accidental relationship but gives strong assurance that expected after-tax net profit of a business is a prime indicator of how effectively the finances of a business are managed. This means for valuation purposes that purchasers of a company's shares expecting net profits to increase on a share basis over the next month, quarter, or longer period will be motivated to demand some of the company's shares even though to assure their purchase a higher price has to be paid than the last sale price of the share. Or this information may cause the present shareholder to refuse to sell his shares except at a higher price than their last sale price. Since the relation is *functional*, we can expect a pattern of continuing direct response to exist between present share value on the one hand and the level of expected net profit on the other. Although this value-determining force may be neutralized or even offset temporarily by uncontrollable and overpowering general market forces, it will nevertheless come to the fore again when general market forces are stabilized.

Another way of looking at it is to assume that two competitive businesses are facing a general declining market. The firm more efficiently managed for net profit will withstand the general force of market decline better than the firm less efficiently managed for net profit. Or, assuming that the same two businesses are facing a general rising market, the firm more efficiently managed for net profit will rise faster with the market than the firm less efficiently managed.

A graphic portrayal of perfect continuity such as the one in Figure 1.1 oversimplifies the relationship between share values and expected net profits in the real market for securities, but it illustrates the meaning of a functional relationship. The straight line in Figure 1.1 symbolizes the pattern of the relationship. The upward slope of the line indicates that a fixed relationship exists between present values of shares and expected net profits; that is, present share values rise in the market when net profits are expected to rise and fall when net profits are expected to fall, other factors being the same. A $4 per-share limit is set arbitrarily, but it could mean that for the time under consideration and with the company's given resources it is practically impossible for decisions to be made that would lead shareholders to expect the company to earn more than $4.

Implicit in Figure 1.1 also is an analytic tool that financial managers can use for guiding their decision-making action internally. For example, assume that the positive relationship indicated by the slope of the line represents something like a typical responsiveness of share values to expected earnings. If financial managers are convinced that this pattern will fit present values in the future, then they can

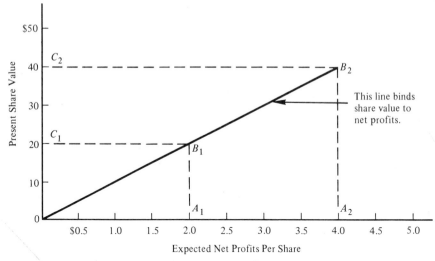

Figure 1.1. Present Share Value: A Function of Expected Net Profit.

control present share values by net profit control. The broken lines A_1, B_1, C_1, A_2, B_2, and C_2 are imposed on the graph to indicate a question and answer technique; The question is: What share value will an expected $2 per share return generate? The answer is that $2 per share will generate a present share value of $20. The process can also be reversed. The question is: What has to be expected in net profits to generate a $20 share value? The answer is that to generate a $20 share value, a $2 share earning has to be expected. The latter is more directly relevant to our goal of maximizing share value. For example, in answer to the question of how much investors have to expect to earn for the company's shares to rise to $25.00, the straight-line function answers $2.50. As pointed out earlier the graph oversimplifies the function of share values; this is done by making after-tax net profit the only variable affecting share value and by making the relationship a continuous one. At least three other variables may interfere with this apparent smooth relationship; one we call the time function, and the others the liquidity function and the solvency function.

PRESENT SHARE VALUE-TIME RELATED

The present value of shares varies directly with the amount of expected net profit, but present value is inversely related to the length of time expected to transpire before the profits are actually realized. This means, for example, that given an expected net profit of $10 per share for a one-year operation, the present value of the company's shares will increase the sooner these $10 net profits are expected to show up in the operating statements of the business. In general if the business is managed so that shareholders expect the income statements to show the net

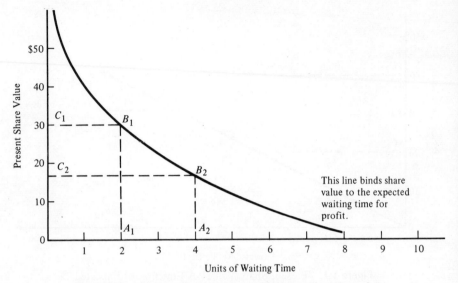

Figure 1.2.   Present Share Value: A Negative Function of the
Waiting Time For Profit.

profits in the next quarter, let us say, rather than in the next year, the present value
will cast this in a favorable light.

Figure 1.2 illustrates this negative functional relationship. The graph implies a
given total quantity of expected future profits expected to be produced at an infinite number of alternative time periods. The vertical axis indicates the resulting
share values and the horizontal axis the alternative time intervals for generating
profit. The function is represented by a curved line that touches the vertical axis
but that never quite touches the horizontal axis. The point at which it touches the
vertical axis indicates the maximum price of the share assuming the unlikely situation in which net profits are expected to be generated instantaneously (at zero
waiting time). At the other extreme, the line never quite touches the horizontal
axis; this means that regardless of how long the investor thinks he will have to wait
for the company to generate the profit, he is still willing to pay something for a
share of the company's stock. The important concept here is the functional relation indicating that an inverse pattern exists between present share value on the
one hand and expected waiting time for net after-tax profits on the other. An
inverse relationship will be noted between the units of waiting time and present
share value; as the expected interval increases from two units to four the present
value drops from more than $30 to less than $20. An inverse relationship exists
also with declining waiting time, so that moving from right to the left on the horizontal axis raises the value function on the vertical axis. Using this graph as a
guideline financial managers are motivated to make decisions that accelerate the
net-profit flow. Together the quantity of the expected net-profit flow and the
timing of the flow are the main independent variables affecting goal attainment.

PRESENT SHARE VALUE-LIQUIDITY RELATED

Liquidity is a condition of fluidity and flexibility in the assets exemplified primarily by the cash balances and cash flows. In addition to cash, a company's investments in short-term securities, particularily United States Treasury Bills, symbolize liquidity of the business. There are various measures of liquidity that will be discussed in Chapter 2; for the present we are concerned just with the general response of share values to the quantity of a company's liquid assets.

Independent of the net profit that a business generates there is a positive functional relationship between the quantity of liquidity, however measured, that a business has and the present value of its shares. As liquidity increases, other factors being the same, the higher the present value of the shares will be. The reason for this is that liquidity is an indication, as mentioned in the first sentence above, of fluidity and flexibility. It indicates the quantitative capacity of a business to take advantage of internal and external investment opportunities. Indirectly there is a relationship between liquidity and expected profit because *present liquid funds are sources of investment for future income.* Figure 1.3 illustrates the general pattern of the relationship between liquidity and the present value of a company's shares.

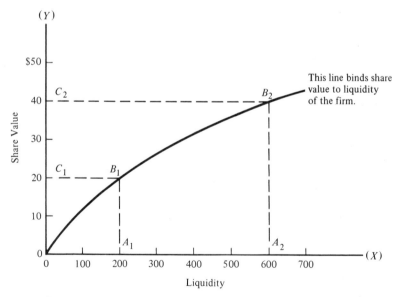

Figure 1.3.   Present Share Value: A Function of Liquidity.

Notice that the relationship is identified by a curved line that loses its steepness as the quantity of liquidity increases. Unlike net profit which increases present value by a straight-line function all the way out on the profit base, liquidity apparently loses some of its force for increasing share values after a certain distance out on that line. This is logical in view of the income-related nature of the assets. If liquidity keeps building up, it is a signal to the securities market of inefficient financial management by having allowed unproductive balances to accumulate. The student should have no problem verifying the pronounced drop-off effect of increasing liquidity on share value on the graph. He will notice that increasing liquidity from 0 to 200 units raises share value from $0 to $20, but that increasing liquidity by 200 from 200 to 400 units causes share values to increase by less than $20.

We need to understand that these are arbitrary values on the two axes of the graph established to illustrate general aspects of the liquidity function. But financial managers may draw on experiences of their business and of other related businesses to construct a graph to suit their own business needs. If such a graph is constructed, then it can be used in the same way that the profit function is used to answer questions about how much liquidity to accumulate for generating certain share values. But it may be rather meaningless to treat the liquidity function independently of the net-profit function.

PRESENT SHARE VALUE-SOLVENCY RELATED

One of the common errors in financial analysis is to improperly identify a business' solvency. Most often liquidity and solvency are confused. Liquidity as stated above simply indicates a comany's state of fluid assets, and this spells out the company's capacity for taking advantage of profitable investment opportunities. Solvency, on the other hand, is the capacity that a business has for paying off its total indebtedness. A company's solvency is indicated more exactly by the quantity of assets that it has on balance relative to the quantity of debts that those assets have eventually to retire. There are numerous refinements, as will be seen in later chapters, when it comes to measuring precisely a company's solvency. Then we sort out the total debts into those that need early servicing and those that need later servicing and offset against those that need early servicing cash and certain other relatively liquid assets that can be called on to retire these debts. Then less liquid assets are matched against debts that need later servicing. Such refinements of debt paying ability play an important part, as will be seen in later chapters, in obtaining financing outside the business, but solvency in the overall view of *total debt-paying capacity is the view that most influences share values.*

For the concept of solvency to be of practical value, financial managers have to identify the functional relationship between the extent of a company's solvency and the value of its shares. The student has enough knowledge of the balance sheet to know what is meant by its total assets and total liabilities and its equity or net worth; the ratio of total assets to total liabilities then should be a meaningful identification mark of a company's solvency. The larger this ratio is, the more solvent a company is, that is, the greater the company's capacity for meeting its total debts. Given the profit and the liquidity functions, the value of a company's shares will increase as this ratio increases but at three different rates. At first, as long as the ratio varies between 0 and 1, shares tend to respond very little to an increase in the company's solvency. When the ratio exceeds 1, however, shares become very responsive to increasing solvency; but after a certain level of safety is reached, the shares again become relatively unresponsive to increasing solvency until it may level off altogether. When the ratio exceeds 1, a margin of safety is developing which plays an important part in its early stages but which later develops a certain amount of superfluity so far as share values are concerned. Figure 1.4 reveals these three stages of responsiveness to solvency.

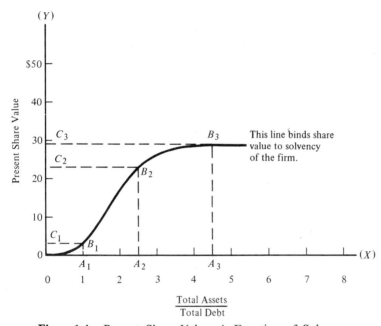

Figure 1.4.   Present Share Value: A Function of Solvency.

Figure 1.4 shows a gradual climb in the value of shares as the solvency ratio increases from 0 to 1. A zero value means that total assets are worthless, while debts with greater than zero value are still outstanding. Legal action may or may not be brought against the business at this stage. As assets increase the ratio inches up to 1, at which time total assets are just enough to cover total debts. This casts the company's shares in a better light because now there is some prospect that ownership in the company may have some worth, at least in the future. The addition to assets in this primary stage could have resulted from issuing more shares of common stock or even from retaining income from profitable operations. But as solvency exceeds 1 attention is called to successful financial management. Response to this is instantaneous, particularly if the growth in assets results from profitable operation; and share values are carried up rapidly until a safe margin is realized in ownership, in this example to a 2.5 ratio, after which added security becomes rapidly less and less meaningful to the owners.

Two points have to be noted in concluding this discussion. First, although the graph is an arbitrary example designed to illustrate the general pattern of functional relationships, financial managers may fit such a curve to the experiences of their own firm. If they can fit such a curve to their own experiences, it may be used in the same manner as net profit and liquidity graphs are used, to plan solvency for maximizing share values. Second, we have to realize that the solvency function is operative jointly with net profit and liquidity. What financial managers seek is the best combination of these three functions to maximize the value of their company's shares. If Figure 1.4 were used we would expand the solvency ratio to 4.5 where the curve flattens out; but considering the fact that benefits to the shares of excessive solvency are much less effective on market price after the ratio reaches 2.5 than are net profits, maybe less effort should be directed to this function and more to the profit function. Excessive solvency may actually conflict with the profit function, measured as it is on a per-share basis, which is true particularily if the margin of assets over debts was increased by issuing more common stock instead of retaining net profits in the business.

THE EVALUATORS

The functional relations described and illustrated in earlier sections are not mechanical operations as the diagrams imply. Human beings are continually relating expected net profits, the timing of these profits, liquidity, and solvency of the business on the horizontal axis of the value graph to present values on the vertical axis. These are the evaluators without whom there would be no functional relationship between the two sets of circumstances. Although the graphs alert financial managers to major issues for analysis and decision making, financial managers cannot afford to lose sight of the importance of the human element in the evaluation process. Knowledgeable investors, who include representatives of financial institutions and investment funds of all sizes and kinds as well as individuals trading in securities on their own accounts, are constantly converting expected profits, time flows, liquidity, and solvency into present share values. The actual value results at any given time from the aggregate demand for and supply of the shares. The final act in the stock market that causes price change is the order to buy shares at a given price and the order to sell shares at a given price. When valuations are favorable, shares will be demanded at higher prices; and when they are unfavorable, shares will be demanded at lower prices. The opposite action from the supply side causes the same price effects. When valuations are favorable, share offerings (supply) will decrease causing prices to rise; and when they are unfavorable, share offerings (supply) will increase causing prices to fall. For this reason it is important that financial managers make public any information that is likely to influence the evaluators' expectations of the quantity and timing of future net profits as well as report to them conditions of liquidity and solvency. Financial managers may participate in the valuation process, but it will not influence their company's shares unless decisions are made and action taken in the securities markets where buy and sell orders are placed for shares of stock.

Finally we will consider a mechanical aid to securities evaluators called the *discounting process*. Discounting is a process by which expected after-tax net profits per share are changed in one simple operation to present values. Discounting has various applications, but the simplest of these is its application to common share valuation. We start with the simple statement:

$$V_p = \frac{P_b}{r}$$
1.1

Where:

V_p = Present value of share
P_b = Budgeted net profit after taxes
r = Discounting rate

Assume that the potential purchaser expects the company to produce a continuing net profit after taxes of $2 per share and that he considers 10 percent a representative discounting rate, then:

$$V_p = \frac{\$2}{.10}$$
$$= \$20$$

Now suppose that the profit is expected to occur at an accelerated rate. The accelerated flow obviously does not affect the size of the expected profits per share; therefore, to reflect its effect on present value the discounting rate has to be lowered, let us say to 8 percent, which reflects the share in a more favorable light. Adjustments may be made in the market in the same manner for the liquidity and solvency of the business increasing liquidity and solvency lowering the discounting rate at certain stages and by variable amounts, and decreasing liquidity and solvency raising the discounting rate at certain stages and by variable amounts.

$$V_p = \frac{\$2}{.08}$$
$$= \$25$$

To illustrate the effect, assume that a decline in the company's solvency raises some doubt in the minds of the evaluators about the future safety of their investment and that the market quantifies this in terms of a 1 per cent increase in the discounting rate from 10 to 11 percent. The effect of this share valuation is illustrated below:

$$V_p = \frac{\$2}{.11}$$
$$= \$18.18$$

The student should not mistake the present value of the profit flow in this case for the present market value of the share as illustrated in the graphs. What is illustrated here is basic mechanism for share valuation which then may affect the demand for, or the supply of, shares in the following way. If the discounted value of the share is greater than present market value, demand may increase for the shares; but if the discounted value is less than present market value, the supply of shares offered may increase. In the former case, prices will tend to increase and in the latter to decrease.

There are numerous extensions and variations of the valuation tool in investments and in financial management theory. Some would substitute dividends for net profits in the numerator; others would combine dividends and net profits in certain proportions in the numerator; some would partition the expected flows in the numerator so that their quantity would vary by time periods; still others would vary the discounting rate in the denominator instead of letting it be constant. These, and modifications of these variations, all have interesting implications for theoretical study, but they unduly complicate the problem of trying to bridge the communications gap in a practical way between financial managers of business and the evaluators of securities.

ROLE OF THE FIRM

The business firm is the vehicle for realizing the common goal of maximizing share values but is clearly the means to an end rather than an end in itself. One of the greatest responsibilities of financial managers is to develop tools and skills for orienting the financial management of the firm to the common goal of maximizing the value of ownership in the business. This means concentrating the skills of financial managers on profit, liquidity, and solvency management because these are the segments of the firm on which the evaluators concentrate. Using the firm as a means to this end takes the approach that financial managers need to understand tools and valuation methods that are used internally by financial managers and takes the stand further that financial managers are responsible for communicating internal accomplishments in managing the firm's finances to the securities market where the valuation process finally takes place. Should dual systems of valuation and decision making exist side by side for financial managers on internal issues and on external issues for investment managers, then financial managers are responsible for reconciling these two systems of valuation and decision making; so that the right decision made internally will not be inconsistent with what is the right decision externally for increasing the market value of the shares.

Finally, a short statement needs to be made about risk in the firm and the role that it plays in share valuation. There are two forms of risk that evaluators consider. One is related specifically to the kind of product or service that the business produces, and the other is related to the financial structure that sustains the organization. At given prices the demand for some products and services is less certain than for others. These firms are rated more risky in the securities market because their quantity and timing of expected net profits are difficult to estimate. Risk in this case implies a condition of less than certainty in making profit estimates. Product and services of this kind may offer possibilities of very high profits but also possibilities of very low profits, both of which make the firm a risky venture for the investor. In Figures 1.1 and 1.2 it was assumed that the market was able to estimate the quantity and timing of net profit with certainty. That meant that there was no risk concerning the ability of the evaluators to forsee the future. In the real world this is not the case, but in some kinds of businesses profit estimates are much more certain than in others. For example, public service companies generally can forecast profits with more certainty than manufacturing firms. But even among manufacturers some can forecast net profits with considerable certainty particularily when goods and services are supplied on fixed contracts. The other risk factor is quite different and is inherently related to the asset, liability, and net worth structures of the business. The firm has different degrees of liquidity risk depending on the quantity of its cash balances and closely related cash items. An inadequate quantity of liquidity reduces the certainty of being able to take advantage of future profitable investments and this creates a liquidity risk. Debts in the financial structure create still another kind of risk, the risk that interest and principal payments on the debt cannot be met with certainty and this creates a solvency risk. The fact that the future is less than certain respecting net-profit flows, availability of funds (liquidity) for taking advantage of investment opportunities, and availability of funds (solvency) for meeting debt obligations causes the securities market to modify its demand for shares.

CONSTRAINTS TO GOAL ATTAINMENT

In making internal financial analyses and decisions for value of shares, financial managers are faced with certain constraining factors. In the long run most constraints can be modified or even removed altogether, but in the short run these constraints have to be accepted and decisions made subject to the constraints. Several of the early chapters of this book deal with showing how to adapt financial operations to short-run conditions of immovable constraints. A very realistic constraint that can neither be displaced nor circumvented in the short run is the constraint of a limited quantity of capital. Admittedly, given a long enough time, the limits of this constraint can be relaxed by financial managers; but at any given time, financial decisions have to be made subject to constraint of limited supplies of capital. The presence of temporary constraints does not make financial managers' problems insoluble, it simply challenges financial managers to identify the constraints, evaluate them, and finally develop tools and skills for optimizing operations subject to these constraints. In fact the ability to adjust to constraints and to cause shares to increase in value in the face of these constraints may be the factor that separates successful from unsuccessful financial managers.

Financial managers' goals internally are dominated by the optimizing principle more than any other single factor. The optimization principle motivates management to make *decisions that are the best possible, subject to given constraints.* Finally, optimal, or the best possible, decisions have to affect favorably the company's share value. Financial managers, more than any other administrative group in the organization, are confronted with numerous challenges to optimize. The variables affecting optimization are not equally easy to isolate and control for all financial issues, and as a result the degree of optimization that can be attained is not the same for every kind of financial issue. In some cases the effects of optimizing are not worth the effort that it takes, but in other instances we are well compensated. A few of the issues that are optimizable and that will be considered in later chapters are income, profits, level of inventory holdings, cash holdings, capital investment, and capital financing.

Optimization is identified typically by *maximum values* in the case of incomes and profits and cash flows and by *minimum values* in the case of costs and expenses, but the important thing to remember in every case is that it represents the best effort possible toward the attainment of goals that converge to affect the company's equity values. Optimizing reduces in most cases to an exact science that requires a certain amount of skill in the use of basic mathematical tools. These tools are described and analyzed in Chapters 3 to 5. It is important finally to recognize that optimization results vary in their importance and influence in the securities market. Some issues like determining the optimal size of cash holdings may be difficult for management to identify with the common goal of raising share values mainly because their results are difficult to communicate in a meaningful manner to the securities market. Then there are other problems like optimizing the amount of net profits or the amount of capital investment, the results of which are readily and meaningfully communicable to the market and exert great influence on share values. In summary it may be said that optimizing is an attempt at precise goal attainment and that, like any worthwhile goal, may not be completely attained. It may be said of optimization that it gives management something tangible to identify with and to hold onto in developing a practical system for analysis and decision making.

METHODOLOGY

A major criteria to effective financial management is methodology. Methodology is an orderly and consistent procedure for approaching and solving problems and resolving issues. Issues cannot be resolved in financial management, or in any other area of management for that matter, if a hit-and-miss method of approach is used. It is our belief that an orderly approach to issues could be standardized to the benefit of the organization and its owners. To this end we establish that the basic methodology of financial management is a fourfold approach. First, it requires research and analysis of all relevant historical data; second, it requires an evaluation of the data; third, and most important, it requires a decision; and finally, the decision requires control. This means that the total methodology needs to be directed to unfolding, solving, planning, and controlling problem issues. Most financial accounting data are historical including statements of income, costs and expenses, and net profits. By studying these elements of operation and applying simple quantitative tool tests, financial managers gain a clearer perspective for planning profitable operations. Financial accounting also supplies balance-sheet data revealing assets, liabilities, and net worth. By studying these elements of financial condition and applying simple quantitative tool tests, the perspective for planning liquidity and solvency is improved. But the end result of this first stage of our methodology is decision oriented; and until decisions are made, financial management issues are not resolved. For this reason special attention has to be given here to the elements of decison making in the total methodology.

THE DECISION

In business finance, and this is true in other areas of management as well, qualifying for decision making implies that a person has the skill for making a high percentage of correct decisions. Theoretically, a correct decision is any decision that causes share values to increase. But a time factor enters the picture: a decision that is interpreted in the market as correct at first may be revalued later as incorrect. If the decision stands the test of time, share values will hold their original gain, but if not they will drop back in value. So if a guiding rule is desired, a reasonable approach may be for management to set a certain attainable share value, then rank decisions first according to what they are *expected* to contribute to this value and later according to what they actually *did* contribute to the value, and keep a record of correct and incorrect decisions in terms of their final effect on the value of the company's shares.

Decisions also vary in degree of importance, so that some may be classified as major, others as minor decisions. The logical basis for distinguishing the importance of the decision is its relative effect on share values. A decision, for example, to make a major plant addition or to introduce a new product line interpreted in the market as a correct decision may, because of its expected effect on net profits, cause a substantial increase in share value. Whereas another decision, for example, to reduce receivables balances by stepping-up collections, also interpreted in the market as a correct decision, may barely cause a ripple in share value. In the latter case, several such correct decisions may have to be made to create an effect comparable to one correct capital investment decision. We are reminded that poor communication between management and the share evaluators may destroy the effects of an important internal decision; for instance, the technical nature of a certain capital investment may be such that its benefits are difficult to communicate and they may have a delayed market effect or no effect at all. Finally, major decisions are also usually riskier decisions which means that we are less certain of their results than we are of most minor decisions; and with the stakes as large as they are, we stand to suffer major losses as is evidenced by larger declines in share values when the decisions turn out to be wrong. Minor decisions have less favorable effects on the market when they are correctly made, but they also have a less unfavorable effect on the market when they are wrongly made.

We assert that in business finance decision making to a large degree is a learnable skill rather than an art and that there are certain tools and methods that increase this skill. This is not saying that anyone studying this book will become a skilled decision maker. Mental and emotional differences and differences in individual interests and capabilities play an important part in the effect that this experience will have on such skills. Some will reach a higher level of skill than others, at which point they can qualify for making major decisions with far-reaching effects on a company's share values in a short time; whereas, others may never reach this level. With the concept of decision making clear in our minds we can move on to three of the applied aspects of decision making.

Organizing For Decision Making.   Organizing is used here in a broad sense as planning to communicate positive attitudes toward decision making within the total management organization. Figure 1.5 is a special kind of organization chart that emphasizes the decision-making character of financial management. This chart divides our subject on the basis of how to approach financial issues on a decision-making basis first through channels of current operations and second through channels of capital management. This is not an organization chart in the ordinary sense of an instrument for defining and delegating authority and responsibility to

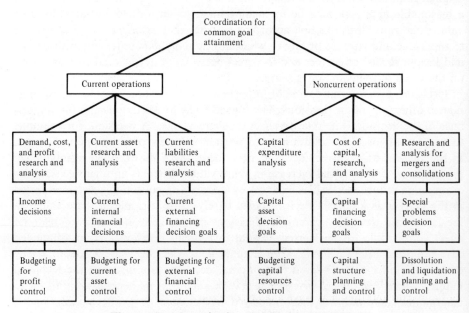

Figure 1.5.   Organization For Decision Making.

specific offices and individuals. It is designed primarily to give the reader a grasp of the total subject of financial management reduced to a decision-making medium. Research and analysis comprise the first block, followed by decision making, and followed in the last by budgeting for financial control as an essential step in the total methodological system. The need for formalizing such an organization in terms of persons, offices, and titles will vary depending on the size and complexity of the business; a small business informally managed could conceivably have a stronger organization than a large business that lacks the subjective prerequisites for communication or the clear perspective that is needed of goals and objectives.

Research for Decision Making. Research is the application of inductive methods to increase the quality of ultimate decisions. In financial management, it includes any form of planned investigation of data contained in the format of the organization chart that may improve the quality of decisions that are made in each area. Research in its simplest form may consist of monthly comparisons of the company's historical statements of income, costs, profits, assets, and liabilities to detect fluctuations and upward or downward trends. In its more sophisticated form research includes applications of various quantitative tools, such as those discussed in Chapters 3 to 5, to collected data to measure stability or flexibility of value changes and fund flows. Research may extend to gathering financial data from other businesses in the industry as a whole of which our business is a part, and it may extend to the business community as a whole and to certain segments of the economy that particularly affect the finances of the firm.

It is a mistake to hold that research is limited to complex corporations that can spend large sums of money on costly equipment, supplies, and salaries. That such programs are in operation is true in product and manufacturing research, but this is not necessary in financial research. With a relatively small amount of equipment and personnel, financial research can be carried on continually by all sizes of businesses and at all levels of current operations and capital management with rewarding results.

Analysis for Decision Making. Analysis of financial data follows two lines of action. First, it is applied to the results of research; quantitative measures of even the simplest forms of research data need to be analyzed before they can be used as the basis for decisions. As part of the analytical process, statistical measurements and tests may be applied to the data that were not employed in the initial research. Examples of this would be determining ratios of one financial value to another, measuring changes in ratios over time, and computing averages of financial values and averages of financial changes. More sophisticated statistical measures may include probabilities and measures of variation from an average. But analysis of researched data, rather than calling for more technical operations, may lead in the opposite direction to a simplification of the initial findings. This happens when tools are applied that result in a less technical restatement of the whole issue in finance. Simplification and interpretation of researched material is vitally important in business finance because of the inherent technical nature of much of the material.

Another important form of analysis, besides that related directly to research, also needs to be mentioned here. This is the deductive or a priori form of analysis. In this approach certain assumptions are made about financial phenomena which seem to be reasonable and acceptable without first carrying on extensive investigation for verification; then, given the assumption or assumptions certain tools are applied and operations performed, and finally conclusions are reached and decisions are made based on these conclusions. The deductive method is easily adapted to financial analysis. As an example of how this method works to come up with useful information for decision making, assume that sales are normally 10,000 units for a given period and that the sales price is $2. By assuming that the unit price will remain the same, we can deduce what total income will be from sales by substituting alternative sales figures that are likely to occur in certain periods. In this manner any possible product sale can be converted into prospective financial income. Another somewhat more sophisticated example is the assumption that the frequency with which certain sales levels are likely to occur form a normal distribution curve, a curve that will illustrate distribution of those sales about their arithmetic average or mean. By performing certain operations that are described in Chapter 3, we can determine the probability that sales will range between certain limits. The deductive method and a priori situations are a vital part of our methodology for several reasons. For one, they are conducive to low-cost analysis compared with research undertakings; two, they are not as time consuming as inductive research; and three, they are highly flexible which makes them applicable to any problem issue regarding which reasonable assumptions can be made. Furthermore, and this is one of the most important reasons for using a priori methods, some projects in finance cannot be researched from the practical viewpoint because by the time the results of the research are compiled and analyzed their usefulness for decision making would have transpired.

This is not to imply that a priori methods are substitutes for research; in fact, the two techniques should be used together whenever it is possible. The single most limiting factor in the use of a priori methods is that complex financial relations may have to be over simplified by assumption to make them soluble, particularly if optimization is sought, in which case their results may have limited practical value. One of the most obvious pitfalls that may result in this direction is the exclusion of certain variables just so that the problem can be fitted into some relatively simple optimizing format. A precautionary note may be sounded also when a priori analysis is used for projecting financial conditions; just because an assumption is reasonable with respect to evaluation of the past does not automatically admit it for analysis and decision making for financial planning. In summary it is suggested that in most problem situations both inductive research and deductive analytic methods have contributions to make.

PLANNING AND CONTROL

Methodology to this point has emphasized research and analysis ending with the decision, but research, analysis, and then what appears to be the correct decision can all lose their effectiveness if they are not put into use with a tangible plan and followed up with internal control. Decision action has to be worked out consciously and deliberately, which calls for tangible plans and detailed budgets for financial action and control. The best way to make the decision work is through a system of budgets applied as indicated at the end of each branch in our organization chart. Budgets perform a twofold purpose. One is to formalize a decision plan by expressing each step of the plan in terms of financial values. The other important purpose that budgets perform is internal control. The method is to check at frequent intervals for deviations from the budget and to force those deviations to remain within stated limits of the budgets. Budgets are applicable as shown in the organization chart to profit, current asset, capital asset, and capital financing control.

SUMMARY

The whole decision-making process in financial management is divided into two parts: decisions subject to capital constraints and decisions altering the capital constraints. It is important in this chapter that the student establish in his mind the concept of a constraint and its implications for financial analysis and decision making. Subject to the limitations of these constraints, the goal in financial management is to maximize the market price of the company's shares.

There must be an established methodology or method also of approaching financial issues for analysis and decision making, and there must be an effective communication between the internal management of an organization and the market place where the evaluators consider the company's prospect for earning profit and the liquidity and solvency risks attending the profit prospects. Discussed under the heading "The Decision" were the problems of organizing for decision making, research for decision making, analysis for decision making, and planning and control for decision making.

PROBLEMS

1. In his effort to communicate the common share maximization goal to marketing and production managers, the financial manager of the ABC Corporation decided to emphasize the expected net profit, present value relationship. Construct a graphic portrayal of the relationship, and indicate how the graph can be used to answer questions about an infinite number of relationships between present value and expected net profits.

2. Figure 1.2 represents the negative functional relationship of the present value of a share and the units of waiting time to realize a given amount of expected income. Disregarding inflation, what factors do you think cause the financial manager to forego increased income in later years for a smaller amount of income in the near future? In other words, why is income valued higher in the earlier years than in later years?

3. In communicating the internal objectives of management to nonfinancial personnel such terms as *optimization goal, capital constraint, methodology* and *organization for decision making* seem to be rather stilted. Putting yourself in the financial manager's position, how would you explain these concepts in language understandable to nonfinancial personnel?

4. Graph and explain the functional relationships between share values and liquidity and solvency of the business. Comment on these functions compared with the profit functions; how do they complement each other?

5. The expected net profit per share of Business A is $3.20 per share. The discounting rate determined in the market for the firm is 10 percent:

    a. Determine the share's present value.

    b. What is the meaning of the 10 percent *discounting* rate?

    c. Distinguish between the resulting value (V_p) and the market value of the share.

    d. Suppose you thought that because of the company's low liquidity there was an unusual profit risk that could be expressed as worth 1 percent; show how you would reconstruct the arithmetic model so that consideration would be given to the liquidity risk in the business.

    e. Suppose you thought that because of the solvency risk in the business, providing there be no liquidity risk, the present value of the share should be less than would be attained by capitalizing $3.20 at 10 percent. Giving a 1.5 percent discounting effect to the riskiness of the shares, what would their value be?

6. Interrelate the various levels of decision making in the chart in Figure 1.5. Where does a priori analysis fit into the picture?

2

Media
for
Market
Communications

Problem issues that confront financial managers internally are often necessarily quite different from the resultant financial reports that are the concern of the securities markets. The reason for this is that internal financial issues are usually only indirectly, and sometimes quite remotely, related to the broader purpose of net-profit, liquidity, and solvency management that are appraised in the securities valuation centers. Throughout the book we attempt to relate internal issues to their broader market context; but before this can be done effectively, we need to take the standard reports of financial conditions such as the operating statement and the balance sheet and analyze them as financial managers do when they recognize the need for bringing about a closer communication between the internal and external aspects of financial management. What we are working with in this chapter specifically is the *mediums for communicating the success and failure of internal decisions, rather than with the substance of the decisions themselves;* the latter must await later treatment.

OPERATING STATEMENT

The operating statement is primarily a summary of historical experience of income, costs, expenses, and net profits. We will examine here the elements of the statement that are significant in the securities market. A three-month (one-quarter) reporting period is used because this is the interval typically used for shareholder reports and is short enough also for certain kinds of internal analysis. The statement below is divided into major operating areas and indicates a relative, as well as an absolute, measure of each area of operation. The purpose of this discussion is to help us firm up in our own minds the scope of the issues that affect market valuations and, therefore, that require close study and attention from financial managers.

COMPANY ——
INCOME STATEMENT
QUARTER ENDING MARCH 31, 1971

		Percent of Net Sales
Gross sales	$300,000	103.0
Less returns and allowances	9,000	3.0
Net sales	291,000	100.0
Cost of goods sold	208,140	71.5
Gross profit	82,860	28.5
Operating expenses	54,000	18.6
Net profit from operations	28,860	9.9
Other net profit (loss)	($600)	(.2)
Net profit before taxes	28,260	9.7
State and federal income taxes (@40%)	11,304	3.9
Net profit after taxes	$ 16,956	5.8

RETURNS AND ALLOWANCES

A general policy of business is to allow customers to return goods that are not acceptable because of inferior quality, poor delivery, or damage. This is the first financial checkpoint and the income statement will show how much income has been lost by shipping goods that have to be returned; these losses can be crucial in determining income flow and net profit and, therefore, bear close watching by management. The net-sales figure gives a financial report of income that has passed the hurdle of returns and allowances. Depending on the kind of business and product or service supplied, the sales figure may represent a cash flow, credit flow, or combination of cash and credit. But whatever the qualitative makeup, net sales signifies a flow of liquid funds into the business that increases cash or receivables from credit sales that will turn over into cash through collections. From the firm's viewpoint the best way to think of net sales is as a continuous addition to the liquid value of the firm.

COST OF GOODS SOLD

Cost of goods sold is a reduction of net sales by the cost of production *allocated to units of goods and services actually sold.* It seldom represents all cash charges, including usually certain charges like wages, salaries and taxes that will be paid in future periods, and depreciation of fixed assets. The term should not be confused with cost of production for the period because sometimes cost of production may produce excess goods and services and in other cases shortages for the period of sale; although cost of goods sold and cost of production will be the same if all goods produced in the period are sold in the same period.

It is best financially to look at the term from two sides; first as a control medium and second as a valuation medium for determining gross profit. As a control medium we relate cost of goods sold to factory operations. For example, the percentage column shows that cost of goods sold were 71.5 percent of net sales for the quarter. By keeping quarterly records of the ratio financial managers can determine whether efficiency at the factory level is changing, and can ask for detailed information when it is needed to improve operating results. The fact that cost of goods sold usually comprises the largest single percentage of net sales is reason enough to keep close records of changing values. Second, as a valuation item cost of goods sold is a reduction in the firm's gross asset through a reduction in finished inventories. This is best illustrated as follows:

$$\begin{array}{l}\text{Beginning} \\ \text{finished} \\ \text{inventories}\end{array} + \begin{array}{l}\text{Additions to} \\ \text{finished} \\ \text{inventories}\end{array} - \begin{array}{l}\text{Ending} \\ \text{finished} \\ \text{inventories}\end{array} = \begin{array}{l}\text{Cost of goods} \\ \text{sold}\end{array}$$

In the manufacturing process *additions to finished inventories* includes raw materials and expenditures made for labor, supervision, and fixed assets used to produce *finished inventories*. *Ending finished inventories* is the sum of all unsold finished inventories, and the difference between this item and the sum of the first two is, therefore, *value of the goods sold*. The valuation concept has another implication as seen below, in computing gross profit.

GROSS PROFIT

The difference between net sales and cost of goods sold is the addition to the value of the firm resulting from current sales less factory costs. It is the first net valuation statement for current operations; it is the addition to liquid assets net of the loss in finished inventory value due to sales. The measure of gross profit to net sales is: $\$82,860/\$291,000 = .285$ or 28.5 percent. This is a relative measure of profits that can be compared with earlier periods of current operations and with percentages of gross profits to net sales of other firms or even with the total industry. The items below summarize the percentage relationship of net sales, cost of goods sold and gross profits:

$$\begin{array}{ccc}\text{Net sales} & - \text{ Cost of goods sold} & = \text{ Gross profit} \\ 100 & 71.5 & 28.5\end{array}$$

$$\begin{array}{ccc}\text{Net sales} & - \text{ Gross profit} & = \text{ Cost of goods sold} \\ 100 & 28.5 & 71.5\end{array}$$

$$\begin{array}{ccc}\text{Gross profit} + \text{ Cost of goods sold} & = \text{ Net sales} \\ 28.5 \qquad\qquad 71.5 & 100\end{array}$$

Action by management to decrease costs below 71.5 percent of net sales will automatically raise the gross profit margin regardless of the dollar values involved. To illustrate the effect of changes in percentages, a decrease in the cost margin by 1.5 percent to 70 percent will increase the gross profit margin by the same amount to 30 percent; and an increase in the cost margin by 1.5 percent will decrease the gross profit margin by the same amount to 27 percent.

OPERATING EXPENSES

The operating expense level in the statement centers on selling and general expenses. Included are commissions and salaries of salesmen and sales managers, advertising expenses, the noncash expense of depreciation of office and sales equipment, salaries paid to executives, personal expense accounts, and depreciation again on administrative building and equipment. The securities market takes a dim view of rising operating expenses because they can cut into profits sharply without contributing correspondingly to net sales.

NET PROFIT FROM OPERATIONS

The net profit from operations is the second net valuation statement for current operations. The profit figures are getting smaller and this one is the net addition to the firm's value resulting from sales for the quarter after all of the costs and expenses of operation are met. Meeting costs and expenses does not necessarily mean they are all paid for; some including wages, salaries, and property taxes may be unpaid on the date of this operating statement ending March 31, and the unpaid portion of these obligations is carried forward in the current liabilities at the end of March. This tells the market how efficient financial management has been in supervising total operations. Relating this to net sales shows that $28,860/$291,000 = .099 or 9.9 percent of the sales income was channeled into net operating profit. Suppose 10,000 shares are outstanding; the net operating profit per share then is $28,860/10,000 or $2.88 for the first quarter's operation. The securities market is vitally interested in this figure for share valuation purposes because in effect this summarizes over a period the success or failure of financial operations. Net profit from operations may be related to net sales and to costs and expenses in a summary as follows:

$$\text{Net sales} - \frac{\text{Cost of goods sold}}{\text{Net sales}} - \frac{\text{Operating expenses}}{\text{Net sales}} = \frac{\text{Net profit from operations}}{\text{Net sales}}$$

$$100 \quad - \quad 71.5 \quad - \quad 18.6 \quad = \quad 9.9$$

Here management can concentrate on either or both of two variables to increase the percentage of operating profits; decrease in the percentage that either or both of the costs and expenses are of net sales will increase the percentage of net operating profit.

So-called nonoperating or secondary income and expense are offset against each other to determine net profit or net loss from nonoperating sources and uses. Income may include interest and dividends on securities investments. Depending on the accounting practice, cash discounts taken on inventory purchases may also be included as other income. Nonoperating income is offset here by nonoperating expenses like interest payments on short- and long-term borrowing. If the purchase practice is to include discounts as other income, then losses from customers taking sales discounts will likely also be included in this section of the statement. In the example above the business lost $600 on net balance which may appear small, but the elements involved could raise a variety of technical financial questions. Net profit before taxes supplies a completed financial picture of the combined results of primary and secondary operations. This figure is of interest to creditors as well as to shareholders. Creditors look on net profits before taxes as the flow of funds for covering interest charges; and whether or not we consider this to be an accurate financial evaluation, financial managers have to acknowledge the creditors' interpretation if negotiations for borrowing are to be carried on with them.

Income taxes are important to financial managers because they are short-term debts that have to be paid in cash and because they cut deeply into the net profits before taxes figure. The residual value added on net balance is $16,956/$291,000 = .058 or 5.8 percent. Since after-tax net profits originate in sales which are cash or credit, net profit does measure in a sense the amount of relatively liquid net value added to the assets of the business for the period. The term "in a sense" is used for the reason that cash generated by sales and collections during the quarter may have been reinvested in less liquid assets by the end of the quarter. But one thing that we are sure of is that solvency of the business is increased by the full force of the after-tax net profit regardless of what quality assets finally result. Reducing this to a share basis for the quarter: $16,956/10,000 = $1.69.

A dynamic element is introduced into operating statement analysis when operations are compared for several periods. For market as well as for internal evaluation, financial managers should make comparative income statements available. Parts of statements, particularly the sales, cost of goods sold, and gross profits, on a plant or departmental basis as well as total statements may be compared. If we look outside the business for comparisons, operating statements of competitive businesses and of the industry as a whole may be available. Comparisons with competitive businesses and with the industry as a whole are valuable media for external and internal use if they are compared on a percentage basis, but in comparing operating items of the same firm for like quarters in two years as is done below, the dollars as well as percentages column is useful. The example below compares operations for the same quarter of 1970 and 1971:

COMPANY ———
COMPARATIVE OPERATING STATEMENTS
FOR QUARTER ENDING MARCH, 1970 AND 1971

	March 31, 1970		March 31, 1971	
	$	%	$	%
Gross sales	360,000	105.0	300,000	103.0
Less returns and allowances	18,000	5.0	9,000	3.0
Net sales	342,000	100.0	291,000	100.0
Cost of goods sold	258,000	75.4	208,140	71.5
Gross profit	84,000	24.6	82,860	28.5
Operating expenses	45,000	13.2	54,000	18.6
Net profit from operations	39,000	11.4	28,860	9.9
Other net profit (loss)	1,500	(0.4)	($600)	(0.2)
Net profit before taxes	40,500	11.8	28,260	9.7
Taxes (@40%)	16,200	4.7	11,304	3.9
Net profit after taxes	24,300	7.1	16,956	5.8

The amount of net sales declined nearly 15 percent from $342,000 to $291,000 over the year and the after-tax profit margin declined roughly 18 percent from 7.1 to 5.8. Now the business had a good start at producing a much better margin of profit than this, as evidenced by its reduction in the cost of goods sold percentage, but it slipped in managing the operating expenses. The securities market quickly detects these unfavorable conditions; whether it will influence the present value of the shares depends on whether or not the market projects this condition to the future because, as was shown in Chapter 1, it is *expected* net profits that affect most present share values.

PROJECTING THE OPERATING STATEMENT

Another communication form that is useful for internal and external financial relations is the pro forma operating statement. This instrument shows what the financial manager expects the company's operating statement to contain on a given future date. The pro forma statement should express the profit goals of financial managers and show how the profits will be attained. To the extent that these goals are grounded in careful analysis and planning the pro forma statement can be a useful communication medium; but if it is based more on wishful thinking than on careful planning, it may be worse than nothing at all. The following example illustrates the use of the pro forma statement: let us say that after careful consideration of all factors, net sales for the second quarter 1971 are expected to increase 10 percent as the cost of goods sold is expected to increase only 6 percent. Operating expenses will increase 3 percent and other income and expenses will be the same as in the previous quarter. Taxes are calculated at 40 percent. The pro forma statement now can be compared with the actual statement for the first quarter of 1971 item by item and evaluations about its effect on present share values made accordingly.

COMPANY ——
PRO FORMA OPERATING STATEMENTS

	Actual Statement Quarter Ended March, 1971	Percent of Net Sales	Pro Forma Statements Quarter Ended June, 1971	Percent of Net Sales
Net sales	$291,000	100	320,100	100
Cost of goods sold	208,140	71.5	220,629	68.9
Gross profit	82,860	28.5	99,471	31.1
Operating expenses	54,000	18.6	55,620	17.4
Net profit from operations	28,860	9.9	43,851	13.7
Other net profit (loss)	($600)	(.2)	($600)	(.2)
Net profit before taxes	28,260	9.7	43,251	13.5
Income taxes (@40%)	11,304	3.9	17,300	5.4
Net profit after taxes	16,956	5.8	25,951	8.1

THE BALANCE SHEET

The balance sheet suggests a wide span of management subjects and helps to suggest general areas as we will see for financial analysis. The balance sheet is a statement of the firm's assets, liabilities, and net worth on a given date. The student should look at asset balances as shareholders do as investments of funds with different degrees of liquidity and on liabilities and net worth as obligations to outsiders with different degrees of financial risk. The hypothetical balance sheet below will serve as a framework for identifying various important decision-making areas in financial management that are communicable to the securities market. Investors are quality conscious in reviewing a company's balance sheet, conscious as we have seen of the liquidity and solvency of the business as it is reflected in the company's assets, liabilities, and net worth.

COMPANY ———
BALANCE SHEET
QUARTER ENDING MARCH 31, 1971
(000's)

Current			Current Liabilities:		
Cash		$ 50	Accounts payable		$ 65
Marketable securities		75	Notes payable		50
Receivables		125	Accruals		4
Inventories		350	Allowances for income taxes		9
Total current assets		600	Total current liabilities		128
Fixed assets:			Long-term liabilities:		
Land and buildings (at cost)	485		Outstanding bonds and notes		120
Less depreciation	100		Pension liability		50
		385	Total long-term liabilities		170
Machinery and equipment	200				
Less depreciation	60		Net worth:		
		140	Capital stock (10,000 shares		
Total fixed assets		525	@ $60 par value)		600
			Paid-in surplus		160
			Retained earnings		67
			Total net worth		827
Total assets		$1,125	Liabilities and net worth		$1,125

CURRENT ASSETS

Current assets include the balances of cash, marketable securities, receivables, and inventories arranged on the balance sheet in this order to signify their relative liquidity. Each of these items will be discussed briefly in this section for the part that they play in communicating conditions of liquidity to the securities market.

Cash, of course, is 100 percent liquid; it is a symbol of fluidity and availability of funds for more permanent and more profitable investment. Cash is not only immediately available for use but we are certain that it will retain its face value during nonuse; we are not certain that it will retain its purchasing value during nonuse. There is no out-of-pocket cost associated with holding cash, but there are foregone profits that are *opportunity costs*, costs of foregoing the opportunity to invest the cash.

Marketable securities are ranked next to cash in liquidity and are usually high-grade, short-maturity, public and private debts. Rather than incurring the opportunity cost of holding too much cash, marketable securities are considered as acceptable temporary investment media. But even within the portfolio of marketable securities wide differences exist in profitability and liquidity of individual security types. In the market where a company's shares are traded, cash and marketable securities may be combined as a measure of the company's liquidity. The market looks favorably on reasonable balances of cash and marketable securities, but large accumulations may raise questions about the efficiency in decision making for increasing the profit flow.

Receivables are related to credit sales, and receivables balances are actually investments in uncollected credit sales. The cost of holding receivables needs to be considered as it is with cash, since it is not actually an income earning asset like market securities are. Several challenging issues are related to credit sales. The market finds a lower degree of liquidity in receivables than in cash or marketable securities, but the investment in receivables is uniquely related to sales which produce profits and tend to increase the value of shares. The range of liquidity is much broader in receivables than in marketable securities, and technical differences in individual receivable accounts require skill in management that is not directly communicable to the market.

Inventories are the least liquid of the current assets; they are more costly to hold than cash and receivables because they take up expensive storage space; and they are subject to price fluctuation and loss in value through deterioration. Financial markets have developed a degree of sensitivity to changes in the quantity of a company's inventory as they have to receivables. Inventory management tests the skill of financial managers on several fronts including raw materials purchasing and processing and holding finished goods for sale.

The quality composition of current assets is indicated in Table 2.1 below. The second column indicates the percentage that each current asset is of the total. The sum of cash and marketable securities is equal to receivables but less than half of inventories; inventories, the least liquid of the four assets, comprises more than half of the total investment. For one period such as this the figures are meaningful; but internal and external analysis are both more effective in comparative statements. For comparison with other firms and with industry averages, the second column alone is relevant.

TABLE 2.1
LIQUIDITY DISTRIBUTION
MARCH 31, 1971

Current Assets	Value ($)	Amount Each Is of Total (%)
Cash	$ 50,000	8
Marketable securities	75,000	13
Accounts receivable (net)	125,000	21
Inventories	350,000	58
Total	$600,000	100

INTERNAL FLOW OF CURRENT ASSETS

Although the flow of current assets is not implicit in the balance sheet, such flow is constantly taking place in the going concern. A diagram like Figure 2.1 is helpful for external as well as internal analysis and understanding. Figure 2.1 illustrates an interchange between income, collections, and payments on the

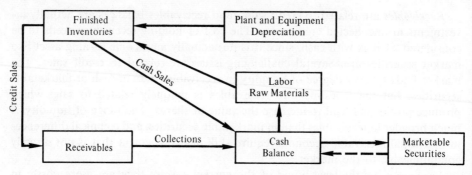

Figure 2.1.   Flow of Current Assets: Internal Sources and Uses.

one hand and balances in the current assets on the other. Plant and equipment which are not included in current asset balances contribute, nevertheless, through depreciation to finished inventory value. The arrow pointing to marketable securities does not mean that all of the cash balance is transferred to marketable securities any more than the arrow to labor and raw materials means that all of the cash balance goes to this use; they indicate that part of the cash balance goes to these uses in the short-run operating cycle. The broken line from marketable securities signifies that marketable securities are convertible back to cash as well as cash is convertible into marketable securities. The most important function of the figure is its educational service suggesting to the outsider as well as the financial organization important problem areas in current asset management, some of which are summarized below:

1. At the plant and equipment level, how much of this kind of capital is needed to support a given level of inventory flow?
2. At the credit sales juncture, what are the costs and returns related to alternative credit sales and cash discount policies?
3. At the receivables level, how large is the balance, how many days have they been held, and what is it costing to hold them?
4. At the collections stage the question is, what would it cost to collect earlier, and what is gained if anything by increasing expenditures for accelerating the collection rates?
5. How much cash is needed, what does it cost to hold it, what does it cost if we run out of cash, and what is gained by investing temporarily in marketable securities?
6. And, finally, what relation if any is there between the flow of current assets and the income and profit goals of the business?

   The student should be able to detect optimization areas in the questions above without necessarily going into the optimizing operation. Optimizing requires more than question asking, although this is necessarily the first step.

CURRENT LIABILITIES

Current liabilities are closely allied with current assets and the current asset flow. In general current liabilities imply debts maturing within one year of the balance sheet, in this case within one year of March 31, 1971. The balances of current liabilities are of special concern to shareholders for the risk that they impose on the company's solvency. Solvency is measured by ability to pay debts; and since any addition to indebtedness is a potential default, current liabilities must create a solvency risk for the firm. Current liabilities in general also create a greater solvency risk than longer term liabilities because of the earlier claim that they have against the company's assets. Let us look more closely at the demands placed by each current debt on the resources of the business.

Accounts payable are unpaid credit purchases, usually of inventories. The amount on balance at any given time is affected by the purchasing and payment policies of the business, larger purchases and slower payments adding to the balances and to the solvency risks for the firm and smaller purchases and faster payments reducing the balances and with it reducing also the solvency risks. An important factor to consider, however, is that collection pressure from the trade creditor may be lessened somewhat by his desire to retain his trade credit accounts and to expand credit sales and net profit.

Notes payable may represent two quite different kinds of debt occurrences. One is the note with an initial maturity of more than one year that is down to its last twelve months or less before it matures and, therefore, has been placed in the current liabilities section of the balance sheet. The other is the note with an initial maturity of less than one year that appears initially in the current liabilities and remains there until it is paid. The original short-term creditor may take a different view toward collecting on his note than the creditor who shifted down from the long-term debt section of the balance sheet to the short. The former in most cases is a commercial bank or some other form of commercial lending institution, while the latter could be a commercial bank, a life insurance company, or a large number of individuals and public and private institutional bondholders.

Accruals and *allowances for income taxes* are unpaid debts related directly to current operations. Accruals may be unpaid wages, salaries, and taxes other than income taxes. Allowances for income taxes are taxes on last period earnings but not due until sometime in the next year or less. Although accruals and tax allowances are not identified by formal debt contracts they imply, nevertheless, the highest level of solvency risk to the business. The shares of a business with large unpaid wages and salaries or a large tax obligation may be more highly discounted than the shares of a firm with its current liabilities concentrated in accounts and notes payable.

The quality composition of current liabilities is indicated in Table 2.2. The second column states the relative size of each current liability. We notice that the reverse of the current assets is true of current liabilities. Relatively low-risk items like accounts payable make up the highest percentage; whereas, high risk accruals and tax liabilities are a relatively small portion of the total debts.

TABLE 2.2
CURRENT DEBT DISTRIBUTION
MARCH 31, 1971

Current liabilities:		Amount Each Is of Total (%)
Accounts payable	$65,000	50.8
Notes payable	50,000	39.1
Allowances for income taxes	4,000	3.1
Accruals	9,000	7.0
	128,000	100.0

SPECIFIC MEASURES OF CURRENT CONDITION

We have seen how to make general measures of liquidity and solvency based on the absolute and relative sizes of the items in the current assets and current liabilities section of the balance sheet. It is a simple matter now for the securities evaluator to make more specific measures of a company's current financial condition, particularly to measure its ability to pay current debts when they come due. An easy indicator for all to understand is the *current ratio:* current assets/current liabilities. Substituting from the balance sheet: $600,000/$128,000 = 4.7. With current assets 4.7 times as large as current liabilities, there is little apparent chance of not being able to pay current debts when they fall due. Another way of looking at this is that the company has a cushion or excess of current assets in reserve for meeting current debts, which is 3.7 percent larger than the amount needed to just cover the debts, determined as follows:

$$\frac{\text{Current assets} - \text{Current liabilities}}{\text{Current liabilities}} = \frac{\$600,000 - \$128,000}{\$128,000} = 3.7.$$

Another important solvency measure is cash and marketable securities and receivables divided by current liabilities. The assets in the numerator of the ratio are also called *quick assets* because they convert relatively quickly to cash. Substituting from the balance sheet: $550,000/$128,000 = 4.3. This measure refines the current ratio by removing inventories from the numerator of the current ratio. For the cushion or excess of quick assets in reserve for meeting current debts, we have 3.3 times the amount of the debt, derived as follows:

$$\frac{\text{Quick assets} - \text{Current liabilities}}{\text{Current liabilities}} = \frac{\$250,000 - \$128,000}{\$128,000} = .95.$$

In any situation where one value is divided into another as current liabilities are in the ratios above, the excess or reserve value over the divisor is 1 less than the original ratio; thus the net working capital ratio is the current ratio minus 1 or $4.7 - 1 = 3.7$. And the excess of quick assets ratio is the quick asset ratio minus 1 or $1.95 - 1 = .95$.

Two other measures of current financial position carry some influence in the securities market. One concerns receivables and net sales in the ratio: Receivables/Net sales. Substituting from the income statement and the balance sheet: $125,000/$291,000 = .43$. This means that the present balance of receivables contains an investment equivalent to .43 quarters of sales. A rising ratio signifies decreasing liquidity which may give rise to collection problems later on. The market could interpret this as inefficient credit management and may accordingly raise the discount rate on the company's shares. If accumulating receivables, on the other hand, marks a credit policy that is designed to increase sales and net profits, this fact should be communicated to the market with the financial statements so that a more equitable valuation may be made of the shares. The other measure of current position is the ratio of inventory to net sales: Inventory/Net sales. Substituting again from the two financial statements: $350,000/$291,000 = 1.2$. This spells out the size of the inventory investment as 1.2 quarters of net sales with an excess over current sales $1.2 - 1 = .2$ times the amount of current sales. The ratio 1.2 indicates that the equivalent to 1.2 quarters of net sales are tied up in inventories. A rising ratio indicates, therefore, a declining liquidity that may be more serious than a rising receivables ratio. Often the inverse of the ratio is used: Net sales/Inventory. This indicates the number of times that a given inventory balance turns over in sales, which is another way of measuring liquidity. In the above ratio: Net sales/Inventory $= $291,000/$350,000 = .83$. The lower this figure becomes the more overloaded the business is with inventory relative to sales and consequently the less liquid it is. The higher the ratio the more liquid the company is; also the higher this ratio, the more intensively financial managers are employing their inventory in sales. For example, in the illustration above the business is carrying on a balance of $1.00 of inventory for every $.83 of quarterly sales. Now if inventories dropped to $175,000 the ratio would double. This indication of more efficient inventory management may cause the company's shares to be discounted at a slightly lower rate in the market.

FLOW OF CURRENT ASSETS—INTERNAL AND EXTERNAL

Now we are ready to expand the current asset flow concept to include short-term external sources that are part of the total operating funds problem. Figure 2.1 left out external financing to center attention on the relation internally of current assets to current operations. Figure 2.2 extends the flow concept to include external sources of funds. Figure 2.2 shows from where outside inventories and cash funds come that get into the mainstream of operations and from where funds come to repay the debts that are created by external financing. Inflow of inventories and cash are marked by the solid lines and repayments by the dotted lines. To con-

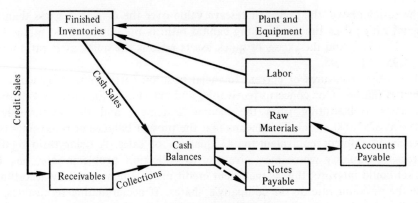

Figure 2.2.   Flow of Current Assets: Internal and
External Sources and Uses.

centrate on the external aspect of the flow, the internal cash flows directly to raw materials, labor, plant, and equipment are omitted. This does not mean, however, that cash funds are not used to these ends at the same time that they are used to repay short-term external debts. In addition to the five questions raised under Figure 2.1 relating to internal fund sources and uses, the following questions may be added that are related to external fund sources.

1. Would it pay to use trade credit for inventory purchases considering the costs of the financing and the solvency risks?
2. What are the costs of trade credit financing, and what do the balances tell about solvency risks?
3. Does it pay to borrow cash, and do notes payable affect the company's solvency risks more than accounts payable?

So that we do not go too far afield at this time on the specifics of the flow of current assets through the business, the student is reminded to look for general applications of the optimization idea to managing external supply sources of funds as he did in considering current asset flows, and to weigh the value of the flow diagram as a communication media in the securities market.

FIXED ASSETS

Fixed assets are funds invested on a permanent basis; permanent means that the asset will not be cashed as long as it is serviceable to the business. Later on the term *fixed capital* will be used to indicate fixed assets. Fixed assets are blended with current assets in the inventory production and sales cycle shown in the two figures. At any given time fixed assets, which can be tangible (plant and equipment) or intangible (patents, franchises, copyrights and goodwill), are carried in the balance sheet at their cost, less depreciation. Depreciation is offset against the cost of the asset to keep investors currently informed of the present book value of the fixed assets and of the book value of outstanding shares. In Table 3.1 the company shows no intangible fixed assets. Notice that fixed assets are divided into land and buildings and machinery and equipment on the quarter-end balance sheet of 1971, with a cumulative depreciation of $160,000 which leaves a net present book value of $525,000. The fixed assets are $46\frac{2}{3}$ percent or almost one half of total assets. Whether this high percentage of fixed assets and the company's relatively low liquidity will have adverse effects on the company's share value depends on what the market expects these fixed assets, in combination with current assets, to contribute to profits. One of the most important problems facing financial managers is how to convert the long service life of fixed assets into expected cash flows and present share values. The details of this issue will be explored in Part VI under the subject of capital budgeting. Because of the large amounts of funds that a company impounds in its fixed assets and their sizeable effect on expected incomes and net profits, fixed asset investment decisions are likely to influence share values more markedly than any single decision relating to current management.

LONG-TERM LIABILITIES

Long-term liabilities include a company's outstanding bonds and notes with maturities of more than one year. As long as debts remain in this section of the balance sheet, the company will not default on its debts, although it may be insolvent measured by the ratio: total assets/total debts. What happens, however, is that when a long-term debt or any installment due on the debt comes within the one-year maturity range, it is shifted down to current liabilities, and if current assets are not on hand to meet the liability, the company will default on its debt. With the $50,000 liability owed its pensioners, the company has a combined long-term debt of $170,000. Long-term liabilities are the *capital* debts of a business because they create net working capital and fixed asset capital.

What concerns the securities market most for share valuation is the total amount of the company's indebtedness and its relationship to assets available for paying off these debts. The first obvious measure of this debt-paying ability is the solvency ratio:

$$\frac{\text{Total assets}}{\text{Total debts}} = \frac{\$1,125,000}{\$128,000 + 170,000} = 3.8$$

This ratio shows that total assets cover total debts almost four times. For more selective coverage of debts by liquid assets the market may look at:

$$\frac{\text{Total current assets}}{\text{Total debts}} = \frac{\$600,000}{\$298,000} = 2.0$$

NET WORTH OR STOCKHOLDERS' EQUITY

The equity section of the balance sheet indicates two other important areas of financial management that are considered in valuing a firm's shares: one is the capital stock, including paid-in surplus, and the other the retained earnings. Long-term debts and net worth together comprise total capital financing, debts representing creditors' capital, and net-worth owners' capital. Net worth is the residual or *net* capital of the business comprised mainly of capital stock and paid-in surplus. Add to this retained earnings and we have the book value of the shareholders' total capital interests; in our balance sheet a value of $827,000 and net worth divided by outstanding shares: $827,000/10,000 = $82.70 book value for each share. Book value of the share may influence present market prices but, if so, more as a foundation value setting a *floor* on their value than accounting for actual current prices. In negotiations between corporations seeking to merge, particularly when one or more of the companies' shares are not actively traded in the market, book values of the respective companies' shares may be important factors affecting exchange ratios.

NET WORKING CAPITAL

Net working capital is the difference between current assets and current liabilities: Current assets — Current liabilities = Net working capital. The importance of net working capital as a liquidity and solvency measure can hardly be emphasized too much as an important market communication medium. What we wish to emphasize here is the relatively permanent nature of the capital. Exchanges between current assets and current liabilities as illustrated in Figures 2.1 and 2.2 are not creative of net working capital nor do they use up net working capital. Changes in net working capital are wrought by exchanges of a noncurrent or capital nature. Illustrated below are two sets of transactions that typically affect the quantity of net working capital: the sources increase net working capital; the uses decrease net working capital.

SOURCES AND USES OF
NET WORKING CAPITAL

Sources Increase Net Working Capital	*Uses Decrease Net Working Capital*
1. Net profits after taxes	1. Net losses from operations
2. Sale of fixed assets	2. Purchase of fixed assets
3. Long-term borrowing	3. Retirement of long-term debt
4. Sale of capital stock	4. Retirement of outstanding stock

The significance of net values of working capital is illustrated in Figure 2.3 which conveys the important message that there is a short- and long-run way of looking at capital funds; the lower rectangular section shows the nonvariable, net-working-capital fund unaffected basically by current transactions such as those in Figures 2.1 and 2.2, and the upper portion shows the variable net working capital affected by noncurrent transactions listed above. The chart shows that a certain quantity of net working capital is constantly available and basically unaffected by typical current transactions, but that in addition to this quantity of capital there is a sum of net working capital that can fluctuate rather widely as capital management

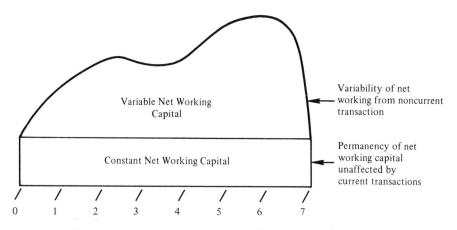

Figure 2.3. Net Working Capital Playing a Dual Role.

decisions are made through the net-working-capital fund. Financial managers are making some effort to bring the message about net working capital to the market by including at least in their annual financial reports statements of capital trans- actions that changed balances of net working capital.

Before leaving this important subject, let us take the net-working-capital reading from our balance sheet and relate it to certain debt classes as is done by knowledge- able investors. Net working capital = Current assets — Current liabilities = $600,000 — $128,000 = $472,000. This is the figure that will remain constant as the business transacts its typical financial operations of securing inventories and cash with accounts-payable and notes-payable financing and as it collects on its receivables and repays its account and notes payable. Net working capital is strong "medicine" for reducing the solvency risks encumbent in current liabilities as it measures the ratio of net current assets to current liabilities:

$$\frac{\text{Net working capital}}{\text{Current liabilities}} = \frac{\$472,000}{\$128,000} = 3.7$$

Add 1 to the net-working-capital ratio, and we have the current asset ratio again: $3.7 + 1 = 4.7$; take 1 away from the current ratio, and we have the net working capital ratio: $4.7 - 1 = 3.7$.

Net working capital is also used in the market to measure a company's long- term or capital debt paying capacity: Net working capital/Long-term liabilities. The reasoning behind this ratio is that since net working capital has current liabili- ties already subtracted from it, the balance is available for covering long-term debt. Substituting: $427,000/$170,000 = 2.5$, denoting that should current debts all be paid, enough liquid assets would remain to cover long-term indebtedness 2.5 times. This measure assures continuing solvency and assures minimum risk and may add value to the company's shares.

Gross capital is the sum of net working and fixed capital. In our balance sheet this is $997,000 ($472,000 + $525,000). It is the mainstay of combined liquid and nonliquid assets that are needed to keep the business on an even keel in the face of changing current operations and current fund flows. This is the sum of the capital creditors' and the capital stockholders' investments in the total assets of the business.

Net capital is the difference between gross capital and long-term liabilities:

(Working capital + Fixed assets) — Long-term liabilities = Net capital
    ($472,000 $525,000) $170,000 $827,000

Net capital is a measure of the shareholders' financial interests in the assets. This is also the equity capital of the business.

THE CAPITAL STRUCTURE

The capital structure of a business is the sum of long-term liabilities and net worth.

It is the sum of long-term liabilities and the net worth on the credit side of the balance sheet:

Long-Term liabilities + Net worth = Gross capital
        $170,000 $827,000 $997,000

We will note that the figure is the same as the *gross capital* on the debit side of the balance sheet. The gross capital refers to the *uses* of funds and the *capital structure* to the sources of the same funds. Attention is called here to the relationships between gross capital and capital structure and equity capital and net worth that will help the student later to understand the true meaning of these important capital concepts:

Gross capital = Capital structure

but

Gross capital $\neq$ Capital structure

The values are equal but they are *not identical;* they are the same quantitatively but not qualitatively. The same is true of the following relationship:

Equity capital = Net worth

but

Equity capital $\neq$ Net worth.

COMPARING BALANCE SHEETS OVER TIME

As the final step in our analysis we will see how comparing the dollar values and the dollar and percentage changes in the items on the balance sheet as a whole can be a valuable, dynamic means of analyzing and evaluating changes in fund balances. The comparative balance sheets illustrated here reflect changes in the company—that occurred during the first three months of 1971.

In the analysis that had gone before we had used one balance sheet, assuming it represented the latest statement of financial conditions. But now we will see how comparing the dollar values and the dollar and percentage changes in the items on the balance sheet as a whole can be a valuable, dynamic means of analyzing and evaluating changes in fund balances for appraising share value. The comparative balance sheets illustrated here reflect changes in the company that occurred between the last quarter of 1970 and the end of the first quarter of 1971.

COMPANY——
COMPARATIVE BALANCE SHEETS

	Balance Ending Dec. 31, 1970	Balance Ending Mar. 31, 1971	Increase ($)	Decrease ($)
Current assets:				
Cash	$ 54,000	$ 50,000		4,000
Marketable securities	150,000	75,000		75,000
Receivables	225,000	125,000		100,000
Inventories	160,000	350,000	190,000	
Others	30,000			30,000
Fixed assets:				
Land and buildings	385,000	385,000		
Machinery and equipment	140,000	140,000		
Total	$1,144,000	$1,125,000		
Current liabilities:				
Accounts payable	$ 95,000	$ 65,000		30,000
Notes payable	66,000	50,000		16,000
Accruals	4,000	4,000		
Allowances for income taxes	7,000	9,000	2,000	
Capital debts:				
Bonds and notes payable	120,000	120,000		
Pension liability	60,000	50,000		10,000
Equity capital:				
Common stock	600,000	600,000		
Paid-in surplus	160,000	160,000		
Retained earnings reserves	32,000	67,000	35,000	
Total	$1,144,000	$1,125,000		

In studying and evaluating this illustration, the evaluator will note unchanged balances; but looking at the current assets of the two balance sheets, it is noted that the more liquid assets, such as cash, marketable securities, and receivables decreased and that inventories, the least liquid of the current assets, increased. This adds up to an overall decrease in liquidity over the past three months, but most important it explains how much each asset contributed to the decrease in liquidity.

Fixed assets, as is often true in this short period of time, were relatively stable. Looking at current liabilities a decrease is noted but not by as much as the increase in inventories absolutely or relatively. The decline in current liabilities decreases the risk to outstanding shares; but when the investor considers it in relation to the decrease in *quick* current assets like marketable securities and receivables, it may not have a net beneficial effect on the shares. In the capital debts we note no change that decreases the risk. Reducing the risk is the addition to retained earnings. The student should place himself in the securities market and translate these balance sheet changes into increases or decreases in demand for the company's shares.

PRO FORMA BALANCE SHEET

Financial managers will have to decide on how much time to spend on projecting the company's balance sheet along with a projection of its operating statement. Projecting the balance sheet goes hand in hand with projecting the operating statement just as analyzing the balance sheet goes hand in hand with analyzing the operating statement. This is logical, since in the financial processes one is the symbol of efficiency in profit management and the other of efficiency in managing the firm's liquidity and solvency. Projecting balance sheets has several purposes, but the most important from the securities market's point of view is its forecast of how management plans to finance and to use its funds in the future. From the financial managers' viewpoint, planning financial balances gives them a time advantage; it gives them time to force their plans into use. It gives the managers time to plan profitable uses of capital funds and time to negotiate external financing on favorable terms to the business.

In general the techniques and problems of converting past experiences to a pro forma balance sheet are pretty much the same as for the operating statement. Rule of thumb methods of forecasting are acceptable for some purposes, but for others detailed budgets may have to be prepared as suggested in Figure 1.5. For the present though we are concerned just with the finished balance sheet as a medium for external financial analysis and, therefore, will not go into procedural details of financial budgeting. The securities market wants to know what major changes in the company's assets, liabilities, and net worth are contemplated by management that will affect the value of the company's shares.

We start with the latest balance sheet March 31, 1971, and adjust these balances to meet plans for the end of the year. Let us assume that the financial condition of the business is expected to be considerably altered by December 31, 1971. These alterations will take the following forms. First, land and buildings will be expanded by $500,000. This expansion will be financed from two sources: net working capital and the sale of common shares of stock. It is estimated that present inventory holdings can be reduced by $100,000 and that the cash from this reduction can be invested in the new plant facilities. Then 4,000 new shares can be sold from $100 each. Second, to accommodate the expansion of land and building the company will need to invest another $200,000 in machinery and equipment; this we hope to finance by expanding retained earnings by $70,000 and by borrowing $100,000 on a long-term note. Allowances for income taxes would increase by $30,000. It was decided at the last minute, however, to borrow $150,000 on the long-term note, so $50,000 could be used to pay off the current liability *notes payable*. Illustrated below are the current balance sheet and the balance sheet for December 31, 1971, demonstrating the changes that are expected to be consummated by December 31.

Investors do not know the details of financial planning that went into the decisions mentioned above as financial managers do, but they have in the balance sheet a picture of what management expects the end results of the planning to be. To clarify the plan investors need to treat these as comparative statements as was done above, summarizing the increases and decreases so that the major policy plans are brought to the fore for those who are appraising the company's shares.

COMPANY ——
PRO FORMA BALANCE SHEET

	Balance Ending March 31, 1971	*Pro Forma December 31, 1971*
Current assets:		
Cash	$ 50,000	$ 50,000
Marketable securities	75,000	75,000
Receivables	125,000	125,000
Inventories	350,000	250,000
Fixed assets:		
Land and buildings	385,000	885,000
Machinery and equipment	140,000	340,000
Total	$1,125,000	$1,725,000
Current liabilities:		
Accounts payables	65,000	65,000
Notes payable	50,000	
Accruals	4,000	4,000
Allowances for income taxes	9,000	39,000
Capital debts:		
Bonds and notes	120,000	270,000
Pension liability	50,000	50,000
Equity capital:		
Common stock	600,000	1,000,000
Paid-in surplus	160,000	160,000
Retained earnings	67,000	137,000
Total	$1,125,000	$1,725,000

SUMMARY

This chapter gives extensive coverage to the commonly used financial statements and reports that help to close the communication gap between decisions made internally by financial management and decisions made in the securities market by investors and potential investors in the company's shares. Comparisons are made between past profits based on prepared operating statements and pro forma operating statements. Second, the balance sheet as an indicator of conditions of liquidity and solvency is examined in some detail. Not only are the individual items in the balance sheet examined, but they are compared over time so that the important items of change are made apparent in the securities market where the company's common stock is valued. The reader is introduced to certain basic ratios and percentages which are common media for communication between the financial organization and the market place for evaluating profits, liquidity, and solvency. Diagrams are included to show the interrelationship between various elements of operation: income, costs and expense, current assets, net working capital, and the capital structure.

PROBLEMS

1. The comparative income statements of Paper Products, Incorporated for the first quarter and the second quarter are as follows:

PAPER PRODUCTS, INCORPORATED
INCOME STATEMENTS
JUNE, JULY, 1971

	1st Quarter	*2nd Quarter*
Gross sales	$28,000	$32,000
Returns and allowances	3,000	2,000
Net sales	25,000	30,000
Cost of goods sold	12,000	18,000
Gross profit	13,000	12,000
Operating expenses	3,000	6,000
Net profit from operations	10,000	6,000
Other net profit	2,000	9,000
Net profit before taxes	12,000	15,000
Taxes (@40%)	4,800	6,000
Net profit after taxes	$ 7,200	$ 9,000

The net profit after taxes for the second quarter is greater than the net profit after taxes for first quarter. In most cases this is a welcomed situation, but what set of figures arouses the concern of the financial manager over operations of the company? Why?

2. The following balance sheet is of a hypothetical company. It is your understanding that an important market communication medium is the balance sheet. Show how each of the questions is significant to share evaluation.

DEPARTMENT STORE, INC.
BALANCE SHEET—JUNE 30, 1971

Current assets:			Current liabilities:	
Cash		$ 9,500	Accounts payable	$ 90,000
Receivables		50,000	Notes payable (to owners)	50,000
Inventories		250,000	Accruals	10,000
Total		309,500	Total	150,000
Fixed assets:			Stockholders' equity:	
Land		200,000	Common stock	
Building and fixtures	600,000		(10,000 shares @ $50)	500,000
Less depreciation	200,000		Capital surplus	200,000
Net value		400,000	Retained earnings	59,500
Total		600,000		759,500
Total assets		$909,500	Total liabilities and equity	$909,500

a. Take liquidity "soundings" from the statement. Suppose that net sales for the past ninety days were $300,000. How could this information be used to further evaluate receivables and inventories?

b. How would you use the balance sheet to measure solvency risks at the present time?

c. Indicate three capital values in the company's assets, and tell what each contributes to an internal financial analysis.

d. Assume that a $100,000 capital debt is created and that the funds are invested immediately in fixed assets. What net effect would this have on: (1) net working capital, (2) gross capital, (3) net capital? Show your work.

e. What capital values on the right side of the balance sheet will match up identically with one or more of the capital values on the left side? What significance is this identity of values in explaining *capital sources* and *capital uses* of funds?

3. Using Figure 2.1 as your guide, assume that plant and equipment supplies 1,000 units to finished inventories and that labor and materials supply another 5,000 units. Prior to adding these units there were 8,000 units of finished inventories. Assume that 4,000 units are sold on credit and 2,000 for cash.

a. Given a $1000 value per unit, what would happen to the finished inventory balance after the sale?

b. If inventories are sold at 30 percent above their carrying value, what is lost in inventory value and what is gained in receivables and cash?

c. What has happened to the total value of the current assets as a result of the sales?

d. Is it likely that current assets will hold these new values in receivables and in the cash balance? If not what will happen to the balances?

e. If receivables and cash, in your answer to d, follow the flow of Figure

2.1 indicate the possible effects on liquidity and profitability of the funds flows.

f. Can profits be related in any way to this flow? If so explain how and where.

4. Using Figure 2.2 as your guide, assume that plant and equipment supplies 1,000 units to finished inventories, that labor supplies 3,000 units, and that 2,000 units of raw materials are needed but are not presently available.

a. How can the raw materials need be met? If raw materials needs are met with external financing, what does this do to solvency risk? Explain.

b. Assume that 2,000 units of raw materials are acquired on a 30-day account payable and that inventories are sold on credit 20 days later at a value well above the amount of the accounts payable debt. What determines whether the business will have to borrow cash to meet its accounts payable? If the business borrows cash to pay off its accounts, has it affected its solvency risks?

c. Aside from borrowing to meet accounts payable, what other use could the business have for cash that is not illustrated in Figure 2.2?

d. Does a large quantity of temporary financing mean that the business is not well managed financially? Explain.

5. Measuring and evaluating the balance sheet components on a given date is one thing, but considering changes in those components over time is another. Comparative balance sheets are a useful tool for showing up significant changes in individual items and in special groups of items over a period of time. To test and improve skill in measuring and evaluating changes, consider the quarterly balances of the Department Store. You are primarily interested in noting which items had changed significantly and which had not. To increase the accuracy of your measurement and evaluation, compute the changes on a percentege basis.

6. Consider the balance sheet as a statement of the *sources* and *uses* of funds, the assets representing at a given time the uses and the liabilities and equity representing sources. Looking at it in this way, the statement takes on a new meaning as a tool for planning future financial needs. The following plans will influence the balance sheet on September 30, 1971. Starting with the balance sheet on June 30, 1971, estimate the value of each of the assets at the end of September, and project the current liability balances which would respond to normal asset investment needs over the same period.

a. Cash on balance would be $10,000.

b. Receivables would be doubled and inventories would be another $150,000 more than they are at the present time.

c. Land would remain at the same value, and combined value of building and fixtures would be increased to $450,000.

d. Accounts payable could finance the increase in inventories.

e. The note payable to the owners and accruals would remain the same.

f. Common stock and capital surplus would not change, but retained earnings are expected to increase by $30,000.

Let a *note payable to bank* in the current liabilities represent the amount of borrowing if borrowing is needed to balance the statement.

DEPARTMENT STORE, INC.

	Balance Sheet March 30, 1971	*Balance Sheet June 30, 1971*
Assets		
Current assets:		
Cash	$ 7,000	$ 9,500
Receivables	60,000	50,000
Inventories	185,000	250,000
Fixed assets:		
Land	200,000	200,000
Building & fixtures (net)	400,000	400,000
Total	$852,000	$909,500
Liabilities & Stockholders' Equity		
Current liabilities:		
Accounts payable	$100,000	$ 90,000
Notes payable (to owners)		50,000
Accruals	15,000	10,000
Stockholders' equity:		
Common stock	500,000	500,000
Capital surplus	200,000	200,000
Retained earnings	37,000	59,500
Total	$852,000	$909,500

PART II

QUANTITATIVE
TOOLS
AND
CONCEPTS
FOR
FINANCIAL
MANAGERS

3

Arithmetic
Tools
and
Skills

Quantitative tools are used to give precise values to financial relationships. They do not change the goals, methodology, and communicative media between the business entity and the market where shares are valued. Tools are developed here primarily for internal use: for developing analytic and decision-making skills that will result finally in more favorable current operating and capital management decisions. Neither do these tools change in any way the purpose and goal of financial management. They are primarily a means of measuring and planning financial accomplishments and setting optimization goals in exact dimensions. If historical experiences and particularly if plans for internal and external financial goal attainments are analyzed quantitatively, decision making will be more objective and less intuitive and impulsive. Quantitative tools for financial managers are mathematical concepts that are applicable to business finance. The writer is departing rather sharply from the conventional practice by developing these fundamental quantitative tools and concepts independently of specific financial issues, but this is done in the expectation of "breaking the ice," so to speak, for the student by reviewing with him some of his high school and college mathematics that are particularly relevant to the decision-making issues that he will confront in normal financial operations. Chapters 3 to 5 explain the rudiments of the tools that are applied to various financial management issues throughout the book without making any attempt to make mathematicians of us.

Arithmetic forms of addition, subtraction, multiplication, and division are used more than any others in research and analysis for financial decision making. Arithmetic is not only an independent tool use, it also plays a major part in solving algebraic problems. Reviewing the mechanical elements of arithmetic operations in this chapter will hopefully enable the student to approach financial issues later on with confidence and assurance.

THE BASIC RELATIONSHIP

The basic arithmetic relationship widely used is the ratio or what we, for reasons that will be apparent later on, prefer to call the *relative value* that one quantity bears to another. Relative value is identified by a numerator and denominator; thus 3,000/5,000 is a relationship of 3,000 to 5,000 and a relative value of 3,000 to 5,000. The line dividing the values is a mathematical symbol ordering the arithmetic operation of division to be performed. Performing the operation: 3,000/5,000 = 0.6/1. This generalizes the relationship and immediately gives management a powerful tool for analyzing the relative value of one quantity to another. The numerator of 3,000 to the denominator of 5,000 is *in the relationship of* 0.6 *to* 1. The value of the tool lies in being able to compare quantitative values of income, costs and expenses, assets, liabilities, net worth, and many combinations of these items relatively. If management wishes to express the relationship in financial values, this can be done simply by expressing the values in dollars and cents as $0.60/$1. This does not change the basic relationship nor does it change the relative nature of the measure.

The utility of this tool is that unlike items can be meaningfully related as long as the substance of the numerator and denominator are related and so long as the financial manager knows how to interpret them. For example, income or net profit in the numerator can be meaningfully related to total units of goods sold. To illustrate, assume that profits are in the numerator and total units sold are in the denominator; then 3,000/5,000 explains that profits are realized *at the rate of* $0.60 of net profit to 1 unit of goods sold. Using the materials of Chapter 2, the student should be able to make other meaningful combinations of unlike items.

Financial items of a business, particularly in the current assets and current liabilities are subject to rapid change which also causes quantitative relationships to change rapidly. There are certain arithmetic rules about changes in these basic relationships that the student needs to learn.

1. A relationship remains the same if a *relative* increase or decrease in one of the members is attended by a *relative* increase or decrease in the other of the same amount. For example, starting with 0.6/1, increasing each number by 0.1 will raise the value to 0.66/1.1, which is the same as the original 0.6/1. Decreasing the original value by 0.1 in the numerator and denominator, results in 0.54/0.9, which is also the same relationship as the original 0.6/1.

2. The relationship changes if a *relative* increase or decrease in one of the members is attended by a *relative* increase or decrease in the other of a different amount. Let the numerator be increased by 0.1 and the denominator by 0.2; this will change the relationship from 0.6/1 to

0.66/1.2, which is smaller than 0.6/1. Reducing the numerator on the other hand by 0.1 and the denominator by 0.2 changes the relationship from 0.6/1 to 0.54/0.8 which is larger than 0.6/1.

3. When both members increase, the resulting relationship will be larger if the *relative* increase in the numerator is greater than the *relative* increase in the denominator, and will be smaller if the *relative* increase in the numerator is smaller than the relative increase in the denominator. The second part of this statement is proven in the example above in which 0.6/1 is decreased to 0.66/1.2 by increasing the numerator by a smaller relative amount than the denominator.

The reason for going into so much detail on these changes and for emphasizing the importance of the relative change is that we often do not understand the importance played by the initial size of the relationship in estimating effects of given changes in the members. The student is sometimes asked the following question: What happens to the financial relationship when the same amount of dollars are added to both members of the starting ratio of 3,000/5,000? Too often the common mistake is made of assuming that the relationship is unchanged because the same absolute values are added to each member.

RATE OF CHANGE

Now that the basic relationship is established as a relative value, the student should have no problem understanding that a *rate of change* is also a relative value comparing the quantity of change in the numerator with the quantity of change in the denominator. The ability to measure change at various levels is an invaluable tool for identifying active and inactive levels of business activity spelled out in financial values.

The mathematical symbol of change is Δ, called *delta*. The relationship of change in the numerator to change in the denominator is actually a comparison of changes in two basic relationships. Let us illustrate this with symbols. Let Y_1 be the original value in the numerator and X_1 be the original value in the denominator. The rate of change in this basic relationship may be expressed then as $(Y_2 - Y_1)/(X_2 - X_1)$. If the new value Y_2 is smaller than Y_1, the Δ value will be minus ($-$) to indicate a negative rate of change. The rate of change may be restated in simpler form now as $(\Delta Y)/(\Delta X)$. This relative value like the relative value of the basic relationship is a directive to divide. But to perform meaningfully, ΔX must be greater than ($>$) or smaller than ($<$) zero; for if it is zero, division will produce a value of infinity: $(Y)/(0) = \infty$. But the opposite situation $(\Delta 0)/(\Delta X)$ can be very meaningful, producing a zero rate of change which means that given a certain change in X there is zero change in Y. To illustrate let X represent time and ΔX equal one year; then we can say that the financial value of Y, let us say net profit, has not responded in any way to one year of operation.

It is important in decision making to consider at what rate total values are increasing and decreasing as well as to know what the resulting total values are. To illustrate the difference, assume that the numerator of the initial terminal rate of 3,000/5,000 is increased by 500 and that the denominator is increased by 1,500; the rate of change is expressed as $\Delta 500/\Delta 1,500$ which reduces to $\Delta 0.33/\Delta 1$. This also creates a new basic relationship after the change of 3,500/6,500 which reduces to 0.54/1, a smaller basic relationship than the original one. One final point needs to be made, namely that the resulting relationship may be negative as well as positive. To illustrate assume that Y_2 is 3,000 and Y_1 is 3,500, then $Y_2 - Y_1 = 3,000 - 3,500 = -500/1,500$ or $-\Delta 0.33/\Delta 1$. The indication is that a decrease of 500 units in the numerator is -0.33 as great as the increase in the denominator. A case in point may be a decrease in cost of goods sold that is 33 percent as large as the increase in sales.

The primary use of the rate of change tool lies in helping us get down to the force that is causing basic relationships to change. It reveals conditions as they are right at the point at which total values are increasing, decreasing, or remaining the same. Research and analytic value of computing rates of change lies in comparing rates of change over time and in comparing rates of change between certain key financial values of our firm with competitive firms and with the industry as a whole. A useful practice is to tabulate rates of change in historical data, to estimate future rates of change, and to tabulate and graph these findings for internal educational purposes. It is important to recognize a limiting factor, however, in the arithmetic expression of rate of change as we have used it here. Consider measuring profit change for example in relation to change in units of sales. The question might be asked: To which particular unit of sale out of the 1,500 is the 0.33 related? There can be only one answer to this: No particular unit of sale, but an *average unit*. Average values are adequate for most purposes in financial management. When this is not adequate and the rate of change is sought at a point, differential calculus is used as the measuring tool. But this is a tool form that is not used in this book.

RELATIVE RATE OF CHANGE

The rate of change is a relative measure as we have seen as the change in the numerator is compared with the change in the denominator, but the *relative rate of change* as we will see is something quite different but very important for evaluating financial change, historical and projected. The tool for measuring the relative rate of change is stated $(\Delta Y/Y_1)/(\Delta X/X_1)$. This indicates three separate dividing operations; first, dividing Y into ΔY, second, dividing X into ΔX, and third, dividing the result of the relative change in X into the result of the relative change in Y. To show how the tool works in practice return to the ΔY value of 500 and the ΔX value of 1,500. Substituting for Y and X, $(\Delta 500/3,500)/(\Delta 1,500/5,000)$. Reducing to a single quantitative value:

$$\text{Relative rate of change} = \frac{\Delta 500}{3,000} \Big/ \frac{\Delta 1,500}{5,000}$$

$$= \frac{0.17}{1} \Big/ \frac{0.30}{1}$$

$$= \frac{0.17}{0.30} \quad (A)$$

$$= \frac{0.57}{1} \quad (B)$$

Specifically the relative increase in the numerator (0.17/1) with respect to the relative increase in the denominator (0.30/1) is in the relationship of 0.57 to 1; the numerator increased just 0.57 as fast as the denominator. As a percentage, if the denominator X increases by 100 percent the numerator Y increases by 57 percent.

The letters A and B are added to the operation to call attention to two independently meaningful levels of analysis. A states that a relative increase of 0.30 or 30 percent in the denominator of the relationship is accompanied by a 0.17 or 17 percent increase in the numerator. If the measure is pushed another step to B still more meaning can be read into the results. The B value is a valuable tool for planning and controlling as well as for researching historical data. For example, if this represents relative rates of change in, let us say, share prices Y to net profits X, we can expect share values to increase at the rate of 0.57 every time net profits increase at the rate 1; or share prices can expect to increase 57 percent every time net profits increase 100 percent. But the value of Y can be adjusted to meet any expected relative increase in X. For example, suppose that profits are expected to increase 0.25, then the numerator and denominator are divided by 4 to get the expected relative increase in share value $(0.57/4)/(1/4) = 0.1425/0.25$, indicating that if profits are increased by 25 percent, share value may be expected to increase 14.25 percent; the ratio $0.1425/0.25 = 0.57/1$, so that the tool structure itself is not altered.

RATE OF GROWTH

A rate of growth is nothing more than a rate of change that is time related, a special application of the rate of change tool to cases in which the X variable is time. The growth rate is usually expressed in relative values, that is as $(\Delta Y/Y)/\Delta X$.

Financial managers are constantly concerned with growth rates of income, costs, net profits, asset balances, liabilities, net worth, and share values over certain time intervals primarily to determine functional patterns for projecting terminal values. Assume that the numerator increases from 3,000 to 3,500 over a three-month period, then the rate of growth $500/3,000/3 = 0.17/3$. This means that the Y value which may be assets, liabilities, or income grew at the relative rate of 0.17 or 17 percent over the past three-month period, or at the average rate of $0.17/3 = 0.057/1$ or 5.7 percent per month. This may have implications to forecasting dollar values; if we know what the starting value is and the monthly growth rate, we can project a terminal total value. We should not limit the use of the tool to internal financial matters, however. Rates of growth in economic values like gross national product, for example, may be translated into financial values for the firm. Technically speaking rates of growth may be negative as well as positive which is a condition that we do not seek except when a negative growth rate would have favorable effects on common goal attainment as it might have when debts or costs are decreasing with the passage of time. A zero rate of growth would result if the condition were $0/3 = 0/1$. A negative rate of growth results, for example, when $(2,700 - 3,000)/3,000/3 = -.10/3 = -.03/1$.

The value of the growth rate tool is further enhanced by selecting pairs of related growth items. For example, when management discovers a functional relationship over time between certain sets of financial phenomena like net sales on the one hand and costs of goods sold on the other, comparing growth rates of this *desirable* and *undesirable* force over the same interval of time can open the door for effective control. Another important comparison may be made between growth rates of economic or social phenomena and the firm. For example, growth rates of the firm's income or share values can be compared with population growth rates, resulting in important measures for analysis and decision making. The student should be aware that examples given here are just a bare sampling of the wide applicability of these tools to both internal and external change. Finally, if financial managers keep continuous records of growth rates and of change, they will continually improve on their evaluations of their companies' financial conditions and will become more and more effective in interpreting this data for others.

SIMULATING CAPITAL GROWTH

Our concern here is specifically with tools that are used continually in managing the capital resources of a business. These tools will serve as valuable references for the student in later chapters. Capital growth is one of the prime capital management issues; in this section of the chapter we will develop the tools for measuring two forms of growth: first, the simpler but very common form of capital growth that is not reinvested and, second, capital growth that is reinvested.

GROWTH NOT REINVESTED

Up to a certain point financial managers may want to consider holding the buildup of funds in liquid balances or even distributing them to shareholders rather than reinvesting them in the business. What we need to do at this time is to develop the tool that financial managers can use to simulate the effect on an initial investment fund and withholding from reinvestment the regular income flow from the initial investment. When a sum of capital is invested in any form of asset and the periodic returns on that investment are not reinvested, the same fixed sum of dollars is added at the end of each period. Without investing the returns, the initial capital sum will accumulate a constant dollar amount each period over the life of the investment. This is *simple* growth as contrasted with *compound* growth; this is arithmetic growth in contrast to geometric growth. Such

TABLE 3.1
GROWTH OF INITIAL VALUE OF 5,000
RETURNS NOT REINVESTED

End of Period	Simple Rate of Growth	Inflow Each Period	Cumulative Inflows	Terminal Values	
1	0.10	500	500	5,500	(5,000 + 500)
2	.10	500	1,000	6,000	(5,000 + 1,000)
3	.10	500	1,500	6,500	(5,000 + 1,500)
4	.10	500	2,000	7,000	(5,000 + 2,000)
5	.10	500	2,500	7,500	(5,000 + 2,500)

growth is illustrated in Table 3.1. The table shows the annual growth of the initial investment, the cumulative growth and the resulting terminal values. Table 3.1 values may be reexamined if we wish in terms of *constant rates of change;* for each unit of change in time X, terminal values Y change at the constant rate of 500 units. Cumulative inflows are important where we seek to show total value accumulated on an initial sum, and terminal values are important because they sum up the total fund of value including the initial investment of 5,000. Table 3.1 identifies the simple rate of growth, dollar inflow, and terminal capital value at the end of any given period. The terminal values column shows the absolute growth of initial value, but no secondary growth of this sum; there is no *compounding* of the initial growth. The reason for no compounding is that there is no reinvestment of the primary growth. Table 3.1 has served our purpose as an explanatory tool, but it is much less cumbersome to project terminal values directly as follows:

$$\text{Terminal value} = P(1 + rn) \qquad 3.1$$

Where: P = Initial value
r = Rate of growth
n = Number of periods of expected growth

Substituting:

$$\text{Terminal value} = 5,000(1 + 0.10 \times 5)$$
$$= 7,500$$

With this tool sums can be projected to any given terminal date quickly and simply. For example, assume that we want the terminal value for an initial sum of 5,000 which is expected to grow at the rate of 0.10 per period for six periods. What will be the value at the end of the sixth period?

$$\text{Terminal value} = 5{,}000(1 + 0.10 \times 6)$$
$$= 8{,}000$$

This tool also has value for analyzing and making decisions about alternative flows when the purpose is to optimize the terminal fund value.

For example, assume that the following alternative flows for projects 1 and 2 are under consideration.

$$\text{Project 1. Terminal value} = 5{,}000(1 + 0.10 \times 6)$$
$$= 8{,}000$$

$$\text{Project 2. Terminal value} = 5{,}000(1 + 0.12 \times 6)$$
$$= 8{,}600$$

Terminal values differ by 600 to the advantage of Project 2 because its growth rate was 20 percent larger than for Project 1. If all that we are seeking is to optimize terminal value, then this tool and its quantifying results make the decision a simple matter; given these results it would be illogical to select the flow of Project 1. But Table 3.2 reveals another important fact about the functional pattern of growth funds. Applying the relative rate of change tool that was described earlier in the chapter, it is noted first that values in Table 3.2 are growing actually at a *decreasing relative rate*, and the reason for this is that there is no secondary or

TABLE 3.2
RATE OF GROWTH OF TOTAL VALUES
AND OF ADDED VALUES

Period	Total Values	$(\Delta Y/Y)/X$	Relative Growth in Terminal Value	Primary Flow	Secondary Flow $(\Delta Y_r/Y_r)/\Delta X$	Relative Growth in Primary Value
1	5,500	$\frac{500}{5{,}000}/1 =$	0.100	500		
2	6,000	$\frac{500}{5{,}500}/1 =$	.090	1,000	$\frac{0}{500}/1 =$	0
3	6,500	$\frac{500}{6{,}000}/1 =$	.083	1,500	$\frac{0}{500}/1 =$	0
4	7,000	$\frac{500}{6{,}500}/1 =$	.077	2,000	$\frac{0}{500}/1 =$	0
5	7,500	$\frac{500}{7{,}000}/1 =$	.071	2,500	$\frac{0}{500}/1 =$	0

compounding growth. The arithmetic progression of 500 comes up looking quite different from 0.10 when it is tested on an increasing value base. To illustrate let Y_r represent the earnings returned on the original 5,000 and ΔY_r the growth each period. The relative growth of column 4 shows a declining rate of growth on a cumulative base, and the last column shows that the secondary growth from the primary flow is zero for each period because the primary flow is not reinvested.

RETURNS ARE REINVESTED

Funds are commonly reinvested in new assets rather than being held in idle cash balances as was implied above or distributed to the shareholders, causing a significant internal growth condition. Reinvestment compounds the growth as a secondary flow is generated. This is geometric growth because the rate of change is a *constant relative amount* instead of a constant absolute amount. Table 3.3 shows what happens over five periods to the 500 received at the end of each year.

TABLE 3.3
GROWTH IN TERMINAL VALUES
RETURNS REINVESTED
(INITIAL SUM 5,000)
GROWTH @0.10

Period	1st 500	2nd 500	3rd 500	4th 500	5th 500	Total Returns	Terminal Value	
1	500.0					500	5,500	(5,000 + 500)
2	550.0	500				1,050	6,050	(5,000 + 1,050)
3	605.0	550	500			1,655	6,655	(5,000 + 1,655)
4	665.5	605	550	500		2,320.50	7,320.50	(5,000 + 2,320.5)
5	732.1	665.5	605	550	500	3,052.60	8,052.60	(5,000 + 3,052.60)

Cumulative returns	3,052
Initial fund	5,000
Terminal value	8,052

The total returns column shows the annual and the total growth of what is earned on the original sum of 5,000 over five periods at 0.10. The terminal value column at the extreme right sums each row and adds the initial 5,000 for a terminal value. Compare this figure 8,052 with the 7,500 when funds are not reinvested, and you have the compounding principle applied to a five-year flow reduced to its simplest arithmetic terms.

Table 3.3, like Table 3.1, is an explanatory tool but now that we understand the underlying arithmetic we can use a more direct way of projecting terminal values. The formula for this puts the n value outside the parentheses performing an exponential or *power* function.

$$\text{Terminal Value} = P(1 + r)^n$$

Where: $P =$ Initial value
$r =$ Rate of growth
$n =$ Number of periods of expected growth

The tool can be used for projecting sums to any given terminal date. Returning to the original example, assume that we are expecting a constant return of 0.10 on an initial sum of 5,000. Substituting in the formula:

$$\text{Terminal Value} = 5,000(1 + 0.10)^5$$
$$= 5,000(1.61051)$$
$$= 8,052$$

Compound interest tables are available with the work done for us in the $(1 + r)^n$ department for many r values and many n values. With these values available we need only multiply the *table factor* by the amount of initial capital to determine the end value of any given present sum. It may help to think of the table factor as the *multiplier* for determining such future value. Illustrated below are two flows illustrating the growth effect of different r values. The multipliers are compound growth factors one at 0.10 and another at 0.12. Projects 1 and 2 are being compared for terminal values assuming reinvestment of current inflows of funds; the choice would be with Project 2 as it was in the earlier example, but the choice is more decisive in this case than in the former because of the geometric growth factor.

$$\text{Project 1. Terminal Value} = 5,000(1 + 0.10)^6$$
$$= 5,000(1.7716)$$
$$= 8,858$$

$$\text{Project 2. Terminal Value} = 5,000(1 + 0.12)^6$$
$$= 5,000(1.9738)$$
$$= 9,869$$

$$\text{Difference} = 1,011(9,869 - 8,858)$$

Table 3.4 is a summary table for illustrating the constant relative growth rate situation when returns are reinvested at $r = 0.10$. This table should be compared with Table 3.2. Table 3.4 shows that when the return on an investment is reinvested at a given rate *this rate identifies the constant relative rate of growth*. The table shows that reinvestment of primary flows causes total terminal values and also the secondary flows from capital investments to increase at a constant rate of 0.10. A great deal of attention has been given here to rate of growth and to projecting terminal values given the growth rates, but this is the foundation to a sound understanding of the basic premises for capital analysis and decision making. The immediate value of the analysis is that it will help us to understand better the

TABLE 3.4
RATE OF GROWTH OF
TERMINAL AND CURRENT INFLOWS

Period	$(\Delta Y/Y)/\Delta X$	Rate of Growth	Period Inflows	$(\Delta Y_r/Y_r)/\Delta X$	Rate of Growth
1	$\frac{500}{5,000}/1 =$	0.10	500		
2	$\frac{550}{5,500}/1 =$	0.10	550	$\frac{50}{500}/1 =$	0.10
3	$\frac{605}{6,050}/1 =$	0.10	605	$\frac{55}{550}/1 =$	0.10
4	$\frac{665}{6,655}/1 =$	0.10	665	$\frac{60}{605}/1 =$	0.10
5	$\frac{732}{7,321}/1 =$	0.10	732	$\frac{67}{665}/1 =$	0.10

explanation and illustrations in the following section dealing with discounting future values to the present.

DISCOUNTING FUTURE VALUES

It goes without saying that in this area of management where the goal of maximizing present share value is clearly spelled out for us, the discounting tool and technique needs to be examined closely for its internal as well as for its external effects. We will be concerned here with general characteristics of the discounting tool and its relation to the conversion of future values to present values, although applications of the tool to specific investment issues are reserved for later chapters. From the methodological viewpoint, expected flows of funds are more tangible for decision making when they are expressed in today's values than when they are expressed in future values; this is true because financial managers as well as share evaluators need to continually offset market prices of capital assets against the present values of the funds expected to be generated by those assets.

The tool for projecting present values to the future has been examined, and now we need a means of bringing future values back to the present; this we call the *discounting tool*. In a single statement, the most important service performed by this tool is to remove the power function, the geometric growth factor, by carrying the operation to the $-n$ power in the following manner.

$$V_p = P(1 + r)^{-n} \qquad 3.2$$

Where: $V_p =$ Present Value
$P =$ Returns expected at some future date
$r =$ Discounting rate
$-n =$ Removal of waiting time

Since $(1 + r)^{-n} = 1/(1 + r)^n$ we can restate the multiplier function as:

$$V_p = P\frac{1}{(1 + r)^n}$$

Substituting values we can see how the operation works to bring back the terminal value 8,052 of the previous section to its original value of 5,000. First let us determine the multiplier by solving the ratio $1/(1 + r)^n$ where $r = 0.10$ and $n = 5$:

$$\frac{1}{(1 + 0.10)^5} = 0.6209$$

The value 0.6209 is the present value of 1 at the end of the fifth period when the discounting rate is 0.10. One simple multiplication by 0.6209 will bring back to the present 8,052:

$$V_p = \frac{1}{(1 + 0.10)^5}$$
$$= 8,052(0.6209)$$
$$= 5,000$$

The five-period compound growth effect is removed and 5,000 is returned to its original state. But the multiplier $1/(1 + r)^n$ is not reserved for this one future value; any future value or values can be brought back in this manner. To illustrate this the following are expected values selected arbitrarily to illustrate the effect of the size of the future value on present value. The multiplier is the same in each case; future values are labeled X and present values Y to emphasize the functional relationship, other factors being the same, between the size of the future values and the size of the present values.

TABLE 3.5
FUTURE VALUES DISCOUNTED TO PRESENT

X Future Values		Multiplier $1/(1 + 0.10)^5$		Y Present Values
3,000	×	0.6209	=	1,863
4,000	×	0.6209	=	2,484
5,000	×	0.6209	=	3,105
6,000	×	0.6209	=	3,725

Figure 3.1 is a graph of the functional relationship between present values on Y and the expected future values on X using the same multiplier (0.6209) for each value. With this tool financial managers and investment managers in the securities market can convert any future X value into present values. Table 1 in the appendix of the book has worked out for us a large number of multipliers for bringing

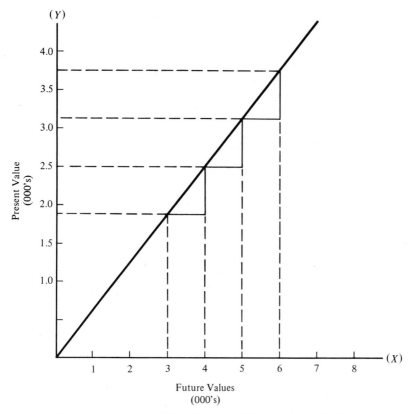

Figure 3.1. Present Value Function Discounting at 0.10 for
Five Periods.

future values back to the present, thus saving us the arithmetic that was done
above.

DISCOUNTING A FLOW OF FUTURE VALUES

In the illustration above a single future value was discounted to the present,
an important operation when management needs to know what the present value
is of one or more different terminal values as was done in Table 3.5. In many cases,
however, a capital investment, or a share of stock is expected to yield a flow of
income over a series of time periods. In this case it is expedient to assume that the
amount is exactly the same for each period so that a simple discounting operation
can be performed, then minor adjustments can be made in the present value to
allow for variations from the constant periodic flow.

The best way to illustrate the effect is to use the same original data as was used
to bring back a single terminal value of 8,052 to a present value of 5,000. This is

done by splitting the 8,052 into a sum of 5,000, which, let us say, is expected to be returned intact at the end of the fifth period, and a series of five flows of 500 each. Table 3.6 returns each of the flows of 500 to the present by the appropriate multiplier to the end of the fifth period and then sums the present values of 5,000 and of each of the steady periodic flows of 500. The fourth column converts the

TABLE 3.6
DISCOUNTING A FLOW AND
A TERMINAL VALUE

(1)	(2)	(3)	(4)	(5)	(6)
Period	$(1 + R)^{-n} = 1/(1 + R)^n$ = Multiplier			Future Flow	Present Value
1	$(1 + 0.10)^{-1} = \dfrac{1}{(1 + 0.10)}$	= 0.909	$\times$ 500 =		454.5
2	$(1 + 0.10)^{-2} = \dfrac{1}{(1 + 0.10)^2}$	= 0.826	$\times$ 500 =		413.0
3	$(1 + 0.10)^{-3} = \dfrac{1}{(1 + 0.10)^3}$	= 0.751	$\times$ 500 =		375.5
4	$(1 + 0.10)^{-4} = \dfrac{1}{(1 + 0.10)^4}$	= 0.683	$\times$ 500 =		341.5
5	$(1 + 0.10)^{-5} = \dfrac{1}{(1 + 0.10)^5}$	= 0.621	$\times$ 500 =		310.5
		Total	3.790	Total	1,895.0

Present value of $500 flow = 1,895
Present value of 5,000 (0.621 × 5,000) terminal value = 3,105
Present value of the sums = 5,000

third to a series of declining multipliers. The fifth is the series of expected returns of 500 each, and the last column shows the decreasing present values of 500 as they extend further into the future. Table 3.6 explains the returning of a constant flow of values to the present given a five-year flow and a 10 percent discounting rate; but notice that the same result is obtained by one act of multiplication: 3.790 × 500 = 1,895. Table 2 in the appendix has worked out for us the multipliers for numerous rates and periods so that we do not need to do the work of column 4.

THE DISCOUNTING RATE

Thus far nothing has been said about the importance of the discounting rate itself in present value calculations. While the subject of the discount rate will be considered again in later chapters, its quantitative significance needs to be examined here. The discounting rate determines how large the multiplier will be for any given period; the larger the rate r in the ratio $1/(1 + 0.r)^n$, the smaller will be the multiplier and, consequently, the smaller will be the product of the multiplication, namely the present value. The *r* value represents the rate at which, over a given time, future value will be reversed to derive a present value; and the higher this *reversal rate* the lower will have to be the present value. The effect of a rising discount rate on a constant value at the end of the fifth period is illustrated in Table 3.7 and in Figure 3.2.

TABLE 3.7
PRESENT VALUE AND
CHANGING DISCOUNTING RATES

Discount Rate	Conversion Rate	Multiplier $1/(1 + r)^n$	Future Value	Present Value
0.06	$\dfrac{1}{(1 + 0.06)^5}$	0.747	500	374
0.08	$\dfrac{1}{(1 + 0.08)^5}$	0.681	500	341
0.10	$\dfrac{1}{(1 + 0.10)^5}$	0.621	500	311
0.12	$\dfrac{1}{(1 + 0.12)^5}$	0.567	500	284

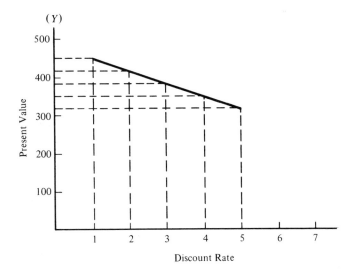

Figure 3.2. Rising Discount Rate and Declining Present Values of 500.

Figure 3.2 brings 500 back from the fifth period at rising discount rates. Notice that the present value function graphs a curved negative sloping line decreasing at a decreasing rate but never reaching zero because regardless of how large the discounting rate is, future values will have some present value. Management has complete control over what rate will be used to bring back future values. Financial managers cannot dictate the rate for investors to use in discounting expected net profits for present share values, but indirectly they can lower this rate in the securities market by reducing the evaluator's expectation of risk incumbent in owning the company's shares. In working to close the gap between internal and external decision making, financial managers should reason that since low rates used in the securities markets will produce high present values for the firm's shares the kind of decisions should be made that will induce the securities market to discount the firm's expected profit flow at lower discount rates. One noteworthy difference exists, however, between the way that financial managers evaluate internal projects and the way investors evaluate expected net profits on shares. This difference is that financial managers usually deal with projects that have definite maturity dates, but net profit flows expected on shares are sometimes assumed to be perpetual. An expected perpetual flow can be discounted in one simple operation $V_p = E_e/r$. Substituting \$5.00 expected earnings per share for E_e and 0.10 for the discounting rate, the present value of the share becomes \$50.00 (\$5.00/0.10 = \$50.00).

But returning to the internal use of the rate, financial managers have to decide on how large this rate should be for each project with an expected long-term flow of funds. The same rate may be used to discount all projects; or fund flows may be discounted by variable rates depending on the certainty with which future flows can be projected. A flow of funds that is difficult to estimate may be discounted by a larger rate than a flow that can be predicted with a high degree of certainty. The riskiness of the former is reflected in a lower present value consequently than the latter.

RISK MANAGEMENT TOOLS

Risk, acknowledges a condition of less than perfect knowledge on the part of management attempting to forecast inflows and outflows of funds. Acknowledging this limitation on forecasting future flows is no complete solution, but in just acknowledging this human shortcoming, management is making important strides forward. We develop the probability tool for two purposes here: first, as a tool for assigning quantitative degrees of certainty with which an event may occur and, second, as a tool for computing expected values. The probability tool is no cure-all to the inevitably present risk factor in financial analysis and planning but does present us with a framework of quantitative values for more precise planning. Also, there are different degrees of effectiveness in probability analysis, depending on how skillful financial managers become in evaluating and applying the tools and in interpreting the results of using the tools. For the sake of clarity in discussion, probabilities are divided into subjective and statistical.

SUBJECTIVE PROBABILITIES

Events such as the demand for a product or service, volume of sales, delivery dates on inventories, and inflows of cash are all practically impossible to predict with certainty. The reason for this is that there is more than one possible occurrence for each of these events. Wherever there is more than one possible occurrence we can subjectively assign probabilities to these occurrences; they are *subjective* probabilities because their quantitative values reflect the judgment in the final analysis of some person or persons. In the section on statistical probabilities we will see how probabilities are assigned mechanically according to a mathematical law.

The number of possible occurrences varies with the kinds of events. Some events have fewer possibilities than others, but in any case we start by arranging the possibilities in a series ranging from the small to the large figure assigning to each possible event a probability of occurrence such that the sum of the probabilities equals 1. The combination of possibilities and their probability assignments together comprise a *probability distribution*. The probability distribution is a tool in which the manager makes his best subjective estimate of the probability of occurrence of each of a series of possible future events. Subjective probabilities may be based on past experience, research, and judgment; but it is still subjective because some person finally decides on the quantitative values of these probabilities.

Table 3.8 is a probability distribution of given terminal values occurring at the end of the fifth period. Instead of projecting a compounded growth value of exactly 8,052 as was done in the capital growth example of Table 3.3, assume that based on past experience and research financial managers expect value ranges somewhere between 7,000 and 10,000 with probabilities as indicated in the table.

TABLE 3.8
PROBABILITY DISTRIBUTION OF VALUES
OCCURRING AT THE END OF PERIOD 5

Possible Values	Probabilities	Expected Values
7,000	0.2	1,400
8,000	0.3	2,400
9,000	0.4	3,600
10,000	0.1	1,000
	1.00	8,400

Column one indicates the range of *possible* values. If we have the range of possible values, that is the smallest and the largest value in a series, the values lying between these two extremes may be selected at random; thus, the column of possible values are sometimes called *random variables*. Column two is the assignment of probabilities that certain possible values will occur; column three is the product of column one and two and is called *expected values*. The sum of expected values (8,400) is the average value, assuming a very large number of actual experiences. The sum of the expected values is the same as the *weighted average* of these values, a term which may be more familiar to the student than expected value. Table 3.9 is just another form of the probability distribution, and we call it a weighted average

TABLE 3.9
WEIGHTED AVERAGE VALUE

(1)		*(2)*	
Possible Values		*Weights*	*(1) × (2)*
7,000	×	2	14,000
8,000	×	3	24,000
9,000	×	4	36,000
10,000	×	1	10,000
		10	

$$\text{Weighted average} = \frac{84,000}{10} = 8,400$$

to remove some of the doubt that the student may have about the former. Finally given the probable terminal value let us convert this as follows at a 10 percent discount rate to a present value:

$$V_p = \frac{1}{(1 + 0.10)^5} \times 8,400$$

$$= 0.621(8,400)$$

$$= 5,216$$

STATISTICAL PROBABILITIES

Statistical probabilities are limited here to a widely used but small segment of the subject called the *normal distribution curve*. The normal distribution tool is not a substitute for the subjective probability distribution, but instead is complementary. For example, *where subjective probabilities are used to determine expected values, the normal curve is used to determine probabilities of given occurring values.*

To use this tool logically an implicit assumption is made that if a much larger number of values than the four in Table 3.7 were included in the series of X variables, the frequency with which the values would occur would form a bell-shaped normal distribution curve. The normal curve is symmetrical, its highest point representing the *arithmetic mean* or weighted average of all possible values. This mean value is the midpoint of the series on the X axis. It is also the modal value, meaning that it is the value that would occur with the greatest frequency. The space under the curve represents all probability distributions with respect to the series of values on the X axis, but it tells us something much more definite than this. Since the curve is symmetrical, 0.50 of the space lies on the left side and 0.50 on the right side of the median line, which means that the values on the X axis have a 0.50 chance of being less than the arithmetic mean and 0.50 chance of being greater than the mean. This is an example of the broadest possible application of a curve as an aid to forecasting X values.

But the range of values for determining probabilities can be narrowed more than to a 50-50 basis. To illustrate this let us consider Figure 3.3, a normal

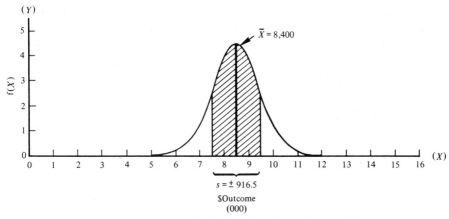

Figure 3.3. Normal Distribution of Possible Values.

distribution based on the weighted values of Table 3.9, where the weights 2, 3, 4, 1 are frequencies of occurrences. Let the weighted average of 8,400 then be the arithmetic mean of Figure 3.3.[1] The reason that the normal curve is so elongated in this case is that such a large percentage of the frequencies in Table 3.3 are clustered around the mean; notice that 7/10 or 70 percent of the frequencies (weights) are X values of 8,000 and 9,000 which are right at the mean. A different distribution of weights like 2, 3, 3, 2 would spread out the curve making it more typically bell-shaped, but it would not shorten the curve. The standard deviation for a frequency distribution like this can be solved in several ways, but the following formula probably offers the most direct solution:

$$s = \sqrt{\frac{\Sigma f(X - \bar{X})^2}{n}}$$ 3.3

f	X	$(X - \bar{X})$	$(X - \bar{X})^2$	$f(X - \bar{X})^2$
2	7,000	−1,400	1,960,000	3,920,000
3	8,000	− 400	160,000	480,000
4	9,000	+ 600	360,000	1,440,000
1	10,000	+1,600	2,560,000	2,560,000
10			$f(X - \bar{X})^2 =$	8,400,000

$$s = \sqrt{\frac{8,400,000}{10}}$$

$$s = \sqrt{840,000}$$

$$s = 916.50$$

[1] To plot this curve ordinates Y of the standard normal curve at z were used: $z = (X - \bar{X})/\sigma$ where X = independent variables 7,000, 8,000, 9,000, and 10,000. $\bar{X}$ = arithmetic mean of 8,400 and σ = the standard deviation.

The shaded portion of the curve marks off the symmetrical area on both sides of the mean corresponding to the dispersion of 916.50 to the left and 916.50 to the right of the mean. Rounding the value slightly, the sum of this area under the curve to the left and to the right of the mean comprises 68 percent of the total area under the curve. We will recall from an earlier statement that the area under the curve represents frequencies of occurrences or probabilities that given X values will occur. Now applying this percentage coverage to the actual case, there is a 0.68 probability that the value, income or whatever it may represent, will fluctuate between 7,483.50 (8,400 − 916.50) and 9,316.50 (8,400 + 916.50). There is a 0.34 probability that it will be below the mean fluctuating between 7,483.50 and 8,400 and also a 0.34 probability that the value will be greater than the mean and fluctuate between 8,400 and 9,316.50. Table 3 in the Appendix is a z table called Areas under the Standard Normal Curve from 0 to z.[2] The first column of the table contains z values which represent distances to the right of the mean stated in standard deviations. The other columns of the table are probabilities of events occurring to the right of the mean. For example suppose we would like to know what probability there is of the value fluctuating 0.20 standard deviation or 183.30 (0.2 × 916.50) above the mean to 8,583.30 (8,400 + 183.30). The table states that there is a 0.08 probability of this; and if we wish to extend this to both sides of the mean, it is simply doubled to probability 0.16.

Standard deviations are stated, as has been seen, in absolute values which make it practically impossible to compare riskiness of projects with competing income or net-profit flows. But a solution to this is found in the *risk relationship*. The formula for this is:

$$R_r = \frac{s}{\bar{X}} \qquad\qquad 3.4$$

Where: s = Standard deviation
$\bar{X}$ = Arithmetic mean

This is a relative measure of dispersion and, therefore, can be used to compare competing projects regardless of their relative size. Substituting the values above in the formula:

$$R_r = \frac{916.50}{8,400}$$

$$= 0.11 \text{ or } 11 \text{ percent}$$

Any project with a larger ratio signifies greater relative fluctuation about the mean and a more risky project for planning, and any project with a smaller ratio signifies less relative fluctuation about the mean and a less risky project for planning.

[2] Murray R. Spiegel, THEORY AND PROBLEMS (New York: McGraw-Hill Book Company, 1968), p. 343. Used with permission of McGraw-Hill Book Company.

SUMMARY

Part II is an important departure from the content of Part I. The first of three chapters dealing with quantitative tools deals with arithmetic tools and skills that are specifically related to financial issues. To some extent this material may be a review for the student, but in most instances because of the application to finance the material should be of practical value for dealing with financial management issues. The reader is introduced to the important concept of the rate of change as a relationship between two variables: one, the independent variable called X and, two, the dependent variable called Y. From the basic rate of change concept we move to the relative rate of change and to basic growth concepts. Much financial information is revealed in dollar values that needs to be converted to rates of change and to relative rates of change to obtain the maximum value from financial experiences for analysis and decision making.

The growth concept in financial analysis is considered; the concept of growth as it applies internally to financial managers and as it applies to the external market for the company's securities. The growth situation is considered from two points of view: one, where the returns from the growth of an asset are not reinvested; and two, where the growth of an asset is reinvested to contribute to further growth. The latter is identified with a common term called *compound interest* and will play an important part particularly in later chapters in which capital management is considered. Discounting operations reverse the growth of assets and convert them to *present values*. This is our application of the basic annuity principle to financial analysis and planning. In this chapter we are also introduced to the concept of risk as it applies to financial analysis. More specifically, we are introduced to probabilities as quantitative risk measures. Considered are *subjective* probabilities and *statistical* probabilities. The technique of computing a degree of variation around an arithmetic mean is illustrated with the standard deviation. The normal distribution curve is introduced as a medium for estimating probability distributions. The reader is informed also of an important table called the Z Table in the Appendix which will be referred to on other occassions when probability measures are sought.

PROBLEMS

1. A relationship remains the same if a relative increase or decrease in one of the numbers is attended by a relative increase or decrease in the other of the same amount.

   a. Beginning with 0.50/1.5 increase the numerator to 0.55. What must the denominator become to maintain the same relationship?
   b. Of the following relationships, three have been increased in the numera-

tor and denominator by the same relative amount. What is the relative value of the increase, and which of the relationships is not maintained?

(1) $\dfrac{0.64}{0.76}$ to $\dfrac{0.80}{0.95}$ (3) $\dfrac{0.72}{0.84}$ to $\dfrac{0.90}{1.12}$

(2) $\dfrac{0.52}{0.68}$ to $\dfrac{0.65}{0.85}$ (4) $\dfrac{1.20}{1.60}$ to $\dfrac{1.50}{2.00}$

2. Heidelberg Manufacturing Company seeks to maintain a ratio of 0.25/1 of net profits to units manufactured. If the firm netted $35,000, how many units would have to be manufactured to maintain the ratio? If the firm manufactured 98,000 units, what net profit could be expected?

3. The numerator of the initial terminal ratio of 3,600/4,800 is increased to 4,000, and the denominator is increased to 5,400. At what rate are the terminal values increasing?

4. Shown below are the figures for net profits and units produced by Better-Made Handbag Company.

Month	January	February	March	April	May	June	
Net profits	$4,200	$4,800	$5,100	$5,600	$6,300	$7,000	= $33,000
Units	1,400	1,800	2,000	2,300	3,000	3,200	= 13,700

During the first six months the company realized $33,000 in net profit on 13,700 units. This is the total picture, but for a more detailed picture of the operation, monthly figures must be analyzed.

a. Using $(Y_2 - Y_1)/(X_2 - X_1)$ where Y represents income and X represents units, determine the relationship of changes in the income to changes in units of production. Reduce the denominator in the relationship to 1.

b. During the month of May income was higher than in any of the previous four months. What value to the financial manager are rates of change in analyzing the May figures?

5. Company A is planning a $100,000 investment in fixed and working capital that is expected to grow at a compound rate of 12 percent for four years. What will be the terminal value? Show the work of determining the multiplier as well as the terminal value.

6. What is the present value of $12,000 discounted five years at 6 percent? 12 percent?

7. The financial manager of a small firm expects to realize a future flow of $11,048 after four years. The discounting rate is 8 percent and the funds are reinvested. Extract the time influence on $11,048 by using $P[1/(1 + R)^n]$. Show the work in determining the multiplier.

8. Graph a situation in which alternative future values of the sixth period are discounted at 12 percent. Let the future values on the X axis range from 0

to 10,000 and the present values on the Y axis range from 0 to just as high as is needed to discount future values.

    a. What is the shape of the curve? What distinguishes the curve in your opinion?

    b. What kind of questions will the curve answer?

    c. Compare the curve to a simple factory tool that shapes and forms plain pieces of metal that are inserted into the machine.

    d. Compare the curve to a simple computer program.

9. Graph a situation in which 800 is brought back from the fourth period at alternative discounting rates ranging from 2 percent to 10 percent. Place discount rates on X axis and present values on Y axis.

    a. What is the shape of the curve? How does the curve differ from Figure 3.3 in the text?

    b. What kind of questions will the curve answer?

    c. Compare the total graph structure to a machine with a tool attachment for converting plain corrugated paper materials into finished containers.

    d. Consider the implications of our quantitative tool to computer programming.

10. Subjective probability distributions may be based on past experiences and research. Assume that past experience shows the following results with respect to the frequency with which sales values occur in the third year of operation.

Expected Income	Frequency
16,000	4 times
17,000	1 time
18,000	2 times
19,000	2 times
20,000	1 time

    a. Set up a probability distribution for expected incomes, and compute the *expected values.*

    b. Using a 0.10 discounting rate, determine the present value of the probability distribution.

    c. Figures in the schedule are for just one year. Suppose that the project is expected to produce for a total of three years. How would you determine present values for the first two years?

11. Financial management estimates that the flow of funds on a proposed project for a given year will probably fall somewhere within the distribution of $5,000, $6,000, $7,000, or $8,000.

    a. Compute the average flow and explain what it means.

    b. Determine the standard deviation of the distribution using the formula:

$$s = \sqrt{\frac{\Sigma f(X - \bar{X})^2}{n}}$$

   c. Assuming a normal distribution, what observations can be made about the probability of the flow?

   d. What is the risk relationship for this one period and what does it mean?

12. In a distribution of data the standard deviation is 1,000 units and the mean is 8,000 units. What is the probability of a selected value being between 7,800 and 8,200 units? Using Table 3 in the Appendix indicate the probability that the data will be *greater* than 8,000 units by 0.5 standard deviation, by 1.5 standard deviations. In each of these two cases, what will be the range in the data starting at 8,000 units?

4

Algebraic
Tools
and
Skills

The treatment here will cover the rudiments of algebraic tools that have significance for financial managers. This in effect builds onto arithmetic tools of the previous chapter. The tools introduced here are selected for the same reason as special arithmetic tools were selected, to increase analytic and decision-making skills of financial managers. Algebra offers some more sophisticated tools than arithmetic for searching out financial problem issues, but, mainly, it offers powerful problem-solving tools that help answer questions about cause and effect relationships in basic financial issues. In general, the greatest contribution made by algebraic tools to our study of financial management is that they establish a format or framework for solving many problems in which we have fixed costs and expenses related to the capital constraint, a coefficient like a constant unit price or unit cost or expense, and an independent variable like volume of output or volume of sale. Finally, they are used when we need to solve for the effect of this financial mix-upon a dependent variable like income, costs and expenses, net profit, or net cash flow. The components of these tools and their total frameworks will be put into use in this chapter; so that even though the student has never had a course in algebra, he should be able to understand and to use the tools when he completes the chapter. It should be emphasized, however, that this is not a crash course in basic algebra but instead is very limited and selective in its coverage. Pertinent elements of the subject analyzed are equations, certain kinds of function, and inequalities.

THE EQUATION

The equation is a statement of equality and is used for solving problems with one or more dependent variables. Typically in financial management we deal with situations of two variables, one an independent variable X and the other a dependent variable Y, with one or more fixed factors. If the term *equation* is too abstract for the student, he may reconsider it in terms of a *program* for problem solving or a model into which he may fit relevant values for problem solving. The solution procedure follows certain established rules, but the usefulness of the solution to financial managers depends on first selecting or constructing the form of equation that meets their special need and second entering the correct values into each niche of the equation.

Here is a very simple example of how the equation can meet the problem-solving needs of business. A condition exists in which Y, the dependent variable, plus 10,000 is equal to 60,000. By applying basic algebraic solution rules the unknown X value is determinable. The answer:

$$Y + 10,000 = 60,000 \qquad\qquad 4.1$$

$$Y = 60,000 - 10,000 \quad \text{(Subtract 10,000 from each side)}$$
$$= 50,000$$

$Y = 50,000$ is the solution. Substitute the value for Y in the original equation to prove that the two sides of the equation are equal; if they are equal, it is proof that the correct algebraic procedure has been used and that the result is mathematically correct. The student will recognize that, although the procedure is algebraic, operations of addition and subtraction are arithmetic. Operations on the original equation have answered the question: What is the value of the unknown Y? As a practical example management may ask: With 10,000 assured from one plant operation, how much does the second plant operation have to produce to reach a total 60,000 operating goal? The solution is 50,000 as worked out above. The effectiveness of the equation as an analytic tool depends on whether it is structured to meet the correct kind of financial issue. For example, if the financial issue were one in which after taking 10,000 away from Y we would still have 60,000, then obtaining 50,000 for Y will not realize our goal. The equation below contains the elements of our problem placed in the proper order and represented by the proper signs, and we cannot emphasize too much the importance of proper tool construction before performing designated operations.

$$Y - 10,000 = 60,000 \qquad\qquad 4.2$$

$$Y = 60,000 + 10,000 \quad \text{(Add 10,000 to each side)}$$
$$= 70,000$$

The answer to the question, how large does Y have to be so that with a 10,000 loss we still have remaining 60,000, is that it has to be 70,000 instead of just 50,000 for goal attainment. With this solution worked out precisely, decisive action will be taken by management for goal attainment.

Next, we consider an equation whose basic form implies somewhat more extensive applications between knowns and unknowns and whose solution operations employ also a wider range of problem-solving rules. The equation meets financial management needs only in problems in which final goal attainment is 60,000.

$$2Y + 10,000 = 60,000 \qquad\qquad 4.3$$

$$2Y = 60,000 - 10,000 \quad \text{(Subtract 10,000 from each side)}$$

$$Y = \frac{50,000}{2} \qquad\qquad \text{(Divide both sides by 2)}$$

$$= 25,000$$

In this case 60,000 must be attained after adding 10,000 to some value of Y. This solution tells us how large Y has to be for goal attainment, and the answer in this case is only 25,000. The equation above may be structured to answer the financial question: With 10,000 assured from flow, how much does each of two other identical flows have to produce? In financial applications these numbers take on various identification marks like dollar signs ($) or units of production and sale, but these are omitted intentionally here to concentrate on the problem issue and on the basic algebraic procedure rules. It should be understood, of course, that the numbers used in all three of the examples are hypothetical and that they are not intended in any way to limit the scope of the tool application to more extensive problem situations.

FUNCTIONAL RELATIONSHIPS—EQUALITIES

The concept of a functional relationship was introduced in Chapter 1, but quantitative detail needs to be developed somewhat further at this time. The student will recall the discussion in Chapter 3, also of various arithmetic relationships sometimes called ratios, in which terminal values Y/X and changes in terminal values $\Delta Y/\Delta X$ were compared and even graphed. We return now to basic relationships with two variables X and Y, in which X is independent and Y is dependent. A functional relationship exists when a given change in X produces a definite continuing (functional) pattern of change in Y. For purposes of financial management, functional relationships may be divided into two general classes of *linear* and *nonlinear* relationships between X and Y with the former commanding more attention than the latter.

THE LINEAR FUNCTION

The equation for the basic linear function is:

$$Y = a + bX \qquad\qquad 4.4$$

This is linear because it signifies a constant rate of change in Y, given the change in X. There are two constants in the equation: a and b. The value a is a fixed quantity of Y or what could be called a starting constant value of Y; it is a constant because it does not vary with changes in X. Graphically a is called the Y intercept because it marks the point at which the graph of the equation $Y = a + bX$ intersects the Y axis; it is also the value of Y when $X = 0$. Already we observe the multivaried features of the linear equation coming to the surface as an analytical tool.

The b value is another constant, but it is a *coefficient* of X. It may also be called a multiplier of X because, whatever value of X is used, it must be multiplied by its coefficient b as part of the total function of generating value for Y. Functionally the b value is extremely important because it is the *constant rate of change* by which the function is identified; and, in the graph of the function, b sets the slope of the line. The constancy of b is what makes the equation linear and distinguishes linear from the nonlinear equations; b is a constant rate of change in the linear relationship but is a variable rate of change in a nonlinear relationship. The rate of change is a pacesetter, and its size actually determines how effectively changes in X will function on Y. In the basic equation of the straight line, it is assumed that the rate of change, $\Delta Y/\Delta X = b$ is known, but b could be unknown when the total relationship Y/X is known; in this case b needs to be determined:

$$Y = a + bX$$

$$a + bX = Y \qquad \text{(Transposing)}$$

$$bX = Y - a \quad \text{(Subtracting a from each side)}$$

$$b = \frac{Y - a}{X} \quad \text{(Dividing both sides by X)}$$

To give the solution value of the linear equation meaning, numerical values need to be substituted; but a financial situation should be simulated in advance, so that outcomes can be tested before managers put real dollars into the operation. For example, without taking any decision action let us solve for Y when a is 10,000 and b is 2. The solution equation is stated as $Y = 10,000 + 2(X)$. We have here a tool that will answer an infinite number of questions about the value of Y, given the fixed value of 10,000, the constant coefficient 2, and varying X. For example, what is the value of Y if X is 1,000, 1,500, 1,600?

$$Y = 10,000 + 2(1,000) \qquad Y = 10,000 + 2(1,500) \qquad Y = 10,000 + 2(1,600)$$

$$= 12,000 \qquad\qquad = 13,000 \qquad\qquad = 13,200$$

The value of such simulation lies in telling financial managers what specific contributions to X, whether as a work force, units of output, or units of sale, will produce in total product, total income, or some other medium of financial value.

Finally management may simulate an optimal value of Y. Whether or not financial action is taken will depend on whether the optimal answer will contribute enough directly or indirectly to share values to justify the costs of goal attainment.

In the examples above the rate of change b was assumed to be positive which meets the facts of the case in some instances but not in others. The general form of a negative relationship is stated as:

$$Y = a + (-b)X \qquad\qquad 4.5$$

This equation states that Y is a negative linear function of X; Y changes negatively by a constant amount given the increase in X. An important financial fact is that the total value of Y becomes smaller as the total value of X increases as is shown in Table 4.1:

TABLE 4.1
SCHEDULE OF DECLINING Y VALUES

Y	$=$	a	$+$	$(-b)X$
8,000	$=$	10,000	$+$	$-2(1,000)$
6,000	$=$	10,000	$+$	$-2(2,000)$
4,000	$=$	10,000	$+$	$-2(3,000)$
2,000	$=$	10,000	$+$	$-2(4,000)$
0	$=$	10,000	$+$	$-2(5,000)$

We can solve for b when it is negative just as we can when it is positive by solving the following equation. Assume that Y and a are known at any given level of X, say at 1,000 units, then solving for b:

$$
\begin{aligned}
b &= \frac{Y - a}{X} \\
&= \frac{8,000 - 10,000}{1,000} \\
&= -2 \qquad\qquad 4.6
\end{aligned}
$$

The student should verify that the negative rate of change for b is constant at every level of X and that the selection of 1,000 units above was a random selection. It is important for us to know by how much unit income or profit will increase $(+b)$ for every given input (X) of production and sale, but it is also important to know how much unit costs and expenses will decrease $(-b)$ for every given input (X) of capital. Financial managers need to watch closely both plus and minus rates of change (b) because it is here in the delta (Δ) region that total Y values are determined, a large positive b value causing Y to grow rapidly and a large negative b value causing Y to decline rapidly with a given increase in X.

The linear graph is a solution tool that has certain advantages for analysis and decision making over the equation. The equation of a straight line is $Y = a + bX$ in which, as mentioned earlier, a is the point of intercept on the Y axis and b is the constant slope of the curve. The degree of the slope is determined by the size of b and, of course, conditions the quantitative values that the Y axis will supply to questions coming from the X axis. In considering the first linear graph assume that $a = 0$, so that the full impact of the X functional relationship will be apparent. If $a = 0$ the graph will start at the origin where X and Y intersect and both equal 0. With the graph starting at 0, any X value can be selected to determine the second point for the line. Let us use $X = 200$, then $Y = 0 + 2(200)$ or 400 for the second point. Where the perpendicular lines to $X = 200$ and $Y = 400$ intersect is the coordinate for the second point. All of the coordinates of X and Y fall on the straight line which is the function of the equation. To check the statement that all coordinates fall on the straight line, several different values of X may be inserted in the equation and plotted on the graph.

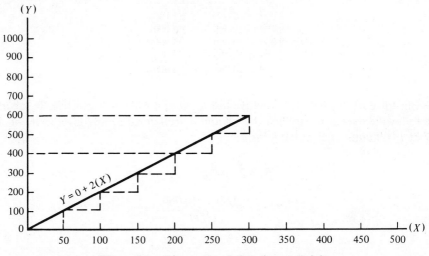

Figure 4.1.   Linear Graph Starting at Origin.

If management has established that $(\Delta y/\Delta x) = (2/1)$ sets the pattern of change in the functional relationship then the particular linear function holds the quantitative answers to an infinite number of X questions. A pertinent question at this stage is: Just how far can Y values be safely projected with the graph? The answer lies in the kinds of financial constraints that limit the expansion of the set function. In Chapter 6 the first practical effect will be seen of placing constraints on X. Figure 4.2 shows what happens when $a = 300$. The line has exactly the same slope as the line in Figure 4.1 except that it is shifted to the left; if the two lines were on

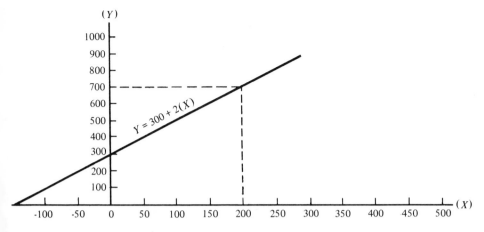

Figure 4.2. Linear Graph, Origin 300 on *Y*.

the same diagram, they would be parallel because their *b* values are the same. The equation for the new line is $Y = 300 + 2(X)$. The slope of the curve is unchanged at $(\Delta y/\Delta x) = (2/1)$. The second coordinate for drawing the straight line is found by substituting the random value $X = 200$, then $Y = 300 + 2(200) = 700$. The slope may appear to be different for Figures 4.1 and 4.2, but that is because the latter had a head start on *Y*. The slopes of the lines can be proven to be the same by showing that the angles formed where the two lines intersect *X* are the same.

Negative *X* values to the left of the origin show that *Y* is linearly related to $-X$ values. The rate of change is the same on the left as on the right of the right side of the *Y* ordinate, but $-X$ values on the left side reverse the process of the right side. As $-X$ values get larger, *Y* values decline; and as $-X$ values get smaller, *Y* values increase. Situations like this are rare in financial management but are conceivable. For example, if *a* represents a fixed sum of cash that came from some source other than net profits, which let us say are on the *X* axis, and if the distance to the left of *O* on the *X* axis represents net losses from operations, as net losses increase cash balances *Y* continue to decrease at a constant rate of 2 units of the initial cash balance for every unit of loss from operations. This is quite different from the equation:

$$Y = -a + bX \qquad \qquad 4.7$$

This starts with a negative value of *Y* which decreases as *X* increases and may be quantified as follows:

$$Y = -300 + 2(X)$$

An example of this could be a cash debt of 300 $(-Y)$ at the start which is reduced by 2 every time *X* increases 1 unit until *X* reaches 150 units after which cash will

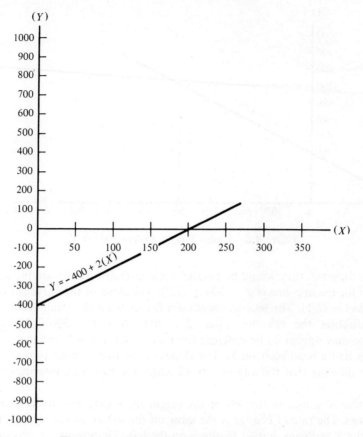

Figure 4.3.   Linear Graph, Origin −300 on Y.

increase positively. Let $Y = 0$ in the equation above and solve for X to get 150 units. The student should verify that the slope is not changed from the slopes of the lines in Figures 4.1 and 4.2, although the line originates in the negative zone of Y.

The equation $Y = a + (-b)X$ is a function in which Y changes at a constant negative rate of 2 for an increase of every unit of X and graphs a declining straight line starting at the upper left of the quadrant and falling off at a constant rate of change $(\Delta Y / \Delta X) = (-2/1)$. Construction of the graph is simple with the given value for a of 1,000. To get the second point for the straight line, solve the equation $Y = 1,000 + -2(X)$, selecting any number at random for X. Letting $X = 200$:

$$Y = 1,000 + -2(X)$$
$$= 600$$

Draw a line perpendicular to 200 on the X axis and perpendicular to 600 on the

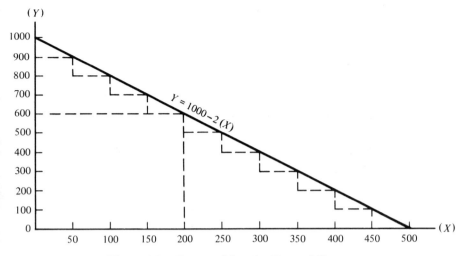

Figure 4.4. Constant Negative Rate of Change.

Y axis; the intersection of these two lines is the second coordinate. Figure 4.4 indicates a negative functional relationship between *X* and *Y* starting at $Y = 1,000$ when $X = 0$. The function defines a situation in which everytime *X* is increased by 50 units *Y* drops by 100 and anytime that *X* is decreased by 50 units *Y* increases by 100. The vertical distance of the dashed lines is the same for every change on the *X* axis, indicating a constant rate. Finally, the 1,000 units of value are dissipated to $Y = 0$, and they would have become negative values on *Y* if the movement had continued out on the *X* axis. Financial managers need to identify the graph with specific problem areas in which the quantity of any current or fixed asset from cash to plant and equipment are dissipated at a constant rate or in which net profits fade away at a constant rate until their value is zero. This function is graphed in Figure 4.4.

SIMULTANEOUS LINEAR EQUATIONS

Any two or more equations that have one set of *X* and *Y* values that satisfy both equations are called simultaneous equations. They are also equations whose graphs cross at only one point, thus identifying graphically the *X* and *Y* values that are common to both equations. Financial managers often need to know the common values of *X* and *Y* that satisfy two linear equations like the sales equation and the cost and expense equation; these may be critical planning points for increasing net profits. Given two financial relationships like the income function and the cost and expense function, each with different rates of change, we may be concerned with the point precisely at which one of these expansion functions overtakes the other. Let us take the two equations $Y = 200 + 2(X)$ and $Y = 0 + 4(X)$ and solve for the only set of *X* and *Y* values that will satisfy both equations simultaneously. The student should be able to follow the logic of the following solution:

$$\text{Since:} \qquad Y = 200 + 2(X)$$

$$\text{And:} \qquad Y = 0 + 4(X)$$

$$\text{Then:} \quad 200 + 2(X) = 0 + 4(X) \text{ at their intersection}$$

$$-2X = -200$$

$$X = 100$$

Now solve for Y by substituting 100 for X in either one of the original equations. Since the second is the simpler of the two, substitute 100 for X in that equation.

$$Y = 0 + 4(X)$$
$$= 4(100)$$
$$= 400$$

To prove that 100 of X and 400 of Y are the correct answers that satisfy both equations simultaneously, substitute them in the original equations as is done below. In step 3, two equations that are equal to the same value (400) at a given point are equal at that point to each other.

$$(1) \quad 400 = 200 + 2(100)$$

$$(2) \quad 400 = 4(100)$$

$$(3) \quad 200 + 2(100) = 4(100)$$

Graphing Simultaneous Equations   The forcefulness of simultaneous equations as tools for analysis becomes even more apparent in graphic form. The values of X and Y that equate both equations at one point can be solved graphically as well as algebraically. It was pointed out earlier that as long as the slope b of two curves is the same the lines will never intersect regardless of their a values. The graphic effect of different b values is, however, that at some level of X they must intersect. The effect of this is shown in Figure 4.5. When two functions flow in the same direction but at different rates, the critical question is: When will the flow at the faster rate overtake the flow at the slower rate? The answer to the question in this case is: When X reaches the level of 100 and Y reaches the level of 400. The graphic tool has the advantage of showing clearly where the two functions intersect and also has the advantage of indicating an infinite number of functional relationships between X and Y above and below the intersection point.

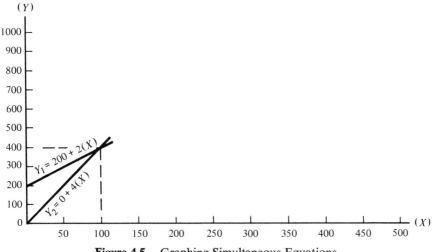

Figure 4.5.   Graphing Simultaneous Equations.

FUNCTIONAL RELATIONSHIPS—INEQUALITIES

In linear relationships, it is a simple matter to solve for Y when X is known, but in the real world X frequently cannot be determined with certainty. In such cases, management has to make decisions based on Y falling within a certain range of X values. Symbols of this language are:

Greater than	$>$
Less than	$<$
Equal to or greater than	$\geq$
Equal to or less than	$\leq$

Let us use inequalities first to define the size of X and then to define Y. The value $X > 400$ means that the X value is greater than 400, which could be an infinitely large value; the only thing we know is that the value is not equal to or smaller than 400. The range is slightly more precise in the expression $X \geq 400$ because this means that X could be exactly 400. Let us limit the range of X even further as follows:

$$500 \geq X \geq 400 \qquad\qquad 4.8$$

This means that X is somewhere *between* 400 at the minimum and 500 at the maximum but can be either one. If we know the b value in this case, we can experiment with different values of X that are realistic to determine possible Y values. Another likely limitation is illustrated below where $X \geq 0$. For example, X could be equal to or greater than 0 but less than 400 stated as follows:

$$0 \leq X \leq 400 \qquad\qquad 4.9$$

Here X has a value of at least 0, but not larger than 400, which makes Y the function of any one of these values of X multiplied by the constant rate of change b.

How and where does the concept of inequality, limits, and range of values fit into financial analysis? First it forces financial managers to realize that functional relationships cannot all be solved as equalities with equations. Second it presents him with a range of functional values that with experience can be narrowed down until solutions to linear problems become more and more accurate. To illustrate, assume that values are given for a range of relationships between X and Y in which a is 0 and b is 2. The solution statement for Y is a range of values somewhere between 0 and 800 expressed as follows:

$$Y = 2(X)$$

Where: $$0 \leq X \leq 400 \qquad\qquad 4.10$$

$$0 \leq Y \leq 800$$

Notice a constant rate of change in Y at the rate of $b = 2$ for the full range 0 $\longrightarrow$ 400. Management now has the basis for decision making: the decision is concerned with whether to act or not to act knowing that Y will be a function of X values ranging from 0 $\longrightarrow$ 800. If this range is too broad for action, management has to narrow it by controlling X; or, if X cannot be *restricted* to a smaller range, then possibly b can be changed. The flow of value is maximized at the outer limit where 400 units are sold to create an inflow of 800 units of Y.

The third and most important use for the inequality perhaps is in the profit optimizing situation that will be explained in some detail in Chapter 7. Here, though, we can introduce the dual product concept of profit optimization. Products X_1 and X_2 share jointly in utilizing a fixed quantity of capital. Two products instead of one bid for a share of the capital at different linear rates until an optimal joint use is determined. We will not solve for the optimal capital use here but will merely introduce the basic quantitative elements for analysis. Assume that 600 units of capital resources are available and that X_1 uses capital at the rate of 2 units for 1 unit of finished product and that X_2 uses capital at the rate of 4 units for 1 unit of finished product. The use rate of capital resource then becomes the rate of change in the linear inequality that may be stated as: $b_1(X_1) + b_2(X_2)$. Substituting for b we have:

$$2(X_1) + 4(X_2) \leq 600 \qquad\qquad 4.11$$

This indicates that X_2 is using capital twice as fast as X_1: so that, if all 600 units of capital were used to produce X_2, only half the number of units of X_2 could be produced as could be produced if all 600 units were devoted to producing X_1.

To graph the inequality, assume first that the two products together always fully use the capital resource; this condition is stated as an equality:

$$2(X_1) + 4(X_2) = 600 \qquad\qquad 4.12$$

By setting X_1 and X_2 alternatively equal to 0, the extremities are set for the linear joint output.

$$2X_1 + 4(0) = 600$$

$$2X_1 = 600$$

$$X_1 = 300$$

$$2(0) + 4X_2 = 600$$

$$4X_2 = 600$$

$$X_2 = 150$$

What we have now are limiting points on the two axis of the graph, one at which $X_2 = 0$ and $X_1 = 300$ and the other at which $X_1 = 0$ and $X_2 = 150$. Connecting the outer limits of these two lines produces a straight line graph of the inequality $2(X_1) + 4(X_2) \leq 600$, indicating the linear relationship between X_1 and X_2 with respect to maximum total capital use of 600. The arrows on the graph indicate that the business can produce anywhere within the constraint of 600 units of capital. The optimizing decision requires that assumptions be made about the unit profit earned by each product; but, since this is not a profit optimizing project, we will not consider that subject now.

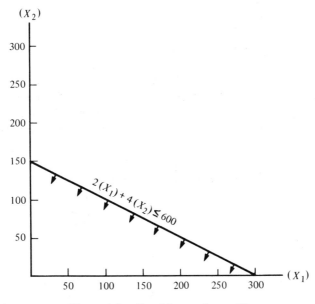

Figure 4.6. Graphing an Inequality.

NONLINEAR FUNCTIONS

A common criticism is that practical financial relations are more often non-linear than they are linear. This may be true, but it is just as dangerous to say that financial relations conform to specific nonlinear patterns as to say that they are linear. In general, this writer believes that, from the analytical viewpoint, it is better to use the linear function as the basic function and then modify this when it is needed to meet the facts of a given case. Nevertheless, we need to examine some of the nonlinear tools to appreciate what is meant when certain financial relationships are said to have nonlinear implications. In concluding this introductory statement, it should be noted that a nonlinear function means simply that the coefficient of X, b in the linear case, is not a constant; that is, $\Delta Y/\Delta X \neq k$, where k represents a constant. Putting it still another way, given the change in X the responding change in Y will be variable. There are numerous nonlinear functional relationships between X and Y, but we will consider here only two of these that have special meaning for us. One the exponential function and the other the parabolic function.

THE EXPONENTIAL FUNCTION

In the exponential function, Y is a function of X as the exponent of a constant and may be stated as:

$$Y = a^X \qquad\qquad 4.13$$

Where: $Y =$ Total value
$a =$ A constant
$X =$ The power function

The rate of change in this case in Y is variable. To illustrate let $a = 2$ and raise X by 1 unit in each equation: $Y = (2)^4 = 16$; $Y = (2)^5 = 32$; and $Y = (2)^6 = 64$. The change in Y grows geometrically rather than arithmetically as b does in the linear function. Table 4.2 illustrates the rate of growth exponential. To determine

TABLE 4.2
EXPONENTIAL RATES OF CHANGE

Base Value	Exponential Value	Y Value	Rate of Change $\Delta Y/\Delta X$	Relative Rate of Change $(\Delta Y/Y)/X$
4	0	1		
4	1	4	3/1	3/1
4	2	16	12/1	12/4
4	3	64	48/1	48/16
4	4	256	192/1	192/64

the relative rate of growth in any such case subtract 1 from the constant value of *a*. The logarithm of a number is the exponent of a base value of that number. The reverse of this is also true; the antilogarithm is the number to which a base value is raised by its logarithm; in the example above, given the base 4, the antilogarithm of 3 is given as 64, and the antilogarithm of 4 is given as 256. The effect of the exponential function is graphed in Figure 4.7; the value of *Y* plots a concave line on arithmetic paper, showing the rapidly increasing arithmetic rate of change, and a straight line on ratio or semilogarithm paper, illustrating the constant relative rate of change. The two graphs show more clearly perhaps than words can describe the true nature of the exponential growth factor. Small investments growing exponentially soon reach immense proportions beyond the expectations usually of even the most optimistic financial managers. For example, $a = 1,000$ growing exponentially for three periods $(1,000)^3$ would reach 1 billion. Such expansion is not commonplace, although there are many cases on record where bright, and sometimes very lucky, persons have parlayed small sums of capital into fortunes of this dimension in the matter of a few years. Aside from the growth benefits of a given sum, management should recognize the accelerating benefits of increasing by a small amount the base value *a*; the student can verify this by varying the size of *a* by 1 unit at a time.

THE PARABOLIC FUNCTION

The parabolic function combines elements of the linear and of the exponential to give a nonlinear relationship such that *Y* will rise or fall with the increase in *X* up to a certain value, level off, and then move in the opposite direction. The basic equation for this function is the quadratic equation:

$$Y = aX^2 + bX + c \qquad\qquad 4.14$$

If $a = 0$, the basic linear equation remains; and if $bX + c$ are removed, we have a modified exponential value in X^2. The rate of change in *Y* increases or decreases at first and then levels off until at the maximum or minimum limit, just before the values change direction, the rate of change is 0. A change in *a* to $-a$ sets up the equation, so that the value of *Y* is a maximum as in income or profit optimization; and a change in *b* to $-b$ sets up the equation for minimizing the value of *Y* as in cost optimization. Table 4.3 illustrates the former and Table 4.4 the latter. The student will notice the important condition of symmetry in the two tables which will be evident also in the graph construction. In Table 4.3, the positive linear function effect was strong enough at first to cause the total value of *Y* to continue to increase; but, finally, squaring the *X* value and multiplying it by $-a$ forced the negative pull to reverse the growth movement. Table 4.4 shows the bottoming-out effect of the tool when signs are reversed in the first two elements with the positive pull from squaring *X* causing the values finally to reverse direction. To keep the minimum value from dropping to negative values, *c* is increased to 90,000 from 10,000. The solution problem in both cases points to the need for

TABLE 4.3
A MAXIMIZING PARABOLIC FUNCTION
$$Y = -1X^2 + 600X + 10,000$$

X	$-aX^2$	$+$	bX	$+$	c	$=$	Y
0	0		0		10,000		10,000
100	$-$ 10,000		60,000		10,000		60,000
200	$-$ 40,000		120,000		10,000		90,000
300	$-$ 90,000		180,000		10,000		100,000
400	$-$160,000		240,000		10,000		90,000
500	$-$250,000		300,000		10,000		60,000
600	$-$360,000		360,000		10,000		10,000

TABLE 4.4
A MINIMIZING PARABOLIC FUNCTION
$$Y = 1X^2 - 600X + 10,000$$

X	aX^2	$+$	$-bX$	$+$	c	$=$	Y
0	0		0		90,000		90,000
100	10,000		$-$ 60,000		90,000		40,000
200	40,000		$-$120,000		90,000		10,000
300	90,000		$-$180,000		90,000		0
400	160,000		$-$240,000		90,000		10,000
500	250,000		$-$300,000		90,000		40,000
600	360,000		$-$360,000		90,000		90,000

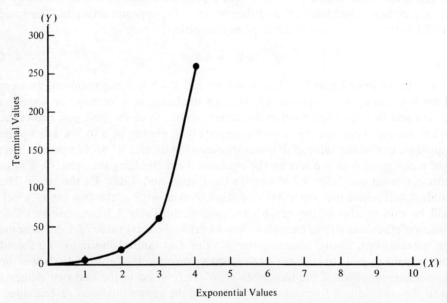

Figure 4.7a. Exponential Values of the Base (4) on Arithmetic Grid.

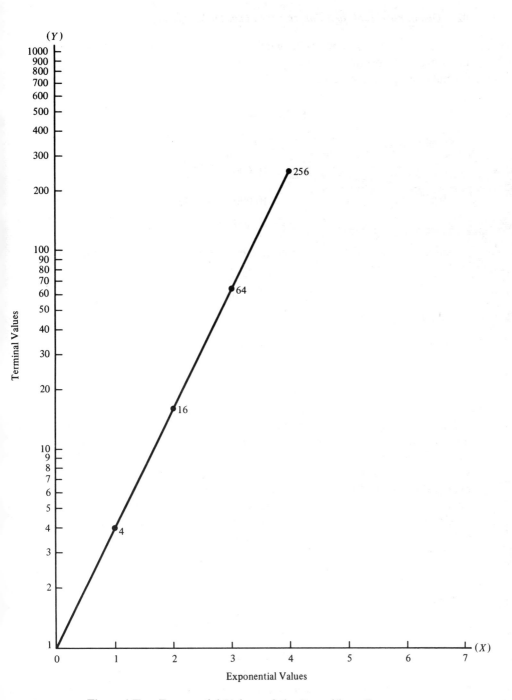

Figure 4.7b. Exponential Values of the Base (4) on Logarithmic Grid.

a tool that will help us determine, with a limited amount of information, how many units of X will produce a maximum or minimum value of Y; and the following formulas supply these needs.

$$Y_{mX} = c - \frac{b^2}{4a} \qquad\qquad 4.15$$

Substituting:

$$Y_{mX} = 10,000 - \frac{(600)^2}{4(-1)}$$
$$= 10,000 + 90,000$$
$$= 100,000$$

To solve for the minimum value of Y, the signs for c and b are reversed.

$$Y_{mn} = -c + \frac{b^2}{4a} \qquad\qquad 4.16$$

Substituting:

$$Y_{mn} = -90,000 + \frac{(600)^2}{4(1)}$$
$$= -90,000 + 90,000$$
$$= 0$$

The distinguishing feature of nonlinear functions is that their rate of change is not constant. Graphically this means, of course, that the graph of the equation cannot be a straight line. As in all forms of graphing, management is provided with a handy tool for answering questions about the effect of an infinite number of X values on Y. Figure 4.8 illustrates the maximizing case in which the graph opens at the bottom and has its vertex at the top. The formula for getting the maximum Y value was illustrated above, but to graph this the X coordinate is also needed which is determined by solving the equation:

$$X = \frac{b}{-2a} \qquad\qquad 4.17$$

Substituting:

$$X = -\frac{600}{2(-1)}$$
$$= 300$$

Now we have 100,000 on the Y axis and 300 on the X. Since the graph starts at the origin of the quadrant, the symmetry of the graph places the second X value 300 units to the right at 600. This is a quick and effective way of building a tool that will answer questions for management about relationships between X and Y.

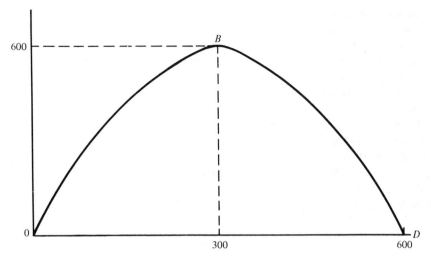

Figure 4.8. Parabolic Function.

Graph construction was simplified by starting Y values at the origin of the quadrant in both of the tables, but some financial operations throw off negative values on the Y axis until X is somewhat larger than 0. When this condition exists, the graph will intersect the X axis both times on the right side of the zero. The quadratic formula is used to solve for the two intersections of X where $Y = 0$. The quadratic formula in this case gives us the two critical points on X for graph construction. In the example below, the parabola will intersect the X axis at 100 and 500 when $a = -1$ and $c = 50,000$.

$$X = \frac{-b \pm \sqrt{b^2 - 4ac}}{2a}$$

Substituting:

$$X = \frac{-600 \pm \sqrt{360,000 - 4(-50,000)}}{2(-1)}$$

$$= \frac{-600 + 400}{-2} = 100$$

$$= \frac{-600 - 400}{-2} = 500$$

SUMMARY

Chapter 4 is a step up from Chapter 3 introducing basic algebraic tools that are used extensively throughout the text. The functional relationships in this chapter are expressed in a quantitative manner, so that the reader is forced to concentrate on details in analysis which will increase his skill as a financial analyst and decision maker. Algebraic tools facilitate the solutions of somewhat more important types of problems than can be handled altogether with arithmetic tools. Algebraic tools, however, are not replacements for arithmetic operations, but they are complements to arithmetic tools and techniques. The greatest value of the tools is in the way that they give precise answers to precise questions relating to financial issues.

An important part of the chapter is the introduction of certain graphic tools indicating linear and nonlinear functional relationships, independent variables X, and dependent variables Y. Although the relationships are expressed in general terms in this chapter, they are related to the concept of value flows; so that the reader can visualize the relationship between ordinary numbers and significant financial data.

PROBLEMS

1. Financial management of the X Company noted that, everytime a unit of net profit appeared, the net working capital of the business seemed to rise by 0.90. The company had no net working capital at the start, but expected net profits to go as high as 20,000 units in the following quarter of operations. The financial manager thought that he recognized in this experience a linear tool relationship that could be used to convert expected net profits into net working capital.

   a. Set up the equation for making this conversion. Identify the *functional* relationship in the equation.
   b. Select four levels of expected net profits and convert them into net-working-capital flows. Now cumulate the net working capital from the four profit figures.
   c. Assume that 10,000 units are in working capital at the beginning of the expected net profit flow and set up the equation for the net working capital function allowing for the beginning balance of 10,000 units.
   d. Does the initial balance of 10,000 units disturb the linear nature of the relationship? Explain.

2. The service station on the corner has linear functions programmed into its regular and premium gasoline pumps.

   a. Supplying arbitrary values for regular and premium, set up the linear equation for each sales flow.
   b. Identify in your equation each of the components: a, b, X, and Y.
   c. How can you justify this as a financial problem?
   d. Graph the two equations on the same chart. What do you observe about the slopes of the two curves? Why the difference?

3. In the plant of Firm A, it is noted that the man on a certain machine turns out 10 units for every hour of work performed. He had a stockpile of 1,000 units at the start of the day.

   a. Set up the equation that will indicate the linear output at any hour of the day.
   b. Identify the functional relationship in the equation. Is this a financial function? If not, how can it be converted to a financial function? Comment on the implications of this to the communications problem existing between financial management and production management.
   c. Convert this to a financial function and project the total value of the worker's output after the third hour of work, the sixth hour, the eighth hour. Suppose you wanted to project the value of the output for the whole department in which five men work on different machines each producing at a different rate. How many linear functions would you need to solve? Suppose that each produced at the same rate. How may functions would you need to solve?
   d. In the example above of one man on one machine, suppose that *b* changed from 10 to 8 units by the middle of the day. How could this have happened? Would it make the function nonlinear? Explain. How would you allow for the change in *b* in planning value of the output for the whole day?
   e. Can you identify a capital constraint in the functional relationships considered above?

4. In the plant of a given concern, raw materials are purchased by the ton with a delivered cost of $100 per ton. Present raw materials stocks are worth $10,000.

   a. Set up the linear equation for determining the sum of raw materials value given any quantity of purchases in ton units.
   b. What is the Y/X value in your answer to question 1? How does this identify the linearity of the problem?
   c. Assuming that no raw materials are used, graph the function and determine the total value of the inventories in stock after any three arbitrary purchases.

5. Finished inventories sell at $3 per unit, out of which the salesman receives a 20 percent commission.

   a. Set up the linear equation that can be used to project sales income.
   b. Set up the linear equation that can be used to project sales commission expenses.
   c. Suppose salesmen are paid a flat monthly sum of $300 and then 20 percent commission. Set up the equation for projecting selling expenses.

6. Company A has a cash fund of $10,000 but expects to be using it up in regular operations at the rate of $400 daily for the next twenty-five days.

    a. Write the equation for determining how much in total will have been used by the tenth day of operations, by the twentieth day.

    b. Now write the equation that will tell management how much will be left in the fund on the tenth day, on the twentieth day.

    c. Graph the equation that will allow management to determine the amount that will remain in the cash balance on *any day* within the twenty-five-day limit.

7. Company X has a bank debt of $5,000 that it hopes to pay off at the rate of $500 monthly for ten months.

    a. Write the equation that will tell management at the end of any given month what is still owed on the debt.

    b. Graph the function that will tell management what will be owed on the debt at the end of any given month.

    c. What advantage and disadvantage does the graphic tool have over the equation? Suppose the equation is programmed in a computer. Does the graph still have the same advantages?

8. Product D generates cash from sales at the rate of $10 per unit and to date has accumulated a balance of $1,000. Product E is new and promises to generate cash at the rate of $20 per unit.

    a. Using simultaneous equations, indicate when product E will overtake product D.

    b. Graph the two functions and verify the *takeover* point in sales for product E.

9. Many important financial problems can be resolved using the single project analysis, but some situations require joint product analysis. Set up the model that illustrates two products using 1,000 units of capital at different linear rates; x, using up the capital at 0.5 times the rate that product x_2 is using it up. Graph this joint linear function. Now arbitrarily draw two sets of perpendiculars to the two axes, and interpret the results with respect to product availability and capital use.

10. The selling price of your product is $40, but you expect to experience a certain amount of resistance to this price in the market after some of the products are sold at $40. You decide to use the parabolic equation to determine under this condition the maximum income from sales. You give the demand resistance to the $40 price a quantitative value of 0.5. Since there is no income, Y value at $X = 0$, the letter c can be dropped from the equation. Also, since this is a maximizing operation, you know that a will be a negative value. The equation of the function then is $Y = -0.5aX^2 + \$40X$. Set up a schedule of X values, indicating the maximum income level. Indicate how this tool can be used to answer questions about expected total income given the units of sales. Graph the function and analyze.

11. Assume a selling price of $30 per unit with (0.2) as a *correction* factor at *a*. Using the formulas: $Y_{max} = -b^2/4a$ and $X = b/-2a$, graph the parabola and set up three questions and answers relating to income and sales.

12. Assume that $c = $2,000$ of fixed costs, that unit variable costs are $30, but that, because of inefficient operations after a certain level of output, unit variable costs will actually rise. To adjust for the inefficiency, *a* is given a value of 0.4; $b = 30, and the equation of the function is $Y = 0.4X^2 - $30(X) + $2,000$. Set up a schedule based on the equation and determine the point of minimum total cost.

5

Finite
Mathematics
and Financial
Management

By definition finite mathematics deals with issues that have definite limits, and the term infinity (∞) is not found in the literature of finite mathematics. In this chapter, some of the basic tools of the mathematics will be described that have a special application to financial analysis. At the same time that the tools add new shapes and forms to our analysis, they also place limitations on analysis specifically for decision making. In exchange for simple and clearly shaped tools, financial managers will find more restricted applications when it comes to optimization and decision-making situations than are found in the applications of ordinary arithmetic and algebra. But these tools should give added insight into financial problem issues, and, hopefully, they will help the reader to understand better some of the more abstract and sophisticated tools and skills that have already been discussed. Included in our discussion are truth tables, switching circuits, sets and subsets, matrices, and decision trees. For students interested in further study of the various subjects that are covered here several outstanding works are available.[1]

TRUTH TABLES

Truth tables are a form of symbolic logic that is used for a limited kind of problem solving. Because our primary interest is financial management, what we are concerned with specifically is the application of the tool to quantifying true

[1] Two widely used texts in this field are: John G. Kemeny, J. Laurie Snell, and Gerald L. Thompson, *Introduction to Finite Mathematics* (Englewood Cliffs, N.J.: Prentice-Hall, Inc., 1957). John G. Kemeny, Arthur Schleifer, J. Laurie Snell, and Gerald L. Thompson, *Finite Mathematics With Business Applications* (Englewood Cliffs, N.J.: Prentice-Hall, Inc., 1961).

and false statements relating specifically to financial issues.[2] This is not a decision-making tool as such; but, by helping to focus attention on important concepts in business finance, truth tables do contribute to a clearer understanding of vital decision-making areas of the subject, which can then be explored in more depth with some of the conventional tools discussed in the previous two chapters. Truth tables contain the basic elements of a special form of algebra that has a constant value of 2, indicating the number of mutually exclusive answers T or F to every simple statement. There is a nonlinear exponential relationship resembling $Y = a^x$ in quantifying the number of possible rows of T and F combinations contained in a truth table. But we need to back up a few steps and look more closely at the components of the simple statement if we are to understand the structure and purpose of the statement for business finance. Let $a = 2$ and the exponential variable $X = n$. The independent variable n indicates the number of statements that are made about a subject and determines the number of columns in the table. Summarizing the quantitative factors in the table structure:

$$Y = (2)^n$$

With 2 as a constant, we determine the size and shape of the table by supplying the value for n. Table 5.1 is the construction in which $n = 2$, that is in which two

TABLE 5.1
POSSIBLE T AND F VALUES
FOR TWO STATEMENTS a AND b

a	b
T	T
T	F
F	F
F	T

statements about some financial problem or issue are put into the table for analysis on a T and F basis. Substituting in the equation:

$$Y = (2)^2$$
$$= 4 \text{ rows}$$

5.1

Here we have a good example of the finite form of this algebra. The row is the key value because it contains the quantitative distribution or possible T's and F's. Three statements would produce a table of eight rows: $2^3 = 8$. Notice the exponential rule in operation here that, while the exponents increase at a constant

---

[2] For applications of the tools specifically to working capital issues see: Louis K. Brandt, "Quantitative Tools for Financial Management," *The Southern Quarterly*, VII, No. 3 (April, 1969), pp. 261–81.

arithmetic rate, the *Y* values increase at a constant *relative rate*, or putting it in another way at a geometric rate. Since we are not testing the content, but just the feasibility of the tool for analysis, any two statements of financial significance such as the following may be substituted for *a* and *b* in the table:

      a. Fixed assets are less liquid than current assets.
      b. Fixed assets are more risky than current assets.

Actually the content of the *a* and *b* statements in the two pairs of statements do not have to be functionally related to each other for the construction of the table to be correct; but, unless they are related, the value of the tool for business finance is limited.

    At this juncture, the mathematical operation has just set the dimensions of the table and has not determined its internal composition; to obtain this, we use algebraic operations that are unique to this kind of tool. What is done specifically is to compound the two simple statements. But to do this certain algebraic operations have to be performed as they are to obtain quantitative results with ordinary algebraic operations, and these operations produce certain interesting and useful results. But first the language has to be identified with *T* and *F* values. First the conjunction $\wedge$ denotes a *T* answer only when statements *a* and *b* are *both* true, and the disjunction $\vee$ denotes a truth value if *either a* or *b* or both are true. Table 5.2 is a compound statement solution resulting from performing the operation of conjunction $\wedge$ first and of disjunction $\vee$ second.

TABLE 5.2
OPERATIONS ON SIMPLE STATEMENTS
PRODUCING COMPOUND STATEMENTS

Simple Statements		*Compound Statements* By: *Conjunction*	*Disjunction*
a	*b*	$a \wedge b$	$a \vee b$
T	T	T	T
T	F	F	T
F	F	F	F
F	T	F	T

The left side of the table contains the initial four rows with eight possibilities of *T* and *F* from Table 5.1 and the right side contains the solutions to the alternative operations $\wedge$ and $\vee$. The first column on the right produces a dearth of *T* values because to get *T, both* statements *a,* fixed assets are less liquid than current assets, and *b,* fixed assets are more risky than current assets have to be true; whereas, the second column produces a generous supply of *T*'s because to get *T either one or both* of the statements can be true. By mathematical law, *T* values under the conjunction of two simple statements *a* and *b* will always be 1 out of 4 or 0.25, and

F values will always be 3 out of 4 or 0.75. It will be noticed, however, that in the *either a* or *b* or *both* disjunction, the opposite results are produced; the *T* values are predominant with 3 out of 4 or 0.75 of the rows, and *F* values are in the minority with only 1 out of 4 or 0.25—both of the statements are false. Since the quantitative count of *T* and *F* is not affected by the content of the statements, *effectiveness of this tool for focusing attention on financial facts depends on how logically the statements are selected.*

A more sophisticated and also a more easily misinterpreted connective is the "if . . . then" known as the *conditional.* Under this rule, the only condition under which the solution statement is false is when, if *a* is *T* then *b* is *F*. The symbol for the conditional is →. We go back to the original truth table with two variables *a* and *b* and now construct a new set of values as in Table 5.3.

TABLE 5.3
THE CONDITIONAL OPERATING ON
TWO SIMPLE STATEMENTS

Compound Statements

a	→	b
T	T	T
T	F	F
F	T	F
F	T	T

The solution to the conditional is in the middle column. The middle value is *F* in the second row because, *b* is *F* when *a* is *T*. We might consider a set of statements like: *a,* net profits are increased and *b,* net working capital is increased. A well established financial relationship like this would give more force to the *T* value under the conditional sign → than under the conjunction and disjunction signs used in Tables 5.1 and 5.2.

In summary, the truth table is simple but nevertheless meets the basic requirements of a tool for identifying various areas for concentration in financial management. Also, it makes a clear move from *possible T* and *F* to *probable T* and *F* values in the shift from simple to compound statements. So far as adapting the proper statements to the tools is concerned, we are reminded as we were in Chapters 3 and 4 that an important rule in using any kind of mathematical tool is to keep the problem statement and the tool selection compatible. But the tables are limited for decision making; although we can perform mathematical operations on the statements, the results are not designed in themselves to convey decision-making messages to management as directly as some of the tools that were discussed in Chapters 3 and 4. Their contribution to the optimizing and share value maximization goals is, therefore, indirect, consisting simply of helping financial managers identify financial problem areas.

SWITCHING CIRCUITS

Business finance borrows here from physical science to pinpoint management issues which are somewhat more functional and practical than those suggested in truth table analysis, despite the fact that they are both rather closely related. A switching circuit is either closed or open. A closed circuit will carry a current; an open one will not. Also, where multiple circuits are used, they may be in series; or they may be parallel. In the example below T_1 is the first terminal of a series which could be the origin of a flow of funds, and T_2 is another terminal which is where the flow ends. The switches are a and b, and the issue is to get the flow of funds from T_1 to T_2.

$$T_1 ----\text{\textbackslash}_a -\text{\textbackslash}_b --- T_2$$

Switches a and b *both* have to be closed to get the flow to T_2 because if either one is open the flow will be blocked. This takes on meaning if a and b are looked on as financial restrictions both of which have to be overcome to get the flow of funds to the business. The truth value of the switching circuit can be quantified as follows. Let the closed switch be T and the open one F, and let the operating connective be the conjunction $\wedge$. Using the earlier example of conjunction, we have just 1 out of 4 chances of both a and b switches being closed. With a third restriction to overcome, the chance of getting the flow through to T_2 is only 1 out of 8, the 8 rows coming from 2^3. The proof of this is found in Table 5.4.

TABLE 5.4
FLOW OF FUNDS TO BUSINESS

Simple Statements			Conjunction
a	b	c	$\wedge$
T	T	T	T
T	T	F	F
T	F	T	F
T	F	F	F
F	F	F	F
F	F	T	F
F	T	T	F
F	T	F	F

But if the restrictions in series are too limiting on the business, a bypass may be found in parallel circuits that will allow the value to come through on an *either/or* basis as illustrated in the accompanying diagram.

$$T_1 ----- \boxed{\begin{array}{c} a \\ \hline b \end{array}} ----- T_2$$

If the *a* constraint is not met, the flow would still come through *b* to T_2; or if the *b* is not met, the value would flow through *a*. The only way that the flow could be stopped would be for restrictions to be placed on *a* and *b* simultaneously. The illustration above shows *a* open and *b* closed to carry the current from T_1 to T_2. The restrictions mentioned above can be likened to a credit restriction placed by the lender on a potential borrower.

USE OF SETS

A truth table is actually a *set* of *T* and *F* elements. A switching circuit is a *set* of switching elements, equations, inequalities, functional relationships, and graphic portrayals discussed in earlier chapters are also sets with elements that are common to the parent set. For example, all of the assets of a business comprise a set of which current assets are a subset; and taken alone current assets are a set with subsets of cash, receivables, and inventories. Further, any one of the current assets like receivables or marketable securities is a set with subsets made up of elements relating to maturity and collectability in each subset. While elements in individual subsets are different, the elements are all common to the set of which they are part. For example, the subset of current assets has different elements than the subset of fixed assets, but the elements in both subsets are contained in the parent set of total assets. The same general approach can be made to liabilities, income, costs, and equity, classifying each as a set with subsets of uniquely distinguishable elements that are common to the parent set. Set tools are part of another special form of algebra with prescribed operations called *intersection* ∩, *union* ∪, and *complement* ∼. Just like operations on simple statements produce *T* and *F* values in truth tables for financial analysis, operations on sets produce subsets with unique combinations of elements for financial analysis.

Skilled operation depends on how effectively management relates tool use to specific financial issues; but, before this skill can be exploited, he needs to know the language of this special form of operation. *Intersection* ∩ produces subsets with elements that are common to two or more sets. For example, intersection of sets *A* and *B* produces a subset *C* with elements common to both *A* and *B*. The value of such operation lies in setting up categories of financial substance, such as the common elements of *A* and *B* contained in *C*, for research and analysis. *Union* ∪ will form subsets containing all of the elements of two or more sets. For example *C* may be a subset formed by combining all the elements in *A* and *B*, its operation being identified as $C = A \cup B$. This operation broadens the scope of the substance; thus, it contains an overlapping of elements that are contained in *either A* or *B* or in both *A* and *B*. Finally, the *complement* is a kind of taking away or subtracting operation. The complement forms a new subset from two or more sets that is void of the elements that are common to both sets. For example, $C = A \cap \tilde{B}$. This says that the subset *C* includes the elements of *A* less the elements of *B* that would be common also to *A* in intersection.

It is always helpful to make comparisons between past and present experiences.

The question and answer relationship between the independent variable X and the dependent variable Y mentioned in Chapter 4 is an important one also in application of set analysis. To illustrate the question and answer relationship, we introduce Venn diagrams. Venn diagrams are graphic tools that illustrate clearly for us the operations on sets of intersection, union, and complement. Suppose that sets A and B represent the company's inventories located in two different warehouses and containing inventory forms $a, b, c, d,$ and e. Illustrated in Figure 5.1 is the universal set of inventory, but we are concentrating on the products at A and B. U represents the universal set; the set of all elements, but the space around A and B and inside the rectangle represents a set of elements outside our subject areas. The effect of performing an intersection on A and B is illustrated by the shaded area in Figure 5.1. The resulting subset C contains c and d, the only elements common to both sets A and B. Subset C singles out the inventories that are common to the two locations that now may be subjected to further study by management. But this area of financial management was selected arbitrarily. A and B could well have represented two portfolios of marketable securities with intersection showing common securities c and d in each portfolio.

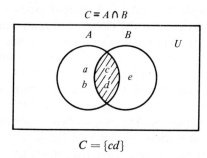

Figure 5.1.   Operation Intersection.

Union of the sets produces a subset with elements a, b, c, d and e as is shown in the shaded areas in Figures 5.2 and 5.3. Operation union broadens the scope of

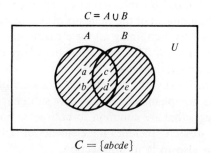

Figure 5.2.   Operation Union.

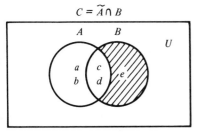
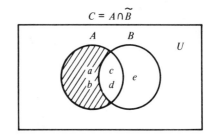

Figure 5.3. Operation Complement.

study rather than isolating a certain area as happens in intersection. Complementing the sets produces a subset with elements removed that are common to the two sets in intersection. Operation complement removes all of the common elements from the new subset and leaves for special study *a* and *b* in *A*, or *e* in *B*. The remaining are marked off by the shaded areas of *A* and *B*.

TREE DIAGRAMS

Like the earlier finite tools, tree diagrams expound the logical deductive process; but they differ in three important respects from the tools discussed thus far. First, they are adaptable to the analysis of events and reactions to events occurring in sequence. Acts are decisions of management, and events are the occurrences on which financial managers act. Second, tree diagrams illustrate a conditional relationship; that is, they reflect the effects of the events and actions of one period on the events and acts of the following period. And, third, tree diagrams are adaptable to probability analysis; that is, they point directly to the correct decision for management to make given certain assumptions about the probability that certain events will occur along the branches of the tree. Figures 5.4 and 5.5 show the quantitative sequence of conditional events; conditional that is because the action at each stage is affected by, or conditioned by, the occurrence of the event of the previous stage. Figure 5.4 is a tree diagram that sets before management the array of logical lines of thought relating to a financial management issue. The financial manager is considering applying for a loan. He is wondering about the directions that such consideration might take and the outcomes that might be expected following one of several alternative paths. The acts that management can control include applying for a loan, quitting the application proceedings, making a financial analysis, and preparing a financial budget.

The tree indicates alternative decisions right at the start: to apply directly for a loan, quit considering the loan prospect altogether, or perform a financial analysis before a decision is made about whether to apply or quit. Self-evaluation is done after the analysis, so that it will not be difficult to grade the analysis as favorable or unfavorable. Again, after the evaluation three alternative courses of action are open to the business: apply for the loan, quit the application altogether, or present

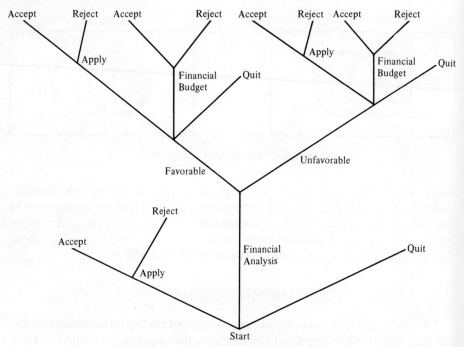

Accept   Reject   Accept   Reject   Accept   Reject Accept   Reject

                    Apply
                                                                Apply
                         Financial   Quit   Financial
                         Budget   Budget   Quit

            Favorable   Unfavorable

                 Reject
    Accept   Financial   Quit
                                          Analysis
              Apply

                          Start

Figure 5.4. The Loan Prospect.

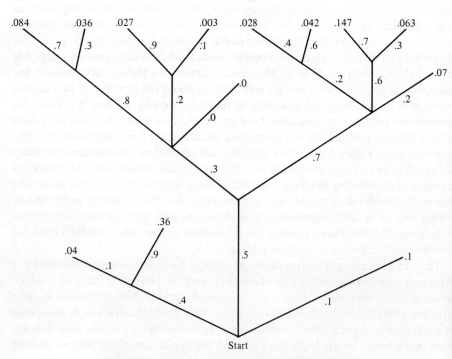

.084   .036   .027   .003   .028   .042   .147   .063
     .7   .3   .9   :1   .4   .6   .7   .3

                                              .0   .2   .6
                                                                                      .07
                      .8   .2   .2
                                    .0

                              .3   .7

                 .36

    .04   .9   .5   .1
         .1   .1
              .4   .1

                          Start

Figure 5.5. Decision Tree with Probability Values.

106

a financial budget to the loan agency. Financial managers have no control over the lender's response to accept or reject the proposal, but they can control their own responses to the events that occur along the branches of the tree before the lender has a chance to make his accept or reject decision.

In its present condition, the tree is not a decision-making tool but can be converted to one by assigning *subjective* probabilities to the occurrence of the acts and events. Figure 5.5 shows the mechanics of arriving at *joint* probabilities, that is, probabilities at the extremities of the branches determined by a series of multiplications. The student will observe that with each multiplication the probability that any one of these paths will be followed to its extremity is less than the size of any one of its component probabilities.

The student will notice also that every time the tree branches out it forms a probability distribution; that is, the sum of the probabilities at any given level on the branches equal 1. For example, at the start three alternative probabilities of $0.4 + 0.5 + 0.1 = 1$. At the next level the probability distribution is $0.7 + 0.3 = 1$. The probabilities that terminal events will occur are indicated in the values at the outer limits of the branches, the largest of which is 0.147 for the second branch from the right at the top of the tree. This is the final event in the path: $0.5 \times 0.7 \times 0.6 \times 0.7 = 0.147$. It will be noted also that the sum of the end values all over the tree equal $1 : 0.040 + 0.360 + 0.084 + 0.036 + 0.027 + 0.003 + 0.028 + 0.042 + 0.147 + 0.063 + 0.070 + 0.100 = 1$.

MATRICES

A matrix is an array of numbers in rows and columns. Matrix algebra is distinguishable in two important ways: first, the physical dimension of the tool, that is the shape of the tool in terms of the number of columns and rows, is a major factor influencing operating procedures. Second, solutions to operations may supply answers simultaneously to numerous unknowns. The Y value that has been brought to the fore so often as a single quantitative value now may consist of a series of answers to a series of questions asked and answered simultaneously.

Addition of matrices is illustrated below. To perform an addition on two matrices each matrix must contain the same number of columns and rows because addition is performed by matching the elements in the matrix sets. Additions are illustrated below. Parentheses are identifying marks of matrices. Analyzing the sum, we may think of the original matrices A and B as sets composed of four elements each, and C as a subset formed by the union of the elements in A and B.

$$A = \begin{pmatrix} 5 & 6 \\ 3 & -2 \end{pmatrix}$$
$$B = \begin{pmatrix} 7 & 3 \\ -1 & 2 \end{pmatrix}$$

$$A + B = \begin{pmatrix} 5 & 6 \\ 3 & -2 \end{pmatrix} + \begin{pmatrix} 7 & 3 \\ -1 & 2 \end{pmatrix} = \begin{pmatrix} 12 & 9 \\ 2 & 0 \end{pmatrix} = C$$

A could have been a matrix of four sources of cash flows for a current period, or it could have been income and expense items of the business at the end of a given period. *B* could have been a matrix of the same items for an earlier or later period than *A*, and matching these matrices gives the solution set showing the cumulative result simultaneously on each of the four elements of the set. The student will notice that there are no addition or subtraction signs in the solution set which means that no more arithmetic operations can be performed, and the reason for this is that the four elements in the subset *C* are not of combinable quality. For example, assume that the four elements include dollars of cash, number of marketable securities, number of receivables accounts, and cases of inventories; these are units of unlike quality and cannot be combined. To subtract, change the signs in set *B* and add algebraically; the student should verify that the resulting matrix is

$$\begin{pmatrix} -2 & +3 \\ +4 & -4 \end{pmatrix}$$

Subtraction gives us simultaneously the difference between two sets of four like quality elements. Again these elements could represent assets, liabilities, income sources, costs, and expenditures for two periods or even for two companies. Although the subset *C* has plus and minus signs, these indicate the net effect on the elements in *A* of subtracting the same quality elements in *B*; and they do not indicate that the remaining unlike elements in *C* can be added and subtracted.

Multiplication is another important operation in matrix algebra; and, again, the shape of the matrix is vital to the operation. Multiplication by one element is relatively easy to understand and to follow. In the example below a single value is multiplied by each value inside the matrix to obtain the solution set.

$$A \times B \quad = \quad C$$

$$4\begin{pmatrix} 5 & 6 \\ 3 & -2 \end{pmatrix} = \begin{pmatrix} 20 & 24 \\ 12 & -8 \end{pmatrix}$$

This could represent a simple operation like raising four separate quarterly income sources to annual values by multiplying each of the sources by 4, or the elements could represent costs and expenses or assets and liabilities. The operation of multiplication is complicated somewhat when set *A* contains several elements; the scope of the solution is greatly expanded when the multiplier is made up of several elements. Let us consider the case in which set *A* contains four elements which are multiplied simultaneously by four elements in set *B* to produce set *C*. We will give the solution to the multiplication first and then consider the steps to arrive at this solution. We can think of the elements in *A* as constants and the elements in *B* as variables.

$$A \quad \times \quad B \quad = \quad C$$

$$\begin{pmatrix} 5 & 6 \\ 3 & -2 \end{pmatrix} \times \begin{pmatrix} 7 & 3 \\ -1 & 2 \end{pmatrix} = \begin{pmatrix} 29 & 27 \\ 23 & 5 \end{pmatrix}$$

The procedure is to multiply each row in *A* by each column in *B*. For multiplication to be feasible, therefore, when each set contains more than one element, the rows in A have to have the same number of elements as the columns in B; or there would be no matching for multiplication. This becomes apparent below where each step is illustrated.

$$(5 \quad 6) \times \binom{7}{-1} = (5)(7) + (\;6)(-1) = 35 - 6$$

$$(3 \quad -2) \times \binom{7}{-1} = (3)(7) + (-2)(-1) = 21 + 2$$

$$(5 \quad 6) \times \binom{3}{2} = (5)(3) + (\;6)(\;2) = 15 + 12$$

$$(3 \quad -2) \times \binom{3}{2} = (3)(3) + (-2)(\;2) = 9 - 4$$

Grouping:

$$AB = \begin{pmatrix} 35 - 6 & 15 + 12 \\ 21 + 2 & 9 - 4 \end{pmatrix} = \begin{pmatrix} 29 & 27 \\ 23 & 5 \end{pmatrix} = C$$

This is a four-way multiplication that can yield valuable results for financial management. For example, suppose that elements of set B are quantitative weights that are assigned to four expected profit sources in A. What we are doing in effect is multiplying the constant (5) by the variable weight (7) and adding to this the product of the constant (6) and the variable weight (−1), giving us a net weighted value of the profit sources 5 and 6 combined of $35 - 6 = 29$. Taking one more example, suppose that the elements 3 and 2 are the weights assigned to the same net-profit prospects 5 and 6 for the next quarter of operations. What we have for that quarter of operations is the net weighted value of the profit sources 5 and 6 combined of $15 + 12 = 27$. We could continue this for two more quarters of operations coming up finally with an expected net-profit flow for each of the four quarters weighted by variable subjective values.

SUMMARY

Chapter 5 is the last of the three purely tool chapters and is somewhat of a departure from Chapters 3 and 4. The term *finite* mathematics introduces to financial analysis certain tools of a less abstract nature than those included in conventional arithmetic and algebra. The tools discribed here make important contributions to analytic techniques in financial management. Truth tables apply symbolic logic to identifying significant financial issues. Switching circuits are introduced to explain the concept of the constraint, particularly with respect to external financial relations. Set analysis is used as a tool for identifying characteristics of certain types of assets and liabilities. The decision tree, as another finite mathematical tool, illustrates a technique for studying more closely the relationship between acts and events that are significant for financial operations. The decision tree also shows

how probabilities can be used dynamically to estimate the probable occurrence
of our event, given the act. Finally, fundamental operations in the use of matrices
are illustrated. Acts of addition, subtraction and multiplication are performed on
matrices to convert raw data to simple summary data for closer analysis and
evaluation.

PROBLEMS

1. The finacial manager of Company *X* decided to use the truth table approach
   to explain to production management personnel the interrelationship between
   production and business finance. This was to be done by making the following two statements relating production to finance.

   a, production generates valuable inventories.
   b, production uses liquid funds.

   To emphasize the positive relationships of the content of the two statements,
   he decided to employ operation disjunction ($\vee$) on the following truth table
   statement of the two statements:

a	*b*
T	*T*
T	*F*
F	*F*
F	*T*

   Perform the operation of disjunction ($\vee$) and explain why this is the appropriate operation to get across his point of strong interrelationship here between
   inventories and liquidity to management personnel. Financial management
   may have to lead production personnel away from a kind of *natural* tendency
   to emphasize that selling the output will restore liquidity and even increase
   liquidity as inventories are sold above their costs.

2. The technique used in problem 1 was so effective that he decided to reverse
   the technique and to use two statements of highly improbable relationships.
   For this purpose he would use the statements:

   a, production generates valuable inventories.
   b, production creates liquid assets.

   To emphasize the negative relationship of the content of the two statements,
   he decided to perform the operation of conjunction ($\wedge$) on the two statements:

a	*b*
T	*T*
T	*F*
F	*F*
F	*T*

Perform the operation of conjunction ($\wedge$) and explain why this is the appropriate operation to get across his point of the improbable nature of the relationship. The same tendency to emphasize the sale of the inventory and its conversion to liquid assets may prevail here as in the case above; management has to distinguish for that purpose between the production of inventories and the sale of inventories.

3. Financial management decided to use truth tables to communicate the interrelationship between sales management issues and financial management issues, so that the two groups would work more closely together for the benefit of the business and its share values. He would do this by using the following two simple statements to emphasize the relationship of sales to liquidity.

   a, inventory sales are increased.
   b, liquidity is increased.

Perform the operaion of disjunction ($\vee$) on the following table to emphasize the positive relationship between sales and liquidity and comment on its quantitative implications. Structural changes in the current assets resulting from sales should be considered specifically.

a	*b*
T	T
T	F
F	F
F	T

4. You use the *disjunction* to emphasize a positive quantitative relationship between two statements. You consider using the following three statements to emphasize to sales personnel the strong relationship between selling and the final common goal in financial management of maximizing share value:

   a, total sales are increased.
   b, net profits are increased.
   c, share values are increased.

The basic truth table for the three statements is reproduced below and has 8 rows $Y = (2)^3$.

a	*b*	*c*
T	T	T
T	T	F
T	F	T
T	F	F
F	F	F
F	F	T
F	T	T
F	T	F

Use the disjunction ($\vee$) operation for your solution and comment on the effectiveness of the results for accomplishing the purpose of emphasizing the role played by marketing in financial goal attainment.

5. The conditional truth table has the following solution assuming two simple statements a and b; the solution is in the middle column.

a	$\longrightarrow$	b
T	T	T
T	F	F
F	T	F
F	T	T

Substitute statements in problem 3 above in the table and evaluate the effectiveness of the tool for convincing the sales personnel of the close relation between sales management goals and financial management goals.

6. Listed at random below are some of the main elements in the substance matter of business finance. Regroup them in terms of sets and subsets; that is, indicate which elements are part of a universal set of elements. What is accomplished by such regrouping so far as clarifying the decision-making areas in business finance are concerned?

current assets	cost of goods sold
notes payable	fixed assets
current liabilities	accounts payables
net profits	operating expenses
net sales	cash
	receivables

7. Company X holds in its marketable securities portfolio 30 short-term securities with the following distinguishable investment elements: 8 are profitable but not liquid; 15 are profitable and liquid; and 7 are liquid but not profitable. Use Venn diagrams to indicate the effect of:

    a. Intersection ($\cap$) of the subsets.
    b. Union ($\cup$) of the subsets.
    c. The complement $A \cap \tilde{B}$.

What does each of these operations on the subsets do for financial management seeking to manage and control the company's temporary securities portfolio for profit and liquidity?

8. Based on the experiences of other firms, you have good reason to believe that the more profitable you are in business during the first year, the better chance you have the second year; and, finally, the better chance still you have of profiting in the third year. You decide to simulate with a decision tree a situation in which you invest $10,000 at the start. The purpose is to project with a decision tree, given certain subjective probabilities, the expected future value

of your business investment over the first three years of operation. Below is the tree that you draw with two probability distributions. Determine the expected values and explain the alternatives available to you at the end of each year. Add to the tree another year of possible operation supplying subjective probabilities and determining possible terminal value for your organization.

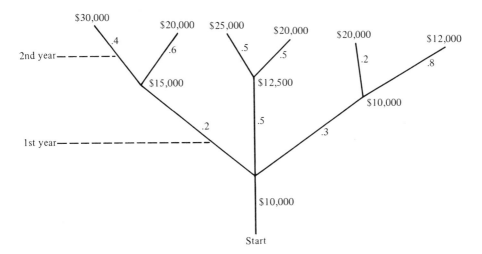

9. Assume that your business has income from the following sources: *a* (sales), *b* (investments), *c* (franchises), and *d* (lease rentals). Listed below are returns from each source expected for the next two years. The matrices are set up for two years as square matrices.

First Year	Second Year
$a = $30,000$	$a = $40,000$
$b = 5,000$	$b = -1,000$
$c = 3,000$	$c = 3,000$
$d = 2,000$	$d = -1,000$

$$\begin{pmatrix} 30,000 \\ 5,000 \end{pmatrix}\begin{pmatrix} 3,000 \\ 2,000 \end{pmatrix} + \begin{pmatrix} 40,000 \\ -1,000 \end{pmatrix}\begin{pmatrix} 3,000 \\ -1,000 \end{pmatrix} =$$

Add and evaluate your financial condition in each of the our areas of management at the end of the second year, then project operations one year further assuming curtailed sales but a moderate improvement in investment income and in lease rentals.

10. Your firm produces products *a*, *b*, and *c* priced at $5, $10, and $15 respectively. Your firm expects to sell 1,000 units of each product the first year,

2,000 the second and 3,000 the third. The multiplication matrix for performing the operations is found below; complete the operation and analyze the result.

$$AB = \begin{pmatrix} \$\ 5 \\ 10 \\ 15 \end{pmatrix} \times \begin{pmatrix} 1\text{st} \\ \dfrac{\text{year}}{1,000} \end{pmatrix} + \begin{pmatrix} 2\text{nd} \\ \dfrac{\text{year}}{2,000} \end{pmatrix} + \begin{pmatrix} 3\text{rd} \\ \dfrac{\text{year}}{3,000} \end{pmatrix} =$$

PART III

**MANAGING
CURRENT
OPERATIONS
FOR
PROFIT**

6

Income
Cost and
Expense
Management

Parts III, IV, and V of this book are all called *current operations*. Current operations has a special meaning in this book: *a scope of decision making in which there are definite capital constraints*. This immediately indicates that decision making in financial management is divisible into two categories: decisions that are made subject to given capital constraints and decisions that are made to alter those capital constraints. Another way of putting it is that managing current operations assumes that the quantity of capital is fixed and, therefore, that decision making concentrates on current or noncapital management issues; whereas, managing noncurrent or capital issues assumes that the quantity of capital is variable and, therefore, that decision making has to allow for changing the quantity of capital of the business. This classification of the issues fits the real world situation and, therefore, should lead to better decisions consistant with the common goal of maximizing share value. Now current operating decisions are directed in some detail at three of the communicating media discussed in Chapter 2: income, costs and net profits, and current assets and current liabilities. In Part III, we are concerned with current operating decisions that are related specifically to profitability; in Part IV, we are concerned with current operating decisions that are related directly to liquidity management and secondarily to profitability; and, in Part V, we are concerned with current operating decisions that are related directly to current debt management and also secondarily to profitability. We seek to apply the tools that were introduced in the three previous chapters where they apply and where they will help to clarify the issues and help us make better decisions. This definition of current operations does not fit exactly any conventional concept. It comes close to the *short-run* concept that the student learned in principles of economics but differs quite noticeably from that concept by limiting the current portion of capital to the *net* portion above current liabilities. In this chapter internal guidelines to income and cost management will be studied, and the reader will be reminded of their applications to the common problem of share valuation. The terms costs and expenses include the conventional financial reporting terms as they appear in accounting statements of costs and expenses.

INCOME MANAGEMENT

Income is the flow of funds that comes from selling goods and services. The term *funds* in income analysis refers to additions to cash and receivables balances in the current assets resulting from cash and credit sales respectively. It is important in managing current operations to recognize at once the interrelationship between values appearing on the reported income statement for profit and liquid current assets. It may be helpful to think of income as an exchange of the least liquid of current assets (inventory) for more liquid current assets (cash and receivables), with the latter adding more to the total value of the company's assets than was lost from the sale of the finished inventories. This is not to imply, however, that the difference in value between cost of goods sold and net sales (gross profit) is all added permanently to the value of the business because operating expenses, *other* expenses, and income taxes all have to be taken out of this liquid reservoir to meet operating needs.

But this makes it even more apparent that income costs and expenses are intimately related to current assets. The student will do well to think of income in this manner as a flow of liquid assets into and out of the business, although the accounting statement of operations, as the investor sees it, does not and cannot reveal this interrelationship. The income statement as we know is strictly a quantitative and not a qualitative statement of value flows; that is, no attempt is made in the operating statement to explain the quality of the income or costs and expenses in terms of qualitative changes rendered in the current assets and current liabilities; and, yet, as financial managers, we need to know what this relationship is. Figure 6.1 is a simple illustration of the basic income-current asset relationship, showing how income flows through sales from inventory values to receivables, and then to cash values. The student will recognize this as a small segment of the flow diagrams in Chapter 2. In Chapter 2 we were illustrating the total flows; here we

Figure 6.1. Income Flow.

are concerned only with the inflow of funds from sales and its convergence into cash. Market valuation of a company's shares, the reader will recall, depends not only on the company's formal financial reports of income and profit but also on the flow reflected in the quantity and quality of resulting current assets and current debts that are a vital part of the total operation. Disregarding all costs for the present for simplification purposes the business will benefit most by maximizing the income flow in Figure 6.1 because this adds the most liquidity to the assets of the firm and, as was stated in Chapter 1, if net profits are given an increase in liquidity will effect favorably the company's share values. Let us consider the optimizing rule and apply some of the tools of Part II to the optimizing goal.

OPTIMIZING OUTPUT SUBJECT TO A CAPITAL CONSTRAINT

The first important challenge to financial managers is to acknowledge and to identify the capital constraint to income maximization. We turn first to the physical law of total diminishing returns. This law states in effect that, if one factor in the production process, like capital, is held constant and the other factors of labor and noncapital financial resources are increased, total output will increase at a decreasing rate to a maximum total output after which additional units of variable factor inputs will cause total units of output to decline. Figure 6.2 illustrates the functional relationship between outputs on the Y axis and the inputs on the X axis. The level of optimal output in units is 500, resulting from combining a given quantity of capital, the capital constraint, with 50 units of variable input. We have

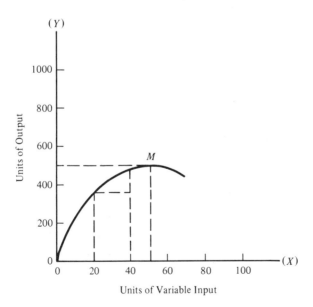

Figure 6.2.   Law of Total Diminishing Returns and Optimal Output.

combined labor and noncapital financial resources on the X axis in a homogeneous unit. This can be done if each unit is a *package* combining a fixed quantity of labor time with a fixed quantity of noncapital financial resources. Noncapital resources are the current assets that increase and decrease through the interchange of current liabilities without affecting net working capital.

It should be noted that the diagram charts a purely physical relationship between inputs and outputs where a capital constraint is existent. Capital consists of fixed assets and net working capital; but it is not necessary to indicate the exact amount because since this is a *current* operation we concentrate just on the variable units of input for final decision making and let the capital constraint be operative in the law of diminishing returns. As a diagram of physical units, it is apparent that to increase inputs of variable factors beyond 50 units would cause the total output to diminish; therefore, the optimization point is where 50 units of input are because, if more units of X variables are applied, the Y readings will decline. The reader will recognize the graphic expression of this functional relationship as nonlinear: a relationship in which the change in Y (output) with respect to a given change in X (input) is not constant. No effort is made to establish a definite rate of change either for the positive or the negative portion of the curve, nor is there any need for extending the curve any farther than it is in Figure 6.2 since the graph has already fulfilled its purpose. It is important to observe, however, the broken lines on the left side of curve becoming shorter as they approach the top of the curve, indicating that output is increasing at a decreasing rate. At point M on the graph the rate of change is zero: $(\Delta Y/\Delta X) = 0$, in which $X = 50$ and $Y = 500$. We will see in the section that follows that the important point on the graph for financial analysis is the 500 units. In moving from a physical analysis to a financial analysis, the vertical axis of Figure 6.2 becomes the horizontal axis of Figure 6.3 and optimizing output gives way to optimizing income.

OPTIMIZING INCOME

We need to distinguish between optimal output and optimal income; and, to do this, a unit selling price has to be introduced. An important assumption needs to be made, namely, that whatever is produced can be sold at the given selling price. Another assumption is that output and sale is either of a single product; or that if the output includes several products, they are closely enough related that the *average product* concept can be associated with them for pricing purposes. Now without giving any consideration to costs and expenses, the capital constraint is clearly identified with the 500 units of output; and the functional relationship between sales income and units of output becomes linear. The student is familiar with the mechanical elements of linearity and so should have no trouble following the quantitative explanation of the optimizing operation.

Let Y equal total income, a equal income at zero sales, b equal price, and X equal units of output and sale. The optimizing tool is the equation $Y = a + bX$, subject to the inequality $X \leq 500$. Linearity and the slope of the curve is implicit in price *b*; *a* is 0 because all income is derived from sales; and there can be no income on *Y* unless there are sales on *X*. But *a* can conceivably have a positive value as is the case when *other* income is forthcoming from sources like dividends and interest on securities investments or from rentals on real estate. Such income is unrelated to operations and gives income a positive value even when output and sales are zero. But since no *other* income is present here the functional relationship is altogether to sales, and *a* must equal 0. Let us assume further that *b* = $10 and that $0 \leq X \leq 500$. We are reminded that sales are limited to 500 units because of the capital constraint that placed a physical limit on output, and it is flatly impossible to sell more than can be produced if all sales come from current output.

Figure 6.3 graphs the income function and the optimal sales level. Since the

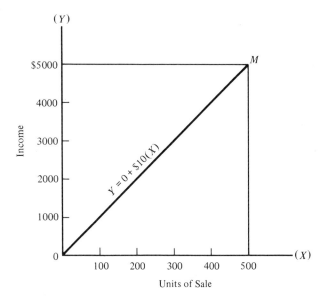

Figure 6.3. Income Optimization.

straight line starts at the origin of the graph, that can be the first point on the graph. The second can be determined by substituting any random value between 0 and 500 for *X* in the equation $Y = 0 + \$10(X)$. Let us substitute 500 for *X*, then:

$$Y = 0 + \$10(500)$$
$$= \$5,000$$

The point is the coordinate of $X = 500$ and $Y = \$5,000$. The coefficient $10 is the slope of the curve indicating that, at any level of total inputs of $X \leq 500$, an addition of one more unit will increase total income by $10 until a limit is reached at $5,000. The summary condition of income optimization subject to the given capital constraint then is as follows:

$$\text{Maximum inputs} \quad = \quad 50$$
$$\text{Maximum outputs} = \quad 500$$
$$\text{Maximum income} = \$5,000$$
$$@ \ \$10 \text{ per unit}$$

But the student will recall from Chapter 4 that a tool such as Figure 6.3 is designed to answer an infinite number of questions about units sold and income derived along the whole range of the graph from $X = 0$ to $X = 500$. We will consider below several items that may cause some variations from the optimal level of income illustrated in the sections above. Considered will be the effect of a demand constraint and price and income elasticity.

Demand Constraint   An assumption was made in the previous section that at $10 total output would be sold, for example, that demand $D \geq 500$. But if $D \leq 500$ it sets up a new force inside the limits of capital constraint, and this smaller limit then becomes the constraint that determines actual income. Attention is called, however, to an important trait of this constraint, namely, that it is an economic force over which financial managers have limited decision-making control. Figure 6.4 illustrates the effect on optimal income of a demand constraint of 400 units. This indicates that at the present price of the product 400 units only can be sold, although the firm is able to produce 500. The constant price of $10 gives the slope to the curve; the slope of the curve is unaffected by the lower sales. The function is extended on the graph from D to M in a broken line, so that income at the point of optimal demand can be compared with income at the point of optimal output.

Price Elasticity and Income Optimization   Price was assumed to remain constant at $10 in the illustrations above, subject first to the limit in output, 500 units, and then to the limit in demand, 400 units. In the real world every business has a range of units that can be sold for a given price. An important income determining factor is the responsiveness of sales to voluntary price changes by management. In Figure 6.4, demand at $10 was limited to 400 units and this limited total income. Without going into detail on the theory of price elasticity, some of the high points of the subject need to be reviewed here for its application to income and profit planning. The law of demand implies a nonlinear continuous negative relationship between price as the independent variable and quantity demanded as the dependent variable giving rise to the familiar downward sloping demand curve. Each such curve has an infinite number of X and Y coordinates with a multitude usually of different degrees of price elasticities along the demand curve.

Specifically, price elasticity is a ratio of the *relative rate of change* in quantity demanded of a product to the *relative rate of change* in its price. We will continue to let X represent price, the independent variable, and let Y represent demand,

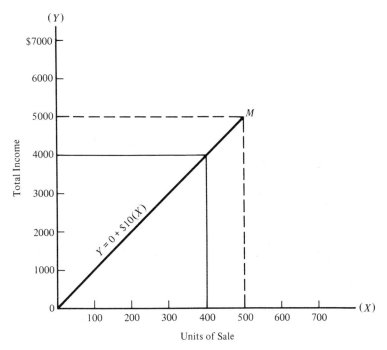

Figure 6.4. Demand Constraint and Optimal Income.

the dependent variable. E_1 is the ratio of elasticity given a decrease in price $(-\Delta X)$, and E_2 is the ratio of elasticity given an increase in price $(+\Delta X)$. The resulting value is a coefficient of elasticity indicating at a given level of sales the change in total demand Y that will result given a change in price X. The effect of this on estimating net sales will be illustrated later in this section.

$$E_1 = \frac{\Delta Y}{Y} \bigg/ \frac{-\Delta X}{X}$$

$$E_2 = \frac{-\Delta Y}{Y} \bigg/ \frac{\Delta X}{X}$$

Elasticity is a matter of degree, and it may vary all the way from zero (0) to infinity (∞). The following illustrates these two extremes. We start at the limit of the constraint at which 400 units are demanded. In the example of no responsiveness (zero elasticity), price changes by $2 from $10 to $8; but there is no change in total demand. As well as calling this zero elasticity, we can also call it *infinite inelasticity* meaning that the market for this product is completely indifferent to its price; the market wants 400 regardless of its price. In the example of infinite elasticity the decline in price of $2 would cause an infinitely large increase in demand. Demand in this case would jump immediately to the maximum output permitted by the capital constraint which in this case is 500 units.

	Zero Elasticity	*Infinite Elasticity*
	$E = \dfrac{\Delta Y}{Y} \Big/ \dfrac{-\Delta X}{X}$	$E = \dfrac{\Delta Y}{Y} \Big/ \dfrac{-\Delta X}{X}$
	$= \dfrac{0}{400} \Big/ \dfrac{-\$2}{\$10}$	$= \dfrac{\infty}{400} \Big/ \dfrac{-\$2}{\$10}$
	$= 0/-0.20$	$= \infty/-0.20$
	$= 0$	$= -\infty$

The decision-making significance of the two cases is quite different. In the first, 400 units would be sold regardless of the price; and, therefore, to lower price by $2 would cause sales income to fall by $800 ($2 × 400). Financial managers should recommend holding the $10 price and possibly even increasing it to maximize income. The second case implies that sales will increase to 500 units immediately by lowering price to $8, which is all that can be produced and sold because of the capital constraint; but, since income is not maximized in this case by lowering the price to $8 ($8 × 500 = $4,000), there is no real incentive to lower the price. But, if lowering the price just $1 to $9 would produce an infinite increase in demand, financial managers should recommend reducing price to $9 to maximize income ($9 × 500 = $4,500). We are reminded again that costs are not considered here; and, therefore, that income maximization may not be the optimal decision for maximizing profits and share values. The effect of raising the price by $2 from $10 to $12 when elasticity is 0 is to increase income from $4,000 to $4,800 ($12 × 400). Infinite elasticity has the reverse affect: raising the price from $10 to $12 causes all demand to vanish and income to fall to 0. The reason for no demand existing at $12 per unit is that all available output will be taken at $10 per unit. What is likely to exist in reality, however, is that elasticity will range between these limits of zero and infinite elasticity.

Only if a relative decrease in price produces the same relative increase in quantity demanded is elasticity *unitary*; at that point income is not affected by a price decrease or increase. Different degrees of elasticity are illustrated below. In I elasticity is unitary because the coefficient of elasticity is −1. In II elasticity is less than unitary with a relative price decline of 0.20 and a relative increase in quantity demanded of only 0.15 causing a coefficient of −0.75. Greater than unitary elasticity is illustrated in III with a price decline of 0.20 causing an increase in quantity demanded of 0.25 and an elasticity coefficient of −1.25. Elasticity coefficients are always negative values because either the numerator or denominator of the ratio, but not both, will have a negative sign.

		I *Unitary* *Elasticity*	*II* *Less than Unitary* *Elasticity*	*III* *More than Unitary* *Elasticity*
$\dfrac{\Delta Y}{Y} \Big/ \dfrac{-\Delta X}{X - X}$	$=$	$\dfrac{80}{400} \Big/ \dfrac{-\$2}{\$10}$	$\dfrac{60}{400} \Big/ \dfrac{-\$2}{\$10}$	$\dfrac{100}{400} \Big/ \dfrac{-\$2}{\$10}$
	$=$	$0.20/-0.20$	$0.15/-0.20$	$0.25/-0.20$
	$=$	-1	-0.75	-1.25

Let us examine more closely the practical financial value of elasticity measures. Start with the example of less than unitary elasticity which produced a coefficient of −0.75 when price is dropped 0.20. This has important implications to financial managers because, if the rate of decline in demand is less than in price, the business would stand to gain by raising rather than lowering price. To illustrate, assume that −0.75 is expected to hold for a price increase of $2 as well as for a price decrease of $2. The result of raising prices by $2 or 0.20 then would cause the following decrease in sales: −0.75[(0.20)400] = −60 units. If sales dropped by 60 units, the new sales figure would be 340 (400 − 60); and income would be maximized: 340 × $12 = $4,080. Some of the questions that financial managers need to ask are: How wide is the range of the −0.75 coefficient above and below the current $10 price? Can sales managers, by advertising activities, broaden the applications of the −0.75 elasticity, so that it will apply also at sales levels above 400 units? Finally, can promotional activities be stimulated to decrease the coefficient of elasticity still further and, thus, make price increases more effective for income maximization?

Now shift to case III where elasticity is −1.25. Here we might stand to benefit by decreasing prices rather than by increasing them. To illustrate the practical application of the tool, assume that the coefficient is expected to hold for a price decrease of $2 as shown in the hypothetical case above. Lowering the price by $2 or 0.20 then would cause the following increase in sales above the initial 400 units: −1.25[(−0.20)400] = 100. Total expected sales now are 500 (400 + 100) units; but income is not maximized because new income is just $4,000: 500 × $8 = 4,000. It is obvious in this example that, with the capital constraint of 500 units, the firm has nothing to gain by lowering prices. The student may recognize a linear relationship in the examples above which, subject to certain simplifying assumptions, allows financial managers to project changes in units demanded, given the relative change in price. We may use for this purpose the equation: $\Delta Y = b(\Delta X)I$, in which ΔY equals the increase or decrease in units of sales resulting from a given relative price change, b the constant elasticity coefficient, X the relative price change, and I the quantity of units sold at the time of the price change. Substituting in the three examples above, we have three different equations:

$$\text{I:} \quad Y = -1(X)400$$

$$\text{II:} \quad Y = -0.75(X)400$$

$$\text{III:} \quad Y = -1.25(X)400$$

To find out how many more or less units will be sold because of a price change, the relative increase (+) or decrease (−) in X is substituted in the equation. To illustrate, assume that with elasticity of −1.25 price is changed relatively by −15 percent. Substituting in equation III:

$$Y = -1.25[(-0.15)400]$$
$$= +75 \text{ units}$$

This brings total sales (475) close to maximum output and at $8.50 per unit would optimize income at $4,037.50: 475($8.50) = $4,037.50. If income optimization is the management goal, this attains it subject to the output constraint. Just how far the linear function can be extended depends on how long the coefficients will hold. That is, will the coefficient −1.25 hold with just a 10 percent price decrease? If the answer is yes to a 10 percent decrease, then the linearity is holding; but, if the answer is no, the linearity is not holding.

Economic Income and Income Optimization   Aside from price changes regional and national incomes can have important effects on how close sales will come to reaching optimal output of 500 units. The income to a business may increase or decrease, without price change when the income and purchasing power of the economic community changes. If management understands relationships between a firm's income and economic income, management can plan to take advantage of these relations. The coefficient of income elasticity is the measure of responsiveness of demand for the firm's product, given changes in the level of income. Unlike price elasticity this is a positive coefficient. The basic statement of elasticity is as follows:

$$E = \frac{\Delta Y}{Y} \bigg/ \frac{\Delta X}{X} \qquad\qquad 6.1$$

Applying this tool, assume that economic income for the area increases from $30 million to $40 million accompanied by an increase in units demanded from 400 units to the limit of the firm's capital constraint of 500 units. Substituting in the formula:

$$E = \frac{100}{400} \bigg/ \frac{10,000,000}{30,000,000}$$
$$= 0.25/0.33$$
$$= 0.75$$

The coefficient 0.75 tells management that, if this measure of elasticity is expected to hold, the relative demand for the firm's product can be expected to increase 0.75 as fast as the relative increase in economic income. The student will recognize this as less than unitary elasticity. The relationship may be restated in the following linear equation: $\Delta Y = 0.75(\Delta X)400$. Assuming that the coefficient has a certain amount of linear holding power, it can be used to make effective income forecasts. To illustrate, assume that economic income is expected to rise relatively by 30 percent when the firm's sales are 400. Substituting in the equation: $\Delta Y = 0.75(0.30)400 = 90$; total sales will increase to 490 units which is still within the limits of the capital constraint. At $10 per unit financial management can translate this into income of $4,900.

Some products are more responsive than others to economic income change just as some are more responsive than others to price change. Financial managers cannot control economic income, but they can research the field for quantitative measures of changes in demand relative to economic income changes as well as they can research changes in demand to changes in price. These analytic methods can then be used to plan and to control income flows.

We have seen that, in estimating demand, management is also estimating sales, subject to the capacity constraint. Income optimization goals finally have to be spelled out in a tangible and detailed sales budget before financial controls can be exercised for income and profit maximization. We will discuss and illustrate below important aspects of the practical job of sales budgeting as the sequel to income optimization analysis such as has been discussed above.

Making the Sales Estimate   The first factor to consider is who in the firm is best qualified to estimate sales. Salesmen in the field who are in close contact with the customer have firsthand information about sales prospects and for this reason may be called for their estimates. Sales managers are further removed from the customer but have a broader view of the firm's sales potential than individual salesmen and, therefore, have something additional to offer. Financial managers with their income goals should serve primarily to orient the estimates of the sales personnel to the general framework of the company's income goals and elasticity conditions discussed above. The second factor to consider is the method of making the estimate. Past sales experience is an important consideration. If several products are sold past sales should be considered of each product, and if sales cover several geographic areas sales experience should be considered for each area. The third factor to consider is professional marketing research services that incorporate economic factors and competetive conditions in statistical forecasting models that may be helpful.

The sales budget finally has to take on definite financial values for effective planning and control. For the budget to serve the purpose of an effective planning and control device, timing the sales is very important. Setting a time schedule on sales makes the selling personnel responsible for producing given quantities of income at definite times and offers a frame of reference for holding the sales personnel responsible for meeting budgeted quotas. Table 6.1 is structured for estimating income from two products in the same hypothetical firm, in which each product has a different selling price. Total expected income is the sum of the net sales of the two products. The total sales volume for each product is the optimization goal after deciding that the prices, $3 and $2 respectively, would come closer than any other prices to responding favorably to elasticity conditions. The budget indicates potential financial loss through returns and allowances, a larger optimal income from the lower priced of the two products, and the expected combined income from the two products. As a control device the budget must be compared with actual sales on short-time intervals such as one month; financial managers are responsible for communicating these levels to sales personnel who are in direct line for remedying this condition.

TABLE 6.1
THE SALES BUDGET

	April	May	June	July	August	September	Six Months
Product *a*:							
Unit price	$ 3	$ 3	$ 3	$ 3	$ 3	$ 3	$ 3
Sales volume	10,270	11,000	11,730	12,469	13,200	14,670	73,339
Gross sales	$30,810	$33,000	$35,190	$37,407	$39,600	$44,010	$220,017
Less 4% for returns and allowances	1,232	1,320	1,408	1,496	1,584	1,760	8,800
Net sales	$29,578	$31,680	$33,782	$35,911	$38,016	$42,250	$211,217
Product *b*:							
Unit price	$ 2	$ 2	$ 2	$ 2	$ 2	$ 2	$ 2
Sales volume	16,500	19,800	21,450	23,100	24,750	26,400	132,000
Gross sales	$33,000	$39,600	$42,900	$46,200	$49,500	$52,800	$264,000
Less 4% for returns and allowances	1,320	1,584	1,716	1,848	1,980	2,112	10,560
Net sales	$31,680	$38,016	$41,184	$44,352	$47,520	$50,688	$253,440
Total gross sales	$63,810	$72,600	$78,090	$83,607	$89,100	$96,810	$484,017
Less returns allowances	2,552	2,904	3,124	3,344	3,564	3,872	19,360
Total net sales	$61,258	$69,696	$74,966	$80,263	$85,536	$92,938	$464,657

Let us look at the sales budget now in a more generalized manner through our linear planning tools. We can think of the sales budget as a linear function of the order of: $Y = bX - [r(bX)]$ in which b equals unit price, X sales volume, and r the rate at which goods are returned by customers. The tool can be used to project net sales income after returns and allowances for each product for an infinite number of unit sales levels instead of just the six months selected for this special budget. The following equations are constructed for products a and b separately. These equations will answer the question of how much income can be expected from each product at any given level of sales. Substituting expected units of sales for X_a and X_b, we can estimate the income flow for each product.

$$Y_a = \$3(X_a) - 0.04(\$3X_a)$$

$$Y_b = \$2(X_b) - 0.04(\$2X_b)$$

By summing Y_a and Y_b the estimated total income for both products is obtained for any period. For example substitute for the next three months the following expected sales of products a and b.

Month	Product	
	a	*b*
1	12,500	16,500
2	14,000	18,000
3	13,000	19,500

Entering these values in the equations the net sales estimates can be solved simultaneously for each product as follows:

Month		Products	
	a		*b*
1	$3(12,500) − 0.04($3 × 12,500) = $ 36,000	$2(16,500) − 0.04($2 × 16,500) = $ 31,680	
2	$3(14,000) − 0.04($3 × 14,000) = 40,320	$2(18,000) − 0.04($2 × 18,000) = 34,560	
3	$3(13,000) − 0.04($3 × 13,000) = 37,440	$2(19,500) − 0.04($2 × 19,500) = 37,440	
	$113,760	$103,680	

Total (a + b) for 3 Months

$113,760
$103,680
$217,440

Risk in the Sales Estimate   The practical value of the sales budget for income planning and control depends on how realistic the sales estimate is. In the previous section, there was no hint that each monthly estimate could be anything but a single quantity which implied certainty in making the estimates. In fact, however, except when sales are contracted for in advance, the risk of estimating the sales figure incorrectly should be acknowledged by applying subjective and/or statistical probabilities to the budget. Table 6.2 illustrates how subjective probabilities can

TABLE 6.2
EXPECTED QUANTITY OF APRIL SALES

Possible Sales (Units)	Subjective Probabilities	Expected Sales (Units)	Cumulative Probabilities
8,500	0.05	425	0.05
9,500	.10	950	.15
10,500	.60	6,300	.75
11,500	.20	2,300	.95
12,500	.05	625	1.00
	1.00	10,600	

be assigned to the risks of not being able to forecast sales with certainty. Illustrated is a probability distribution for units of sales of product *a* for the month of April, the first month of the six-month planning period. The row of possible sales graduates sales by 1,000 units between the lowest sales that the company had experienced (8,500) for this month over the past three years and the highest sales experienced (12,500) for this month over the past three years. Each of the probabilities may represent the relative frequency with which the sales figure is expected to occur in the future, and this may be closely tied to the frequency with which the experience occurred in the past. The outcome differs from the 10,270 units projected for April in Table 6.1. The resulting expected sales volume for April of 10,600 is the weighted average sales estimate and the quantity most probable to occur in a large number of experiences given these subjectively assigned probabilities.

Given the distribution of possible sales in Table 6.2, the normal curve analysis can be applied to determine the statistical probability of dispersion about expected sales of 10,600 units. The 10,600 units is an anchor value, as a symbol of long run tendency, around which all other possible sales will fluctuate. It is helpful to financial managers budgeting operations to know how widely sales will fluctuate about this average. We use the standard deviation to measure the *risk* that management is taking in attempting to make an accurate estimate of sales and, of course, sales income. The student will recall that the procedure for measuring the standard deviation was illustrated in Chapter 3. Here we will modify the formula slightly to lessen the amount of arithmetic that is required. The following formula is suggested for this purpose:

$$\sigma = \sqrt{\sum (s - \bar{S})^2 p}$$ 6.2

Where: σ = Standard deviation
s = Each possible sales volume for April
$\bar{S}$ = Expected sales volume for April
p = Probability of each possible sales volume occurring

Values from Table 6.2 are substituted below in the formula above.

$(s - \bar{S})$	$(s - \bar{S})^2$	$(s - \bar{S})^2 p$
$8,500 - 10,600 = 2,100$	$4,410,000 \times 0.05 =$	$220,500$
$9,500 - 10,600 = 1,100$	$1,210,000 \times .10 =$	$121,000$
$10,500 - 10,600 = -100$	$10,000 \times .60 =$	$6,000$
$11,500 - 10,600 = 900$	$810,000 \times .20 =$	$162,000$
$12,500 - 10,600 = 1,900$	$3,610,000 \times .05 =$	$180,500$
	$\Sigma(s - \bar{S})^2 p =$	$690,000$

$$\sigma = \sqrt{690,000}$$
$$\sigma = 830 \text{ units}$$

Interpreting the results in terms of probability of occurrences, there is a 0.68 probability that sales will range between one standard deviation above and one standard deviation below 10,600 units or between 9,770 units (10,600 − 830) and 11,430 units (10,600 + 830). On the positive side alone, this means that there is a 0.34 probability that sales will be between 10,600 units and 11,430 units. As we narrow the range of possible sales around the mean, the probability of these sales occurring also becomes less. To determine these probabilities, we can turn to Table 3 in the Appendix, the z table. From the z table, we can determine the probability that sales will be greater than 10,600 units by a certain fraction of a standard deviation. For example, the probability that sales will exceed 10,600 units by 0.10 σ or 83 units (0.10 × 830) is 0.039 which may be rounded to 4 percent. Since the curve is symmetrical, there is the same 4 percent probability that sales will be less than 10,600 units by 0.10σ. Financial managers are concerned with the actual sales estimate at 0.10σ above and below the average because this helps plan sales income. For example, they can plan on sales fluctuating above the average to 10,683 units with a 4 percent probability, and they can plan on sales fluctuating below the mean to 10,517 units with a 4 percent probability. The student should see the z table to determine the probability of other ranges above and below the mean.

COST AND EXPENSE MANAGEMENT

We have concentrated on sales income thus far, so that the full impact of this important flow would be understood for the part that it plays in the current operation. The matter of income optimization was also examined independently of costs and expenses to force us to concentrate on the relationship between income and various constraints. But now we need to introduce cost and expense variables which are factors to contend with in the real world of current operations.

OPTIMIZING COSTS AND EXPENSES

The optimization goal, given the level of sales income, is to minimize the sum of costs and expenses. We will consider costs and expenses in isolation from income as income was considered in isolation from costs and expenses; and, in the next chapter, the two will be brought together in the net profit analysis. To understand the constraining role that capital plays, we need to analyze two different cost and expense forms: fixed costs and expenses and variable costs and expenses.

FIXED COSTS AND EXPENSES

Capital assets, and capital debt contracts used to finance those assets, have attached to them costs and expenses that are fixed in total amount until another capital management decision is made, but in any given operating period decisions have to be made subject to the constraints of fixed costs and expenses. Financial managers are challenged to minimize *total* costs and expenses despite the fixed costs and expenses that result from capital management decisions. Although little can be done to alter these charges without making a capital management decision, financial managers need to identify them before they can be coped with effectively. First costs and expenses relating to capital assets include depreciation on buildings, machinery, and equipment. Sound principles of financial accounting require that depreciation be treated as a cost of doing business even though such charges are not cash expenditures. The important point here, however, is that depreciation is related to the value of the investment and not to the volume of production and sale. Other asset-related fixed costs and expenses include lease rentals paid for using other companies' fixed assets. Still other asset-related fixed charges are property insurance and property taxes. Like depreciation and lease rentals, these last two charges are related to the value of the fixed capital rather than to the level of their use in operations. All of the above charges except depreciation require cash expenditures, but *that does not make depreciation any less of a fixed cost and expense.*

Finally, interest charges on capital debts like long-term notes and bonds, that were issued to acquire current and fixed capital assets, are fixed expenses. They are fixed because although they appear in the operating statement, they are not affected by the level of operation. Repayment of the debt itself, however, either in installments or in a single payment are not found in the operating statement and are not fixed costs and expenses.

Now we can put all fixed costs and expenses together regardless of whether they are related to capital assets or capital liabilities and regardless of whether or not they incur cash expenditures. The reason we can do this is that fixed charges are all expressed in a common dollar unit of value. The larger this total sum the greater the burden on financial managers to hold down *total* costs and expenses; and, given a certain net sales level, the harder it is for financial managers to produce net profits. But this is getting slightly ahead of the narrative. Returning again to the basic concept of fixed charges, it may be clarified further by reconsidering linear equations; let us look at fixed costs and expenses in the context of the linear equation to see whether or not they are indeed independent of operations. By assuming that all output is sold, we can substitute, as was done in the income analysis, *units of sale* for units of output below.

$$C = a + cX \qquad\qquad 6.3$$

Where: C = Total cost
a = Fixed costs and expenses
c = Unit variable cost
X = Units of sale

C replaces Y and c replaces b in the basic linear equation $Y = a + bX$. C is a function of X, and c is the coefficient of X which sets the rate of change that takes place in C. If the *change* in C results from the constant unit variable cost c, then fixed charges a can render no change in total costs C. They render no *change* in C, but that does not mean that fixed charges do not affect the size of total costs and expenses. Another way of looking at fixed costs and expenses is as a fixed burden on total costs. This can be illustrated by assuming that sales $X = 0$ and rewriting the equation as:

$$C = a + c(0)$$

$$C = a$$

Figure 6.5 graphs total costs C as a function of fixed costs and expenses a. The equation $Y = \$2,000 + 0(X)$ indicates that the slope of the line $c = 0$. A function with no coefficient is easily drawn because it is a horizontal line perpendicular to C at one point, in this case at \$2,000. It is observed that moving out on the X axis

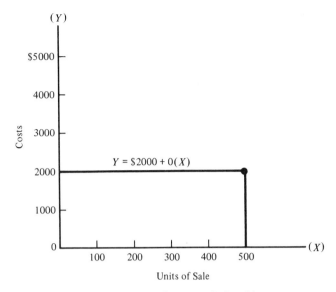

Figure 6.5.   Fixed Cost Relationship.

to 500 units total cost is still $2,000. There is no slope to the curve; total fixed costs and expenses do not change with the level of output and sale; there is no control over the item; and there is no optimizing issue. But considering variable costs and expenses is quite a different condition.

The first point on the total cost function is fixed costs and expenses of $2,000. The second point can be found by substituting any value between 0 and 500 for X. The second point is connected to the first point at $2,000 on the C axis and the total cost function is formed. To get the second point the largest sales figure was used with the following result:

$$C = \$2,000 + \$3(500)$$
$$= \$3,500$$

This means that when total units produced is 500 on the X axis, total fixed and variable cost is $3,500 on the Y axis. The variable portion of total costs lies above the fixed cost line. At any point on X it is the difference between total costs and fixed costs: $TVC = C - a$. In the example above it would be:

$$TVC = \$3,500 - 2,000$$
$$= \$1,500$$

VARIABLE COSTS IN THEORY AND PRACTICE

There may be some question in the student's mind between what he learned in economic theory about the nonlinear nature of unit variable costs and the linear nature of total variable costs discussed here, but this question can be answered if we are allowed some flexibility in the theory. The student will recall from economic theory that the shape of the unit variable cost curve conforms closely to a parabola with a cost minimizing vertex, that is with the vertex or the limit of the parabola pointing downward. If we are allowed to modify this by letting minimum unit costs of $3 continue for a range of X values instead of for a single X value, the two approaches can be reconciled. This would indicate the more realistic situation wherein financial managers find the minimum unit variable cost and then are able to increase output and sale within a given range of units without causing unit costs and expenses to increase significantly.

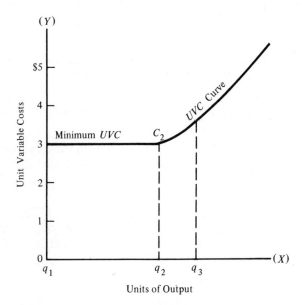

Figure 6.6.   Unit Variable Costs and Expenses Minimum Cost Range.

Figure 6.6 illustrates this minimizing condition. By starting minimum unit costs at the origin of the graph, we assume that output and sale will not begin until the level of optimal unit variable costs and expenses are determined. When this level is found, production and sale will begin; thus minimum costs and expenses begin right at the C axis and hold all the way to q_2. From that point on they rise sharply because of the capital constraint and the law of diminishing returns. The sudden increase in unit costs beyond q_2 cannot be resolved unless the capital constraint itself is removed by new investment. But returning now to the main issue of identifying total variable cost and expense, if it is reasonable to assume that unit variable charges can be held constant from q_1 to q_2, then the equation for total variable charges can be stated as a linear function of output and sales for the range q_1 to q_2.

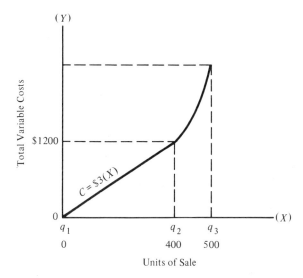

(Y)

Total Variable Costs

$1200

$C = \$3(X)$

0

q_1
0

q_2
400

q_3
500

(X)

Units of Sale

Figure 6.7.   Optimal Variable Costs.

Figure 6.7 shows total variable costs increasing at a constant rate of $3 per unit from 0 to 400 units of output and sale. Optimal total variable charges are at C_2 where they start rising sharply because of pressure from the fixed quantity of capital. We will recall that without considering costs and expenses the law of diminishing returns would allow output to reach 500 units. But considering variable costs alone, it would not be expedient to produce for sale after total variable costs and expenses start their rapid increase right after 400 units. The optimal level of output X and sales, from the total cost viewpoint C, can be decided on the basis of total variable costs alone because fixed costs are not affected as we have seen by the size of output and sales. Anticipating Chapter 7 somewhat, it may be noted that it is the difference between unit price and unit variable costs and expenses that decides finally how much has to be sold to cover fixed charges and to make net profits.

Figure 6.8 is an optimal operations graph without noting specifically net profit effects. It combines the total sales income, Figure 6.3, and total variable costs and expenses, Figure 6.7. Figure 6.8 illustrates both the total sales income function $(Y = 0 + \$10X)$ with a potential maximum of 500 units and the total cost and expense function $(C = \$2,000 + \$3X)$. *A* marks the intercept of the total cost function at $2,000 of fixed costs and expenses by capital investment. The slope of the total cost curve reflects the $3 unit variable cost. *B* marks the intersection of total costs and total income, the level of sales at which total costs and total sales are equal. *C* is the controlling point in operations determined by 400 units of sales and by reaching the limit of the $3 minimum unit variable charge. *D* would have been the point of operation if maximizing sales income alone had been the goal. The line *CE* indicates rapidly rising total costs because of increasing unit variable costs. More will be said about the income, cost, and expense relationship and their effect on net profits in the next chapter.

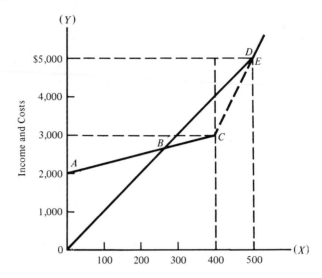

Figure 6.8. Optimal Operations.

The simplest way of budgeting total variable costs and expenses is to relate each item individually like direct labor, direct materials, and sales commissions to one unit of sales and then project each total variable cost month by month. Substitute for *C* the unit variable cost for each of the items that is clearly variable with sales then insert the expected units of sale for each month of the budgeting period. It is suggested that, since several linear equations would need solving simultaneously, management employ a multiplication matrix as illustrated in Table 6.3. Table 6.3

TABLE 6.3
VARIABLE COST BUDGET
MATRIX METHOD

Units Costs		*Monthly Sales Estimate (Units)*		
			Months	
		1st	*2nd*	*3rd*
Direct labor	$4			
Direct materials	$3	1,000	2,000	3,000
Sales commissions	$2			

$$1{,}000\begin{pmatrix}4\\3\\2\end{pmatrix}\ +\ 2{,}000\begin{pmatrix}4\\3\\2\end{pmatrix}\ +\ 3{,}000\begin{pmatrix}4\\3\\2\end{pmatrix}$$

Direct labor	$=$	$\begin{pmatrix}4{,}000\\3{,}000\\2{,}000\end{pmatrix}$	$+$	$\begin{pmatrix}8{,}000\\6{,}000\\4{,}000\end{pmatrix}$	$+$	$\begin{pmatrix}12{,}000\\9{,}000\\6{,}000\end{pmatrix}=\begin{pmatrix}24{,}000\\18{,}000\\12{,}000\end{pmatrix}$

projects the monthly cost for each variable cost factor and gives the three-month total for each of the three items. Fixed costs do not vary with sales and, therefore, create no budgeting problem in current operations. Table 6.3, however, oversimplifies the final budgeting operations. Costs and expenses are not always clearly fixed or variable. In some instances variability is combined with fixed qualities. *Overhead* costs and expenses, for example, that are primarily fixed in nature may have a degree of variability but not enough to be perfectly linear. Shadings like these do not discredit the tools and analytic techniques that have been discussed, but put financial managers on notice that in a budgeting situation quantitative generalizations may need modifying with personal experience and individual judgment. If the general and the specific are combined the result is likely to produce a final cost and expense budget like the one in Table 6.4.

TABLE 6.4
COST OF GOODS SOLD BUDGET

Part I
Direct Costs

	April	May	June	July	August	September	Total
Product a:							
Direct labor	$ 5,916	$ 6,336	$ 6,756	$ 7,182	$ 7,603	$ 8,450	$ 42,243
Direct materials	8,873	9,504	10,135	10,773	11,405	12,675	63,365
Product b:							
Direct labor	7,920	9,504	10,296	11,088	11,880	12,672	63,360
Direct materials	11,088	13,306	14,414	15,523	16,632	17,741	88,704
Total direct labor	13,836	15,840	17,052	18,270	19,483	21,122	105,603
Total direct materials	19,961	22,810	24,549	26,296	28,037	30,416	152,069
Total direct labor and materials	$33,797	$38,650	$41,601	$44,566	$47,520	$51,538	$257,672

Part II
Overhead Costs

	April	May	June	July	August	September	Total
Product a:							
Fixed overhead	$ 4,000	$ 4,000	$ 4,000	$ 4,000	$ 4,000	$ 4,000	$ 24,000
Variable overhead	1,479	1,584	1,689	2,514	2,661	2,958	12,885
Product b:							
Fixed overhead	6,000	6,000	6,000	6,000	6,000	6,000	36,000
Variable overhead	1,901	2,281	2,471	3,548	3,802	4,055	18,058
Total fixed overhead	10,000	10,000	10,000	10,000	10,000	10,000	60,000
Total variable overhead	3,380	3,865	4,160	6,062	6,463	7,013	30,943
Total fixed and variable overhead	$13,380	$13,865	$14,160	$16,062	$16,463	$17,013	$ 90,943
Cost of goods sold	$47,177	$52,515	$55,761	$60,628	$63,983	$68,551	$348,615

Part III

Sales Expense Budget

	April	May	June	July	August	September	Total
Product *a*:							
Direct selling expense, commission @15%	$ 4,437	$ 4,752	$ 5,067	$ 5,387	$ 5,702	$ 6,338	$ 31,683
Product *b*:							
Direct selling expense, commission @5%	1,584	1,901	2,059	2,218	2,376	2,534	12,672
Salaries	4,654	4,654	4,654	4,654	4,654	4,654	27,924
Total selling expense	$10,675	$11,307	$11,780	$12,259	$12,732	$13,526	$ 72,279

SUMMARY

Chapter 6 is the first of two chapters in Part III dealing with current operations for profit and subject to certain capital and demand constraints. The capital constraint is shown to be the main restricting force in planning for maximum income and minimum cost and expense. Demand is also a constraint affecting income. The optimization concept is applied for the first time in this chapter as a tool for income maximization. The demand constraint is introduced, and price elasticity and income elasticity are also discussed. By careful analysis of a company's demand elasticity and income elasticity, financial managers are able to make more precise estimates of income on the way to income optimization. The key variable is the elasticity coefficient which can be fitted into simple linear relationships to project quantitative effects on sales. In the final analysis, practical application is made of tools and quantitative techniques to budgeting income and cost on a month-by-month basis. Multiplication is worked on the matrix to project simultaneously variable costs: direct labor, direct material, and selling expenses. In the concluding section of the chapter we see how the quantitative tools and techniques that were developed earlier can be applied to the final stage in financial planning called the cost and expense budget.

PROBLEMS

1. Construct an input-output diagram indicating the effect of the capital constraint and the law of diminishing returns on optimization of output.
    a. What is the optimal number of output units?
    b. Construct an income optimizing situation based on a hypothetical optimal output. Give a value to b and indicate the equation of the function.
    c. Now condition this to a situation where demand $<$ capital constraint; to a situation where demand $>$ capital constraint.

2. You computed the elasticity coefficient of your firm at 5,000 units of sale and found it to be −1.2.

    a. Write the equation for determining the effect on demand for the firm's product given a certain relative change in price. Explain each item in the equation.

    b. What would total demand for the products be if ΔX were: −0.08, −0.12, and .10?

    c. Determine total income at the new level of demand and sales in each case in *a* above, assuming price before the change was $1 per unit.

    d. Suppose that capital resources of your firm limit output to 6,000 units. Would the demand for your product in any of the cases above exceed the capital constraint?

    e. How can this tool and skill help in budgeting income?

3. At 1,000 units of sale, demand elasticity for your firm's output relative to change in economic income is 0.62. This makes the sales-determining tool: $\Delta Y = 0.62(\Delta X)1,000$.

    a. What is the functional meaning of the equation?

    b. Substitute 0.30 for ΔX and solve. What would total income be of your firm before and after the change in economic income assuming your products sold for $2 each?

    c. Assume a capacity limit of 1,200 units. Could you meet demand? Suppose the elasticity coefficient were 0.70 and $\Delta X = 0.30$. Could you meet the demand? If not, what remedy is open?

4. You produce products *a* and *b* with the following income experience:

	Product	
	a	*b*
	Price $6	Price $8
Gross sales	$10,000	20,000
Returns and allowances	200	400
Net sales	$ 9,800	19,600

    a. Set up equations for forecasting net sales income for each product.

    b. Capacity output for product *a* is 2,500 units, for *b* it is 3,000. Which product is operating nearer to capacity?

    c. What is optimal net sales income for the firm?

5. The financial manager of Firm A forecasts units of sale for the next two quarters to be 3,000 and 4,000 respectively.

    a. This is called sales forecasting under certainty. What does this mean?

    b. Draw up a subjective probability distribution for sales during the next two quarters. How do the expected values compare with the estimates above?

    c. Under what conditions might this method of income budgeting be more meaningful than the former; when less meaningful?

6. A firm has fixed and variable costs to contend with in finally planning for profit.

    a. What is meant by total costs being a function of output and sales, given unit variable costs?

    b. Fixed costs are not a function of output and sales. Why not?

    c. What is the relationship between fixed costs and the constraint?

    d. How can the economic theory of nonlinear total variable costs be adapted to the financial management tool of linear total variable costs?

7. There is an important relationship between the general theory of variable cost planning and the specifics of the cost and expense budgeting. Why does fixed cost not create a budgeting problem? Explain how cost planning tools and skills and the everyday budgeting techniques complement each other.

8. The decision is to use matrix algebra in solving simultaneously three linear cost equations. It is reasoned that this can be done conveniently because direct labor, direct materials, and sales commissions are all linearly related to sales. The equations in effect for the three items are indicated below with the Y subscripts identifying the costs:

$$Y_1 = \$10(X)$$

$$Y_m = \$15(X)$$

$$Y_c = \$8(X)$$

Sales for the next three months are expected to be $10,000, $15,000, and $20,000 respectively. Construct the model and multiply. Interpret your results.

7

Profit
Management

The profit-management function is usually associated with high-level financial management, and some large businesses even set up special profit-planning committees and departments to formulate policy rules and tools for profit analysis, planning, and control. But unless the communication line is kept open all the way down the line of financial organization and to sales and manufacturing, profit management will not be effective. The end result of profit management will automatically be communicated to the securities market. Some businesses realize the goal of profit attainment; others do not, and the reason for this is twofold. First, the quantity of capital is a constraining factor of great importance in profit realization. Some businesses have relaxed their capital constraints to permit large profits to be earned, and other firms have held to a restricting quantity of capital. Managerial skill in the use of analytic and decision-making tools and methods is the second important reason for the difference in net profits realized by business. We are continuing to be concerned in this chapter with the second factor affecting net profits; we are continuing, as was done in the previous chapter, to analyze *current operating issues* which assume fixed quantities of capital. In this chapter we conclude what was started in Chapter 6 and finalize the results of internal management of current operations with the profit budget. The reader will find in this chapter tool uses that are also more communicable to the securities markets than those used in Chapter 6. The format of the chapter follows the basic methodological format of analyzing historical profits and then of applying simple quantitative tools to profit planning and control.

MAKING USE OF PAST EXPERIENCES

Financial managers need to study their own and other companies' profit reports as the major source of information for keeping abreast of significant profit changes and trends and as the first step in successful profit planning. Historical experiences are extremely important to the management team in planning for the future as well as for grading themselves on their success or failure in the past. In the grading process various quantitative measures of profitability are used. Each of these measures makes some contribution to a better understanding of what the profit goal actually is, the extent to which the profit statement actually measures efficiency in management; and, finally, the extent to which it communicates relevant information to the securities market. Several of these important profit-measuring and interpreting media are: the sources and uses of net profit statement, profit margins, profit earned on capital investment, and, finally, rate of profit earned per share of stock.

SOURCES AND USES OF INCOME

A report of the sources and uses of income for producing profit will single out the important and unimportant items that caused profits to increase and decrease over a given operating period. This kind of a report is easily understood by outsiders as well as by the management group itself. Any statement like this which registers the amount of, and the factors affecting, change in net profit is an important analytic tool. To construct this statement, all we need is operating information for two or more periods.

Table 7.1 is divided into Parts I and II. Part I contains comparative operating statements for the years 1970 and 1971 with changes that occurred in each item during 1971. Part II groups the critical income and cost and expense items showing

TABLE 7.1
PART I
COMPARATIVE OPERATING STATEMENTS

	Year Ended Dec. 31, 1970	Year Ended Dec. 31, 1971	Changes Increase	Decrease
Net Sales	$893,000	$970,000	$77,000	
Cost of goods sold	644,500	693,800	49,300	
Gross profit	$248,500	$276,200	$27,700	
Operating expenses	178,200	180,000	1,800	
Net operating profit	$ 70,300	$ 96,200	$25,900	
Other income	6,000	6,000		
Other expenses	10,000	8,000		$2,000
Before-tax profit	66,300	94,200	27,900	
Income taxes	28,976	43,484	14,508	
After-tax profit	$ 37,324	$ 50,716	$13,392	

PART II
SOURCES AND USES OF PROFIT

Change in sources:	
Increase in sales	$77,000
Decrease in other expenses	2,000
Total sources	$79,000
Change in uses:	
Increase in cost of sales	$49,300
Increase in operating expenses	1,800
Increase in taxes	14,508
	$65,608
Addition to net profit	13,392
Total uses	$79,000

whether their effect was to increase or decrease after-tax net profits. Part II gives meaning to the changes in Part I; notice that the decrease in *other expenses* is a source of net profit and is added to the increase in net sales. Any decrease in a cost or expense is a *source* of net profit; any increase in a cost or expense is a *use* of net profit. The addition to net profit during 1971 resulted because the increase in net sales and decrease in other expenses together more then offset the increases in cost of goods sold, operating expenses, and income taxes. For effective internal control, financial managers should single out the items that have had the greatest effect on net profits positively and negatively. The items that increase net profit will want to be increased and those that decrease net profit decreased.

PROFIT MARGINS

Profit margins are the measures of profit levels stated as percentages of net sales. These measures indicate to financial managers the amount of each sales dollar that was retained at each profit level. As relative values, whether in decimals or in percentages, the profit standing can be compared with earlier periods and, more important, with profits of competitors and even with profits of the whole industry to gain a closer insight into the effectiveness of past decision making by financial managers. Table 7.2 is the same statement of operations used in Chapter 2 but identifies specifically the profit margins at four strategic levels of the company's operations. Gross profit shows that 28.5 percent of total sales (28.5 cents of each sales dollar) is profit generated at the factory level. If there were no further costs or expenses, this would also represent the percentage of net operating profit returned on net sales; but usually there are operating expenses of selling and administration with which to cope. The net operating profit margin shows that, after allowing for what are designated as operating expenses plus the cost at the factory, 9.9 percent of original sales (9.9 cents on each sales dollar) remains. *Other* charges being larger than *other* receipts, the *other* profit (loss) has caused the net profit margin before taxes to decline from 9.9 to 9.7 percent. The margin before taxes is a summary of primary and secondary operating efficiency stated as a

TABLE 7.2
OPERATING STATEMENT WITH PROFIT MARGINS
QUARTER ENDING MARCH 31, 1971

Net sales	$291,000	100.0	
Costs of goods sold	208,140	71.5	
Gross profit	82,860	28.5	Gross profit margin
Operating expenses	54,000	18.6	
Net operating profit	28,860	9.9	Operating profit margin
Other profit (loss)	(600)	(0.2)	
Before-tax profit	28,260	9.7	Net margin before taxes
Income taxes (@ 40%)	11,304	3.9	
After-tax profit	$ 16,956	5.8	Net margin after taxes

proportion of sales. Net profit after taxes shows that the combined primary and secondary efforts of management after an assumed 40 percent tax rate left the shares with a net increment of 5.8 percent (5.8 cents on each dollar of initial sales). This is the percentage of the total inflow left from sales after all costs, expenses, secondary operating gains and losses, and income tax charges are deducted.

Comparing profit margins for several periods makes them more valuable media for profit planning. Table 7.3 is a statement of profit margins compared for three

TABLE 7.3
COMPARATIVE PROFIT MARGINS

	Quarter Ended September 1970 %	Quarter Ended December 1970 %	Quarter Ended March 1971 %
Gross profit	27.5	17.1	28.5
Net operating profits	12.5	1.5	9.9
Other profit (loss)	(0.6)	(0.1)	(0.2)
Before-tax profits	11.9	1.6	9.7
After-tax profits	7.1	1.0	5.8

quarters, but some knowledge of costs and expenses is needed to give these figures meaning. For example, the sharp drop in gross profits for the quarter ended December, 1970, tells us that cost of goods sold for that month had to be relatively a much larger portion of net sales than it was in the quarter before. This is a signal for the financial manager to trace operations back to the factory for the source of the trouble. It is apparent in the report for the quarter ending in March that corrective action had been taken or the gross profit margin would not have increased so sharply from 17.1 to 28.5. By identifying and correcting such problems, financial managers may prevent them from occurring again and may establish from this experience a policy for budgeting future profit at this level of operations. Although such evaluations are primarily for internal use, statements of comparative margins may also serve a valuable external use.

PROFIT EARNED ON CAPITAL INVESTMENT

Profit margins are primarily for internal analysis, planning, and control; but comparing net profits with capital investment serves a double purpose of helping to evaluate operations internally and externally. The rate of return on investment is no substitute for the internal analysis of the profit margins which we have just discussed, but it does have certain advantages for measuring efficiency. First, the investment base is relatively stable; and, second, creditors and stockholders have an easier time identifying profit with their investments in the business than they do with sales. We will examine briefly four investment concepts that are currently used for evaluating short-run profits: total assets, gross capital assets, and net capital assets. Asset values will be taken from the balance sheet in Chapter 2. Total assets are less the estimate made for bad debt losses on receivables and less the allowances made for depreciation of fixed assets. Net profits are on an after-tax basis for the convenience of outsiders and are taken from the report for December, 1971, in Table 7.1.

$$\text{Return on total assets} = \frac{\text{Net profits}}{\text{Total assets}}$$

$$= \frac{50,716}{1,125,000}$$

$$= 4.5\%$$

The return of 4.5 percent may seem low, but to properly evaluate it requires that comparisons be made with earlier periods and with returns earned by competitive businesses and by the industry as a whole. If it is used comparatively, it can be a useful indicator of how effectively financial managers are employing the company's total resources. Investors may use this same indicator even though it does not relate profits to their investment. The following measure removes the noncapital portion of total assets from the denominator but keeps the same value in the numerator, causing the return to increase.

$$\text{Return on gross capital} = \frac{\text{Net profits}}{\text{Gross capital}}$$

$$= \frac{\$50,716}{\$1,125,000 - \$128,000}$$

$$= 5.1\%$$

For this measure to be effective it has to be compared with ratios of like elements; it cannot be compared with the first ratio if the evaluation is to be of any use. In the second ratio, $128,000 was removed from total assets, the noncapital portion of current assets that would just cover current liabilities. Now, if another portion of total assets is removed, the $170,000 supplied by capital debts, the denominator

return per share can be restated as a relative value. To do this a dollar value for the share is needed. The dollar value can be the *book value* of the stock or, better still, its market value. The book value is determined by dividing total common shares into the company's net worth or more accurately common equity. The term common equity warns us that, if preferred stock is outstanding, it will be subtracted from the net worth of the business before dividing by the number of common shares. The book value of our company's common stock is $827,000/ 10,000 = $82.70. Using this book value the return per share is:

$$\frac{\$\ 5.07}{\$82.70} = 6\%$$

PROFIT PLANNING

Historical analysis of net profit can be useful for profit planning. From the applied viewpoint each segment of the profit plan needs to be presented to the proper operating division far enough in advance so that it can be consummated. For example, sales personnel are given the optimal sales plan in time to organize the sales force to plan sales strategy and to make the best use of the limited capital resources. Production personnel are given the optimal production plan for meeting finished inventory needs at the sales level. The production department now follows the same general policy as sales in planning its labor force and raw materials needs in advance; so that, operations will go on uninterrupted, and the best use can be made of the limited capital resources budgeted to production use. Even the general administrative staff is given advance notice so that the office force and supplies can be increased or decreased on favorable terms. The profit plan may even be presented to stockholders, and in some cases to creditors, showing them what profit prospects lie ahead. Shareholders want to know how much profit is expected to be generated, and creditors want to know what is expected to be realized in profits for paying interest and principal on outstanding debts.

THE PROFIT FUNCTION

But before preparing the details of a specific profit plan, management needs to have a general plan of action establishing the functional relationships between volume of output and sales and potential net profits from operations, remembering that, with the quantity of capital given, certain costs are fixed. The reader should have developed by now considerable skill in using linear planning tools so that he can go directly to the substance of the profit function as a general planning tool. The first equation expresses the functional relationship between net profits before taxes and in a function of volume of sales. The profit equation below assumes that income taxes are not yet assessed against income. This is, therefore, *net operating profit*, assuming for the moment at least that there are no *other* net gains or losses.

$$P = bX - (a + cX) \qquad\qquad 7.1$$

Where: $P =$ Before tax net profit
$b =$ Unit price
$c =$ Unit variable costs and expenses
$X =$ Number of units sold
$a =$ Fixed costs

Net operating profit is the dependent variable with the rate of change in profit measured by the difference between net sales (bX) and total fixed and variable cost $(a + cX)$. Substituting, let fixed costs a equal \$2,000, price b equal \$10, and unit variable costs and expense c equal \$2 and assume that the maximum units (500) are sold.

$$P = \$10(500) - [\$2,000 + \$2(500)]$$

Since capital costs a are fixed regardless of the level of output and sale, *What management is really concerned with in profit planning is maximizing net profits after total variable costs and expenses.* This important objective is more apparent in the equation:

$$P = X(b - c) - a \qquad 7.2$$

This equation restates the profit plan more clearly by isolating the two critical elements b and c in the profit set. We can verify that by substituting in equation 7.2 the values used in equation 7.1 the same profit of \$2,000 will result. Here we have constant rates of change in income b and constant rates of change in variable costs c. The difference in the two rates of change determines the pattern of the profit function; the greater this difference the greater the profit flow, and the smaller the difference the smaller the profit flow. Another *functional* characteristic of equation 7.2 is that it shows the *contribution* made to fixed costs by net profits over variable costs. In the equation $P = X(b - c) - a$, the contribution to fixed costs and expenses on a unit basis is the difference between the constant rate of change in total income (\$10) and the constant rate of change in total variable costs and expenses (\$2). The larger this difference the more profits over variable costs that are contributed to fixed charges with each unit of sale. Multiplying the difference by X expresses the contribution in total dollars. To illustrate let X equal 200.

$$\text{Contribution} = X(\$10 - \$2)$$
$$= 200(\$8)$$
$$= \$1,600$$

At sales of 200 units, profits above variable costs and expenses is short \$400 of meeting fixed costs and expenses: fixed costs and expenses equal \$2,000, and contribution to fixed costs are \$1,600. Management should realize, however, that since fixed costs (\$2,000) have to be met regardless of the output, *it is better to sell where some contribution is made to fixed costs than to discontinue sales altogether just because fixed costs are not covered completely.* This should be the policy so long as the capital investment decision is made, and the constraint cannot be reduced. This, of course, is a current operating decision; a later capital management decision can contract the quantity of capital investment to reduce the fixed charges. The final stage in planning is setting up a detailed profit budget that serves the dual purpose of supplying a tangible plan for putting the profit function into action over a stated time period and of supplying a tangible instrument for financial control. But the budget will be considered in a later section. First, let us look more closely at the important point at which the contribution of profits over variable costs just covers fixed charges, in other words, the *break-even point* at which before-tax profits are zero, reduced sales would cause a loss, and increased sales would cause a net taxable profit.

THE BREAK-EVEN POINT

The break-even point reveals how many units have to be sold to just cover total costs and expenses (fixed and variable). This is not the optimal level of operation because no net profits are realized here, but it is the first step to planning optimal profits. Simultaneous equations can be used to determine this point. To do this, the income and cost equations contained in the profit function need to be separated. Let Y equal sales income and C equal total fixed and variable costs and expenses; at the break-even point, Y has to be equal to C. If $Y = C$ at the break-even point, then at this point:

$$bX = a + cX$$

Substituting:

$$\$10(X) = \$2,000 + \$2X$$
$$\$8X = \$2,000$$
$$X = 250 \text{ units}$$

To prove this substitute 250 units for X in the two equations:

$$bX = a + c(X)$$
$$\$10(250) = \$2,000 + \$2(250)$$
$$\$2,500 = \$2,500$$

GRAPHIC ANALYSIS

Graphic analysis of the profit function is a useful tool for general profit planning. It has an advantage over the equation of showing the whole range simultaneously of units of sale from the point at which negative profits occur (fixed

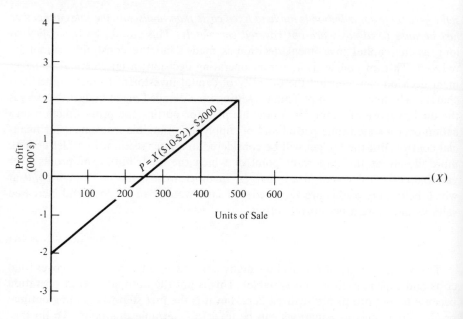

Figure 7.1.   Profit Optimizing Illustrated.

costs are not totally covered) to the point at which optimal profits occur at the limit of the controlling constraint. Figure 7.1 illustrates optimal profits as they would be under two alternative constraints: one the variable cost and expense constraint of 400 units and the other the output and sale constraint of 500 units. The demand constraint is another factor to consider, but this subject was developed at some length in Chapter 6. Only one of these constraints can be effective, of course, and that must be the smaller of the two. The break-even point is at *b*, where the profit function line intersects the units of sale line at 250 units. To the left of this point, profits are negative because sales of less than 250 units would not con-tribute enough profit to fully cover the $2,000 fixed cost. Variable costs and expenses are always covered because income provides from the very first unit of sale a $10 income which is $8 greater than unit variable costs and expenses. Mov-ing to the right from the break-even point, profits can be read off of the *Y* axis for an infinite number of alternative sales levels subject to the governing constraint; optimal output is 400 units and optimal profits are $1,200 where sales are 400 units.

THE PROFIT BUDGET

After reviewing past experiences and developing general skills in the use of the profit optimizing tools, financial managers are ready for budgeting details. The methodology of goal attainment will be explained here for a hypothetical plan which is structured first as a sample budget and then as a finalized budget.

The sample budget is the simulation of a number of operating periods to attain the basic structure of the profit plan. Budget construction requires first research and application of simple arithmetic indicators like those that were applied to profit statements earlier in the chapter mainly to evaluate past experiences. Second, it requires forecasting sales for selected periods using elasticity coefficients and subjective and statistical probabilities wherever they promise to improve the quality of the sales forecast. Finally, the sample budget should offer enough information for setting up a general profit-planning equation. Complex problems like these are always easier to visualize if first they are reduced to simple mathematical models. It cannot be emphasized too strongly that going through the sample budgeting procedure entails considerable detail as was pointed out in Chapter 6. For example, estimating units of sales and sales prices are challenging tasks in themselves. Their costs of goods sold may include a complex of wages paid hourly, cost of goods by the piece, and different prices paid for varied kinds of raw materials. It always includes wear and tear (depreciation) of capital facilities. Administrative expenses may require estimating several commission rates on different products and even different rates paid different salesmen selling the same product. These are a few of the details that are worked out under the leadership of the financial organization. Table 7.4 is the sample budget.

TABLE 7.4
COMPANY———
SAMPLE MONTHLY PROFIT BUDGET
APRIL TO JUNE, 1971

	April	*May*	*June*	*Total*
Gross sales	$63,810	$72,600	$78,090	$214,500
Returns and allowances	2,552	2,904	3,124	8,580
Net sales (Units @ $2.50 each)	$61,258	$69,696	$74,966	$205,920
Cost of goods sold	24,503	27,878	29,987	82,368
Direct labor	13,836	15,840	17,052	46,728
Direct materials	19,961	22,810	24,549	67,320
Overhead	13,380	13,865	14,160	41,405
Total cost of goods sold	$47,177	$52,515	$55,761	$155,453
Gross profit	$14,081	$17,181	$19,205	$ 50,467
Operating expenses:				
Direct selling	$10,675	$11,307	$11,780	$ 33,762
Administrative	1,600	1,600	1,600	4,800
Total operating expenses	$12,275	$12,907	$13,380	$ 38,562
Net operating profit	$ 1,806	$ 4,274	$ 5,825	$ 11,909
Other income (expense) net	832	367	418	1,617
Before-tax profit	$ 2,638	$ 4,641	$ 6,243	$ 13,522
Taxes (@ 40%)	1,055	1,856	2,497	5,408
After-tax profit	$ 1,583	$ 2,785	$ 3,746	$ 8,114
Net profit per share (10,000 shares)	$.16	$.28	$.37	$.81

Table 7.4 contains the income, cost, and expense estimates for each month and for the sum of the three months in the second quarter of 1971 for Company—. It states the average unit selling price and the total sales expected to be made each month and for the total three months. Finally, it gives a breakdown of after-tax net profit on a per share basis. But this budget does not yet reflect the effect of the optimizing technique which will be considered at this time. Nevertheless, from the information contained in Table 7.4 a definite profit program can be shaped. To illustrate how this is done, certain assumptions have to be made. First, assume that the present profit record is not satisfactory and that the goal is to expand operations in the framework of present capital. To make the varied costs and expenses fit into a planning model, a certain amount of regrouping of costs and expenses is necessary. First, variable costs and expenses are combined to get an average unit variable cost figure that is meaningful for the second quarter of 1971. This is done in the following manner:

COMPANY———
BUDGETED COSTS AND EXPENSES

Direct labor	=	$ 46,728
Direct materials	=	67,320
Direct selling	=	33,762
Total	=	$147,810
Unit Variable Cost	=	$\dfrac{147,810}{82,368} = \$1.7945$
Units of Sale	=	

This implies that no change is planned in the basic structure of capital that would alter optimal unit variable charges. We assume, in other words, that the business will be able to operate at a somewhat higher level of sales without raising unit variable charges above $1.7945; so that, applications of the profit function will be correct to the cents per share of stock. In the following calculations, we will not round this figure. Elasticity of demand is assumed to be infinite so that *within certain limits* the customers will take whatever added output is offered at the current price level of $2.50.

Now we have two of the basic values in the profit function: price, $b = \$2.50$, and unit variable costs and expense, $c = \$1.7945$. *Other* expected income d is expected to remain at $1,617 for the planning period.

Overhead costs	$41,405
Administrative expenses	4,800
Total fixed costs and expenses	$46,205

The profit function is expanded slightly now as follows to include *other* expected income:

$$P = [X(b - c) + d] - a$$

Substituting, now we have the profit equation for the sample budget:

$$P = X(\$2.50 - \$1.7945) + \$1,617 - \$46,205$$

The key to profit optimization is increasing sales in this case to the limit of maximum unit variable charges, to the point at which total variable costs and expenses start increasing sharply. Suppose that, after applying a probability distribution to possible sales as was done in Chapter 6, *expected sales* would be increased by 10 percent from 82,368 units to 90,605 units. Entering this in the equation, before-tax net profits are expected to be $19,334 which becomes $11,600 and $1.16 per share after a 40 percent tax:

$$
\begin{aligned}
P &= [X(b - c) + d] \\
&= [90,605(2.50 - 1.7945) + 1,617] - \$46,205 \\
&= 63,921 + 1,617 - 46,205 \\
&= \$19.334
\end{aligned}
$$

Assuming a 40 percent tax rate, the profit figure is adjusted to an after-tax basis by multiplying the before-tax figure by $(1 - 0.4)$.

$$\text{Optimal after-tax profit} = (1 - 0.4)19,334 = 11,600$$
$$\text{Per share net profits} = \$11,600/10,000 = \$1.16$$

The break-even point between total sales and total costs and expenses is determined as follows:

$$Y = \$2.50(X) + \$1,617$$
$$C = \$1.7945(X) + \$46,205$$

Since

$$Y = C \text{ at the break-even point:}$$
$$2.50X + 1,617 = 1.7945(X) + 46,205$$
$$2.50(X) - 1.7945(X) = -1,617 + 46,205$$
$$.7055X = 44,488$$
$$X = 63,200 \text{ units}$$

If 90,605 units of sale are optimal, we can restate the break-even point now as a certain percentage of the optimal level of sales; our firm will break even at 70 percent of optimal: $63,200/90,605 = 0.697$ which rounds to 70 percent. The relative break-even point should tell management that the unit contribution margin $(\$2.50 - \$1.7945) = 0.7055$ is narrow and that control action is needed either to increase unit price or to decrease unit costs and expenses. Since demand was assumed above to be infinitely elastic for the present range of sales, we have no control over price; an increase in price would cause a very large loss in sales and would possibly cause the business to lose all of its sales. But unit costs and expenses may be reduced. If we find that the contribution margin cannot be increased, the only solution may be to reduce capital costs and expenditures which entails a capital management decision.

THE FINAL PROFIT BUDGET

An operating budget is constructed finally incorporating the optimization goal in the detailed plan of operations. The plan calls for goal attainment which would increase after-tax net profits from $0.81 to $1.16 per share, a gain of $0.35 over what was planned in the sample budget. All of this is expected to be realized by increasing the volume of sales. Given the fixed costs and expenses of $46,205 and unit profit of $0.7055 ($2.50 − $1.7945) above variable charges, it is obvious that the more units we can sell after covering fixed charges the more total net profits will be realized by the business. Getting back again to the present budgeting problem, we will notice that the optimization plan is directed to a total quarter of operations. For the final budget to be effective for internal control purposes though, the plan should be restated in detail on a monthly basis. A monthly profit plan will give financial managers a chance to correct variations from the final budget before it has had time to have damaging effects.

Table 7.5 is the final profit budget for the second quarter, 1971, stated on a monthly basis. The final step in control is to compare monthly budgeted operations with actual monthly operations and to exert influence where it is needed at different levels of the budget at the end of each month. Each item on the actual statement for April will be compared with its corresponding item in the budgeted statement. If actual gross sales are less than planned for April or if returns and allowances are larger, financial managers need at least to communicate with the sales managers. It may have resulted from economic, social, or psychological factors over which sales managers have no control; but it may have resulted from sales management factors that can be controlled. Financial managers are responsible for detecting these differences, and also for communicating them to those who are directly responsible and who can make the corrections. At the cost of goods sold level with its specialized control areas of direct labor and direct materials, financial managers need to challenge the actual costs just as they do actual sales when they do not conform to the budget. Financial managers are not responsible for making corrections but are responsible for seeing that the corrections are made to prevent this from recurring in May. The same procedure is used on operating expenses and administrative expenses and for each month in the planning period.

We assumed in the paragraph above that actual operating values were *adverse*, that is, sales were lower and costs and expenses were higher than the budgeted

TABLE 7.5
FINAL MONTHLY PROFIT BUDGET

	April	May	June	Total
Gross sales	69,936	79,570	85,587	235,093
Returns and allowances	−2,552	−2,904	−3,124	−8,580
Net sales	67,384	76,666	82,463	226,513
Cost of goods sold				
Direct labor	15,220	17,424	18,757	51,401
Direct materials	21,957	25,091	27,004	74,052
Fixed overhead	10,000	10,000	10,000	30,000
Semifixed overhead	3,380	3,865	4,160	11,405
Total cost of goods sold	50,557	56,380	59,921	166,858
Gross profit	16,827	20,286	22,542	59,655
Operating expense	11,743	12,438	12,958	37,139
Administrative	1,600	1,600	1,600	4,800
Total operational expense	13,343	14,038	14,558	21,939
Net operating profit	3,484	1,248	7,984	17,716
Other income	832	367	418	1,617
	4,316	6,615	8,402	19,233
Tax (@ 40%)	−1,726	−2,646	−3,362	−7,712
After-tax profit	2,590	3,969	5,040	11,599
Net profit per share (10,000 shares)	0.259	0.397	0.504	1.16

figures. But what if actual sales are higher than the budgeted and costs and expenses are lower than the budgeted. At first this may seem to be the ideal situation; but, if the budget had considered output, income, cost, and expense factors before the optimizing procedure was undertaken, then an increase in output and sales may have disparaging effects. For example, excess sales, with a given quantity of net working capital, could cause inventory shortages and long-run loss of customers. To meet the added sales, the whole production organization may have to be geared to a point at which inefficiency in manufacture caused by limited fixed and working capital resources may cause total costs to rise sharply.

THE JOINT PRODUCT SITUATION

Profit optimization becomes somewhat more complex when two or more products bid for the use of limited capital resources. In this section, we will consider the profit optimization problem when a given quantity of fixed and working capital is rationed to produce two products. The special method of attaining this goal is called *linear programming*. Linear equations are basic optimizing tools as they are in the single or the average product case that has been pursued in Chapters 6 and 7 thus far, but underlying the analysis is the *inequality* as a quantitative tool for indicating the rate at which the products use up jointly a given limited quantity of capital resources. The prime issue before management is how to ration limited capital resources to maximize profits from joint production and sale. In our example, we assume a two-product optimizing situation.

Assume that two products X_1 and X_2 are manufactured by a firm which has available $6,000 cash and other liquid asset funds of net working capital, that is, $6,000 above total current assets that would be needed to just cover current liabilities. This sum of working capital must be shared by products X_1 and X_2 during a given operating period. The firm has $5,000 available in fixed capital also to be shared in producing products X_1 and X_2. It is noted further that net working capital will be used by X_1 and X_2 at the linear rate of $10/1 and $15/1 respectively. That is, every time one unit of X_1 is produced, $10 of net working capital is drawn into use; and every time one unit of X_2 is produced, $15 worth of net working capital is drawn into use. With respect to fixed capital, that is plant and equipment, the linear use rate is $20/1 for X_1 and $10/1 for X_2. This means that, every time one unit of X_1 is produced, $20 worth of fixed assets is used; and every time one unit of X_2 is produced, $10 worth of fixed assets is used. If breaking down fixed capital into $20 and $10 units respectively is puzzling us, we can think of these as units of fixed assets time expressed in dollar values.

Now going back to the linear function as it applies to inequalities, we summarize what was explained in the paragraph above with the two quantitative relationships:

$$\$10X_1 + \$15X_2 \leq \$6,000$$
$$\$20X_1 + \$10X_2 \leq \$5,000$$

The values on the right side of the inequality signs, the dollar values of net working capital and fixed capital respectively, are related to the Y values in single product linear equations. Values to the right of the inequality signs are linear functions of the quantities X_1 and X_2 with coefficients of $10 and $15 respectively in the first inequality and of $20 and $10 respectively in the second. If the student analyzes this carefully, he will see that the first function states that products X_1 and X_2 can be produced using up any quantity of net working capital at the constant rate of $10 and $15 respectively but not to exceed $6,000. For example, terms of the inequality could be met by producing 100 units X_1 and 100 units of X_2 because:

$$\$10(100) + \$15(100) = \$2,500$$

Only a little over 1/3 of the net working capital would be used up in this operation Or they could be produced in different quantities such as 100 of X_1 and 200 of X_2 which would use up $10(100) + $15(200) = $4,000 of the capital. There is no point in continuing the illustrations because there are an infinite number of combinations of X_1 and X_2 quantities that could be produced with $6,000 of liquid working capital. In applying the operation to fixed capital, the principle is exactly the same; but, since the coefficients are different, total capital use will be different. Let us substitute the same quantity of X_1 and X_2 variables of 100 and 100 in the fixed asset function:

$$\$20(100) + \$10(100) = \$3,000$$

This is a feasible operation because only 3/5 of the fixed capital would be used up. At the production rate $X_1 = 200$ and $X_2 = 100$. $\$20(200) + \$10(100) = \$5,000$; and the full quantity of fixed assets would have expired. But an infinite number of combinations of X_1 and X_2 values can be used provided not more than $\$5,000$ is used.

The equations for the upper limits of the inequalities are as follows:

$$\$10(X_1) + \$15(X_2) = \$6,000$$
$$\$20(X_1) + \$10(X_2) = \$5,000$$

Using the limiting equations above, we can portray graphically the linear relationships of the inequalities. We do this in four stages, first, using the $\$6,000$ working capital and, second, the $\$5,000$ fixed capital limit, setting X_1 and X_2 alternately equal to zero and solving the following equations.

$$
\begin{array}{rrl}
(1) & \$10X_1 + \$15X_2 = & \$6,000 \\
\text{Setting } X_2 = (0) & \$10X_1 + \$15(0) = & 6,000 \\
& X_1 = & 600
\end{array}
$$

$$
\begin{array}{rrl}
(2) & \$10X_1 + \$15X_2 = & \$6,000 \\
\text{Setting } X_1 = (0) & \$10(0) + \$15X_2 = & 6,000 \\
& X_2 = & 400
\end{array}
$$

$$
\begin{array}{rrl}
(3) & \$20X_1 + \$10X_2 = & \$5,000 \\
\text{Setting } X_2 = (0) & \$20X_1 + \$10(0) = & 5,000 \\
& X_1 = & 250
\end{array}
$$

$$
\begin{array}{rrl}
(4) & \$20X_1 + \$10X_2 = & \$5,000 \\
\text{Setting } X_1 = (0) & \$20(0) + \$10X_2 = & 5,000 \\
& X_2 = & 500
\end{array}
$$

The first equation shows that, if product X_1 alone is produced, there is working capital enough to produce 600 units; and this is the limiting point on the X_1 axis. The second equation shows that, if product X_2 alone is produced, there is working capital enough to produce 400 units; and this is the limiting point on the X_2 axis. Connecting these two points produces line *BE* which is the *limit* of the joint production function of products X_1 and X_2 subject to the working capital constraint of $\$6,000$ and the use rate of $\$10$ and $\$15$ respectively by X_1 and X_2. The third equation shows that, if X_1 alone is produced, there is fixed capital enough to produce 250 units; and this is the second limiting point on the X_1 axis. The fourth equation shows that, if product X_2 alone is produced, there is fixed capital enough to produce 500 units; and this marks the second limiting point on the X_2 axis. Connect-

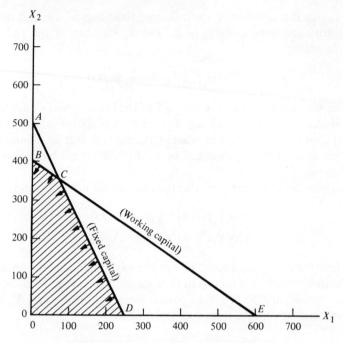

Figure 7.2. Graphing Inequalities.

ing the two points produces line AD which is the linear joint production function of products X_1 and X_2 subject to the fixed capital constraint.

The shaded area on the graph represents the set of all possible combinations of X_1 and X_2 output and sales that are possible without violating one or more of the capital constraints. For example, if X_1 were produced beyond 250 units, it would be violating its fixed capital constraint even though there is still enough working capital to produce 600 units. And X_2 is *frozen* at 400 units because after that its working capital constraint would be violated even though fixed capital could have let it go on to 500 units. To meet all of the constraints the products have to be produced jointly within the outer limits of the shaded area $OBCD$. Again, an infinite number of combinations of X_1 and X_2 are possible within these limits, but the optimal combination is the one that maximizes profit.

PROFIT MAXIMIZATION—A GRAPHIC SOLUTION

We have learned that, with the quantity of capital given and subject to output, cost, and expense limitations, net profits are a linear function of sales. Unit operating profit we will recall is equal to $b - c$. In the example used here of X_1 and X_2, we assume that unit profits are \$20 and \$60 respectively with the profit maximization equation for the joint products stated as:

$$P_{mx} = \$20(X_1) + \$60(X_2)$$

At first the maximizing solutions would appear to be infinite since the more units of X_1 and X_2 that are produced jointly the higher would be their joint profit, but this does not hold as we have seen because operations have to be contained within the limits of the two capital constraints outlined by $OBCD$. A graphic operation will locate for us the optimal output and sales combination of products X_1 and X_2 given the profit maximizing function above. Figure 7.3 has all of the elements for answering the question: Given the profit function, what combination of X_1 and X_2 will maximize profit? The procedure is to plot the points on the X_1 and X_2 product axes at which net profits for each product are equal, that is, plot a point on the X_1 axis which when multiplied by $20 will give the same result that the point selected on the X_2 will give when multiplied by $60. Since unit profits for product X_2 are 3 times as large as unit profits for X_1, the quantity selected on X_1 has to be three times as great as the one on X_2 for profits to be the same. In Figure 7.3, we select points 50 and 150 on X_2 and X_1 respectively and draw a profit function line through these points. To prove that profits are the same at each point, let:

$$X_1 = 0 \qquad\qquad\qquad X_2 = 0$$
$$X_2 = 50 \qquad\qquad\qquad X_1 = 150$$

Then: $\$60(50) = \$3{,}000$ \qquad And: $\$20(150) = \$3{,}000$

Any coordinate on this profit function line will produce a sum of $3,000 profit for the joint output and sale; but, as the profit function line is moved in the direction of

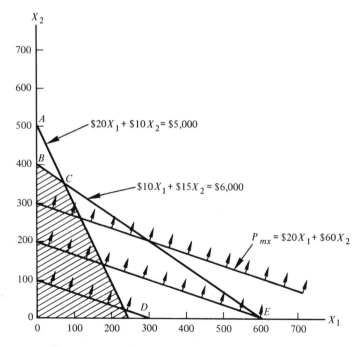

Figure 7.3. Optimizing Output: A Graphic Solution.

the arrows, the coordinates produce larger joint X_1 and X_2 profits with each movement of the line toward the limit of the feasible profit set $OBCD$. To illustrate this, we let the new line intersect X_2 at 80 units and X_1 at 240 units. The student should verify that any combination of products X_1 and X_2 on the new line will produce a profit of \$4,800. The point of maximum profit is found finally by moving this function to the outer limit of the profit set $OBCD$. Because of the great profit advantage of X_2, more of this product will be produced than of X_1; in fact, the last point in $OBCD$ touched by the profit function line is at point B where 400 units of X_2 are produced and 0 units of X_1 are produced. Total profits are: \$60(400) = \$24,000.

This is the extreme case used to illustrate the important role played by the unit profit margin in determining the product mix. Now suppose that profits are the same on each unit of X_1 and X_2 and that the profit maximization function is:

$$P = \$60(X_1) + \$60(X_2)$$

Then the points selected on the X_1 and X_2 axes would be the same in setting the profit functions. This would put a different slope on the profit function curve and would dictate a different product mix for profit maximization. Taking a straight edged instrument and starting at $100X_1$ and $100X_2$, the student can verify that the outermost point in this case is at C. Whenever the last point is out in space, as it is in this case, instead of on one of the axes, the X_1 and X_2 values can be more accurately located by solving simultaneously the X_1 and X_2 values.

$$10X_1 + 15X_2 = 6,000$$
$$20X_1 + 10X_2 = 5,000$$

Multiplying by 2: $\qquad 20X + 30X_2 = 12,000$

Multiplying by -1: $\qquad -20X - 10X_2 = -5,000$

Adding algebraically: $\qquad\qquad\quad 20X_2 = 7,000$
$$X_2 = 350 \text{ at } C$$

Substitute in first equation: $\quad 10X_1 + 15(350) = 6,000$
$$10X_1 = 6,000 - 5,250$$
$$X_1 = 75 \text{ at } C$$

Total profits should be somewhat larger in this case than in the former even though fewer units of X_2 are produced because the reduction in output of X_2 by 50 units $(400 - 350)$ is more than offset by the added output of X_1 by 75$(75 - 0)$ with the same unit profit of \$60. Substituting the quantities in profit maximizing function:

$$P = \$60(75) + \$60(350)$$
$$= \$25,500$$

The student may want to experiment with different product mixes using the $\$60(X_1) + \$60(X_2)$ profit function to verify that there is no more profitable product mix than the one of $X_1 = 75$ and $X_2 = 350$.

SUMMARY

This chapter has covered a wide scope of subjects related to the important problem of profit management. First, methodology in management was emphasized: historical analysis and comparative profit analysis are important methods for gaining an insight into segments of operation that need closer control. Historical analysis can also lend assistance to the profit-planning operation, and it is the profit-planning operation that is of main concern to financial managers. The importance of the capital constraint and the importance of linear planning tools was emphasized as the first step in effective profit planning and control, not as an end product but as a complement to the budgeting operation.

Implicit in most of the optimizing analysis is the single product firm or the firm producing products that are similar enough so that they can be fitted into the single-product profit function. But some companies produce such diverse products that they do not readily fit into the single-product model; the linear programming technique was used to illustrate profit planning in a two-product operation. In summarizing this section, the following factors should be noted. First, there are product forms that are so different in their physical composition and in their rate of capital consumption that they do not fit well into the one-product profit planning situation analysis that was developed earlier in the chapter. Second, linear programming serves the purpose very well of quantifying the concept of a capital constraint and of showing how decision making for net profit is limited by the quantity of capital resources. Third, this analysis emphasizes the importance of simulating and planning operations with profit budgets before making action decisions. Fourth, the examples that were used above reaffirm for us that in current operations unit net profits times the volume of sales are the main variables in planning net profits from current operations. As a sidelight on this, the graphic illustrations are effective media for showing how by increasing capital investment the perimeters of the decision set $OBCD$ are moved out to permit a larger volume of output and sale. Finally, the question of the relationship between this kind of internal analysis for profit and the market analysis for maximizing share values needs to be mentioned. Break-even points such as were discussed earlier in the chapter are clearly understood and, accordingly, should be treated as mediums for communicating profit-management goals and procedures to the securities market. Presently, linear programming media are not part of the typical investor's kit of value indicators, but this does not mean that they will not be part of the analytic equipment in the future.

PROBLEMS

1. The board of directors of the Adams Manufacturing Company decided to launch an aggressive program of profit management and control. Specifically, the program was to provide realistic profit management that would be a source of motivation for the nonfinancial as well as the financial personnel. The finan-

cial manager decided to start by setting up a kind of educational program in which certain simple tools could be used to give reported profits a dynamic meaning and, thereby, help to motivate operating efficiency. He began by explaining the functional meaning of each of the basic profit figures: a. gross profit, b. net operating profit, c. other profit (loss), d. before-tax profit, and e. after-tax profit. He felt that most of the personnel were unaware that financial management decisions consider simultaneously several profit levels on the operating statement. He thought this could be best illustrated by plotting the tabulated profits for the business at three levels of operations for the past six months.

ADAMS MANUFACTURING COMPANY
PROFIT SUMMARY
JULY 31————DECEMBER 31, 1970

	Jul.	*Aug.*	*Sept.*	*Oct.*	*Nov.*	*Dec.*
Gross profit	$85,000	$95,000	$110,000	$110,000	$70,000	$60,000
Before-tax profit	70,000	75,000	90,000	90,000	50,000	40,000
After-tax profit	35,000	37,500	45,000	45,000	25,000	20,000

    a. Construct a line graph on arithmetic paper. Explain the graph so that it will be understandable to nonfinancial personnel.

    b. Construct a cumulative profits table for the six-month period and plot the cumulative monthly figures on an arithmetic graph with an explanatory paragraph.

2. Using the figures in Problem 1, determine the rate of change at the three levels of profit, using the rule: $(Y_2 - Y_1)/(X_2 - X_1)$. Now determine the relative rate of change in the three profits figures using the rule: $(Y_2 - Y_1/Y_1)/(X_2 - X_1)$. Evaluate the two profit measures. Let X equal the number of months.

3. In order to learn more about the profit factors in the business, the financial manager of the Adams Manufacturing Company compared the sources and uses of profits during the current year. As the first step to securing and comparing the information, he completed the following form. Explain how the results

ADAMS MANUFACTURING COMPANY
COMPARATIVE INCOME STATEMENTS

	November 1970	*December* 1971	*Increase*	*Decrease*	*No Change*
Net sales	$233,333	$200,000			
Cost of goods sold	163,333	140,000			
Gross profit	70,000	60,000			
Operating expenses	21,000	21,000			
Net operating profit	49,000	39,000			
Other profit (loss)	1,000	1,000			
Before-tax profits	50,000	40,000			
State & Federal taxes	25,000	20,000			
After-tax profit	25,000	20,000			

of working out this form and preparing a *sources* and *uses* of profit can be used as the first step toward an effective investigation for profit control.

4. Below is a comparison of three different value sets. You are the financial manager of the Adams Company. How can you compare these unlike amounts to evaluate your own company's profit experience?

MAKING PROFIT COMPARISONS FOR FOUR QUARTERS
ADAMS MANUFACTURING COMPANY

	3rd Quarter 1970	4th Quarter 1970	1st Quarter 1971	2nd Quarter 1971
Gross profits	$ 290,000	$ 240,000	$ 280,000	$ 350,000
After-tax profits	117,500	90,000	105,000	110,000
Net sales	2,000,000	2,000,000	1,500,000	1,500,000
Competitor				
Gross profits	$ 370,000	$ 380,000	$ 390,000	$ 400,000
After-tax profits	150,000	160,000	150,000	200,000
Net sales	1,500,000	1,500,000	1,000,000	1,000,000
Industry				
Gross profits	$1,500,000	$1,800,000	$2,000,000	$2,500,000
After-tax profits	600,000	600,000	650,000	650,000
Net sales	10,000,000	10,000,000	12,000,000	12,000,000

5. Complete the following table of operating information. Each unit of product sells for $2.00, and unit variable costs are 0.6 of the price.

OPERATING INFORMATION

Sales Volume	Value	Change in Sales Volume	Unit Variable Costs	Fixed Costs and Expenses $1,000	Total Costs and Expenses	Change in Total Costs and Expenses
500						
1,000						
1,500						
2,000						
2,500						
3,000						
3,500						
4,000						

a. Write the equations for the profit function.

b. Graph the profit function, omitting the income and cost functions.

c. Compare the rates of change in sales and in total costs and expenses. If numerical relationships of this kind between sales, costs, and expenses are plotted on arithmetic graph paper, what kind of lines will result when the points are connected?

d. What significance does the capital constraint and the demand constraint have on determining optimal profits?

6. Assume that you produce two differently priced goods and that different manufacturing costs are incurred in producing them. You feel that graphing their profits individually would give you a closer grasp of their planning and control potentials than combining them and averaging their profits. The following basic information is summarized for the two products.

> Product *A*—Price $4 per unit.
>   Maximum sales capacity 7,000 units
>   Present sales volume 5,000 units.
>   Unit variable cost 70 percent of sales price.
>   Fixed costs and expenses $3,000.
> Product *B*—Price $8 per unit.
>   Maximum sales capacity 5,000 units.
>   Present sales volume 3,000 units.
>   Unit variable cost 60 percent of sales price.
>   Fixed costs and expenses $6,000.

Chart the operating information for Products *A* and *B* on two separate graphs.

   a. Illustrate the break-even points for each product on the graphs. Check this by the formula method.
   b. What is the ratio of the break-even point in sales for each product to its maximum sales capacity? What does this tell you about the risk in producing each product?
   c. Compare the contribution rate of each product toward fixed costs.
   d. Which of the two products do you recommend promoting for greater profit? Can anything be done about the capital constraints?

7. Put yourself in the position of a financial manager working closely with the manufacturing and selling personnel to budget a six-month operating plan. The reason for using six months is that past experience shows six months to be a typical operating cycle for your organization. You realize the futility of trying to plan the profits for so complicated an operation as manufacturing without knowing the details of expected sales and production. From the sales division, you learn that 10,000 units of finished goods are in stock, that 100,000 units are expected to be sold, and that the stocks of finished goods at the end of the period will be increased to 20,000 units. You discover that the production manager took his cue from the sales estimates and planned accordingly to manufacture a total of 110,000 units of finished goods: 100,000 for sale and 10,000 to be added to finished stocks. You learn that he expects goods in process of production to be unchanged at the end of the period but that he plans to double the raw materials holdings from 5,000 units to 10,000. He indicated that one unit of raw materials would produce one unit of finished goods so that his purchases of raw materials need to equal the sum of finished goods for sale and for addition to finished stocks. As financial manager, you now summarize the information that you think will be relevant to profit planning.

Expected sales volume .... 100,000 units
Expected manufacturing volume .... 110,000 units
Expected purchases volume .... 115,000 units

To convert this to dollars you need monetary values. This does not prove difficult because the sales price had been set at $10 per unit. Each unit of raw mate-
rials going into finished goods will cost $2, and each unit of finished product
will contain in addition $2 of direct labor service and $1 of capital depreciation
in combination with other forms of overhead.

   a. Given this information, construct the cost-of-goods-sold estimate and
      the gross profit estimate of the sample profit budget.

   b. You still have the operating expenses and income taxes to consider.
      With the following information, complete the forecast all the way to
      after-tax profits. Sales commissions are 10 percent of sales value; sales
      and administrative salaries are $40,000; and other selling and admin-
      istrative expenses are to be $10,000. Other profits (losses) are expected
      to be ($4,000), and income taxes are expected to be paid at the rate of
      40 percent.

   c. What will the expected return per share of stock be, assuming that
      40,000 shares are outstanding?

   d. In one paragraph, state how this projection of your operations will
      help to attain your profit goal.

   e. After examining capital facilities, you decide that 120,000 units can be
      sold instead of 100,000. Determine the optimal profit at the higher
      sales level.

   f. Construct an optimal profit budget based on the sample budget and
      your optimization plan.

8. You are trying to optimize the output of two very different products that use
   jointly the same limited fixed capital facilities which are spelled out as a maximum of 3,000 service hours available at stage A in production and a maximum
   of 2,000 service hours at stage B. The two products X_1 and X_2 use these capital
   facilities at the rate of 6 and 8 units respectively at stage A and 2 and 3 units
   respectively at stage B. The profit maximization functions for the two products
   is: $P_{mx} = \$2(X_1) + \$3(X_2)$

   a. Write the functions for the inequalities at stage A and stage B.
   b. Graph the inequalities.
   c. Using the graphic method, determine joint output and sales.
   d. Use simultaneous equations to verify that your graphic solution is
      correct.
   e. Comment on this as a profit planning technique, incorporating in your
      discussion the role of the capital constraint in short- and long-run
      decision making.

PART IV

**CURRENT
OPERATIONS:
INTERNAL
FUNDS
MANAGEMENT**

8

Inventory
Management

In Part IV current operations are carried to funds management. This means managing the current assets including inventory, receivables, cash, and near cash assets. We still analyze and make decisions subject to a capital constraint but shift our optimizing emphasis to individual current assets. Although we treat the assets in isolation, several current assets may be involved at the same time in managing current operations; not only several assets but current assets and current income costs and expenses.

SCOPE OF INVENTORY MANAGEMENT

First, let us consider what is not a concern of this chapter. The chapter is not concerned with sales revenue from inventory because this has been covered in Part II. Neither is inventory management specifically concerned with financing inventory purchases. This is not to say that financing of inventories is not an important part of the total current flow problem; but inventory financing, because of its varied nature, is necessarily reserved to Part V. What this chapter is concerned with is problems that arise because of special kinds of financial management issues that arise from purchasing, holding, and processing this asset. These are special kinds of problems for several reasons. First, the asset lies right in the center of current operations for profit. Second, because of the low liquidity compared with other current assets, inventories subject the business to more than a proportionate amount of risks. Third, because of sizeable costs connected specifically with ordering, holding, and being short of inventories, considerable benefit may be realized for the business and its shares by optimizing the quantity of inventories held in stock. Various aspects of these three problem areas are explored in this chapter.

LIQUIDITY FACTOR IN INVENTORY MANAGEMENT

Let us define liquidity as the amount of flexibility and fluidity in the current assets to take advantage of future profitable operating opportunities. Liquidity factors in inventory management relate to the extent that this quality of fluidity exists in inventory investments. Liquidity risk in any asset is the chance that management takes of not being able to turn over that asset into cash or some other relatively fluid asset like marketable securities or receivables for added operations. In inventory management, that risk can be related to the chance that inventories cannot be turned over into cash through normal sales channels. The desire to realize the cash investment value from inventories does not set aside the objective of realizing net profits from the sale of inventories. Profits are concerned altogether with the *net value* added in the disposition of inventories. Inventories, as has been pointed out earlier, are not as liquid or fluid as other current assets; and there is also a range of liquidity within the inventory class itself. Inventories that are readily convertible to receivables and cash through normal sales channels can be considered *intrinsically* liquid; while, if it returns its value quickly through forced sales, it can be considered *extrinsically* liquid. Management is concerned primarily with the former although there are some conditions when extrinsic liquidity needs to be evaluated. The risk of loss in cash value of inventory is associated with holding inventory and more definitely with losses resulting from price decline, style-change product deterioration, and seasonality.

GENERAL LIQUIDITY FACTORS

Price decline is a prime risk factor associated with decreasing liquidity, and, unfortunately, financial managers often have limited control over this important variable. A common cause of price decline is competition from other businesses, which increases the market supply when demand stays about the same. The only way to reduce this kind of risk is to increase control of the market, but this is a capital management problem and lies outside the scope of this immediate problem. New competitive products also threaten present prices, and even more risky is outright price cutting by competitiors during a general economic crisis.

A significant common characteristic of all of these supply factors is that they are not usually controllable in current operations. Instead they are risks that financial managers have to live with and counteract as much as possible by controlling the quantity of inventory that they hold. Then there are decreases in demand due to changes in seasons and changes in buying habits. All of these demand factors deserve special attention from financial managers particularly when considering price elasticity, but often the only recourse is to anticipate their occurrence and to restrict inventory investment.

Style change decreases liquidity particularly of finished consumers' goods. Companies holding inventories that have gone out of style could suffer major losses in liquidity as their inventories return in cash just a fraction of their initial cost. This is apparent for hard goods such as automobiles and appliances as well for soft goods like clothing.

Product deterioration also ranks high among factors affecting a product's liquidity. All products are subjected to this risk, but in widely varying degrees. The rate of deterioration in fresh foods and medicines is much faster than for other inventories like textiles, metals, timber, and lumber. Exceptions to the rule of deterioration are certain inventories like cheeses, wines, and works of art. Deterioration varies in degrees, but in any case it usually prevents selling the product through normal channels. Often the product is forced into a new lower grade market and in extreme cases into a salvage market where even extrinsic liquidity is greatly impaired. One important fact should be noted in conclusion, namely, that the basic causes of deterioration lie within the scope of internal control.

Seasonality of goods affects their saleability. Changing weather conditions in the northern and southern hemisphere countries create seasonal demands for goods which cause losses in intrinsic and extrinsic values to inventories held during off seasons. This is remedied partly by carrying goods through interim seasons. Where surplus storage space is available this can be done, but more often end-of-the-season sales are held to realize as much liquidity as possible from the inventories by forced sale.

LIQUIDITY FACTORS—INTERNAL

Aside from general liquidity risks that apply to multi-industry inventories, there is a special liquidity classification distinguishing the liquidity of inventories in a given producing firm. The basis of liquidity classification here is the nearness of inventory to the point of sale. In manufacturing, inventories go through three stages from raw materials to goods in process to finished goods, each with a different degree of certainty as to their convertibility to receivables and cash.

Raw Materials Raw materials are the least liquid of the three inventory types in a production enterprise because they are farthest away from sales. Another way of stating this is that the far distant *maturity* date of raw materials decreases their liquidity. Then there is the low liquidity of raw materials coming from forced sales of goods that cannot be absorbed in the manufacturing process. In speaking of the low liquidity of raw materials, we are referring to materials purchased specifically for manufacture and not of futures contracts purchased for speculation in the commodities markets; futures contracts, while exposed to some risk of loss in value, nevertheless are more flexible and, therefore, have greater liquidity than raw materials awaiting processing by a given firm.

Liquidity risks increase directly with stockpiling of all inventories but probably increase faster with raw materials than with the other two forms. Besides the purchase price, management stands to lose from the costs of storing raw materials;

and this part of the problem will receive special attention later in our optimization analysis. Counteracting the risks of price decline in quantity holdings of raw materials is the prospect for greater profits resulting from discounts on quantity purchases. One final point should be mentioned, namely that the amount of risk that management can afford to take through inventory holdings to increase profits is a variable factor that differs widely among individual businesses.

Goods in Process   Goods in the process of manufacture bring raw materials one step closer to sale. The liquidity risk of these goods is decreased over raw materials because of the shorter time before sales which wipes out most of the general liquidity risks discussed in the previous section. It is noteworthy, however, that the risk of loss from forced sale of goods in process of manufacture may be greater than for raw materials because of the limited scope of their market; it is not an easy matter to dispose of goods either in the normal course of sales, or under forced sales, that are worked on but not finished.

Finished Goods   Finished goods are ready for sale and often are already sold by the time they reach the end of the production line. But whether they are sold or not, they are usually more liquid than raw materials and goods in process. They are more liquid because of the shorter time before normal sale serves to avoid the mishaps of price change and the other general liquidity risks, and, also, they are more liquid than the other forms in those cases of forced sales. There are risk of errors in sales scheduling however, which may develop serious surpluses of finished goods, causing added costs for insurance, shelter, taxes, spoilage, and deterioration, greater usually than for raw materials. Financial managers are confronted with the same decision-making issue in finished goods management as in raw materials and partly finished goods, that of compromising between small quantities of finished goods to reduce liquidity risks and related holding costs, and large quantities as a preparedness measure for meeting forthcoming demand.

RESEARCH AND ANALYSIS

Financial managers need to research and to quantify their past inventory management practices like they do their profit management practices for effective liquidity management and control. Financial managers are urged to keep a constant vigil over inventory levels for reasons that should be clear by now. A few basic measuring tools are suggested here for researching and analyzing historical data and for planning inventory balances for the future.

Relative Share of Current Assets   The most fundamental quantitative expression of this low-liquidity current asset is the measure of its relative share of total current assets. Current assets are composed fundamentally of cash, marketable securities and inventories. The relative measure of inventories is: Inventory balance/Total current assets. Thus if inventories are $50,000 and current assets $150,000, the relative value is 0.33/1. Numerator and denominator can be taken right off of the balance sheet whenever the financial managers desire. The worth of this measure increases when comparisons are made over time and also with competitive firms and with the total industry. Rates of change are interesting and useful media indicating the increase or decrease in the inventory balance given a certain quantity increase in total current assets. An important question needing an answer is: How important relatively is this risky asset? And is it increasing or decreasing in importance in our business? Whichever direction it is taking, does it need curbing or expanding? Financial markets as well observe this ratio, but financial managers should penetrate their inventory balances more intensively and measure the balances: Raw materials/Total inventories, Goods in process/Total inventories, and Finished goods/Total inventories. Any changes over time in these values should be closely noted. Evaluation of these ratios is such that an increase in the first and second ratios, compared with the last, may be more reason for concern than if the situation were reversed.

Inventory Turnover   The turnover of the inventory investment on a given date into net sales or cost of gods sold will show how large the inventory investment is on the average compared with the volume of business transacted. The turnover ratio, Net sales/Inventory balance, expresses liqudity in terms of sales (liquid assets like cash and receivables) generated with a given inventory investment. Let us substitute in the ratio: $200,000/$100,000 = 2/1$, two dollars of sales related to a $100,000 inventory investment. If sales increase to $450,000 and inventories to only $150,000, the turnover increases to $3/1$, indicating more efficient asset use for liquidity through sales. The latter induces a less risky condition for the business; but, if the ratio becomes extremely high, financial managers may be sacrificing sales and profitability for too much safety and security. There needs to be an optimal ratio established by financial managers that balances profitability prospects with liquidity needs.

AVERAGE AGE OF INVENTORIES

As a governing rule, financial managers can expect that the longer funds are invested in any given inventories, the less chance there is of fully recovering those funds either through regular or forced sales. The average age of inventories is a relationship between the dollar quantity on hand at the beginning or end of an operating period, or an average of these two, and the quantity purchased or manufactured over the whole period: purchased when management is concerned with the age of raw materials and manufactured when he is concerned with the age of finished goods. The general relationship for raw materials is stated as follows:

$$\text{Average age of raw materials} = \frac{RM}{P} \times D \qquad 8.1$$

Where: RM = Raw materials balances
P = Total purchases during the period
D = Number of days in the purchasing period

Substituting, assume that $8,000 in materials are on hand at the end of a two-month operation and that purchases during the two months were $40,000; the average age of the inventories is 12 days: ($8,000/$40,000) × 60 = 12. The key value is the basic relationship of $8,000/$40,000. This states that 1/5 or 20 cents on each dollar of purchases on the average is held in the inventory balance. Multiplying this ratio by the days in the operating period simply restates the relative size of the inventory balance in terms of days. Thus 0.20 × 60 = 12 days. The same relationship can be stated as *the number of average day's purchases contained in the raw materials balance: RM/(P/D)*. Substituting, $8,000/($40,000/60) = 12, and the equivalent of twelve average days of purchases are invested in the present raw materials.

The average age of raw materials is a linear function of the ratio: RM/P. In the linear equation $Y = b(X)$, Y is the average age of raw materials, b is the days in the purchasing period, and $X = RM/P$. The average age will function linearly with RM/P. The coefficient is the constant number of days in the purchasing period; given a sixty-day purchasing interval the equation is $Y = 60(RM/P)$. Average ages can be projected now for any value of X, and the whole range of relationships is contained in the graph of the equation as illustrated in Figure 8.1. The slope of the line is Y/X which is a constant 60, an increase in the average age of inventories by 60 every time that the ratio increases by 1 or an increase in the average age of 6 days every time the ratio goes up by 0.1. The Y axis is a quantitative measure of liquidity risk with risk increasing as the average age increases; and, since average age is a function of the X variable, risk becomes a linear function of the ratio RM/P. How far out on the X axis the business dare go depends on how much risk it can afford to take in return for the profit it will produce, and the risk that it can *afford* to take is directly related to the quantity of capital that it

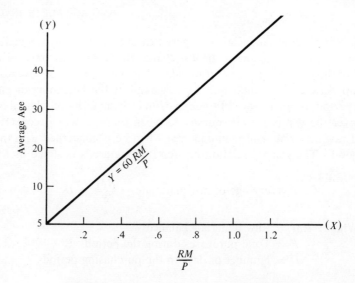

Figure 8.1.   Raw Materials Aging Function.

has in relation to inventories, in this case, the quantity of net working capital that it has over the inventory balance: Net working capital/Raw materials. Let current assets be $300,000, current liabilities $100,000 and raw materials $150,000; the relationship is $200,000/$150,000 = 1.33. The working capital constraint is the limiting factor determining how much of this asset of low liquidity can be supported by current assets in total, after setting off against the current liabilities. An increasing ratio signals the business that more of the working capital fund is free now for investment in raw materials for profit attainment and that less has to be held in a liquid state for future investment. The effect on the ratio, of such a transfer of funds can be illustrated as follows. Assume that the ratio Net working capital/ Raw materials = $1,000/$200 = 5/1 and that a turnover of 2.5/1 is considered adequate liquidity for net working capital. By transferring 200 more units of cash into raw materials the ratio becomes: $1,000/$400 = 2.5/1. Notice that the quantity of capital is not reduced by the transaction but that the liquidity of the business is reduced by doubling the size of the least liquid of the current assets. The effect should be to accelerate net profits. If the ratio had been held as it was originally at 5/1, it would have indicated that liquid funds were being held awaiting more favorable investment prospects for the future.

OPTIMIZING FACTORS IN INVENTORY MANAGEMENT

Taking the three basic current operating assets, inventories, receivables, and cash, inventories most of all have been researched for optimizing costs of handling and holding at each of the levels of raw materials, goods in process, and finished goods. In this discussion, emphasis is placed on raw materials because of the risky nature of the investment and because methods of optimizing raw materials are also applicable to goods in process and to finished goods. Three critical issues will be considered: one, optimizing the holding quantity of raw materials; two, optimizing lead time in placing raw materials orders; and, three, optimizing the quantity of safety stocks.

OPTIMIZING RAW MATERIALS HOLDINGS

In Figures 2 and 3, two different average holding quantities are illustrated; but there are many more than just two alternative holding levels for financial managers to consider. In the optimizing operation, the average level of holdings, of course, has to be calculated. For the full year 20,000 units are needed. The optimizing problem is to order those units in such a way that the average quantity of raw materials on balance will minimize the sum of two cost forms: total *carrying costs* and total *ordering costs*. Total carrying costs decrease the smaller the average quantity of raw materials held, and total ordering costs increase the smaller the average quantity of raw materials held. With two costs working in opposite directions as these are, optimization will occur at the level of average inventory holdings where the sum of the two costs are at a minimum. Since the two costs move in opposite directions, optimization is also identified as the *level of average raw materials holdings where total carrying costs and total ordering costs are equal.*

Nature of Holdings   An important assumption is made of uniform raw materials use in the production process, so that the size of a raw materials order can be conveniently expressed in *average* raw materials holdings. This assumption is reasonable because business managers can control internally the raw materials use rate and often do just that to attain the financial advantages of level production. If raw materials are put into production at a steady rate, the average raw material holdings over the use period may be stated as:

$$\text{Average holdings} = \frac{\text{Starting quantity}}{2}$$

Suppose the starting quantities are a series of alternatives 5,000, 10,000, and 12,000 units. The average holdings in units then are 5,000/2 = 2,500, 10,000/2 = 5,000, and 12,000/2 = 6,000 respectively. We will see at once that the average holdings increase at the same relative rate as the starting quantity. When the relative rate of increase $\Delta X/X$ in the starting quantity went up by 1 or 100 percent from 5,000 units to 10,000 units the relative rate of increase $\Delta Y/Y$ in average holdings also increased by 1 or 100 percent from 2,500 units to 5,000 units. The reader should verify that the same relationship holds when the starting quantity increases from 10,000 units to 12,000 units. The importance of this analysis is that it establishes the functional pattern for average inventory investment given the starting size of the inventory.

Now an important step forward is taken toward cost minimization if we let the starting quantity in the numerator of the ratio be the *order quantity* of raw materials. That is, assume that the quantity of raw materials put into use at the start is the quantity that was *ordered* for use during that period. This does not mean necessarily that the goods were ordered on the starting date but that they were on hand in full strength at the start of the period. The ratio of average holding then is: Average holdings = Order quantity/2. One of the critical problems in raw materials management is determining the optimal ordering time, but this problem is reserved for later. Figures 2 and 3 below illustrate graphically what we have been saying here, that, at a constant use rate, the average size of inventory holding during the use period is determined by size of the variable order quantity. The diagrams illustrate 20,000 units of raw materials use over one year; 2 illustrates orders of 5,000 units starting one each three months, and 3 illustrates orders of 10,000 units starting one each six months. Total units needed, however, over the year are 20,000.

Carrying Costs   The significance of Figures 2 and 3 for optimizing purposes is the effect that they have on total holding costs. Raw materials holding costs include storage, insurance, personal property taxes, and interest on the inventory investment that are all unit variable costs. Totaling these costs and dividing by the number of units held will give a unit variable carrying cost. The unit cost is a

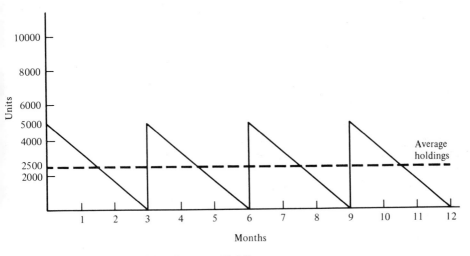

Figure 8.2. Average Holdings—
Four Orders, 20,000 Units Total.

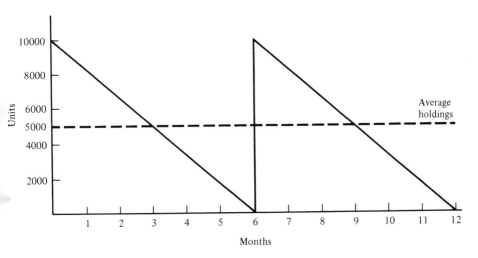

Figure 8.3. Average Holdings—
Two Orders, 20,000 Units Total.

constant value, and total carrying cost is a linear function of the quantity of inventories held. The total variable cost function may be designated:

$$H_{c_1} = c_1(X) \qquad\qquad 8.2$$

Where: H_{c_1} = Total variable holding costs
c_1 = Unit variable carrying cost
X = Average number of units held

H_{c_1} is the C equivalent of the standard variable cost equation used in Chapter 6. Assume that $c_1 = \$0.075$; then the linear holding cost function is

$$H_{c_1} = \$0.075(\bar{X})$$

Table 8.1 shows the constant rate of increase of $75 in raw materials holding costs with each increase of 1,000 units of average raw materials holding. We start arbitrarily at a 4,000-unit average assuming that to hold less would subject the company to the risk of inventory shortages that would offset the advantages of holding inventory balances. Technical aspects of the *safety stocks* issue will be discussed in a later section; for the present, we need just to recognize the linear nature of total variable costs. The capital constraint is implicit in setting the upper limit of 8,000 units of inventory holdings; that is, given the net working capital, 8,000 units of raw materials are the maximum that financial managers can allow production to carry.

TABLE 8.1
HOLDING COST FUNCTION

c_1		$\bar{X}$		H_{c_1}	ΔH_{c_1}
$0.075	×	4,000	=	$300	
.075	×	5,000	=	375	75
.075	×	6,000	=	450	75
.075	×	7,000	=	525	75
.075	×	8,000	=	600	75

Ordering costs   Now that carrying costs have been related to average holdings, we need to relate ordering costs also to the average quantity of inventory holdings. Figures 2 and 3 illustrated that the same objective of using 20,000 units of raw materials can be attained in two different ways. The level of raw materials use over the period then becomes a constant value. The problem is, how much of this inventory should be held on balance on the average? Given a constant use rate, larger and less frequent orders not only increase the average quantity of inventory holdings for meeting demand but they also decrease the portion of total inventory holding costs that are related specifically to ordering operations. The ordering portion of holding costs referred to here includes salaries for clerical, secretarial, and managerial services and long-distance telephone bills, postage, and stationery expenses incurred every time an order is placed for raw materials regardless of how large or how small the order happens to be. Relating this specifically now to the decision by management to hold certain quantities of raw materials, the larger the average quantity desired on balance the lower the total ordering cost. Financial managers in the last analysis can decide whether to raise or to lower their average raw materials investment balance and can determine in advance the amount expended not only on carrying the balance but also the amount expended on ordering it. The ordering cost function is different from the carrying cost function in two important ways: first, it is a negative function, and, second, it is a nonlinear function. It increases at a decreasing rate of change, which is stated as:

$$H_{c_2} = c_2\left(\frac{K}{2\bar{X}}\right) \qquad 8.3$$

Where: H_{c_2} = Materials order portion of total holding cost
c_2 = Cost of each order
K = Total units needed for the financial period
$\bar{X}$ = Average holding quantity

Table 8.2 shows the inverse relationship between holding costs (H_{c_2}) and the size of the order where: $c_2 = \$200$, $K = 24{,}000$ units, and X is the variable average holding quantity. Again we start at an average ordering size of 4,000 units. The number (2) in the denominator of the ratio raises the average holdings considered by management to the actual quantity that would be ordered to attain the desired average. This has to be done because the total quantity is ordered rather than the average holdings. Table 8.2 indicates also the inverse relationship between total ordering costs and the average holding size, decreasing from $600 when 4,000 units are held on the average to $300 when 8,000 units are held. Notice, however, that, with average holdings increasing by 1 or 100 percent, $8{,}000 - 4{,}000/4{,}000 = 1 = 100$ percent, total ordering costs decreased only 0.5 or 50 percent, $600 - \$300/\$600 = 0.5 = 50$ percent.

Optimal Holding Size Now that both cost schedules are available, combining them will produce the minimum cost combination or approximately the minimum. It will produce the approximate minimum in our example because of the wide intervals of 1,000 units between alternative average raw materials holdings. Table 8.2 combines significant total costs to illustrate the approximate optimal holding quantity. It will be observed that total costs decline and then rise and that the rate

TABLE 8.2
OPTIMAL QUANTITY OF RAW MATERIALS HOLDINGS

$\bar{X}$	$H_{c_1} = \$0.075(X)$	$H_{c_2} = \$200\left(\frac{24{,}000}{2\,(\bar{X})}\right)$	$H_{c_1} + c_2$
4,000	$300	$600	$900
5,000	375	480	855
6,000	450	400	850
7,000	525	342	867
8,000	600	300	900

of change decreases and then increases in size. The approximate optimal point is accurate enough for practical operating purposes, although this is not quite mathematically correct. For the mathematically correct figure, we ask the question: What is the optimal average holding quantity? Since the point at which the sum of carrying and ordering costs $H_{c_1} + _{c_2}$ are at a minimum is the point also at which carrying costs $c_1\bar{X}$ are equal to ordering costs $c_2(K/2\bar{X})$, we can derive the solution formula as follows:

$$\text{Carrying costs} = \text{Ordering cost:} \quad c_1\bar{X} = c_2\left(\frac{K}{2\bar{X}}\right)$$

$$\text{Multiply by } 2\bar{X}: \quad 2c_1\bar{X}^2 = c_2 K$$

$$\text{Divide by } 2_{c_1}: \quad \bar{X}^2 = \frac{c_2 K}{2_{c_1}}$$

$$X_{op} = \sqrt{\frac{c_2 K}{2_{c_1}}} \qquad\qquad 8.4$$

The optimal average raw materials holdings are 5,657 units determined by substituting in the formula as follows:

$$\bar{X}_{op} = \sqrt{\frac{\$200 \times 24{,}000}{2(\$0.075)}}$$

$$= \sqrt{\frac{\$4{,}800{,}000}{0.15}}$$

$$= \sqrt{32{,}000{,}000}$$

$$= 5{,}657 \text{ units}$$

If 5,657 units is the optimal quantity to hold, on the average the optimal order quantity will be 11,314 ($2 \times 5{,}657$) units, and this quantity will have to be ordered 2.1 times ($24{,}000/11{,}314 = 2.1$) during the planning period. Over a 180 day planning period, the inventory order would be placed every 85 days: $180/2.1 = 85$.

Figure 8.4 is the graphic solution of the optimal holding quantity which, like Table 8.2, is not as precise as the formula. Figure 8.4 is somewhat more exact than the table because it indicates a continuous relationship between the average quantity of holdings on the X axis and the total cost of holding on the Y axis. (H_{c_1}) is the increasing portion of total holding costs, (H_{c_2}) is the decreasing portion of total holding costs and $H_{c_1} + _{c_2}$ is the sum of the two costs. The intersection of H_{c_1} and H_{c_2} marks the point at which the constant rate of change of H_{c_1} and the changing rate of H_{c_2} are equal. The graph indicates that the quantity of optimal inventory holdings lies between 5,000 units and 6,000 units, which may be accurate enough for most raw materials planning situations.

Economic Order Quantity   Our approach to the inventory management problem has been directed at the average size of the inventory balance which is consistent with the initial premise that inventory investments, particularly raw materials, need special attention from financial managers. This attention is needed as we have seen because of the low liquidity of raw materials, which results from the nature of the manufacturing process itself that takes raw materials and runs them all the way through the production line before they are ready for sale. This

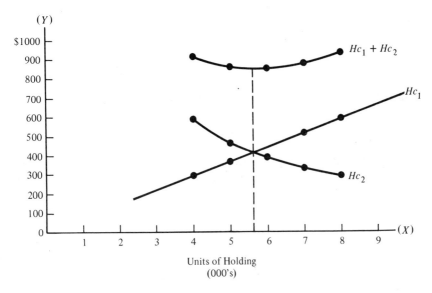

Figure 8.4. Graphing Optimal Raw Material Holdings.

is why average *holdings* of raw materials have been emphasized over *acquisitions* in the optimizing operation.

More often than not, however, the analysis points to inventory acquisitions rather than to optimal holdings. Acquisitions or the optimal order size of raw materials is what was called earlier the order quantity of raw materials put into use at the beginning of each time interval. The optimizing goal in this case is to select the most economic order quantity, that is, the starting quantity that minimizes the sum of carrying and ordering costs. The formula for determining the economic order quantity is:

$$EOQ = \sqrt{\frac{2(c_2 K)}{c_1}} \qquad 8.5$$

The only difference between this formula and the one for determining optimal average ($\bar{X}$) holding quantity is that the numerator under the radical sign is multiplied by 2, and the 2 in the denominator is dropped. EOQ is twice the size of $\bar{X}$; thus:

$$EOQ = 2(\bar{X})$$

Substituting from our original solution: $EOQ = 2(5,657) = 11,314$ units. And $\bar{X}$ is, therefore, 1/2 of EOQ so that EOQ is determined then:

$$\bar{X}_{op} = \frac{1}{2}(EOQ)$$

The decision for finished inventory holdings is made independently of the decision for raw materials holdings, although the optimizing method is much the same. There is an important difference, however, in the control exercised by management in the disposition of raw materials and in the disposition of finished inventories. For purposes of analysis, we will assume that finished inventories are disposed of at a uniform rate like raw materials, realizing that there are some businesses that would have to modify this assumption considerably to make it fit reality. By assuming that finished inventories are disposed of at a constant rate, we can proceed with the cost analysis and with developing the basic model for optimizing the average holding size of inventories.

Variable Carrying Costs   Finished goods carrying costs include unit variable costs for storage, insurance, property taxes, and interest on the inventory investment whose total values vary linearly with the average number of units held. In the finished state inventories are more valuable and will, therefore, incur higher unit carrying costs than raw materials. To illustrate the linear nature of the equation, assume that it costs \$0.15 per unit to carry the finished goods; then finished inventories carrying costs are the solution to the following equation:

$$H_{c_1} = \$0.15(X)$$

The rate of increase in H_{c_1} is \$0.15 given an increase of one unit in finished inventories holdings. Instead of costing \$75 for every 1,000 units of finished inventories held, it will cost \$150:

$$H_{c_1} = \$0.15(1,000)$$
$$= \$150$$

In manufacturing, the supply of finished goods is controllable by financial managers. Assuming that the rate at which finished inventories are sold is a constant one, the quantity of finished goods in stock is also controllable. Average finished inventory holdings are then controllable by planning the size of the production run. The production run for finished goods inventories is comparable to the order size of raw materials purchases. For example, suppose that 10,000 units of finished inventories are produced in four runs of three months each and that the rate of sale is constant; then 2,500 units are manufactured in each run, and average finished inventory holdings are:

$$\text{Average holdings} = \frac{\text{Finished inventory run}}{2}$$
$$= \frac{2,500}{2}$$
$$= 1,250 \text{ units}$$

But if the total 10,000 units are produced in two runs, average holdings are doubled to 2,500 units for the same reason that doubling the order size of raw materials doubles the average holdings. Consider Figures 2 and 3 for the graphic illustration of the doubling effect on average holdings. The significance of these examples should be apparent; namely, that, since carrying costs are linearly related to inventory holdings, the total cost of holding finished inventories is proportional to the quantity that management desires to hold.

Set-Up Costs   Set-up costs are fixed for each production run and include the costs of planning the production run and the sales budget, setting up machinery, and equipment and raw materials inventories. Set-up costs are similar to ordering costs in their effect on total holding costs. Since it costs about the same each time the plant is set up for a finished inventory run, the more often this is done the larger is the total cost; and the less often it is done the smaller the total set-up cost. This function is negative and nonlinear. It is negative because total set-up costs decrease the larger the production run, and it is nonlinear because total set-up costs decrease at a decreasing rate the larger the production run.

The negative nonlinear relationship is stated as:

$$H_{c_2} = c_2 \left(\frac{K}{2(\bar{X})} \right)$$

There is no reason why c_2 in planning a production run should be any more or less costly than c_2 in placing a raw materials order, but K in finished inventories will be less than K in raw materials except when just 1 unit of raw materials goes into each unit of finished goods. In our hypothetical case, assume that $c_2 = \$200$, but that $K = 10,000$. Now total set-up costs will vary inversely with changes in average inventory balances $(\bar{X})$ in the relation of:

$$H_{c_2} = \$200 \left(\frac{10,000}{2(\bar{X})} \right)$$

Optimal Holding Quantity   Table 8.3 combines the c_1 and c_2 holding costs in finished inventories management and indicates the general area of the optimal average holding quantity. Let the range in average units of finished inventory holdings be between 1,000 units and 5,000 units, the capital constraint setting the

TABLE 8.3
OPTIMAL QUANTITY OF FINISHED INVENTORY HOLDINGS

$\bar{X}$	$H_{c_1} = \$0.15(\bar{X})$	$H_{c_2} = \$200\left(\frac{10,000}{2(\bar{X})}\right)$	$H_{c_1} + c_2$
1,000	150	$1,000	$1,150
2,000	300	500	800
3,000	450	334	784
4,000	600	250	850
5,000	750	200	950

upper limit of 5,000 units. Where the average quantity of raw materials starts with 4,000 units, financial managers feel that average finished holdings can be dropped safely to 1,000 units. Table 8.3 indicates that the optimal average holding quantity is 3,000 units and that the corresponding minimum cost is $784. The range of optimization is between holding 2,000 units and 3,000 units. Graphing the functions will come close to showing us the optimal point as is seen in Figure 8.5. For the exact point of optimization, however, we work the formula.

$$\bar{X}_{op} = \sqrt{\frac{c_2 K}{2c_1}}$$

$$= \sqrt{\frac{\$200 \times 10,000}{2(0.15)}}$$

$$= \sqrt{\$6,666,666}$$

$$= 2,582 \text{ units}$$

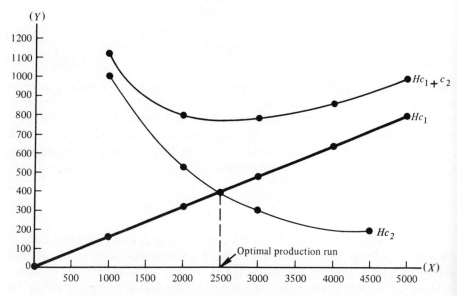

Figure 8.5.   Graphing Optimal Finished Goods Holdings.

Lead time is the time allowed for a raw materials order to arrive. Planning for the delivery of raw materials cannot be synchronized perfectly with the time that they are needed, but the next best thing to a perfectly synchronized delivery date is to have the order arrive early. The question is just how early should management plan to have the inventories arrive. Early arrivals incur added carrying costs that were not provided for in selecting the optimal holding quantity. Figure 6 indicates

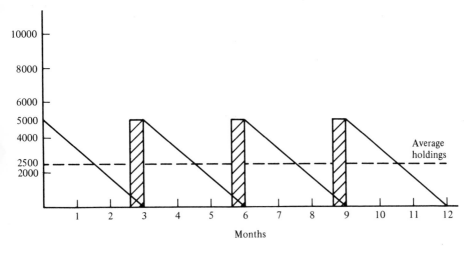

Figure 8.6. Average Holdings Four Orders, 20,000 Units Total
Early Inventory Arrival.

the general complementary nature of early arrivals of raw materials to the order quantity and to average inventory holdings. Three items are apparent in the figure. First, the optimal order quantity of 5,000 units is not affected by the early arrival of raw materials. Second, average holdings are unaffected by the early arrival. Third, there is overlap between raw materials of the previous period and the new order of raw materials except right at the end of the raw materials use.

Optimizing the lead time is not as simple and direct as optimizing the average holding quantity and the order quantity. The reasons for this are that financial managers: (1) cannot be sure when their order will reach the supplier, (2) cannot be sure that materials will be available to fill the order when it does arrive, and (3) cannot be sure when the materials will arrive after they enter the transportation system. All of these factors prevent financial managers from predicting with certainty whether a given raw materials order will arrive right on time, late, or early. The risk factor suggests that arrival dates be estimated with probabilities of occurrence. In the last analysis, the optimizing decision is a cost minimizing decision in which *costs of being late are equated with costs of carrying early inventory arrivals.*

Costs of Being Late Costs of being late result from depleting safety stocks if any had existed, slowdowns in machine use, layoffs, and temporary shutdowns. Costs of being late can be stated as constant costs for each day that a *given order size* will be late. There is a linear relationship between the number of days late that a raw material order arrives and the daily cost of being late if the arrival date can be predicted with certainty. But being unable to predict the date with certainty, the cost of being late has to reflect the risk of a probability distribution.

Table 8.4 indicates the probabilities that an order will be late from zero to seven days assuming that orders are placed from five days to ten days before stockout. Stockout is the day that the previous order of raw materials is used up.

TABLE 8.4
PROBABILITY OF BEING LATE

Days Ordered	*Days Late*							
Before Stockout	*0*	*1*	*2*	*3*	*4*	*5*	*6*	*7*
5	0.36	0.30	0.10	0.06	0.05	0.03	0.0	0.0
6	.30	.10	.06	.05	.03	.0	.0	.0
7	.10	.06	.05	.03	.0	.0	.0	.0
8	.06	.05	.03	.0	.0	.0	.0	.0
9	.05	.03	.0	.0	.0	.0	.0	.0
10	.03	.0	.0	.0	.0	.0	.0	.0

We assume that the latest date that an order would be placed prior to stockout is five because experience has shown that any order placed four days or fewer before stockout has an extremely small probability of arriving on time. An order placed five days before stockout has a 0.36 probability of being exactly on time, zero days late, and a 0.54 (0.30 + 0.10 + 0.06 + 0.05 + 0.03) probability of being late from one to five days. The sum of these probabilities (0.90) is the probability that the goods will arrive on the day that they are put into use or that they will arrive late, given a five-day lead time. The balance of the probability distribution, 1 − 0.90 = 0.10, is the probability that the goods will arrive early. An order placed six days before stockout has a 0.30 probability of being right on time and a 0.24 probability of being late which is distributed among the next four days. The difference in the probability distribution, 1 − 0.54 = 0.46 is the probability that delivery may arrive early. Notice that, when inventories are ordered ten days before stockout, they will arrive right on time with probability of only 0.03 and will have no probability of being late.

Table 8.5 is a table of late delivery costs adjusted to the risks of the respective probability distributions. The first column is the days late column and was the days late row in Table 8.4. The column is the cost of being late from zero days (being right on time) to being late as many as five days. The number of units ordered does not need to enter the picture because the economic order quantity was determined earlier to be 11,314 units, and *this is the order quantity for which the optimal lead time is sought.* For each order placed five days or more before stockout, there is a series of costs; these are the costs adjusted for the probability that the order with a certain lead time will be late a given number of days. The sum of each cost column is the expected value (*EV*) or the most probable cost of being late for each lead time. It should be noted that costs of being late diminish as the days ordered before stockout increase but that they are nonlinear because of the variable probability coefficients. The general order of the relationship may be stated as:

$$EV = \sum_{X=0}^{8} (X_n P_n c)$$

8.6

TABLE 8.5
COST OF BEING LATE

		Days Ordered Before Stockout (Lead Time)										
		5 Days		6 Days		7 Days		8 Days		9 Days		10 Days	
Days Late	Cost @ $100 Per Day	Prob.*	Value	Prob.	Value	Prob.	Value	Prob.	Value	Prob.	Value	Prob.	Value
0	$ 0	0.36	$ 0	0.30	$ 0	0.10	$ 0	0.06	$ 0	0.05	$0	0.03	$0
1	100	.30	30	.10	10	.06	6	.05	5	.03	3	.0	0
2	200	.10	20	.06	12	.05	10	.03	6	.0	0	.0	0
3	300	.06	18	.05	15	.03	9	.0	0	.0	0	.0	0
4	400	.05	20	.03	12	.0	0	.0	0	.0	0	.0	0
5	500	.03	15	.0	0	.0	0	.0	0	.0	0	.0	0
6	600	.0	0	.0	0	.0	0	.0	0	.0	0	.0	0
7	700	.0	0	.0	0	.0	0	.0	0	.0	0	.0	0
Expected Value			$103		$49		$25		$11		$3		$0

*Abbreviation for Probability

Where: EV = Expected value of being late for each lead time from five to ten days before stockout

$\sum_{x=0}^{8}$ = Summation of costs of being late from zero to seven days for each lead time

X_n = Number of days late

P_n = Probability of being late

c = Daily cost of being late

Costs of Being Early   There is also a cost related to the chance that raw materials orders will arrive before they are needed. Carrying costs due to early arrival include storage costs, wages of extra work force to handle the inventories, and insurance and property taxes. Under conditions of certainty, these costs are linearly related to the number of days that the inventories are held; but variable probability coefficients make the costs nonlinear.

TABLE 8.6
PROBABILITY OF BEING EARLY

Days Ordered Before Stockout	Days Early							
	0	1	2	3	4	5	6	7
5	0.36	0.05	0.05	0.0	0.0	0.0	0.0	0.0
6	.30	.40	.05	.01	.0	.0	.0	.0
7	.10	.30	.40	.05	.01	.0	.0	.0
8	.06	.10	.30	.40	.05	.01	.0	.0
9	.05	.06	.10	.30	.40	.05	.01	.0
10	.03	.05	.06	.10	.30	.40	.05	.01

Table 8.6 is a subjective probability distribution for early arrivals of the 11,314 unit optimal order size. Special attention should be paid to the probability values under zero days early. It will be noticed that these are the same as for zero days late because in either case they represent arrivals on the day that they are put into use. The student should verify also that the sum of the probabilities that an order will arrive late and that it will arrive early, plus the common probability of arriving on time, will equal 1. The final table illustrates the combined costs of arriving late and of arriving early. The latter places the optimal lead time between six and

TABLE 8.8
OPTIMAL LEAD TIME

Cost of Being	Days Ordered Before Stockout					
	5 Days	6 Days	7 Days	8 Days	9 Days	10 Days
Early	$ 3.50	$26.50	$62.50	$107.50	$145.00	$201.50
Late	104.00	50.00	26.00	12.00	3.00	0
$EV =$	$107.50	$76.50	$88.50	$119.50	$148.00	$201.50

TABLE 8.7
COST OF BEING EARLY

Days	Cost	5 Days		6 Days		7 Days		8 Days		9 Days		10 Days	
Early	@ $50 Per Day	Prob.*	Value	Prob.	Value	Prob.	Value	Prob.	Value	Prob.	Value	Prob.	Value
0	$ 0	0.36	$0	0.30	$ 0	0.0	$ 0	0.06	$ 0	0.05	$ 0	0.03	$ 0
1	50	.05	2.50	.40	20.00	.30	1.50	.10	5.00	.06	3.00	.05	2.50
2	100	.01	1.00	.05	5.00	.40	40.00	.30	30.00	.10	10.00	.06	6.00
3	150	.0	0	.01	1.50	.05	7.50	.40	60.00	.30	45.00	.10	15.00
4	200	.0	0	.0	0	.01	2.00	.05	10.00	.40	80.00	.30	60.00
5	250	.0	0	.0	0	.0	0	.01	2.50	.05	7.50	.40	100.00
6	300	.0	0	.0	0	.0	0	.0	0	.01	3.00	.05	15.00
7	350	.0	0	.0	0	.0	0	.0	0	.0	0	.01	3.50
Expected Value			$3.50		$26.50		$64.50		$107.50		$145.50		$202.00

Days Ordered Before Stockout (Lead Time)

*Abbreviation for Probability

189

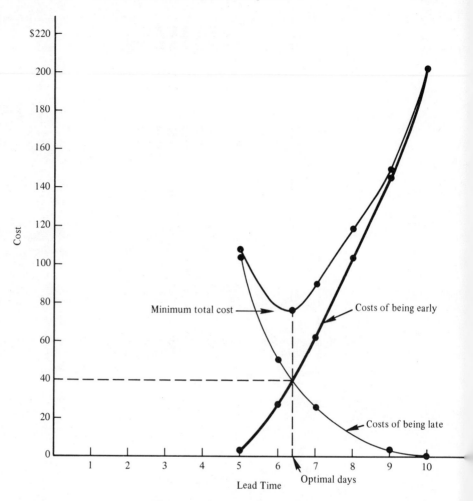

Figure 8.7. Optimal Lead Time.

seven days. Figure 8.7 graphs the relationship and provides us with a more accurate statement of the optimal lead time of about six and a half days before raw materials are put into use.

OPTIMIZING SAFETY STOCKS

We have considered the problem of optimizing lead time as a complement to the decision to hold an average of 5,657 units of raw materials and to the decision to order twice this amount or 11,314 units. Nothing has been said thus far, however, about preparing for the contingency of being short of raw materials during the period of raw materials use. The need for safety stocks arises from the risk in the real world situation, that the negative linear raw materials use implied in

Figures 2, 3, and 6 may suddenly accelerate leaving the business with raw materials shortages that would disrupt operations at any stage of raw materials use. For operations to be disrupted would not require that the total 11,314 units of raw materials be used, but any acceleration above what is budgeted for a given date may disrupt operations. If we are dealing with finished inventories, market demand may suddenly accelerate causing shortages at any period during finished goods holdings. Another cause of shortages in raw materials, at the end of the operating period at least, is failure of the order to arrive on time. Although the optimal lead time is about six and one half days from the cost minimizing viewpoint, this does not mean that raw materials will never run out before the new stock arrives. The cost optimizing table indicates probabilities of being late from one through four days, and any one of these occurrences could disrupt operations. The risks of not being able to meet the raw materials budget may be offset in part at least by holding a given safety stock. If the safety stock itself is depleted to meet temporary shortages, new orders must be placed to replenish them. The effect of a 1,000 unit safety stock on the average holdings and economic order size is illustrated in Figure 8 below.

It should be noted that the order quantity of 5,000 units and the average raw materials holdings of 2,500 units are the same in Figure 8 as they are in Figure 2 drawn earlier in the chapter and that the decision to hold 1,000 units of safety stocks is not related at all to the decision to optimize the order size at 5,000 units or to optimize the average holdings at 2,500 units. The reader should also note the difference in the shaded areas of Figures 6 and 8, the former illustrating the effect of lead time on the timing of inventories and the latter illustrating the effect of safety stocks on the quantity of inventories. When the quantity of safety stocks

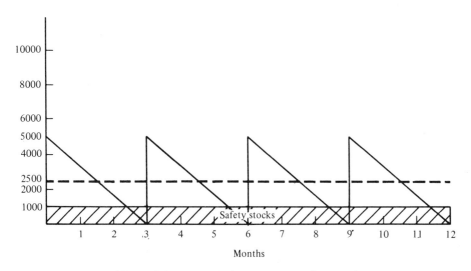

Figure 8.8.   Four Orders, 20,000 Units Total
Safety Stock 1,000 Units.

needed cannot be estimated with certainty, financial managers may employ probability distributions to improve the quality of their estimates. In the last analysis, however, the optimal safety stocks decision is a cost minimizing function as the optimal holding quantity and the optimal lead time decisions are. The optimizing goal is to *carry the quantity of safety stocks that will minimize the sum of the short costs and the safety stock carrying costs.*

Short Costs　Safety stocks are carried to offset the costs of being short of stocks during the budgeted raw materials run. The number of units carried depends on what the shortage is expected to be. The shortage cannot be predicted with certainty because it relates to the demand that the production department places on raw materials; and production depends on demand from the sales department. A probability distribution for demand needs to be set for a quantitative estimate, therefore, of shortages.

TABLE 8.9*

COST WHEN NO SAFETY STOCK IS HELD

1 Possible Average Demand	2 Probability of Average Demand	3 Optimal Raw Materials	4 Possible Shortage	5 Probable Shortage	6 Cost of Being Short @ $0.50 Per Unit
5,657	0.70	5,657	0	0	$ 0
5,857	.17	5,657	200	34	17
6,057	.07	5,657	400	28	14
6,257	.04	5,657	600	24	12
6,457	.02	5,657	800	16	8
	1.00				†EV = $51

*The author wishes to acknowledge that Chapter 6 of *Basic Managerial Finance* by Adolph E. Grunewald and Erwin E. Nemmers, (New York: Holt, Rinehart and Winston, Inc., 1970) was helpful in structuring the safety stock tables of this chapter.
†Expected Value

Table 8.9 needs some explanation. Column 1 is a range of possible average demands starting at the optimal holding quantity of 5,657 units of raw materials determined earlier in the chapter. Demand referred to here is connected directly with the production process. Increased demand for the finished product either in the warehouse or in the product market will be reflected back to production and to the demand for raw materials. Column 2 is a probability distribution of demand for raw materials during the use interval. Probability of average demand being the same as the optimal holding quantity of 5,657 units is 0.70. There is a relatively high probability also that there might be a demand for 5,857 units, but *possible* shortages will exceed 200 units. Column 4 is the difference between possible demand in column 1 and average optimal holdings in column 3. Column 5 is the product of possible shortages and the probability distribution of demand, and finally column 6 converts column 5 to costs and their sum to an expected value. Table 8.10 determines for us expected values of being short when the quantity of

TABLE 8.10
COST WHEN 200 TO 800 UNITS OF
SAFETY STOCK ARE CARRIED

Probability of Demand	200 Units Carried			400 Units Carried			600 Units Carried			800 Units Carried		
	Poss.* Shortage	Prob.† Shortage	Cost	Poss. Shortage	Prob. Shortage	Cost	Poss. Shortage	Prob. Shortage	Cost	Poss. Shortage	Prob. Shortage	Cost
0.70	0	0	$ 0	0	0	$ 0	0	0	$ 0	0	0	$ 0
.17	0	0	0	0	0	0	0	0	0	0	0	0
.07	400	28	14	0	0	0	0	0	0	0	0	0
.04	600	24	12	600	24	12	0	0	0	0	0	0
.02	800	16	8	800	16	8	800	16	8	0	0	0
			EV = $34			EV = $20			EV = $ 8			EV = $ 0

*Abbreviation for Possible
†Abbreviation for Probable

extra holdings ranges between 200 and 800 units. The same probability distribution of demand is applied to each of the possible shortages.

Carrying Cost   To offset short costs, financial managers recommend carrying a constant margin of raw materials in excess of the optimal holding quantity of 5,657 units. Doing this will incur carrying costs just as carrying costs were incurred in arriving at the average holding quantity. Carrying costs in this case are a certainty; management can add to its average holdings any quantity that it desires, paying a constant unit cost without any probability adjustment. Since the same kind of raw materials are carried for safety stocks as are carried for normal operations, we can state the linear equation for carrying safety stocks as:

$$S_{c_1} = 0.075(X)$$

Where: S_{c_1} = Total cost of carrying safety stocks
0.075 = Unit carrying cost
(X) = Number of units carried

We are concerned with total order quantities of safety stocks instead of average quantities for carrying because we do not expect safety stock to be used up at a steady rate. Carrying costs are a linear function of the total quantity purchased for safety stocks, therefore, to indicate that the total quantity of safety stocks is held on balance all of the time. In our hypothetical case where average holdings are 5,657 units, we will assume that safety stock holdings are graduated by units of 200. Table 8.11 below indicates the schedule of resulting costs from carrying such quantities.

Optimizing Safety Stocks   The optimal quantity of safety stocks is the quantity

TABLE 8.11
COST OF CARRYING SAFETY STOCKS

S_{c_1}	0.075	(X)
$ 0	0.075	0
15	.075	200
30	.075	400
45	.075	600
60	.075	800

TABLE 8.12
OPTIMAL SAFETY STOCKS

	Number of Units Carried				
	0	*200*	*400*	*600*	*800*
Out-of-stock costs	$51	$34	$20	$ 8	$ 0
Carrying costs	0	15	30	45	60
Total costs	$51	$49	$50	$53	$60

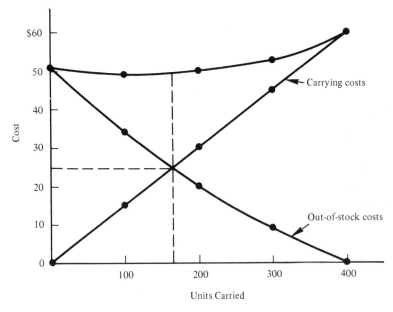

Figure 8.9. Optimal Safety Stocks.

that minimizes the sum of out-of-stock costs and carrying costs. Table 8.12 summarizes the two sets of costs. The optimal safety stocks would appear to be between 200 and 400 units. But Figure 8.9 is a graphic solution that tells us that the optimal safety stock is about 162 units; the point at which the two costs are equal is $25; and total cost at this minimum point is between $48 and $49.

SUMMARY

This is the first of three chapters that deal with important problems of current asset management. Quantitative measures for determining the liquidity of inventories ranging from raw materials to finished goods are applied. The single most important problem in inventory management deals with the optimizing techniques that result in plans for holding optimal quantities of inventories, plans for timing the orders and plans for carrying the optimal quantity of inventory safety stocks. All three inventory optimizing goals are interrelated. Extensive use is made of probability distributions when financial managers are unable to estimate with certainty the arrival dates of inventory orders and the application rate of raw materials to the production process. The analysis is an orderly development for determining first the optimal average holding quantity. From there is determined the optimal quantity of safety stocks by comparing the cost of being out of inventory with the cost of carrying added stocks. In this chapter, the reader sees an application of practically all of the quantitative techniques and tools that were developed and applied earlier. Several graphic tools are used to illustrate the optimizing method for analysis.

PROBLEMS

1. Your attention has been called in this chapter to quality differences in inventories and their effect on liquidity. Assume you are considering several combinations of a $10,000 inventory investment for your company. Investments can be made in units of $2,500; and, to give objectivity to the comparisons for decision making, you weight the inventories on a liquidity basis as follows: raw materials = 1, goods in process = 2, and finished goods = 3. Now rank the alternatives appearing below in the order of their weighted average liquidities.

   a. What is the basis for weighting the inventory classes differently as was done above? How are the different liquidity ratings related to risk?
   b. Suppose that the business is a bakery, a garment manufacturer, or a frozen fruits processing concern. Would you consider altering the weights given above for any of these three businesses?

ALTERNATIVE INVENTORY INVESTMENTS

	I	II	III	IV	V	VI
Raw materials	$ 5,000	$ 2,500	$ —	$ 2,500	$ 2,500	$ 7,500
Goods in process	2,500	5,000	2,500	2,500	—	2,500
Finished inventories	2,500	2,500	7,500	5,000	7,500	—
Total	$10,000	$10,000	$10,000	$10,000	$10,000	$10,000

2. To prevent investments in any one class of inventories from getting out of balance with the volume of trade transactions, the financial manager of the Zilker Manufacturing Company runs tests on the average ages of the raw materials and the finished stocks every three months. The last five tests produced the following results:

ZILKER MANUFACTURING COMPANY

Raw Materials

	1st Test	2nd Test	3rd Test	4th Test	5th Test
Ending raw materials	$ 5,000	$ 7,000	$ 9,000	$12,000	$12,000
Purchases	$10,000	$14,000	$24,000	$36,000	$36,000

Finished Inventories

	1st Test	2nd Test	3rd Test	4th Test	5th Test
Ending finished goods	$10,000	$12,000	$15,000	$20,000	$25,000
Total costs of manufacture	$30,000	$30,000	$35,000	$40,000	$40,000

a. Set up the equation for determining the average ages of the inventories.
b. Determine the average ages of raw materials and finished goods and evaluate each from the liquidity viewpoint.
c. Suppose that the average ages of raw materials and finished goods for the industry as a whole are twenty-one days and twenty-nine days respectively. Indicate the variance of each test from the industry average for raw materials and finished goods. Which of the two inventory classes needs the closer control using the industry standards?

3. Where several clearly different kinds of inventories are bought or manufactured, risk of loss may be reduced further by pinpointing the slow moving inventories. The manager of the Davis Hardware has noted that the average age of inventories has increased over the past year and has decided that checking the ages of the present inventories would offer a fair basis for locating the source of the trouble. The inventory types listed below are a grouping of the major inventory classifications handled by the store. Complete the schedule below and make recommendations for improving the liquidity conditions for the business.

DAVIS HARDWARE
CLASSIFYING INVENTORY TYPES
NOVEMBER 20, 1965

Age Classification (Days)	Date of Purchase	Inventory Type	Amount $	Percentage Each is to Total
1 to 30	November	D	$ 1,000	
31 to 60	October	A	5,000	
61 to 90	September	C	2,000	
91 to 120	August	E	10,000	
Over 120	Earlier	B	14,000	

4. Being convinced that a general overstocking of inventories can be a major risk to share values, you are interested in developing some kind of inventory planning tool that will keep this risk exposure to a minimum. You consider raw materials planning first and then finished goods. Your production and raw materials use budgets are already set to maximize profits the next six months, but your raw materials purchases budget is still not settled. Your goal is to stock enough raw materials so that the production flow will not be impaired. In seeking an optimal quantity, your goal is to minimize total holding costs $H_{c_1 + c_2}$. In all you will need 30,000 units of raw materials for a given period; the problem is to decide on how many units to stock on the average over the period. Average carrying sizes would conform to the range from 2,000 units to 6,000 units with 1,000 unit intervals.

a. Construct a schedule of average holdings and total H_{c_1} costs assuming that each unit costs $0.10 to hold.
b. What is the linear holding cost equation, and what function does it perform that the schedule does not perform?

   c. Assume it costs $100 to place an order for these inventories regardless of the size of the order. Using the formula: $H_{c_2} = \$100\,K/2\bar{X}$, construct a schedule of H_{c_2} costs at each purchase level.

   d. Combine the H_{c_1} and H_{c_2} schedules and determine the general area of optimization.

   e. Now graph the two cost functions showing more precisely where the optimization point is.

   f. Check the graph with the formula:

$$H_{c_1} + _{c_2} = \frac{1}{2}\sqrt{\frac{2Kc_2}{c_1}} \quad \text{or} \quad \sqrt{\frac{c_2 K}{2c_1}}$$

5. Very similar to the raw materials holding problem is the finished inventories holding problem. The sales budget is geared to maximizing profits, but the cost of stocking or holding finished inventories still needs to be considered. In place of H_{c_2} representing variable ordering costs, you are going to let it represent inventory scheduling and setting-up costs on the production line. To store finished inventories will cost $0.20 per unit, and to plan and set up for a production run will cost $120. Average carrying sizes for finished inventories range from 1,000 units to 5,000, and the total units needed for sale during the period is 20,000 units. Perform the same operations as you were asked to perform in problem 4.

6. Assuming a firm has determined its economic order quantity and order interval, it still must determine when to place the order. Lead time is the interval between placing an order and requiring the goods. The method of placing the order, work load of the supplier, inventory being available, and the transportation method used in shipping the order will determine the interval between placing the order and actual receipt of the goods. The longer the lead time the greater the chance of increasing inventory holding costs. The shorter the lead time the greater the chance of increased costs due to production slowdown and lost sales. Given the probabilities of being early in the table below and a cost of $50 per day, compute the expected values of being early.

DAYS LEAD TIME AND PROBABILITIES
OF BEING EARLY

Days Early	1	2	3	4	5	6	7	8
0	0.0	0.02	0.08	0.60	0.50	0.15	0.08	0.02
1	.0	.0	.02	.08	.15	.50	.15	.08
2	.0	.0	.0	.02	.08	.15	.50	.15
3	.0	.0	.0	.0	.02	.08	.15	.50
4	.0	.0	.0	.0	.0	.02	.08	.15
5	.0	.0	.0	.0	.0	.0	.02	.08
6	.0	.0	.0	.0	.0	.0	.0	.02

7. Given the probabilities of being late in the table below and a cost of $100 per day, compute the expected values of late costs.

DAYS LEAD TIME AND PROBABILITIES OF BEING LATE

Days Late	1	2	3	4	5	6	7	8
0	0.00	0.02	0.08	0.60	0.50	0.15	0.08	0.02
1	.02	.08	.15	.05	.15	.08	.02	.0
2	.08	.15	.50	.15	.08	.02	.0	.0
3	.15	.50	.15	.08	.02	.0	.0	.0
4	.50	.15	.08	.02	.0	.0	.0	.0
5	.15	.08	.02	.0	.0	.0	.0	.0
6	.08	.02	.0	.0	.0	.0	.0	.0
7	.02	.0	.0	.0	.0	.0	.0	.0

8. Optimum lead time is determined when the sum of early and late costs is at a minimum. Plot the early and late costs on a graph and determine the optimum lead time.

9. Problems 6-8 were concerned with minimizing costs related to inventory delivery risks. Now we need to consider minimizing costs related to inventory safety stocks. Below is a probability distribution of average inventory demand. The cost per unit of being short is $0.80 and the optimal average holdings are 5,000 units. Complete the schedule determining the expected values of being short for the probability distribution in which no safety stock is held.

EXPECTED VALUES OF BEING SHORT NO SAFETY STOCKS

Average Demand	Probability of Aver. Demand	Optimal Average Holdings	Possible Shortage	Probable Shortage	Cost of Being Short @ $0.80 Per Unit
5,000	.60				
6,000	.20				
7,000	.08				
8,000	.06				
9,000	.04				
10,000	.02				
	1.00				

10. Now consider the case where safety stock is held; safety stock in amounts ranging from 1000 units to 5000 units. Determine the expected values of being short of inventory at each level of safety stocks. The same probability distribution is used in problem 9. The structure of the expanded schedule is reproduced here.

EXPECTED VALUES OF BEING SHORT
SAFETY STOCKS ARE HELD

Probability Distribution		1000 Units Carried			2000 Units Carried			3000 Units Carried		
Units	Proba-bility	Possible shortage	Probable shortage	cost	Possible shortage	Probable shortage	cost	Possible shortage	Probable shortage	cost
5,000	.60									
6,000	.20									
7,000	.08									
8,000	.06									
9,000	.04									
10,000	.02									

Probability Distribution		4000 Units Carried			5000 Units Carried		
Units	Proba-bility	Possible shortage	Probable shortage	cost	Possible shortage	Probable shortage	cost
5,000	.60						
6,000	.20						
7,000	.08						
8,000	.06						
9,000	.04						
10,000	.02						

11. Now that we have looked at the cost of demand exceeding our optimal inventory of 5000 units, we need to compare these costs with the costs of carrying extra inventories—the safety stocks. Assume that carrying costs including insurance, storage, interest and taxes amount to $0.15 per unit.

    1. Set up the equation for the carrying costs. Why does a probability distribution not have to be devised for these costs? Why do we not use the term "expected value" when referring to these costs?

    2. Set up a schedule of costs using Table 8.11 in the text for an example.

12. Finally complete the schedule below, and graph the costs. How many units should be carried in safety stock?

OPTIMAL SAFETY STOCKS

	Number of Units Carried					
	0	1000	2000	3000	4000	5000
Out-of-stk. costs						
Carrying costs						
Total costs						

9

Credit
Sales and
Receivables
Management

Receivables are current assets arising from credit sales. Our concern here is with the internal problems of managing these assets as part of the total problem of managing current operations for net profits. Managing receivables means making decisions relating to the investment of funds in this asset that contribute directly or indirectly to share values. In keeping with the general liquidity objective, financial managers should use cash funds as economically as possible in expanding receivables, at the same time considering the benefits from the profit of expanded credit sales. The student needs to relate receivables to the total current operation for net profit and to apply basic analytic and decision-making tools for income and cost analysis wherever this is possible for optimizing receivables holdings.

SCOPE OF THE SUBJECT

Inventory management, as was seen in Chapter 8, is not concerned with sales transactions as receivables management is, and receivables management is not concerned with external supply channels for getting assets into the business. In a later chapter, we will see how receivables are used externally to bring cash funds into the business, but this is a form of external financing that falls under the heading of cash borrowing rather than receivables management.

Figure 9.1 illustrates the scope of this subject as related to credit sales and its relationship to cash flow through collections. Notice the dual relationship between credit sales, income, and net profits on the one hand and credit sales and receivables on the other. A profit margin of 10 percent is assigned arbitrarily to show how the income stream is reduced from credit sales to net profit without affecting

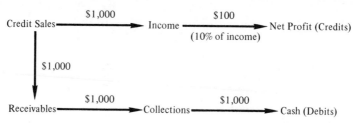

Figure 9.1.   Credit Sales and Receivables Management.

the flow of funds to receivables and cash. There is a conflict here that is not apparent in the diagram, namely that the same factor, easy credit terms, that motivates income and profit potential also creates liquidity risks at the point of receivables because long credit terms could deter operations and actually reduce profits. The parallel rather than intersecting relationship between terminal net profits in one case and cash in the other is important because it brings out the fact that cash and net profits are independent of each other despite their common origin in credit sales. Considered in the following sections are the effects of changes in credit sales policies on a firm's net profits and the effects of changes in credit sales and collections policies on receivables balances.

CREDIT SALES POLICIES AND NET PROFITS

The capital constraint sets ultimate output and sales limits on current operations, but it was seen that demand can be the determining constraint and that it can be affected by price elasticity. The following sections will consider the effect on demand and profit of cash discount and credit policies.

CASH DISCOUNT POLICY: SALES EFFECT

A firm's cash discount policy is usually stated on the sales invoice as a given amount, say 4 percent, if the account is paid within ten days from the purchase date. The importance of the cash discount from the financial manager's viewpoint is its effect on price, income, and net profit. It will be recalled from Chapter 6 that, given the price elasticity, an increase or decrease in demand can be derived for any given price adjustment. Now, to the extent that a cash discount is a decrease in price, the elasticity tool can be applied to credit sales estimates. For example, assume that, at 400 units of sales, price elasticity is greater than unitary (−1.4). Given this information Table 9.1 indicates the number of *added* units that will be sold, increasing the size of the discount from 0.02 to 0.05. Think of a 0.02 cash discount as a price decrease of 0.02 or 2 percent and each cash discount as a price discount of an equivalent amount. The negative sign before the discount rate indicates an equivalent price decline. The equation for the quantity of incremental sales is $\Delta X = -1.4(d_r)400$, where ΔX is the net addition to sales resulting from the combined lowering of price and the price elasticity coefficient at 400 units of sale.

TABLE 9.1
INCREMENTAL SALES EFFECTS
OF
RISING DISCOUNT RATES

ΔX	=	$-1.4(d_r)$	$\times$	*400*
11	=	$-1.4(-0.02)$	$\times$	400
17	=	$-1.4(-0.03)$	$\times$	400
22	=	$-1.4(-0.04)$	$\times$	400
28	=	$-1.4(-0.05)$	$\times$	400

CASH DISCOUNT: PROFIT EFFECT

Assume that unit price is \$10 and that a 4 percent discount is allowed for early payment; the adjusted price of the product now is $10(1 - 0.04) = \$9.60$. Given the price, income is a linear function of the units of sale. Allowing customers to take discounts does not change the basic linear income equation $Y = b(X)$ but simply modifies the b value. Letting d_r equal the discount rate, the equation for the income function is $Y = b(1 - d_r)X$. This offers management a modified program for determining incomes for an infinite number of sales volumes subject to capital and demand constraints. Let us go one step further to the profit function. Let $c = \$2$ and $a = \$2,000$. The effect of the cash discount is shown below in comparing P_1 and P_2 in which the latter offers a 4 percent cash discount and in which $X = 400$ in each case.

$$P_1 = (b - c)X - a \qquad\qquad 9.1$$
$$= (\$10 - \$2)400 - \$2,000$$
$$= \$1,200$$

$$P_2 = [b(1 - d_r) - c]X - a$$
$$= [\$10(1 - 0.04) - \$2]400 - (2,000)$$
$$= \$1,040$$

The examples above suggest that P_1 is the preferred selling policy. But this results from the condition of zero price elasticity; that is, the lower price caused by the cash discount does not motivate sales. To make this more realistic, assume a -1.4 price elasticity; then, Table 9.1 can be used to determine the total sales effect of a given cash discount rate. Pick any discount rate (d_r) and add the incremental value X to 400 for the total sales effect. For a 0.04 price decrease at 400 units of sales, incremental sales are 22 units. Add this to 400 and substitute in the profit equation:

$$P_2 = [\$10(1 - 0.04) - \$2]422 - (\$2,000)$$
$$= \$7.60(433) - \$2,000$$
$$= \$1,207.20$$

This raises profits above the original (P_2) function in which elasticity was zero and more than offsets the effect of the cash discount. The reason for this is that the positive profit effect of sales elasticity is greater than the negative profit effect of the cash discount. It should be noted that P_2 is also larger than P_1 in which no cash discount was offered. The reader may wish to experiment with the same set of discount rates appearing in Table 9.1 but with different elasticity coefficients. The importance of the above illustration for analysis and decision making is that there are two variables that actually affect profit optimization; one is the cash discount which decreases net profits, and the other is sales elasticity which increases net profits subject to the capital constraint that affects the volume of output and sales. The former of the two variables, sales elasticity, is not easily controlled even in the long-run operation but the latter, cash discounts, is subject to internal financial control.

CREDIT PERIOD POLICY: COST EFFECT

When a cash discount is not offered, management, nevertheless, will indicate on the sales invoice the *net* period for the payment of the credit account. One of the important decision issues in credit sales management turns on whether or not to extend the *net* period to promote sales; and this is a more difficult problem to research and to analyze than the cash discount because it does not fit right into a simple model. To give meaning to the credit term policy for profit analysis, we have to follow the path of cost analysis rather than price. Whereas cash discounts will decrease net profits except for favorable conditions of price elasticity, extending the net payment period on credit sales increases opportunity costs of holding larger receivables investments. We may also look at this as the opportunity cost of decreasing liquidity. The reader will recall that liquidity is a condition of fluidity evidenced primarily by growing balances of cash and marketable securities that can be directed quickly to profitable asset investments. Funds tied up in receivables are at least temporarily deprived of profitable investment and, therefore, incur an opportunity cost that is linearly related to the length of time that a given quantity of receivables are withheld from more profitable investments.

Let us illustrate the nature of this cost and its effect on prospective profits with a few simple examples. Assume that credit terms are extended to ninety days from thirty. The cost relationship can be illustrated quantitatively using the basic linear cost equation: $C = cX$ and adjusting it for the added opportunity cost as follows:

$$C = [c + (rbt)]X \qquad\qquad 9.2$$

In this equation, unit variable cost c is \$2, unit price b is \$10, opportunity cost r is 1 percent per month, credit time t is three months, and X is the quantity of sales. X is the number of units of inventories sold at a unit variable cost of \$2 plus the opportunity cost of carrying the receivables.

$$\begin{aligned} C &= [\$2 + (0.01 \times \$10 \times 3)]X \\ &= (\$2 + \$0.30)X \\ &= \$2.30(X) \end{aligned}$$

The equation indicates that to the regular $2 unit variable cost is added a receivables *carrying* cost that is linearly related to the length of time that the receivables are held. Expanding this to a profit function we have:

$$P = [\$10 - (\$2 + 0.01 \times \$10 \times 3)]X - (\$2,000)$$

The size of the profit will depend on the size of X, which is the financial managers' expectation of net sales resulting from extending easier credit terms. Before considering the effect of variable sales on net profits, let us determine the break-even point in sales as an indication of where net profits begin. We observe that a substantial contribution toward fixed costs is made by each unit of sale despite the carrying cost of receivables:

$$\begin{aligned} \text{Contribution} &= b - c \qquad\qquad\qquad 9.3 \\ &= \$10 - \$2.30 \\ &= \$7.70 \end{aligned}$$

To solve for the break-even point, we set the cost equation equal to the income equation and solve for X:

$$\begin{aligned} \$10X &= \$2.30X + \$2,000 \\ \$7.70X &= \$2,000 \\ X &= 260 \text{ units} \end{aligned}$$

Management can tell now that profits can be made by selling more than 260 units, but more important to know is whether or not extending credit will generate enough new sales to justify the added opportunity cost incurred by extending the credit. Management wants to know first what it would take in higher cost sales to attain the profit that is already earned on a cash sales basis. For this purpose, assume that 400 units can be sold without offering any credit terms. The profit equation under this condition is $P = (\$10 - \$2)400 - \$2,000$, and net profits are $1,200. For the new higher cost condition to attain this level of profit, 416 units need to be sold. The solution is found to this problem by setting the new profit equation equal to $1,200.

$$\begin{aligned} X(\$10 - \$2.30) - \$2,000 &= \$1,200 \\ 10X - \$2.30X &= 3,200 \\ 7.70X &= 3,200 \\ X &= 416 \text{ units} \end{aligned}$$

Any sales over 416 units resulting from extending credit will earn more net profits after fixed charges than would have been earned by selling for cash 400 units. To know whether profits can be optimized by extending credit terms depends on a kind of coefficient of credit-term elasticity. *Credit-term elasticity is the quantitative measure of customer responsiveness to credit extension.* If the customer is likely to be very responsive to credit extension, credit sales may easily exceed 416 units; but, if he is not responsive, sales may barely increase over what they would be on a cash basis. Some of the factors that determine this elasticity are the liquidity of the customer, short-term investment opportunities of the customer, and nature of the credit terms offered by competitors.

Financial managers cannot estimate with certainty the effect of easier credit terms on sales and net profits and, therefore, may resort to a probability analysis. It was seen in Chapter 6 how subjective probabilities are applied to allow for the risks of sales estimates. If the business has had no experience with extending credit terms, it may be difficult to assign probability weights to possible sales. Experience of other firms in this case may be helpful, and the normal frequency distribution will be helpful for estimating the degree of fluctuation in sales around their average. A cautionary note needs to be sounded, however, about the risk of overexpanding receivables investment. With a given quantity of capital, automatic limits are set on the quantity of receivables that a business can safely carry. It is a temptation for a firm to expand credit sales without considering the limits of its capital constraint, particularly its working capital constraint. The conflict is forever present between the desire on the one hand to maximize net profits through credit extension and the realization on the other that in current operations certain very definite capacity limits are set by capital which cannot be resolved except by relaxing the constraint and considering a capital investment decision. Aside from profit maximization factors, there are internal management problems related to carrying, and collecting on receivables, that will be considered in the following section.

OFFSETTING LIQUIDITY RISKS OF RECEIVABLES HOLDINGS

Liquidity risks of holding receivables are of two kinds: one is the risk that they will not be collected on the date that they are due; the other is the risk that they will not be collected at all. With the quantity of capital fixed for current operations, financial managers seek to maintain a balance of receivables that is commensurate with the company's profit objective and its goal of maximizing share values, without exposing the company's shares to unfavorable discounts in the securities market from the delay in cash flow from receivables collections. In general, it may be said that the larger portion, at the end of any given operating period, that receivables balances are of total sales for the period the more risky this asset is to the firm and its shareholders. This is logical because, as a larger proportion of sales go into receivables balances instead of directly into cash, the more difficult it is to plan the cash flow that is needed to meet current operating needs. Also, the larger the receivables balance the more difficult it is for other working capital resources to withstand the shock of mass delays in collections and possibly the shock of defaulting accounts. Granting longer credit terms may induce larger sales and more net profits as was suggested earlier, but this increases the average maturities of receivables balances and increases the risk of cash shortages until more working capital resources are acquired by the company. To some extent the risks of receivables holdings can be avoided by establishing receivables management criteria.

SELECTING CREDIT CUSTOMERS

The job of managing and controlling receivables can be made somewhat easier by a careful selection of credit customers. While careful customer selection is no guarantee against delinquency and loss, it does reduce the probability of loss. The credit worthiness of customers is established by their debt-paying experiences in the past and by conditions of their current and capital finances that reflect debt-paying capabilities for the future. To check on past debt-paying experiences, financial managers can turn to those who have extended credit to these prospective customers in the past. Inventory suppliers are one main source of information because suppliers of inventories are the firms that create receivables; and these businesses are confronted with the same problems as we are in creating our own receivables. Other sources of information include commercial banks, credit bureaus, and credit rating agencies.

AVERAGE AGE OF RECEIVABLES

By assuming that receivables are created at a uniform rate over time, we can convert a given ratio receivables/sales to an average age of receivables. It may be easier to understand the *average* age concept if we think of the resulting age as representing the number of days of average credit sales contained in the receivables balance. Thus, if receivables are $10,000 and average daily credit sales are $200, the quantity of average daily credit sales contained in the receivables balance is:

$$\text{Number of days of average daily credit sales} = \frac{\$10,000}{\$\ 200} = 50$$

The simplifying assumption of the even daily flow of credit sales into receivables balance is made as the first step to obtaining a useful measure of liquidity. Planning credit sales and receivables balances is necessarily preceded by researching and analyzing the quantity of current receivables balances on an average age basis. It offers an effective method of comparing the relative quantity of receivables today with the relative quantity in the past and with relative quantities of receivables held by competetive firms and by the industry as a whole. The formula for computing the average age of receivables is the following:

$$Y = D\left(\frac{R}{S}\right) \qquad\qquad 9.4$$

Where: Y = The average age of receivables
R = Value of the receivables balance at the end of a given operating period
S = Value of net sales or credit sales for the current period
D = Number of days in the operating period

Substituting:

$$R = \$10,000 \qquad S = \$20,000 \qquad D = 90 \text{ days}$$

$$Y = 90\left(\frac{\$10,000}{\$20,000}\right)$$

$$Y = 45 \text{ days (average age or average days' credit sales)}$$

Average age (Y) is a function of X which is ratio R/S. The value of Y in this case is determined by the relative value of R to S and not by the size of receivables or sales independently. This factor of a relative X value is important to the financial manager. The ratio alone has a value of $10,000/20,000 = 0.5/1$. Think of the total relationship above as a linear function, and it will have more meaning for analysis. Where $b = 90$ and $X = R/S$, then $b = 90$ is the coefficient of X, the constant rate of change and the slope of the curve on a linear graph. Figure 9.2 contains two curves, one representing the functional relationship between average ages and the ratio of receivables balances to sales in a ninety-day sales situation and the other the functional relationship between average ages and the ratio in a

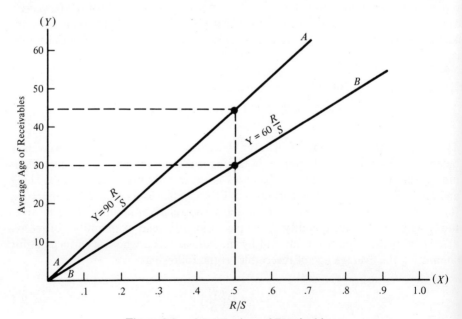

Figure 9.2. Average Age of Receivables.

sixty-day sales situation. Both curves AA and BB begin at the origin of the graph where the ratio is zero. At this point, there are no receivables which is the only condition that can produce a zero ratio: $R/S = 0/S = 0$. The graph will tell quickly what the average age of receivables is for any R/S value between 0 and 1. It is interesting and important to note that, for both coefficients of 60 and 90, the average age of receivables increases linearly as the R/S variable increases on the X axis and decreases linearly as the R/S variable decreases on the X axis. It is also interesting to notice that given any R/S value, for example 0.5, the average ages produced by the AA function given the same X values are longer in every case than the average ages produced by the BB function. The X axis could have been carried further to the right to the point at which $R/S > 1$. Ratios in excess of 1 indicate that receivables balances at a given time exceed sales for the current operating period. This condition can easily result by arbitrarily selecting a short sales period with a correspondingly small total sales, but this will not affect the average age of receivables if the decline in sales is at the same rate as the decline in time. For example, assume that the sales period selected for analysis is changed by 50 percent from sixty to thirty days and that sales are less by the same relative amount of 50 percent:

$$\text{Using a 60-day operation:} \quad 60\left(\frac{10,000}{10,000}\right) = 60 \text{ days}$$

$$\text{Using a 30-day operation:} \quad 30\left(\frac{10,000}{5,000}\right) = 60 \text{ days}$$

If receivables balances had been larger in the second than in the first case, the average age of receivables would have been more than thirty days; and, if receivables balances had been smaller in the second than in the first case, the average age of receivables would have been smaller than thirty days.

Historical analysis of average ages sheds light on receivables management practices and may be helpful guides to credit sales and collections policies for the future. Table 9.2 compares average ages over four quarters; this is a hypothetical example illustrating the effect of different relative rates of change in receivables and net sales on changes in average ages of receivables. Illustrated below Table 9.2 is a comparison between the *relative* rates of change in receivables in the numerator and the relative rates of net sales in the denominator. For a review of

TABLE 9.2
AVERAGE AGES COMPARED
$D(R/S)$
$D = 90 \text{ DAYS}$

	1st Quarter	*2nd Quarter*	*3rd Quarter*	*4th Quarter*
Receivables balance	$ 75,200	$135,700	$275,400	$250,800
Net sales	150,400	280,500	310,100	300,200
Average age (days)	45	44	80	75

the mechanics of these operations, the reader is referred to Chapter 3. When the relative rate of increase in receivables is greater than the relative rate of increase in net sales, the ratio and the average age of receivables will increase. But, when the relative rate of decrease in receivables is greater than the relative rate of decrease in net sales, the ratio will decrease and the average age of receivables will decrease. Both of these conditions are evident in the schedule below and are verified in Table 9.2 above. The third row of values tells us how the relative rate of change in receivables compares with the relative rate of change in net sales. The first figure in the third row states that the relative rate of growth in receivables through the second quarter was 0.93 or 93 percent as great as the relative rate of growth in net sales. As this figure is less than 1 the average age of receivables will fall. The second value states that receivables increased relatively almost ten times as fast as net sales, and this should produce a major increase in the average age of receivables. The last value indicates that the relative decrease in receivables balances was 2.78 times as great as the relative decrease in sales, and this should produce a noteworthy decrease in the average age of receivables. The reader can verify each of these items and their corresponding effect on average age of receivables by referring to Table 9.2.

RELATIVE RATES OF CHANGE
IN RECEIVABLES AND NET SALES

	1st to 2nd Quarter	2nd to 3rd Quarter	3rd to 4th Quarter
Receivables	$\frac{\Delta 60,500}{75,200} = \Delta 0.804$	$\frac{\Delta 139,700}{135,700} = \Delta 1.03$	$\frac{\Delta -24,600}{275,400} = \Delta -0.089$
Net sales	$\frac{\Delta 130,100}{150,000} = \Delta 0.865$	$\frac{\Delta 29,600}{280,500} = \Delta 0.105$	$\frac{\Delta -9,900}{310,100} = \Delta -0.032$
Comparative relative changes	$\frac{\Delta 0.804}{\Delta 0.865} = 0.93$	$\frac{\Delta 1.03}{\Delta 0.105} = 9.80$	$\frac{\Delta -0.089}{\Delta -0.032} = 2.78$

CLASSIFYING AGES OF RECEIVABLES

Classifying receivables by age groups gives management closer control over the quality of the individual accounts than does the measure of average ages. A schedule of classified receivables ages is illustrated in Table 9.3. The first column sets up the age groups by thirty-day intervals. The second shows the months of sales, and column three shows the quantity of each month's sales still uncollected. Column four shows the percentages of receivables in each age class. To evaluate receivables for taking control action, information in the table above has to be compared with earlier age classifications. A comparison with earlier classifications will show specifically where control action should be taken. Table 9.4 shows clearly that the liquidity structure of receivables has improved over the past three months as the portion of the sixty-day or younger class increased from 33 percent of the total at the end of September to almost 80 percent three months later.

TABLE 9.3
CLASSIFIED AGES OF RECEIVABLES
DECEMBER 31, 1970

Age Classes (Days)	Months of Sale	Balance of Receivables	Percentage of Total
1 to 30	December	$100,000	22.7
31 to 60	November	250,000	56.8
61 to 90	October	48,000	10.9
91 to 120	September	40,000	9.1
121 to —	Earlier	2,000	0.5
Total		$440,000	100.0

TABLE 9.4
COMPARATIVE AGES OF RECEIVABLES
SEPTEMBER 31, 1970 AND DECEMBER 31, 1970

Age Schedule (Days)	Month of Sale		Receivables Balances		Percentage of Total	
	(A)	*(B)*	Sept. 31 *(A)*	Dec. 31 *(B)*	Sept. 31 *(A)*	Dec. 31 *(B)*
0 to 30	September	December	$ 41,500	$100,000	11.9	22.7
31 to 60	August	November	74,200	250,000	21.4	56.8
61 to 90	July	October	185,600	48,000	53.4	10.9
91 to 120	June	September	35,300	40,000	10.2	9.1
121 to —	Earlier	Earlier	10,800	2,000	3.1	0.5
			$347,400	$440,000	100.0	100.0

NUMBER OF DAYS TO MATURITY

Just as important in liquidity analysis as knowing how long receivables have gone uncollected is knowing how much time they still have to run before they mature for collection. As the average time a business has to wait to collect its receivables increases, the less liquid they are and the shorter the time the more liquid they arc. Comparison of average maturities should be made with earlier periods for a dynamic analysis of expected cash flows. Comparing maturities of receivables with receivables ages, we approach the account balances from two different vantage points. Maturities state the number of days remaining between the present date and the date when the receivables are due for collection, whereas, the age of receivables states the number of days that have transpired from the time that the credit sale was made and the present date. Both are important liquidity measures, the former as a measure of how long we have yet to wait before cash inflow is available and the latter as a measure of how long we have already waited. But the same receivables may be included in both measures, *their age measuring how long they have been owed us to date and their maturity measuring how long those same receivables have still to run.*

It is a relatively simple matter to go one step farther as was done in aging receivables to locate the predominant maturity class or classes that need special attention: either shortened to increase liquidity or lengthened to increase sales and profits. An illustration based on fifteen-day time intervals is found in Table 9.5. The

TABLE 9.5
CLASSIFICATION OF MATURITIES
OF RECEIVABLES

Maturity Classes (Days)	Cash Values	Percentage of Total
0 to 15	$205,000	53
16 to 30	85,600	22
31 to 45	99,000	25
Total	$389,600	100

fact that such a large portion of the receivables will produce cash in fifteen days or less throws a favorable light on receivables management practices. At the same time the fact that as much as 25 percent of the accounts are due in more than thirty days could be a signal for reconsidering the credit sales policies. The main service of the comparisons can now be made with earlier balances to see whether the current relationships are consistent with earlier periods or whether maturities have shifted. The procedure for comparing maturities of receivables currently owned with receivables owned at the end of some like period is basically the same as for comparing receivables ages except that the intervals used for maturity classes may differ as they do above from the intervals used for receivables ages.

BUDGETING RECEIVABLES

Budgeting receivables is a dynamic aspect of offsetting liquidity risks of receivables management that is concerned essentially with future relationships between credit sales, liquidity in receivables investments, and profitability. We will budget receivables under two different conditions: first, with given credit terms and varying sales and, second, with a change to easier credit terms and the same varying sales. The purpose of the budget is to project the effect on receivables of changing net sales and changing credit terms. Table 9.6 assumes credit terms of net thirty days from the end of the month (E.O.M.) in which the sale is made.

Sales are increased 20 percent in the second month, 10 percent in the third, and 5 percent in the fourth. Seventy percent of total sales are on credit, and customers will comply universally with the payment terms of thirty days net E.O.M. With credit sales collected in the month after sales, the month-end receivables are always equivalent to the current month's credit sales. Aggregate receivables increase with sales, but the risk of liquidity in terms of their average age is not impaired holding

TABLE 9.6
INVESTMENT WITH INCREASING SALES
SALES TERMS: NET 30 DAYS E.O.M.

	1st Month	2nd Month	3rd Month	4th Month
Net sales	$100,000	$120,000	$132,000	$138,600
Receivables B.O.M.	—	70,000	84,000	92,400
Credit sales (70%)	70,000	84,000	92,400	97,020
Total receivables	$ 70,000	$154,000	$176,400	$189,420
Collections	—	70,000	84,000	92,400
Receivables E.O.M.	$ 70,000	$ 84,000	$ 92,400	$ 97,020
Average age of receivables $D(R/S)$	21 days	21 days	21 days	21 days
Net profit @ 6% of sales	$ 6,000	$ 7,200	$ 7,920	$ 8,316

at twenty-one days. The significance of the table is that enforcement of given credit sales terms, in this case thirty days E.O.M., in the face of rising sales, will allow an increase in net profits without increasing liquidity risks measured by the relative age of receivables.

But financial managers want to consider also the effect on receivables and profits of changing the terms of credit sales as well as varying just the sales volume. Table 9.7 compared with Table 9.6 shows what would happen if easier payment terms

TABLE 9.7
RECEIVABLES INVESTMENT WITH EASIER CREDIT TERMS
SALES TERMS: NET 60 DAYS E.O.M.

	1st Month	2nd Month	3rd Month	4th Month
Net sales	$100,000	$120,000	$132,000	$138,600
Receivables B.O.M.	—	70,000	154,000	176,400
Credit sales (70%)	70,000	84,000	92,400	97,020
Total receivables	$ 70,000	$154,000	$246,400	$273,420
Collections	—	—	70,000	84,000
Receivables E.O.M.	$ 70,000	$154,000	$176,400	$189,420
Average age of receivables $D(R/S)$	21 days	38 days	40 days	41 days
Net profit @ 6% of sales	$ 6,000	$ 7,200	$ 7,920	$ 8,316

were offered given the sales schedule. Easier credit terms have the effect of increasing receivables balances sharply at first; but after the sixty-day collection policy goes into effect, liquidity measures tend to stabilize. Table 9.7 shows easier credit terms increasing liquidity risk but not increasing sales or profitability. If we see this taking shape in simulating future operations, it should be a warning to institute a tighter credit policy because we are taking a greater risk and incurring more receivables *carrying* costs without being compensated with higher sales and profits.

General descriptive illustrations such as those above are vital tools for understanding and studying the functional relationship between independent and dependent variables. But these underlying factors have to show up finally in tangible budgets of some kind if they are to be put into practical use. Budgets force financial managers to test their policy plans and to give advance notice of what has to be done and what controls have to be exercised to meet liquidity and profitability needs. Suppose that the ratio R/S for a representative period was \$30,000/\$300,000 making receivables on the average equal to 10 percent of sales but that now a cash discounting plan is expected to be introduced that will reduce receivables balances from \$30,000 to an average of \$24,000, or 8 percent of \$300,000 sales. If this ratio is expected to hold for a series of different sales levels, it is a simple matter to forecast receivables balances by multiplying expected monthly sales by 0.08. The assumption made here that the representative ratio of 0.08 will hold regardless of the sales volume may be true in some businesses but in others the ratio may increase or decrease with changing sales. A more dependable way to budget receivables is to consider each period on its own merits. To accomplish this objective, collections of credit sales on a monthly basis are also considered. Table 9.8 is a

TABLE 9.8
COLLECTIONS FORECAST

Estimate of Credit Sales		April	May	June	July	August	Sept.	Total
March	$ 77,600	$62,080	$14,744					$ 76,824
April	49,006		39,205	$ 9,311				48,516
May	55,757			44,606	$10,594			55,200
June	59,973				47,978	$11,395		59,373
July	64,213					51,370	$12,200	63,570
August	68,429						54,743	54,743
September	74,350							
Total	$449,328							$358,226
Total Collections		$62,080	$53,949	$53,917	$58,572	$62,765	$66,943	$358,226

collections forecast prepared in March based on estimated collections. Let 80 percent of sales be expected to be collected in the month after sales, 19 percent in the second month, and 1 percent expected to be lost in bad debts. Table 9.10 is a summary of the plan for receivables balances resulting from expected sales and collections.

A receivables budget is a plan for investing funds in receivables, but it is also a control tool setting standards of performance. Departures from these standards should be corrected the first month that actual performance departs from budgeted performance. Critical elements for control are credit sales, collections, and bad debt losses. Credit sales *above* the planned portion will increase receivables balances and the average age of receivables beyond the budget and require action from financial managers to restore the balance between cash and credit sales. Collections below the planned portion will also increase the investment in receivables and the average age of receivables beyond the budget, and this also requires corrective action from financial managers to stimulate collections. Bad debt losses above the planned portion will affect the company's liquidity in a more drastic manner than by increasing receivables balances and will, therefore, receive special attention in the following section.

TABLE 9.9
SUMMARY BUDGET

	April	May	June	July	August	Sept.	Total
Receivables	$ 77,600	$ 64,036	$ 65,286	$ 70,742	$ 75,741	$ 80,721	$ 77,600
Credit sales	49,006	55,757	59,973	64,213	68,429	74,350	371,728
Total receivables	$126,606	$119,793	$125,259	$134,955	$144,170	$155,071	$449,328
Collections	62,080	53,949	53,917	58,572	62,765	66,943	358,226
Net receivables	$ 64,526	$ 65,844	$ 71,342	$ 76,383	$ 81,405	$ 88,128	$ 91,102

BUDGETING OVERDUE ACCOUNTS

In the receivables budget just completed, bad debt losses were estimated arbitrarily at 1 percent of net sales. This figure could have been based on actual experience, or it could represent a conventional value common to a certain class of business. But we will consider here a somewhat broader treatment including the whole group of accounts that are overdue. We will use matrix algebra in this case to project receivables simultaneously in four categories of overdue accounts. This tool is used primarily to supply quantitative information about the distribution of accounts in the overdue budget. With this information, financial managers can broaden their scope of receivables decisions for analysis and control.

We illustrate the application of the tool to the budgeting situation in a general problem where overdue accounts (Y) are a function of variable credit periods: X is thirty, sixty, ninety, and more than ninety days. Experience combined with a priori assumption, we will say, accounts for the schedule or coefficients contained in Table 9.10. These coefficients indicate the number of accounts overdue for each time span listed in column 1, related to the variable terms of sale under which they originated. This table indicates model relations that are permanent enough to provide a format for projecting future receivables balances. The first value in the

TABLE 9.10
PAST-DUE ACCOUNTS PER 100 SALES TRANSACTIONS

Days Past Due	30-Day Terms	60-Day Terms	90-Day Terms	More Than 90 Days
1 to 10	1	2	4	2
11 to 20	0	1	6	4
21 to 30	0	2	4	2
31 to 40	0	1	3	2

second column states that out of every 100 sales transactions on thirty-day payment terms one is overdue one to ten days. The first value in the third column states that, out of every 100 sales on sixty-day payment terms, two accounts will be overdue one to ten days. The first value in the fourth column states that, out of every 100 sales transactions made on ninety-day payment terms, four accounts will be overdue one to ten days; and the first value in the last column states that, out of every 100 sales transactions made on more than ninety-day payment terms, two accounts will be overdue one to ten days. Each figure in the matrix can be explained by using the same procedure. In looking at column three, one sees that ninety-day credit terms have a predominance of delinquent accounts of all ages, even more delinquency than sales made on terms longer than ninety days.

Mathematically, the values in Table 9.10 are coefficients indicating rates of change (b) that will occur in the total number overdue accounts in each *past-due* classification. If these (b) values result from a substantial amount of researching of past experiences and of researching the experiences of other firms and the industry as a whole, they should serve a valuable purpose in budgeting delinquencies and bad debt losses. As a planning and control tool, however, they need to be adjusted and corrected from time to time as more empirical knowledge about the responses of customers to their financial obligations is determined. Next, the independent variables, estimated credit sales transactions, are brought into the analysis. Table 9.11 is the *estimate of the number of sales transactions* (in 00's), expected to be made in the ensuing budgetary period offering credit terms ranging from net thirty days to more than ninety days. Thus, X_1 indicates 100 sales transactions offering thirty-day credit terms will be made in the budgeting period; X_2 indicates 200 transactions offering sixty-day terms; X_3 indicates 400 transactions offering ninety-day terms; and X_4 indicates 100 transactions offering longer than ninety-day terms. The two zeros are dropped in each case for convenience in arithmetic.

TABLE 9.11
PLANNED SALES TRANSACTIONS
(IN 00'S)

X_1 = 30-day terms	= 1
X_2 = 60-day terms	= 2
X_3 = 90-day terms	= 4
X_4 = More than 90 days	= 1
Total transactions	8

The solution to the number of accounts resulting from these sales transactions that will be delinquent for each of the periods (1 to 10) through more than ninety days is found by solving the equations in Table 9.12. The Y values in the equations are the resulting number of accounts that are expected in each delinquency class. For example, Y_1 equals one to ten days delinquent for all sales transactions with terms from thirty days to over ninety days; Y_2 equals eleven to twenty days delinquent for all transactions with terms from thirty to over ninety days; Y_3 equals

TABLE 9.12
RECEIVABLES EQUATIONS IN LINEAR FORM

$Y_1 = 1(X_1) + 2(X_2) + 4(X_3) + 2(X_4)$
$Y_2 = 0(X_1) + 1(X_2) + 6(X_3) + 4(X_4)$
$Y_3 = 0(X_1) + 2(X_2) + 4(X_3) + 2(X_4)$
$Y_4 = 0(X_1) + 1(X_2) + 3(X_3) + 2(X_4)$

twenty-one to thirty days delinquent for all transactions with terms from thirty to over ninety days; and Y_4 equals thirty-one to forty days delinquent for all transactions with terms from thirty to over ninety days.

Y_1 is the solution to the sum of the products of X_1 multiplied by the first constant in the first row in Table 9.10, (X_2) multiplied by the second constant (2) in the first row, (X_3) multiplied by the third constant (4) in the first row, and (X_4) multiplied by the fourth constant (2) in the first row. They are multiplied in this manner because the transactions (the X's) are expected to contain the same delinquency ratio (one to ten days) as indicated in the descriptive Table 9.10. Thus, the constants and the variable of the Y_1 function are correctly formulated for a logical and meaningful quantitative solution. In the second row the same X variables are used as were used in equation Y_1; but the coefficients in this row are different than in the first because different kinds of delinquent accounts are being quantified. Y_2 accounts in the second row are delinquent from eleven to twenty days as against one to ten days in the Y_1 equation. Viewing Table 9.13 in total, one sees a universal *set* containing four *subsets*, Y_1 through Y_4, with four *elements*, X_1 through X_4, of variable values in each of the subsets.

The solution to the problem of how many total delinquent accounts to expect in each delinquency class given the number of transactions in each credit term offering from thirty days to above ninety days, is found by the multiplication of matrices. The solution procedure is illustrated in Table 9.13. It is relatively simple to perform the multiplication because the set of X variables is a single column matrix, and the multiplication procedure is a matter merely of matching this column with each of the rows of delinquent accounts illustrated in Table 9.13 and then multiplying.

TABLE 9.13
MULTIPLYING RECEIVABLES VALUES

Matrix of Delinquent Accounts Per 100 Sales Transactions	Matrix of Credit Sales Transactions (In 00's)	Number of Past-Due Accounts (In 00's)	Days Past Due
1 2 4 2	1	$23 = Y_1 =$	1 to 10
0 1 6 4	2	$30 = Y_2 =$	11 to 20
0 2 4 2	4	$22 = Y_3 =$	21 to 30
0 1 3 2	1	$16 = Y_4 =$	31 to 40
	Total delinquent accounts	91	

Table 9.13 shows that out of a total of 91 delinquent accounts resulting from 800 credit sales transactions, 23 or 25 percent are expected to be delinquent one to ten days; 30 or 33 percent are expected to be delinquent eleven to twenty days, 22 or 24 percent are expected to be delinquent twenty-one to thirty days; and 16 or 18 percent are expected to be delinquent thirty-one to forty days. Suppose that company practice is to classify accounts that are delinquent for twenty-one days or longer as *bad debts*; then, out of future sales transactions, management can expect 38 or 42 percent of its delinquent accounts to be bad debts. The student should be able to see at once the potentialities of this technique for simulating not only bad-debt budgets but also for simulating any budgeting situation in receivables management in which variable traits like receivables ages and maturities can be incorporated into a matrix model such as the one above. In the example above, certainty was assumed in budgeting the quantity of sales transactions, so that the basic principle of analysis would not be overshadowed by arithmetic. In cases where transactions cannot be forecast with certainty, however, a probability distribution can be set up for the number of sales transactions $X_1 - X_4$, thus producing more realistic values for multiplication. If management is convinced that a risk situation exists, then the procedure is to set up probability distributions for each credit term $X_1 - X_4$. This means setting up probability distributions for the number of possible sales transactions offering thirty-day terms, sixty-day terms, ninety-day terms, and terms over ninety days. If this procedure is followed, then each item in a series of possible sales transactions offering thirty-day terms is multiplied by the probability that each number of transactions will in fact be realized. The sum of these multiplications will give the expected number of transactions offering thirty-day credit terms. The same procedure is followed to get the expected number of transactions offering sixty-day terms and longer. When the expected number is determined for each of the four classes of credit terms $X_1 - X_4$, these values then are entered in the transactions column of values in Table 9.13 instead of the values 1, 2, 4, and 1 that were used in our illustration. The procedure from this point on is the same as under conditions of certainty. Values in the resulting transactions column of the matrix are multiplied by matching values in each row in the delinquency section of the matrix, and the solution will be a summary column of expected accounts for each delinquency category. The class may wish to apply the above technique to a set of hypothetical values to verify that this procedure is effective using probability distributions.

An interesting variation of the operation explained above for determining the distribution of delinquent accounts on the basis of their overdue periods is to invert this data for an estimate of the number of sales transactions given the delinquency distribution. The example below assumes conditions of certainty in estimating the number of past-due accounts. Now, given the number of delinquent accounts in each overdue period, the sales transactions that would produce just such classification of overdue accounts can be determined by an operation called *inverting* the matrix. To use the technique, we need the original set of delinquency coefficients of Table 9.10. Arithmetically this is a long operation compared with simple multiplication performed earlier, even for a 4 × 4 matrix. For speed and accuracy a computer-programmed inverting procedure is almost a necessity. Any set of variables can be used then to forecast sales transactions. To illustrate the procedure, the inverted matrix will be multiplied by the *Y* values from Table 9.13. The lengthy part of the operation is inverting the delinquency matrix to produce the values in the left part of Table 9.14 unless they are obtained with the computer.

TABLE 9.14
DETERMINING FUTURE CREDIT TRANSACTIONS
INVERTED MATRIX METHOD

Inverse of *Delinquency Matrix*					*Delinquent Accounts* *Original Y Values*		*Budgeted Transactions* *(In 00's)* *X Values*
1	−0	−1	−0		23		1
−0	−1	−0	+2	×	30	=	2
−0	+1	+1	−3		22		4
0	−1	−1.5	+4		16		1

Notice that the resulting *X* values in this case are the expected sales transactions of Table 9.11. This is true because values in the delinquent accounts column were taken from solution Table 9.13. These values were used to simplify the illustration, but in practice this column of values could vary widely from the solution figures in Table 9.13 with the result that a different set of budgeted transactions figures would appear in Table 9.14. The value of this method of sales transactions planning should be at once apparent, producing as it does the estimates of how many sales transactions need to be executed under each credit term from thirty days to over ninety days if the business is to maintain an optimal delinquent account distribution established in the original matrix Table 9.10. As a control tool, financial managers are responsible for enforcing the sales transactions budget on sales managers if financial managers are to optimize the delinquent account distribution. Finally, however, it is noted that the inverting operation is not limited to situations of delinquency; any matrix of receivables traits such as average ages and average maturities can be inverted and used to extract sales estimates that may even be the basis for income and profit planning.

SUMMARY

Chapter 9 is a financial analysis related specifically to credit sales and receivables balances. In this chapter again, we see numerous opportunities for applying the basic quantitative tools of financial analysis and planning to receivables management. It is shown how cash discounts on credit sales in effect are the same as a price reduction which influences quantity of sales subject to the amount of price elasticity. Important measuring tools are considered for determining the ages of receivables and for quantifying the maturities of receivables. The concept of a receivables budget is developed for planning receivables balances. In the final section on receivables analysis, the matrix tool is applied to the analysis of delinquent accounts receivables. The purpose of this operation is to indicate how to estimate the distribution of receivables balances with respect to the number of days that the accounts are past due. It is also shown that, by using the inverse of the matrix, a given experience in the delinquency of accounts can project the number of trade credit sales that are likely to occur in each delinquency category.

PROBLEMS

1. Company A has reason to believe that 70 percent of its total sales up to $10,000, will be credit sales and that from $10,000 to $20,000, 80 percent, of its sales will be on credit.

   a. Construct an equation for each range of sales that will allow management to determine by simple computation the quantity of credit sales at any level of total sales up to and including $20,000.
   b. Are the credit sales a linear or nonlinear function of total sales in this problem? Explain, identifying the rate of change and the slope of the curve(s) if this equation were graphed.
   c. The following is a profit equation for the operations of Company A. Analyze the equation in detail.

$$P = 0.8X[1 - 0.2] - \$1,000$$

2. You are considering offering a cash discount of 4 percent to stimulate sales and would like to know what effect it will have on present volume of 1,000 units. From researching the market and considering past experiences, you deduce that the elasticity coefficient at 1,000 units is -1.4.

   a. Determine the effect on sales volume of setting the discount rate at 4 percent.
   b. Apply your answer in question a to the following profit equation assuming price is $10; unit variable cost is $4; and fixed costs are $500:

$$P = X[(b - d_r b) - c] - \$500.$$

   c. Would it be advisable to offer the discount or to sell without the discount?

3. Your firm has been selling on a cash basis, and you are hoping to offer sixty-day credit at no charge to the customer. You feel that an opportunity cost of 0.015 per month is incurred, however, if the terms are extended.

   a. What is the meaning of opportunity cost in this case?
   b. Letting opportunity costs be included, set up the equation for determining total variable cost assuming that unit variable costs are $4, that price is $10 and that the credit will be extended for sixty days.

c. Analyze the profit equation: $P = X[\$10 - (\$2 + 0.015 \times \$10 \times 2)]$ $- \$2,000$. Determine profit for a sales level of 400 units, 420 units.

4. The average age of receivables is a linear function of R/S. Suppose that the coefficient of the linear function is 30 and that the quantity of capital resources limits the R/S value to 0.8.

    a. Set up the equation.
    b. What is the meaning of the coefficient in this case?
    c. Graph the function.
    d. What value is the graphic tool for measuring receivables ages?
    e. Suppose the coefficient is increased to 60. What does this mean? Where would this appear on the graph?
    f. Given an X value of zero, what will the Y value be? Will this always be true? Explain.

5. Management observes that the dollar investment in trade receivables is increasing rapidly from month to month and becomes concerned with whether this is a mark of declining liquidity or just a normal receivables growth. It is decided to test this in two ways: first, by the investment in receivables relative to current assets and, second, by the investment in receivables relative to sales.

    a. Illustrated below are figures for receivables and total current assets for the past five months. Calculate the percentage of receivables to current assets at the end of each month and evaluate.
    b. Below are credit sales figures stated on a monthly basis. Compare your findings with the results in a and evaluate. For a more vivid picture for evaluation and decision making, plot two line graphs comparing R/CA and R/S where the horizontal axis indicates the months and the vertical axis indicates percentages.

MONTH-END RECEIVABLES AND CURRENT ASSETS

	April	May	June	July	August	September
Receivables	$5,000	$7,000	$10,000	$12,000	$12,000	$15,000
Total current assets	30,000	30,000	35,000	40,000	45,000	40,000
Percentage R/CA						

MONTH-END RECEIVABLES AND CREDIT SALES

	April	May	June	July	August	September
Receivables	$5,000	$7,000	$10,000	$12,000	$12,000	$15,000
Credit sales	8,000	9,000	10,000	15,000	20,000	20,000
R/S						
Average age						

6. After checking the average ages of receivables, you find that they are increasing. But you want to locate, if possible, the age classes that are causing the average increase so that closer collection control can be exercised. To accomplish this, you construct the following schedule on the last days of June.

CLASSIFIED AGES OF RECEIVABLES

Age (Days)	Month of Sale	Balance of Receivables	Percentage of Each Class to Total	Expected Collections (%)	Net Cash Values
1 to 30	June	$10,000		100	
31 to 60	May	15,000		99	
61 to 90	April	30,000		80	
91 to 120	March	5,000		10	

a. Complete the schedule above, including the net cash value.
b. What control action do you recommend, if any, assuming that your sales are all made on a net sixty-day basis?
c. How would you compare current conditions with the previous year?

7. Overly liberal credit terms, as well as poorly managed collections, may have accounted for the increasing average age of our receivables. For a closer look at this side of the issue, we must work out the average and the classified maturities of the existent receivables. Complete the table and compute the weighted and unweighted average days to maturity.

DETERMINING AVERAGE MATURITY

Account Number	Days to Maturity	Cash Values	Weighted Cash Values
1	10	$ 5,000	
2	23	20,000	
3	30	10,000	
4	21	10,000	
5	20	15,000	
6	28	15,000	
7	5	5,000	

Average days (unweighted) =
Average days (weighted)   =

a. How would you set up a classified schedule of maturities?
b. What would a classified schedule show us that the average would not?
c. Suppose credit terms are eased causing receivables balances to rise. Under what conditions would this rise in receivables balances result in a shorter average age of receivables?
d. Would you evaluate a condition like this as favorable or unfavorable? Explain.

Account Number	Days to Maturity	Cash Values	Weighted Cash Values
1	20	$ 5,000	
2	30	5,000	
3	28	10,000	
4	10	35,000	
5	10	25,000	

8. You wish to forecast receivables investment as well as to measure prospective profit. The typical short-run problem is to project simultaneously receivables

balances and profits. In trying to solve this problem, assume that sales are expected to decrease by 10 percent each month and that 80 percent of the sales are on credit with terms of net thirty days. With this information, complete the joint statement of receivables and profits.

RECEIVABLES INVESTMENT PLAN
CREDIT TERMS: NET 30 DAYS

	January	*February*	*March*	*April*
Net sales	$30,000			
Receivables B.O.M.	5,000			
Credit sales (80%)				
Total receivables				
Collections				
Receivables E.O.M.				
Average age of receivables				
Net profit @ 6% of sales				

a. Now prepare a statement of the same kind proposing that credit terms be relaxed to net sixty days and sales remain at $30,000 monthly. On the basis of your new findings, what would happen in each case to the ratio R/S? Evaluate the liquidity and profitability effects of easing up on the credit terms.

b. Does the fact that goods are sold on terms such as those illustrated above mean that collections will always be made in exactly that pattern? Explain.

9. The following matrix indicates the range of average ages of classified receivables balances and the number of accounts in each age class by terms of sale.

ACCOUNTS IN AGE CLASS FOR EACH 25 SALES TRANSACTIONS

Age Range (Days)	30-Day Terms	60-Day Terms	90-Day Terms
1 to 30	5	4	6
31 to 60	1	8	4
61 to 90	0	2	6

a. Analyze the matrix.
b. The following sales transactions are planned (in 25's):

$$X_1 = \text{30-day terms} = 2$$
$$X_2 = \text{60-day terms} = 3$$
$$X_3 = \text{90-day terms} = 1$$

c. Set up the matrix of simultaneous equations solving for variables Y_1, Y_2, and Y_3.
d. Find the number of accounts expected in each age class given the expected sales transactions.

10

Cash
Management

This chapter is concerned with managing cash funds in their relation to other current assets as part of the total current operation for profit. Like inventories and receivables, cash is a costly asset to hold; and, like these two assets, cash does not earn profit. Like inventory, but not necessarily like receivables, a certain quantity of cash nevertheless has to be held if the business is to operate profitably. The reader can sense the general nature of the cash management problem: to hold enough on balance to meet operating requirements, at the same time not to hold cash in such large quantities as to incur excessive holding costs. In the analysis that follows, cash management issues will consider separately cash balances and cash flows. Although this division of the material is somewhat arbitrary from the practical operating viewpoint, it will serve for the present to identify the major problem areas of this difficult far-reaching subject.

CASH BALANCES

There are two clearly distinguishable cash balances: one, the balance that is held for normal transactions purposes and, two, the balance required to meet basic safety requirements. We will approach this subject much as we did inventory management from the optimizing viewpoint considering, first, that important balance held for transactions purposes and, second, the balance held as safety stocks to meet minimum cash requirements.

But before going into the details of these analyses, let us consider the role of the capital constraint in cash management. The capital constraint is felt in managing both the cash balance and the cash flow. The capital constraint is implicit in the level of current operations that cash balances and flows are geared to serve.

The reason that one firm holds only $5,000 for transactions while another holds $10,000 is that the former, because of limited net working capital and fixed capital, is confined necessarily to a lower level of operations. Larger capital resources would have permitted more expansive operations and required larger cash balances and flows. Financial managers are confronted with this realistic situation wherein capital resources are limited, and cash funds, therefore, like other current assets seek an optimal level. Looking back at income and profit management, one sees that the capital constraint clearly limited output for sale and profit. With inventories it was the issue of how to optimize inventory holdings and order quantities subject to given capital constraints, and with receivables it was the problem of optimizing given capital constraints affecting credit extension and receivables holdings.

THE TRANSACTIONS BALANCE

The transactions balance is much the larger of the two balances, and it is subject also to wider and more rapid fluctuations than cash balances of safety stocks. As cash holdings are not income producing assets regardless of how large or how small they may be, the only approach left is for financial managers to optimize at minimum total costs. It is specifically through minimizing cash holding costs that financial managers hope to increase expected profits and share values. The transactions balance raises a major problem for financial managers seeking an optimal cash holding size. The optimizing procedure examined here is operative under certain rather limiting assumptions. After this procedure is extended to its logical conclusion, the assumptions will be relaxed and modified to fit less rigid conditions of cash management. It is specifically through minimizing cash holding costs that financial managers hope to increase expected profits and share values. This analysis will apply the cost minimizing tools and skills to the decision goal of determining how many units of cash should be held on balance to meet transactions.

Carrying Costs Carrying costs are positively related to the quantity of cash held on balance during a given period, but they are not a carrying cost in the same sense as inventory carrying costs. Cash balances are an altogether different kind of asset than inventories, consisting primarily of demand deposits in commercial banks for which no storage costs, insurance charges, or taxes are paid usually by the depositing firm. Cash holding costs are opportunity costs; by holding cash on balance for future transactions, the opportunity is foregone of earning profits by investing the funds in near-cash assets like marketable securities.

The opportunity cost of holding cash is the going market rate or return on the kind of investment that would meet the combined profit and risk needs of the business. The equation for the opportunity cost function is:

$$H_{c_1} = c_1 \bar{X} \qquad\qquad 10.1$$

Where: H_{c_1} = Total opportunity costs
c_1 = Unit holding costs
$\bar{X}$ = Average units of cash held

By assuming that cash is used at a steady rate during each holding period, the average quantity of cash held during any transactions period is equal to 1/2 of the amount ordered at the beginning of the use period. The subscript 1 in H_{c_1} prepares us for another holding cost which will be encountered later as H_{c_2}. Assume that opportunity costs for the planning period is \$0.04 per dollar held. The equation for the function then is:

$$H_{c_1} = \$0.04(\bar{X})$$

H_{c_1} tells management what it is costing in foregone profits for any number of alternative cash holdings. The \$0.04 will be recognized as the constant rate of change in total variable costs and as the slope of the graph of the equation. Table 10.1 is a schedule of costs starting with an average cash balance of 1,000 units and increasing each interval by 1,000 units. The last column indicates the constant rate of change in total carrying costs of \$40 for each change of \$1,000 in the quantity of cash holdings.

TABLE 10.1
VARIABLE HOLDING COST FUNCTION

c_1	$\bar{X}$	H_{c_1}	ΔH_{c_1}
0.04	1,000	\$ 40	
.04	2,000	80	40
.04	3,000	120	40
.04	4,000	160	40
.04	5,000	200	40
.04	6,000	240	40

NONLINEAR HOLDING COSTS

Nonlinear costs in this case are negatively related to the quantity of cash budgeted to any given period. It may be helpful to think of budgeting or planning a given quantity of cash in terms of an inventory *order*; that is, budgeting cash is in effect ordering a certain sum of cash. Costs of budgeting are related to time spent by financial managers analyzing past conditions and planning future needs. It also includes the clerical and stenographic services and supplies and may even include time spent setting up a line of credit with commercial banks. But it does not include interest or service charges of any kind levied by the bank in case a cash loan is obtained. The total of these cash planning costs is about the same regardless of how much cash is planned for the transactions balance. The declining cost function is expressed as follows:

$$H_{c_2} = c_2\left(\frac{K}{2\bar{X}}\right) \qquad 10.2$$

Where: H_{c_2} = Cost of securing cash for the total operating period
c_2 = Cost of planning to obtain a single order of cash

K = Total cash needed for a given operating period
$\bar{X}$ = Average quantity of cash holdings

The $K/2\bar{X}$ variable will decrease with an increase in the average units of cash ($\bar{X}$) budgeted to the balance, with the result of decreasing the total cost (H_{c_2}) of the funds over the operating period. Table 10.2 shows this relationship, starting with $\bar{X}$ = $1,000. The maximum sum of cash required for use over the operating period is 12,000 units; $2(\bar{X})$ at the limit = $2(6,000)$ = 12,000 units.

The observing student will be looking for the optimal cash balance, the level of average cash holdings that minimizes the sum of carrying and ordering costs. Table 10.3 is the sum of carrying and ordering costs at each level of average cash

TABLE 10.2
NEGATIVE CASH HOLDING COST FUNCTION

c_2	$\times$	$\dfrac{K}{2\bar{X}}$	$=$	H_{c_2}
$60		$\dfrac{\$12,000}{2,000}$		$360
60		$\dfrac{12,000}{4,000}$		180
60		$\dfrac{12,000}{6,000}$		120
60		$\dfrac{12,000}{8,000}$		90
60		$\dfrac{12,000}{10,000}$		72
60		$\dfrac{12,000}{12,000}$		60

TABLE 10.3
OPTIMAL CASH HOLDING

	Average Cash Holdings (Units)					
	1,000	*2,000*	*3,000*	*4,000*	*5,000*	*6,000*
Carrying cost (H_{c_1})	$ 40	$ 80	$120	$160	$200	$240
Ordering cost (H_{c_2})	360	180	120	90	72	60
Total cost	$400	$260	$240	$250	$272	$300

holdings, indicating that 3,000 units of cash ($3,000) is the optimal holding amount, where $H_{c_1} + H_{c_2}$ = $240. Checking the table against the formula shows that the minimum cost on the table of $240 is exactly correct.

$$\bar{X}_{op} = \sqrt{\frac{c_2 K}{2c_1}} \qquad\qquad 10.3$$

$$= \sqrt{\frac{\$60(12,000)}{2(0.04)}}$$

$$= 3,000 \text{ units}$$

The reader is reminded of the capital constraint that has implicitly played an important part in the analysis that has gone before. The role of the capital constraint becomes very clear the moment a question is asked such as: Why are only $12,000 of cash balances planned for transactions during the next financial accounting period? The answer to this, which is found in Chapters 6 and 7, also gives the answer to the question of why the optimal planning size of the transactions balance is $6,000 and why the optimal average holding quantity is $3,000. If the optimal holding quantity is 3,000 units and cash is used at a constant rate over time, the optimal order quantity of cash is 2 × $3,000 = $6,000. The final question now is: How many times do financial managers have to order cash to be assured of a constant $3,000 average balance? The answer to this question will give us the optimal number of orders to place during the financial operating period. The answer to this question is found in the solution to the equation that follows. The optimal number of times to budget and to negotiate for cash is 2. If the financial accounting period over which 12,000 units of cash are to be used is one quarter, then the quantity ordered is $6,000 every six weeks; or, if $12,000 of cash is used every month, it will need budgeting every two weeks.

$$\text{Optimal orders} = \frac{K}{2\bar{X}_{op}} \qquad\qquad 10.4$$

$$= \frac{\$12,000}{6,000}$$

$$= 2$$

OPTIMIZING LEAD TIME

Lead time is the time that is allowed to offset the lag between the *start* of cash budgeting and negotiation for the cash and the time that it is available for use in transactions. In our example of optimal average cash holdings, no allowance was made for possible lags between the time that the decision was made to plan for the $6,000 cash acquisition and the time that it is needed to be put into cash transactions. Knowledgeable financial managers are not only aware that such lags do in fact exist, but they are also aware of the consequences of insolvency and financial failure that may result from such lags. In recognizing the need for cash planning to bridge this gap, we will consider cost factors connected with budgeting cash requirements at different time intervals prior to the date that the balance is expected to be put into use.

Cost of Being Late   Whether financial managers plan to secure the cash from sales and from collection of receivables or plan to secure it from external sources like commercial banks and other business lending agencies, there is some measureable degree of risk as to the day that the funds will become available. There are many random factors that could cause a late access date that are related to the flow of cash sales, paying habits of credit customers, and lending practices of financial institutions. The important fact for analytic purposes is that, because of the random nature of these factors, financial managers' control over cash acquisitions is far from being a certainty.

If the use rate of the cash balance can be predicted and controlled as is assumed in the earlier optimizing example, even though the *access date* of the cash balance may not be known with certainty, the risk of late access is quantifiable and convertible to expected costs. If the cash is accessible right on the day that the previous funds are used up, it incurs no cost; but, if it arrives late, a daily cost is incurred that is related directly to the value of the lost transactions. This cost is a linear function of the number of days that the cash order arrives late and is related to the optimal average cash holdings of $3,000. Such costs include losses from not being able to take advantage of cash purchase discounts, quantity purchase discounts, and penalties for not being able to pay on time accounts payable arising from inventory purchases and notes payable arising from bank loans and the creation of other forms of commercial paper and tax accruals. There is also an intangible cost in the form of loss of goodwill which may result if the business should be delinquent on wage and salary payments. Past experiences of this and related businesses enable financial managers to establish a daily *late access cost* that under conditions of certainty is linearly related to the number of days late but that under risk conditions in nonlinearly related, such that the sooner the cash planning begins prior to when the funds are needed the lower the expected value of being late.

Referring specifically to the optimal average holding quantity of $3,000, let us assume that the daily late cost is determined to be 0.005 of the average balance or $15(0.005 + $3,000). Total late costs under certainty are the products of the number of days that the cash will be late and $15, but the risk situation requires a somewhat more detailed statement. Time and space will not permit us to go through the details again of converting probabilities of being late to total expected costs of being late, although the problem at the end of this chapter relating to this subject should be worked by the reader. For details of setting up a risk situation problem, we are referred to Tables 8.4 and 8.5 of the text.

Cost of Being Early If the only cost connected with early planning and negotiating for transactions balances were late costs, financial managers would simply start seeking cash funds on the date that expected value of being late is at a minimum. But decreasing late costs accompanying earlier cash accesses are offset at a certain point by rising costs of early cash accesses.

Early access to cash means that funds are waiting to be put into current transactions. The same random variables, (1) the flow of cash sales, (2) paying habits of credit customers, and (3) the lending practices of financial institutions, that can cause a delay in cash access can also cause the cash *order* to arrive before it is needed. Costs of being early are opportunity costs resulting from carrying the cash rather than investing it in liquid income-earning assets like marketable securities. The first response may be to invest it in transactions rather than in lower-yielding marketable securities, but this kind of reasoning has two flaws. First, there is no room for more cash in the present transactions plan; and, second, if there were room, transactions imply investments in assets with much greater liquidity risk like receivables and inventories. Under conditions of certainty, the cost of early access to cash is linearly related to the number of days that the order will be early. Under risk conditions such as often prevail, however, the cost of planning for cash balances a certain number of days or weeks in advance is adjusted to the probability that such early planning will be one, two, three, or more days or weeks early. Instead of being simply a linear function then of the number of days early, the cost of being early becomes a nonlinear function of the product of the numbers of days early that it is possible for the cash to be and the probability distribution of it being early those numbers of days. The resulting expected values will in general increase at an increasing rate.

Referring specifically now to our earlier optimizing problem, carrying costs of early cash arrivals are figured on the total order quantity of $6,000 because the full amount of the order instead of the average balance of $3,000 will be available for the full time before it is put into transactions. To illustrate, suppose that 0.05 percent or $3 could have been earned daily on $6,000 ($0.0005 \times \$6,000$) had it been invested in marketable securities instead of being held in idle cash balances; then, the daily opportunity cost of holding the $6,000 is $3, and the expected value of planning for the cash balance a certain number of days before it is needed is the sum of the $3 times each number of days early that it could possibly arrive times the probability that it will arrive early each of these days. Instead of going any further into the details of cost determination under such risk condition, the student is referred to Tables 8.6 and 8.7 of the text. Reviewing the pattern of inventory costs in these tables, one observes that cash carrying costs would increase rapidly the earlier that financial managers acquire the cash.

Optimal Lead Time   The reader is reminded that the optimal number of days lead time is indirectly if not directly affected by the capital constraint under which financial managers are operating. The indirect effect is asserted through the size of optimal cash acquisitions $6,000 and optimal average cash holdings $3,000. As pointed out earlier, the answer to why the optimals must be limited in size to $6,000 and $3,000 is because of the limitations on capital resources for planning current operations (Chapters 6 and 7). Daily late costs and early costs are directly affected by the size of optimal cash holdings and by the optimal cash order quantity which are affected by the total cash needs for the period which is affected by the level of operations.

Getting back now to the immediate optimizing issue, financial managers seek that lead time in planning and negotiating transactions balances that will minimize the sum of the costs of being late with cash and the costs of being early. Another way of putting it is that financial managers seek the lead time which would equate late costs and early costs. Graphically portrayed, the optimal lead time is the number of days or weeks on the X axis that would cause the declining curve of late costs and the increasing curve of early costs to intersect right below the vertex of the total lead time cost curve. All three of the curves on this graph would be nonlinear because of the risk adjustment spelled out quantitatively in probability distributions.

We need to return again to the initial goal of optimizing the average cash holdings for transactions purposes if we are to follow logically this section of the cash balance analysis. First it should be noted that lead time in planning and negotiating transactions balances does not solve the important problem of determining the quantity of cash safety stocks that a business should hold on balance. The latter is the problem specifically of determining how large the safety stock of cash should be to cushion errors in planning the use rate for the transactions balance. It is easy to confuse the effect of lead time with the effect of safety stocks of cash with respect to the transactions balance. The big difference is that lead time does create a possible temporary overlapping of old and new optimal acquisitions near the end of the transactions period, the chance of this occurring being indicated by the probability that the new order for the optimal transactions balance will be consummated early. Safety stocks of cash play quite a different role for two reasons: first, safety stocks are an addition to the optimal transactions balance; and, second, the balance is expected to remain intact always, and if it is used in part or in total to meet shortages in the transactions balances, it will be immediately replaced. The solution to the problem of what size safety stocks to carry can be found with the cost minimizing technique which entails a consideration, first, of short costs and, second, of carrying costs.

Short Costs   Safety stocks of cash are carried to offset the probability that sometime during the operating period of say four weeks, the transactions balance will be used at a faster rate than initially planned. Factors that cause this condition are random variables that are all related to an acceleration in the use rate of the transactions balance. Some of the factors over which management has little control that would cause this are: (1) decision by creditors to accelerate their collections or to shorten the *net* dates of their accounts receivables (our accounts payables), (2) refusal of a lending agency to renew a maturing note, (3) increased prices for goods, services and taxes, and (4) contingency losses resulting from property damage and lawsuits. Notice that all of these factors are related to the rate at which the transactions balance is used; whereas, the factors affecting late costs (the lead time problem) are all related to a delay in the availability of the transactions balance. The former is concerned with factors affecting the use rate of the balance, the latter with acquiring the balance at the start of the transactions period. Short costs are costs that will be incurred if the reserves of safety stocks are not great enough to meet temporary shortages in the transactions balance caused at any time during operations by one or more of the items listed above.

The number of units carried in the cash safety stocks will depend on what the shortages in the transactions balances are expected to be. The shortages cannot be predicted with certainty because of the factors listed above, but financial managers do know with certainty that the larger the safety stocks of cash that are carried the lower the probability of running out of the total quantity of cash. This effect of large safety stocks on the probability of being short of cash for transactions is of primary concern because of its favorable cost effect. Cash shortage costs are the costs of obtaining under emergency conditions funds to offset shortages caused by one or more of the four factors listed above. Such costs are directly and linearly related to the size of the shortage under certainty conditions. Under risk conditions as usually prevails, however, the costs are nonlinearly related to the size of the shortage. Since the larger the safety stock is the less chance there is of being short, it follows that the larger the safety stock is the smaller the short costs. By carrying enough safety stocks, one can eliminate cash shortage costs altogether. Table 10.4 is the probability distribution that the demand will be equal to or exceed the

TABLE 10.4
EXPECTED VALUE———NO SAFETY BALANCE

Possible Average Demand	Probability of Average Demand	Optimal Cash Balance	Possible Cash Shortages	Probable Cash Shortages	Cost of Cash Shortages @ $0.40 Per Unit
$3,000	.65	$3,000	0	0	0
3,200	.20	3,000	200	40	$16.00
3,400	.09	3,000	400	36	14.40
3,600	.05	3,000	600	30	12.00
3,800	.01	3,000	800	8	3.20
	1.00				EV = $45.60

optimal average cash holdings of $3,000 in the transactions balance. The table also shows costs, assuming that no safety balance is carried and that the emergency rate of securing cash replenishment is $0.40 per dollar short. Table 10.5 shows the effect on expected value of carrying between $200 and $800 in the safety balance. Tables 10.4 and 10.5 show the range of expected values, probability adjusted short costs, given alternative quantities of cash in the safety balance. The cost of being short of cash when an average of $3,000 is carried in the transactions balance and $800 is carried in the safety balance is 0. This does not mean though that $800 will be held in the balance. For the answer to the question of how much to hold in safety stocks, we need to examine cash carrying costs and then seek the minimum of the two costs.

Carrying Costs   Carrying costs are the same for holding safety balances as they are for holding transactions balances. Cash carrying costs are the opportunity costs of not investing the cash in liquid securities. Carrying costs for the transactions balance were $0.04 per dollar held and the cost of the holding is linearly related to the quantity of dollars held in the safety balance under conditions of certainty which is the condition under which all cash is carried. Since we do not expect to use up the safety balance as we do the transactions balance, the cost is obtained simply by multiplying the quantity of dollars held in the safety balance by $0.04 as indicated in Table 10.6. The quantity of holdings ranges from $0 to $800 as was seen in Tables 10.4 and 10.5. Table 10.7 is the total cost table indicating the optimal cash safety balance.

TABLE 10.5
EXPECTED VALUE—CARRYING FROM $200 TO $800 SAFETY BALANCE

Prob. Dist.*	$200 Balance			$400 Balance			$600 Balance			$800 Balance		
	Poss. Short.†	Prob. Short.‡	Cost @ $0.40 Per Dollar	Poss. Short.	Prob. Short.	Cost @ $0.40 Per Dollar	Poss. Short.	Prob. Short.	Cost @ $0.40 Per Dollar	Poss. Short.	Prob. Short.	Cost @ $0.40 Per Dollar
0.65	0	0	0	0	0	0	0	0	0	0	0	0
.20	0	0	0	0	0	0	0	0	0	0	0	0
.09	400	36	14.40	0	0	0	0	0	0	0	0	0
.05	600	30	12.00	600	30	12.00	0	0	0	0	0	0
.01	800	8	3.20	800	8	3.20	800	8	3.20	0	0	0
			EV = $29.60			EV = $15.20			EV = $ 3.20			EV = $ 0

*Abbreviation for Probable Distribution
†Abbreviation for Possible Shortage
‡Abbreviation for Probable Shortage

233

TABLE 10.6
CARRYING COSTS OF SAFETY BALANCE

Quantity Held	Unit Cost	Total Cost
$ 0	$0.04	$ 0
200	.04	8
400	.04	16
600	.04	24
800	.04	32

TABLE 10.7
OPTIMAL SAFETY BALANCE

	$0	$200	$400	$600	$800
Expected short costs	$45.60	$29.60	$15.20	$ 3.20	$ 0
Carrying costs	0	8.00	16.00	24.00	32.00
Total costs	$45.60	$37.60	$31.20	$27.20	$32.00

Table 10.7 indicates that the optimal level of safety balances is right at $400 where total short costs and total carrying costs come closest together. Minimum total costs, however, are at $600. When this condition prevails a more accurate reading can be obtained by graphing the values. The graph would indicate that the optimal quantity of cash to hold in the safety balance is slightly over $400. The student should verify this.

SOME SUMMARY OBSERVATIONS

The subject of cash balances is often dismissed with a discussion of descriptive materials on the grounds that cash balances are too much a part of the basic input and output operations and too unsteady and unpredictable to attempt to fit into a formal analytic framework such as has been done here. Although the treatment may need to be rather heavily guarded by assumptions that are not always applicable, the descriptive approach leaves much more to be desired as a useful method for financial analysis.

The most delicate of our assumptions is the one that allows cash to be treated pretty much as a commodity like raw materials that financial managers seek out and optimize by combining ordering costs and carrying costs. Admittedly there are uncontrollable inflows of cash that are difficult to foresee and to control and that would detract from the validity of the ordering technique as it was developed here for some businesses. Nevertheless, by emphasizing acquisition techniques, attention is directed to the important area of cash budgeting and negotiation of cash loans. The concept of lead time applied to cash management further emphasizes the need for planning to avoid liquidity risks at the end of a transactions period. Finally the safety balance concept is formalized so that a clear line can be drawn from the conceptual viewpoint between the fluctuating transactions portion of the total cash balance and that relatively stable balance held as a kind of emergency fund against the risk of unusual losses in the transactions balance.

CASH FLOWS

In the previous section various aspects of the cash balance were considered with a view to optimizing the holdings for transactions purposes, optimizing the lead time on planning to acquire transactions balances, and optimizing the quantity of safety stocks. All of these issues are relevant to the total issue of cash management and are difficult to separate from cash flow issues. In this portion of the chapter, however, we will pay special attention to the flow of cash and to the specific management issues that are identified therewith.

FLOW OF CASH TO NEAR-CASH ASSETS

Very closely related to cash balances are highly liquid income earning assets called marketable securities. These assets occupy an important place in cash management because they offer a source of profit for intermittent excess funds in the transactions balance. For example, if the lead time for an order of cash results in an early acquisition of funds, marketable securities offer the logical temporary investment outlet for the funds; or, if transactions expenditures lag behind the cash use schedule, temporary excesses of cash should find their way into liquid income earning assets such as marketable securities. Following is a brief discussion of the investment alternatives offered in this market and the advantages and disadvantages of each to the business.

Regular Treasury Bills Regular Treasury bills are direct obligations of the United States Treasury that are issued weekly at a discounted value to mature in ninety-one days. These bills mature every Thursday at the Federal Reserve Bank of New York at face value. Like all of the other United States debts, Treasury bills are secured by the general credit of the central government and are generally looked on as the nearest thing to a completely riskless, highly liquid investment. If bought on the day of issue, they must be held for ninety-one days to be certain of realizing their full intrinsic liquidity. However, since large blocks of the securities mature every week, it is possible to invest continuously in securities with maturities of not more than one week. And, by purchasing a maturing issue on Wednesday, the investment can be made for as short a time as one day. Regular Treasury bills possess a high quality of intrinsic liquidity because of certainty of payment and because of the chances they offer for very short investment holdings. There is seldom any problem of finding bills that meet almost every maturity need of the business. At the same time, there is little risk of loss if the business finds itself in need of cash and has to market them before they mature. The market facilities for Treasury bills are highly developed and responsive to demand and supply conditions. As we would expect, however, these are the lowest yielding of all investments.

Special Treasury Bills   Besides the regular Treasury bills that are issued weekly, the Treasury issues bills from time to time to meet special cash needs. One common form, the *tax anticipation bill,* is sold to provide the Treasury with cash in advance of income tax receipts. Business investors can buy these bills at a discount and then use them at their full face value to meet their income tax obligations as they come due. Returns on the investment are somewhat higher than on regular bills, but their infrequent issuance widens the gap between dates of maturity and reduces their liquidity somewhat. Their longer maturities also increase the risk of fluctuation in their market values. There is no question about the bills being fully valued when they mature; but, as we can see now, this is not the only factor affecting liquidity.

Dealers' Repurchase Agreements   Nonbank securities dealers sometimes sell government securities with the obligation to repurchase the securities on demand from the holder. The repurchase price is set in advance, but the date of repurchase or sale date is left open for the investor to decide. This is, in effect, an advance of cash by the investor to the securities dealer in exchange for the dealer's promise to return the cash plus a fixed rate of interest on demand to the investor. The financial manager may buy any investment security for this purpose that the dealer will agree to repurchase, although usually relatively active government securities are used. But this kind of contract is bought usually for its higher yield to the business and not for its short maturity. The risk occurs if the dealer is financially unable to meet the call for cash from the investor. The chance for profit actually depends on the form of security we can get the dealer to agree to repurchase and the terms under which he agrees to make the repurchase.

Commercial Paper and Bank Acceptances   *Commercial paper* is the term applied to discounted, unsecured promissory notes of private corporations that mature from four to six months after their issue date. The notes are drawn in multiples of $2,500, and total issues sometimes reach several million dollars. They are bought outright by commercial paper dealers for resale in the money market. These notes are issued by manufacturers, distributors, and personal and commercial finance companies with exceptionally strong national credit standing. Commercial finance companies, like the Commercial Investment Trust (C.I.T.), Commercial Credit Company (C.C.C.), and General Motors Acceptance Corporation (G.M.A.C.), have supplied the money market with large quantities of "finance paper" of this kind. The fact that commercial bank dealers do not usually handle this form of security, however, limits its availability for temporary investment purposes. Two factors that bear unfavorably on the liquidity of commercial paper are its irregular issuance, and the tendency for commercial paper dealers to offer notes to regular clients—usually large commercial banks. The history of these security forms has shown that they are paid off without fail by the issuers when they mature; but, in case the corporation fails to pay the debt at maturity, the holder has no recourse against the commercial paper dealer.

Bank acceptances are unsecured bills of exchange growing out of domestic and international trade transactions in which commercial banks allow their credit to be substituted for the credit of their customers. The intrinsic liquidity of these investments is somewhat higher than for commercial paper for two reasons: first, the liquidity of commercial banks in general is greater than the liquidity of business enterprises; and, second, the maturities of these contracts are usually somewhat shorter than those of commercial paper. In addition, there is a strong and active open market for these investments supported by the Federal Reserve Banks that will usually buy unlimited quantities of bank acceptances at favorable rates to the sellers.

Other Security Forms   Other security forms include Treasury notes and bonds, state and municipal bonds, and private corporation bonds. These are long maturity instruments but may meet the liquidity needs for temporary investment if they are purchased a short time before they mature. It would be risky to buy these instruments long before they mature with the expectation of cashing them in at a profit in the open market. Market activity is limited in the securities, and they are subject to wide fluctuations in value in the face of changing quantities of investment funds in the capital market.

Near-Cash Assets: Quantity Analysis   For this purpose all of the near-cash assets that the firm holds comprise a set of marketable securities with subsets of these securities distinguishable by the three traits of profitability, intrinsic liquidity, and extrinsic liquidity. Intrinsic liquidity is marked by very short maturity of the security and a high degree of probability that the security will be cashable at maturity without loss. Extrinsic liquidity indicates that the security, although not necessarily of very short maturity, is very marketable, so that cash funds can be recovered quickly in the market without much risk of loss. Assume that our business has in its marketable investments portfolio 38 securities with 7 exclusive sets of traits and combinations of traits of profitability and liquidity. Table 10.8 lists

TABLE 10.8
SETS OF MARKETABLE SECURITIES

Number of Sets	Number of Securities	
1st	7	Profitable
2nd	1	Intrinsically liquid
3rd	3	Extrinsically liquid
4th	10	Profitable and intrinsically liquid
5th	8	Profitable and extrinsically liquid
6th	4	Intrinsically and extrinsically liquid
7th	5	Profitable, intrinsically and extrinsically liquid
	Total 38	

the number of securities in each set. The purpose of the analysis is to create subsets of securities which contain profitability and liquidity traits that may affect the total profitability and liquidity of the business and its resulting share values. The procedure is to perform operations of intersection ($\cap$), union ($\cup$), and complement

($\sim$) on the subsets for more complete and detailed information about the portfolio makeup for evaluation and decision making. The intersection of sets forms a subset with exclusive elements. The union of sets forms a subset containing the sum of the elements, and the complement is a subset of elements common to two or more sets removed. Figure 10.1 portrays with Venn diagrams the basic information con-

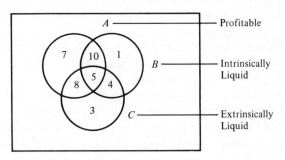

Figure 10.1.   Quantitative Portfolio Analysis.

tained in Table 10.5. The comprehensiveness of the solutions will depend specifically on the questions that are asked. Below the diagram is a series of questions, and answers that are easily checked out using the Venn diagrams. The universal set of securities could conceivably include more than 38, but these would have to be securities without liquidity and without profitability. This would have to be a set of securities that are both nonprofitable and nonliquid; but, since we are considering here a marketable securities portfolio, it is highly improbable that such securities would be found in this set.

1. How many securities are intrinsically and extrinsically liquid? This required an operation in intersection $B \cap C$. The solution is 9 (5 + 4) or 24 percent of the total of 38 securities.
2. How many are either intrinsically or extrinsically liquid or both? The answer is found in $B \cup C$, and the solution is 31 (10 + 8 + 5 + 4 + 3 + 1) or 82 percent of the total number of securities. But some of these 31 are profitable as well as liquid.
3. We may want to look at the securities in the group of 31 that are just liquid but not profitable, which means removing the ones that are profitable. This subset is created by the operation:

$$(B \cup C) \cap \tilde{A}$$
$$= 31 - 23$$
$$= 8$$

Checking this in the Venn diagrams 1 + 4 + 3 = 8 which are in sets B and C but are not intersected by A.
4. How   many   are   profitable?   The   answer   is   all   of   the   securities

$(7 + 10 + 5 + 8) = 30$. Most of these (23) are also liquid $(10 + 5 + 8)$. Just 7 are profitable but not liquid as can be seen in Venn diagram A.

5. Regarding the securities in question (4), additional details can be obtained. For example, we can determine how many of the profitable securities are intrinsically but not extrinsically liquid. Expressed symbolically, $[A \cap (B \cup C)] \cap \tilde{C}$ implies that profitable and extrinsically liquid securities are taken away leaving us with just 10 securities that are profitable and intrinsically liquid:

$$[A \cap (B \cup C)] \cap \tilde{C}$$
$$= 23 - 13$$
$$= 10$$

6. Or management may want to know how many of the 23 profitable and liquid securities are not intrinsically liquid. This is symbolized as $[A \cap (B \cup C)] \cap \tilde{B}$, performing the operations:

$$[A \cap (B \cup C)] \cup \tilde{B}$$
$$= 23 - 15$$
$$= 8$$

The implications of these operations to financial managers should be apparent. First, they describe the portfolio of marketable securities by bringing to the fore important security traits. Second, they suggest a simulation technique for classifying and identifying securities with specific important traits; and, finally, they provide a focal point for planning an effective security mix for balancing liquidity and profitability.

Net Sources and Uses of Cash An important cash flow concept for historical analysis with management is the statement of net sources and uses of cash over one or more time intervals. Net cash flows count just the transactions that require net transfers of cash. This eliminates transfers of cash that are cancelled out. The only source of cash that is recorded is that which is not over a given period of time offset by an equivalent use of cash, and the only use of cash that is recorded is that which is not over a given period of time offset by an equivalent source of cash. This type of statement may be prepared conveniently since it is based on changes in the balance sheets. The following changes in the account balances show the net sources and uses of cash.

Sources of Cash	*Uses of Cash*
Decrease in assets	Increase in assets
Increase in liabilities	Decrease in liabilities
Increase in capital stock	Decrease in capital stock
Increase in retained earnings	Decrease in retained earnings
Increase in surplus reserves	Decrease in surplus reserves

A net decrease in an asset over the period means that more cash has been received from the asset in the period than has been expended on it. Table 10.9 shows how comparative quarterly balance sheets are used to prepare a statement of cash sources and uses for two quarters of operations.

Table 10.9 is a net cash flow summary of a small business given two consecutive quarters. Part I shows the changes in the comparative balance sheets, and Part II summarizes the *sources* and *uses* of cash based on the changes in Part I. Net increases in the flows increase the cash balance, and net decreases decrease the cash balance. This should help to emphasize the continuity that exists between cash balances and cash flows. The value of the comparison lies in evaluating changes

TABLE 10.9
PART I
COMPARATIVE QUARTERLY BALANCE SHEETS

	End of 1st Quarter	End of 2nd Quarter	Increase (Decrease)	End of 3rd Quarter	Increase (Decrease)
Assets					
Current assets:					
Cash	$ 6,000	$ 17,500	$11,500	$ 7,500	$(10,000)
Temporary investments	3,500	1,500	(2,000)	7,600	6,100
Receivables	22,750	35,750	13,000	26,350	(9,400)
Inventories	41,500	44,500	3,000	19,700	(24,800)
Prepaid expenses	3,000	1,000	(2,000)	4,000	3,000
Fixed assets:					
Long-term investments	12,000	12,000		12,000	
Real estate	22,000	22,000		22,000	
Machinery and equipment	8,150	9,000	850	15,000	6,000
Intangibles	2,100	2,100		2,100	
Total assets	$121,000	$145,350	$24,350	$116,250	$(29,100)
Liabilities and Net Worth					
Current liabilities:					
Notes payable	$ 7,500	$ 22,000	$14,500	$ 4,500	$(17,500)
Accounts payable	13,000	23,650	10,650	15,250	(8,400)
Wage accruals	1,500	1,500		500	(1,000)
Tax accruals	5,250		(5,250)	500	500
Long-term liabilities:					
Long-term note	6,200	6,200		2,000	(4,200)
Bonds payable	21,550	21,550		21,550	
Depreciation allowances	8,000	9,000	1,000	10,000	1,000
Net worth:					
Capital stock (3,000 shares @ $10 par)	30,000	30,000		30,000	
Capital surplus	6,000	6,000		6,000	
Retained earnings	22,000	25,450	3,450	25,950	500
Total liabilities and net worth	$121,000	$145,350	$24,350	$116,250	$(29,100)

PART II
SOURCES AND USES OF CASH

2nd Quarter Sources of Cash		3rd Quarter Sources of Cash	
Temporary investments	$ 2,000	Receivables	$ 9,400
Prepaid expenses	2,000	Inventories	24,800
Notes payable	14,500	Tax accruals	500
Accounts payable	10,650	Depreciation reserves	1,000
Depreciation allowances	1,000	Retained earnings	500
Retained earnings	3,450	Reduction of cash balance	10,000
Total sources	$33,600	Total sources	$46,200
Uses of Cash		*Uses of Cash*	
Receivables	$13,000	Temporary investments	$ 6,100
Inventories	3,000	Prepaid expenses	3,000
Machinery and equipment	850	Machinery and equipment	6,000
Tax payment	5,250	Notes payables	17,500
Additions to cash balance	11,500	Accounts payable	8,400
		Wage accruals	1,000
		Long-term notes	4,200
Total uses	$33,600	Total uses	$46,200
Beginning cash balance	$ 6,000		$17,500
Addition (losses) in cash balances	11,500		(10,000)
Ending cash balances	$17,500		$ 7,500
Cash turnover	11.2 times		5.3 times

hat have occurred in the past. A sharp decline will be noticed in the rate at which he beginning cash balance for the second quarter was turned over in total cash handled, compared with the rate at which the beginning cash balance of the third quarter was turned over in total cash handled. Total cash handled is the sum of he sources and uses of cash in each quarter. Some specific questions that financial managers might ask are: (1) Are the cash balances impaired by the net loss in this ast quarter? (2) Did the additions to notes and accounts payables in the second quarter add substantially to the risks of insolvency? (3) Does the large cash flow rom current assets in the third quarter signify seasonality of operations?

BUDGETING THE CASH FLOW

The general purpose of a cash budget is to give advance notice of: (1) how much cash will probably be needed to realize a given short run profit objective, 2) how much cash can be expected from current income to meet these needs, and 3) how the cash balance will be increased or decreased by these flows. Advance notice is an invaluable service of cash budgeting if this notice is used constructively. An important responsibility of financial managers lies in communicating the cash budgeting goals to the operating personnel whose cooperation is needed for these goals to be realized. The collections personnel are, for example, affected and with advance notice can be expected to execute the scheduled collections on credit sales. The same applies to managers in charge of inventory purchases; with advance notice of their financial manager's cash plan, they are responsible for timing their terms of purchase so that cash resources will not be strained.

Budgeting the Sources   One of the most important sources of cash is cash sales. Businesses selling wholly on a cash basis have this source automatically determined for them in their sales estimate. Transportation and certain personal service businesses usually fall into this category. But most businesses sell both on cash and credit terms which complicates the planning problem. This creates the problem of estimating what portion of total sales will be cash and what portion will be credit. Some businesses, like electric and gas utilities and telephone communication services, have built-in collection controls in their facilities for discontinuing services when payments are not made on time. Most businesses have to resort to less direct means of stimulating collections. One is to offer the customers cash discounts for paying within a set time. Collections experiences are valuable guides for planning future collections, but financial managers may wish to set up higher standards for the future and use new techniques to improve on past experiences.

Planning interest, rental, and dividend receipts is a simple matter because the capital facilities producing these funds are fixed. Incidental sources of cash from the sale of assets may also be planned easily. If the business has a good reserve of marketable securities, it may not have to plan quite as closely on its cash from operations; and, finally, good credit ties with commercial lending agencies may relieve the business of temporary cash shortages from operations.

Budgeting the Uses   Budgeting the uses of cash means, primarily, estimating cash needs for employment services and, except in service businesses in which inventory purchases are relatively minor items, for inventory payments. Requirements for cash payments are much more responsive in some businesses than in others to changes in production and sales. Public utilities and transportation companies, for example, with heavy investments primarily in fixed capital can expand current operations greatly without increasing their outflow of cash to operations; while manufacturing and merchandising businesses depending heavily on working capital will find their cash balances declining quickly with increased operations. An offer of high purchase discounts will stimulate us to pay for our inventories at an early date and may even induce us to borrow for this purpose when commercial credit services are available.

Other payment problems involve taxes and insurance on fixed properties; or, if businesses rent their fixed capital facilities, lease rental payments. In any case, payments revolving about the fixed properties are directly related to the quantity of those properties being employed. If the properties are owned by the business, they will frequently be financed with long-term debts or capital stock. If financed by long-term debts, the interest and principal payments on the debts also have to be included in the budget. If financed by capital stock, dividend payments have to be budgeted. Finally, cash payments have to be planned for meeting income tax payments.

Function of the Cash Balance   Transactions balances and particulary safety balances serve as leveling factors to absorb temporary excesses of cash inflows and to compensate for temporary excesses in the cash outflow. Because of the risk and cost of being out of cash this reservoir of cash can never be allowed to go dry. It has also been seen, however, that because of the cost that it incurs we cannot afford to keep it filled to the brim. Optimization theory was employed earlier in the chapter to show how to attain the most efficient cash balance.

The more closely we can coordinate cash inflows and outflows from operations the less cash we need to keep in the balance. Eventually, the two flows will balance; but, in the very short run, financial managers have to face the reality of an imbalance between the two flows. It is this imbalance that we seek to compensate for in our cash balance. The cash budget will supply advance warnings of expected excesses and shortages in cash which can be met by planning for the appropriate adjustments to the balance. Budgeted cash excesses can be met by investing in temporary securities, building up inventory stocks, granting easier credit terms, purchasing fixed assets, or paying off indebtedness. If cash shortages are imminent, then selling securities, pressing for more cash sales and earlier collections on credit sales, dumping if necessary some of the inventories, and even selling fixed assets or borrowing funds outside the business may be resorted to.

Constructing the Budget In constructing the cash budget, financial managers should bring into use all of the tools and analytic skills that they have developed to this time. Setting up the sales and collections schedule is an important part of cash budgeting. Either an over- or underestimate of cash inflow from this source can have serious effects on future operations. Accurate forecasting of collections requires keen evaluation of customers' paying habits and capabilities. While past experiences are important, we are looking ahead now and cannot afford to be bound too closely to what has happened in the past. After the plan of sales and collections is finally decided on, it will serve as a major tool for estimating cash receipts.

Differences between fast and slow collections, which are disregarded in planning operations for profit, create important problems when it comes to budgeting cash for liquidity. Table 10.10 summarizes on a monthly basis the expected receipts from collections. Assume that on March 31 the Company had $125,000 in receivables due to mature in three installments: $50,000 in April, $50,000 in May, and $25,000 in June. But, the business expects $3,000 loss on the last installment of receivables reducing them to $22,000. No discounts are allowed for early payment of the $125,000, but management has recently initiated a new policy allowing 2 percent discount on sales collected in the first month after sale and requiring all remaining sales to be paid in the second month after sale. Of future sales assume that 30 percent will be collected in the first month after sale, and 70 percent will be collected without loss in the second month after sale. This policy will be put into effect in April, so the first results will be felt in May with the collection of 30 percent of April's sales less 2 percent discount. Table 10.10 projects collections of present receivables of $125,000, and of expected new sales. Inventory payments by manufacturing and merchandising businesses require major expenditures of cash.

TABLE 10.10
COLLECTIONS ESTIMATE

	April	May	June	July	August	September	Total
Net sales	$61,257	$69,697	$74,967	$80,264	$85,537	$86,500	
Receivables							
(March 31, 1971)	$50,000	$50,000	$22,000	($3,000 loss on last installment)			$122,000
April		18,377	42,880				61,257
May			20,909	$48,788			69,697
June				22,490	$52,477		74,967
July					24,079	$56,185	80,264
August						25,661	25,661
Total receivables	$50,000	$68,377	$85,789	$71,278	$76,556	$81,846	$433,846
Less 2% discount	—	368	418	450	482	513	2,231
Net collections	$50,000	$68,009	$85,371	$70,828	$76,074	$81,333	$431,615

Practically all purchases are on short-term credit, and often a cash discount for early payments is obtainable. Assume that there was $65,000 in the accounts payable balance March 31. Of this amount, $38,800 less 3 percent discount will be paid in April; and the $26,200 balance without benefit of discount will be paid in May. To this payment in May will be added the payment for all of April's purchases less 3 percent discount. For the remaining four months, discounts will continue to be taken by paying for raw materials in the month following their purchase. The estimated month-by-month cash-payments effect of this plan is illustrated in Table 10.11.

TABLE 10.11
COMPANY ———— PAYMENTS FOR PURCHASES

	April	May	June	July	August	September	Total
Purchases	$24,503	$27,878	$29,986	$32,105	$34,214	$37,175	$185,863
Gross payments:							
March purchase	38,800	26,200					65,000
April purchase		24,503					24,503
May purchase			27,878				27,878
June purchase				29,986			29,986
July purchase					32,105		32,105
August purchase						34,214	34,214
Total gross payments	$38,800	$50,703	$27,878	$29,986	$32,105	$34,214	$213,686
Less discounts @ 3%	1,164	735	836	900	963	1,026	5,624
Net payments	$37,636	$49,968	$27,042	$29,086	$31,142	$33,188	$208,062

Aside from raw materials payments, the largest single monthly outlay of cash is for the services of direct labor. In addition, there are cash outlays for factory overhead that include indirect materials, indirect labor, supervision, property taxes, and utilities which are cash costs that we will assume the business pays in the month in which they are incurred.

TABLE 10.12
COMPANY ——— PAYMENTS FOR DIRECT LABOR
AND FACTORY OVERHEAD

	April	*May*	*June*	*July*	*August*	*September*	*Total*
Direct labor	$13,836	$15,840	$17,052	$18,270	$19,483	$29,122	$113,603
Factory overhead	8,380	8,365	9,160	11,062	11,463	14,013	62,443
Total payments	$22,216	$24,205	$26,212	$29,332	$30,946	$43,135	$176,046

Direct selling outlays are mainly salesmen's commissions and salaries. Administrative payments require payments for office and executive salaries and traveling expenses and utilities; this portion of the cash budget is contained in Table 10.13.

TABLE 10.13
COMPANY ——— PAYMENTS FOR SELLING AND ADMINISTRATION

	April	*May*	*June*	*July*	*August*	*September*	*Total*
Direct selling	$10,675	$11,307	$11,780	$12,259	$12,732	$13,526	$72,279
Administration	1,600	1,600	1,600	1,600	1,600	1,600	9,600
Total payments	$12,276	$12,907	$13,380	$13,859	$14,332	$15,126	$81,879

Other cash income that the business expects to receive includes $350 in interest and dividends in April and in July. Other cash expenditures include $100 interest in April and September. Table 10.14 itemizes these special inflows and outflows of cash.

TABLE 10.14
COMPANY ——— OTHER INCOME AND EXPENDITURES

	April	*May*	*June*	*July*	*August*	*September*	*Total*
Other income:							
Interest and dividend	$350			$350			$700
Other expenditures:							
Interest	100					$100	200
Net income (expenditure)	$250			$350		($100)	$500

Summary of the cash budget is the master plan for projecting and controlling the cash flows and balances. The cash budget serves the same purpose in relation to liquidity planning and control as the operating budget does in profit planning and control. Some of the key terms in the budget should be considered. The *source of cash* is the forecast of monthly receipts expected to be secured primarily from collections on sales. *Uses of cash* is the forecast of monthly disbursements expected primarily for purchasing raw materials and for meeting wages, salaries, and commissions. The net *increase (decrease)* is the difference between total expected receipts of cash and total expected disbursements. The net figure shows how much the cash inflows and outflows are expected to be out of balance each month. The master budget reveals important facts in Table 10.15 about both cash flows and cash balances for the next six months. It is shown that more cash will be needed in each of five months than is expected to be generated through operations. As indicated in the totals column, the sum of the monthly cash losses is expected to be greater than the sum of the monthly gains by $33,872. In the months of May and September, the optimal safety balance of $20,000 is expected to decline; but, in all other months, it is expected to exceed $20,000. This temporary cash decline is the kind of situation that often develops in seasonal businesses getting ready for an expanding sales period in the following season.

TABLE 10.15

COMPANY ——— CASH BUDGET SUMMARY

	April	May	June	July	August	September	Total
Sources of cash:							
Collections							
(Table 10.10)	$50,000	$68,009	$85,371	$70,828	$76,074	$81,333	$431,615
Other income							
(Table 10.14)	350				350		700
Total sources	$50,350	$68,009	$85,371	$71,178	$76,074	$81,333	$432,315
Uses of cash:							
Purchases							
(Table 10.11)	$37,636	$49,968	$27,042	$29,086	$31,142	$33,188	$208,062
Factory costs							
(Table 10.12)	22,216	24,205	26,212	29,332	30,946	43,135	176,046
Selling and administra-							
tion (Table 10.13)	12,276	12,907	13,380	13,859	14,332	15,126	81,879
Other expenditures							
(Table 10.14)	100					100	200
Total uses	$72,228	$87,080	$66,634	$72,277	$76,420	$91,549	$466,187
Monthly increase							
(decrease)	($21,878)	($19,071)	$18,737	($ 1,099)	($ 346)	($10,216)	($ 33,872)
Beginning cash	50,000	28,122	9,051	27,788	26,689	26,343	
Ending cash	28,122	9,051	27,788	26,689	26,343	16,127	
Optimal safety balance	20,000	20,000	20,000	20,000	20,000	20,000	
Cash margin	8,122	(10,949)	7,788	6,689	6,343	(3,873)	

Now let us see how serious the liquidity management problem actually is considering the overall cash condition of the business. It will be noted that the business has a *beginning cash* balance of $50,000. Financial managers feel that this balance can be reduced during the next six months of operations to a $20,000 optimal emergency fund without impairing operations for profit in any way. While management is not prohibited from using the optimal safety balance, they are expected to use it with caution. The beginning cash is increased or decreased by the net change from the current month to produce the *ending cash* for the month. The ending cash is expected to be above the $20,000 emergency fund in four out of six of the months, but in May and September it is expected to be less by $10,949 and $3,873 respectively. This excess or deficit figure is what is called, for lack of a better term, the *cash margin*; considering all the inflow and outflow factors, it indicates the margin by which cash on hand is expected at any month end to be greater or less than the optimal safety balance. No borrowing would be necessary by this business over the six months except perhaps at the end of September to replace the $3,875 reduction in the safety balance. If management insists on maintaining the balance right at $20,000, positive action could be taken on the basis of the information in the budget, to level off the negative margins that are expected in May and September, possibly by selling marketable securities, trade receivables, inventories, or even fixed assets. If the assets are not to be disturbed, management might plan to borrow the funds at the beginning of the month, paying them off at the end as excess funds are available. Or better still, action may be taken to reduce cash outlays and to accelerate collections.

The final purpose of cash budgeting is to provide control tools—particularly in the individual budgets for cash sales and collections, payments for inventory purchases, and employment and other cash expenses. The planned flows do not just work themselves out automatically and spontaneously just because they are planned and written down in these budgets. They have to be guided and directed by financial managers with the aid of personnel in production, sales, and general administration.

Assuming that our best skills have been used to form the budget, we are now ready to enforce it, which means turning again to the individual budgets of cash receipts and payments. Variances from the sales and collections schedules that produce more cash than planned are less serious than variances that produce less. The former reduces liquidity risks but increases opportunity costs, and the latter increases liquidity risks but decreases opportunity costs.

Control emphasizes enforcement of the budget; but, whereas this is the main purpose behind the budget, it does not rule out using *variable* budgets. Variable budgets provide for a margin of error in the master plan and in the individual cash-flow schedules before remedial action is taken through control channels. For example, a 5 or 10 percent variation may be allowed in the budgeted items or in certain key items before the communication system is put into action between the financial and nonfinancial managers. Although the estimates in the final budget are considered relatively fixed for the short run, they may be subjected to periodic review and even to revision if changes occur, such as increases in inventory prices or in wage rates.

SUMMARY

Cash management is the last of the three chapters on current asset management. The reason for placing it in this position is that, in the normal operating cycle of funds flowing from inventories to receivables and then to cash, we have in the cash a reservior of funds for transactions. Some of the same tools and optimizing techniques used in inventory analysis are applied to the cash balance analysis. Although rather limiting assumptions have to be made to enable us to apply these tools, it is thought that the value of being able to make exact statements about optimal levels of cash holdings, cash ordering dates, and cash safety stocks far more than offsets the disadvantages of the limiting assumptions. Particularly important regarding the optimizing technique is the establishment of a safety stock of cash. Cash balances are related to cash flows in the cash budget; both concepts of cash balance and cash flow are brought together in the cash budget. The cash budget provides a practical planning tool and a control device for financial managers. The cash budget is a detailed instrument that prepares schedules indicating individual sources and uses of cash to provide financial managers with an effective means of avoiding shortages of cash and excess of cash in the future. Excess quantities of transactions funds should be invested in marketable securities such as Treasury bills and high quality debts of private enterprises. In considering alternative investment opportunities and marketable securities, set analysis can be applied to gain a closer insight into the company's investment portfolio from the viewpoints of profitability, liquidity, and solvency.

PROBLEMS

1. From the month-end information given below, indicate the trend in liquidity measured a. absolutely in dollars, and relatively b. in the percentage of cash to current assets, c. in the turnover of cash in total sales, and d. in the turnover of an average day's sales in the cash balance. Use a thirty-day month. Explain each of the measures and evaluate as indexes of liquidity.

MONTH-END VALUES

	1st	2nd	3rd	4th	5th	6th
Cash	$ 2,000	$ 3,000	$ 5,000	$10,000	$ 8,000	$ 8,000
Other current assets	6,000	10,000	15,000	15,000	15,000	14,000
Total	$ 8,000	$13,000	$20,000	$25,000	$23,000	$22,000
Net sales	$15,000	$21,000	$18,000	$28,000	$30,000	$30,000

2. In any given period excess sources of cash over cash used in operations increase cash balances, and excess uses over sources decrease cash balances. Complete the schedule below and indicate significant changes that have taken place in the major a. operating sources of cash, b. operating uses of cash, and c. velocity of cash turnover in total cash handled. Evaluate what has happened.

MONTHLY FLOWS

	1st	2nd	3rd	4th	5th	6th
Cash sales	$12,000	$16,000	$18,000	$25,000	$31,000	$30,000
Collections	4,000	4,000	7,000	10,000	4,000	—
Total sources	$16,000	$20,000	$25,000	$35,000	$35,000	$30,000
Wages and salaries	$ 5,000	$ 6,000	$ 7,000	$ 8,000	$10,000	$10,000
Inventory payments	10,000	15,000	20,000	25,000	30,000	30,000
Other payments	1,000	2,000	3,000	2,000	—	—
Total uses	$16,000	$23,000	$30,000	$35,000	$40,000	$40,000
Beginning cash	$40,000					
Increase (decrease)	—					
Ending cash	$40,000					
Total cash handled	$32,000					

Velocity of cash turnover $= \dfrac{\$32,000}{\$40,000}$

3. Your firm has decided to keep $5,000 in its bank balance all of the time as an emergency fund and to keep additional balances not to exceed $20,000 for transactions purposes. Since the $20,000 is not required to be held on balance all of the time, you decide to set narrower limits for cash holdings; so that the balance of the funds can be invested in temporary securities based on minimizing cash holding costs.

    a. Set up a schedule of transactions balances ranging from $0 to $20,000 by $4,000 intervals.

    b. Assume that you can invest these funds in temporary securities earning 3/4 percent monthly. What is the linear holding cost equation?

4. Your operations are expected to be at a level at which a total cash flow of $40,000 will be needed for the following quarter. You are going to plan a quantity of cash holdings for these transactions that will reduce as much as possible the total cash holding costs. As a solution to this problem total cash holding costs are divided into unit variable costs and fixed cash planning costs. The former is estimated to be 2 percent per dollar of cash for the planning period, and the latter costs $200.

    a. Distinguish between the two cost forms mentioned above.

    b. Using the equation $H_{c_1} = 0.02(\bar{X})$ and $H_{c_2} = c_2(K/2\bar{X})$, schedule the total variable and total fixed costs for a range of cash balances from $10,000 to $40,000. Let the intervals increase by $5,000.

    c. Graph the two schedules and determine the optimal cash holding.

5. You realize that although an optimal cash balance can be determined for a given operating period actual cash balances may vary somewhat from the optimal. One of your main concerns is with investing excess cash above the optimal.

a. What investment opportunities are there for offsetting the temporary cash excesses?

b. Suppose that you expect to hold as many as 20 securities at one time and that you expect them to vary in profitability, intrinsic liquidity, and extrinsic liquidity something like the following:

Number of Securities

5	Profitable
4	Intrinsically liquid
5	Extrinsically liquid
3	Profitable and intrinsically liquid
2	Profitable and extrinsically liquid
1	Intrinsically and extrinsically liquid

Draw the Venn diagrams illustrating the various profit and liquidity combinations listed above, labeling the diagrams A, B, and C.

c. Using the Venn diagrams in b, answer for yourself the following questions:

(1) How many securities would be profitable *and* intrinsically and extrinsically liquid?

(2) How many securities would be profitable *or* intrinsically *or* extrinsically liquid?

(3) How many securities would be intrinsically *or* extrinsically liquid but *not* profitable?

(4) How many securities would be profitable *or* intrinsically *and* extrinsically liquid?

(5) Evaluate the results of your simulation for cash management.

6. The Capital Supply Company manufactures electrical supplies mainly for home construction. Sales are very seasonal, with the rush season extending from February through August. Manufacturing is primarily custom order which enables the business to hold finished inventories to a minimum. During peak production, the business needs large quantities of cash. Therefore, near the end of January each year Mr. Thomas, the financial manager, prepares a detailed cash budget to help him determine and plan for monthly cash needs. In addition to the cash budget, Mr. Thomas also forecasts profits and prepares a pro forma balance sheet for the end of August; but he is particularly concerned at this time with whether or not the company will be able to finance its cumulative cash needs without resorting to borrowing. He hopes to accomplish this with his accumulated cash and marketable securities presently on hand. Putting yourself in Mr. Thomas' place, complete the unfinished exhibits including the cash budget appearing in the problem.

Exhibit 10.1 is the company's balance sheet brought up to date for January 31, 1971. The relatively large cash marketable securities balances are typical for this season. Cash will drop sharply during the early stages of manufacture, but the financial manager does not want it to fall below $30,000. Receivables are at a low ebb, and the $80,000 in inventories are all raw materials. Receivables and raw materials inventories at the end of the seven-month operation are usually larger than they are at the beginning. Mr. Thomas expects to collect in February the receivables now on balance and to pay his accounts in the same month, taking an allowable 4 percent discount. The note payable to officers bears 5 percent interest; it is due in June, with interest for nine months. Although payment of the note could probably be delayed, the present plan is to pay it on schedule.

Exhibit 10.2 is a monthly raw-materials-payment schedule. Purchases are based on a two-month lead time for production, and are 40 percent of expected sales two months ahead. The purchases are made on a 4 *percent, ten days E.O.M.*

EXHIBIT 10.1
THE CAPITAL SUPPLY COMPANY
BALANCE SHEET
JANUARY 31, 1971

Assets		Liabilities and Stockholders' Equity	
Current assets:		Current liabilities:	
Cash	$ 100,000	Accounts payable	$ 40,000
Marketable securities	200,000	Note payable	35,000
Receivables	25,000	Accrued wages—salaries	10,000
Inventories of raw materials	80,000	Income taxes payable	10,000
Total current assets	$ 405,000	Total current liabilities	$ 95,000
Fixed assets:		Stockholders' equity:	
Land	$ 500,000	Common stock	$ 800,000
Machinery and equipment		Capital surplus	200,000
(net of depreciation)	320,000	Retained earnings	130,000
Total fixed assets	$ 820,000	Total stockholders' equity	$1,130,000
Total assets	$1,225,000	Total liabilities and equity	$1,225,000

EXHIBIT 10.2
THE CAPITAL SUPPLY COMPANY
INVENTORY PAYMENTS SCHEDULE

	Planned Sales	Planned Purchases	Less 4% Purchase Discount
February	$ 100,000	$ 60,000	$ 38,400
March	100,000	60,000	57,600
April	150,000	100,000	57,600
May	150,000	100,000	96,000
June	250,000	80,000	96,000
July	250,000	80,000	76,800
August	200,000	40,000	76,800
Total	$1,200,000	$520,000	$499,200
September	200,000		
October	100,000		

EXHIBIT 10.3
THE CAPITAL SUPPLY COMPANY
CASH PAYMENTS OTHER THAN FOR PURCHASES

	February	March	April	May	June	July	August	Total
Factory wages	$30,000	$30,000	$50,000	$50,000	$40,000	$40,000	$20,000	$260,000
Factory salary	1,000	1,000	1,000	1,000	1,000	1,000	1,000	7,000
Power	500	500	750	750	600	600	350	4,050
Factory rental								
Sales commissions								
Sales and administrative salaries	4,000	4,000	4,000	4,000				
Income taxes			10,000					
Note payable with interest					36,313			
Total								

basis, and the business will pay according to schedule to take advantage of the discount.

Exhibit 10.3 is a list of the monthly expected cash payments other than raw materials purchases. About $0.20 out of every sales dollar is expected to go to factory wages, but it is important to note that production precedes sales by two months so that the wage expenditures in any given month are based on the sales estimate for two months in the future. Sales commissions, on the other hand, are 15 percent of the current sales estimate. Factory salaries are $1,000 monthly with sales and administrative salaries $4,000 monthly. The exhibit also shows the income-tax payment of $10,000 in April and the $35,000 note payment to the officers in June at 5 percent per annum.

Exhibit 10.4 is a schedule of cash receipts from collections on credit sales. Sales are made on terms of *net thirty days*. About 90 percent of the sales will be collected in the month after sales, and the other 10 percent will be collected in the month following. Losses on bad debts are expected to be negligible.

EXHIBIT 10.4
THE CAPITAL SUPPLY COMPANY
SALES AND COLLECTIONS SUMMARY

Planned	February	March	April	May	June	July	August
Sales	$100,000	$100,000	$150,000	$150,000	$250,000	$250,000	$200,000
Collections:	25,000						
90%		90,000	90,000				
10%			10,000				
Total							

Exhibit 10.5 is the cash budget summarizing the expected monthly cash receipts and disbursements. It also shows the expected monthly and cumulative excesses and deficits in cash. Putting yourself in the financial manager's position,

determine whether your cash on hand and your investments in marketable securities combined at the end of January are large enough to finance the cumulative deficits and to maintain at all times a $30,000 cash balance.

EXHIBIT 10.5
THE CAPITAL SUPPLY COMPANY
CASH BUDGET
SEVEN MONTHS ENDING AUGUST 31, 1971

	Feb.	Mar.	Apr.	May	June	July	Aug.
Receipts	$ 25,000	$ 90,000	$100,000				
Payments	96,900	116,100	153,850				
Increase (decrease)	(71,900)	(26,100)	(53,850)				
B.O.M. cash	100,000	28,100	(2,000)				
E.O.M. cash	28,100	(2,000)					
Minimum cash							
needed	30,000	30,000					
Cumulative excess							
(deficit)	(1,900)	(28,000)					

7. Ace Novelty Company wishes to have access to $100,000 on November 1, 1971. Based on past experiences it takes a minimum of five days to arrange for their cash requirements. Should the cash become available before November 1, the cost is .04 percent per day. If the cash is not available until after November 1, the cost is .20 percent per day.

    a. Given the probabilities of being early in the table below, compute the expected values of being early.

DAYS LEAD TIME AND PROBABILITIES

Days Early	5	6	7	8	9	10
0	0.0	0.05	0.20	0.50	0.20	0.10
1	.0	.0	.10	.20	.50	.20
2	.0	.0	.0	.10	.20	.50
3	.0	.0	.0	.0	.0	.20
4	.0	.0	.0	.0	.0	.10

    b. Given the probabilities of being late in the table below, compute the expected values of being late.

DAYS LEAD TIME AND PROBABILITIES

Days Late	5	6	7	8	9	10
0	0.0	0.05	0.20	0.50	0.20	0.10
1	.05	.20	.50	.20	.10	.0
2	.20	.50	.10	.0	.0	.0
3	.50	.20	.10	.0	.0	.0
4	.20	.05	.0	.0	.0	.0
5	.05	.0	.0	.0	.0	.0

c. Plot the expected values for being late, being early, and their totals on a graph. Determine the optimum lead time.

8. Most firms carry a minimum cash balance.

    a. Given the data below and the knowledge that being short of cash will cost the firm $0.50 per year per dollar short, compute the expected values of being short of cash.

Possible Average Demand	Probability Distribution of Demand	Optimal Cash Balance
$100,000	0.65	$100,000
$130,000	.25	$100,000
$160,000	.08	$100,000
$190,000	.02	$100,000

    b. Given the knowledge that it costs $0.04 per day per dollar carried, compute the cost of carrying from $30,000 to $90,000 as a minimum cash balance.

    c. Plot the shortage and carrying costs on a graph. What is the optimal minimum cash balance?

PART V

CURRENT
OPERATIONS:
EXTERNAL
FUNDS
MANAGEMENT

11

Unsecured
Financing

Part IV dealt with the internal management of funds invested in current assets individually. Part V deals with obtaining inventory credit and cash on formal contracts from outside sources for meeting these current asset needs. External financing is all part of the same general problem of managing a business to keep it supplied with inventories and cash, so that operating budgets and cash flow budgets can be expedited for profit, liquidity, and solvency. Contractual relations in external financing vary in complexity depending on whether the company can negotiate unsecured financing, that is financing without pledging some of its assets to the creditor, or whether the company has to secure its financing with a pledge of some of its assets. In this chapter, we will examine current forms that lend themselves to unsecured financing after considering policy goals in current financing.

POLICY GOALS

Final goals are the same for secured and unsecured borrowing, namely, to gain the use of inventories and cash that will have favorable effects on the company's share values. Inherent in unsecured financing are the effects on liquidity, solvency, and profit that each form of financing has.

LIQUIDITY CONSIDERATIONS

The liquidity goal is to obtain from the financing source all of the inventories or cash that are needed to execute the profit plan. After the asset reaches the business, it becomes an internal management problem (Chapters 8 and 10). The term liquidity risk has an important meaning to unsecured borrowing; *liquidity risk is the probability that the planned borrowing will not meet the liquidity requirement for optimizing inventory and cash holdings.* For example, financial managers are taking a risk that the financing will be inadequate whenever there is a chance that, because of the terms of the financing itself, the quantity of the assets required for optimizing is not forthcoming at the time and the place where the funds are needed. Internal plans to order and to use the funds, in other words, are subjected to a risk in financing which may cut off the flow of the asset and prevent the business from reaching the optimizing goal. Although more will be said about this later on, it is important to note at this time that the quantity of a company's capital, particularly its net capital (total assets—total liabilities) and its net working capital (total assets—current liabilities), are important factors affecting the extent of the liquidity risk associated with current financing. Finally, it should be noted also that a successfully executed financing could be offset by inefficient management of the assets after they enter the business, and so from the practical viewpoint it is difficult to draw a line between where external management of current financing ends and where internal management of the assets themselves begins.

SOLVENCY CONSIDERATIONS

Solvency is the ability of a business to pay its debts as they mature, and the solvency risk is the probability that the business will be unable to meet its current debts when they mature. Unsecured current debts have different degrees of built-in solvency risk which are related to (1) the length of their maturities, (2) their repayment schedule, and, last but not least, (3) the kinds of creditors holding the debts. Short maturities are more risky than long because they are a constant challenge to the company's ability to pay. If debts could be continually long maturities, never shifting to the short-term debt category it is *certain* that there would be no cash shortage for paying the debts, and, therefore, there would be no risk of default.

Remember that decisions to optimize inventory balances for normal operations, to optimize lead time, and to optimize safety stocks and decisions to optimize cash balances for normal operations, to optimize lead time, and optimize safety stocks of cash are made independently of solvency risks connected with their related financing. After the optimizing decision is made, however, the evaluation standards listed above need to be considered. The specific form of financing then is decided on its own merits. As a general policy matter, financial managers prefer the longer to the shorter debt contracts. This policy may have to be modified, however, to meet special situations, such as when the operating cycle of the inventory or cash transaction is shorter than the number of days that would be optimal considering the financing contract independently. As a general policy matter, financial managers prefer also the easier repayment schedule, the schedule that allows the business to retain its cash as long as possible for internal reinvestment between payment dates and that allows the business to reserve the larger payments to the end of the payment schedule. This policy preferring the delayed repayment schedule may be modified when the current investment project terminates prior to the initial budget enabling the debt to be repaid at an early date for minimizing solvency risk. Finally, as a general policy of minimizing solvency risk, it is beneficial for the business to obtain financing from businesses that depend on selling goods and services as well as on extending inventory credit and lending money because the supplier is then dependent on the debtor for sales as well as the debtor is dependent on the creditor for funds. More specifically, trade creditors in general are lenient because they are concerned with continuing credit sales for profit, and commercial banks in the area where the business is located are more likely to admit flexibility in their collection demands on the business than are banks in outlying areas that make loans only in isolated cases.

PROFIT CONSIDERATIONS

Profit considerations are present in short-term financing only by indirection through cost considerations. Financing in itself creates costs and expenses for the business rather than creating net profits, just as holding inventories, receivables, and cash creates costs rather than generating profits. Profit considerations are evident only when relative cost factors are being considered as when mutually exclusive forms of financing are considered or when negotiations are taking place between the business and the financing agency. Special attention is given in this section to the cost elements in current financing with no explicit references being made to their profit effects.

Internal costs result from time spent planning the financial budget. In addition to planning and negotiating time spent by higher level financial personnel, there are secretarial services and supplies connected with budgeting financial needs that are also part of internal costs. Like inventory ordering costs and cash budgeting costs, the more often such external financing is planned the larger their total costs. For example, planning once for $10,000 would cost just about half as much as planning twice for $5,000 each time. The student will recognize here the elements of the nonlinear cost function that was used in Chapter 10. The other side of the cost of financing is the interest rate which will command our attention at this time. The interest rate is the external cost that needs to be understood by financial managers if they expect to react in a way that will be to their own benefit. We will consider here briefly two elements in the short-term interest rate: the prime interest rate over which financial managers have little or no control and the risk adjustment factor in the interest rate over which they may develop considerable control.

The prime interest rate is the portion of the total borrowing rate paid the lender to induce him to part with his cash and is equivalent to what the lender could have earned by extending his credit to basically riskless borrowers like the United States Treasury or some other *prime* commercial borrower. The rate is determined in the central money market where large borrowers go for short-term unsecured funds with contracts like Treasury bills, commercial paper, and banker's acceptances.

The actual rate on any given day is determined by the interaction of the supply of cash and the demand for cash in the central money markets. Most important to the borrowing firm is that this portion of his total interest rate is not alterable by the firm. The firm can strive, through efficient management of its finances, to meet the standards required in the money market to obtain funds at costs approaching the *pure* rate; *but it cannot, regardless of how efficiently it is managed, change the prime rate of interest.* The functional relationship between the *dollar amount* of interest and the prime interest rate is linear and may be represented by:

$$I = r_1(X) \qquad\qquad 11.1$$

Where: $I =$ Dollar interest
$\quad r_1 =$ Pure interest rate
$\quad (X) =$ Quantity of dollars borrowed

Although a firm cannot individually affect the size of the pure interest rate, the firm can aspire to attain this riskless state as pointed out above so that at the limit of risklessness his actual interest rate may approach the prime rate. In a practical sense, however, no enterprise, public or private, that is unable to create its own means of payment as the central government is, should be considered altogether riskless.

Now the risk adjustment is the portion of the firm's interest rate that is paid to compensate the lender for the *chance* that he takes of not collecting the interest and principal sum of the firm's debt on the dates that they are due. A very important fact needs mentioning at this time regarding this short-term risk-adjustment rate, namely, that the rate reflects more than any other single factor the condition of the firm's solvency and liquidity. The reason that this fact is mentioned here is to note that the points of emphasis are quite different between the cost of equity (stock) financing, which will be considered in Chapter 17, and debt financing. Profitability considerations which are major factors, as we have seen, affecting share values are of minor importance when it comes to valuing a firm's position for short-term unsecured financing.

It is doubtful even that liquidity conditions reflect directly on the rate of interest as solvency conditions do in current or long-term debt financing. There are several measures of solvency as was seen in Chapter 2, but the one that is more generally acceptable perhaps than any other for this purpose is the one that tests a company's capital position relative to its total current and long-term debts. At the risk of being somewhat arbitrary on this matter but for the sake of clarifying the basic relationship, we make the risk portion of the borrowing rate a function of the relative importance of the total debts or liabilities of the business (current debt + long term debt) to its net capital (total assets − total debts). Since net capital equals net worth equals equity, we will use the last and simplest of these terms to represent net capital. The relationship of total debt to equity may be stated in either of the following two ways: D/E or $1/(E/D)$. Both will produce the same quantitative value. For example, assume that total debt is $60,000 and that the equity of the business is $100,000:

$$1. \quad \frac{D}{E} = \frac{60,000}{100,000} = 0.6$$

$$2. \quad \frac{1}{E/D} = \frac{1}{1.67} = 0.6$$

Let us use the ratio D/E to illustrate how this variable affects the risk rate. Let r_2 be the risk charge in the total interest rate and let (r_1) be the coefficient of the function, then:

$$r_2 = r_1 \left(\frac{D}{E}\right) \qquad\qquad 11.2$$

Substituting, assume a pure or prime rate of interest of 6 percent, equity of $100,000 and debt of $60,000:

$$r_2 = 6 \left(\frac{60,000}{100,000}\right)$$
$$= 3.6\%$$

The r_2 value will increase linearly with the ratio of debt to equity until after a certain ratio, let us say 1.2, is reached after which the financing may be cut off altogether. A ratio of 1.2 would produce an r_2 rate of 7.2 percent. Suppose that $D = 0$, then r_2 would also equal 0 because $6 \times 0 = 0$, indicating a pure or prime interest rate. The assumption of linearity here was made to simplify the tool and to help identify the main variables in this important problem. In the practical world, it is better to start with a simplified model of this kind and let the financial managers of each business modify it if it is necessary to fit their own special case.

Now the total interest rate relationship may be summarized as $R = r_1 + (D/E)(r_1)$ or just as $R = r_1 + r_2$. Substituting from the example above in which $D = \$60,000$ and $E = \$100,000$:

$$R = 6 + 3.6$$
$$= 9.6\%$$

Finally we need to affirm the constraining function of capital in short-term interest rate determination. The effect of the capital constraint on the risk rate finally needs to be observed. In the illustration above, net capital was held constant, as in fact it is in current financial analysis. But notice that, if the quantity of net capital had been $150,000 instead of $100,000 in the example above, a $60,000 debt would have added instead of 3.6 percent to the risk charge only 2.4 percent:

$$r_2 = 6 \left(\frac{\$ \ 60,000}{\$150,000}\right) = 2.4\%$$

The larger capital balance not only reduces the risk rate, but it also extends the perimeter for more total financing. Thus, if creditors set a limit on borrowing such that $D/E \leq 1.2$, net capital of \$150,000 compared with the initial \$100,000 allows the company to expand its current financing to \$180,000 (1.2 × \$150,000) from \$120,000 (1.2 × \$100,000) before its financing is cut off.

INVENTORY CREDIT

Inventory credit implies that inventories are purchasable without the immediate need for cash. They are purchased *on credit* which creates payables in the financing firm's current liabilities. Financial managers seek inventory credit so that raw materials and finished goods will be available as planned to meet their optimizing goals. We will consider trade credit now from the financing company's viewpoint and its implications for liquidity, solvency, and cost.

LIQUIDITY EFFECT OF TRADE CREDIT FINANCING

Inventory can be purchased with cash on hand or with trade credit. Table 11.1 shows that trade credit, whatever form it may take, preserves liquidity temporarily. Liquidity measured by the ratio cash/current assets is actually decreased by trade credit financing, but it is decreased at a much slower rate than when inventories are bought with cash. This is a temporary condition, of course, but the important thing is that it preserves cash at its higher present value rather than at its lower future value.

TABLE 11.1
CASH AND CREDIT PURCHASES OF INVENTORIES

	I Before Purchase	II Purchase with Cash	III Purchase with Credit Trade
Cash	\$ 30,000	\$ 10,000	\$ 30,000
Receivables	40,000	40,000	40,000
Inventories	30,000	50,000	50,000
Current assets	\$100,000	\$100,000	\$120,000
	Ratio: $\frac{Cash}{Current\ assets}$ $\frac{30}{100} = 30\%$	Ratio: $\frac{Cash}{Current\ assets}$ $\frac{10}{100} = 10\%$	Ratio: $\frac{Cash}{Current\ assets}$ $\frac{30}{120} = 25\%$

SOLVENCY EFFECT OF TRADE CREDIT FINANCING

If the same quantity and quality of goods are available with the same inventory delivery service and at the same financing expense, financial managers should take the credit that offers the easiest payment terms. The degree of external control from trade credit sources is a minor consideration. Trade credit financing is noted and, in fact, sought after partly at least because of the informal manner in which the supplier treats his customer. The debt is evidenced in the buyers' *accounts payable* except when a financial institution supplies the financing. There are usually no signatures on the open book accounts to formally acknowledge the debt, nor is this kind of financing secured by pledges of specific assets. The inventories are saleable as soon as they arrive even though the payables created by the purchases are still unpaid. The buyer will not usually be pressed for payment if he continues to buy from the supplier and if he continues to pay his debts if not sooner then later.

COST FACTOR IN TRADE CREDIT FINANCING

Financial expenses vary considerably in obtaining trade credit. Inventory suppliers do not usually charge an interest rate on open book accounts, except that an opportunity cost may be calculated when a business does not take advantage of cash discounts offered by the inventory supplier. For example, a business which is offered a 4 percent discount if its bills are paid in thirty days with a *net* date of sixty days is in effect paying interest at the rate of 4 percent for thirty days of credit. The first thirty days is without charge because 4 percent discount is received through the first thirty days; the next thirty days though cost 4 percent. Converting the thirty-day 4 percent charge to an annual rate:

$$I = 0.04\left(\frac{360}{30}\right) = 48\%$$

Or if you look on this as 4 percent for sixty days, the rate is cut in half to 24 percent. Whichever way we look at it, however, the rate is exceedingly high for failing to take advantage of a cash discount. With reference to the interest rate analysis of the previous section in which $R = r_1 + r_2$, the annual discount rate of say 24 percent is the R value, most of it representing r_2 at a high risk cost because of the open book and unsecured nature of the financing.

QUANTITATIVE ANALYSIS OF ACCOUNTS PAYABLE

In special cases, as when dealers finance the purchase of machinery and equipment, automobiles, or appliances for resale, formal financing documents are used to execute the purchase; but these are secured forms of financing. The most common form is the account payable which is unsecured and is the subject of close study by financial managers. These obligations are related directly to inventory purchases; and, like inventories, they make up usually a large portion of the total current liabilities of most commercial and manufacturing companies. Because of the solvency risk implicit in the accounts, they need to be analyzed at regular intervals for closer control and for more effective planning of future financing. We will consider here applying the same kind of analysis to accounts that was applied in Chapter 10 to marketable securities.

We assume that the basic traits that need analyzing are discountability of the accounts for cost analysis, size, and age of the accounts for solvency analysis. There are manageable traits in accounts other than these three, but these three are the main traits that concern financial managers at the present. Included in this group are sixty accounts that are divisible into seven sets of A discountable accounts, B accounts $\geq$ $5,000, and C accounts that are overdue. The distribution is as follows among the seven sets of accounts. Venn diagrams are used to show how intersection, union, and complement can be used to bring added significant facts about the accounts to the fore. The questions asked here will supply quantitative information needed for evaluating the condition of the accounts.

TABLE 11.2
SETS OF ACCOUNTS PAYABLE

Subsets	Number of Accounts	Sets of Accounts Payable
1st	20	Discountable
2nd	10	$\geq$ $5,000
3rd	8	Overdue
4th	6	Discountable and $\geq$ $5,000
5th	6	Discountable and overdue
6th	7	Overdue and $\geq$ $5,000
7th	3	Discountable, overdue and $\geq$ $5,000
	Total 60	

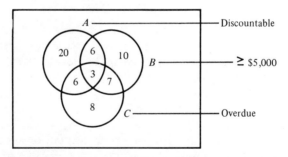

Figure 11.1.   Quantitative Accounts Payable Analysis.

1. How many accounts are $\geq$ $5,000 and discountable? This is an operation in intersection (A $\cap$ B), and the answer is 9 (6 + 3) or 15 percent of the total number of accounts. This reveals information about the chance for saving money by taking discounts on large accounts.
2. How many of the accounts are $\geq$ $5,000 and overdue? This also requires an operation in intersection, and the answer is 10 (7 + 3) or $16\frac{2}{3}$ percent of the total number. This reveals useful information about the solvency risks spelled out in the size of the accounts and in the willingness of the creditors to carry us on large overdue accounts.

3. How many accounts are discountable? The answer is 35 (20 + 6 + 6 + 3). Twenty of these are exclusively discountable, and 15 are either or both ≥ $5,000 and overdue. The student should extend this question and answer the exercise further.

The summary results point out to financial managers first, the basic problem areas in managing accounts payable. Second, they quantify past accounts management practices for evaluation and control and, third, accounts payable practices may be planned for the future.

CASH BORROWING

The discussion of unsecured cash borrowing describes briefly the institutional services available for obtaining unsecured cash loans, the instruments used in the loan transactions, nature of the capital constraints in short-term unsecured borrowing, and, finally, the plan for financial budgeting.

INSTITUTIONAL SERVICES

Current loans are made almost altogether by commercial banks and commercial paper companies. In negotiating for loans, financial managers consider the quantity of loan funds available to the lending institution itself, cost to the borrowing business, repayment terms in proposed contracts, and special capital-related restrictions placed by the lending agencies on the total amount of borrowing. All of these factors can be restated in terms of their liquidity, solvency, and profitability effects on business.

National banks are the primary unsecured source of cash borrowing to meet optimal transactions balances and safety stock requirements. But these institutions are legally restricted to lending not more than 10 percent of their net capital (total assets — total debts) to any one borrower on a secured or unsecured basis. Thus, financial managers of a given company seeking a loan from a national bank with $2 million of net capital are limited by banking laws to a $200,000 loan. It is interesting to note that, although this is done in a legal instead of a physical way, the capital constraint nevertheless restricts income and profit of individual banks as well as of nonbanking firms. Still another way of looking at this from the business firm's point of view is that a double capital constraint is placed on the borrower; one resulting from the limited quantity of net capital within the firm and the other resulting from the limited quantity of net capital within the lending agency. The loan limit of the bank may force a cutback on a current operation that would make operations fall below the optimal. In practice, however, financial managers will not limit their borrowing to one bank; or they may go to a bank with larger capital resources and, therefore, with greater loan potential; or they may even go to the money market for a prime loan if their r_2 rate is extremely low.

It is sound practice for financial managers to sample the market by contacting more than one bank before making loan committments. It is generally true that interest rates on unsecured loans are lower than secured rates, but this is true because only companies with very high credit standing and very low r_2 values can borrow in the unsecured loan market. But some banks have minimum service charges that others do not have. Repayment terms are written into the loan contract, but some banks insist on shorter maturities than others. Management should negotiate for loan contracts that are long enough to avoid unusual maturity risks. Risk charges tend to increase in rate with the lengthened maturity of bank loans, however, which may offset some of the solvency gained by the longer maturity. A common restrictive feature of commercial bank loans that may vary considerably among individual banks is the requirement that a portion of the business loan be held on deposit with the bank during the life of the loan. This is called a *compensating balance* and may range between 10 and 20 percent of the loan. This is to *compensate* the bank for the risk of losing cash reserves at their reserve banks through check clearances. This is understandable from the lender's viewpoint, but it is a handicap to the business needing a certain quantity of cash funds to attain optimal cash balances for transactions and for maximizing share values.

Some banks give better lending service than others. But most of them do supply numerous services to business customers in addition to regular lending which may include: (1) holding and paying interest on savings deposits; (2) writing letters of credit to facilitate domestic and foreign trade; (3) accepting bills of exchange for regular customers; (4) collecting checks, drafts, and notes for customers; and (5) supplying credit information to customers. Costs of bank loans are affected by a combination of factors. Policy decisions of the Board of Governors of the Federal Reserve System are bound to affect the supply of funds and the cost of r_1 in the money market, but neither financial managers of business nor managers of member banks have any control over these policies. If r_1 is increased by such action from the Federal Reserve or from the other side by the Treasury demand for a large sum of short-term cash funds, the R value for all business will automatically increase even though r_2 is unchanged. The best response to this by financial managers is to improve their condition (D/E) so that r_2 will be a minimum.

Commercial paper companies are nonbanking institutions specializing in discounting unsecured promissory notes (paper) that mature in four to six months from their date of issue. The companies are concentrated in the New York financial district where they are generally called *discount houses*. This title identifies them with the instruments they handle that are purchased on a discount basis and are payable on maturity at their face values. In their unsecured financial services to business, they are competitive with commercial banks.

The quantity of funds obtainable from a commercial paper company may be less than the quantity of funds obtainable from a bank with the same capital resources because they are not allowed to "create" deposits on a fractional reserve basis as commercial banks are. In practice, however, discount houses may actually be able to advance more funds to individual businesses because they are not restricted by the 10 percent rule on loans as are commercial banks. A commercial paper company with $500,000 in net capital could advance the full amount to a single business, while a bank restricted by the 10 percent rule could lend only $50,000. Actually, a commercial paper company with this much more capital to lend might be able to supply even more cash because it can borrow easily in the open money market and even directly from commercial banks for expanding its loan base. More important than any other factor in determining the quantity of funds that a business can get from a commercial paper company is the business's own general credit standing. Since commercial paper companies make advances only on unsecured contracts, the business is obligated to have an "A-1" credit rating before it can borrow. In addition, the supplier is not too interested in a customer's business unless the borrowing reaches a certain minimum amount. Neither are they interested usually in maturities of less than four months or more than six months.

Discount houses do not create deposit credits with a checking account as commercial banks do. Nor do they offer supplementary services in savings accounts, letters of credit to facilitate foreign and domestic trade, accepting of bills of exchange, collecting on checks and drafts, or any of the other services offered by commercial banks. But these companies shine when it comes to lowcost lending. But to qualify for this low rate means that the company's debt ratio D/E has to be relatively low which is another way of saying that r_2 has to be very low.

Repayment terms on commercial paper are fixed at the time of the financing and are payable to whomever presents the notes when they mature. The notes are seldom in the hands of the commercial paper company when they mature. We can expect them to be presented by commercial banks, individuals, and businesses in and outside the financial district. This makes for very impersonal relations between the borrower and the creditor and forces prompt repayment on the date that they are due which may create a solvency risk. Finally, less control is exercised by commercial paper companies over business operations of the borrower than by any other short-term supply source. The reason for this is that the selection process in this market is so keen that whoever qualifies is strong enough financially to be spared any outside interference.

FINANCIAL INSTRUMENTS

One of the reasons for using unsecured borrowing is its relative simplicity and lack of formality. Although this is true, there are still a certain number of instruments that have to be prepared and signed by the borrower. The following information has to be supplied in the application for a loan.

1. Name and address of the applicant.
2. Type of business and date of organization.
3. Amount and length of loan request.
4. Purpose of the loan and in some cases a financial budget to show how and when it will be repaid.
5. Previous borrowings: dates and amounts.
6. Recent audited balance sheets and operating statements.

7. The following ratios for the past few years. These ratios may be request-
ed on a quarterly or semiannual basis.
   Net worth/Total debts or Total debts/Net worth
   Net working capital/Current liabilities
   Current assets/Current liabilities
   Quick assets/Current liabilities
   Cost of goods sold/Inventories
   Net profit after taxes/Net sales

The instrument that identifies a short-term unsecured borrowing usually is
a promissory note which may be a single-payment note or an installment note.
The single-payment note allows the business to use the cash for the full period of
indebtedness. The single-payment form of note is used extensively in business
borrowing from both commercial banks and commercial paper companies, with
this important difference that commercial bank notes are usually *interest bearing*
whereas commercial paper company notes are *discounted*. If an interest-bearing
note is used, the borrower receives the face amount of the loan which he returns
with interest at maturity. If a discounted note is used, the borrower receives the
face amount of the loan less the discount; and at maturity he returns the face
amount of the note.

The installment note requires repayment in part soon after the borrowing takes
effect. On short-term notes, the payments are usually made in uniform amounts
each month until the debt is fully paid at the end of the year; or they may be in
small uniform amounts until a final large payment is made. The latter is a *balloon
note*. A *telescoped note* has larger initial payments with later payments diminishing
in size. The installment note reduces liquidity and increases solvency risks for the
borrower. The liquidity effect of installment payments can be illustrated as follows.
Suppose that $6,000 is borrowed repayable in six equal installments commencing
one month after date. The average fund holdings during the period are only $3,000
as shown below.

$$X = \frac{(a + b)}{2} \qquad\qquad 11.3$$

Where: X = Average cash holdings
        a = Amount of cash received
        b = Balance on hand at end of contract period

Substituting:

$$X = \frac{(\$6,000 + 0)}{2}$$

$$X = \frac{\$6,000}{2} \quad \text{or just} \quad \$3,000$$

Financial managers need to consider the effect of the installment note on the optimal transactions and safety stock balances; one thing that they are assured of in this case is that their beginning cash balance acquired for transactions purposes will be used at a constant monthly rate to meet maturing debt requirements.

CAPITAL CONSTRAINTS AND THE QUANTITY OF UNSECURED FINANCING

We have already seen that the size of a company's net capital is a primary determinant of its cost of obtaining trade credit and cash funds on unsecured contracts. It was noted briefly that the total quantity of a company's financing could be restricted by the size of its net capital. This last item will be explored somewhat further in this section illustrating the application of simple algebraic tools for more exact statements and solutions to the quantitative problem.

The creditor looks on net capital as a measure of debt-paying capacity in case of forced liquidation. In liquidation unsecured creditors have a prior claim to the assets over the shareholders, and they consider the net worth of the business as a good cushion to fall back on. Shareholders and potential shareholders are interested primarily in the market value of a company's shares which reflect primarily earnings and earnings potential of the business. The equity of a business, measured by the total market value of its shares, may be larger or smaller than the book value of the company's equity as it appears in the balance sheet; the instability of this value is one reason why creditors do not use it as a loan valuation constraint. Another closely related reason for creditors using the book-value figure is that they are concerned with liquidation value of the company's net capital in case they are required to bring legal action for collection of their loan. Finally, and this may be a more important factor than one may suspect affecting the creditor's preference for book values, it is much easier to come up with a definite loan limit for the applicant if clear-cut book values of net capital are used in preference to market values. What is the maximum amount that can be borrowed if the capital constraint is expressed so that after the loan the company's total debts must not exceed its net capital? Assuming that total assets are $40,000 and total debts are $10,000, the constraint is stated by the lender as:

$$\text{Net capital} = \text{Present debt} + \text{New lending}$$
$$\$30,000 = \$10,000 + X$$
$$X = \$20,000$$

X is the unknown value of allowable unsecured borrowing from the company's viewpoint. This answers the question of how much borrowing is permissible given $30,000 of net capital. Increasing net capital may seem a simple matter, but it would require an important capital management decision to increase the company's supply of net capital. Can the student see what kind of capital management decision would be required here?

The net capital structure is a quantitative symbol of debt-paying capacity in case of liquidation, but the measure does not consider the quality of the underlying capital assets. By turning to net working capital, the lender is able to impose a qualitative as well as a purely quantitative capital constraint on unsecured financing by the firm. Suppose that the net-working-capital constraint is stated so that it has to be 1.5 times the size of current liabilities after the loan is made. Assume that current assets are $45,000 and that current liabilities are $20,000, making net working capital $25,000 ($45,000 − $20,000). To determine how much financing can be secured without violating the constraint financial managers quantify their borrowing capacity as:

$$\$25,000 = 1.5(\$20,000 + X)$$
$$\$25,000 = \$30,000 + 1.5X$$
$$-1.5X = \$30,000 - \$25,000$$
$$X = -\$3,333$$

No new borrowing would be allowed in this case, in fact $3,333 is the amount by which the present current debt has to be decreased to restore the required relationship of net working capital being 1.5 times as great as current debts. Lower values on the right side of the initial equation may qualify the business for obtaining cash from unsecured borrowing. For example, if the lender reduced his coverage requirement from 1.5 to 1, then our working capital of $25,000 could support a $5,000 loan. Or, if the 1.5 requirement is retained and current liabilities are reduced to $15,000, the solution would allow $5,000 more of financing. The test of the solution is whether or not the net working capital is in the ratio to current liabilities that is required after the financing. Let us test the case where $X = -\$3,333$ by trying to borrow $2,000 instead of reducing current liabilities by $3,333.

$$\$25,000 = 1.5(\$20,000 + \$2,000)$$
$$\$25,000 = \$30,000 + \$3,000$$
$$\$25,000 \neq \$33,000$$

Next let us test the case in which current liabilities are reduced to $15,000 which would permit $5,000 of new financing. In this case, working capital is $30,000 ($45,000 − $15,000); and $5,000 is the correct solution to the amount of allowable financing.

$$\$30,000 = 1.5(\$15,000 + \$5,000)$$
$$\$30,000 = \$22,500 + \$7,500$$
$$\$30,000 = \$30,000$$

The quality differences of current assets are also relied on to reveal details of debt-paying capacity that cannot be supplied in the total current assets or in the net working capital. This is done by selective grouping of the highly liquid assets for comparison with current debts. Cash and marketable securities, for example, are compared with current debts; and the well-known *acid test* is applied to the current assets to see whether cash, marketable securities, and trade receivables together will be large enough to cover the current liabilities after the proposed borrowing.

Institutional lenders are likely also to single out certain current assets that have special significance for debt-paying purposes, like marketable securities, that will mature at about the same time as the proposed loans. Receivables balances, average ages, and average maturities are important as well. Businesses whose receivables are decreasing in average age and decreasing in average maturities are considered to be improving as credit risks. Businesses whose inventory balances are decreasing in proportion to total current assets and in proportion to net sales and cost of goods sold are also looked on favorably for obtaining unsecured financing.

In the last analysis, financial managers want to acquire funds with the minimum of restrictions standing in their way. Sometimes competition among lenders will help them realize this goal, but competition needs to be discovered by the financial managers themselves. First though, they have to have a clear picture of the structure of competition in the short-term loan market, which can be illustrated briefly with switching circuits. Assume that T_1 below is a source of borrowing such as a commercial bank, and T_2 is the borrowing firm. The goal is to get funds from T_1 to T_2, that is from the lender to the borrowing firm:

$T_1 \longrightarrow a \longrightarrow b \longrightarrow T_2$

Figure 11.2. Creditor Restriction in Series.

Let us assume that the creditor placed the following requirements on borrowing such that: *a* current assets/current liabilities after borrowing must be $\geq 3/1$ and *b* cash + marketable securities + receivables/current liabilities after borrowing must be $\geq 1.5/1$. Funds will flow into the business only if both restrictions *a* and *b* are met. We can quantify the possibilities of meeting the external constraints with the truth table. Let the closed switch be *T* and the open switch *F*, and let the connective be the conjunction $\wedge$. The truth values of the two statements are illustrated below with only one possibility that both *a* and *b* will be closed. It should be apparent also from what we know about truth tables that, as more restrictions are added, the less possibility there is of getting cash flowing into the business from the bor-

TABLE 11.3
TRUTH VALUE OF A SERIES OF CONSTRAINTS

a	*b*	*a*	$\wedge$	*b*
T	T		T	
T	F		F	
F	F		F	
F	T		F	

rowing sources. For example, with a third constraint like *c*, total borrowing must not exceed $100,000 only one *T* out of eight would be possible. But if this circuit is too restrictive, management can search the loan market for less demanding sources where *either* one *or* the other of the constraints will bring forth the cash.

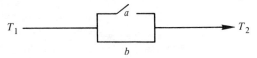

Figure 11.3.   Creditors Parallel Constraints.

Competition in lending gives the business an *either-or* situation such that, if restriction *a* cannot be met, cash will still flow from T_1 to T_2 if *b* can be met and vice versa. Now we can quantify the possibilities of getting cash using the disjunction tool $\vee$. Let *T* be the closed switch, *F* be the open switch as above, and the operating connective be the disjunction $\vee$, showing that the *either-or* restrictions are met in three out of four possibilities.

TABLE 11.4
TRUTH VALUE OF PARALLEL RESTRICTIONS

a	*b*	*a* $\vee$ *b*
T	*T*	*T*
T	*F*	*T*
F	*F*	*F*
F	*T*	*T*

ALTERING THE DEBT STRUCTURE FOR UNSECURED FINANCING

In one of the last algebraic solutions above, it was shown how by reducing the company's starting current liabilities from $20,000 to $15,000 the company's net working capital was increased from the original $25,000 to $30,000 and its borrowing potential was increased from $-$3,333 to $+$5,000. A few words are in order now showing how net working capital can be increased by reducing current liabilities but not disturbing current assets. Assume that net working capital is $20,000 and that current liabilities are $20,000; paying off a $10,000 current debt will reduce current liabilities to $10,000 and will decrease current assets by the same amount causing net working capital not to change. But another way of decreasing current liabilities, at the same time increasing net working capital, is to shift the current liability to long-term liabilities, which may be designated *secondary financing*. Such transfers lengthen the debt structure by exchanging long-term debts for short-term debts and lengthens the debt structure as former short-term payables now become long-term payables. The result is reduced solvency risk to the business by clearing away some of its current liabilities, and this sets the stage for increased unsecured borrowing. Net working capital can actually be created in this way for the business as illustrated below where $50,000 in current debts are transferred to long-term debts.

TABLE 11.5
EFFECTS OF DEBT TRANSFER

	Before Transfer	*After Transfer*	*Per Cent Increase*
Current assets	$300,000	$300,000	
Current liabilities	150,000	100,000	
Net working capital	$150,000	$200,000	
Net working capital/current liabilities	1/1	2/1	100
Current assets/current liabilities	2/1	3/1	50

THE FINANCIAL BUDGET

Unsecured lenders are paying more and more attention to tangible plans for borrowing and debt repayment as admissible evidence in applying for unsecured financing. Even more important, lenders in some cases are using these plans to determine precisely how much a business is qualified to borrow. To the extent that these budgets are accepted, we might even say that the borrower is allowed, within certain limits, to determine for the lender the amount of the financing, the timing of the financing, and the timing of its repayment. A business that cannot qualify for borrowing because of limited amounts of capital may be able to qualify using proper budgeting materials. In other cases, budgeting may give that extra little push to put a firm over in negotiations for unsecured borrowing. A hypothetical financial budget is produced below to show how this tool can be used by financial managers to obtain cash without pledging other assets for collateral. But before deciding definitely on this technique, assume that management decided to make a joint probability analysis of the borrowing issue for reassurance before entering the loan market.

A decision tree with the same probability distributions as the one illustrated in Chapter 5 is used in Figure 11.4 to show the logical sequence of an unsecured borrowing plan. The purpose of the tree is to show what an important part the financial budget can play in debtor-creditor borrowing relations where no assets are pledged to secure a debt. Alternatives available to the business are quitting the application, performing a financial analysis, and preparing a financial budget; the rest is up to the lending agency. Without introducing monetary values, we can determine the joint probability of coming up with an Accept along each of the probable borrowing paths. For example, the probability of acceptance of a borrowing request along the short path at the left is just 0.04 (0.4 × 0.1), while the probability of a rejection on this path is very high 0.36 (0.4 × 0.9). If management submits to a financial analysis, interesting results may follow. A good rating from the analyst sets up a high probability that management will apply directly for the loan, but it sets up a low probability that financial budgets will be prepared. The

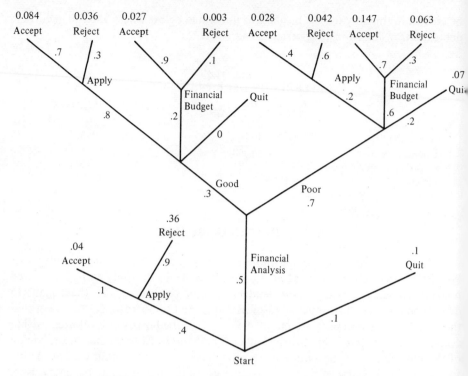

0.084   0.036   0.027   0.003   0.028   0.042   0.147   0.063

Accept   Reject   Accept   Reject   Accept   Reject   Accept   Reject

.7   .3   .9   .1   .4   .6   .7   .3

Apply   Apply   Financial   .07

Financial   Quit   .2   Budget   Qui

Budget

.8   .2   .6   .2

0

Good   Poor

.3   .7

.36

Reject

.04   Financial   .1

Accept   .9   Analysis   Quit

.1   .5

Apply

.1

.4

Start

Figure 11.4.   Borrowing Tree with Probability Values.

path, Financial Analysis → Good → Financial Budget → Accept, has a small
probability of 0.027, the implication being that a budget may be superfluous if
the financial analysis of historical condition proves Good. But the results are
reversed on the right side of the tree following a Poor rating from the analysis:
Financial Analysis → Poor → Apply → Accept, which gives a joint probability
of only 0.028 ($0.5 \times 0.7 \times 0.2 \times 0.4$). But following the path from a Poor analysis
to the Financial Analysis → Poor → Financial Budget → Accept is 0.147 (0.5
$\times 0.7 \times 0.6 \times 0.7$) exceeding all other probabilities. Financial managers know
that, if an acceptance is highly prized, a different course of action will be followed
if the financial analysis is poor than if it is good; and this course of action is to
prepare and present a financial budget.

Borrowing is in multiples of $1,000 rounding the notes to the next highest
$1,000 each month that funds are borrowed. Interest charges are to be paid at the
end when the debt is closed out, and money is borrowed on the first of the month
and repaid at the end of the month. A minimum of $20,000 is expected to be kept
in the cash balance. It is not necessary to go into the cash schedules to show the
source of each receipt or the use of each cash disbursement since that procedure
was illustrated in detail in Chapter 10. The cash budget and the financial budget
have to be coordinated, however, to get the overall picture of what is planned.
The cash budget shows heavy cash deficits right up to July when the cash flow is

expected to reverse. These key figures are found in the row "Monthly increase (deficit)" of the cash budget. Funds for repaying the debt are expected to rise rapidly in August and September.

The financial budget deals with cash transactions that are associated with current operations. The financial budget is actually the cash budget extended to include the details of proposed borrowing and repayment. Below Tables 11.6 and 11.7 illustrate separately the cash budget and the financial budget for a hypothetical company which has no relation to the hypothetical cash budget illustrated at the end of Chapter 10. The purpose of Table 11.6 is to show how the cash shortages are expected to develop, and the purpose of Table 11.7 is to show the plan of the borrowing and are accordingly to be used to repay the debt so that "Borrowing

TABLE 11.6
CASH BUDGET
(APRIL TO SEPTEMBER)

	April	May	June	July	August	September
Cash receipts:						
Sales and collections	$80,000	$50,000	$40,000	$70,000	$90,000	$100,000
Other net receipts	500	200	200	100	300	500
Total cash receipts	$80,500	$50,200	$40,200	$70,100	$90,300	$100,500
Cash disbursements:						
Inventory	$48,000	$50,000	$60,000	$50,000	$40,000	$ 20,000
Noninventory	30,000	30,000	30,000	20,000	30,000	20,000
Total disbursements	$78,000	$80,000	$90,000	$70,000	$70,000	$ 40,000
Monthly increase (deficit)	$ 2,500	($29,800)	($49,800)	$ 100	$20,300	$ 60,500
Beginning cash balance	25,000	27,500	(2,300)	(52,100)	(52,000)	(31,700)
Month-end cash balance	27,500	(2,300)	(52,100)	(52,000)	(31,700)	28,800
Required cash balance	20,000	20,000	20,000	20,000	20,000	20,000
Cumulative excess (deficit)	$ 7,500	($22,300)	($72,100)	($72,000)	($51,700)	$ 8,800

TABLE 11.7
FINANCIAL BUDGET
(APRIL TO SEPTEMBER)

	April	May	June	July	August	Sept.
Cumulative excess (deficit)						
(Table 11.6)	$ 7,500	($22,300)	($72,100)	($72,000)	($51,700)	$ 8,800
Borrowing required B.O.M.	—	$23,000	$50,000	—	—	—
Borrowing retired E.O.M.	—	—	—	—	$21,000	$52,000
Cumulative borrowing	—	$23,000	$73,000	$73,000	$52,000	—
Service charge on line of credit						
@ 1/4 of 1% of $80,000						$ 200
Monthly interest @ 8% per year*		$ 153	$ 487	$ 487	$ 487	$ 359
Cumulative interest charges		$ 153	$ 640	$ 1,127	$ 1,614	$ 1,973
Total financial charges						$ 2,173
Cumulative excess (adjusted for service						
charge and interest)						$ 6,627

*Monthly interest 1/12 of year.

retired E.O.M." wipes off the cumulative borrowing altogether, pays service and interest charges, and has $6,627 remaining in the balance. The difference between the balance in the cash budget of $8,800 and the balance in the financial budget of $6,627 is accounted for by service and interest charges.

SUMMARY

Chapter 11 is the first of the three chapters in Part IV dealing with external financing for current operations. The chapter deals specifically with unsecured financing as distinguished from secured, the purpose being to establish certain policy goals concerning liquidity, solvency, and profitability in short-term financing. Unsecured financing means obtaining funds on the general credit of a business, without pledging specific assets, that is. The first unsecured financing form is inventory credit. A brief analysis is made of the accounts payable in the company's current liabilities. These are obligations owed as a result of purchasing inventory on credit; and set analysis is applied to these accounts to classify the payables in terms of those that are discountable, those that represent $5,000 or greater indebtedness, and, finally, those that are over due in their payment date.

Capital constraints are indicated which affect the quantity of allowable unsecured cash borrowing. Here we can see how the quantity of capital not only constrains the operating activities of a business but also constrains the short-term financing activities. Again we return to the use of some of the finite mathematical tools developed in Chapter 5 to illustrate the existence of constraints and possible methods of removing or relaxing those constraints on short-term unsecured financing. Finally, practical application is made of the quantitative tools to the financial budget. The financial budget is a plan for borrowing cash and for returning the cash with interest to the creditor. The purpose of the budget is primarily to facilitate obtaining cash borrowing by presenting the plan to the lending agency. The decision tree is employed as a tool for analyzing the probability that the business will be able to obtain the cash that is sought in the financial budget.

PROBLEMS

1. Your loan request is rejected by a bank on the basis that your accounts payable balance is too large. This causes you to make a quantitative review of the balances in terms of three special traits: a. cash discounting opportunities, b. size of the individual accounts, and c. overdue status of the accounts in total which fit into these three categories:

A	Discountable	20
B	$\geq \$4,000$	10
C	Overdue	10
	Total	40

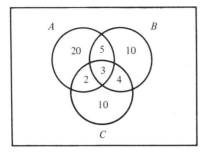

The Venn diagram shows how some of the accounts have intersecting traits. Using the diagram, you seek answers to the following questions about the accounts:

    a. How many are discountable *and* ≥ $4,000?
    b. How many are ≥ $4,000 and overdue?
    c. How many are discountable, ≥ $4,000, and overdue?
    d. How many are ≥ $4,000 *or* overdue?
    e. In the diagram above, where is the set of accounts that are exclusively not discountable, not ≥ $4,000, and not overdue?
    f. Construct three more questions and give the answers letting at least one employ the complement (∼).

2. The rate of interest that a business pays for short-term unsecured borrowing includes costs for pure interest and a risk charge.

    a. Distinguish between the two rates.
    b. Write the equations for each of the two functional relationships and distinguish them. Assuming that the pure interest rate is 7 percent, what would your borrowing rate be for a range from $6,000, to $20,000, by $2,000 intervals?
    c. It might be argued that the risk rate should increase at an increasing rate. What does this mean and do you think that the logic of this is well-founded?

3. The Acme Company manufactures high-quality draperies, curtains, bed and furniture coverings. The owners' investment in the business plus current income supplied enough funds in the past to meet the normal cash requirements. But the general management of the business is considering introducing a new line of competitive merchandise that would be sold under a new trade name. While the business has been earning a reasonable return for the present owners, it is the general feeling that considerably more profits could be made by extending operations in the direction of the competitive product. The extra profits are expected to come mainly from more fully utilizing present capital facilities. Because of the nature of the products, the demand would be seasonal, requiring extra large purchases of textile materials and large payrolls two or three times

yearly. The goods would then be sold to customers who are accustomed to relatively easy credit terms ranging between sixty and ninety days. But before the venture can be undertaken, plans would need to be made for extensive seasonal borrowing.

While the treasurer of the Acme Company was considering the general subject of short-term financing, he saw published in the local newspaper two balance sheets, one of the Commercial Discount Company and the other of the First National Bank. He noted that the two institutions were similar in total size; and, therefore, he examined the two statements closely from the viewpoint of a potential borrower, looking for clues, primarily, of the financial institutions' lending practices and capacities.

First National Bank Statement of Condition		Commercial Discount Company Balance Sheet	
Assets:		Assets:	
Cash & due from banks	$ 4,500,000	Cash	$12,500,000
U.S. Govt. securities	2,200,000	Notes receivable	4,560,000
Other bonds & securities	1,500,000	Repossessions	20,000
Stock of Fed. Res. Bank	50,000	Fixed assets	1,250,000
Loans & discounts	12,450,000	Deferred charges	250,000
Letters of credit & acceptance	28,000	Other assets	150,000
Income accrued	80,000		
Furniture & fixtures	20,000		
Total	$20,828,000	Total	$17,730,000
Liabilities:		Liabilities:	
Deposits	$15,200,000	Bonds payable	$ 5,500,000
Letters of credit & acceptance	28,000	Notes payable	250,000
Other liabilities	75,000	Mortgage payable	250,000
Deferred income	80,000	Unearned interest	800,000
Capital stock	2,500,000	Common stock	9,000,000
Surplus	2,500,000	Retained earnings	1,930,000
Undivided profits	445,000		
Total	$20,828,000	Total	$17,730,000

a. Compare the quantity of loans outstanding of the two companies. Which of the two companies is likely to have the larger portion of secured loans?

b. Compare the liquidity of the two companies' assets. What effect could this have on the potential borrower?

c. Compare the maturity dates of the two companies' liabilities. What is the significance of the comparison from the solvency viewpoint? What effect could this have on the potential borrower?

d. Suppose the treasurer of the Acme Company were granted a $30,000 loan. In what form would the funds be paid by the two companies?

e. What is the largest unsecured loan that the commercial bank would ordinarily make to the Acme Company? Could the company borrow more on a secured basis?

f. Assuming that the legal reserve requirement for the commercial bank is 20 percent, how much, if any, can it expand its present loans?
g. Can you tell by looking at the Commercial Discount Company's balance sheet how much it can expand its total loans? Explain.
h. Suppose that both financial institutions sold another $1 million worth of common stock; consider the possible effect on each one's lending capacity.

4. Aside from considering the capabilities of the lending and inventory supply sources, the financial manager of Acme realizes that the condition of his own business is vitally important. Realizing that credit standards would differ in details among individual suppliers, he knows that in all cases a great deal of attention would be given to the capital status and to the past operating experiences of his business. Keeping this in mind, he plans to reexamine the company's latest statements of financial condition included below.

ACME COMPANY
COMPARATIVE BALANCE SHEETS

	Balance Sheet Six Months Prior	Balance Sheet Current
Assets		
Current assets:		
Cash	$ 12,000	$ 7,500
Receivables	68,000	120,000
Inventories	165,000	140,000
Prepaid expenses	2,000	1,000
Total	$247,000	$268,500
Fixed assets:		
Land	$ 50,000	$ 50,000
Building & equipment	350,000	320,000
Intangibles	50,000	30,000
Total	$450,000	$400,000
Total assets	$697,000	$668,500
Liabilities and equity		
Current liabilities:		
Accounts payable	$ 47,000	$ 20,000
Notes payable	5,000	—
Accruals	1,000	1,000
Total	$ 53,000	$ 21,000
Long-term debts	$100,000	93,500
Common stock	400,000	400,000
Capital surplus	100,000	100,000
Retained earnings	44,000	54,000
Total liabilities and stockholders' equity	$697,000	$668,500

ACME COMPANY
COMPARATIVE INCOME STATEMENTS

	Previous Six Months	*Present Six Months*
Net sales	$350,000	$310,000
Cost of goods sold	225,000	250,000
Gross profit	$125,000	$ 60,000
Operating expenses	75,000	40,000
Before-tax profits	$ 50,000	$ 20,000
Taxes at 50%	25,000	10,000
After-tax profits	$ 25,000	$ 10,000

a. The financial manager decided to apply several basic tests to the company's capital structure to get some idea of his total borrowing capacity. He had learned that commercial banks and trade creditors in the area did not like to see the total debts of the business exceed 50 percent of its stockholders' equity. The following model would serve this purpose:

$$Y = 2(Z + X)$$

Where: $Y =$ Equity
$Z =$ Present debt
$X =$ New debt

b. Next, the treasurer wanted to see how closely these figures would compare based on another general policy of the creditors, that net working capital should not be less than $1\frac{1}{2}$ times the size of the current liabilities. This is expressed as:

$$Y = 1.5(Z + X)$$

Where: $Y =$ Present net working capital
$Z =$ Present current debts
$X =$ New borrowing

5. Another way for management to look at capital and other constraints that lenders place on an unsecured borrowing is as open-switching circuits. You realize that an interesting analogy exists between a borrowing constraint and the open switch; and, as the top financial manager of the business, you decide to use this analogy to explain to the board of directors why your firm is unable presently to borrow $40,000 on a short-term unsecured note because one lender from whom your firm has been borrowing requires both that your net working capital be two times current liabilities and that equity in the business be two times total indebtedness after borrowing. Present condition of the business is as follows:

Assets		Liabilities and Net Worth	
Current assets	$200,000	Current liabilities	$100,000
Fixed assets	500,000	Fixed liabilities	100,000
		Capital stock	300,000
		Retained earnings	200,000
Total	$700,000	Total	$700,000

a. Diagram the switching circuit showing the board what the present situation is and illustrate the probability of success using a compound statement truth table employing the *and* connective ($\wedge$).

b. Explain the situation above in terms of capital constraints.

c. Diagram the switching circuit showing the board how the capital constraint might be avoided. Indicate the probability of success with a compound statement truth table employing the *or* connective ($\vee$).

6. You wish to simulate alternative courses of borrowing action on a borrowing tree to determine the net dollar value of a $40,000 borrowing proposal. Using the tree structure below, follow the most remunerative path, assuming that to make a financial analysis costs $400. If the analysis is good, it costs $200 to prepare a financial budget; if the analysis is poor, it costs $300. To apply for the loan costs $100.

a. Complete the probability distributions at each level of the tree.

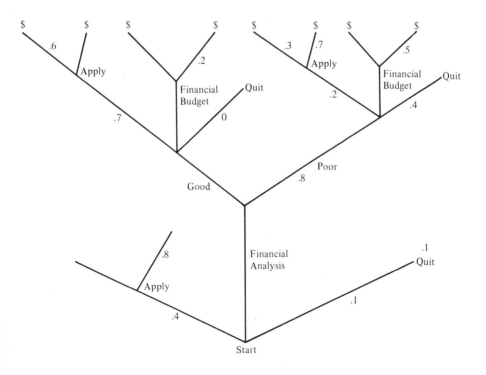

b. Determine the *expected values* of the various borrowing paths and determine the most advantageous path to follow.

c. Is it worthwhile to go ahead planning the details of the borrowing, or should it be given up altogether?

d. In general, what capital condition is likely to be at the basis of the 0.8 probability of a Poor result from the financial analysis?

7. Company A's financial analysis did not show the company in a strong light; that is, its narrow capital margins would prevent the company from borrowing the cash that was needed. Illustrated below is the company's current balance sheet. Conventional capital requirements are that net current assets have to be $1\frac{1}{2}$ times current liabilities and equity has to be equal to total debt.

COMPANY A

Current assets	$200,000	Current liabilities	$150,000
Fixed assets	400,000	Fixed liabilities	150,000
		Capital stock	250,000
		Retained earnings	50,000
Total	$600,000	Total	$600,000

a. Using the statement above, indicate what is meant by a narrow capital margin in this case. Why with the present capital is management unable to borrow $50,000?

b. Management has a large order that will yield a generous profit margin if operations are managed efficiently and on this basis has decided to use the financial budget as a "last-ditch" stand to apply for a $50,000 six-month loan. The following condensed financial budget is taken to the bank in support of the application for the loan. Interest at 8 percent will be paid at the end of the sixth month.

	Future Months					
	1st	2nd	3rd	4th	5th	6th
Expected receipts	$10,000	$10,000	$15,000	$30,000	$40,000	$20,000
Expected expenditures	20,000	30,000	30,000	20,000	10,000	10,000
Excess cash	(10,000)	(20,000)	(15,000)	10,000	30,000	10,000
Cumulative excess cash	(10,000)	(30,000)	(45,000)	(35,000)	(5,000)	5,000
Interest						$ 2,000

(1) What details about cash receipts and expenditures should management be prepared to offer the loan officer of the bank as supplementary schedules to the summary statement above?

(2) According to the interest charges, when does management plan to borrow the $50,000? When will management repay it? On the basis of the expected flow, what modification of the repayment

plan could management offer that might make the lender more willing to grant the loan?

(3) What is the *expected value* in your opinion of the $50,000 loan request?

(4) Without explaining how it could be done, what capital management decision might be considered to relax the present constraints? What are the limitations of the capital management approach to a problem like this?

12

Receivables
Financing

Cashing receivables, like unsecured borrowing, is an integral part of cash management. Often in considering the details of the financing, this is likely to be forgotten. Chapter 9 dealt with receivables and their internal relationships to income and profit; now we will show how the external management problem is related specifically to cash flows for liquidity and profit. The term *receivables financing* is used in the customary sense here to mean selling, and pledging open-account trade receivables in exchange for cash.

REASONS FOR RECEIVABLES FINANCING

This is a secured form of financing; but, like unsecured borrowing, the basic purpose is to obtain the maximum cash funds at the lowest possible solvency risk and at minimum cost. These are general goals for all forms of external financing, but they do not tell us why businesses use their trade receivables particularly for this purpose. One important reason for financing with receivables is that market facilities are highly developed, so that almost any kind of manufacturing and merchandising business can get cash by pledging or selling its accounts receivable. Included in the markets are financial services of factoring companies, commercial finance companies, and commercial banks. While at one time the market serviced textile manufacturers almost altogether, today manufacturers and distributors of iron and steel, furniture, leather goods, toys, sporting goods, tools and light machinery, and many other products may benefit from the services.

Receivables financing is the only form of financing that offers the business a choice between selling the assets outright or borrowing on their collateral to get

284

the cash. Financial managers see freedom for action in this kind of financing that is present nowhere else.

No other asset reflects more directly the level of current operations than receivables. When credit sales increase, the investment in receivables increases; and, when sales decrease, the investment decreases. The tendency is for businesses to be short of cash when operations expand and to be long on cash when contraction takes place. Borrowing on receivables security or selling receivables offers the flexibility that financial managers may need to meet this dynamic fluctuating operation, borrowing during peak production and sales and returning the funds to the cash balance and to the financial agency when operations are contracted.

Receivables financing was considered in the paragraph above as a passive rather than an aggressive factor in operations, the result rather than a cause of increasing credit sales. We can see the latter effect, however, if we think of credit sales as part of the total operating cycle in which receivables financing in period one supplies the cash for raw materials purchases and finished inventory purchase and manufacture in period two.

A study of the forms for receivables financing has much to offer toward understanding better the benefits and limitations of this kind of financing. We will consider the forms for factoring receivables first and then for borrowing on the pledged assets.

FACTORING

The selling or *factoring* form is called the factoring agreement which is a mutual acceptance of the sales terms and conditions in which the factoring agency is the *sole* purchaser of all the credit sales.

Before financial managers decide to sell receivables outright, they should understand the terms of the contractual relationship between the business and the financial agency. First the sale of receivables is directly tied to the credit sales. Ownership of the receivables is absolute in the factoring agency, and the receivables sale contract is completed when the goods are delivered to the customer. A completed sale means that the factoring agency assumes the responsibility for ledgering the accounts, collecting on them, and taking the losses on bad debts.

One of the most important provisions from the liquidity viewpoint deals with the price or return the selling business gets from the receivables sale. The purchase price is stated as a percentage of the cash discount value of the credit sale. If $10,000 in merchandise is sold, for example, on terms 2/10 net 60, the factor's purchase price and the receivables selling price is $9,800, $10,000(1 − 0.02) = $9,800. The *advance payment* to the business may be a stated percentage up to 90 percent of their cash discount value. This is called an *advance payment* because it is paid to the business before the accounts mature. The balance *less charges* for services of financing, adjustments for returned or damaged merchandise, and adjustments resulting from late deliveries is returned to the business later at a time called the *average due date.*

To show how the purchase price operates, suppose that receivables with a $10,000 invoice price are sold on a discount basis of 2 percent, 90 percent of the value to be advanced immediately and 10 percent at a later date. The business will receive a first check for $8,820 immediately: 90(0.98 × $10,000). Assuming that there are no merchandise returns, the business will receive a check for $980 ($9,800 — $8,820) later on the average due date of the accounts, less interest and service charges.

The average due date is an important term for financial managers to understand because it is used for two different purposes. It sets the date for the receipt of the final installment from the sale of receivables, and it sets the terminal date for computing interest charges on the 90 percent advance received from the factor. The average due date is a weighted average based on the days that each account has to run from the time it is sold to the factor until the day that it matures. The method of averaging the due date including the ten days for check clearance is illustrated in Table 12.1. Assume that these accounts are sold on April 15, 1971, which in this case we will call the *focal date*.

TABLE 12.1
COMPUTING AVERAGE DUE DATE
FOCAL DATE APRIL 15, 1971

Account Number	Net Value of Receivable	Date Due	Days from Focal Date	Cash Discounted Value (4%)	Weighted Cash Value
1	$ 10,000	4/20/71	5	$ 9,600	$ 48,000
2	2,000	4/20/71	5	1,920	9,600
3	6,000	4/30/71	15	5,760	86,400
4	10,000	5/10/71	25	9,600	240,000
5	8,000	5/15/71	30	7,680	230,400
Total	$36,000			$34,560	$614,400

Weighted average days to maturity: $\frac{\$614,400}{\$ 34,560} = 18$ days to May 3

Weighted average-	18 days
Check clearance period	10 days
Total days	28 days

Average due date May 13 (April 15 + 28 days)

Interest charges are paid by the business on the 90 percent advance of funds from the date of the receivables sale, to their average due date. Using a 6 percent interest rate on an advance of 90 percent, the interest will be 28/365 × $31,104(0.06) = $143.14.

Factoring charges, or *commissions* as they are also called, are the major financing expenses for the business. Charges range from $1\frac{1}{2}$ percent to as high as 3 percent every time receivables are sold. In general, account charges on short maturities are less than on long. The rate is based on the cash discounted value of the accounts, and total commissions are a linear function of the value of the sales. The function of a 2 percent rate is $C = 0.02(X)$, and a \$10,000 sale will cost the business \$200.

$$C = c(X) \qquad\qquad 12.1$$
$$= 0.02(\$10{,}000)$$
$$= \$200$$

If accounts are sold at this rate every 35 days, the annual charges using 365 days would be \$2,000 or 20 percent of the \$10,000 receivables value. This may seem like an exceptionally high rate, but it is not necessarily so if it is compared with what it would have cost the business to maintain its own services of credit analysis, ledgering, collecting, and risk taking.

When a business decides to factor receivables, it will have to notify its customers that the accounts are payable directly to the factoring agency. This explains the term *notification financing* that is used in referring to factoring. Notification is made by way of a stamped notice on the sales invoice that the account obligations are payable directly to the financial agency.

THE SPECIAL BORROWING FORM

The special borrowing form is patterned somewhat on the factoring agreement and is often called a *sale* of receivables but is interpreted legally as a loan rather than as a sale. Some of the most important provisions of the agreement will be summarized here.

A factoring company, commercial finance company, or commercial bank may use this special agreement, although the form was developed originally by commercial finance companies. No commitments are made by either party to buy or sell all receivables as they are in factoring. But the business agrees to offer receivables of its choice to the finance company from time to time, and the finance company agrees to buy from time to time the accounts that are acceptable to it. While the finance company prefers to be the sole purchaser of these accounts, there is actually nothing to prevent the business from offering them to competing financial agencies or to hold onto some of the receivables themselves. An interesting fact is that the receivables that are *sold* never leave the premises of the business nor are the customers notified that their accounts have been sold. This form of financing, therefore, is *nonnotification* financing.

There is no intention on the part of the financial agency to assume the risk of loss on these receivables; the financial agency has the right of recourse against the financing business in case the customer defaults on the receivables.

The purchase price is usually the net value of the receivables rather than their cash discount value, and withholdings are usually about 20 percent of their net value. This withholding is a margin of security to protect the lender against losses on receivables.

The agreement states that the total financing charge is a single daily charge that may vary between 1/40 and 1/20 of 1 percent per day. These are the only charges for the financing, and they are simple to compute. A $10,000 cash advance on receivables at 1/20 of 1 percent per day and maturing in twenty days will cost the business $100. Cost of the financing is a linear function of the number of days to maturity:

$$C = kr(X) \qquad\qquad 12.2$$

Where: C = Total cost of borrowing
k = value of receivables
r = Daily rate
X = Number of days to maturity

Substituting:

$$C = \$10,000[0.0005(X)]$$
$$= \$10,000[0.0005(20)]$$
$$= \$100$$

To simulate total costs at different maturity levels financial managers need merely to substitute the number of days to maturity in the equation each time in place of X. The student may want to verify this by graphing the function, putting number of days to maturity on the X axis and total cost of borrowing on the Y axis. This equation can be changed slightly by letting the constant k be a given maturity like twenty days and letting receivables be the independent variable X. This will give us a "program" for determining total financing costs for an infinite number of alternative quantities of receivables of a given maturity.

The Collateral Note Form   The collateral note has had a long and successful history as an instrument for secured receivable borrowing, and the form was well established legally and financially long before the special receivables borrowing agreement was developed in this country. This is one of the simplest and yet most versatile of all financial forms. The note identifies the financing as borrowing and not as the sale of receivables. The note may be made payable on demand or on a stated date. The whole securing contract may be written on one side of the instrument, or the monetary transactions portion may be contained on its face with the collateral pledge on the back.

Since this is not a sale agreement, we do not usually think in terms of the sale price of the receivables. But there is a more-or-less fixed loan policy on this kind of financing that is comparable to that in the special agreement. The general policy is to lend up to 70 or 80 percent of the net value of the invoices. This might be called the "price" of the receivables, and also becomes the amount of the debt stated on the note. A commercial bank will set up the full amount, let us say 80 percent, as a deposit credit for the business available for withdrawal immediately, although the bank may require the business to hold 10 percent or more of the loan in a "compensating" balance. Suppose that $10,000 (80 percent) is advanced on $12,500 of receivables and that $1,000 (10 percent) has to be held in a compensating balance. The actual working fund of cash then becomes $9,000 on $12,500 of receivables collateral.

Repayment of the debt is related directly to the terms of the note and not to the maturities on the receivables, although it can be expected that the maturity of the note will be geared to the maturities of the receivables. All financing charges are stated in a single interest rate on the face of the note. They are stated as annual rates and are limited in amount by state laws. In the illustration above, this would be figured on the $10,000 base, even though a portion of the loan has to be kept on balance. Interest is usually paid at maturity but in some cases is deducted from the amount of the advance as a discount at the time the loan is made.

The struggle by commercial finance companies and their business clients to obtain favorable court rulings acknowledging the legality of assigning accounts receivables for borrowing has been a long but now a successfully concluded one. Almost every state acknowledges either by statute or by court decision that creditors receiving properly executed assignments of receivables have prior financial rights to the exclusion of all other creditors.

In *validation* states, the title to the receivables is valid just by executing the agreement or collateral pledge and by conveying the assignment form with a schedule of accounts to the financial institution. In *recordation* states, title to the accounts is secured for the creditor if the business records in the clerk's office show notice of assignment or intent to assign receivables accounts with a certain financial agency. A few states have bookmarking laws, requiring that the receivables ledger of the business be marked indicating assignment. Even when not required by law, financial managers may want the books marked, and the creditor wants them marked sometimes, to prevent the business from making duplicate assignments of the same accounts.

QUALIFYING FOR RECEIVABLES FINANCING

Qualifying to sell receivables as compared with borrowing on them requires quite a different manner of preparation. A great deal of overlap exists in the services performed by financial institutions. Commercial banks buy receivables outright on factoring agreements as well as make loans on receivables collateral; factoring companies lend money on special receivables financing agreements as well as purchasing receivables outright on a factoring contract; and large commercial finance companies now have factoring departments and divisions in addition to lending on special sales contracts and on collateral notes. Financial managers, therefore, would do well to qualify on the basis of the kind of financing desired, such as sales of receivables or borrowing, rather than on the basis of the institution supplying the funds.

QUALIFYING TO SELL RECEIVABLES

The purchaser of receivables is interested in a company's capital position but not for the same reason as are unsecured or secured lenders. The purchaser of receivables is concerned with the size of the firm's net capital, net working capital, and its profit experience mainly because he wants to deal with a going concern for continuing financing. But qualifying to sell receivables without recourse on a factoring contract requires first of all that the seller's customers who become directly and wholly responsible for paying the receivables meet the standards of high credit standing. The first step in qualifying to sell receivables outright then is to select credit customers who will be acceptable to the factoring agency. The following questions might be asked about the prospective customer: Does he have capital stability for continuing operations? Does he pay his accounts promptly? Is the business efficiently managed as evidenced by its profitability?

Ages of the receivables at the time they are offered for sale also affects their acceptability. After the factoring agreement is completed, this is not a problem, however, because each credit sale has first to be approved by the factor. But, when existing accounts on the company's books are factored, their ages do affect their marketability. Receivables that have exceeded in age the cash discount period, may be difficult to sell to a factor.

Maturities of the receivables have a very important effect on their qualifications for outright sale. Accounts with short maturities generally are favored over longer maturities because shorter maturity means more rapid turnover of the accounts, less risk, and more commission fees for the factor.

Finally, the type of merchandise sold has some effect. Merchandise with stable prices qualify better than products with unstable prices, and products subject to sudden style change and fluctuating demand do not produce the most saleable kinds of receivables.

QUALIFYING TO BORROW ON RECEIVABLES SECURITY

In borrowing on receivables security, more emphasis is necessarily placed on the general credit of the business that is doing the borrowing than it is in factoring; and less emphasis is placed on the credit standing of their customers whose receivables are pledged to secure the borrowing. Capital qualifications of the borrower are emphasized because this will tell whether the business can pay its debts in case the customer defaults on receivables obligations. The ratios total debt/net capital, current assets/current liabilities, quick assets/current liabilities, and net working capital/current liabilities are basic credit analyzing tools that are used by the creditor. Still the ratios in this case are used primarily to indicate to the creditor general rather than specific borrowing capacity. The maximum loan limit for example is not likely to be related directly to the quantity of the company's net capital or net working capital as it is in unsecured lending. The most important item setting the debt limit is the *quantity* of pledgeable receivables. Age and maturity of the receivables are important primarily for what they indicate as to prospective cash flows into the borrowing firm. In the last analysis in a loan situation, it is the borrower's total ability to pay that is the important factor; although indirectly this is affected by the quality of the pledged receivables.

LIQUIDITY, SOLVENCY AND PROFITABILITY

The goal in receivables financing is to maximize cash receipts, which means getting the maximum amount of cash from the given quantity of receivables sold or pledged. Given a certain quantity of receivables then, the decision as to which of the three methods of receivables financing to use would turn on which form could supply the largest sum of cash in the shortest period of time.

The illustration in Table 12.2 is a comparison of the liquidity effects on the business of cashing $36,000 in receivables accounts in three different ways: by factoring, by using the special financing agreement, and by using the collateral note. Assumptions about specific terms of the contracts are arbitrary because this is not intended to show that one method of financing is superior to the other two. Different receivables buying and lending policies of financial agencies means that

TABLE 12.2
LIQUIDITY COMPARISON
FACTORING AGREEMENT
FACTORING CHARGE 2%
INTEREST 6% ANNUALLY

Invoice value of receivables		$36,000	
Less 4% discount on invoice		1,440	
Value on shortest selling terms		$34,560	
Advance April 15 @ 90% of $34,560			$31,104
Gross balance on average due date			
($34,560—$31,104)		$ 3,456	
Less factoring charge (2% of $34,560)	$691		
Less interest for 28 days on $31,104	143		
Total financing charges		834	
Net receipts on average due date			2,622
Total cash receipts			$33,726

SPECIAL FINANCING AGREEMENT
DAILY INTEREST RATE 1/25 OF 1% DISCOUNTED ON APRIL 15
BALANCE OF CASH ON MAY 13
CASH RECEIPTS APRIL 15

Net value of receivables		$36,000
Advance April 15 @ 80% of $36,000		28,800
Gross balance on May 13 ($36,000—$28,000)	$7,200	
Less financing charge @ 0.0004 daily for 28 days:		
$36,000 (0.0004) 28	403	
Net receipts May 13		6,797
Total cash receipts		$35,597

COLLATERAL NOTE PLEDGE
ANNUAL INTEREST CHARGE 6% DISCOUNTED ON APRIL 15
80% CASH ADVANCE AT TIME OF BORROWING
BALANCE OF CASH AS RECEIVABLES MATURE

Net value of receivables		$36,000
Advance April 15 @ 80% of $36,000		28,800
Less 10% compensating balance		2,880
Advance April 15		$25,920
Gross balance on May 13 ($36,000—$25,920)	$10,080	
Less annual interest charge of 6% for 28 days		
(365-day year): $28,800 (0.000164) 28	133	
Net receipts May 13		9,947
Total cash receipts		$35,867

COMPARATIVE CASH RECEIPTS

	4/15	5/13	*Total Cash Receipts*
Factoring	$31,104	$2,622	$33,726
Special financing	28,800	6,797	35,597
Collateral note	25,920	9,947	35,867

this decision has to be made separately on the merits of each case. The purpose of the example is to provide a model approach to the general decision-making problem that can be applied to any specific case. The following assumptions are relevant to this one model. First, the net value of the receivables is $36,000. Second, each account is discountable at 4 percent, so that the total accounts have a cash value of $34,560 [$36,000(1 — 0.04)]. Third, interest rate is 6 percent for a 365-day year. Fourth, the date of financing is April 15, and the average maturity for the accounts is 18 days from April 15 to May 3, see Table 12.1. This last item is important; factoring adds 10 days to the 18 days making it 28 days to May 13.

In summarizing the liquidity effect of the three forms of financing, several observations are apparent. First, the factoring arrangement supplies the largest sum of cash at the outset on April 15, but the total received is less than under the other two forms. The large sum at the beginning of the period results from the 90 percent advance, and the smaller total sum results from limiting the receipts to their cash discounted value. The smallest beginning cash flow accompanies collateral note financing. The reason for this is the 10 percent compensating balance requirement. If the compensating balance were not required, the collateral note would yield about the same quantity of funds as the special borrowing form on April 15.

Timing is an important factor to consider, however, in evaluating alternative sources of cash and may spell the difference between successful and unsuccessful liquidity management. The larger quantity of funds at the beginning of the period reduces the risks of cash shortages and even provides funds for further expansion of operations. In comparing the special receivables financing form and the collateral loan form, one sees that they both return about the same total quantity of funds over the twenty-eight days.

Solvency considerations concern the debt-paying problems imposed on the business by receivables financing. The goal in management is to *use the form with the minimum risk of default*. This lends itself to precise quantitative measurement as do the two factors of liquidity and profitability discussed earlier. Table 12.3

TABLE 12.3
COMPARATIVE LIABILITIES

Factoring agreement	$——
Receivables financing agreement (80% of receivables value)	$28,800
Collateral note pledge (80% of receivables value)	$28,800

illustrates the comparative current liabilities created by the three different forms of financing. The factoring agreement providing for outright sales of the receivables relieves the business of all debt obligations, and this clearly is the method of financing with the lowest solvency risk to the business. The two borrowing forms contain the same risk quantities. Theoretically, the liability to the business is less direct on the special borrowing agreement than in the collateral note pledge because of the shield offered by the receivables. In practice, however, using this kind of borrowing makes the business even more vulnerable as the creditor can exercise his right of recourse against the business any time a customer is delinquent without waiting for a note to mature. In a note with a fixed maturity, on the other hand, the maturing of individual accounts does not affect the paying date of the debt.

In all three forms of financing the ratio of cash/current liabilities increases; but it increases much faster in factoring than in the other two forms because factoring does not increase current liabilities. The ratio of current assets/current liabilities and of quick assets/current liabilities are basically unchanged by the outright sale of receivables but may increase or decrease in the other two forms, depending on whether the ratios were smaller or larger than 1/1 at the time of financing.

There is no profit in financing. This statement holds true for secured borrowing as well as for unsecured trade credit financing and unsecured borrowing. As stated in Chapter 11, the profit feature of financing is altogether relative. Profits are earned by efficient management of assets, and lower financing costs leaves more of that profit for the business. This necessitates turning to the cost problem for profit considerations. In Chapter 11, a model interest rate equation was set up for unsecured borrowing: $R = (r_1 + r_2)$, in which r_2 represented the risk charge. The same model is applicable to receivables and inventory borrowing. The r_1 factor is no problem to determine because that is the prime money market rate and is the same whether borrowing is unsecured or secured. Where the secured effect enters is at r_2. It would seem that this would be lower when security like receivables are pledged to secure the promissory note or whatever specific debt form is used; but this does not necessarily follow because there are other important variables, mainly the D/E ratio and the NWC/CL ratio that are important solvency measures affecting risk conditions. One way of looking at it is that companies pledging receivables on borrowing contracts pay higher interest rates than borrowers on unsecured contracts because they are more tightly constrained by limited capital resources than firms that can borrow on their capital strength alone. It would be safe to say, however, that given the r_2 risk factor of a firm that can borrow without security, the same firm might be able to reduce r_2 slightly by the pledge of receivables.

On the matter of the three forms of receivables financing, profitability considerations are based on a comparison of the financial charges of the three forms; and this should not be difficult to determine now that the liquidity comparison is worked out above. Net financial expenses are the contractual charges plus secondary financing charges and minus savings. The most profitable form is the one with the lowest net financial expenses. A case in point is the special borrowing agreement that could, by its rigid terms, cause extra credit investigation, book-keeping, and collection charges to be imposed on the business. Factoring has the opposite effect in that it saves the business the expenses of credit investigation, bookkeeping, collection, and losses on bad debts. We assume that factoring $36,000 in receivables over a twenty-eight-day period saves the business $12 daily on credits, collections and bad debt losses but that using either one of the two bor-

TABLE 12.4
COST COMPARISON

Factoring agreement:		
$34,560 @ 2% factoring charge	$691	
Interest on $31,104 @ 6% for 28 days	143	
Gross financial charges	$834	
Less $12 daily savings for 28 days	336	
Net factoring charge		$498
Receivables Financing Agreement:		
@ 1/25 of 1% daily	$403	
Plus $3 daily extra services for 28 days	54	
Net borrowing charge		$457
Collateral Note Pledge:		
6% annually on $28,800 for 28 days	$133	
Plus $3 daily extra services for 28 days	54	
Net borrowing charges		$187

rowing forms requires extra internal expenditures of $3 daily to raise the quality
of the receivables to the level at which they are acceptable for sale or for use on
a collateral loan. Table 12.4 is a cost comparison of the three forms given the
same $36,000 net value of receivables discountable at 4 percent as was used in
the liquidity and solvency analysis. Recall that the 2 percent factoring charge is
based on the discounted value of the receivables and not on their net value of
$36,000.

Using the models in the table, any business can easily substitute its own figures
and arrive at a meaningful comparison of the alternative forms. There can be
little doubt that the note form of financing will usually be the cheapest; even if,
as shown in the previous section, it is not the most liquid form. But there is another
factor in computing the costs of borrowing that was not considered above. By
assuming that the business would be satisfied with whatever quantity of funds is
made available, we did not have to impute a cost to the compensating balance.
The compensating balance reduced the fund from $28,800 to $25,920. But suppose
that the business needs a minimum borrowing of $28,800. Then the total amount
of borrowing must be increased to the X quantity:

$$(X - 0.10X) = \$28,800$$
$$X = \$32,000$$

To prove that $32,000 is the correct amount of borrowing that will give the business
$28,800 substitute in the equation:

$$X - 0.10X = \$28,800$$
$$\$32,000 - .10(\$32,000) = \$28,800$$
$$\$28,800 = \$28,800$$

Substitution is a test to determine whether holding a 10 percent compensating
balance against the $32,000 loan will leave $28,800 for transactions: $32,000 −
$3,200 = $28,800.

A final aspect of the three alternative forms of financing that should be considered, although it may be difficult to quantify, is the internal control over credit
sales and receivables that is affected differently by each of the three forms. In
factoring, the seller usually has to have every credit account approved by the
factoring agency, which is understandable since the risk is transferred altogether
to the factoring agency. Fortunately, the factor assumes responsibility for the
credit analysis and investigation of new accounts, but freedom in decision making
for the seller is impaired somewhat by this requirement. Directly related to the
loss of control is the notice to the customer telling him to pay his accounts to the
factor instead of to the seller. This may disturb some customers, and it deprives
the seller of control over the cash for transactions. The special financing agreement
does not deprive the business of complete control over its credit sales, nor are
payments made directly to the financial agency by the customer. We will recall

that this is nonnotification financing and that the customer may not even be aware that the financing is taking place. But the lender requires a detailed assignment form from the borrower indicating precisely when every securing receivable matures; so that funds from their collection are channeled to the lender as they are collected, and, if a customer defaults on a receivable, the borrowing firm is liable immediately for its payment. Thus, receivables are controlled indirectly by the lending agency for cash flow purposes, as well as approving receivables before they are "bought" from the business at the start. Borrowing on the collateral note involves less external control than either one of the other two forms. This is the case for the reason that most of these loans are made by commercial banks, and commercial banks rely heavily on the borrower's capital resources even though specific receivables accounts are assigned to the bank to secure the loan. There is no notification to the customer of the receivables pledge; the customer's payments are made directly to the business, and the receipts may be held or used internally in any way the financial managers desire until the promissory note matures. The item of first importance in the collateral note contract is the signature of the financial officers who bind the business to repay the debt; then the receivables collateral figures are only secondary if the company defaults on its note. There is a big difference between this secondary kind of control reserved pretty much for cases of default and the primary kind of control exercised from the time of the credit/sale in a factoring arrangement and to a lesser extent in the special receivables financing agreement.

SUMMARY

Chapter 12 considers the ways in which receivables can be used to obtain cash. Various technical forms of receivables financing are examined. The primary purpose of the analysis is to evaluate the forms of financing and the markets for receivables financing in terms of their effect on the company's liquidity, solvency, and profitability. Three model illustrations are set up that could be applied to any business organization enabling it to select between using factoring facilities, special receivables collateral forms, and standard bank borrowing forms. The model forms identify the liquidity, solvency, and cost factors related to alternative sources of the financing.

PROBLEMS

1. Company A is a medium-sized manufacturer of women's leather gloves, purses, and shoes. The business is located in a city with 50,000 population. It operates with a small amount of equity capital relative to its total sales during peak seasons and has had a policy of financing its needs as much as possible out of income. Most of its sales are made to women's shoe stores and to small and medium-sized department stores on sixty-to-ninety-day credit with no discount

allowance. Its customers are often slow and irregular in their payments, making it difficult to budget cash; but bad debt losses are very low. The company is owned by five persons, three of whom are considered well-to-do but who do not want to put more capital into the business even though a shortage of funds in some periods prevents the business from taking advantage of purchase discounts. With this information, review the receivables financing prospects for the business.

2. Mr. Ford, the financial manager of a wholesale grocery, decided that if a financial budget is useful to qualify for unsecured borrowing the same tool might be used to help qualify for receivables financing. He expects 80 percent of his monthly sales to be on credit. He expects that 30 percent of the credit sales will be collected in the month of sale and that the remainder will be collected in sixty days from the end of the month. The sixty-day lag in collections would create a need for borrowing. He thought that his receivables would be in demand and that he could borrow from his bank or local finance company and get an 80 percent cash advance. The financing could be done at the end of each month using receivables generated by each month's sales. The receivables that he had on hand at the present were not large, and he would leave those out of the borrowing plan. In addition, he would let his collections of 70 percent be budgeted to retiring the debts to see how long it would take to retire the accumulated indebtedness. Complete for him the following receivables financing budget. Assume that 1 percent is charged on the monthly balance of outstanding debt for the total financing services.

RECEIVABLES FINANCING BUDGET

	January	February	March	April	May	June	July
Sales estimate	$10,000	$15,000	$20,000	$40,000	$50,000	$15,000	$10,000
Credit sales (80%)	8,000	12,000					
Less collections (30%)	2,400	3,600					
Available for borrowing	5,600	8,400					
Borrowing @ 80%	4,480	6,720					
Cumulative borrowing	4,480	11,200					
Collections for repayment @ 70%	—	—					
Cumulative repayments	—	—					
Balance due on debt	4,480	11,200					
Monthly interest	44.80	112.00					
Cumulative interest	44.80	156.80					

a. Is Mr. Ford's point well taken that the same basic tool used to qualify for unsecured borrowing might help to qualify him for receivables financing? Explain the similarities and differences in the two kinds of borrowing situations.

b. What is the maximum borrowing?

c. When will the debt be fully retired?

  d. Is the 70 percent collection the only source of funds available for paying off debts of this kind?

3. Fiscal Fitness, Incorporated manufactures sporting goods for a year-round market. In an effort to maintain level production, the business often runs out of cash near the end of the month. As a result, purchase discounts often have to be foregone; and on some occasions the business is even late in making its trade credit payments. Conditions improve for the first fifteen or twenty days of the next month as collections pick up, but then it is the same story over again. Mr. Mims, the financial manager, has observed a gradual increase in the average age of the accounts and an increase in the number of bad debts. He has in the past avoided borrowing by letting his trade creditors carry the extra weight, but recently he decided that a major financial problem was taking shape in his organization. He felt that in admitting that this condition existed, the first step had been taken toward solving it. He consulted his company's banker about a flexible, unsecured, short-term loan program but was told that more capital would be needed for this purpose. He realized that this would not be practical because of the size of the business, the local nature of its operations, and the lack of proper financial contacts and experiences. The banker had heard of a financial agency in a nearby larger city, however, that was advertising a factoring service. He volunteered the opinion that while these agencies' charges tend to be higher than bank loan rates, it would be justifiable in this case to pay the higher rates temporarily until more capital could be obtained for unsecured borrowing. Mims went straight to the factoring company and was given a copy of the factoring agreement for further study.

   He studied the form looking specifically for answers to the following questions. How soon could the cash be secured after the financing is approved? What percentage of the receivables could be turned into cash? When would the "debt" have to be repaid? What effect would the financing have on his current financial condition and on his capital in case he should want to do unsecured borrowing in the future? Would the factoring agency, because of its financing practices, do anything to reduce the business' future sales and profits? What would he be getting in the way of financial services for the fees that he would have to pay? Lastly he wondered whether the factor would come in and try to run the business. Advise Mr. Mims on these points.

4. The financial manager of Company *X* has been factoring his company's receivables for several years. Over these years the company has expanded its capital. It has improved its general credit rating, and the manager is wondering whether the owners of the business would not benefit from borrowing on the security of the receivables instead of selling them outright to a factor. Under the present factoring agreement the business is charged a 2 percent fee on its total credit sales and 6 percent interest on the advance of funds to the average due date. The company has been receiving a monthly advance of 90 percent on the discounted value of the receivables at the end of each month and the balance on their *average due date*. A commercial finance company is offering cash advances,

on the other hand, of 80 percent on the credit sales with the balance payable when the last receivable matures. But a service charge of 1/30 of 1 percent would be charged on the invoice price of the receivables. At the same time, a local bank offered to lend up to 80 percent on the receivables but would require a 10 percent compensating balance on the amount loaned. Interest at the annual rate of 7 percent would be charged by the bank without any additional charges. The financial manager expects his monthly credit sales to average about $40,000 with their maturities checking out in a pattern something like the following, and he expects to offer the customers at the same time 4 percent discounts.

Account Numbers	Amount	Days of Maturity
21	$ 8,000	20
10	6,000	25
15	10,000	30
20	16,000	30
Total	$40,000	

a. Compare the amount of cash that would be received from each of the three different methods of receivables financing.
b. Compare the costs of the various forms of financing, assuming that the monthly cost of operating a credit and collections division would be $300. Include the interest charge for replacing the compensating balance.
c. Compare the effects of the respective financing forms on the: (1) current ratio, (2) acid test ratio, and (3) working capital ratio.

13

Inventory Financing

Inventory financing means borrowing on inventory security. The general purpose is the same as that of receivables financing, namely to use pledgeable assets to correct temporary maladjustments in cash. Receivables financing is done when management cannot wait for account collections to supply cash needs in the normal course of business, and inventory financing is done when management cannot wait for inventory sales to supply either receivables or cash in the normal course of business. In the early days of inventory financing, the physical properties themselves served to secure the debts; but today inventory collateral is used in place of the inventories to accommodate trade, thus leaving the physical inventories free for processing, storage, display, and sale.

INSTITUTIONAL SERVICES

Commercial banks supply most of the cash for inventory loans made to business and banks often make loans starting with inventory collateral to loans on receivables and unsecured loans. Inventories are popular collateral because (1) inventory is tangible and easily identifiable; (2) there is almost always some kind of market for inventories in case they have to be reclaimed; and (3) making such loan requires a minimum of credit analysis and evaluation.

Management may be wise to examine different inventory financing services. Some banks specialize in certain forms of inventory lending, like lending on factory inventories or on warehoused goods. This specialization may even extend to certain kinds of goods, like furniture, textiles, or steel just to cite a few. Specialization while an advantage to some businesses, may be a disadvantage to businesses handl ing several kinds of inventory. In weighting different lending services, the business may find that some are more generous than others in their valuations of inventories or in the percentages of cash advances granted on the collateral. Some may allow longer maturities than others, although maturities are usually closely tied to the expected sale date for the inventories. Still others may be noted for charging slightly lower interest rates than other lenders, although here again the type of inventory pledged may have some influence.

Less important quantitatively than commercial banks in this field of lending are factoring companies and commercial finance companies. These may combine inventory and receivables financing. Thus, funds may be advanced on goods in the process of manufacture or in storage. Then, when the inventories are sold on credit, inventory collateral will be replaced by receivables collateral to continue the lending; or, in the case of a factor, inventories in the process of manufacture may serve as security until the credit sale and then receivables can be substituted.

QUALIFYING TO BORROW

Most businesses at one time or another depend on inventories to secure short-term loans. Some seasonal businesses depend on them regularly; others depend on them intermittently to supplement unsecured borrowing; and still others use them only to meet emergency borrowing needs. In any case, definite requirements must be met if the business is to borrow on favorable terms. Terms of borrowing include a statement of financial charges on the loan and a statement of the maturity of the loan. We will consider first, the general requirements and, second, the specific inventory requirements for obtaining favorable borrowing terms.

GENERAL CREDIT REQUIREMENTS

The key question for financial managers to consider is: What general credit standards are we expected to meet to secure favored treatment from creditors on the inventory borrowing? Commercial banks are likely to emphasize general credit factors more than commercial finance companies and factors; and certain kinds of loans, such as loans on factory inventories and on "floored" inventories, are likely to emphasize general credit of the borrower more than loans on warehoused inventories and inventories in transit for reasons that will be explained below. But all forms of inventory lending look in the first instance for certain standards of capital strength in the borrower. For example, the net capital relative to total debt, the ratio of working capital/current liabilities, and the net profits ratios are all considered by the creditors as measures of debt-paying capability of the business and general operating efficiency of management for inventory financing. The size of the debts contracted and repaid in the past are also important considerations; in general, large loans promptly repaid convey more general credit strength to the borrower than small loans paid promptly.

General credit standing is important for inventory financing but the actual amount of the borrowing for which a business is able to contract will depend among other things on the value of the inventory and the facility with which the inventory can be converted to cash to meet a defaulted note, namely, its marketability.

The quantity of inventory security is the first factor affecting the amount of borrowing. Other factors being the same, businesses that hold large balances of inventories to maintain production and distribution goals have a chance to borrow larger sums than businesses with small amounts. With the loan margin at 70 percent, for example, an inventory balance of $10,000 would permit $7,000 of borrowing; while a balance of $5,000 would support only $3,500. The borrower may obtain not only a larger dollar loan but a larger margin of loan; thus, in the former instance the business may obtain a 75 percent loan or $7,500 on the $10,000 base but only 70 percent or $3,500 on the $5,000 base.

A second factor of much importance to the lender is the marketability of the inventory in case he is forced to claim it for a quick cash sale. Marketability of goods depends pretty much on how close they come to qualifying as staples. Staples are commodities that are produced in agriculture, mining, and manufacture that form the main inventory element in the production of finished goods. In general, these items make up the raw materials of industry. In discussing the liquidity of inventories in the normal production process in Chapter 8, raw material was placed below goods in process and finished goods because it was farther from the point of normal sale. Now, however, the creditor is concerned not with the normal but the abnormal condition of sale; he is concerned with the *extrinsic* liquidity rather than the intrinsic liquidity of the inventory. Because of the universal demand domestically and internationally for such commodities as cotton, grain, steel, lumber, and nonferrous metals, an active commodity market has developed in which these items can be readily sold by the creditor. As raw materials are combined with labor and fixed capital to produce specialized finished goods, they lose this marketability. This is not to imply that raw materials should be withheld from production to facilitate borrowing, but this is mentioned to give the reader a view of the active area for inventory financing.

Aside from the two qualifying factors of high value and marketability mentioned above, there are two other inventory characteristics that determine their qualifications for borrowing. One of these is price stability. We can be holding a large quantity of valuable merchandise that would appear to be a good potential source of borrowing; but, if price conditions in this particular goods market are unstable, creditors will shy away from making cash advances on such security except perhaps on a very narrow margin. Untested consumer goods may fit this category but so may some of our staples whose output is subject to wide fluctuation.

Products following a seasonal or even cyclical price pattern, on the other hand, are not in this class because their price changes are predictable; and the creditor can make allowances for these changes when setting the loan maximum and the maturity dates. Large businesses can regulate their prices to some extent and thus improve their borrowing conditions, but unfortunately small and medium-sized businesses that seem to depend most on inventory borrowing cannot do much to solve the problem. Some protection is offered small businesses by the commodity market; there the market mechanism not only helps to level out commodity prices but also offers the creditor a place to sell the collateral contracts that he receives from defaulting borrowers. The other of these secondary qualifying characteristics is the "storability" of the inventory. Some financing is secured by inventories while they are right in the factory being processed, in shipment, or even on the display floor for sale; but much of the financing is advanced on goods that are being stored in some warehouse. Some goods lend themselves more readily to long periods of storage than other, and those goods are also more favorable security for borrowing. Goods that need to be stored under certain temperature conditions are not ruled out altogether; they may just automatically set a short limit on the term of the borrowing.

FORMS FOR INVENTORY FINANCING

Forms for inventory borrowing cover a much wider area than receivables financing. We will approach the use of inventory forms by showing how they can be used to meet cash needs of business at different levels of production and sales, starting at the factory, going from there to the warehouse, then to the public carrier, and finally to the display floor.

Borrowing on Factory Inventories   The form for turning factory inventories over into cash is the *factor's lien* that will be discussed here. In 1823, the first legislative act was passed in England giving the creditor a lien on the inventories while they were on the manufacturer's premises, provided a notice was posted at the location of the inventories and provided a notice was filed in the clerk's office stating that the inventories were pledged to secure a loan. The English law became the model for legislative acts of a similar kind enacted later in this country. In 1911, New York State passed the first factor's lien law patterned on the early English law. This law has been broadened and clarified but even to this day serves as the model for our state factor's lien laws. The substance of the laws now in effect assert that:

1. Lenders may obtain a lien on all goods consigned from time to time to the debtor under a blanket agreement, and the liens are valid against all creditors from the date the notice is filed.
2. A sign is required to be posted on the premises of the debtor stating that a given lender has a lien on all of the inventories on the premises.

The factor's lien is the most flexible of all forms of inventory financing used today. The contract between the manufacturer and the financial agency is an agreement that the business will borrow from time to time from the financial agency and that the financial organization will at its discretion lend to the business on a promissory note or other evidences of debt. The inventory may include raw materials, goods in process, and finished goods. As new raw materials are brought onto the premises, they add to the borrowing base. The percentage of cash borrowing may vary between 60 and 80 percent of the inventory value.

The factor's lien is a functional approach to borrowing. As more raw materials come onto the premises, more cash may be borrowed; and, as raw materials are processed into finished goods, they become more valuable and increase the security base for more cash borrowing.

Figure 13.1 summarizes the flow of the debt instrument, inventory collateral, and cash in a typical factor's lien form of borrowing and repayment.

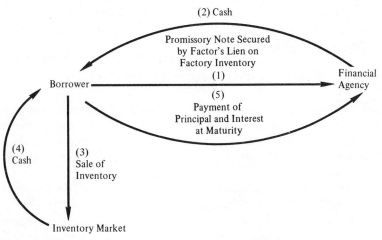

Figure 13.1. Borrowing on Factory Inventories.

Borrowing on Warehoused Inventories   Warehouse receipts are issued by public and field warehousing organizations. Public warehousing facilities, also called *terminal warehouses*, are usually located in large cities near railroad, trucking, and port terminals. There are terminal warehouse specialists that store petroleum products, vegetable oils, dairy products, and so on. The warehousing firm has the legal right to issue warehouse receipts to businesses depositing their goods. The warehouse receipt is a relatively simple instrument, the primary purpose of which is to acknowledge receipt of specific inventory items available for secured borrowing.

Field warehousing concerns, however, supply the bulk of all commercial warehouse receipts collateral for short-term borrowing. This field service is supplied when licensed warehousing firms take their storage and warehouse services directly to the premises of the business for generating financing collateral. The idea of taking the warehousing service to the business gained great impetus during the depression years of the 1930's as commercial banks, smarting from their losses on unsecured loans and on loans secured by real estate and stock market collateral, turned to inventory as a more reliable loan base. During this time also, the United States Agricultural Department through its surplus crop loans developed a widespread interest in warehousing services and warehouse receipts as a medium for agricultural and commercial borrowing; and by 1950 the Uniform Warehouse Receipts Act had been adopted by all of our states. The cost to the borrower of terminal and field warehousing services are unit variable fees that are based on the value of the product or on the number of cubic feet occupied by the product.

Negotiable Warehouse Receipts   Warehouse receipts may be negotiable or nonnegotiable. Negotiable or *order* receipts are issued to the business and are endorsed in blank on the back, like an ordinary check or note, when it is used to secure a loan. Commercial banks do most of this lending, but commercial finance companies and factors also make loans on negotiable receipts. From the moment the goods are warehoused, the business can (1) keep the receipts and reclaim the goods from the warehouse at any time, (2) sell the receipt in the commodity market, or (3) borrow on the security of the instrument. When the instrument is used for borrowing, it gives the lender a title-bearing instrument that can be sold at any time in the commodity market to recover on a defaulted note. On the other hand, if the debt is paid on time, the instrument has to be released to the business borrower who can then recover his goods. Or the lender can release the receipt from time to time to the borrower so that he can withdraw inventories from storage for further processing and sale. Because of the risk of releasing the negotiable receipt, a nonnegotiable receipt is more often used.

Nonnegotiable Warehouse Receipts   The nonnegotiable receipt is issued directly to the bank or some other financial institution instead of to the business depositing the inventories, thereby making the financial agency the registered owner of the instrument. The only way that the goods can be released under such an instrument is on written order from the financial institution. Without risking the loss of inventories, the financial agency can accommodate the business by issuing a written order to the warehouseman to release from time to time inventories that need processing or that need to be delivered to complete a sale. If they need processing, the business can then substitute a factor's lien and give this to the bank for the portion of the inventories released from the warehouse. If the inventories are sold, then the seller can simply give the bank a trade bill drawn against his customer to replace the warehouse receipt.

Figure 13.2 illustrates the flow of inventories, warehouse receipt, and cash in a nonnegotiable warehouse receipt financing. Had this been a negotiable warehouse receipt, it would have gone first to the borrower and second to the financial agency.

Borrowing on Goods in Transit   One of the oldest and most widely used forms of collateral is the *bill of lading*, used to secure creditors' interests in inventories that are in transit by land, water, or air. Actually the bill of lading is very similar to the warehouse receipt in the way that it originates. It is a *receipt* given by a bonded carrier. The purpose of the financing is to release the funds that are tied

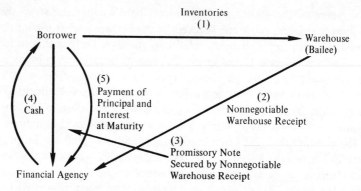

Figure 13.2.   Borrowing on Warehoused Inventories.

up in the inventories while they are transported from the factory, from a factory to a warehouse, or from a warehouse to a processing plant some distance away. The longer the transportation time the more important this kind of borrowing service becomes to the business; long shipments of two weeks or more may cause serious shortages in the inflow of cash unless the bill is used to bring in cash. Figure 13.3 shows the flow of inventories in transit as a source of borrowing using the negotiable bill of lading.

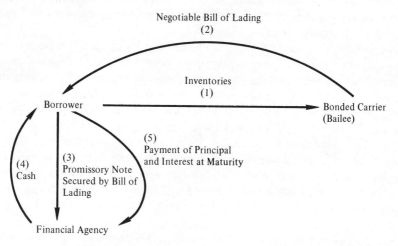

Figure 13.3.   Borrowing on Inventories in Transit.

Floor Plan Inventory Financing   The trust receipt is the collateral instrument used by dealers to secure financing to display and sell finished inventories like automobiles, household appliances, radios, television, and farm and road construction machinery and equipment. In these industries, the financing is known as *floor plan* or *factory to store* financing because it is used to get finished inventories onto the dealer's floor ready for sale. The services of a financial middleman, such as a commercial bank or finance company, are needed to carry the debt; so that the manufacturer or distributor can be paid in cash immediately when the goods are shipped. This is called *wholesale* financing to identify it as commercial or business financing and to distinguish it from financing the sale of the merchandise later on to the consumer. To distinguish the two kinds of financing, let us consider an automobile dealer. The dealer obtains wholesale financing using a trust receipt form of collateral which enables him to obtain automobiles for display and sale. Then when an automobile is sold, the customer secures financing on a collateral contract like a conditional sale instrument or a chattel mortgage, and the dealer retires his debt on the trust receipt note. We are concerned here only with the commercial or business side of the financing. Figure 13.4 illustrates the major steps in the financing. Figure 13.4 shows the release of inventories by the factory

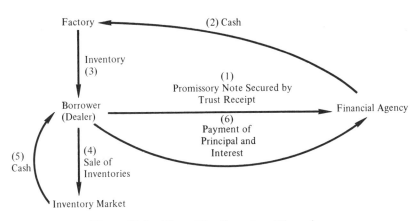

Figure 13.4. Floor Plan Inventory Financing.

as soon as the financial agency representing the borrower makes the cash payment. The dealer repays the debt to the financial agency as the inventories are sold and, thus, retires his notes.

The trust receipt offers a strong instrument for creditor control over inventory purchases. The only assets qualifying for this kind of financing are assets that are easily identifiable by serial, motor, and model numbers as indicated above. The sale price contains the markup over cost, and the business is not allowed to sell the objects below this price without the consent of the creditor. The creditor depends on the margin between their cost and their sale price as an extra cushion of cash. The creditor attempts to exercise close control over all of the cash received from the sales. The financing business is not the owner but merely the trustee holding the properties *in trust* for the entruster, the financial institution. The financing business adds the inventories to its assets and adds a note payable to its current liabilities. This form of financing can return a high rate of profit on a small capital investment. Suppose, for example, that a dealer with $20,000 of net capital investment turns over in one year $100,000 of floor planned financing, on which 10 percent is earned after taxes. In one year this business has earned 50 percent ($10,000/$20,000 = 50 percent). We have illustrated here how the inventory on the floor provides the security for purchasing it on credit. If the dealer owns the inventory on his floor outright, then he can use the same kind of contract (promissory note secured with a trust receipt) to borrow cash on his inventory and use that cash to buy more inventory or for any other need that he has in operating his business. Figure 13.5 shows how this kind of transaction would be executed. Figure 13.5 shows how owned and paid-for inventories on the retail dealer's floor can be used to raise cash. The trust receipt form of collateral is transferred to the financial agency until the inventories are sold, and then the debt is repaid with cash from the sale. The purchaser in the inventory market, however, is not affected by the financing between the borrower and the financial agency.

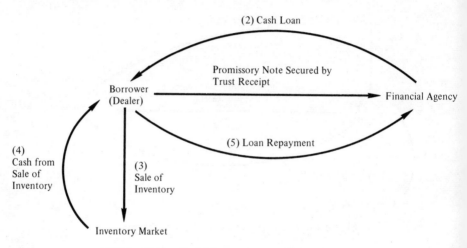

Figure 13.5.   Cash Borrowing on Floored Inventories.

MAKING THE DECISION

Decision-making issues are not as clear-cut in inventory financing as in receivables financing because the different inventory forms are not always competitive or easily substituted. For example, the bill of lading may have desirable features for financing which we cannot take advantage of unless we are shipping goods, and we are not likely to ship goods just to be able to take advantage of this kind of financing. Let us consider each of the above-described forms briefly now from the viewpoint of liquidity, solvency, and profitability.

LIQUIDITY CONSIDERATIONS

Financial managers should use the borrowing that will yield the largest sum of cash for a given quantity of inventory. Lenders extend larger margins of cash on some loans such as bills of lading and warehouse receipts than on factor's liens and trust receipts. Financial managers may benefit, in some cases, by shifting inventories from the factory to the warehouse for larger cash borrowings if production is not unfavorably affected thereby. Even the retail dealer in certain products may benefit by shifting some of his stock from the display floor to a bonded warehouse to obtain larger loan margins. Since we are concerned with the net cash effects of such decisions, we have to consider also the cash charges for storage and issuing warehouse receipts that would not be encountered as long as the goods are on the production line.

While we are searching for larger cash returns from inventory financing, we should not overlook the prospect of unsecured borrowing and receivables financing or of a combination of two or more forms of borrowing to gain the maximum cash return. The margins on inventory borrowing may range between 60 and 80 percent of the cost of the product, whereas receivables financing usually starts at 80 percent and goes up to 95 percent in some cases. Furthermore, the base value to the business of inventories after they are sold and become receivables is greater than before their sale.

SOLVENCY CONSIDERATIONS

To the extent that one inventory form can be substituted for another, management should try to use the form that exposes his business to the lowest possible solvency risk. We do not find the clear-cut difference here either that we find in receivables financing; the borrower on inventory collateral has a current liability added to his books in every inventory borrowing. But the different forms have different effects on the risks in case the business is hard pressed to pay its debt.

Factory inventories are not the most accessible to the creditors because of their changing location, their changing form, and finally because they may be sold in the ordinary course of business. This makes them difficult for the creditor to assemble; and, even when they are assembled, they may be difficult to sell at the factory site without taking a great loss. The risk of heavy loss compels the creditor to take his chances that the inventories will bring a better return if they are allowed to remain in production. Not so, however, with goods stored in a licensed warehouse. It is a relatively simple matter to sell a negotiable warehouse receipt through a commodity broker, and thus dispossess the borrower of his income-earning assets. Goods in transit also may easily be repossessed by the lender, or more simply the negotiable bill of lading can be sold in the same manner as the warehouse receipt.

PROFITABILITY CONSIDERATIONS

Financial managers seek the type of borrowing that will net the largest profit for the business. Just how can the form of financing affect sales and profits? Financing on warehoused inventories can supply cash to expand production, sales, and profits. This works in two ways. Buying raw materials in quantity lots reduces the purchase price, and the purchased inventories properly warehoused can be turned into cash for continuing or expanding operations. The same general principle is in operation for goods in shipment from their point of manufacture to marketing areas. Financing with bills of lading on goods in shipment provides the cash to continue and to expand profitable operations.

More complicated is making decisions to borrow from the most economical sources. In general, the charges for inventory borrowing are less than the charges for receivables financing; but charges vary within the class of inventory financing itself. Some of these factors are controllable by financial managers; others are not. Custom plays an important part: it may be customary to charge 8 percent on some kinds of loans and 6 percent on others. The quantity of the underlying inventories also plays a part in the borrowing cost; up to a certain point, it will cost less to borrow as the quantity of the securing inventory increases. Of some significance also is the size of the loan. Larger loans up to a point tend to bear lower rates of interest than small loans until a saturation point is reached.

On top of financial charges are incidental expenses that vary according to the method of borrowing. Borrowing on factory inventories requires filing a legal notice, which will have a small fee attached, and posting a sign at the entrance to the premises which is some added expense. In addition, there is inventory counting, sorting, and reporting in some cases to meet the creditor's demands. Warehousing creates expenses of storing and insuring the goods and paying the warehouseman's expences of issuing receipts that affect financing expenses and profits. This all reduces to saying that borrowing on inventories that are in the process of manufacture is less likely to deprive the business of income and profit than borrowing on warehoused inventories or on inventories in the hands of a public carrier. But these conditions of inventory financing are not altogether mutually exclusive as the alternative forms of receivables financing are: a given business may need to use the whole series of financial transactions from factory financing to warehouse receipts to bonded carrier, to floor plan financing.

CONTROL CONSIDERATION

Financial managers desire the form of financing that has the minimum amount of external constraint over decision making. Control over factory inventories is necessarily relatively loose; it has to be because of the changing character and location of the goods. Warehoused inventories are controlled by the warehouseman, as long as they are in his possession to the exclusion of all others even those with title to the inventories. As a bailee, his control is relinquished only after his charges have been paid; and then the control passes to the owner of the warehouse receipt. The borrower loses all control over the warehoused inventories unless they are released to him by the lender. Control over goods in transport also rests first in the public carrier which relinquishes its possession and control only after transportation charges are fully paid. Secondarily, they are controlled by the lender and the borrower can only regain possession and control if the accompanying debt is paid and the bill of lading given to the borrower.

INVENTORY FINANCING BUDGET

An inventory financing budget is a forecast for several months of the quantity of inventory expected to be generated by the business for borrowing purposes. Like the basic financial budget illustrated in Chapter 11, the inventory financing plan will also include the schedule for paying the principal and interest on the borrowing. Table 13.1 puts the inventory financing budget into practice subject

TABLE 13.1
INVENTORY FINANCING BUDGET

	January	February	March	April	May	June
Sales estimate	$10,000	$15,000	$ 30,000	$60,000	$100,000	$100,000
Level of production	36,000	36,000	36,000	36,000	36,000	36,000
Cost of goods sold	7,000	10,500	21,000	42,000	70,000	70,000
Addition to finished inventories	29,000	25,500	15,000	(6,000)	(34,000)	(34,000)
B.O.M. inventories:						
Raw materials	10,000	10,000	10,000	10,000	10,000	10,000
Goods in process	5,000	5,000	5,000	5,000	5,000	5,000
Finished goods	20,000	40,000	74,500	89,000	83,500	49,000
E.O.M. inventories	$64,000	$80,500	$104,500	$98,500	$ 64,500	$ 30,500
Available for borrowing	$29,000	$25,500	$15,000	$ —	$ —	$ —
Month-end borrowing	23,200	20,400	12,000	—	—	—
Cumulative debt	23,200	43,600	55,600	55,600	49,600	15,600
Month-end repayment	—	—	—	6,000	34,000	15,600
Debt balance	23,200	43,600	55,600	49,600	15,600	—
Interest @ 8%*	—	154.67	290.67	370.67	330.67	104

*Monthly interest computed at 1/12 of yearly rate.

to our assumptions. It is assumed first that production is a level amount and that cost of goods sold represents how much of the level production is expected to be sold. The balance between the production and sales plan is the amount of inventory available for financing. Assume that we can borrow 80 percent of the value of the "Addition to finished inventories." The peak financial needs will be reached by the end of March, after which time more inventories are expected to be sold than are produced; and the excess sales over production will be used to repay the debt in multiples of $1,000. Interest at 8 percent per annum will be paid monthly. Maximum indebtedness is expected to be $55,600 at the end of March. The first evidence of retiring this is in April, and the last $15,600 is repaid in June. The financial basis of repayment is sale of the finished inventory at cost. This is not a cash budget; and, therefore, we do not have to account for the flow of funds to other uses.

SUMMARY

Chapter 13 shows us how to use the current asset inventory as a pledge for borrowing cash to meet temporary operating needs. The approach to inventory financing is somewhat different than to receivables financing because of the different parts played by the assets in current operations. The purpose is to review alternative forms of inventory financing and to select the forms and institutional services that will give the business the best possible balance of liquidity, solvency, and profitability from the financing. Inventory financing is unique in that it may start at the factory level. It may move on from there to the warehouse form of financing, then to borrowing on inventories on transit and borrowing to secure inventory for the display floor and for sale. Finally, we consider the use of inventories on the floor that are owned by the business as a source of collateral for additional cash borrowing. No small item in inventory financing is the planning of inventory balances available for borrowing purposes. The inventory financing budget is a useful means of estimating the quantity of inventories that will be available for borrowing on collateral note contracts. A total inventory financing budget indicates the quantity of inventories available for borrowing each month and the quantity of funds that they will finance. It includes also a plan for retiring indebtedness including interest payments.

PROBLEMS

1. The Wanakee Manufacturing Company produces a high quality of cutlery, cases for wrist watches, and costume jewelry. While sales are rather sea onal and reach their peak around the Christmas and Easter holiday seasons and in the graduation and wedding months of late spring and early summer, an effort has been made by management to maintain a relatively level production schedule. Mr. Haynes, who is in charge of finances, had resorted to short-term borrowing in the past. In some cases the borrowing was on an unsecured basis, but more often on inventory collateral because the company's capital was relatively small in comparison with its temporary cash needs. This year Haynes decided to keep a monthly plan in advance for inventory security out of current operations and to project in an inventory financing budget the potential monthly borrowing. He felt that with a definite plan of this kind made well in advance he would be in a favorable bargaining position for cash. With this he proceeded to review the prospective sales, production, and financing relationships in the company.

    Purchases were planned so that raw materials supplies would be unchanged at $10,000, and production was planned so that partly finished goods would remain unchanged at $5,000. Cost of goods sold would be 70 percent of sales. Production of finished inventories would be in level monthly amounts of $40,000. Haynes reasoned that excess production of finished inventories could be used each month for financing on a borrowing margin of 80 percent. This would enable him to plan his monthly and cumulative borrowing potential. He was wondering about the sources of funds for repaying his borrowing and decided that this could be handled by selling off inventory investments from April through June. Complete the financial budget for him and evaluate.

INVENTORY FINANCING BUDGET

	January	February	March	April	May	June
Sales estimate	$10,000	$15,000	$30,000	$50,000	$80,000	$100,000
Level production	$40,000	$40,000	$40,000	$40,000	$40,000	$ 40,000
Cost of goods sold	7,000	10,500				
Addition to finished inventories	33,000	29,500				
B.O.M. inventories:						
Raw materials	10,000	10,000				
Goods in process	5,000	5,000				
Finished goods	20,000	53,000				
E.O.M. inventories	68,000	97,000				
Available for borrowing	33,000	29,500				
Month-end borrowing	26,400	23,600				
Cumulative	26,400	50,000				
Funds for payment	$	$				

2. The financial manager of the Commercial Tire and Rubber Manufacturing Company purchases raw rubber and certain costly chemicals for about two months of production at full capacity. The forming and molding process is relatively fast so that materials are usually run through the whole process in one or two days. Then the finished products are stored in a field warehouse for as long as a month in some cases after which they are shipped to company stores in outlying retail marketing areas. Write a paragraph describing the forms of financing that the company could have used to free its cash from the inventory investment from the time that the raw materials are purchased to the date of final sale.

3. Below is a group of remnants of diagrams indicating the transference of inventory and inventory collateral for secured borrowing. Complete the diagrams numbering each step and telling what kind of financing is represented by each.

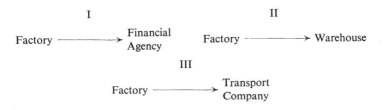

PART VI

CAPITAL
BUDGETING
THE
INVESTMENT
DECISION

14

Capital
Concept
for
Investment

From a practical viewpoint capital budgeting is a method of relaxing or un-coupling capital constraints to current operations, and we must not lose sight of the current operating goals of maximizing present share values as details and various ramifications of the investment decision are considered throughout Part VI.

In this chapter in particular, the basic principle of the uncoupling function of the capital variable is explained and illustrated showing how capital, which is constant for current operating analysis and decision making, changes to become the X variable in certain capital relationships. If we can condition ourselves to think of capital as a variable for conditioning current operations for profit and for efficient current asset and current debt management, then we will have dis-covered the single most important role played by capital budgeting in the whole field of financial management. Capital in its basic financial form refers to assets of a company that are constant for decision making in what has been described in this book as current operation situations. The corollary of this is that capital refers to assets that are variable for decision making in what we will learn to refer to as noncurrent or capital budgeting operations. Aside from its implications to method-ology in financial management, capital also has a very materialistic character that was discussed briefly in Chapter 2 and will be identified again below.

CAPITAL COMPONENTS

Capital components include net working capital and fixed capital.

NET WORKING CAPITAL

Net working capital is the difference between current assets and current liabilities (current assets — current liabilities = working capital). The constant nature of the capital during current transactions is illustrated in the simplest form below.

CURRENT OPERATIONS AND NET WORKING CAPITAL

Current Assets	Current Liabilities	Working Capital
$500,000	$128,000	$372,000
	Cash is used to purchase $50,000 in inventory	
$500,000	$128,000	$372,000
	Short-term bank loan of $25,000 is made	
$525,000	$153,000	$372,000
	Accounts payable in amount of $75,000 are retired	
$425,000	$ 53,000	$372,000
	Note is given to trade creditor in exchange for an open account in the amount of $30,000	
$500,000	$128,000	$372,000
	Sale of $50,000 in inventories at cost	
$500,000	$128,000	$372,000

Net working capital is the liquid part of the total capital and includes tangible assets altogether. It is not earmarked specifically in the current assets, but each current asset is capable of containing a capital value and a current value as will be shown later on, just as total current assets have a capital portion and a current operating portion.

FIXED CAPITAL

For the most part, fixed capital includes land, buildings, machinery, and equipment, the assets that are relatively stationary in point of physical structure and location. These are all tangible forms of capital; then there are intangibles like franchises, copyrights, and goodwill. But included in fixed capital are also common stocks held by one company to control another's assets. Individually and collectively fixed capital assets are low in liquidity compared with net working capital and for this reason are also often called "sunk" capital.

GROSS CAPITAL

Gross capital is the sum of net working capital and fixed capital: gross capital = net working capital + fixed capital. The following relationships are also significant: gross capital = capital structure, but gross capital ≠ capital structure. This means that gross capital is equal in quantity to the capital structure, but that it is not an identity (≠) to capital structure. It is important to distinguish between the equality of the two which is a quantitative relationship, and the identity of the two which is a qualitative relationship. In quantity they are the same, but in quality they are different: gross capital identifies the use of capital contained in the assets, and capital structure identifies the source of capital contained in the long-term liabilities and net worth. Part VI is concerned with the former and Part VII with the latter.

EQUITY CAPITAL

Total assets less total liabilities leaves equity capital, also called in financial management *net capital*. It is net because it represents the unencumbered part of total assets. It represents the owners' total share in the capital and, therefore, may also be expressed as:

$$\text{Net capital} = \text{equity capital} = \text{net worth}$$

Equity capital is the portion of gross capital remaining for the owners in case of a company's liquidation. This is another case of an equality but not an identity. As equalities, it may be helpful to think of net capital as the quantity *applied* of owners' capital and equity or net worth as the *quantity supplied* of owners' capital. The sources side of the issue will be considered, as pointed out above, in Part VII, although it is important to understand clearly the difference between these capital concepts before proceeding any further with the capital concept for investment.

CAPITAL BUDGETING AND PROFIT MANAGEMENT

From the financial viewpoint, capital investment decisions are designed to relax the constraints on current operations. In this section, we can go into some detail showing how capital investment decisions are related to the three areas in current operations: profit management, current assets management, and current debt management. The function of the two general categories of fixed and working capital will be identified as the discussion progresses.

PROFIT MANAGEMENT ISSUES

Profit management issues revolve about the profit set $P = X(b - c) - a$. In this section, each element of this equation which was considered constant in current profit management will be treated as capital variables for the special purpose of showing how capital investment decisions can alter one or more of the elements in the universal set individually and jointly. Considered separately here are capital budgeting decisions to change price b, unit variable cost c, quantity of output and sale X, and fixed charges a.

Price Control Decisions The student will recognize $b - c$ in $P = X(b - c) - a$ as the measure of unit profit contribution to fixed charges and expenses in current operations when the capital resources are fixed. He will recall also that the profit margin $(b - c)$ is a coefficient of the volume of sale X in the linear profit function.

Let us assume that capital is budgeted now to increase price for the duration of a planned new capital investment, that price elasticity is *less* than unity, and that all other factors are unchanged; the result then is an increase in the unit profit margin and an increase in expected optimal profits for a stream of future current operations. If these expectations are successfully communicated to the securities market the company's present share values will increase.

It is one thing to raise or lower a price which is completely at the mercy of price elasticity because the quantity of capital is constant as was shown in Chapter 6 and quite a different thing to make a capital investment decision suggested here to raise and to maintain the higher price *b*. To successfully attain the latter requires that financial managers evaluate their company's position in the industry before making costly investment decisions that may not be effective for increasing price. A good example of this is the firm producing under conditions of pure or nearly pure competitive conditions in which it does not have enough capital for overcoming price elasticity that would exceed unity. If the firm truly operates under conditions of pure competition, then it would, in fact, be useless to direct its capital investment to increasing profit through price control.

But in most risk categories of business, capital applications to tangible and intangible assets is effective for some price maintenance and control. The goal is attained by developing product and service images that will sustain price increases by causing demand not to respond unfavorably in the market place to slight price increases. Image-creating assets may consist mainly of intangible fixed assets like copyrights, trademarks, and advertising copy. To support the image-making action, however, requires increasing the capital balance of inventories, cash, and receivables. In addition to demand considerations price maintenance may be realized by controlling supply by investing in plant and equipment, patents, copyrights, and franchises which may all serve to give the business more control of output and of the total market in an oligopolistic manner that will support a limited price increase.

UNIT COST CONTROL

Starting with the profit function again: $P = X(b - c) - a$, capital expenditures are directed now to reducing and maintaining a lower unit variable cost (c) over the life of the capital investment. The effect is the same as in a price increase, to increase the unit size of the profit contribution; but this is a more practical approach with more long-lasting effects for most business than the former case. Other factors in the equation being unchanged, financial managers can expect to raise the level of optimal profits by investing in new capital that will reduce unit variable costs. Inflexible raw materials prices and fixed hourly wage rates challenge financial managers to employ greater quantities of capital to attain this lower level of unit variable costs rather than to attempt to attain this goal altogether within the confines of bargaining, negotiating, and corner-cutting with a fixed supply of capital.

Goal attainment may be reached through different decision paths. One course is to replace less efficient machinery and equipment with more efficient. Given more efficient capital facilities, productivity of labor and management is increased, spelling out lower unit variable costs. But to accommodate the new form of fixed assets, the optimal quantity of inventory, receivables, and cash holdings may have to be increased. Aside from replacing old facilities production efficiency may be increased by making net additions to total plant, equipment, and net capital margins of the current assets. The proportion in which fixed and net working capital are employed in an expansion decision compared with a replacement decision depends on the kinds of goods and services that are supplied by the firm. Capital expansion by a merchandising firm may consist mainly of placing larger orders and stocking larger quantities of inventories. Additions to storage space may have to accommodate the larger inventory holdings; if the new storage facilities save renting storage space, unit carrying costs of inventories will be decreased. Manufacturing firms may require a somewhat closer balance in expansion between what is needed in fixed and working capital to reduce and to maintain lower unit variable costs; while, in mining and exploration companies and in public utilities and transportation companies, unit costs are reduced almost altogether through tangible fixed capital investment.

QUANTITY CONTROL DECISIONS

In the goal of exercising greater control over the quantity of output and sale, financial managers seek to extend the output and sales (X) to higher levels in the function $P = X(b - c) - a$. The goal specifically is to extend the output and sale limits without changing substantially any other element in the profit set, thus, extending the limits of optimal profits for higher present share values.

One way of attaining this is by investing in advertising, market research, and direct selling facilities with possible departmentalization of sales services requiring additions to floor space, machines, sales, and research facilities. To complement investment for sales expansion, net investments will also need to be made in inventory, receivables, and cash balances. But sales expansion requires in most cases an increase also in plant facilities to accommodate the wider market for the goods. A new product or service may open up a whole new market for output and sales which inevitably requires new plant and equipment as well as added working capital.

FIXED COST CONTROL DECISIONS

Included in fixed costs are salaries of management, property taxes, insurance, and wear and tear and obsolescence of tangible and intangible fixed assets. This is the fixed cost factor a in $P = X(b - c) - a$ that, although subject to some reduction in value through new investment, will almost always increase with every one of the capital investment decisions suggested earlier. Investments can be made for price increase without unit variable costs increasing, and investments to increase volume of sale can be made without unit variable costs increasing. But neither form of decision can usually be made without fixed costs rising, nor could decisions to decrease unit variable costs likely be executed without fixed costs increasing. Usually the best that management can do is to minimize the increase in fixed costs when capital investment decisions are made to increase X or to decrease c. Exceptions to this case might occur should severe competition develop between suppliers of capital equipment thus enabling the business to buy new equipment of equal quality at a lower price than the old, resulting in a lower a value for future profit planning. Or an economic recession could cause capital facilities and accompanying fixed costs and expenses to decrease. Financial managers are not advised, however, to sit back and wait for either one of these two phenomena to occur. Since both of these are economic phenomena over which financial managers have no control, they do not have to be examined further. There is still one chance, however, that fixed costs resulting from new capital investment may be less than fixed costs related to old capital investment, and this may result from increased efficiency of fixed assets experiencing benefits of technological research. If new machines are more productive, for example, two machines may do the work where formerly three machines were needed. If two machines costing \$12,500 each produce as much as three machines costing \$10,000 each produced formerly, fixed costs are actually reduced by buying new and more costly assets.

MULTIPLE INVESTMENT DECISIONS

In the paragraphs above the investment effect was considered independently for each element in the profit function. This was done to help make the transition from the simple current operating decisions where all factors in the profit equation are constant except X, to the capital management decision where any one of the elements except fixed costs could conceivably be favorably affected and controlled by capital investment.

But actually any two or more of the profit factors can be influenced simultaneously by capital investment decisions. For example, a decision to invest in sales promotion X may at the same time enable the business to raise price b, thus increasing profits from both sources: increased unit price and increased volume of sale. It is not uncommon, since the planning and preparation itself for capital budgeting entails considerable expenditures, to budget expenditures simultaneously to two or more segments of the profit function. Multiple investment decisions benefit profits from two directions, but so will each of the plans simultaneously increase fixed costs and expenses. There is one general way of stating the capital budgeting goal from the investment side and that is to plan capital projects so long as the present value of their expected net returns are increased for share value maximizations.

A SUMMARY ILLUSTRATION

By now the interrelationship between the capital decision and the current operating decision for income and profit should be clear. Each capital budgeting decision is designed to place the business in a more advantageous position than in the past for expected future current operations and consequently for present share values. The uncoupling effect of a plant expansion decision on prospective sales and profits is best illustrated with graphs like those in Figures 14.1 and 14.2. Figure 14.1 graphs prospective income, costs, and profits; and Figure 14.2 graphs only the profit effect of the expansion.

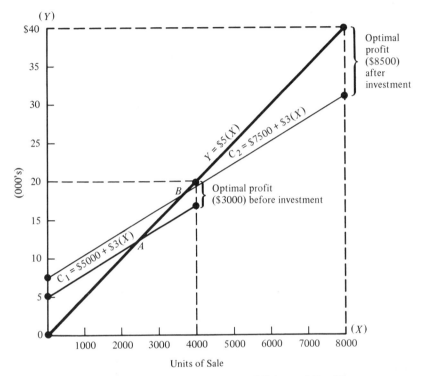

Figure 14.1. Budgeting Increased Sales and Profit.

In the figure above, price will remain at $5 after the investment, and unit variable costs will remain at $3 after the investment; but fixed costs and expenses will rise by 50 percent from $5,000 to $7,500. A marks the break-even point before expansion and B the breakeven point after expansion. Management believes, in other words, that by increasing fixed costs 50 percent output and sales can be increased 100 percent from 4,000 units to 8,000 units and net profits 183 percent: ($8,500 − $3,000)/$3,000 = 1.83 or 183 percent. One question that might have been raised, whether or not demand is great enough at $5 to allow the business to expand sales, apparently has already been answered by management in the profit optimizing function: $P = 8,000(\$5 - \$3) - \$7,500 = \$8,500$. Figure 14.2 is a conversion of the sales function to a profit function. The starting point is a negative $7,500 after the 50 percent increase in investment and is increased from $5,000

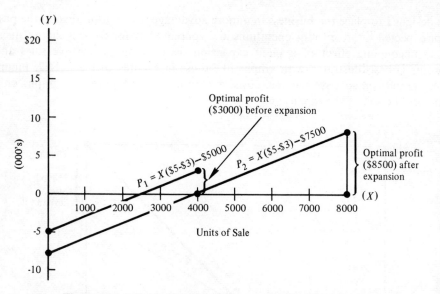

Figure 14.2. Profit Function Before and After Plant Expansion.

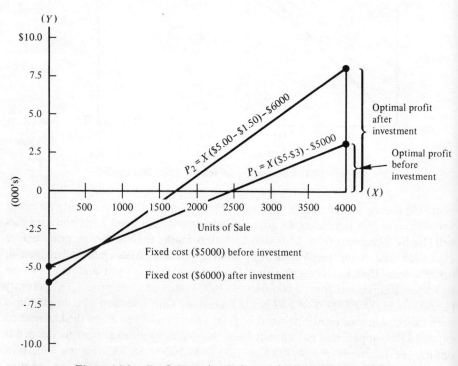

Figure 14.3. Profit Function Before and After Reducing Unit Variable Cost.

324

to $7,500 by dropping the point of origin of the profit function in Figure 14.2. It is very important for us to see that the capital investment decision has simply extended the scope of decision making for optimizing profits in future current operations. There is no assurance that optimal profits will be attained in the future just because capital is budgeted toward that goal. The factor that determines whether or not optimal profits will be attained and share values increased depends finally on how efficiently financial managers allocate the capital to internal use and how efficiently income, costs and expenses, current assets, and current liabilities are managed subject to the new capital constraint.

Figure 14.3 graphs a situation in which new investment has two effects simultaneously, one to reduce unit variable costs from $3.00 to $1.50 and the other to increase fixed costs from $5,000 to $6,000. Notice that output is still restricted to 4,000 units despite budgeting capital to unit variable cost reduction and to increased fixed charges. In this graph the X and Y scales are increased compared with Figures 14.1 and 14.2, so that the critical section of the graph is more apparent to the reader.

CAPITAL BUDGETING AND INTERNAL FUNDS MANAGEMENT

This section relates capital budgeting decisions, specifically, to internal and external current funds management. The student will recall that internal and external funds management were discussed in Parts IV and V assuming that the quantity of capital was given.

INTERNAL FUNDS MANAGEMENT

We relate here capital investment decisions to optimization goals in inventories, receivables, and cash management, the purpose being to show that capital invested in the net values of these assets in effect loosens quantity constraints and sets the stage for expanding levels of future current operations. Budgeting to each of these balances has the effect of increasing net working capital.

Inventory Effect In the case of inventories, this means that the total number of inventory units (X) used during a given period is increased. It means also that optimal average holdings ($\bar{X}$) of inventories is also increased without giving up other current assets like cash or receivables in exchange for the inventories, and without giving a trade credit payable in exchange for the inventories, as in inventory financing. The capital investment in inventories could have come only from exchanging fixed capital for inventories or, what is more likely, from capital structure financing, that is, by financing with long-term debts or with capital stock in this case to raise the net balance of the working capital. Without considering the specific capital structure source of the funds in detail, which is left to Part VII, the net working capital effect of an $10,000 capital increase in inventories is illustrated in Table 14.1.

TABLE 14.1
BUDGETING CAPITAL TO INVENTORIES

	I Before Capital Expansion		*II* After Capital Expansion	
Current assets:				
Cash	$10,000		$10,000	
Receivables	20,000		20,000	
Inventories	30,000	$60,000	40,000	$70,000
Current debts:				
Accounts payable	$15,000		$15,000	
Notes payable	10,000		10,000	
Others	5,000	$30,000	5,000	$30,000
Net working capital		$30,000		$40,000

Increasing the capital balance in inventories can have several favorable effects on future operations. First, it is a substitute for going to inventory financing on short-term open account or on a secured or unsecured account, which consequently avoids solvency risks that would accompany the growth of current debt balances. Second, should current sources of inventory credit or cash borrowing be needed in the future, this addition to the capital balance of inventory makes larger amounts of inventory credit available faster and more economically. The distinguishing feature of the working capital addition does not lie in the fact alone that larger quantities of inventories are being held but that they are held specifically as capital assets to raise future current operations to a new higher and relatively permanent level of operations. This is a relatively permanent higher level of operations because, since they were not financed internally out of the existing cash balance or externally with trade credit, they do not have to be contracted in the near future to restore cash or to repay current debts.

Receivables Effects   Budgeting capital to receivables also has a net-working-capital effect. This means that receivables increase is planned through expanded credit sales, the capital portion of receivables being the uncollected credit sales above cost of goods sold. In any given sales transaction, the capital value of receivables is equal ($=$) to but not an identity ($\neq$) to the gross profit on credit sales; and the net-working-capital value of receivables at any given time is equal to the cumulative gross profit from credit sales less the portion of those receivables that have been collected. This is a true capital-budgeting effect because these net capital funds in the receivables are related directly through gross profits to internal financing through net worth in the capital structure. To confirm this statement, Table 14.2 shows the net-working-capital effect of selling $20,000 of inventories from Table 14.1 for the sum of $30,000. All $30,000 is added to receivables, but only $10,000 is capital; and this increases net working capital from $40,000 to $50,000. The $10,000 addition to net working capital is balanced by a $10,000 addition for the present to net worth in the capital structure, although this is not illustrated in the table which deals just with capital assets.

TABLE 14.2
BUDGETING CAPITAL TO RECEIVABLES

	I Before Capital Expansion		*II* After Capital Expansion	
Current assets:				
Cash	$10,000		$10,000	
Receivables	20,000		50,000	
Inventories	40,000	$70,000	20,000	$80,000
Current debts:				
Accounts payable	$15,000		$15,000	
Notes payable	10,000		10,000	
Others	5,000	$30,000	5,000	$30,000
Net working capital		$40,000		$50,000

Increasing the capital value of receivables has several important favorable effects on the business. It places current internal funds on a level for higher optimal profits. The reason for this is that the capital portion ($10,000) of the total receivables is internal capital growth, not to be collected and repaid to the factors of production as the noncapital portion of receivables is. This makes a permanent addition to capital as long as it is not lost by management, not only increasing on a relatively permanent basis future profit potential but also decreasing liquidity and solvency risk in future current operation. It decreases liquidity risk because, when the capital value of the receivables is collected, the cash balance is increased; and solvency risk is decreased because the current debt paying capacity of the business has been increased by a rise in the ratio of net working capital over current debts (net working capital/current debts).

Cash Effect   Budgeting capital to the transactions balance of cash has very much the same long-run effects as budgeting it to receivables; namely, it creates net working capital base for a relatively permanent expansion of future current operations for increasing expected profits and for reducing liquidity and solvency risks. This means that cash balances are increased without decreasing inventories or receivables by an equivalent amount and without increasing current liabilities. Selling inventories above their cost on a cash transaction has the same capital effect on the cash balance as the credit sale of inventories has on the capital value of the receivables balance and the capital addition to cash is balanced by an equivalent addition to net worth in the capital structure. Collecting on receivables shifts the net capital value of receivables to the cash balance but does not add to net working capital. Capital can be budgeted to the cash balance also by liquidating fixed assets or by incurring capital structure obligations in the same manner that this can be done to the inventories. Table 14.3 shows capital increases in cash without changing the inventory balance from what it was in Table 14.2. The capital balance of cash is increased by $10,000 to $20,000, and again net working capital is increased by $10,000 to $60,000. The source of the capital addition has to be fixed assets or the capital structure because inventory balances are unchanged.

TABLE 14.3
BUDGETING CAPITAL TO CASH

	Before Capital Expansion		After Capital Expansion	
Current assets:				
Cash	$10,000		$20,000	
Receivables	50,000		50,000	
Inventories	20,000	$80,000	20,000	$90,000
Current debts:				
Accounts payable	$15,000		$15,000	
Notes payable	10,000		10,000	
Others	5,000	$30,000	5,000	$30,000
Net working capital		$50,000		$60,000

Uncoupling the capital constraint in cash in this manner has a very important effect on profit prospect, liquidity, and solvency risks. Increasing the capital portion of the cash balance opens the door to larger inventory purchases, a larger employment force, and a more intensive use of fixed capital facilities. Or the cash may even be invested in fixed capital facilities for a better balance between working and fixed capital. Solvency risk is reduced, of course, by a higher net-working-capital ratio, net working capital/current debts, and also because of the higher acid test ratio, (cash + near-cash assets + receivables)/current debts. The fact that the cash balance was not increased by short-term borrowing means that current debt claims were not increased against cash at least for the duration of the capital holdings.

CAPITAL BUDGETING AND EXTERNAL FUNDS MANAGEMENT

EFFECTS ON UNSECURED BORROWING

It was shown in earlier chapters how, given a certain amount of net capital and net working capital, the quantity of debts can usually be expanded to some fraction of that capital. In this section, we will let the quantity of net capital and net working capital vary and note the effect on optimal borrowing of varying that quantity of capital.

Variable Net Capital   The quantity of current and capital borrowing is a function of the size of the net capital. Another more descriptive way of putting it is that the quantity of current and unsecured borrowing is a function of the equity funds budgeted to capital assets. Net capital equals total assets minus the total debt. Therefore, net capital must be financed with equity funds. Net capital is no certain combination of fixed and working capital; it may be all of one or the other or a combination of both. In this respect net capital is a quantitative and not a qualitative constraint. Letting X be the independent variable net capital, letting Y be the dependent variable amount of borrowing, and letting the coefficient b be the rate of increase in borrowing, the total quantity of borrowing can be stated as $Y = bX$. Assume that for every $1 of equity capital $0.50 can be borrowed on an unsecured contract, then the borrowing function is:

$$Y = \$0.50(X)$$

The optimal quantity of borrowing is infinity so far as this one relationship is concerned, the only constraint being limits on available quantities of net capital. Since the source of net capital is necessarily equity financing, then it is the same thing as saying that the only limit on borrowing is the quantity of available equity financing. Thus, subject to the constraint of equity capital X, debt financing Y is a linear function of the quantity of equity capital. We assume that $0.50(X)$ will satisfy the debt market; but, with the extension in the dollar amount of borrowing (Y) beyond a certain point, other variables besides net capital, such as the quantity of income available for meeting interest payments, may lower the b coefficient below $0.50.

Variable Net Working Capital Another capital variable that may have to be relaxed by management to expand debt financing is net working capital. Net working capital may have to be budgeted independently of equity capital to meet the needs of the debt market. This is saying that it is not only the quantity of the capital but its liquidity that affects the availability of external financing. Up to a certain point at least, we may expect the functional relationship between quantity of unsecured borrowing and the net working capital variable to take the same shape as borrowing with the net capital variable. Let X be the independent variable quantity of net working capital, and let Y be the dependent variable of all possible borrowing and b be the borrowing coefficient. Suppose that for every unit of net working capital the firm can borrow $0.75; then the borrowing function is stated as:

$$Y = \$0.75(X)$$

The optimal quantity of borrowing is infinity assuming that net working capital is unlimited; but this, like equity capital, has quantitative limits after a certain dollar amount of borrowing, as other variables enter the scene to lower the borrowing coefficient below $0.75.

Double Variables When creditors make continuing lending contingent on the company's expansion of both equity and the net working capital, financial managers have double variables to consider in decision making. With double rates like the ones above of $Y = \$0.50(X)$ and $Y = \$0.75(X)$, financial managers may wonder which one is the limiting factor.

The answer is that it is the equation with the lower coefficient because this is the one that will require the greater cushion, given the debt limit. If $100,000 is

set by the lenders as the debt limit of the business, this limit will need mor
net working capital variable than it will net capital variable; to illustrate:

$$\$100,000 = 0.75X$$
$$X = \$133,000$$

but:

$$\$100,000 = 0.50X$$
$$X = \$200,000$$

The effect of capital budgeting on secured borrowing is more specific tha
in unsecured borrowing. Equity capital and net working capital have mor
limited applications to secured borrowing than to unsecured; in secured borrow
ing, it is the quantity of capital invested in the specific asset that is the quantitativ
basis for borrowing.

Current Assets Of the current assets, primarily inventories and receivable
are used for secured borrowing. If management had budgeted capital to inventor
balances, then immediately a new source of borrowing is created that may b
exploited to expand future operations. This means that the present capital con
straint on secured inventory financing has been lifted for increasing profits an
share values. Capital budgeted to receivables balances opens the door to variou
forms of receivables financing that were discussed in Part IV of the book. Th
capital share of receivables value exceeds the value of the inventories that create
them as was seen earlier, and this jump in the value of current assets immediatel
increases borrowing potential above the amount allowed on the inventories befor
they created receivables capital through credit sales.

Fixed Assets Any time capital is budgeted to fixed assets, secured borrowin
feels the full impact of the budgeting. Fixed capital is converted to cash mainly b
borrowing secured by a mortgage on the fixed assets. Cash from this kind of bor
rowing increases net working capital and can be retained in cash balances investe
in temporary securities or invested in finished inventory by combining raw mate
rials and labor at the production level. Or the cash borrowed on fixed asset securit
can be rebudgeted to other fixed assets for increasing output and sales and/or fo
reducing unit variable costs (c).

CAPITAL BUDGETING AND
COST OF BORROWING

In the previous section, discussion of capital budgeting and external funds man
agement models were set up to show how the quantity of borrowing is relate
functionally to the net capital equals the equity variable. Now we need to conside
the effect of continuing borrowing on the cost of borrowing. The cost of borrow
ing function $R = r_1 + r_2$ that was introduced in Chapter 11 is the introduction t
the cost of unsecured borrowing is basic to the issue. We will recall that, given th

quantity of net capital, r_2 is, within certain limits anyway, a positive linear function of the ratio D/E. It was also noted that, since net capital equals equity is fixed in the short-run decision, the cost of borrowing becomes a linear function up to a certain point again of the debt variable in the numerator of the ratio.

Turning our attention to capital budgeting, however, both elements of the ratio D/E become variable; equity in the denominator and debt in the numerator. This makes the risk cost factor r_2 a function of two variables instead of one, both of which are budgetable in capital management:

$$r_2 = r_1(D/E).$$

Table 14.4 shows the effect on R of, first, holding the debt constant and increasing equity, second, increasing both debt and equity by the same dollar amounts, and, third, by increasing debt and equity by the same relative amounts. Equity will increase by $10,000 in each of the three illustrations. Debts will increase by $10,000 in the second set of values and by a value that will give the same relative increase in debts in the third set of values as the $10,000 represents of equity. Since r_2 is the pure rate of interest over which financial managers have no control that value will remain at 6 percent.

TABLE 14.4
BORROWING COSTS
DEBT AND EQUITY VARIABLE

Debt Held Constant	Debt and Equity Vary by Same Amount	Debt and Equity Vary by Same Relative Amount	
$r_1 + r_1(D/E) = R$	$r_1 + r_1(D/E) = R$	$r_1 + r_1(D/E)\dfrac{\Delta D}{D}\bigg/\dfrac{\Delta E}{E} = 1 = R$	
$6 + 6\left(\dfrac{10,000}{20,000}\right) = 9.0$	$6 + 6\left(\dfrac{10,000}{20,000}\right) = 9.0$	$6 + 6\left(\dfrac{10,000}{20,000}\right)$	$= 9$
$6 + 6\left(\dfrac{10,000}{30,000}\right) = 8.0$	$6 + 6\left(\dfrac{20,000}{30,000}\right) = 10.0$	$6 + 6\left(\dfrac{15,000}{30,000}\right)$	$\dfrac{.50}{.50} = 9$
$6 + 6\left(\dfrac{10,000}{40,000}\right) = 7.5$	$6 + 6\left(\dfrac{30,000}{40,000}\right) = 10.5$	$6 + 6\left(\dfrac{20,000}{40,000}\right)$	$\dfrac{.33}{.33} = 9$
$6 + 6\left(\dfrac{10,000}{50,000}\right) = 7.2$	$6 + 6\left(\dfrac{40,000}{50,000}\right) = 10.8$	$6 + 6\left(\dfrac{25,000}{50,000}\right)$	$\dfrac{.25}{.25} = 9$
$6 + 6\left(\dfrac{10,000}{60,000}\right) = 7.0$	$6 + 6\left(\dfrac{50,000}{60,000}\right) = 11.0$	$6 + 6\left(\dfrac{30,000}{60,000}\right)$	$\dfrac{.20}{.20} = 9$

The message of Table 14.4 should be quite apparent; the first section emphasizes the favorable effect on borrowing costs, of reducing a firm's solvency risks measured by the ratio of debt to equity and indicating a negative functional relationship decreasing at a decreasing rate. Benefits in borrowing costs are large in the early stages as net capital increases. But the benefits of adding more net capital, that is the excess of assets over liabilities, has a diminishing favorable effect on borrowing rates which will never eliminate the risk element altogether as long as some debt, short- or long-term, remains in the financial structure. This would exclude this company from ever quite attaining prime borrowing status; the only way to accomplish this would be to retire the debt so that $r_2 = r_1(D/E) = 0$.

The second set of figures shows the reverse effect of increasing indebtedness by the same dollar amount as equity is used to increase net capital assets; the borrowing rate will increase because of the increasing solvency risk to the borrower; it will increase at a decreasing rate but will never double the prime rate because the ratio D/E will never reach 1. What is likely to happen in this case is that some qualitative capital constraint like net working capital or *quick assets* which is not keeping pace with the growth in equity capital, because some of the capital is being diverted to fixed assets, will force the business to quit borrowing before the rate approaches 12 percent. Or some special cutoff factor may be introduced like net profits before interest as a signal in the debt market that the company is not generating enough income flow to cover interest charges by some arbitrary ratio such as 2/1 or 3/1. But increasing to the net capital base in Table 14.4, the rate of increase in R can be decelerated and the approach to 12 percent delayed, thus allowing a larger absolute quantity of dollar borrowing unless the highly unlikely condition results in which liquid capital and net profits before interest remain constant with the expansion of the capital budget.

The third set of data indicates a stationary borrowing rate in the face of increasing debt and equity capital. By restricting the relative increase in debt capital to the same rate as equity capital, the proportion D/E remains constant and the solvency risk of the financial structure is the same after each new financing. Expressed as comparative relative rates of change $(\Delta D/D)/(\Delta E/E)$, the relationship remains equal to 1. An interesting fact should be noted, namely that the value of r_2 is determined in this case by the size of the initial ratio D/E which in this case was 0.5/1. Whatever the resulting relative rates of increase in debt and equity capital after the initial ratio, the value of r_2 will remain the same as long as the relative rate of increase is the same for both forms of financing. The student may want to test this by letting debt and equity capital increase each time at a constant relative rate of 0.5 instead of a declining relative rate to guarantee that R will remain at 9 percent. By the same token, if the initial ratio had been 10,000/30,000, the R value would have remained at 8 percent as long as $(\Delta D/D)/(\Delta E/E) = 1$. The limit to this kind of borrowing, obviously, finally has to be found in the total dollar amount of the borrowing relative to a liquid capital constraint like net working capital or relative to the net profit flow available for interest payments.

CAPITAL CONCEPT: A RESTATEMENT

If there is any such thing as a set of general rules that identify the capital investment decision in capital budgeting, this chapter can probably be considered as such a set. The purpose of the chapter has been to place the concept of capital management in its proper perspective to the whole subject of financial management. This chapter should hopefully have helped to clarify the following three facts of financial management. First, it should serve to reemphasize that current operating decisions in the last analysis are the decisions that determine profitability, liquidity, and solvency for their effect on the market value of a company's shares. To add tangibility to this concept, the basic profit function $P = X(b - c) - a$ was reexamined allowing capital investment decisions to set new limits on the variables. The same method was used in returning to current assets and current liabilities individually and collectively to illustrate the effect of capital management decisions on foundations for current operations. Second, this chapter should have illustrated clearly that limits to goal attainment in current operations are controllable through the capital budgeting decision, and that this decision has implications for external as well as for internal financing, both with respect to the quantity of borrowing and the cost of borrowing. The relationship of the capital investment decision was shown not to be an independent financial management decision but simply a decision for extending the limits of future current operating decisions. Finally, this chapter has sought to simplify the borrowing-equity capital relationship by carrying forward to capital management the function established in current operations. Debts were considered in total rather than in segments of current debts and long-term debts in considering the general function of net capital in the business, although some attention will be given, later to quality differences between debt forms in the capital structure and the effect of these differences on the capital financing decision and present share values. We will also have an occasion in considering the individual debt forms to consider criteria used by financial managers for increasing their borrowing potential besides the basic net capital and net working capital criteria discussed in this chapter.

SUMMARY

Chapter 14 is the first chapter of Part VI dealing with the whole subject of capital management as it relates to the capital investment decision. Chapter 14 specifically deals with the capital concept for investment and, thus, lays the groundwork for the next two chapters. The concept of capital is developed as a means of relaxing the constraints on current operations. Capital investment decisions constantly confront financial managers when they become concerned over the restrictiveness of certain capital facilities. The chapter points out clearly the relationship between the quantity of capital and the current operation and emphasizes that, for profit management purposes, relaxing of the capital constraint may open the door to much wider horizons of profit, which in turn will affect shareholders' evaluations of the company's expected net profits and share values. Graphic portrayals give the reader a visual overview of the functional relationships that exist between the three basic valuation items and the present value of a company's share. The chapter establishes that capital investment decisions are complements to short-term operations rather than substitutes.

PROBLEMS

1. The profit function $P = X(b - c) - a$ is given.

   a. Identify the constraints in this as a current operating model.
   b. As a current operating model, comment on the status of capital as a constraint on future profits.
   c. Apply the concept of capital budgeting in general as an uncoupling force to the profit function in general.

2. The present profit function of your business is $P = X(\$6 - \$2) - \$1,000$ with an output and sales capacity of 500 units. You wish to expand the profit potential of your business.

   a. One possibility is to invest to double output and sales capacity without disturbing the price or unit variable cost. But you estimate that such investment will double fixed costs and expenses, and you are wondering whether it would pay for you to undertake the investment. Do you recommend the project? Compare the break-even points of the business in terms of units of sale before and after the investment.
   b. An alternative to the condition above is to spend the money on machinery and equipment and sales facilities that would allow you to raise and maintain price at $7 per unit at the same time decreasing unit variable costs to $1 and increasing fixed costs to $1,200. Would you recommend this approach in preference to the budget in a above? Identify optimal profits in each case and indicate its use for decision making.
   c. Consider as a third alternative a situation in which expenditures could increase output and sales to 800 units, increase price from $6 to $7, decrease unit variable cost from $2 to $1, and increase fixed costs to $1,500.

3. Your goal is to increase future profits by increasing your profit function: $P = X(\$10 - \$4) - \$4,000$. You are a producer in a purely competitive industry.

   a. Because of your industry class, which, if any, of the above elements in the profit set are unalterable as far as your individual firm is concerned? Which, if any, can be changed by capital budgeting?
   b. Say that you produce and sell a differentiable product; where would you direct your capital budgeting emphasis and why?
   c. Suppose your firm has potential as an oligopolist. Where would capital budgeting be directed? Illustrate the effect of what you propose on the profit function.
   d. Under what unusual conditions might the value (a) in the function be reduced at the same time that capital is budgeted to decrease (c)? Do financial managers have control in any way over these conditions?

e. How is optimal profit determined in each of the three industry situation above?

4. As financial manager of a business, you feel that the general effects of your capital budgeting plan should be illustrated graphically to nonfinancial management personnel. Subject to the present capital constraints, your profit function is $P = X(\$10 - \$4) - \$1,000$.

   a. Graph the present profit function in which X is limited to 500 units. Identify the break-even point on the chart.
   b. Graph the profit function in which X is expanded by capital budgeting to 1,000 units at no additional fixed costs. Identify the break-even point and optimal profit. Now identify the break-even point and optimal profit at which the expansion would add $1,000 to fixed costs and expenses.
   c. Divide the original profit function of your business into two separate functions: one, the income function and the other the cost function. Now graph these functions indicating the break-even point. Check this break-even point with the one on the profit graph that you drew in a above. Now graph the effect of raising X to 1,000 units and a to $2,000 from $1,000. Compare optimal profits and the new break-even point with the same values in b above.

5. The table below illustrates the current internal and external funds condition of Company A before budgeting additional net working capital to the current assets.

COMPANY A
BEFORE BUDGETING NET WORKING CAPITAL

Current assets:		
Cash	$20,000	
Receivables	40,000	
Inventories	30,000	$90,000
Current debts:		
Accounts payable	20,000	
Notes payable	20,000	
Others	5,000	$45,000

   a. Simulate the effect on your new condition of budgeting $20,000 to the capital values of your inventories. Prove the capital nature of the inventory expansion and explain its effect on future borrowing operations for profit and on c_2 in inventory holding costs.
   b. Starting again with the original position of the company, budget $20,000 in capital to receivables. Prove the capital status of the change and explain its effect on future borrowing operations and operations

for profit. Evaluate the resulting long-run financial effect of budgeting the $20,000 to inventories relative to budgeting it to receivables.

c. What long-run benefits are realized and what problems are created by budgeting capital to cash instead of to inventories or receivables?

6. You are a financial manager of Company D, and you believe that the loan market will extend unsecured loans to your business at the rate of 0.4 of your gross capital.

   a. Set up the equation for determining how much can be borrowed with no limit on the quantity of gross capital. Identify the symbols in the equation and indicate the allowable amount of borrowing assuming gross capital of: (1) $30,000, (2) $50,000, and (3) $80,000.
   b. What are the components of gross capital?
   c. Suppose that equity capital were the independent variable in the equation rather than gross capital. Would you expect the coefficient to be larger, smaller, or the same as the 0.4 in the original? Explain.
   d. Suppose that net working capital were the independent variable in the equation rather than gross capital. Would you expect the coefficient to be larger, smaller, or the same as the 0.4 in the original? Explain.
   e. What importance is the double variable situation when it comes to simulating maximum debt financing?

7. Our basic model for indicating the effect of capital budgeting on cost of borrowing is: $R = r_1 + r_1(D/E)$.

   a. Identify the symbols in the equation.
   b. Solve the equation assuming that $r_1 = 7$ percent, $X = $40,000$, and $D = $20,000$.
   c. New set up a schedule starting with $D = $10,000$ and $E = $30,000$. Show the effect on borrowing cost for five intervals of: (1) increasing each form of financing by $10,000, (2) increasing equity capital by $5,000 each time but holding debt constant, and (3) increasing each kind of financing by the same relative amount. Interpret each cost effect in terms of solvency risk.

15

Foundations
for
Decision
Making

Foundations for making capital investment decisions rest firmly on neoclassical marginal value analysis which was first placed on an exact science basis in the late nineteenth century by the British economist Alfred Marshall. Since the 1950's students of corporation finance, business finance, or financial management, whatever we prefer to call it, have reshaped, extended, and redefined the basic precepts of neoclassical marginal analysis to meet capital investment theory of financial management and have presented it as the present discipline of the investment side of capital budgeting. This chapter will examine the theoretical economic foundations for the kit of tools and criteria for analysis and decision making that will be developed in detail in Chapter 16. The investment side of capital budgeting, as business knows it today, is still a combination of predominantly rule-of-thumb and more-or-less scientific decision-making indicators. Some of the rule-of-thumb criteria for decision making will be critically examined considering the theoretical backgrounds of our present system for analysis and decision making.

INVESTMENT INDICATORS

The following criteria cannot be called theories because they are not complete statements of cause-and-effect relationships for decision making. Yet neither can they be left out of the discussion of capital investing because they are still widely used by many apparently successful businesses. The main feature that characterizes all of them is that they are fragmentary systems that serve as guidelines or indicators for making capital investment decisions. For example, the treatment usually plays on a limited segment of capital like fixed assets or machinery and equipment specifically, seldom incorporating the net working capital. By the time we complete reviewing these techniques, the student will be inclined to choose one and perhaps wonder how there can be anything left for further consideration. Rules for decision making are more clearly formed for some in this group than for others. They are understandable for the most part, but their applications in some cases are somewhat vague. Their main weakness from our point of view is that they are not part of a total integrated system of financial management. They do not relate, in other words, the capital investment decision to the current operating decision as was done in Chapter 14; and they do not relate specifically or generally to a common goal in management such as share value maximization. In reviewing these indicators, we will start with the simplest form and will gradually move up to somewhat more technical media. The review of the various forms will be somewhat critical to call attention to the primary problem areas in capital budgeting, rather than to belittle the thought and effort that has gone into developing these indicators.

REPLACE AN ASSET WHEN WORN OUT

This method would replace buildings, machinery, and equipment when they are worn out—when repairs will no longer restore the fixed asset to its normal level of efficiency. This poses several problems and questions, not the least important of which is deciding when an asset is actually "worn out" or what is its normal level of efficiency. With modern methods of servicing and repair, some forms of capital may never reach this stage completely. Then, too, who will make the decision as to when the capital is worn out: an engineer, a salesman for a machinery and equipment company, or a financial manager? The considered opinions of all of these "experts" are inclined to vary widely. It might be answered that an asset is worn out when it would take more cash to repair or rebuild it than it is worth. This is a kind of insurance adjuster's yardstick and means that it would be cheaper in some cases to replace the asset with a new or used one than to repair and rebuild the present one. The term *worth* is also difficult to define in general terms; although, we will see later that, applying the discounting principle, expected net cash flows can be used to establish present worth or *present value* of an asset. Using a rule-of-thumb indicator of this kind has a tendency to turn to depreciation allowances for income-tax purposes as a guide to replacing worn out fixed assets. Using income taxes as a guide, fixed assets may be replaced when their period of allowable depreciation or even their period of "accelerated depreciation" for tax purposes has expired. If the depreciation approach is used for conserving on income tax payments, it may also explain some of the large quantities of investing in plant and equipment that have taken place in the past; but it can hardly be accepted as a rational theory of capital investment.

As a decision-making approach, this would suggest a passive rather than an active attitude toward investment which says to get along with what we have as long as possible rather than to search out new capital budgeting opportunities that will raise the sights of the business for future returns and for higher present share values. Opportunities to invest profitably will be passed by simply because capital assets now in use are still operative with some degree of efficiency. Nor is this method effective for selecting between competing assets, since it relates just to assets already in use. Thus, if assets B and C compete to replace the worn out asset A, the method is of little use except to reaffirm to the financial manager that A is worn out and needs replacing. Present share values may increase in spite of this investment practice but hardly because of it.

INVEST WHEN RETAINED EARNINGS BECOME EXCESSIVE

A good safe policy according to some business managers is to invest in capital assets only the *excessive* portion of a company's retained earnings. Long-term creditors sometimes impose this or similar restrictions on the use of working capital funds, stating that fixed asset purchases must be limited to situations in which retained earnings exceed a given dollar amount or when they exceed a certain percentage of a base value like capital stock or net working capital. Such restrictions protect creditors' property interests in the business, but this does not make it acceptable as an investment policy if the goal in management is to increase share values. That this is safe and conservative cannot be denied because it rules out the risks of borrowing money or even of issuing capital stock to raise funds for capital investment. The risk of being unable to meet interest and principal payments that attends capital borrowing and the embarrassment to financial managers of being unable to pay dividends on capital stock financing can be avoided by using the retained earnings guideline for making investment decisions.

The fact that some of the large corporations have used this method in the past to build capital empires out of retained earnings has caused it to command a certain amount of prestige and respect in the management community, but it falls far short for many reasons of meeting the needs of the modern philosophy of capital management. First, it contains a basic error by implying that retained earnings on the right side of the balance are matched by cash or other highly liquid assets awaiting plant and equipment investment on the left side. Second, because the decision to invest would depend on past savings rather than on expected earnings puts this method out of step with the present way of thinking of financial managers. This may very well raise the question of whether investment should be related at all to the "thriftiness" of the business as evidenced by its retained earnings. Third, most businesses would not make enough net profit to accumulate for capital investment if they were not allowed to invest with capital secured from the open capital market. Fourth, of course this method has nothing to offer that would help us to allocate a given sum of capital among competing projects. This is a passive approach as the former indicator is to decision making; although, the passiveness consists of *waiting* for funds to build up for investment, whereas the former consists of waiting for the assets to wear out. Aside from its passiveness, the main weakness of the indicator is that it puts the "cart before the horse." It is a generally sound principle in budgeting investment decisions to base the decision on the merits of the capital project itself, independent of the availability of funds for financing the project, then to seek the funds to execute the project.

The cost-savings approach to decision making has much to offer over the two methods discussed before, although it is also limited because it disregards the income potential of a new investment. The approach is forward-looking in that decisions are based on *expected* costs of production rather than on costs of investment projects of the past. Probably the most important contribution made by this indicator is the opportunity it offers of comparing and choosing between competing capital assets. The simplest method of comparing investment alternatives is by their average annual costs. The arithmetic is simple, but there are never enough facts to avoid errors altogether. As a matter of expediency, the normal depreciable life of the asset may be used as its service life. No distinction is made between cash and noncash costs and, therefore, depreciation may be a substantial factor in decision making even though it does not incur cash expenditures. If use of raw materials is the same for the competing machines, materials costs do not need to be included in the cost comparison; and any other costs that are the same for the competing projects can be cancelled out for decision making.

Table 15.1 compares the machine in use with two competing assets. Past experiences along with advice from machinery and equipment manufacturers may be

TABLE 15.1
COMPARATIVE COSTS FOR ALTERNATIVE INVESTMENTS

Operating Costs	Asset in Use	Asset A	Asset B
Direct labor	$ 5,700	$ 5,800	$4,800
Maintenance	900	300	700
Depreciation	5,000	4,000	4,100
Taxes and insurance	30	140	50
Power	200	200	150
Total	$11,830	$10,440	$9,800
Cost savings over asset in use:		$ 1,390	$2,030

relied on by financial managers in this case for estimating additional costs for making comparisons. Assets A and B are compared to see which, if either, can save on the costs of operation for the business. The alternatives are to: (1) keep the asset now in use, (2) replace the present asset with A, or (3) replace the present asset with B. Assets A and B have expected service lives of four and five years respectively and perform the same quality of service. We can see that the asset in use should be replaced by asset B, which offers the larger cost saving of $2,030.

Cost-savings methods of decision making are simple and feasible, but they are limited in certain ways. First, they are pointed primarily at machinery and equipment replacement decisions. Second, and more important perhaps, they do not allow for the possible effect of a capital investment on future income. If income were unaffected by investment decisions, this question would not be raised; but the quality and quantity of work produced may differ widely between individual assets which could affect the volume of sales, net profits, and share values. For example, the quality of packaging services supplied by a new machine may make the product more saleable, or the speed with which a machine turns out the finished product may increase X as well as decrease c in the profit function $P = X(b - c) - a$. Asset A which is rejected altogether because its operating costs are higher than B may have generated enough additional income from added sales to more than offset the higher costs, with a favorable effect on share values. Another factor of considerable importance is the treatment given here to depreciation. No consideration is given to the income producing potential, through reinvestment, of noncash expenses like depreciation nor is the discounted present value of those funds considered in the decision as they could have been since the funds were not actually expended.

THE MAPI SYSTEM

A more sophisticated cost comparing method of making investment decisions is found in the MAPI (Machinery and Allied Products Institute) replacement procedure. Every fixed asset in use is called a *defender*, and every prospective new asset is called a *challenger*. Each defender and challenger incurs (1) capital costs and may have (2) operating advantages or (3) operating disadvantages over other challenging assets. Capital costs are the sum of the loss in market value of the machine owing to its age and imputed interest owing to the opportunity cost of holding the capital instead of investing the funds in some relatively riskless security. Capital costs of new investment proposals are usually higher than for the older existing assets because of the greater loss in market value during early years of a new investment. But the proposed new machine is also likely to have an advantage in producing larger net operating income which results from cost savings but also from qualitative or quantitative advantages in sales. Financial managers should continually challenge the existing machinery and equipment to offset the operating advantages of new machines and equipment with their lower capital costs. But unless an existing machine can meet the challenge, it should be replaced for the benefit of the business.

The MAPI system has been used widely in the machine tool industry for making replacement decisions, and it has contributed much to making business managers, and financial managers in particular, aware of the practical aspects of fixed asset investment decisions. Although this is not intended as a complete capital budgeting theory, it has contributed much to the use of simple quantitative tools for making evaluations of investment opportunities for making precise decisions to invest or not to invest. This method has elevated the subject of capital investment to an active, and even an aggressive, science in applying it to machinery and equipment analysis. There is no *waiting* for machinery and equipment to wear out and no *waiting* for earnings to accumulate before an investment is made. The method recognizes that investments can have sales effects that have to be taken into consideration in evaluating projects. The aggressiveness of the method in searching out new investment opportunities is a considerable innovation over the three indicators previously discussed; in fact, if any one of these indicators can be considered more than a rule-of-thumb method of analysis, it is the MAPI system. Its limiting features are that it is primarily an asset replacement technique; it is confined primarily to tangible fixed assets and machinery and equipment in particular; it does not attempt to estimate net income flows over the life of the investment; and it does not attempt to relate the specific machinery and equipment decision to the broader issue of the company's share values.

INVEST FOR EARLY PAYBACK

A practice in widespread use by businesses today and one that can be adapted to almost any form of fixed asset is to invest in an asset whenever the *net cash flow* that the asset is expected to generate is large enough *to pay back* the initial investment in a relatively short period of time. This policy may be applied to machinery and equipment replacement and additions and sometimes to complete plants and production lines and comes closer to being a general capital investment theory than any of the other plans thus far discussed. In applying this method, the cash flow rather than the net profit is the basis of decision making. Cash costs connected with the project are subtracted from sales expected to be generated by the project to arrive at a net-cash-flow figure. The resulting average annual net cash flow is then divided into the cost of the asset. To illustrate, assume that an asset costing $10,000 is expected to generate average annual net cash flows of $4,000. The investment would be paid back then in two and one half years: $10,000/$4,000 = $2\frac{1}{2}$, which is a 40 percent average annual rate of return on the investment ($4,000/$10,000 = 40 percent) for the two and one half years of payback.

Whether the investment will be made in this case depends on what management's *cutoff period* is. If the cutoff period is less than two and one half years, the proposed investment will not qualify; but if the cutoff period is more than two and one half years the investment will be made. The cutoff period may be an arbitrary figure, the purpose of management being mainly to make it as short as possible to display conservative investment policy without being so conservative as to deprive the business of undertaking profitable projects. Theoretically, this method keeps the rate of return on capital at a high level by requiring the cash flow from the investment to pay for itself in a short period and based on the assumption that the high rate will continue throughout the remaining life of the asset.

Suppose several investments are competing for adoption by the business. Those that cannot meet the cutoff requirement are eliminated right off; and, of the remaining projects, the one with the shortest payback period will be selected. To illustrate how this operates, suppose that three machines A, B, and C are competing for acceptance. Their purchase prices are $8,800, $10,000 and $12,000 respectively. Assuming a required pay-back period of two and one half years, machines A and B will qualify; and, if just one investment is finally allowed, it will be A.

TABLE 15.2
SHORT PAY-BACK METHOD ILLUSTRATED

	A	B	C
Net sales	$10,000	$10,000	$14,000
Cash costs and expenses	5,000	4,000	5,000
Depreciation	1,000	1,000	1,200
Before-tax profit	4,000	5,000	5,800
Taxes (@ 40%)	1,600	2,000	2,320
After-tax profit	3,400	3,000	3,480
Purchase price	8,880	10,000	12,000
Net cash flow:			
Net profits	3,400	3,000	3,480
Depreciation	1,000	1,000	1,200
Payback period	$\dfrac{\$8,800}{4,400} = 2$	$\dfrac{\$10,000}{4,000} = 2.5$	$\dfrac{12,000}{4,680} = 2.6$

As we can see, this is a clean-cut tool for decision making. It is easy to understand, is easy to apply, acknowledges cash flow as a decision factor, and contains a strong air of conservatism that is cherished by financial managers generally. Manufacturers and distributors of machines and equipment are often well prepared with figures for showing that their products have short pay-back periods. This method of decision making is favored by many because it reduces the chances of making mistakes from overinvesting. Limitations of this method in meeting general capital budgeting needs are as follows. First, like the other indicators, decision making concentrates on fixed assets. Second, the approach is basically a defensive one. The key words are caution and conservatism instead of research and experimentation. Third, the technique itself of basing decisions on the first few years of operations may very well be questioned. The implication is that the investment can be paid out in the first few years; all after that will be profitable years for the business. Of course, this does not follow; and, if management inadvertently assumes that the first few years are representative of the future, serious errors in decision making are likely to result. The matter of the length and regularity of income flow over the life of the investment proposal, and its effect on the investment decision, is one of the major issues for consideration in Chapter 16.

ECONOMIC FOUNDATIONS OF CAPITAL BUDGETING THEORY

Capital in neoclassical economic analysis includes fixed assets and any form of working capital that contributes to production. No attempt is made in economic analysis to distinguish as we do in financial analysis between the capital and the noncapital portion of individual current assets. The optimization goal is to invest in new capital projects until expected future profits are maximized. When profits are maximized, investment decisions are in equilibrium. There is no reason for increasing or decreasing investment because moving in either direction would be detrimental to the business. The equilibrium concept is valuable for its contribution to a precision form of decision making that is prevalent in a somewhat modified form in modern capital budgeting. Two classic examples of profit optimization analysis applied to the investment decision are found in the marginal productivity theory of investment and the marginal efficiency theory of investment. These two theories are closely related in some respects and quite different in others. The former is a long established theory, the latter a more contemporary theory; but both have made valuable contributions to the foundations of capital budgeting and will accordingly be discussed here in some little detail.

MARGINAL PRODUCTIVITY THEORY

The marginal productivity theory of capital is a model for explaining the demand schedule and the demand curve of a firm for capital funds to finance capital investment projects. The term marginal refers to *incremental profit* before allowing for interest charges and taxes.

The Term Explained Quantitatively, marginal productivity of capital is, as mentioned above, the increment or increase in net profit before interest and taxes resulting from investing another increment of capital. But if marginal productivity analysis is to be a useful tool for optimizing investment, the incremental dollar return must be restated as a relative value as the ratio of incremental profit before interest and taxes to the increment of capital that produces the profit. Using the

TABLE 15.3
DECLINING MARGINAL PRODUCTIVITY
OF CAPITAL

Y	X	ΔY	ΔX
$100	$100		
200	200	$100	$100
280	300	80	100
310	400	30	100
320	500	10	100
325	600	5	100

delta values with which we are familiar, let ΔY be an increment of net profit before interest and taxes; and let ΔX be an increment of investment that created the profit. Then the ratio $\Delta Y/\Delta X$ equals the incremental ratio or the *marginal rate of return.*

The law of diminishing returns causes the marginal increments of profits to decline with fixed marginal increments of capital. Marginal productivity of capital is thus a diminishing value that can best be explained and illustrated with a table such as the one below. Table 15.3 illustrates the declining nonlinear nature of marginal productivity of capital. Think of Y values as total profit before interest and taxes, X as units of capital, ΔY as incremental profits, and ΔX as incremental inputs of capital.

The Optimal Capital Budget Returning to the ratio $\Delta Y/\Delta X$, or what was called earlier the marginal rate of return, we can restate the incremental profits as declining rates of return and even as declining percentage rates of return as follows in Table 15.4.

TABLE 15.4
DECLINING MARGINAL RATES OF RETURN

Y	ΔY	ΔX	$\dfrac{\Delta Y}{\Delta X}$	%
$100				
200	$100	$100	$\dfrac{\$100}{\$100} = 1.0 =$	100
250	50	100	$\dfrac{80}{100} = 0.8 =$	50
280	30	100	$\dfrac{30}{100} = 0.3 =$	30
290	10	100	$\dfrac{10}{100} = 0.1 =$	10
295	5	100	$\dfrac{5}{100} = 0.05 =$	5
297	2	100	$\dfrac{2}{100} = 0.05 =$	2

This sets the framework for the marginal productivity theory of investment. Given the market rate of interest and the schedule of declining marginal productivity of capital, *financial management will set the level of investment at the point at which marginal productivity of capital equals the market rate of interest.* The most important feature of the theory is its implication that investment decisions are motivated by the need to equate two rates, the rate of return on an increment of investment and the interest, the latter being the rate of return required by the lender of debt capital. Another way of stating the theory is that a business will invest in new projects until the rate of return before interest and taxes is equal to the cost of borrowed capital. The optimal investment level is the point at which the two values equate, and this is where the firm is at investment equilibrium. This condition is

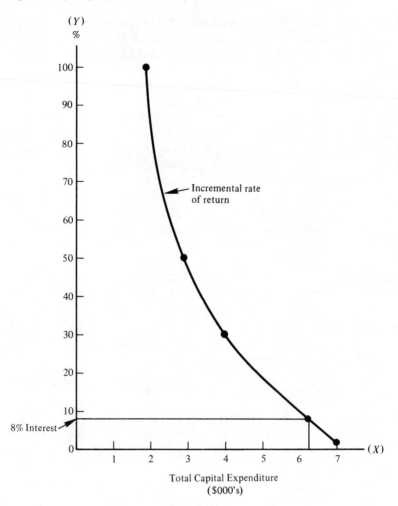

Figure 15.1.   Optimal Level of Investment.

best illustrated graphically. Figure 15.1 is a graph of Table 15.4 with an 8 percent fixed interest rate. We will call this the optimal capital budget. The functional importance of the theory should be at once apparent. It is a clear-cut precision tool that is practical if the rate of decrease can be determined for the marginal rate of return; that is, it is practical if financial managers can determine the slope of their nonlinear demand curve for capital.

Evaluating the Theory   In evaluating the marginal productivity theory of investment, we should keep in mind that we are talking about a foundation theory for capital budgeting and not the total theory of capital budgeting. It should be noted first that a valuable framework is established for identifying variables such as the marginal rate of return on capital and the market rate of interest which indeed are important factors in the investment decision. The implication is, however, that unlimited quantities of capital are available at a fixed market rate of interest. It should be noted that management can control the level of investment but that it cannot control the interest rate. In this theory, the market rate of interest is a uniform *cost of capital* and a cutoff rate for setting the level of investment. It is interesting that a single interest rate, that prevailing in the capital funds market, is the common cutoff rate for all businesses. There is some question as to whether this is the interest rate r_1 or $r_1 + r_2$. If it is just the former, then investment would proceed to the prime interest rate which is applicable only to a relatively few businesses in the whole economy, and most firms using this rate as their cutoff point would be budgeting capital to projects that were earning less than they have to pay for the funds that they are putting into the project. If the rate represents $r_1 + r_2$, then it is the current borrowing rate of the firm which is more realistic; although, we are not saying that the borrowing rate of the firm is necessarily the correct cutoff point for making new investments.

MARGINAL EFFICIENCY OF CAPITAL

The marginal efficiency of capital (MEC) theory is identified with the work of the late John M. Keynes in his *General Theory*.[1] Marginal efficiency of capital differs from the marginal productivity theory in one important respect. It spells out clearly the importance of the discounting principle or what has been called the *time value* concept of money in determining the rate of return on the marginal unit of capital. An earlier British economist, Alfred Marshall, who wrote his classic *Principles of Economics* near the turn of the twentieth century, recognized the time value concept of money and its general discounting effect on present values; but he did not incorporate this in his basic investment theory. He states, nevertheless, that:

> Every element ... which dates from a time anterior to that day, must have a compound interest for the interval accumulated upon it: and every element, which dates from a time posterior to that day, must have compound interest for the interval *discounted from it*.[2]

The Term Explained and Illustrated   Nevertheless, it remained for the marginal efficiency of capital theory to refer to the discounting principle, as it is used today for computing present values, as a vital factor in the capital investment decision. Keynes states the meaning of the marginal efficiency of capital as follows:

> More precisely, I define the marginal efficiency of capital as being equal to the rate of discount which would make the present value of the series of annuities given by the returns expected from the capital-asset during its life equal to its supply price.[3]

---

[1] John Maynard Keynes, *The General Theory of Employment Interest and Money* (New York: Harcourt, Brace & World, Inc., 1936).

[2] Alfred Marshall, *Principles of Economics*, 8th ed. (London: Macmillan and Co., Limited, 1936), p. 353. Italics in the quote are mine.

[3] Keynes, *General Theory*, p. 135.

Returns referred to in the definition are expected net profits before interest and taxes and will henceforth be called PBIT. The *supply price* is the installed cost of a fixed asset. To illustrate what is meant by the marginal efficiency of capital, we will select some values from the present value Table II in the Appendix, and make certain other simple assumptions. Assume that PBIT or *returns* referred to in the quotation are expected to be $1,000 for each of five periods on an asset which would cost installed $4,212, the *supply price* of the asset. Now it is a simple matter to determine from the table the *marginal efficiency of capital* which is 6 percent, for this is the only one of the three rates that would equate the expected flow for five periods of $1,000 to $4,212. The manner of finding the rate is illustrated in the table below in which the table factor at the end of each of the five-year periods is multiplied by $1,000. The other rates miss the mark as we can see; 4 percent misses it on the high side by $240 ($4,452 − $4,212), and 8 percent misses it on the low side by $219 ($4,212 − $3,993). Another way of looking at the equating effect of the rate is as a ratio of 1:

$$\text{Present value} = \frac{\$4,212}{\$4,212} = 1$$
$$\text{Supply price}$$

TABLE 15.5
MARGINAL EFFICIENCY OF CAPITAL INCOME STREAM
OF $1,000 EACH PERIOD FOR FIVE PERIODS

4%	6%	8%
0.962	0.943	0.926
1.886	1.833	1.783
2.775	2.676	2.577
3.630	3.465	3.312
4.452 × $1,000 = $4,452	4.212 × $1,000 = $4,212	3.993 × $1,000 = $3,993

In still another way, the marginal efficiency of capital is the rate which causes the algebraic sum of the PBIT stream and the price of the asset to equal 0. To illustrate this we use present values of 1 received for five periods, taken from Table I in the Appendix. The negative value given to the supply price of the asset means that $4,212 is expended right at the start for the asset before any profits are expected from it. It is not stated explicitly in the definition that delayed payments for the asset should be discounted as well as delayed receipts, although it is logical to assume that this would be the case.

There is also the important phrase in the Keynesian definition of marginal efficiency of capital *during its life*. This means that the expected PBIT over the *whole life* of the asset has to be brought back to the supply price of the asset by the MEC (marginal efficiency capital). The reason this is called the *marginal* efficiency is that each increment of capital has such an expected PBIT over its whole prospective life. And the reason the whole life of the asset concept is so important

TABLE 15.6
ALGEBRAIC SUM OF
PBIT AND SUPPLY PRICE OF ASSET IS ZERO (0)

6% *Present Vaue of PBIT*
$1,000 × 0.943 = +943 1,000 × .890 = +890 1,000 × .840 = +840 1,000 × .792 = +792 1,000 × .747 = +747

Present value of income =	+ $4,212
Supply price of asset =	− 4,212
Algebraic sum =	0

is that it marks a clear break from the use of a simple average profit figure or simple marginal profit figure as the basis for decision making; the MEC refers to a *stream* of profit on marginal or incremental capital and does not mean average marginal profit on marginal or incremental capital.

Since marginal efficiency of capital is such an important fundamental concept and since it is used so frequently in capital budgeting, we may do well to reconsider it in one of its other more popular guises. Most often it is called the *internal rate of return*, internal because it is derived from evaluations of income and net profit rather than from phenomena in the external capital supply markets. It is an efficiency measure, *efficiency* with which business managers make decisions that pertain to income, costs and expenses, and net profit related to specific capital expenditures. Whereas, there is some evidence in the Keynesian writing that the MEC equates *net cash flow* rather than PBIT with the supply price of the asset; his application of MEC to optimal investment analysis leads us to believe that his "returns expected from the capital-asset" refers to the same PBIT figures used in the typical marginal productivity of capital analysis. But it is not our purpose here to attempt to interpret what Keynes really meant; the point raised here is that the term *internal rate of return*, which will be used frequently in Chapter 16, refers specifically to net cash flow rather than to PBIT, the former representing net sales minus all cash costs and expenses including taxes.

The Optimal Capital Budget In the MEC theory of investment, the optimal capital budget marks the point of maximum PBIT. The diminishing rates of return, the diminishing MEC, forms the firm's demand schedule for capital. In terms of discounting rates this means that as added units of capital are budgeted producing smaller expected profit streams over the whole life of the incremental unit of capital, smaller and smaller discounting rates are needed to equate the smaller stream with the fixed supply price of the asset. Table 15.7 illustrates the fact that smaller expected PBIT streams also have smaller MEC rates, given the same supply price of the asset.

TABLE 15.7
DECLINING MARGINAL EFFICIENCY OF CAPITAL
FOR SIX INCREMENTS OF INVESTMENT
(ANNUALLY FOR FIVE YEARS)

	1 $1,168	*2* $1,111	*3* $1,055	*4* $1,000	*5* $ 946	*6* $ 894
	1,168	1,111	1,055	1,000	946	894
	1,168	1,111	1,055	1,000	946	894
	1,168	1,111	1,055	1,000	946	894
	1,168	1,111	1,055	1,000	946	894
	1,168	1,111	1,055	1,000	946	894
Total	5,840	5,555	5,275	5,000	4,730	4,470
Supply price of asset	$4,212	$4,212	$4,212	$4,212	$4,212	$4,212
Equating rate (MEC)	12%	10%	8%	6%	4%	2%

Figure 15.2 summarizes graphically the MEC theory of investment. *When the quantity of capital is unlimited, management will continue to budget capital to operations until the MEC and the market rate of interest are equal.* In this case equilibrium of the firm is reached with the third unit of capital whose expected profit flow of $1,050 discounted at 8 percent (also the market rate of interest) will equal $4,212. Observe that the incremental values are $4,212 on the X axis and that the functional relationship between ΔX and ΔY is linear. The linear function is a graph of Table 15.7 values whose five-year profit streams were selected arbitrarily so the MEC ratios would fall on even rates of return simply for convenience in using the present value tables. Although this is acceptable for illustrative purposes, the reader should realize that the function may not necessarily be linear. As an experiment, he may wish to alter the five-year flows in Table 15.7; so that the rate of return function will be nonlinear decreasing at a decreasing rate as the marginal productivity graph Figure 15.1.

The optimal capital budget is the one in which $12,636 worth of capital is purchased, three $4,212 incremental units, that is, with MEC of 8 percent equating the rate of interest on the third application of capital. This is the point of equilibrium also because to invest less would mean that the discounted rate of profit on incremental units of capital is still above the cost of borrowing the capital; and to invest more would bring down the discounted rate of profit below the cost of borrowing the capital. Keynes, because of the depression era in which he wrote, recognized the important possibility of the MEC becoming trapped below the level of the market rate of interest. Such trapping effect may result from a price (b) decline, resulting from a general decline in spending power and demand for the output of industry. To make matters worse, in a recession period unit variable costs (c) and also fixed costs (a) in the profit function are likely to remain relatively stable rather than decline with the decline in demand; and this combined set of circumstances,

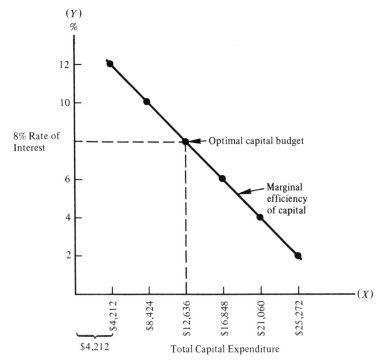

Figure 15.2.   Optimal Capital Budget.

declining demand and sticky costs and expenses, could cause the business to be trapped with capital that is returning less than the going market rate of interest.

Uncertainty of Expected Profits   In developing his investment theory, Keynes took note of the risk that attends estimating of future flows of net profits. Psychological factors are explicitly called on in explaining risk conditions associated with trying to estimate future incomes and profit; at best, future incomes are *prospective* and *expected* rather than *certain* so far as the decision maker is concerned. There is a hint at least in his analysis of the need for quantifying the risk of making estimates of future values as a guard against budgeting too much or too little capital to specific projects, and he acknowledges that the decision maker (financial manager) himself must have "doubts in his own mind as to the probability of his actual earning the prospective yield for which he hopes."[4] In this same tone, the writer did not believe that financial managers of business could promise rational responses in the securities market to rational investment decisions made by financial managers of business. The propounder of the theory asserts further that there is practically no relationship between the market value of a company's shares and the rationality with which financial managers make investment decisions. Thus, whereas the value of a company's shares has a place in the total theory of capital

---

[4] Keynes, *General Theory*, p. 144.

investment, their evaluation is thought to be dominated by basically irrational behavior and by fluctuations in mass psychology more than by trying to give present values to financial managers' budgeting decisions as we have asserted.

Management Aspects of the Theory   The MEC theory represents an important breakaway from the typical neoclassical approach to capital investment by asserting that the level of the marginal efficiency of capital is subject to some degree of internal control, thus bringing the theory closer to the concept of capital investment as set forth in Chapter 14, despite the air of pessimism that prevailed generally during the depression era. The analysis acknowledges, for example, that there may be some hope for increasing PBIT even during a general economic recession by more efficient internal planning and control of income and costs and expenses, which would raise MEC. Or if PBIT cannot be increased, MEC may be raised by negotiating a lower supply price for the investment asset subject to certain practical control limits which are related to the degree of oligopsony and oligopoly existing in the firm and in the supplier of the assets. Table 15.8 is a hypothetical example of how

TABLE 15.8
INCREASING MARGINAL EFFICIENCY OF CAPITAL
BY INTERNAL CONTROL

| | Table Values | |
Period	6%	10%
1	0.943	0.909
2	1.833	1.736
3	$2.673 \times 1,000 = \$2,673$	$2.487 \times 1,075 = \$2,673$

certain forms of internal operating control could increase MEC. Table 15.8 assumes first that an investment expenditure of $2,673 will yield annual profits before interest of $1,000 for three years; the stream of income will equate with $2,673 at 6 percent according to the present value table. Assume further that the going market rate of interest is 7 percent, so that the marginal efficiency of capital is below the rate of interest and that the firm is, therefore, out of equilibrium. The firm does not need to be trapped at this point if management can raise its PBIT above $1,000 for each period as was done in the second situation. By raising PBIT to $1,075, the stream equates with the supply price of the asset at a MEC of 10 percent. The business now is at the equilibrium point, and it has an inducement to do more capital investing. Some of the specific internal control action that might have caused this are the following: sales (X) might have been increased by better sales promotions practices and price b might have been increased slightly if the price elasticity coefficient had been less than 1. PBIT might have been increased also by lowering b if price elasticity had been greater than 1. There is always some chance of lowering unit variable costs c by careful raw materials buying practices and to some extent by increasing the efficiency of labor. If drastic action had been needed, liquidation of certain obsolete capital assets might have been effected to decrease fixed costs and expenses (*a*).

The other way of increasing the marginal efficiency of capital is by lowering the supply price of the asset. This may be less probable than the former course of action; nevertheless, it is possible to negotiate a lower supply price for the asset if the buyer enjoys a position of some considerable degree of oligopsony. Any action on the part of management to lower the price of the asset automatically raises the marginal efficiency of capital, even though expected PBIT are not affected. The effect of this is illustrated in Table 15.9. The income stream remains at $1,000, but the *supply*

TABLE 15.9
INCREASING MARGINAL EFFICIENCY OF CAPITAL
BY EXTERNAL NEGOTIATION

| Period | Table Values | |
	6%	*10%*
1	0.943	0.909
2	1.833	1.736
3	2.673 × $1,000 = $2,673	2.487 × $1,000 = $2,487

price of the asset is reduced by negotiation from $2,673 to $2,487. Where formerly the marginal efficiency of capital was 6 percent, now the lower investment expenditure raises the rate to 10 percent. It must be implicitly assumed, of course, that the quality of the capital asset was not adversely affected by the lower price.

INTERPRETIVE REMARKS

For several reasons the marginal efficiency of capital theory continues to hold a status position in capital budgeting theory. First, it recognizes the time value of money and the reinvestment opportunities that are tied in with the compound interest principle. Second, it has done much to discredit *certainty* in forecasting income as is evidenced in the frequent use of such terms as *prospective yield* and *expected income* when referring to future profit streams. Third, and this follows from the second, the theory implies that weights or probabilities could be assigned to expected incomes and prospective yields because of the risk factor inherent therein. Fourth, by explaining that disequilibrium conditions can exist for extended periods during an economic depression, this is, nevertheless, a challenge to financial managers to counteract this condition by internal financial planning and control and by "shopping" for lower supply prices of capital assets. For techniques of income, cost, and profit planning to raise PBIT, the business manager is referred to Chapters 6 and 7 of this text.

Certain shortcomings are apparent in the theory that cause it to fall short of meeting our needs for a complete theory of capital budgeting. First, the firm and its individual share values and shareholders are secondary in importance in the theory, to the purpose of developing a general theory of how to optimize the use of all employable resources in the economy as a whole. Increasing the MEC is a means to the end of increasing the level of the employment of all natural and manufactured resources in the economy, of which capital is just one. This goal for the economy as a whole is quite different from the common goal of the firm to increase its share values. Second, and in a similar vein, no attention is given to internal organization for capital budgeting. Terms like *capital budgeting, financial manager,* and *decision making* have been supplied at times by this writer, but they are not found in the literature of the theory developed here. Third, although Keynes implicitly recognizes the interplay between business managers, he discounts greatly the idea that there is anything like a communication line between the decisions of financial managers and the decisions by investors in the securities market to bring the market value of the shares into line with the discounted value of their expected net returns. As pointed out earlier, there is presumed to be a kind of mass psychology in the securities market, quite independent of financial managers' decisions and actions, that dominates buying and selling actions that determine share values. Fourth, there is no rationing of capital to the individual firm; that is, the quantity of funds for capital investment is unlimited, the only constraint being the market rate of interest. This implies that the company's borrowing rate is immune to the debt already in the company's financial structure and the attending solvency risk that is apparent in the debt market. Fifth, like the marginal productivity theory, the MEC theory implies that the firm's cost of capital is the market rate of interest and that this serves as the cutoff rate for new investment. If the market rate is the prime rate (r_1), then there is no allowance made for the risk factor in individual projects with the result that many projects will be undertaken where the MEC is below the true risk of borrowing. But if the market rate is $r_1 + r_2$, then it will be above the prime rate and will eliminate projects whose MEC does not exceed the market borrowing rate. Despite these questions raised about the validity of the market rate of interest as a practical cutoff to a firm's investment, it is interesting to note that our governmental monetary authorities do attempt to control the quantity of capital investment in the nation as a whole by taking direct action that changes the prime rate (r_1) of interest. The reason that this is effective, as will be explained in Chapter 17, is not because the prime rate is the actual cutoff for new investment but because *it is one of the major items in the cost of capital,* which in turn is the cutoff rate for new investment.

SUMMARY

This chapter is divided into two major parts. The first part is a survey of what we call investment indicators. These are the rule-of-thumb methods still commonly used by business organizations as guidelines to capital investment. Some of the common guidelines are as follows: replace an asset when it is worn out; invest when retained earnings become excessive; invest for cost savings; and, finally, invest for an early payback. The last of these is one of the most generally used techniques for decision making where machinery and equipment are involved.

The second part of the chapter establishes a theoretical foundation on which current capital budgeting theory is based. Financial management theory is deeply indebted to economic theory for the basic models and tools used in making capital expenditure decisions. First of these is the marginal productivity theory of neo-classical economics. Second is the important theoretical work of John M. Keynes and the exposition of the marginal efficiency of capital concept. The main contribution made in the marginal efficiency theory lies in its recognition of the need for applying the discounting principle to expected net profits. This concept defines the rate of return as the discounting rate which equates the expected profit from a proposed investment project, with the supply price of that project. The optimal level of investment under the marginal efficiency concept is the level at which the marginal efficiency of capital is equal to the market rate of interest. Although this earlier theory could not anticipate all of the problems that arise in applying such theory, it established the basic methodology for approaching capital investment expenditures and provided us with a tool for effective analysis and decision making.

PROBLEMS

1. Financial managers of Company A are considering organizing for capital budgeting. After discussing the matter with managers of other small firms, they found no actual organization for capital budgeting; instead, it was found that the following methods were among those used for decision making.

   a. Replace capital equipment when it is worn out.
   b. Invest when retained earnings exceed the average net working capital for the past three years.
   c. Replace an asset when the average annual cost of a proposed new asset is less than the average cost of the present asset.

   Comment briefly on the limitations of each of these three investment indicators.

2. The Cole and Miller Manufacturing Company produces precision instruments for sea and air transport and for outer-space research and travel. To accommodate the rapid developments in these fields, plant machinery and equipment and attachments sometimes become obsolete over night. The company, therefore, maintains a regular budget for capital investment which is expanded both for replacements and additions to fixed capital. King and Warner, major stockholders in the firm, expressed the view that because of the relatively fast turnover of capital, the early payback factor should be seriously considered in making capital expenditure decisions. To illustrate how this would work, they looked at one of the problems confronting management at the present time. One of the present machines has become obsolete.

   Three machines A, B, and C would perform about the same kind of services and would cost $6,000, $7,000, and $8,000 respectively. The sales, costs, expenses, and profits allocated to the machines are illustrated below. The policy of management is to reject any machine that does not meet a three-year pay-back, and to choose from the qualifying machines the one with the shortest payback.

	Machines		
	A	*B*	*C*
Net sales	$8,500	$7,500	$10,000
Cash costs and expenses	5,500	2,500	6,000
Depreciation	1,000	1,500	1,500
Before-tax profit	2,000	3,500	2,500
Taxes (@ 40%)	800	1,400	1,000
After-tax profits	$1,200	2,100	1,000

    a. Complete the comparison, eliminating competitors that do not meet a three-year payback.

    b. Using this method of decision making, which machine will the company buy?

    c. What is the simple average rate of return earned by your first choice machines over the period in which its investment is returned?

    d. Is the rate of return in *C* a net profit earned on investment? If not what is it?

    e. What advantage and disadvantages does this method of decision making have?

3. The foundations of our modern-day capital budgeting theory are rooted in economic theory.

    a. What is meant from the financial manager's point of view by the marginal productivity of capital being a demand schedule for capital?

    b. With the following information prepare a schedule showing (1) incremental profits and (2) incremental capital inputs.

	Capital
PBIT	*Inputs*
100	1
200	2
280	3
350	4
410	5

    c. Assume that 1 unit of capital investment costs $800; set up a schedule of marginal rates of return and a column of constant interest rates of $70 per unit of capital. Indicate the optimal level of capital investing given the interest charge.

    d. What assumption is made in the theory about the quantity of capital funds available?

e. Comment on management control as it might affect marginal productivity of capital through the elements of the profit function: $P = X(b - c) - a$.

f. What is meant by equilibrium between the marginal rate of return and the rate of interest? What significance does the equilibrium concept have for financial managers seeking to maximize share values?

g. Suppose you are trying to choose between alternative investments to perform a given job. How would the MEC technique be used for decision making?

h. What limitations if any does the theory have in our present system of financial management?

4. As a warm-up exercise, try in your own words to define the marginal efficiency of capital and tell why it is called an internal rate of return.

a. Using the present value Table II in the Appendix, determine the marginal efficiency of capital of the following proposed capital investments. When the supply price is less than $1,000, you will "round" to two places beyond the decimal point.

Supply Price	Expected PBIT	Life of Asset (Years)
$5,019	$1,000	10
4,160	1,000	7
4,111	1,000	6
379	100	5
361	100	5
856	100	15

b. Use the present value Table I in the Appendix, and set up a schedule showing that the algebraic sum of the expected PBIT and the supply price of the asset is equal to zero for the first three investments.

c. Select any three of the investments and show that the ratio of the present value of PBIT and the supply price of the asset is unity.

5. From the schedule below, determine the schedule of declining marginal efficiency of capital using Table II in the Appendix. The supply price of the asset expected to yield these declining profits is $3,312.

DECLINING MARGINAL EFFICIENCY OF CAPITAL

	1	2	3	4
	1,136.58	1,090.55	1,000	955.84
	1,136.58	1,090.55	1,000	955.84
	1,136.58	1,090.55	1,000	955.84
	1,136.58	1,090.55	1,000	955.84
Supply price of asset	$3,312	$3,312	$3,312	$3,312

Graph the declining marginal efficiency of capital and indicate the optimal level of investment assuming that the market rate of interest is: 6 percent, 10 percent.

6. Using the model $P = X(b - c) - a$, indicate what kind of corrective investment action on these items would increase the marginal efficiency of capital. Use the present value Table II in the Appendix to answer the following questions.

   a. Suppose that the market rate of interest is 8 percent and that the present expected profit flow on a $3,312 capital investment for four years is $955.84 yearly. Is the MEC of the business equal to, greater than, or less than the market rate of interest?

   b. Assume that financial managers figure out a way to raise the expected profit flow to $1,044.80 annually. Would it profit the business to make the investment? Explain.

   c. If the expected flow from the investment for the next four years is expected to be $955.84 annually, but there is a chance to negotiate the supply price of the asset down to $3,030, what is the MEC and should the investment be made? Use Table II.

16

Structure
for
Decision
Making

In this chapter a format is established for analyzing and for making capital investment decisions. The basic premises of capital budgeting and their relation to future profitable operations that were developed in Chapter 14 are carried forward to this chapter on theoretical foundations developed in Chapter 15. As a conclusion to the investment management portion of capital budgeting, this chapter should provide the tools and skills that will assist in bringing financial managers closer to their goals of maximizing share values.

METHODOLOGY

Reconsidered first are the precepts of methodology in financial management defined in Chapter 1 as they apply specifically to capital investment decisions. The large expenditures for capital investments and the corresponding risks that they incur is the reason for financial managers needing to establish a method for reviewing investment proposals before making committments.

ORGANIZING FOR CAPITAL INVESTMENT

One thing noticeably lacking in the theoretical foundations of capital budgeting discussed in Chapter 15 is a financial organization for decision making. Although decisions are made less often in capital management than at the current level of operation, the magnitude and the relative complexity of the individual decision places a premium on making the correct decision. Futhermore, to be organized for making current operating decisions and not for making capital investment decisions is like planning for one course at a time in a college career without a master plan for the total program. Instead of treating capital expenditure decisions as incidental, they need to be admitted to the mainstream of financial management. This means creating an awareness of the capital management issue including involvement of personnel outside the financial organization as a whole to the purpose and intent of capital planning.

Communications exist in the organization to let financial management receive ideas from line personnel who are in direct contact with working and fixed capital needs. The function of financial personnel should be to motivate investment proposals in the areas of sales and production and to screen the proposals by applying to them financial tools and skills for analysis and decision making. Sales management may best be able to suggest ways of increasing X and b in the profit equation through capital investment; production management may suggest ways of decreasing c and in special cases even of decreasing a through capital investment; and financial managers should be qualified in the use of measuring tools and skills for screening these proposals and for coordinating them to put the business on a higher plane for common goal attainment. Capital planning should not be confined to periods of prosperity just because profits and retained earnings are increasing and fixed assets are wearing out more rapidly. Aside from being concerned with projects that immediately change the limits of the profit function, projects should be considered that have more remote benefits and that have indirect as well as direct profit effects like safety programs and programs to protect the health of the employees.

It takes organizational skill to set up a theory of capital budgeting and standards to determine which investments are profitable and which are not. And when a fixed sum of budgeted capital has to be rationed, it requires the ranking of projects to decide which should command higher priority and which lower. Finally, financial managers should organize to see that the investment budget is executed on schedule. It is one thing to budget capital to investment proposals and still another to see that funds are available and properly applied to execute the budget. Although the flow of capital funds may have been implied in the investment budget, securing them raises problems that are part of the total subject but quite different from the investment decision.

RESEARCH AND ANALYSIS

Organizing for capital budgeting means continually considering capital investment to broaden profit horizons and to increase the company's long-run share values. Such opportunities have to be sought through research and then analyzed through the use of simulation technique. We will consider this analytic approach to the subject in some detail.

Simulation means projecting the effects of investment proposals to the components of the profit function before making commitments for capital expenditures or for capital financing. This is a powerful tool for analysis in view of the possible long-term adverse effect on share values of making poor investment decisions;

financial managers cannot afford to make capital expenditure commitments because of possible long-lasting adverse effects on a company's share values without first testing their effects in simple simulation models. To illustrate how this can be done, we start with the profit model: $P_e = X(b - c) - a$, letting P_e be *expected* profits. Then we enter the values as they would be with the company's present capital facilities and determine optimal expected profits. Then we enter the change or changes that would occur in the elements of the profit structure given the proposed investment and determine expected optimal profits. The additional expected profit is the marginal profit from the first increment of investment. Then this can be repeated with subsequent increments of investment until no incremental profits are realized. This is an oversimplified form of simulation from the practical viewpoint and, therefore, needs sweeping adjustments to make it applicable to the real situation in which it would be expedient to extend investment to the limit at which incremental profits are zero. Not only would this be overextending the company's risks in many cases, but it might be impossible to attain by most businesses because of the limitation of internal and external funds.

CASH FLOW APPROACH

Accounting for the expected income from capital investment and the expenditure for the assets are both put on a cash basis in making capital investment decisions. One reason for this is that over the long run investment income flows are turned over through the cash balance. For example, credit sales that in the current operation build up the receivables of a business over the life of a capital investment are collected and turned into transactions through cash balances; likewise, accruals that are current liabilities at certain stages in operations in the long run are paid off with cash funds. More important than these two factors are the noncash costs and expenses like depreciation, depletion, and amortization that are used to compute net profits in the income statement. Noncash costs and expenses like these, while significant for reporting current profits, are of no significance as a cost or expense factor in estimating cash flows. Success or failure in the last analysis is measured by the total quantity of cash that an investment proposal would generate over its life compared with the cash that would be expended on the investment. In general terms, the optimization goal is to maximize the inflow of cash from the investment proposal relative to its outflow. But before going further into the goals, we need to examine the components more closely on both sides: the cash inflow and the cash outflow.

NET CASH INFLOW

It is the *net* cash flow expected from the investment project that financial managers compare with the supply price of the investment for decision making. Net cash flow is the difference between cash income and cash costs and expenses related to individual budgeting proposals. The initial profit function of Chapter 14 was

$P = X(b - c) - a$. This is basically a current operating tool and is applied to the total enterprise. Although there is no discrepancy between the profit function as it relates to the current operating goal of the total business and the net cash function as it relates to an individual investment, certain qualitative changes and additions have to be made to the factors in the initial model. Income taxes, which are cash expenses, are deducted; and noncash costs and expenses like depreciation and amortization charges that are included in *a* above to determine net profits for income tax purposes have to be returned to the net cash flow. The model is adjusted easily to a net cash flow basis as follows:

$$NCF_e = [X(b - c) - a](1 - t_r) + nc \qquad 16.1$$

NCF_e equals the expected net cash flow. The value $[X(b - c) - a]$ is the same as in the original function. But $1 - t_r$ converts before-tax profits to an after-tax net profit; and *nc*, as depreciation and other noncash costs and expenses, converts after-tax profit to a linear net cash flow. Why change from a net profit analysis which is applicable to the firm as a whole to a net cash flow analysis when individual capital assets are concerned? The answer to this is twofold: first, cash is tangible, liquid, easy to identify and easily reinvested; and, second, because of the long periods involved in the analysis, all of the inflows and outflows of value will have turned over through cash.

Getting back to the form of the statement once more, what we have finally is a net after-tax profit figure $[X(b - c) - a](1 - t_r)$, with noncash charges (*nc*) added back. When the only noncash charge against income for tax purposes is depreciation as it often is, the net cash flow can be simply stated as the sum of after-tax net profits in the operating budget plus depreciation.

$$NCF_e = \text{After-tax net profit} + \text{depreciation} \qquad 16.2$$

Table 16.1 shows that the measure of net cash flow is the same using either the *direct* method or the *indirect* method of stating the flow.

This tabular tool is awkward for extensive analysis but it does show which factors are involved in a cash flow statement. For most purposes, the original equation 16.1 is a more effective tool. To illustrate, suppose that management wants to know how much cash will be generated annually from an investment that will have the following results: sales $X = 120,000$ units, price $b = \$1$, unit variable cost $c = \$.70$, noncash fixed charges $a = \$10,000$ and the tax rate $tr = 0.4$. Substituting:

$$NCF_e = [120,000(\$1 - \$.70) - \$10,000](1 - 0.4) + \$10,000$$
$$= [36,000 - 10,000](0.6) + 10,000$$
$$= \$25,600$$

It is simple arithmetic to convert any set of expected values into expected net cash flows in this manner. Equation 16.1 is useful also for showing that there is no inconsistency between the net cash flow standard for internal financial manage-

TABLE 16.1
COMPANY Z
CURRENT OPERATING STATEMENT

Net sales	$100,000
Cash costs and expenses	70,000
Cash profits	30,000
Noncash charges	10,000
Before-tax profits	20,000
Taxes (@ 40%)	8,000
After-tax profit	$12,000

Net Cash Flow

Direct Statement			*Indirect Statement*	
Net sales		$100,000	After-tax profits	$12,000
			Noncash charges	10,000
Cash charges:				
Cost and expenses	$70,000			
Taxes	8,000	78,000		
Net cash inflow		$ 22,000		$22,000

ment, and the net profit standard as communicated to the securities market. When the securities market is sophisticated, as it is today, the NCF_e equation could be used to supplement the regular net profit statement for better communication and a more complete evaluation of our shares.

In conclusion to this section, a feature of the cash flow that needs mentioning is that, in making investment decisions, net cash flows are projected over the whole life of the asset. Depending on how the flow is expected to be returned, it may be all projected to one terminal date several years into the future; it may be projected as a steady or irregular annual stream; or it may be projected as a combination flow: steady or irregular annual amounts plus a terminal amount at some distant date. With a given time schedule, the optimization goal in its simplest terms is to maximize the total net cash flow from a given project. This is just stating the simple fact that, if the time schedule of the net cash flow is set, the greatest benefit is realized from maximizing the future flow of cash. But the facts of net cash flows are that they do vary widely in individual cases, and the time schedule as well as the total quantity of the net cash flow can be a major value-determining factor as will be recalled from Chapter 3. But aside from the total size of the cash flow and the timing of the flow, capital investment decisions have to consider the expenditure side of the issue or what, in a more limited sense, is the supply price of the asset.

THE CASH OUTFLOW

Now we can extend the optimizing goal of capital investment to a relative basis, to the relationship of expected net cash flow, and to what has to be expended to attain the flow. A more complete statement of the decision-making goal can be stated then to maximize the excess of the net cash flow from an investment over the cash expenditure for the investment. To fit the actual case, consideration has to be given to different time schedules both for paying and for receiving.

Controllable factors that the financial manager needs to consider before making capital expenditure decisions are twofold. First, he should explore the chance of negotiating with the supplier for lower capital expenditures; this applies to items like inventories in net working capital as well as to fixed capital. Second, there is the chance of paying for the asset in the future, in part at least, instead of paying for all of it today. Some commonly used deferred payment plans require a down payment with the balance paid in equal installments until the asset is paid for in full. The precise form of the payment schedule has important effects on the actual value of the expenditure; other forms of expenditure include large installments in the first years *telescoping* to smaller payments near the end. With the extensive treatment that was given to the time value of money in Chapter 3, the student may already be speculating about the present cash value of alternative payment streams and their effect on the investment decision. In the remainder of the chapter, two approaches to decision making will be developed: one, the internal rate of return which is a relative statement of net cash flow to capital expenditure and, the other, the present cash value which is the present dollar value of the expected cash flow compared with the dollar value of the capital expenditure. The internal rate of return method is discussed first because it grows out of the marginal efficiency of capital theory of investment discussed in Chapter 15; and, because in point of time, it was the first method adapted to the practical problems of capital budgeting.

INTERNAL RATE OF RETURN FOR DECISION MAKING

The reinvestment growth rate developed in Chapter 3 is a good starting point for identifying the internal rate of return. The internal rate of return is an inverted growth rate. It is the rate that discounts a given future net cash value back to a given cash value in the present. At the same time, it is the growth rate that causes the discounted present cash value to attain the dimension of a given future cash value. More specifically for investment purposes, *it is identified as the rate that equates an expected net cash value with the investment proposal that would pro duce that value.* It differs from the definition of the marginal efficiency of capital only in identifying the expected flow of income definitely with a net cash flow rather than with profit before interest and taxes. The basic tools for determining the internal rate of return are present value Tables I and II in the Appendix. Table I supplies internal rates of return that equate a single net cash value with a cash investment. Table II supplies internal rates of return that equate a constant stream of net cash flows with a cash investment. Although both tables are based on $1 they are adaptable for solving investment problems of any magnitude. First the internal rate of return will be determined given net cash flow as a single terminal value, and then the rate of return will be determined given net cash flow as a stream of regular and irregular values.

The simplest kind of problem is determining the internal rate of return realized when, in exchange for a given cash investment today, a single cash sum will be received at a stated time in the future. This could be a case of a company buying an asset like land, research equipment, or even securities with definite expectations of what the asset will return in a single sum of cash at some stated future date. The internal rate of return is the discounting rate in Table I that will equate the single future sum with the present price of the investment.

In financial management, we deal primarily with future values that contain growth, which means that they evidence a future net cash flow. To illustrate the single net cash flow case, assume that, by investing $10,000 today in research equipment, we expect to develop a patented process that can be sold after three years for net cash of $13,322; that is net cash flow after cash costs and expenses on the project have been fully covered. This means that the *initial investment*, plus $3,322 of after-tax net cash profits, will be returned. To determine the measure of the internal rate of return, we need to first state the relationship of the present capital expenditure to the net cash flow.

$$\frac{\$10,000}{\$13,322} = 0.751$$

Reading across period 3 in Table I, we find 0.751 in the 10 percent discounting column; this means that, with the net cash flow reinvested annually for three years, this project would yield an average internal rate of return of 10 percent. Looking at this internal rate of return now as a reinvested or compound growth rate, we see the rate at which $10,000 would have to be invested today for it to grow to $13,322 three years in the future.

The amount $13,322 is selected arbitrarily so that the rate could be read right off the table without interpolating. Any value at the end of the third year other than $13,322 would not have been exactly 10 percent; and, to get the exact internal rate of return, we would have had to interpolate as is done below. To illustrate this, suppose that $13,000 had been expected from the $10,000 investment of $13,322. The procedure of interpolation is as follows: $10,000/$13,000 = 0.769, which is somewhere between 8 percent (0.794) and 10 percent (0.751) on Table I, and the following model is used to get the correction factor:

$$\text{Correction factor} = \frac{A - B}{A - C}(R_1 - R_2) \qquad 16.3$$

Where: A = Table factor for the lower of the two rates
B = Table factor for the unknown rate for which we are solving
C = Table factor for the higher of the two rates
R_1 = Higher of the two rates
R_2 = Lower of the two rates

Substituting:

$$\text{Correction factor} = \frac{0.794 - 0.769}{0.794 - 0.751}(2)$$

$$= 0.58 \times 2$$

$$= 1.16 \text{ percent}$$

$$\text{Corrected rate} = 8 + 1.16 = \underline{9.16} \text{ percent}$$

Whether the return is 10 percent or 9.16 percent, the same question has to arise in the minds of financial managers: Is this return high enough to justify the investment? The answer depends on how high financial managers place their required rate, their cutoff rate; in essence how high they set the *cost* of tying up the $10,000 for a three-year period. We cannot go very far into capital budgeting decisions without considering the cutoff rate and what is called the company's cost of capital. Analysis of the cost of capital is reserved for the following chapter; for this discussion of capital budgeting it is enough to recognize it as a cutoff rate for deciding on acceptable and nonacceptable investment projects.

CONSTANT STREAM OF NET CASH FLOWS

In a simulated capital investment after the adjustment is made to sales volume X and the other factors, especially b and c, that affect $NCF_e = [X(b - c) - a](1 - tr) + nc$, it may be assumed that the project has a constant net cash flow effect over the life of the investment. In making each flow constant, financial managers are looking for the internal rate of return that will equate the following with a present investment value.

$$NCF_e \sum_{t=0}^{t=n} = [X(b - c) - a](1 - tr) + nc \dots n \qquad 16.4$$

A model like this will fit any proposal that is expected to have a stable flow of cash. Illustrating, assume that an investment costing $23,220 is expected to yield $10,000 annually in NCF_e for three years. The table value for this three-year flow is found as follows: $23,220/$10,000 = 2.322. The rate of return in this case must be read from Table II. Reading across row 3, we find that 2.322 is in the 14 percent discounting column, meaning that the project would yield an average annual internal rate of return of 14 percent for three years on the initial investment. Another way of stating it is that $23,220 invested for three years at a reinvestment growth rate of 14 percent would yield a net cash flow of $10,000 for each of the three years.

Interpolation is necessary when the quotient above does not result in an exact matching table factor. Suppose that the capital expenditure had been $20,000 instead of $23,220 and that the table factor therefore had been $20,000/$10,000 = 2. Reading across row 3 of Table II, the table factor is 2.042 for a 22 percent rate of return and 1.981 for a 24 percent return with 2 lying somewhere between these two extremes. This illustrates how a decline in the supply price of the investment can cause a sharp rise in the internal rate of return. Interpolation:

$$\text{Correction factor} = \frac{A - B}{A - C}(R_1 - R_2) \qquad\qquad 16.5$$

$$= \frac{2.042 - 2}{2.042 - 1.981}(2)$$

$$= 0.69 \times 2$$

$$= 1.38$$

$$\text{Corrected rate} = 22 + 1.38 = \underline{23.38} \text{ percent}$$

VARIABLE NET CASH FLOW

In still other investment plans, sales volume may be expected to vary over the life of the investment so widely that the assumption of a constant net cash flow would be unrealistic. Or, instead of sales X varying, the proposed investment may cause other elements like b or c in the NCF_e model to vary. In making the net cash low estimate in this case, certain values in $NCF_e = [X(b - c) - a](1 - tr) + nc$ have to be varied each year of the forecast; but this model adjusted for annual change will fit any variable net cash flow situation. The patterns of the flows will depend on the purpose of the investment. For example, the investment may be designed to increase net sales X, to raise b, or to decrease c a given amount each year, or even to change two or more of the capital variables simultaneously with the effect of creating irregular expected net cash flows. To illustrate the rate of return techniques, we turn to Table I. Suppose that a $10,000 investment is expected to return over three years $3,000, $5,000, and $7,000 respectively for a total of $15,000. First, we average the expected cash flow, $15,000/3 = $5,000, and divide this value into $10,000 for the table value: $10,000/$5,000 = 2. This figure will locate the general vicinity of the rate of return. It tells us that the rate of return somewhere around 22 and 24 percent on Table II. We go back now to Table I to compute the actual rate because each of the expected values is different. Checking the 24 percent and the 22 percent columns, we see that both produce present values for the three-year flows of less than $10,000 which means that both rates are too high. Moving to the 20 percent column, we see that the rate produces a present value very close to $10,000, too close to need interpolating.

The problem can now be extended to include the case in which, on the termination date of the project, cash funds are expected to be returned from unused net working capital or from the salvage value of fixed capital. To illustrate this, assume that $500 in net working capital is expected to be intact on the termination of the project and also that another $500 can be expected from the salvage value of fixed assets. This additional $1,000 must raise the rate of return above 20 percent. The computation is illustrated below. First, the expected average annual flow is $5,333 instead of $5,000: $16,000/3 = $5,333. Dividing $5,333 into $10,000 we get a table factor of 1.875 which falls in Table II between 26 percent and 28 percent. Again we turn to Table I to work out the details of the rate because each year has a different quantity of the irregular flow. The present values of the flow at 26 percent and at 28 percent are both below $10,000, so we know that the rate of return must be less than 26 percent. By trial and error, we find that the rate is between 22 percent and 24 percent. Interpolation determines the exact rate of return.

TABLE 16.2
RATE OF RETURN WHEN THE FLOWS ARE IRREGULAR

Year	Table Factor	22%	Table Factor	20%
1	0.820 × $3,000 =	$2,460	0.833 × $3,000 =	$ 2,499
2	.672 × 5,000 =	3,360	.694 × 5,000 =	3,470
3	.551 × 7,000 =	3,857	.579 × 7,000 =	4,053
	Total present value	$9,677		$10,022
	Approximate rate of return		20%	

TABLE 16.3
RATE OF RETURN WHEN THE FLOWS ARE IRREGULAR
AND A TERMINAL VALUE IS RECEIVED

Year	Table Factor	24%	Table Factor	22%
1	0.806 × $3,000 =	$2,418	0.820 × $3,000 =	$ 2,460
2	.650 × 5,000 =	3,250	.672 × 5,000 =	3,360
3	.524 × 7,000 =	3,668	.551 × 7,000 =	3,857
	.524 × 1,000 =	524	.551 × 1,000 =	551
	Total present value	$9,860		$10,228

$$\text{Correction factor} = \frac{A - B}{A - C}(R_1 - R_2)$$
$$= \frac{\$10,228 - \$10,000}{\$10,228 - \ \ 9,860}(2)$$
$$= 0.62(2)$$
$$= 1.24$$
$$\text{Corrected rate} = 22 + 1.24 = \underline{23.24}$$

NEGATIVE NET CASH FLOW AND DUAL RATES OF RETURN

The internal rate of return is the rate that equates the expected net cash flow with the capital expenditure. It is also the rate that causes the algebraic sum of the investment expenditure, a negative value, and the net cash flow, a positive value, to equal zero. It is the latter of the two definitions of internal rate of return that will be applied to an unusual kind of situation in which a reversal of the normal net cash-flow condition causes a negative net cash flow to appear somewhere along the otherwise normal positive flow. Normally, capital budgeting projects produce positive net cash flows from operations even though for a given period a net loss from operations may be expected; this will still produce a positive net cash flow because added back into the flow is the depreciation equivalent of cash funds from sales.

But this does not allow for another situation that may arise in the middle of the stream, figuratively speaking, namely the need for making another investment to execute the total project for profit. An example of this type of project could be some kind of land development, exploration, or land exploitation project in which an initial investment (negative net cash flow) is to be made which will produce a stream of cash income for a certain number of periods, after which another cash investment is required (another negative net cash flow) to execute the remainder of a profitable project.

Let us assume that we are budgeting capital to a land development project requiring a small initial investment of $300 which is expected to produce a positive net cash stream for four periods; but that, in the fifth year a new investment of $12,000 (negative net cash flow) will have to be made to realize the final goal of operation. In the fifth year, operations were expected to yield $2,000; but, with the offsetting $12,000 capital expenditure, the net cash flow for the fifth period is expected to be − $10,000. The expected net cash flow for the project including the middle-of-the-stream expenditure plan is illustrated in Table 16.4. The table shows that two internal rates of return result: one between the 1- and 2-percent rates and the other between the 16- and 17-percent rates. The exact rates at which the algebraic sums of the two sets of values are equal to 0 are 1.14 and 16.69 percent. The correct rate is the one following which the net present values are negative values, and the preceding net present values are positive.[1] The rate that meets this test is 1.14 percent; it is preceded by a positive value of $37 and followed by a series of negative values. The 16.69-percent rate of return cannot be the correct one because it is preceded by negative values and followed by positive values. It is difficult to conceive of a situation wherein the cost of capital would be less than 1.14 percent, so a project proposed of this kind will be rejected.

Figure 16.1 graphs Table 16.4. Notice that the internal rate of return function crosses the 0 net-present-value line at two points: at 1.14 percent and at 16.69 percent. The graph relates also an infinite number of combinations of net present value on the Y axis with an infinite number of internal rates of return on the X axis.

A DEFERRED OUTFLOW

We have been concentrating on the rate of return assuming that the investment expenditures were made all at the beginning of the investment period. This was done to center attention on appraising future net cash flows as the variables effecting the internal rate of return. But many capital expenditures such as long-run sales promotion programs, research and development projects, lease contracts, and installment purchases of real properties spread capital payments over several

---

[1] John G. McLean, "How To Evaluate New Capital Investments," *Harvard Business Review*, XXXVI (November-December, 1958), p. 59.

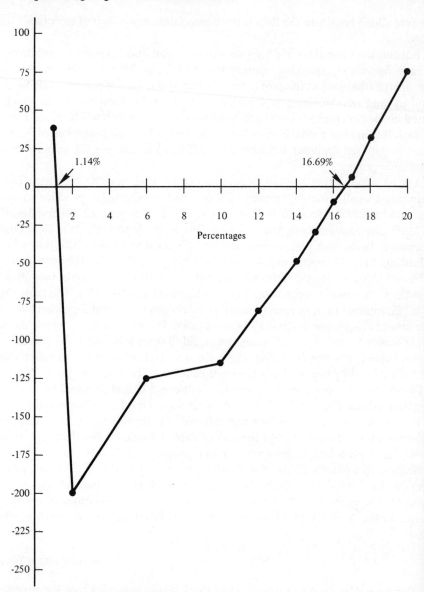

Figure 16.1. Negative Net Cash Flow Produces Two Internal Rates of Return Initial Investment $300.

years. We will consider briefly deferred payments as means of increasing the internal rate on investments assuming that no external financing charges are levied on the deferred payments. With this assumption the economy of deferred payment results from having the funds on hand in the business for internal reinvestment until the deferred payment is due. To show how this affects the rate of return on

TABLE 16.4
NEGATIVE NET CASH FLOW PRODUCES TWO INTERNAL RATES OF RETURN
INITIAL INVESTMENT $300

Net Cash Flow		Discounting Rates										
Period	*Amount*	*1%*	*2%*	*6%*	*10%*	*12%*	*14%*	*15%*	*16%*	*17%*	*18%*	*20%*
0	$ -300	$ -300	$ -300	$ -300	$ -300	$ -300	$ -300	$ -300	$ -300	$ -300	$ -300	$ -300
1	1,000	990	980	943	909	893	877	870	862	854	847	833
2	1,500	1,470	1,442	1,335	1,239	1,196	1,154	1,134	1,115	1,095	1,077	1,041
3	1,000	971	942	840	751	712	675	658	641	624	609	579
4	1,000	961	924	792	683	636	592	572	552	533	516	482
	-12,000											
5	2,000	-9,510	-9,060	-7,470	-6,210	-5,670	-5,190	-4,970	-4,760	-4,560	-4,370	-4,020
6	1,800	1,696	1,598	1,269	1,015	913	821	778	738	700	666	603
7	1,000	933	871	665	513	452	400	376	354	333	314	279
8	600	554	512	376	280	242	211	196	183	171	160	140
9	1,000	914	837	592	424	361	308	284	263	243	225	194
10	1,500	1,358	1,041	817	579	483	405	371	341	312	287	243
Net present value =		+37	-204	-124	-117	-82	-47	-31	-11	+5	+31	+74

Net present value =   0 (at 1%)   0 (at 17%)

Internal rates of return =   1.14%   16.69%

project, we will assume that a $10,000 capital expenditure is payable over a three-year period and that $2,000 is invested at the end of the first year and $4,000 a the end of each of the next two years. These outflows can easily be converted to present values, but there may be some question as to what discounting rate to use The higher the rate the lower the present value of the expenditure and the highe the internal rate of return will be. We do not know what rate will be earned on the proposed investment, so we turn elsewhere for the discounting rate.

Let us use 12 percent which we assume is the firm's borrowing rate $(r_1 + r_2$ for this amount of capital if the business were charged for the deferral. The presen value of the payments is computed using Table II. The first payment of $2,000 ha a present value of $1,786 ($2,000 × 0.893) and the last two payments a combined present value of $6,036 ($4,000 × 1.509), giving a total present value of $7,822 Assume that $4,000 annually will be generated in net cash flow. The same proce dure is used as before. Since this is a constant net cash flow of $4,000 the rate of return table factor is: $7,822/$4,000 = 1.955 which falls almost on 25 percent in Table II. If the $10,000 investment had been paid for at the beginning of the period the student should verify that the actual internal rate of return after interpolating would have been only 9.71 percent. In some cases in the financial world deferral can be obtained without charge when the supply of capital assets is greater than the demand; and, in this case, the method illustrated above is a valid one for deter mining internal rate of return. In other cases, there will be some charge for the deferral, in which case this rate should be used for discounting the payments to the present. The danger lies in selecting a discounting rate that is too high, as may have been done in the illustration above to overstate the internal rate.

THE OPTIMIZING DECISION: INTERNAL RATE OF RETURN

The examples that have been presented thus far were used to show how to convert expected net cash flows and given capital expenditures into measurable internal rates of return. These are elements that had to be described before a meaningful theory of capital budgeting could be developed. The basic premise of the theory is that financial managers will budget capital *to investment projects so long as the internal rate of return exceeds some designated cutoff rate.* This premise will have to be modified in some ways and expanded in others as will be seen in developing a complete theory that will meet the facts of the financial world. Start ing with the basic premise, the optimal budgeting level is reached when the last increment of investment meets that cutoff point. The best way to explain the optimizing principle is to let the cutoff point be zero; that is, we assume that capital will be budgeted until the internal rate of return on the incremental unit reaches zero. If we can understand the optimizing method of obtaining a zero incremental rate, it is a relatively simple matter from there to fit the analysis to variable cutoff rates.

The diminishing marginal efficiency of capital sets the basic pattern for illustrat ing the optimizing operation except that we substitute internal rate of return for

MEC. We assume that the only constraint placed on investment for the present is the cutoff at zero rate of return. Financial managers cannot stop investing until this point is reached because they do not know where the optimal investment point is until they actually reach the zero rate. To avoid misunderstanding, the reader is cautioned, however, that we are talking now about an investment model or simulation for all budgets are simulations of what *may* be done. Capital budgets are first of all plans for future action that are studied, evaluated and then finally actually applied. So now we can construct a general optimizing capital budget such as Table 16.5. Table 16.5 shows the diminishing rate of return effect of budget-

TABLE 16.5
OPTIMAL LEVEL OF INVESTMENT
DIMINISHING INTERNAL RATE OF RETURN

(1) Investment Project	(2) After-tax Net Profit	(3) Depreciation	(4) NCF$_e$ (2) + (3)	(5) Capital Expenditure	(6) Conversion Factors	(7) Internal Rate of Return (%)
a	$2,400	$1,000	$3,400	$10,000	2.941	32.0
b	1,600	1,000	2,600	10,000	3.846	23.2
c	800	1,000	1,800	10,000	5.555	12.2
d	0	1,000	1,000	10,000	10.000	0
e	−800	200	−600	10,000	−16.667	−rate

ing five $10,000 increments of investment, each with a life span of ten years. Elements in the budget are identified by the column heads: (1) lists the number of independent investment projects, (2) is the after-tax net profit expected to be added to total profits by each increment of investment; (3) is the constant annual depreciation allowance for each project over a ten-year period; (4) is the sum of expected net profits and depreciation; (5) is the price of each investment proposal; (6) is the conversion factor for each ratio (5/4); and (7) is the internal rate of return for each of the flows for ten years. The rates have been interpolated for accuracy.

The whole schedule of Table 16.5 is a simulation of internal rates of return. Column (7) contains *the diminishing rates at which a diminishing marginal NCF$_e$ over the life of each investment proposal equates with each $10,000 incremental expenditure.* The table shows the internal rate of return declining for each subsequent investment until it reaches 0 where the expected net cash flow just covers the $10,000 spent for the capital asset. Special attention is called to project *d* with its 0 rate of return. It will be noted that, although the project would yield a net cash flow of $1,000 for each of the five periods, there is no internal rate of return. *This is a nonprofitable project because it just returns its initial investment; but it is not a negative return because it does not return less than its initial investment.* It may be helpful to identify the 0 rate of return in the following manner with the present value ratio: $P_n[1/(1 + r)n]$. Substituting in the ratio from the table where *r* equals the internal rate of return of 0 and P_n equals the $1,000 expected return for each of the ten years:

$$\text{Present value} = \frac{\$1,000}{(1+0)} + \frac{\$1,000}{(1+0)^2} + \frac{\$1,000}{(1+0)^3} + \dots 10n$$
$$= \$10,000$$

The optimal level of the budget is discovered at the fourth level of $40,000. If the budget had stopped before this, it would have foregone profits, and to have gone beyond this would have netted a loss. The reason it has to go as far as 0 is that we do not know where the optimal level is until the simulation has been carried all the way to 0. It is noted that profits are maximized at $4,800 which is the sum of the three profitable investments (see column 2). Since this is a capital budget, it designates to financial managers not to invest $40,000 but to go directly to a $30,000 investment for the maximum profit. If the size of each increment had been smaller, the optimal investment level would have been somewhat different but, when we assume too small applications of capital, the theory departs from reality and loses its usefulness for decision making. As a guiding principle management should make each unit of investment just as large as is consistent with the size of investments ordinarily made by the business. Carried to its logical conclusion, the model schedule above could be applied to any division or department within the business organization.

This important model has two limiting features. One, it implies that unlimited capital resources are available for management to invest as much as is needed to reach the 0 rate of return. In the example above, it means only $30,000; but, in other examples, it may mean much more. Although capital financing is practically unlimited for some businesses, in most cases financial constraints do limit the availability of funds. Two, in assuming a 0 cutoff rate, the budget also implies a 0 cost of capital. With a zero cost of capital, investment will be made so long as the return is above the 0 rate. This is a dangerous implication because it could result in incremental investments below the company's cost of capital and this could have serious repercussions on the value of the company's shares. If the above premise is modified then by allowing, first, for the constraint of limited capital financing and, second, for the constraint of a cost of capital above 0, it becomes adaptable for making practical capital budgeting decisions. The cost of capital is reserved for more detailed consideration in the following chapter, but we will consider below a typical problem situation in which the quantity of available funds limits the scope of the capital budget.

BUDGETING CAPITAL SUBJECT TO A FUNDS CONSTRAINT

If the business is organized for capital budgeting, as was suggested earlier that it should be, investment proposals will come to the fore from sales, production and from other departments of the business with nonhomogeneous forms of capi tal that entail a wide range of capital expenditures. Let us assume, as is typically true in most concerns, that capital funds are limited and in this case limited to $100,000. The following projects have been submitted by different departments of the business. Each proposal includes an estimate of its service life, an estimate of the annual net cash flow over its service life, and a computed internal rate of return.

TABLE 16.6
ALTERNATIVE INVESTMENT PROPOSALS

Investment Project	Expenditure	Service Life (Years)	Net Cash Flows	Years	Internal Rate of Return
a	$ 40,000	10	$10,000	(1 to 5)	16.4
			5,000	(6 to 10)	
b	40,000	10	5,000	(1 to 5)	11.2
			10,000	(6 to 10)	
c	30,000	5	8,000	(1 to 5)	10.4
d	20,000	4	8,000	(1 to 4)	21.9
e	20,000	4	2,000	(1 to 3)	14.1
			26,000	(4th)	
	$150,000				

Project a splits its flow with $10,000 yearly for the first five years dropping to $5,000 yearly for the second five years. Project b splits its flow also but reverses it with the small returns expected in the first five years and the larger ones the second five years. Notice the premium in the internal rate of return on the first project because of the earlier large returns. The method of obtaining the rate for project a is discussed here. Determine the average net cash flow ($10,000 + $5,000/2 = $7,500) and then divide the average into $40,000: $40,000/$7,500 = 5.33. This is very rough; but, on Table II, 5.33 in the tenth row indicates a rate between 12 percent and 14 percent. Checking 14 percent on Table II gives a present value of $43,245 which is too far above the $40,000 expenditure; the rate of return has to be higher than this to equate the irregular flow with $40,000. By trial and error the rate is found to be between 16 percent and 18 percent. Interpolating is done to obtain the exact rate of 16.4 percent which is illustrated in Table 16.7. The rates 11.2 and 14.1 percent for projects b and e were obtained in the same manner.

The important decision of ranking still lies ahead. Table 16.8 ranks the projects in terms of their internal rates of return showing how the $100,000 of funds would be used up. None of these projects is operating at the margin where the rate of return would be 0, but some project or projects have to be dropped if management is to stay within the financial constraint of $100,000. If projects are not divisible, project b has to be dropped or more capital sought. Assume at first that the ceiling on capital budgeting is fixed at $100,000 which has been appropriated by the business to this purpose. Table 16.8 shows a very realistic possibility for this kind of situation. It shows projects d, a and e using up $80,000 of the $100,000,

TABLE 16.7
INTERNAL RATE FOR PROJECT A
NET CASH FLOW IS SPLIT

	16%				*18%*		
Years	*Table Factor*	*Net Cash Flow*	*Present Value*	*Years*	*Table Factor*	*Net Cash Flow*	*Present Value*
1 to 5	3.274 ×	$10,000 =	$32,740	1 to 5	3.127 ×	$10,000 =	$31,270
6 to 10	1.559 ×	5,000 =	7,795	6 to 10	1.367 ×	5,000 =	6,835
		Total	$40,535			Total	$38,105

$$\text{Correction factor} = \frac{A - B}{A - C}(R_1 - R_2)$$

$$= \frac{\$40,535 - \$40,000}{40,535 - 38,105}(2)$$

$$= 0.44$$

$$\text{Corrected rate} = 16 + 0.44 = \underline{16.44} \text{ percent}$$

TABLE 16.8
RANKING INVESTMENT PROJECTS
CAPITAL RESOURCES OF $100,000

Project	Internal Rate of Return	Size of Investment	Cumulative Investment
d	21.9	$20,000	$ 20,000
a	16.4	40,000	60,000
e	14.1	20,000	80,000
b	11.2	40,000	120,000 ($100,000 limit)
c	10.4	30,000	150,000

the rate of return on the incremental $20,000 project e being 14.1 percent. Not enough capital is available to undertake the fourth project (b) that would yield 11.2 percent; and so financial managers may hold the funds temporarily in liquid income earning assets like marketable securities, seeking at the same time another profitable $20,000 investment or seeking another $20,000 to invest in project b. Nothing is said in this case about the cost of capital cutoff rate; but, if the cutoff rate is set at say 16 percent, only $60,000 of the fund will be invested, and this in projects d and a.

PRESENT VALUE FOR DECISION MAKING

Present value was explained and illustrated in Chapter 3, so that the mechanics of determining present value of an expected net cash flow does not have to be illustrated in detail as was done with the internal rate of return. Nevertheless, there is a decision-making framework that is related uniquely to present value analysis that needs to be considered and compared with the internal rate of return analysis. First, let us review the substance of the present value framework for decision making. The guiding principle for decision making is to budget capital to projects whose expected net cash flows have present values exceeding the expenditure for the projects. This assumes an existing discounting rate which is the company's cost of capital. If a company's net cash flow discounted at its cost of capital produces a present cash value that is exactly equal to the expenditure for the project, that project is not profitable; the flow of cash will replace the investment, but it will not generate value above the investment. Present value is actually a much simpler term than internal rate of return because it assumes a discounting rate rather than solving for one and simply uses this rate to convert NCF_e to present cash values. It is important to understand the optimization goals of capital budgeting stated both from the rate of return side and from the present value side. In the former, given an unlimited quantity of available financing, funds will be budgeted to new projects until the incremental internal rate of return equals the company's cost of capital. In the latter, given the cost of capital as the discounting rate, funds will be budgeted to new projects until the present dollar value of the incremental NCF_e equals the expenditure for the project. Limits of investment in the real world may be less than optimal as was pointed out earlier if capital resources are restricted, but this does not alter the general optimization theory. It will become apparent as we compare the two optimizing techniques that for most purposes the two situations are interchangeable. Later, we will consider special cases in which the two methods are not compatible.

A SINGLE NET CASH FLOW

The same net cash flow and cash investment figures are used here as were used in the rate of return analysis to show the similarities and differences between the two methods. It was assumed in the rate of return analysis that an investment of $10,000 today in a research project would yield a net after-tax cash flow at the end of the third year of $13,322. The rate of return method tells management exactly what rate of return would be earned on such an investment, an answer which the present value method is not designed to give.

The present value approach to this problem is to discount the future sum of $13,322 by the company's cost of capital to determine whether the present value exceeds the investment of $10,000. If the present value exceeds the price of the investment, then the project yields more than the cost of capital; and funds should be budgeted to the project. We recall that the internal rate of return on the project, the rate that equated the terminal value with the capital expenditure was 10 percent. Assuming that the cost of capital is 10 percent, we turn to the third row in Table I in the 10 percent column where the table factor is 0.751 and 0.751 × $13,322 = $10,000 after rounding. At a cost of capital of 10 percent, there would be no incentive to invest because the present value of $13,322 is just equal to the price of the investment. Neither would the investment be made if it yielded a 10-percent rate of return because then the investment would not be yielding more than its cost of capital cutoff rate, and both methods produce the same result. Likewise any cost of capital smaller than 10 percent will cause present value to exceed $10,000 making this a profitable investment and any cost of capital larger than 10 percent would cause the present value to be less than $10,000 making this an unprofitable investment. Suppose that the cost of capital in the example above were 8 percent with a Table I coefficient of 0.794. Bringing the future value back to the present:

$$\text{Present value} = 0.794 \times \$13,322$$
$$= \$10,577$$

This will not tell us what the rate of return is on the investment but it does indicate that its present value is above the price of the investment by $577 or 5.8 percent: $577/\$10,000 = 0.058 = 5.8$ percent. Applying an 8-percent cost of capital cutoff rate to the rate of return method will also be a signal to invest, because then its 10-percent rate of return will have been 2 percent above its cost of capital. It may be noted, however, that in either method close consideration needs to be given to determining what the firm's cost of capital is because, if it is understated, it may result in overbudgeting of capital which may cause fixed costs (a) in the profit function $P = X(b - c) - a$ to rise so high that profits and share values will be adversely affected. And, if the cost of capital is overestimated, capital may be underbudgeted which may cause output and sales to be unduly restricted and may cause variable costs (c) in the profit function to rise so high that profits and share values will be adversely affected.

Interpolation is needed to determine present value when the company's costs of capital is not found in the present value tables. The formula for correcting present value is the same as for correcting the rate of return, but the symbols are defined differently.

$$\text{Correction factor} = \frac{A - B}{A - C}(T_1 - T_2) \qquad 16.6$$

Where: $A =$ Discounting rate above cost of capital
$B =$ Cost of capital
$C =$ Discounting rate below cost of capital
$T_1 =$ Table factor for rate below cost of capital
$T_2 =$ Table factor for rate above cost of capital

Substituting a 9-percent for an 8-percent discounting rate and multiplying the corrected table factor by the terminal value of $13,322, we have the following result showing that at the higher cost the margin over the price of the investment is cut almost in half; but the investment will still be made.

$$\text{Correction factor} = \frac{10-9}{10-8}(0.794 - 0.751)$$

$$= 0.0215$$

$$\text{Corrected table factor} = 0.751 + 0.0215 = 0.773$$

$$\text{Present value} = 0.773 \times \$13,322$$

$$= \$10,298$$

CONSTANT STREAM OF NET CASH FLOW

Table 3.6 illustrates the arithmetic principle underlying the discounting of a constant five-year flow back to its present value using a 10 percent discounting rate. Table II in the Appendix gives the multipliers for selected discount rates where an investment is expected to yield a steady stream of $1 net cash flows. The table factor for a $1-stream for three periods discounted at 8 percent is 2.577. Put this coefficient in the linear equation $Y = bX$ and the present value of the flow is determined. Substituting $10,000 for X:

$$Y = 2.577(\$10,000)$$

$$= \$25,770$$

The importance of this model is at once apparent; the present value can be determined for any three-year steady cash flow substituted for X.

Using the internal rate of return method, a $10,000 three-year net cash flow resulting from a $25,770 investment equates with the investment at 8 percent. If 8 percent is indeed the company's cost of capital rate, there will be no investment. But even if it is 8 percent, any investment priced below $25,770 expecting to produce annual net cash flows of $10,000 is recommended. If the investment expenditure is reduced it will also require more than an 8 percent rate of return to equate the $10,000 cash flow with the new investment, thus driving the rate above the company's 8 percent cost of capital and giving the signal to invest. As pointed out in the previous section, the present values of an expected cash flow may not be found in the table values, so that interpolation may be necessary. Assume that the cost of capital is 9 instead of 8 percent and notice its effect on present value.

$$\text{Correction factor} = \frac{A-B}{A-C}(T_1 - T_2)$$

$$= \frac{10-9}{10-8}(2.577 + 2.487)$$

$$= 0.045$$

$$\text{Corrected table factor} = 2.487 + 0.045 = 2.532$$

$$\text{Present value} = 2.532 \times \$10,000$$

$$= \$25,320$$

Variable net cash flows are much easier to convert to net present values than they are to convert to internal rates of return. Table I is used when net flows are expected to change annually or every few years; but, if for several years the flow is expected to be constant and then change and remain constant again, present value Table II makes the solution easier. A cash terminal value may be net working capital or salvage value at the end of any one of the net cash flows. This figure is brought back in a single operation by multiplying the expected value at the end of the period by the factor for that year from Table I. Illustrated below is a nine-year expected net cash flow discounted at a 10 percent cost of capital. The flow is expected to change at three-year intervals and $5,000 in working capital is expected to be on hand at the end of the ninth year. The operation for determining present value is easy and direct.

TABLE 16.9
PRESENT VALUE OF CHANGING LEVEL FLOWS
(10 PERCENT DISCOUNT RATE)

Year	Net Cash Flow		Table Factors 10% Column		Present Values
1	$ 5,000				
2	5,000				
3	5,000	×	2.487	=	$12,435
4	8,000				
5	8,000				
6	8,000	×	1.868	=	14,944
7	10,000		(4.355 − 2.487)		
8	10,000				
9	10,000	×	1.404	=	14,040
			(5.759 − 4.355)		
			Total		$41,419
	(Working capital) $5,000 × 0.424			=	2,120
			Total Present value	=	$43,539

Now that we have the present value of the sum of irregular cash flows, we need to know how much cash such as an investment would require before a budgeting decision can be made. If the project requires less than $43,539 in cash, it could be undertaken; but, rather than just invest in any project that yields the company's cost of capital, it may be desirable to make a risk allowance by setting some minimum relative spread between the present value of the net cash flow and the price of the assets. For example, suppose that financial managers set as the company's policy the investment in any project that is priced at 20 percent or, in this case $8,708 ($43,539 × 0.2 = $8,708$) below the present value of the expected flow. Using the internal rate of return method, the reader should verify that the expected irregular flow in Table 16.9 will equate with $43,539 at a 10 percent rate of return.

A DEFERRED OUTFLOW

The present value gap over capital expenditure is wider, other factors being the same, when the capital expenditure is made in installments than when it is made at the beginning of the investment period. The decision-making significance of this is that an investment that may be marginal or submarginal, paid for in cash at the beginning of the investment period, may become supermarginal when it is paid for in installments. Let the payment schedule include a $10,000 down payment at the start followed by five payments of $7,000 each starting in the second year. Since this is a constant cash flow after the initial payment, Table II will supply the proper multiplier. But a new problem arises here. At what rate should the payments be discounted? Should it be the company's cost of capital or some other rate? If the company has had recent installment financing experiences, the most current borrowing rate would be acceptable. The size of the rate is very important because the present value of the outlay, as well as of the inflow, can be a decisive factor determining whether an investment should or should not be made. An 8 percent discounting rate is used to convert the expected outflow of $45,000 to a present value.

	Table Factor		Present Value
Down payment $10,000	1.000		$10,000
5 payments @ $7,000 each	3.697 × $7,000	=	25,879
(Starting in second year)			
		Total	$35,879

The margin between the present value of the outflow ($35,879) and the present value of the inflow ($43,903) is $8,024 or 18 percent: $8,024/$43,903 = 0.18 = 18 percent. Total cash outlays in the above illustrations are $45,000 which is larger than the present value of the expected cash flow, but discounting the outflow by 8 percent reduces it to a present value of $35,879 which as pointed out above is 18 percent less than the present value of the inflow.

THE OPTIMIZING DECISION: PRESENT VALUE METHOD

The structure of the optimizing function is essentially the same using the present value method of analysis as using the internal rate of return. We assume that there is no restriction on funds, that the cost of capital is 12 percent, and that investment will be made in any project whose net cash flow discounted at the cost of capital exceeds the investment expenditure. The same net cash flows are used in Table 16.10 below that were used in Table 16.5 with the internal rate of return method so that the student can see that the optimal investment level is the same for both methods. Columnar headings are as follows: (1) enumerates the projects; (2) is the expected ten-year net cash flow for each of the investment proposals; (3) is the table factor for a ten-year discounting period at a cost of capital of 12 percent; (4) is the capital investment; (5) is the present value of the net cash flow from the

TABLE 16.10
OPTIMAL LEVEL OF INVESTMENT
DIMINISHING PRESENT VALUES
(12 PERCENT COST OF CAPITAL)

(1)	*(2)*	*(3)*	*(4)*	*(5)*	*(6)*
Investment Projects	*Expected Net Cash Flow*	*Table II Factor for Ten-Year Constant Flow*	*Capital Expenditure*	*Present Value Net Cash Flow*	*Cumulative Excess Over Expenditure*
a	$3,400	5.650	$10,000	$19,210	$ 9,210
b	2,600	5.650	10,000	14,690	13,900
c	1,800	5.650	10,000	10,170	14,070
d	1,000	5.650	10,000	5,650	8,420
e	−600	5.650	10,000	−3,390	5,030

investment; and (6) is the cumulative excess of present value over the cumulative investment. The student should verify that a lower cost of capital will stimulate further investing. As pointed out in summarizing the rate of return technique, to be an effective program this should be applied on a departmental basis or at least on a divisional basis. Executed at each level of the management organization, it will optimize capital investment for business as a whole. The approach implicitly assumes that, at the cost of capital of 12 percent, the business is able to get enough funds to reach its optimization goals. Unlimited funds may be obtained at this cost, or a definite restriction may be placed on the funds, the effect of which will be illustrated in the next section. Another factor should concern financial managers, and that is, whether by pushing investments to the optimum, funds will continue to be available only at higher costs of capital. If this is the case, then the discounting rate has to be increased to reflect rising costs with the effect of reducing present value and curbing investment.

BUDGETING CAPITAL SUBJECT TO A FUNDS CONSTRAINT

A typical problem is to determine how to allocate a fixed sum of capital among alternative investments to maximize returns. Since the size of investment proposals will vary, decisions in the final analysis have to be based on the relative advantage of one investment compared with another. Assume that $100,000 is budgeted for capital investment and that the following proposals have been made by different departments. Each investment includes an estimate of its service life, an estimate of the annual net cash flow, and a ratio of present value over capital expenditure. The expenditure sizes and the flow rates are the same as those used in a comparable example using internal rates of return (Table 16.8). Part I contains basic computations for determining present values, and Part II ranks the projects on the basis of relative advantage. Again it will be noted that the projects selected for using up the $100,000 are the same as they are in the internal rate of return. It should be noted, too, in comparing the rankings with the rates of return that the two projects

(2) and (3) whose net-cash-flow/capital expenditure were less than 1, at the bottom of the ranking in Table 16.11, were the projects that would not meet the test of a 12 percent cost of capital at the bottom of the internal rate of return rankings in Table 16.8. In summary then, as long as the cutoff for the internal rate of return is the same as the discounting rate used for the present value method, the two methods are interchangeable.

TABLE 16.11
PART I
ALTERNATIVE INVESTMENT PROPOSALS
(12 PERCENT COST OF CAPITAL)

Investment Project	Capital Expenditure	Service Life (Years)	Annual Flows	Years of Flow	Table Factors	Present Net Cash Flow	Net Cash Flows / Capital Expenditure
a	$40,000	10	$10,000	(1 to 5) × 3.605 =	36,050	$\frac{46,275}{40,000} = 1.15$
			5,000	(6 to 10) × 2.045 =	10,225	
b	40,000	10	5,000	(1 to 5) × 3.605 =	18,025	$\frac{38,475}{40,000} = 0.962$
			10,000	(6 to 10) × 2.045 =	20,450	
c	30,000	5	8,000	(1 to 5) × 3.605 =	28,840	$\frac{28,840}{30,000} = 0.961$
d	20,000	4	8,000	(1 to 4) × 3.037 =	24,296	$\frac{24,396}{20,000} = 1.21$
e	20,000	4	2,000	(1 to 3) × 2.402 =	4,804	$\frac{21,340}{20,000} = 1.06$
			26,000	(4th) × 0.636 =	16,536	

PART II
RANKING INVESTMENT
CAPITAL RESOURCES OF $100,000

Project	Net Cash Flow / Capital Expenditure	Size of Expenditure	Cumulative Investment
d	1.210	$20,000	$ 20,000
a	1.150	40,000	60,000
e	1.060	20,000	80,000 ($100,000 limit)
b	0.962	40,000	120,000
c	0.961	30,000	150,000

SPECIAL PROBLEMS OF ESTIMATION

Cash flow figures have been supplied arbitrarily to illustrate important principles of decision making using the internal rate of return and present value techniques. Before this, no special consideration was given to the risk factor inherent in the sales estimate (X) in the function: $NCF_e = [X(b - c) - a](1 - tr) + nc$.

A single value has been assigned to X letting the model above generate the cash flow, implying that such estimates of sales can be determined with certainty. It is apparent that, if X the independent variable in the NCF_e is determinable with certainty, then decision making becomes rather mechanical. But not being clairvoyant, one may attach considerable risk to the sales estimate. For a review of the basic tools of subjective and statistical probability as they relate to quantitative data, the student is referred to Chapter 3.

SUBJECTIVE PROBABILITIES

Because of the past experiences of sales managers and financial managers, subjective probability distributions can be established for each competing project for each year of its service life in the hope of obtaining an estimated sales X and estimated NCF_e figure that reflects several market variables not apparent in the single estimate. Table 16.12 illustrates a model procedure for adjusting sales

TABLE 16.12
EXPECTED SALES (X)
PROBABILITIES AS INDEPENDENT VARIABLES

	First Year	Second Year	Third Year
Possible Units of sales (000's)	10 20 30 40 50	10 20 30 40 50	10 20 30 40 50
Probabilities	0.1 0.2 0.4 0.2 0.1	0.1 0.1 0.2 0.5 0.1	0.3 0.2 0.2 0.2 0.1
Adjusted estimates (000's)	1 4 12 8 5	1 2 6 20 5	3 4 6 8 5
Expected sales (000's)	$1 + 4 + 12 + 8 + 5 = 30$	$1 + 2 + 6 + 20 + 5 = 34$	$3 + 4 + 6 + 8 + 5 = 26$

estimates to subjective probabilities. The same range of possible sales is used for each of the three service years with a different probability distribution for each year. The sum of the adjusted values in the last row is the expected sales for each year. The expected sales values are inserted in the NCF_e, and the final step is to determine the internal rate of return on the project.

In Part I of Table 16.13, NCF_e is determined based on expected sales in Table 16.12 above. In Part II, NCF_e is discounted at 12 percent to obtain present values. Decision making from this point on is the same as under assumptions of certainty; if the present value of a proposal exceeds its supply price, discounting at the cost of capital, the investment should be made. In this example, the investment should be made if it would cost less than $156,810.

Whether or not to employ this technique in place of a single sales estimate for each year depends on the kind of sales contracts the company has. Contracts with governmental agencies and with large corporations may be certain enough to justify a single estimate, but in most cases the market for sales is less than certain. Assigning a probability distribution to sales does not remove the risk altogether of acting on the wrong estimate; it just makes quantitative allowances for those risks in the expected sales estimates.

TABLE 16.13
PRESENT VALUE OF EXPECTED SALES
ADJUSTED FOR SUBJECTIVE PROBABILITIES
PART I

Year	Expected Net Cash Flow
1	$NCF_e = [30,000(\$6 - \$2) - \$10,000](1 - 0.5) + \$10,000 = \$65,000$
2	$NCF_e = [34,000(\$6 - \$2) - \$10,000](1 - 0.5) + \$10,000 = \$73,000$
3	$NCF_e = [26,000(\$6 - \$2) - \$10,000](1 - 0.5) + \$10,000 = \$57,000$

PART II
PRESENT VALUE OF NET CASH FLOW
(12% COST OF CAPITAL)

Year	NCF_e	Table Factor	Present Value
1	$ 65,000	0.893	$ 58,045
2	73,000	.797	58,181
3	57,000	.712	40,584
	$195,000		$156,810

STATISTICAL PROBABILITIES

Assuming that the frequency distribution of expected net cash flows forms a normal curve, we are able to deduce certain facts about the probability that net cash flows will range within certain limits which may be useful in making capital investment decisions. Table 16.14 uses measures of *central tendencies* to predict the probability of expected net cash flows ranging within one standard deviation and 2/3 of one standard deviation of the arithmetic mean of expected net cash flows. The arithmetic means in Table 16.14 are not taken from the sales figures of

TABLE 16.14
STATISTICAL PROBABILITIES OF EXPECTED SALES

(1) Year	(2) Arithmetic Mean ($\bar{X}$)	(3) Standard Deviation (σ)	(4) Range Between Mean and Plus One σ (0.34 Probability)	(5) Range Between Mean and Plus 2/3σ (0.25 Probability)
1	$40,000	$6,000	$40,000 < X \le $46,000	$40,000 < X \le $44,000
2	30,000	3,000	30,000 < X \le 33,000	30,000 < X \le 32,000
3	30,000	1,500	30,000 < X \le 31,500	30,000 < X \le 31,000

Table 16.12 but are selected arbitrarily as are their standard deviations: the purpose of the table is to illustrate how statistical probabilities are used to improve estimates of net cash flow rather than to emphasize performing the statistical operations. The table has several useful applications to decision making as indicated by the column heads: (1) represents the three service years of the proposed investment,

(2) the arithmetic mean of possible expected net cash flows for each of the years, and (3) the standard deviation for each year's sample of net cash flows. The standard deviations tell us that the first year will be dispersed twice as widely about the mean as in the second year and four times as widely the first year as in the third. We ask the question specifically for the first year: What is the probability that sales will range between $40,000 and $46,000? Our answer is somewhat roundabout. The probability of sales being ± one from the mean, from $34,000 (40,000 − 6,000) to $46,000 (40,000 + 6,000) is 0.68268 which may be rounded to 0.68. Table 16.14 limits the range to probabilities of sales being larger than the means. Column (4) indicates the range in sales that will occur with a probability of 0.34 (0.68/2). This does not give the exact sales estimate; but it will give assurance to financial managers, for example, that sales will be between $40,000 and $46,000 with a probability 0.34 and that sales for the second year will be between $30,000 and $33,000 with a probability 0.34. Setting the range in this manner should help financial managers finally set a precise subjective probability on a specific sales figure. Column (5) helps even more to limit the range for more careful subjective probability analysis. It states, for example, that in the first year sales will range between $40,000 and $44,000 with probability 0.25 and that in the second it will range between $30,000 and $32,000 with probability 0.25. If closer ranges than 2/3 are desired, they may be obtained, from Table III in the Appendix.

The riskiness of making sales estimates in general is reduced as has been seen by using the measure of the standard deviation for estimating probable sales. But the effectiveness of the tool varies according to the size of the *relative* dispersion: $Cv = \sigma/\bar{X}$. The larger the value $\sigma/\bar{X}$ the less reliable the arithmetic mean will be as a sales estimate. The $\sigma/\bar{X}$ measures the *relative* amount of the dispersion around the mean or the *risk relationship* (see Chapter 3) with the results summarized in Table 16.15. The last column in the table indicates a much narrower relative range

TABLE 16.15
RELATIVE SALES DISPERSION

Year	Arithmetic Mean ($\bar{X}$)	Standard Deviations (σ)	Risk Relationship (Cv)
1	$40,000	$6,000	$6,000/$40,000 = .15
2	30,000	3,000	3,000/ 30,000 = .10
3	30,000	1,500	1,500/ 30,000 = .05

of probable *error* from the mean in the third year than in the first or second. Not only is the dollar dispersion expected to be smallest in the third year, the relative dispersion is also expected to be smallest in that year. Another way of looking at it is in terms of rate of change: if the relationship 0.05/1 is representative for the third year, it would indicate that, for every dollar increase in the mean, the standard deviation would be only $0.05; whereas, in the second year the rate would be $0.10 and in the first year $0.15. The role of the statistical measures of probability and risk is to temper with quantitative measures what would otherwise be a purely qualitative judgement of sales. The final purpose is to provide management with expected sales (X) to enter into the NCF_e function that will be realistic for determining present values and internal rates of return. The writer is not implying that statistical techniques are applicable to all situations. But they are just another set of working tools that financial managers should be acquainted with; so that, when the condition presents itself, managers will be prepared to apply the tools skillfully.

SUMMARY

Lying at the basis of the current capital budgeting theory is the important concept of the net cash flow. Net cash flow is the difference between net sales and total cash expenditures. A common method of measuring this using the regular financial accounting statements is to add net profits after taxes to depreciation expenses for the cash flow period. After considering the concept of the net cash flow, we identify the other side of the investment decision, the capital expenditure. Given the expected net cash flow over the life of the capital expenditure and the cost of the capital expenditure, we seek the internal rate of return which equates the present value of the expected net cash flow with the capital expenditure. This is the rate also that causes the algebraic sum of the expenditures and cash inflows to equal zero.

Cash flows take numerous forms. First, the flow may consist of a single sum of cash receivables at some future date. The internal rate of return equates that sum with the capital expenditure producing that sum. Second, many investment projects generate a constant stream of net cash flows received at regular intervals in the future. The discounting rate that equates this stream of expected net cash flows with the capital expenditure is the internal rate of return on the investment that generates that stream. Third, some net cash flows fluctuate, which makes the discounting operation somewhat more difficult; the discounting rate that equates the variable net cash flow stream with the capital expenditure is also the internal rate of return for that proposed investment expenditure.

Not all capital investment expenditures are paid for in cash at the time of the purchase. In case an asset is allowed to be purchased on a deferred payment basis, those payments must be discounted back to their present value to obtain the capital expenditure value of the investment. The resulting present value of the deferred outflow is then equated with the expected net cash flow from that project. The internal rate of return that brings these two values together is the internal rate of return on the investment proposal that would produce that stream. One of the most important considerations in capital budgeting is the optimizing decision. The optimizing decision illustrated in its simplest form would cause capital investment to continue at a declining internal rate of return until that return is equal to zero. This somewhat oversimplifies the problem of optimization from the practical point of view because a zero rate of return is set as the cutoff rate. From the applied viewpoint, it would not be profitable for the business to continue making incremental investments to the point of a zero rate of return because then any cost of capital above a zero would exceed the internal rate of return on the incremental unit. Nevertheless, unless a simulation model is extended to the point of zero return, financial managers may be unable to establish just where the rate of return begins to exceed zero.

A common situation in capital budgeting is the one in which a firm has a certain fixed sum of cash for capital investment forming an automatic capital constraint on new investment. Given such a constraint, the firm is confronted with having to rank investment projects, so that the projects will be ranked in the order of their internal rates of return until the funds are all committed. In most cases the net cash flow can be expected to be a positive flow over the whole life of the investment. In some cases, however, supplementary investments may be planned somewhere along the net-cash-flow stream with the effect of producing a negative net cash flow. Table 16.4 and Figure 16.1 in the text showed that, under this condition at which a negative net cash flow appears in an otherwise positive stream of cash, there are two internal rates of return that equate the positive and the negative cash inflows and outflows. There can be only one internal rate, however, for decision making, and the correct one is that one which has been preceded by positive present values and is followed by negative present values. This kind of illustration is sometimes given to discredit the use of internal rate of return method for decision-making purposes; but, if the method suggested here is followed, there is no reason for rejecting the use of the rate of return technique because of dual rates. What it may require, however, is somewhat more work at the machine to determine what the two rates are.

The *present value method* may be used as an alternative to the internal rate of return for decision making. It was shown in the chapter that, if the discounting rate used for the present value method is also used as the cost of capital cutoff rate for the internal rate of return method, then the decisions to invest or not to invest will be the same with either of the two methods. Finally, special problems of estimation are considered. Issues were considered in which probability distributions were applied to the estimates of net cash flows. It was shown that, first, by using subjective probabilities and, secondly, by using statistical probabilities, more meaningful estimates of net cash flows were possible.

PROBLEMS

1. Identify each of the following terms:
   - a. Simulating investment proposals.
   - b. Net cash flow.
   - c. Deferred expenditure.

d. Internal rate of return.
e. Diminishing internal rate of return.
f. Interpolation.
g. Optimal level of investment.
h. Present value of NCF_e.
i. Subjective probabilities.
j. Statistical probabilities.
k. Variable net cash flow.

2. An investment proposal is made to you in which you would have to invest $20,000 for scientific equipment to search for sunken treasure off the coast of Florida. It will take about three years of planning and exploring, at the end of which time you hope to "strike it rich" and cash in on your investment for $40,000.

   a. What rate of return would you be realizing?
   b. Before making a final decision, you decide to set up a subjective probability distribution for the return expected at the end of the third year. After searching your past experiences for risky investment experiences, you assign the following probability distribution:

Expected net cash flow:	10,000	30,000	40,000	50,000
Probability:	0.2	0.3	0.4	0.1

   c. What is the risk-adjusted expected value, and what internal rate of return are you most likely to realize? Should the investment be made? Explain.

3. A $5,000 investment today will yield an annual net cash flow of $2,500 for two years.

   a. What does Table II in the Appendix tell about the rate of return?
   b. Using the model, present value $= P[1/(1 + r)] + P[1/(1 + r)^2] \ldots n$ indicate the rate of return earned on the investment.
   c. Explain your findings in terms of after-tax net profits.
   d. Assume now that you expect the investment to have $1,000 in net working capital left at the end of the second year. What would this do to the internal rate of return if anything? Show your work.

4. You are considering budgeting $80,000 to new capital that promises to add 20,000 units annually to sales for five years. Unit price is $6 and unit variable cost is $4. Fixed charges connected with operations will be $20,000, $12,000 of which will be depreciation. The tax rate is 40 percent.

   a. Set up the NCF_e function and determine the annual NCF_e, assuming a constant stream.
   b. Determine the internal rate of return, interpolating if necessary.
   c. The cost of capital of the firm is 14 percent. Should capital be budgeted to the investment?

d. Assume that the supply price of the machine could be paid for in two installments, $40,000 immediately and $40,000 at the end of two years.
e. Some would say that new investment should be made in this case when the internal rate of return reaches zero. What is your comment about this?

5. A plant extension costing $120,000 is being considered. Net cash flows from the project are expected to be $15,000 annually for the first four years and $30,000 annually for the last six years.

   a. What is the internal rate of return on this variable net cash flow? Interpolate to find the exact rate of return.
   b. This company's cost of capital is 10 percent. Should the investment be made?
   c. Another construction and equipment supply company will do the same plant extension job for the same price but offers to let the company pay for this in two equal annual installments bearing interest at 5 percent. Usually the company pays 6 percent interest on its capital debts. Determine the present value of the capital expenditure allowing for the 5-percent interest charge. Without computing the new internal rate of return, indicate whether, given with the NCF_e mentioned above, this would be a better "deal" than the one requiring a cash payment of $120,000.

6. As financial manager of Company X, you have been assigned the responsibility of screening investment proposals and selecting the ones each year that will do the most for the business. This time the sales and production departments submit the following proposals. A total of $60,000 has been budgeted to capital investment. Prevailing lease rate is 6 percent.

Project	Kind of Expenditure	Amount of Expenditure	NCF_e (Annual)	Life Span (Years)	Terminal Value
1	Two trucks	$30,000	$10,000	4	$ 2,000
2	Workers' lounge	10,000	0	10	0
3	Lease of office equipment	10,000 annually	14,000	5	0
4	Warehouse extension	40,000	5,000	10	5,000
5	Advertising	30,000	12,000	3	1,000
6	Research equipment	15,000	0	2	25,000

7. You are considering replacing a machine. You have found the one best suited to perform the job, but you want to get some idea of what it is worth to you today. The machine is expected to generate net cash at the rate of $1,200 annually for four years.

   a. What is the maximum price that you would pay for the machine, assuming that you expect your investments to return net cash flows at the rate of 8 percent? At 10 percent?

b. Assuming that the machine will have a $300 scrap value at the end of the fourth year, what is the maximum that you would be willing to pay, assuming that you expect your investments to produce net cash flows at the rate of 12 percent?

c. Later on you consider two competing machines each costing $8,000. The first promises to generate cash at the rate of $4000 annually for five years, and the second promises to generate $5000 for four years. The prevailing flow rate generated is 12 percent. Which one should you buy?

8. The Selfridge Chain Stores Company was considering investing between $150,000 and $200,000 in a new store to be located either in city X or Y. After studying the alternative locations for some time, the financial manager divided the findings into two parts, the first indicating information about the capital expenditure requirements and the second information about expected annual income and expenditures.

	Capital Expenditure Data	
	Store X	*Store Y*
Fixed investment	$175,000	$200,000
Expected service life	10 years	10 years
Sale price at terminal date	$25,000	$50,000
Working capital required	$50,000	$60,000

	Expected Annual Income Data	
	Part I: Years 1 to 3	
	Store X	*Store Y*
Annual net sales	$150,000	$160,000
Cash operating expenses	80,000	120,000
Depreciation (straight-line)		
Before-tax profit		
Taxes (@ 40%)		
Annual net profit		

	Part II: Years 4 to 6	
	Store X	*Store Y*
Annual net sales	$180,000	$200,000
Cash operating expenses	100,000	130,000
Depreciation (straight-line)		
Before-tax profit		
Taxes (@ 40%)		
Annual net profit		

	Part III: Years 7 to 10	
	Store X	*Store Y*
Annual net sales	$200,000	$200,000
Cash operating expenses	110,000	100,000
Depreciation (straight-line)		
Before-tax profits		
Taxes (@ 40%)		
Annual net profit		

a. Determine the present values of the two capital expenditures, using an 8 percent discount rate and assuming that store X is paid $75,000 now and $100,000 in five years and that the $200,000 store is paid for in four years $50,000 each year.
b. Determine the present value of the net cash flows from operations and the values of fixed and working capital recoveries on the terminal date.
c. Compare the relative present values for the alternatives and make the investment decision.

9. The management of the Z Department Store had budgeted $100,000 to capital expenditures and was considering two alternatives: one a store renovation and modernization and the other the purchase of a $100,000 interest in a radio and TV station. The first would include installation of an escalator, wall-to-wall carpeting, air conditioning, and a new lighting system. The total investment would be depreciated by the straight-line method over the next ten years, and there would be no scrap value at the end of that time. Annual net sales could be expected to increase by about $25,000 and cash expenses by $3,000. Taxes are 40 percent of net income. The radio and TV venture would be depreciated by the straight-line method over the same number of years but is expected to have a $40,000 scrap value at the end of the period. Net sales at the store were expected to increase by $10,000 yearly for the first five years, and income from the sale of radio and TV time was expected to return another $8,000 for each of the first five years. Annual expenses before depreciation were expected to increase $6,000 for the ten-year period. Net sales at the store could be expected to increase to $12,000 for the last five years, with the sale of radio and TV time also increasing from $8,000 to $15,000 for the second five years. Taxes were 40 percent of net income.

a. Compare the present values of the two competing streams of net cash flows using a 10 percent discounting rate. Is this a sufficient basis for decision making?
b. Suppose that the investment in the broadcasting station could be paid for at the rate of $10,000 annually over ten years but that the store investment had to be paid for all in cash at the beginning of the period. Using a 6 percent discounting rate for the capital expenditure, compare the investment.

PART   VII

CAPITAL
BUDGETING
THE
FINANCING
DECISION

17

Cost of
Capital and
Market
Structure

It was shown in Part VI that budgeting for investment is logical and feasible without making capital financing decisions, but it is capital financing decisions and the capital markets that supply capital resources for actually relaxing the constraints caused by a scarcity of capital. This chapter develops the cost of capital considering conceptual factors in the cost of capital, quantitative relationships in the cost of capital, underlying financial rates, and, finally, the institutional structure of the markets where cost of capital is determined.

CONCEPTUAL FACTORS

The concept of the cost of capital as it is applied to capital budgeting is quite different from the notion of cost of capital as an outlay of cash for paying interest on long-term debts and dividends on capital stock. There are several underlying rates. There are financing rates that are contractual rates that are very specific like the rates of interest for secured and unsecured capital borrowing, and there are fixed dividend rates assessed the business for going to the market with *preferred* shares of stock. These clearly formed market costs underlie the cost of capital and are important factors affecting the cost as will be seen in discussing market rates later on. But cost of capital as it is used in this analysis refers to a single rate that is related specifically to return on net capital or what may be called the return on common equity capital. This rate is not contractual and often it is not specific; but, conceptually, it plays a major part in determining what the level of investment will be and what the value will be of the company's common shares of stock.

395

RELATION TO MARKET PRICE OF COMMON SHARES

The cost of capital is related uniquely to the market price of common shares. First, the cost of capital is the rate of return that investors in a company's common stock *expect* of the stock to warrant paying its current market price. Second, the term *expects* has a special meaning in that it carries with it a kind of ultimatum that, unless financial managers can communicate (Chapter 2) to the market convincing evidence that these expectations will be realized, the present price of the company's shares in the market is not assured. But the reader should not confuse expected return (E_e) with expected dividend receipts. The definition of the cost of capital may thus be stated in terms of the market value:

$$d = \frac{E_e}{P_m} \qquad\qquad 17.1$$

where: d = Cost of capital
$\quad\quad E_e$ = *Expected* dollar return per share of common stock
$\quad\quad P_m$ = Present market price of the share

Substitute $3 for E_e and $20 for P_m; then $d = 0.15$ or 15 percent.

AS AN INTERNAL RATE OF RETURN

Another way of thinking of the cost of capital, which follows from the paragraph above, is as an internal rate of return to the investor which equates for him a perpetual stream of *expected* net earnings with the market price of the share. Using the terminology that was used in Chapter 16 in discussing internal investment policy, it is the rate that causes the algebraic sum of the outflow of cash to purchase the share of stock, and the present value of the stream of E_e, to equal zero. This latter statement, of course, is the same as the former; and the expression for this can be derived from the basic equation above:

$$d = \frac{E_e}{P_m}$$

$$P_m = \frac{E_e}{d} \qquad\qquad 17.2$$

Assume in the second equation that E_e equals $3 and that P_m equals $20, the same as was assumed above. Now we can solve for d as follows:

$$\$20 = \frac{\$3}{d}$$

$$\$20d = \$3$$

$$d = 0.15 = 15\%$$

If we give a negative sign to the $20 to indicate that it is an expenditure of capital and a positive sign to net income, we can see that the cost of capital is the equating value that causes their algebraic sum to be zero.

$$-\$20 = \frac{\$3}{0.15}$$
$$-\$20 = +\$20$$
$$= 0$$

CONCEPT OF NET CAPITAL

The cost of capital refers specifically to net capital: total assets — total debts equals net capital. The book value of net capital appears in the net-worth section of a company's balance sheet, but the cost of capital is related to the market value necessarily of net capital or common equity. But the market value of a company's net capital is also equal to the sum of the values of its outstanding shares. The total cost of capital for the business then is the aggregate return that the evaluators (Chapter 2) *expect* the business to earn on the market value of its equity. This is a very important concept because it reemphasizes the role of the securities market in setting the cost of capital. If E_e were expressed as an aggregate amount of earnings demanded on the market value of the equity, however, it would give us the same d value as using an individual share; and the latter is more directly relevant to the common goal of maximizing share values.

OPPORTUNITY COST CONCEPT

The important fact should be noted however that in the last analysis the E_e/P_m rate that the market imposes on a business is an opportunity cost to the business; it is a cost measured by the cost of attracting investors away from other almost equally desirable investment opportunities. Each company has to compete with investment opportunities in the capital market as a whole with its wide range of investment opportunities of which common stock is just one of many related opportunities including purchasing government and private corporation bonds and preferred shares.

DISCOUNTING BUDGETED NET PROFIT

Given the cost of capital, the market also has for itself a rate by which budgeted net profits per share of stock can be discounted to the present. In the example above in which the cost of capital is 15 percent based on E_e equals $3.00 and P_m equals $20.00, suppose that as the result of effective communication (Chapter 2) the market foresees the business generating a perpetual flow of *budgeted* net profit (*pb*) (Chapter 7) equals $3.45. Present value (*V$_p$*) of the share then is determined as follows:

$$V_p = \frac{pb}{d}$$ 17.3

$$= \frac{\$3.45}{0.15}$$

$$= \$23.00$$

Notice that the cost of capital is not changed but that the present value of future net profit has gone above the current market price of $20.00. This does not increase the market price above $20.00 automatically; but, by possibly increasing demand for the shares, it may indirectly increase the market price of the shares.

THE RATE AS A FINANCING COST

The cost of capital is mainly a factor to consider in the daily market place, but it is also a factor in raising new capital for relaxing its capital constraints. This may be done with other forms of capital besides common stock. But, on some occasions, common stock financing is considered; and financial managers then need to compare the cost of common stock financing with the cost of alternative forms like borrowing and preferred stock financing. It is no great problem to make such comparisons when a company's shares are traded actively in the market, but companies with inactively traded shares may have difficulty determining the cost of their equity capital. Consequently, this subject requires close consideration.

INTERNAL CONTROL CONSIDERATION

Finally, we need to consider in the general concept of the cost of capital the important matter of internal control. Although the securities market in the last analysis determines the costs based on alternative investment opportunities, there is hope for financial managers seeking to control their company's cost of capital. Financial managers would want to reduce their cost of capital because this would reduce the discounting rate for determining present share values. To illustrate, suppose that *pb* increased above the $3.00 minimum required to maintain the $20.00 market price, to $3.45 as illustrated earlier, but that other favorable factors in the company also converged on the market to reduce the company's cost of capital from 15 percent to 12 percent, causing the present value of the share to rise to $28.75.

$$V_p = \frac{pb}{d}$$

$$= \frac{\$3.45}{0.12}$$

$$= 28.75$$

Financial managers seek to reduce their cost of capital for two reasons. One is to raise the market valuation of the shares and hopefully the market price. As a secondary factor, since decreasing the cost tends to increase market value, a given sum of funds can then be raised in the primary stock market by issuing a fewer number of shares.

QUANTITATIVE RELATIONS IN THE COST OF CAPITAL

Let us consider now the controllable and the noncontrollable variables in the cost function. The cost of capital is a positive linear function of the ratio E_e/P_m, which means that its equation is $d = b(E_e/P_m)$. More important it means that, given the change in the ratio E_e/P_m, d will change by a constant amount. But it will be more meaningful to us if the numerator E_e and the denominator P_m are considered separately. It will be noted in Table 17.1 that a positive linear relation-

TABLE 17.1
COST OF CAPITAL

Linear Function of E_e				Nonlinear Function of P_m			
b	E_e/P_m	d	Δd	b	E_e/P_m	d	Δd
1	1/10	0.1		1	1/13	0.0776	
1	2/10	.2	0.1	1	1/12	.0833	0.0057
1	3/10	.3	.1	1	1/11	.0909	.0076
1	4/10	.4	.1	1	1/10	.1000	.0091

ship exists between the net return E_e expected by the market on the company's shares and the cost of capital (d) but that a negative nonlinear relationship exists between the market price of the company's stock (P_m) and the cost of capital d. Referring to the left side of the table, why would more earnings E_e be expected of a business with the market price of its stock remaining unchanged? Why, in other words, would the market demand more earnings per share without being willing to pay more for the company's stock? There are two possible answers to this question. One is that alternative investment opportunities for the stock of companies in the same risk class are relatively better than they had been; and, two, financial managers of this concern may have relaxed their controls over profit, liquidity, and solvency compared with other firms to increase the riskiness of investing in the firm. In short, the financial image of the business has lost some of its glow relative to other firms that are competitive in the securities market. On the right side of the table, how can a company's shares drop in market price causing the cost of capital to rise when expected earnings are holding the same value? The answer is that market prices P_m are determined by the valuation in the market of the company's profits liquidity and solvency package which in this case was apparently becoming increasingly unfavorable; the reason that the market continued to expect (demand) $1 of the business was because its stock relative to the stock of competitive firms in the financial market had deteriorated over the intervals. The reader should verify with the tables that a constant *decreasing* market price for the stock causes the cost of capital to rise at an increasing rate; whereas, a constant *increasing* market price causes the cost of capital to decline at a decreasing rate.

Returning now to the original equation for the cost of capital, $d = E_e/P_m$, we derived earlier the equation $P_m = E_e/d$. The second equation enables financial managers to determine what market price their shares would need to attain a given cost of capital goal. To illustrate, suppose that the market expects of a given company that earnings on its shares be $1 if the market price is $10, $2 if the price is $20, and $3 if the price is $30. In other words, the company is so constituted relative to other firms that it is expected to return *10 percent to the investor on whatever its market price happens to be.* Given the 10 percent cost of capital financial managers can, by discounting budgeted net profits of the firm by that rate, arrive at the present value of their firm's stock and compare V_p with P_m. More will be said about this in the following section.

MARKET PRICE, COST OF CAPITAL, AND VALUATION OF SHARES

The reader's attention is called to an important relationship between the market price of a company's shares and the company's cost of capital. It will be noted in the examples above that market price was given in both of the basic cost of capital equations: $d = E_e/P$ and $P = E_e/d$. If we substitute the values E_e equals $3 and P equals $20 in each of the equations, we will come up with the same cost of capital of 15 percent but just stated in two different ways. The important factor, however, is that cost of capital determination premises a given market value of the stock.

The market is continuously performing two operations. One is to determine the cost of capital for a company by equating what the market sets as a required return per share of stock with the market price of the stock: $P_m = E_e/d$. The other operation is to use the cost of capital d to derive present values for the company's shares based on their budgeted profit: $V_p = pb/d$. The latter may be restated as: $V_p = (1/d)(pb)$. This converts the cost of capital from a percentage to a turnover ratio and changes the operation from division to multiplication. Referring to the earlier example where the cost of capital was 15 percent, the multiplier now becomes $1/0.15 = 6.67$. Substituting this value in the equation we have:

$$V_p = 6.67(pb) \qquad\qquad 17.4$$

Any budgeted net profit per share is then raised by 6.67 to determine its present value. Since cost of capital (in this case the multiplier 6.67) is not affected directly by the present value of the share V_p, financial managers can convert any number of budgeted net profit flows into present share values (not into market prices). If the reader will learn to distinguish the present value formula $V_p = (1/d)(pb)$ from the market value formula $P_m = E_e/d$, his understanding of the cost of capital concept should be considerably enlightened. The earnings that the market expects the business to produce E_e should be identified with a wide scope of economic and financial factors which are closely tied to alternative investment opportunities. The profits pb that the market expects the shares to earn on the other hand are a function pretty much of information communicated (Chapter 2) to the market by financial managers. It is the historical record of past performances and the budgets of future performances that enable the securities market to make estimates of probable pb values for discounting, and this is the more controllable value of the two. Indeed pb is what much of our emphasis has been directed toward thus far throughout the book. But the fact that the dependent variables in the two situations are different does not mean that the market value and the *valuation* of shares are mutually exclusive because market prices which are basic to determining a company's cost of capital are determined by supply of, and demand for, a company's shares which is determined largely by the capitalization process which depends on the cost of capital for discounting. A high cost of capital will tend to devalue shares relative to their budgeted profits pb through the discounting process and will in turn cause their market prices to decline; whereas, a low cost of capital will tend to raise the value of the shares relative to their budgeted profits pb which will in turn cause their market prices to rise. A lower present value for the shares may cause *market price to fall* and the *cost of capital to rise*, and the cost of capital will not decline unless there is some underlying reason why in view of alternative investment opportunities the market should consider as acceptable a lower net earnings E_e. By the same reasoning, a higher present value for the shares may cause *market price to rise* and the *cost of capital to fall*, and the cost of capital will not rise unless there is some underlying reason why in view of alternative investment opportunities that the market should not consider as acceptable the present net earnings E_e.

But as pointed out earlier in the chapter d is controllable to some extent by financial managers working on efficiency in operations to influence E_e. Thus, while the market value of the company's shares may be declining because of unfavorable market reaction to the company's short-run profit prospects, financial managers may be altering the asset and liability structures of the business (liquidity and solvency) so that from the long-run point of view the market may look more favorably on the business and lower its earnings demand so that part at least of the adverse effect on market price may be offset by a lower E_e value.

An adjustment for probability

In the theory developed here of the cost of capital, *certainty* is assumed in illustrating the important E_e variable. If it is an oversimplification to assume that financial managers can determine with certainty what the securities market "expects" our shares to earn, let it be known that this was done intentionally to implant the concept firmly in our minds and to place it in its proper perspective to the current operating concept of budgeted net profit pb that was hinted at in Chapters 1 and 2 and developed in Chapter 7.

Nevertheless, it is suggested that in making applications of the theory of the cost of capital we recognize that the probability distribution may be a valuable tool for use. The procedure is as follows. First, set up a range of possible E_e values; let us say $3, $4, $5, $6, and $7 with probabilities of occurence of 0.1, 0.1, 0.4, 0.3, and 0.1 respectively. Multiply and sum the products: $0.1 \times \$3 = \$0.30$; $0.1 \times \$4 = \$0.40$; $0.4 \times \$5 = \$2.00$; $0.3 \times \$6 = \$1.80$; and $0.1 \times \$7 = \$0.70$. The sum of these products is $5.20, which is the expected E_e; the weighted average expected earnings or the earnings per share that the securities market will most probably demand of our shares if they are to hold their present value P_m. To measure the fluctuation around this expected value, we may return to the schedule of possible E_e values and determine their standard deviation from the $5.20 mean and make a statistical probability analysis of the fluctuation according to the rules developed in Chapter 3 and using Table III in the appendix.

UNDERLYING FINANCIAL RATES

Considered here are the financial rates that underlie the cost of capital. It was stated earlier in the chapter that, although borrowing rates and preferred dividend rates are not costs of capital, using capital as a net value, they do have an effect as opportunity costs on the cost of capital. Considered first is the market rate of interest, and considered second is the dividend rate on preferred stock. Through these two charges, we should obtain a better understanding of where the cost of equity capital fits into the total framework of financial charges and how it differs from the others for decision making in capital budgeting.

MARKET RATE OF INTEREST

The market rate of interest is determined by the interaction of the supply of funds and the demand for funds in the capital loan market. The point at which the supply schedule of funds and the demand schedule for funds are equal is the equilibrium rate of interest. Figure 17.1 illustrates the two forces of demand and supply determining a market rate of interest. The independent variable is put on the Y axis and the dependent variable is on the X axis to follow the procedure used ordinarily in interest theory analysis. The supply curve S_2S_2 marks an increase in the quantity of loan funds coming into the market at a given schedule of interest rates. Shifting the supply curve to the right creates a new equilibrium rate of interest dropping from r_1 to r_2. The reader should verify that shifting the demand curve for funds down and to the left accomplishes the same thing of establishing a new lower equilibrium rate of interest.

The reader will recall that, in the marginal productivity theory of capital investment, this market rate of interest is the cutoff to further capital investment. Although the last term "cutoff" is not included usually in developing conventional interest theory, at the point of equilibrium: marginal productivity = market rate of inter-

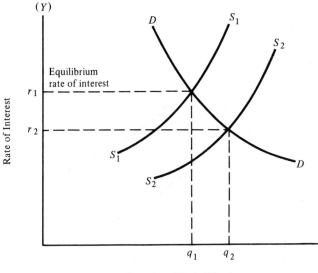

Figure 17.1. Market Rate of Interest.

est = cost of capital. The prime market rate interest becomes a universal cutoff rate for all capital budgeting projects. The weakness of the analysis is twofold. First, for explaining cost of capital, this is a prime interest rate which is apparently applied to all forms of capital investing without regard to the form of financial contract that is used; and, second, this is a uniform rate applied to all businesses regardless of the composition of debts and equity in their capital structures.

The above-mentioned theory of the market rate of interest is modified somewhat by the *liquidity preference* theory of the market rate of interest which makes the market rate of interest the reward for parting with idle cash balances and putting funds into an interest-earning, risk-taking debt security. Figure 17.2 lets the supply of loanable capital funds in the economy be a constant, making the rate of interest vary with the demand schedule for liquidity. The shift in the demand curves from $D_1 D_1$ to $D_2 D_2$ indicates an increase in the preference for cash instead of capital investment securities which causes the prime interest rate to increase. This is still a demand and supply theory but emphasizes that the supply of loan funds is perfectly inelastic, so that changes in the rate are attributed altogether to changes in the liquidity preference of the investing community.

It should be verified that shifting the SS curve can also affect the market rate of interest. The liquidity preference theory, like the previous theory, channels all costs of capital to riskless borrowing giving no consideration to risk problems related to either the contractual form of the financing or the structure of debt and equity in the financial structure of the borrower. Although the last of the three terms below is not included in the development of the theory, at the equilibrium

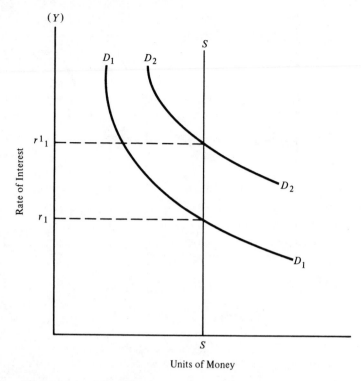

Figure 17.2. Liquidity Preference and Market Rate of Interest.

point: marginal efficiency of capital = market rate of interest = cost of capital. The prime market rate of interest is still treated in this theory as a universal cutoff rate for all capital budgeting projects.

The market rate of interest is still viewed by many as a cost of capital for all firms and as a cutoff rate for new investment. Let us look at this rate a little more closely now from the practical viewpoint of where it fits into our more restrictive theory of cost of capital related specifically to equity capital. The rate of interest in the prime debt market is truly the return that can be earned by a capital investor for simply parting with his liquidity but not taking any risk. The prime capital market is open to all investors, and this is where the market rate indirectly affects the cost of capital d that financial managers have to withstand in equity financing. The prime borrowing rate r_1 has to be borne by all companies' shares because all investors in common shares have the alternative of withdrawing their funds from the shares and putting them in these riskless debts. As a discounting rate r_1 is the rate that equates future net profit on a riskless debt with the purchase price of the debt, it is also the rate which will cause the algebraic sum of interest and capital inflows from the security, and the price paid for the security, to equal zero. Another way of looking at this from the cost of capital viewpoint is as *the opportunity cost to the business of investors preferring a riskless debt to the risky common shares of their business.* There is no fundamental error in admitting the market rate of interest to a firm's cost of capital; the danger lies in presuming that this is the cost of capital for all firms. In using the market rate of interest as an inflationary control tool, the Federal Reserve recognizes this as a foundation rate on which rest other borrowing rates and even the cost of equity capital. It should be apparent that financial managers have no control over this first segment of their cost of capital.

RISK CHARGES

Added to the prime market rate of interest are two risk charges that every company has to bear in its cost of capital, *even though it does not have debts in its own capital structure.* The first of these charges is related to the risk class to which the company belongs. The basis of risk is the type of product or service that the group of companies supply and the resulting quality of its capital assets. The important point made here is that the risk class is identified by the product and service and by the accompanying composition of liquid and nonliquid assets. *Risk for the class as a whole is identified, in other words, with production and sales and the attending asset structure more than with measures of solvency for the class as a whole.* Classes whose assets are invested primarily in net working capital are subjected to less risk in borrowing than companies whose assets are primarily fixed, and classes whose fixed capital suffers from rapid depletion and/or depreciation are more risky to the investor than companies whose fixed capital has a relatively stable value. Also classes producing highly specialized goods and services are more risky to the investor than producers of staples, necessities, and goods that are adaptable to multiple uses.

The other part of the risk charge is related to individual firm status. Here both sides of capital are considered by the investor: the assets or the uses side and the capital structure or the sources side. A company, because of its size, and quality of assets, may be more or less risky to the investor than the whole group of which it is a part. We can think of the group of companies as a whole setting a kind of average risk charge; and the individual firm within the class, because of its own unique form of capital assets and financial management skill, causing this charge to be greater or smaller than the average for the group. The other factor entering the risk charge at the firm level is the solvency risk. Solvency risk is related to the composition of the capital structure. The extent to which this affects a company's cost of capital depends on how the market reacts to the composition of a firm's capital structure. This also is related to how a firm's capital structure compares with the average for the risk class as a whole. Thus a public utility or railroad company with a given debt/equity ratio may not be penalized with a high risk charge because it is in a risk class that has a large amount of debt in its capital structure; whereas, another company with the same debt ratio in a class of companies that carries on the average a smaller debt ratio may be severely penalized in the securities market.

To show the relation of the risk charge, combined with the charge for parting with liquidity, to the cost of capital, let r_2 represent the combined internal and external risk charge assigned to a company's borrowing costs, the total cost of which is $R = r_1 + r_2$. R is the rate of return that the investor has to have to meet his combined costs of parting with liquidity and of assuming the risks of losing interest and principal on a loan contract. This is an opportunity cost to the firm even though it does not borrow money because, to attract investors to its common share market, the company has to induce the investor away from the loan market. What management needs to do is to convince the investor to exchange an internal rate of return that will equate an expected constant cash interest flow with the price of a capital debt for a rate of return of greater risk that will equate an expected net-earnings flow E_e with the price of common stock. This has important implications to the cost of capital and capital investment policy; for, if the securities market requires a higher rate of return for discounting expected share earnings than it would require to induce investment funds into capital debts, then the company's capital borrowing rate cannot be its cost of capital. It follows from this that, if a company's borrowing rate were used as its cost of capital the company would budget funds to projects that yield internal rates of return below the company's true cost of capital on equity capital, causing budgeted profits and its share values to decline. The question of whether reducing capital borrowing costs can reduce the cost of capital is frequently raised. In answer to this, we need to look at the cost components r_1 and r_2. First, r_1 is the prime rate and cannot be changed by management. Second, r_2 reflects a combined risk class and individual firm risk charge. The risk class, as a whole, cannot be controlled, but the firms' risk elements in r_2 can be controlled by more efficient budgeting of capital assets and by giving more careful consideration to the capital structure. To the extent that r_2 can be lowered, there is some chance that E_e and consequently d can be lowered; and, with the lower discount rate, the present value and the market value of the shares may increase.

DIVIDEND CHARGES

Dividend charges on preferred stock is still another important element affecting indirectly the cost of capital. Every company has to bear this charge, as it does prime interest and risk charges, as opportunity costs whether the company issues preferred stock or not. Dividends are usually paid annually out of net profits after interest and taxes. They are quasi-fixed charges. They are not part of a in the profit function, but they are contractual obligations of the business that have to be met before the company's net profits accrue to common shares. Preferred dividends in a given company have to be larger than interest payments because of the added risk to the investor of not collecting the dividends and of having no legal recourse against the business if it fails to pay the dividends.

Indirectly preferred dividend charges increase the cost of a firm's capital because investors have a choice of buying preferred shares in a given risk class at a higher rate of return than could be realized on capital debts. Being a form of capital stock and having no maturity date, the present value of a share is determined by the same simple process as is used for capitalizing expected common share earnings. To illustrate, let a company be committed to a $6 annual dividend with a discounting or capitalization rate for the company in the preferred share market of 0.08; the present value of the share is $6/0.08 = $75. The internal rate of return required to equate a perpetual annual $6 stream with the purchase price of the security is 0.08. This affects the cost of capital of companies in the same risk class because, unless the expected rate of return (cost of capital) on common shares of the company is enough higher than 8 percent to compensate for the added risk of holding common shares, investors will put their funds in preferred rather than in common stock. But if preferred dividend charges had been used as the cost of capital for new equity investment, capital would be budgeted to projects that yield rates of return below what is required on common shares; and such investment would actually cause a decline in common share prices. Only a limited amount of control exists over preferred dividends as a method of reducing the cost of capital. The reason for this is that the preferred dividend rate has at its base the whole structure of debt rates as opportunity costs for issuing preferred shares; debt rates account for most of the preferred stock dividend being what it is. But this does not rule out altogether the benefits of more efficient capital budgeting to capital assets and more careful planning of the capital structure as ways of reducing preferred dividend charges. To the degree that this goal of reducing preferred share rates is attained, the rate of return required by investors in the preferred shares market will be lowered as will the internal rate of return required to be earned on common stock.

SUMMARY STATEMENT

Cost of capital can be summarized now as a cumulative opportunity cost that the firm has to overcome to finance new investment projects with common shares without experiencing a decline in share prices. This is logical because it would be unreasonable to assume that any common equity financing can be done unless the investor can foresee a return on the present value of the shares above what could be realized by buying any of the lower-risk securities. The cost of capital is the rate of return needed by the investor to induce him to hold onto his shares instead of putting his funds in slightly lower yielding securities at a correspondingly lower risk. This theory comes closer to being a marginal cost of capital theory than anything else because cost of capital is determined at the margin at which opportunity costs to the investor of holding onto the shares is just barely more than the expected return from parting with the share. If there is no buying action of a given common stock, its value will not increase. Should investment opportunities in less risky securities deteriorate by, let us say, declining interest and preferred stock dividend rates, this would actually cause the investor to discount the present budgeted stream of net profit *pb* at a lower rate causing common stock to be bought and sold at a higher price. As a concluding remark, there are some very clear areas in which financial management action can be taken to reduce the company's cost of capital; and these areas are primarily in managing capital assets and secondarily in managing the capital structure.

INSTITUTIONAL STRUCTURE OF THE MARKETS

Frequent reference has been made in this and in the previous chapter to the securities market where the price P_m is determined for a company's traded securities. This is the secondary market where securities are traded and market prices are determined in contrast to the primary market where the company secures its cash from the initial securities sales. Each of these two markets will be discussed briefly here as machinery for security pricing that financial managers need to be acquainted with.

THE SECONDARY CAPITAL MARKET

The secondary market is the one in which the investing public exchanges capital funds and securities without directly affecting the inflow of cash to the business. This *securities market* is distinguished from the primary market where the business gets its funds for capital investment. The secondary market is a valuation facility for the business that provides a valuable guide to future capital stock and capital-debt financing, provided financial managers have an open market where the investing public comes to offer funds in exchange for investment securities and to offer securities in exchange for capital funds. The funds offered comprise the market supply of capital, and the securities offered comprise the market supply of securities. The value of the securities at any given time is determined by the ratio of capital funds to capital securities. In general, an increase in the ratio tends to increase value and a decrease tends to decrease market values. The structural makeup of the secondary market includes the organized exchange and the over-the-counter market.

The Organized Securities Market   If our securities are traded in an organized market, they have to be listed. They are called organized exchanges because they possess all of the characteristics of a business organization with charters and by-laws, governing bodies, officers, and rules and regulations for internal operations. These enterprises are *places* for carrying on securities trading, but the organized exchange itself does not participate in securities buying and selling.

Examining the structure and operation of the organized exchanges may indicate good reasons for financial managers' wanting to list rather than letting their companies' securities be traded in less formal markets. The New York Stock Exchange and the American Stock Exchange are both located in lower Manhattan in the center of the financial district and are called *national* exchanges because the securities that are traded are issued by nationally known companies and companies with nationwide interest to investors.[1] These are auction markets held on the floor of the exchange where only members with *seats* are allowed to buy and sell securities for themselves or, if they are brokerage firms, for their customers. Memberships, which are called seats on the exchange, are bought and sold very much like commodities are; although, their turnover is low by comparison. A seat or membership on the New York Stock Exchange sold in 1869 for $3; between 1920–1925 resale prices averaged about $100,000, and in 1929 at the height of stock market activity one membership was sold for $625,000.

In the last instance, prices of securities are determined by transactions by members on the actual floor of the exchange. The most active of these members in terms of volume of business transacted is the *commission broker* which is a firm that has its main office near the trading floor itself and has a direct wire service to its member or members on the floor of the exchange and to its branch offices in different states. These agencies are important intermediaries reflecting supply and demand. They handle odd-lot buy and sell orders, that is, in blocs of less than 100 shares, and round-lot orders in units of 100. Thus, the demand and supply forces of thousands of small traders are felt daily and weekly in the market, and they help to create an orderly price structure reflecting net profit expectations E_e. On the floor also are the *floor trader* and the *specialist*. The floor trader accomplishes this by roaming from one trading *post* to another buying and selling securities with his own funds and for his own account instead of for regular customers. He sells primarily to commission brokers thus helping them to fill customers' orders. The stabilizing effect results from his trading on a narrow margin and for a short period, usually buying heavily when a stock falls slightly and selling again when it regains its strength. The specialist accomplishes about the same results for stocks, but he is the prime risk taker on the floor of the exchange. Instead of acting at his option, he is required by the exchange rules to help create and maintain a fair and orderly market in the stocks that are his specialty, even though it may mean heavy personal losses.

The mechanical aspects of the transactions themselves that investors can execute through their commission brokers have important effects on a company's share values for future financing. One of these is *margin buying*, which is customers' buying on credit supplied by commission brokers. The New York Stock Exchange allows its broker members to lend up to a certain percentage of the market value of a security. This creates an accelerated effect on buying securities, but the broker's right to liquidate his customer's holdings in case of a sharp decline in price may have an accelerating effect in the opposite direction of selling. The Federal Reserve Board is allowed to temper the effect of marginal buying by limiting the amount of cash that member banks in the Federal Reserve System may lend to brokers

---

[1] Regional exchanges include the Midwest Exchange in Chicago, the Pacific Coast Exchange in San Francisco, Philadelphia-Baltimore Exchange in Philadelphia, and the Boston, Detroit, Cincinnati, Pittsburgh, Salt Lake City, Spokane, and the San Francisco Mining Exchange, which is the smallest but one of the oldest exchanges, having been organized in 1862.

and others pledging capital-stock collateral for their customers' margin accounts. *Short-selling* is done usually for regular gains but also to hedge against the risk of loss on an ordinary purchase order. In a short sale, the investor directs his broker to sell for his account stocks that he does not yet own but that have risen high enough above their "normal" price to indicate a profit. The short seller expects to realize his profit by buying the stock at a lower price for future delivery. The price-stabilizing effect occurs at both ends of the transaction: the sale first checks the incline, and the purchase later to cover delivery checks the decline. Finally, the technical operation of *arbitrage* may have a stabilizing effect on a more limited scale. Arbitrage takes place when options to buy stocks, such as stock purchase *rights*, are *out of parity* with the market price of the stock that they are authorized to buy.

Before deciding whether to list a stock on a particular organized exchange, financial managers should realize that chances of being rejected are generally better than they are of being accepted. Although the regional exchanges are not as strict, neither are their benefits as pronounced. Age, quantity of assets, profits, dividends, and then, finally, the important national interest test has to be met. The applicant also has to agree to report to its stockholders at least fifteen days before its annual stockholders' meeting, and all listed companies are required to submit financial reports of condition to the SEC (Securities and Exchange Commission), to the stock exchange, and to its stockholders. An initial listing fee is charged. In some cases, this is a flat dollar amount. In others, it is based on the quantity of shares outstanding, decreasing per share as the number of shares increases.

The benefits that are realized from listing can be traced to the structure and operation of the exchange facilities mentioned above. First, the auction-market situation enables the supply and demand forces of capital and of capital securities to be quickly and accurately reflected in the exchange value of the securities. For example, if we develop a new product or service, if our sales increase, if we develop a method of cutting our costs, or even if we hire certain key management personnel, these factors will all quickly show favorable effects on the market price of the shares and on the sale of future issues. Second, the exchange is constructed and operated to allow the maximum freedom in trading the shares, so that price fluctuations tend to be relatively small amounts. Third, the transactions and services rendered by its members are geared to promoting the maximum participation by small and large investors alike, making it hard for any one group of investors to manipulate the market and allowing the market evaluations of the small holders to be reflected. Fourth, listed securities are always before the public in the daily newspapers and in radio and television reports. This enables management to keep in close communication with the investor's evaluations of their business, and it gives the business a certain amount of free advertising. Fifth, some investors, particularly some financial institutions, as a general policy matter will not buy unlisted securities because they are hard to market on short notice.

Over-the-Counter Market   The over-the-counter market is any place where securities are exchanged with some regularity. In picturing this service, we must discard the notion of a centralized marketing place with a highly organized institution providing trading facilities for its members. There are no organized *places* of this kind where members come together regularly to buy and sell; and, therefore, there can be no memberships or seats as there are in the organized market. The over-the-counter market exists in the office of any securities dealer who simultaneously offers to buy and sell certain stocks and bonds. These markets exist all over the nation in cities of all sizes, but the securities traded usually have a local and regional flavor. On the other hand, new securities issues also find their way into the secondary market through over-the-counter securities dealers. Securities dealers usually *make a market* for the securities that they buy and sell. The dealers will buy from anyone desiring to sell, and they will sell to anyone desiring to buy. Many more different securities are traded in this market than in the organized exchanges.

An important stabilizing factor in the structure and operation of the over-the-counter markets today is the NASD (National Association of Securities Dealers). About 3,000 securities dealers and broker-dealers operating in this market belong to the NASD. The NASD was organized under a 1938 law requiring formation and registration of such an organization with the SEC. This is a nonprofit organization that derives its income from dues and fees from its members, and the activities of its members are closely supervised and regulated by the organization. Members are expected to observe high standards of commercial honor and *just and equitable principles of trade.* The association has the tools for enforcing strict disciplinary action against its members if such action is needed. The NASD is making a special effort to develop better public understanding of and interest in the over-the-counter markets. The National Quotation Bureau of the NASD prints what are called the *Pink Sheets* containing bid and asked prices of all actively traded stocks and bonds. Daily newspapers in larger cities will publish the prices of local as well as national securities. We should note that unlike the organized exchanges that publish completed transactions, these exchanges never report the price at which transactions are completed.

Decision-Making Factors While most businesses have no chance of listing on one of the two national exchanges, many can qualify for listing on the regional organized exchanges that compete with trading in the over-the-counter market. Financial managers are pressed, in this case, into making a decision between listing and not listing. Advantages of the former have already been considered. We can now examine the advantages of remaining unlisted. First, there are no listing charges. Second, financial statements and reports are not required of unlisted companies as they are of listed, although dealers will require these statements of companies for whose securities they make a market. Third, a strong feeling exists that small and medium-sized businesses receive more attention from over-the-counter dealers than they do from brokers in the organized exchanges for the following reasons: (1) with relatively few accounts to handle, a dealer can give more attention to each; (2) since the dealer makes a market for the securities, it is to his interest to see that the securities are actively traded; and (3) dealers in local markets are likely to be well acquainted with the industry and the products of the businesses in their region.

PRIMARY CAPITAL MARKET

A primary capital market is any place that we can go to secure capital funds. The general structure of this market resembles the over-the-counter facilities more than the organized exchange. The market place for these funds is any financial institution that participates in making direct capital investments in business in exchange for security instruments. The relationship of the primary market to the secondary markets should be noted. First, day-to-day trading in the secondary markets sets values on securities that determine the sale price for capital financing in the primary market. Second, the wholesale section of the over-the-counter market absorbs new capital issues from the primary market, and from there they find their way into the markets of the organized and unorganized exchanges. There are actually two divisions of this market that financial managers have to consider before making capital-financing decisions; one is the private placement services and the other is the underwriting or investment banking services.

Private Placement Services   The private placement market is the one in which complete capital-debt issues or capital-stock issues can be placed with a small number of investors for long-term holdings. The term *private placement* distinguishes this as a market in which capital can be sought with the maximum speed, and minimum expense.

Capital in this market comes primarily from commercial banks and life insurance companies. Supplementing these are mutual savings banks, investment companies, and pension funds. Commercial banks supply the shorter capital loans with intermediate maturities ranging between two and ten years, while life insurance companies make the longer advances of up to twenty-year maturities and in some cases more. There is some chance of aligning the institution with the use to which the funds are put. Thus, if capital for fixed assets is needed, we would probably get better response from a life insurance company or mutual savings bank than from a commercial bank which is primarily interested in supplying funds for working-capital expenditures. When combined working- and fixed-capital uses are planned, services of the two types of financial institutions may be combined to supply the needs.

This market is primarily for borrowing. Secured and unsecured promissory notes with a loan agreement that can be shaped to individual borrowing needs are used. If bonds are used, just a few instruments need to be printed in large denominations. Instead of printing 1,000 bonds in $1,000 denominations to borrow $1 million, a single instrument for that amount may be printed, or ten may be printed for $100,000 each. Private placement creditors usually intend to hold the capital debts until they mature. Even if this were not the intention, it would have to be the general case since secondary market facilities are not designed to handle intermediate and long-term promissory notes in the large denominations held in this market.

Most of this borrowing can be done in the local market, which allows the business to deal with financial representatives who are familiar with local financial problems. Communication is likely to be clear and meaningful between financial managers and the capital suppliers. This helps to get the capital contract custom designed to meet special financial needs and may make it easier to get adjustments and alterations in case that financial difficulties occur later on. The objection to the local supplier is that his funds may be too limited in meeting extensive capital expenditures. The supply of capital in this market can be expanded to some extent by getting the suppliers to pool their lending resources. While the market may have limitations for the large capital borrowers, this is not true for medium-size and small borrowers. Institutions in this market would not usually hesitate in making a loan because it was too small. In the underwriting or investment banking market, on the other hand, the costs of preparation, handling, and risk taking cost more than the small borrower can stand.

Investment Banking Services   The investment banking or underwriting services are sought when new capital-stock issues and capital debts are placed for further public sale and distribution. *Underwriting* is a term that comes to us from the insurance business and means undertaking for another business the risks of financial loss for a premium or what in this case is called the underwriting *spread*. Whereas in the private placement market we deal throughout the financing period with the original capital supplier, in the underwriting market the supplier is on the scene only temporarily. Much of the personal touch and local flavor of the private placement is absent in this market, but in return it offers other benefits. Investment banking services include the following:

1. Origination, registration, underwriting, and syndicating of new corporate stock and bond issues.
2. Public distribution of issues through wholesale and retail channels.
3. Extensive trading as principal and broker in many unlisted and some listed issues, including securities of banks, insurance companies, public utilities, and industrial corporations.
4. Purchases of large blocks of listed or unlisted stocks for secondary distribution through security marketing channels.
5. Participation as agent in arranging private financing with insurance companies, banks, investment trusts, and other institutional accounts.
6. Arrangement of contracts for sale and lease-back of properties.
7. Participation as agent in negotiating purchase and sale of controlling or major stock interests in going business concerns.
8. Consultation and assistance in corporate mergers, consolidations, liquidations, and recapitalizations, and the like.
9. Purchase of temporary investment of entire or substantial equity interests in going concerns for subsequent public or private sale.
10. Large-scale buying and marketing of bonds of states, municipalities, and other government bodies.

The closer a company's securities issues come to a public distribution, the more certainly they must be registered with the SEC, and in some cases also with state securities commissions as well. Private placements of securities are not affected, but all underwritings of stocks and bonds have to run the full gamut. The more important laws affecting the issuance of securities are the Securities Exchange Act of 1933, the Public Utility Holding Company Act of 1935, and the Trust Indenture Act of 1939. Some of the state laws are actually older than the federal laws. These laws are more regulative and restrictive in most cases than the federal laws, but state laws are lax by comparison in enforcement. Compliance with the federal laws in some cases also serves to fulfill the state requirements. The Securities Exchange Act of 1933 was the first general federal securities regulating law in the United States. The law of 1933 supplies the instrumentality for preventing, by forcing registration, the fraudulent issuance of stocks and bonds. For registration, management is required to supply a "full and fair disclosure" of all material information relating to issuance of stocks and bonds destined for the open markets. The SEC created by the law is not concerned with evaluating or rating securities for investment purposes, just with enforcing full disclosure of all information that if withheld or misrepresented might result in misinforming and in defrauding the public. The 1933 act lists thirty-two items that are required for registering public issues. Compliance with all of these requires many hours of work, costly legal and financial accounting and auditing reports, and expensive printing services. The issuing company is assessed a registration fee based on the sale price of the securities. Financial managers and other company officials connected with a public issuance, including board members, accountants, engineers, and every investment banker having anything to do with the issue, are liable in civil and criminal suits for violations of the law.

In some cases, an issue of securities will be underwritten on a *best-effort* basis by the investment bank. This is not a true underwriting contract since the investment banker does not take the risk of loss for unsuccessful sales, just so long as his best effort was used in trying to distribute the issue. The typical purchase agreement, however, is a *firm commitment*. In this the investment banker or syndicate of bankers agrees to pay a fixed sum of cash to the business for the total issue on delivery or to stand by and pay to the business a sum of cash equal to the market value of the unsold portion of the issue. The *standby agreement* is often used when a business offers a new issue of common stock to its present stockholders at a *privileged* subscription price; the investment banker agrees for a cash fee to purchase at the subscription price all shares not taken by the stockholders. Terms of the typical *purchase agreement* go into effect as soon as the business agrees to the net-cost conditions. When the purchase is syndicated to spread the risk of loss, the investment bankers are all bound to the terms of the contract through their manager or representative underwriter who is responsible for collecting the purchase funds from the other members and delivering them all at one time to the company. The underwriters' compensation is the spread between the price paid to the business and the retail price at which the underwriter and his affiliated retail dealers expect to market the securities to the public. The amount received by the issuer is called the *net proceeds* from the sale. The buyers promise to pay for the securities within a given period (usually three to five days) after the issue is fully registered with the SEC. The date set for the payment is known as the *closing date*, and it marks the time when the company has to deliver the securities to the underwriters. Each underwriter in a syndicate is individually liable to the issuer for his own share of the securities but not for the others. The issuing company warrants that it has filed the necessary information with state and federal offices. It then promises: (1) to amend its registration statement with the SEC so the public sale can begin; (2) to pay all expenses connected with preparing and filing the registration statement and prospectus, issuing and delivering the securities, printing and selling the prospectus, listing the securities on an exchange in some cases, and paying state and federal security taxes and fees; (3) to apply the proceeds from the sale to the purposes for which they were stated in the registration statement and prospectus; (4) to use its best effort to qualify under the "blue-sky laws" of the various states where the securities are to be sold; and (5) to pay the filing and recording fees required in the states. The investment banker's obligation to take and pay for the securities at a specified time is determined by the company's fulfilling these promises and on the purchasers' receiving a favorable opinion from the company's legal council stating that the company has complied with the proper laws and has executed and authenticated the securities and prepared them for delivery. It is not uncommon to let the underwriters withdraw within twenty-four hours after the completed registration if the market generally has reacted so adversely as to make an offering at the expected price impracticable.

SUMMARY

In the two previous chapters, the concept of the cost of capital was used freely indicating its use as a cutoff rate for making capital-expenditure decisions. This chapter explores in some detail the subject of the cost of capital and to a more limited extent the market structure in which financial managers seek funds for capital investment. The conceptual factors relating to the cost of capital included the: relation of cost to the market price of common shares, cost of capital as an internal rate of return, concept of net capital, opportunity cost concept, cost of capital as a discounting rate in the securities market, cost of capital as a borrowing rate, and internal control factors affecting the cost of capital.

Next was considered the quantitative relationships in the cost of capital. The cost of capital is, as is shown, a linear function of the quantity of per share net earnings *expected* of the business in the securities market. The cost of capital is the ratio of this expected dollar earnings per share of stock E_e to the current market price of that stock E_e/P_m. Emphasis was placed on the meaning of E_e as a dollar return required of the business to maintain the current market price. Increasing E_e while holding P_m constant causes the cost of capital to increase at a constant rate. At the same time, it was shown that by holding constant E_e and decreasing current market price of the stock, the cost of capital increases at an increasing rate. This establishes that the cost of capital is a linear function of E_e but not of the market price of the share P_m. The present value of the share of stock in the market is a function of budgeted net profits pb and not of E_e. It is important to distinguish between the roles played by pb and E_e, both in determining the present value of a share of common stock and in determining the cost of capital. Since pb is not a direct determinate of the cost of capital, it is a valuation symbol which, when discounted by the cost of capital, produces a present value V_p, and only if the present value V_p of the share exceeds the current market price of the share for a continuing period will the market price be affected.

The underlying financial rates affecting the cost of capital need to be considered for a full understanding of the role played by opportunity costs. The underlying financial rates include first the market rate of interest, which is a prime rate equal to r_1. The financial charge of the prime rate of interest is an opportunity cost that every corporation has to bear in computing its net capital cost. In addition to the prime rate, most businesses also have added a risk charge designated as r_2. Total borrowing cost is $R = r_1 + r_2$. R is the rate of return that the investor has to have to meet his combined costs of parting with liquidity and of assuming the risks of losing interest and principal on a loan contract. This is an opportunity cost to the firm affecting its cost of capital. Finally the opportunity cost of preferred dividends is also included in the foundation rates paid for financing with net capital.

The institutional structure in which corporations seek capital funds consists of two basic institutions: the secondary financial market which includes organized securities marketing services and the over-the-counter marketing services. The second institutional structure includes the primary market where the corporation takes its new issues of common stock and other forms of securities to raise cash funds for investment. Included in the primary market are institutions that advance funds directly to the corporation without going through the central marketing services, such as commercial banks, life insurance companies, and others. Then there are the investment banking institutions that purchase complete issues of new securities from corporations advancing them the cash funds and marketing the securities through their own marketing facilities in the secondary markets.

PROBLEMS

1. Start with expected after-tax net earnings per share of $2, increase by intervals of $2, and graph the effect of this on the cost of capital when the share price is $40. Graph also the Δd line on the same graph.

   a. What do the two lines reveal?
   b. Does this reveal a favorable or unfavorable condition for the business? Why?
   c. What conditions in the economy could account for this?

d. Using the formula $P = (1/d)(E_e)$, show that a rising cost of capital prevents the share from increasing. Use data given above.

2. Set up a schedule showing E_e constant and cost of capital of the firm decreasing by 0.01 and price of the stock changing accordingly.

   a. Set up the formula where price of the stock is the dependent variable. Show with the formula how a decrease in cost of capital raises the price of the stock.
   b. In view of the definition of cost of capital as the ratio of the expected earnings to the market price of a share of common stock, how do you explain the increase in share value without E_e increasing?

3. Draw two diagrams illustrating the variables affecting market rate of interest according to market supply of and demand for capital and changes in liquidity preference.

   a. In the supply and demand diagram, show the effect on the rate of interest of increasing demand, of increasing supply. What does each mean?
   b. In the liquidity preference diagram, show the effect on the rate of decreasing liquidity preference, of increasing the supply of money.
   c. What basis do we have for calling these rates the cost of capital?
   d. What inconsistency is there in using the market rate of interest to explain the cost of capital and cutoff rate for all firms?
   e. If the market rate of interest is not a complete explanation of the cost of capital, where does it fit into the theory?

4. Assume that the prime rate of interest is 6 percent and that the average risk rate on borrowing by the firm is 2 percent.

   a. How does the above information help to explain a company's 12 percent cost of capital?
   b. The Federal Reserve takes action which causes the prime rate to increase to 8 percent. What effect could this have on a company's cost of capital? Explain.
   c. The product of the risk class to which your business belongs suddenly is found to have harmful effects on the consumers' health. What effect if any will this have on your company's cost of capital? Explain.
   d. Your company recently has developed a new product that promises to have a lasting effect on the market. What resulting changes in the cost of capital equation would produce: (1) increase cost of capital, (2) decrease cost of capital, (3) cause cost of capital to remain the same?
   e. Your firm has just gained control of certain strategic patents which will increase considerably the quality of your product compared with the product of other companies in the same risk class. What effect will this have on r_2 in the $C_{min} = r_1 + r_2$ equation? What effect if any will this have on your cost of capital? Explain.

5. Assume that the prime rate of interest is 6 percent, and the average risk rate for the firm's borrowing is 2 percent and the risk charge for issuing preferred stock is another 2 percent.

   a. E_e for Company A's shares is $4, and its price is stable at $40. What is the company's cost of capital?

   b. Now E_e remains at $4, but the prime rate of interest decreases by 2 percent. What happens to the company's cost of capital? Why and how will the change in the cost of capital be reflected in the common stock market?

   c. There is a sudden demand in the market for preferred shares in Company A's risk class. What effect will this have on the discounting rate for preferred dividends in the risk class? What effect will this have on the company's own cost of capital and its share values?

   d. Assume that the investment market steers away from preferred shares in a given risk class but offsets this completely with more interest in the corporate bond market. What effect, if any, will this have on a company's cost of capital? Explain.

   e. Why does a company want to decrease its cost of capital? Can financial managers do anything to decrease their company's cost of capital?

18

Planning
the
Capital
Structure

The capital structure contains at any given time the balances in capital financing accounts. Some writers limit their discussions of the capital structure to the costs indicated for the various security forms, using the average of these as the company's cost of capital. Our purpose is much broader; it is to give the student an overall view of the capital financing problem and to prepare him for a more detailed consideration of various capital financing forms in the chapters that follow. Cost of capital is one of the considerations, but only indirectly through the effect of the capital structure mix upon budgeted profits and solvency risks.

FORM OF THE CAPITAL STRUCTURE

It is important to understand the relationship between capital which is comprised of long-run assets, and the capital structure which is a composite of long-term financial obligations. This will help us to understand further the fundamental difference in the two areas of financial management for managing share values. First, it is important to distinguish between the relationship of equality and identity in the two areas of management.

$$\text{Gross capital} = \text{Capital structure}$$
$$\text{Gross capital} \neq \text{Capital structure}$$

Quantitatively, gross capital and capital structure are the same; qualitatively, they are not the same. They are equal ($=$) but are not identities ($\neq$). Qualitative differences result because gross capital is the sum of capital assets (net working capital and fixed capital), and the capital structure is the sum of credit balances incurred in obtaining capital assets. General debt and ownership relationships in the capital structure are:

$$\text{Capital structure} = \text{Net worth} + \text{Capital debt}$$
$$\text{Capital structure} - \text{Capital debt} = \text{Net worth}$$
$$\text{Capital structure} - \text{Net worth} = \text{Capital debt}$$

A further classification follows:

$$\text{Net worth} = \text{Common stock} + \text{Preferred stock} + \text{Retained earning}$$
$$\text{Capital debt} = \text{Liabilities with maturities over one year}$$

RISK PATTERN WITHIN THE STRUCTURE

The last classification above reveals important qualitative differences within the capital structure itself that will be discussed in the following chapters. The debt portion of the capital structure signifies high risk, the net worth portion low risk from the company's point of view, and just the opposite from the investor's viewpoint as was shown earlier in the basic theory of cost of capital. Measures of the quantitative portions of high- and low-risk elements in the structure are necessary to understanding how the capital structure affects the cost of capital, if it affects it at all.

TABLE 18.1
COMPANY X
CURRENT CAPITAL STRUCTURE

	Amount
Note payable (due in 10 years)	$ 200,000
Bonds	400,000
Common stock (200,000 shares @ $10 par)	2,000,000
Preferred stock (10,000 shares @ $100)	1,000,000
Retained earnings	1,400,000
Total capital structure	$5,000,000

Significant relationships include the following:

Capital debts/Capital structure = $600,000/$5,000,000 = 0.12
Net worth/Capital structure   = 4,400,000/5,000,000 = 0.88

Total   1.00

These ratios reveal the general risk pattern contained in the structure showing that 0.12 of the balance of capital has been financed at high solvency risk and 0.88 at low risk. Any action to increase the first relationship adds to solvency risk; any action to increase the second decreases solvency risk. For a closer view of relative solvency risks:

Net worth/Capital debts = $4,400,000/600,000 = 7.3
Capital debts/Net worth = 0.14

    The first measures the relationship directly of low- to high-risk capital financing, showing that low-risk financing is 7.3 times as large as high-risk financing. Reversing the order, the company has 0.14 as much high-risk financing on balance as it has low-risk. Any financing that increases the first relationship lessens risk in the capital structure, and any financing that increases the latter increases risk in the capital structure. One final classification is suggested because of the treatment given later to these forms in cost of capital analysis.

Common stock/Net worth = $2,000,000/$4,400,000 = 0.45
Preferred stock/Net worth = $1,000,000/$4,400,000 = .23
Retained earnings/Net worth = 1,400,000/4,400,000 = .32

                                                  Total   1.00

Preferred stock is the most risky of the three net-worth forms of capital from the company's viewpoint and retained earnings are the least.

SOLVENCY RISK

    We are concerned with the effects on solvency risks and, consequently, on the r_2 and E_e elements in borrowing by changing relative quantities of debt and equity in the capital structure. Its effect on cost of capital as defined in Chapter 17, however, at best is indirect. Assuming that the riskiness of debts relative to nondebt obligations are recognized in the capital structure, financial managers need to establish usable tools then for expressing standards of attainment in the capital structure mix that will meet the needs of the firm. We are more concerned here with the tools and skills for measuring and planning the standards than we are with setting the actual standards. Two model tools are suggested: first, capital structure ratios and, second, income and fixed charges ratios.

CAPITAL STRUCTURE RATIOS

    One way of planning the capital structure is to make it fit into a model compiled from a number of different experiences by the business. Supplementing this may be the experiences of competitive businesses; of the industry as a whole; and of securities analysts, underwriters, investors, and government commissions who have their own ideas about how debts and equities should be combined in the capital structure. There is no such thing as *the* model capital structure for all businesses, but there are common characteristics that seem to typify certain risk groups. Some with relatively stable income, costs, and net cash flows may operate safely with high-debt ratios, but these are subjected to more public regulation than businesses with fluctuating flows of funds.

In the last analysis, financial managers have to set up the actual proportions of the high-, low-, and medium-risk capital forms for their own firm. An example appears below. Suppose that the following model ratios are established: capital debts 20 percent, preferred stock 30 percent, common stock 40 percent, and retained earnings 10 percent. How will this model affect R_2 and E_e/P_m cost? If we have already reached these proportions, new financing will have to be in the same proportions for the model to be maintained. With an $800,000 expansion planned for the capital structure, solving the following equation will answer the question of how to ration the new financing without disturbing the present ratios. When $1X$ represents the amount of planned internal financing all others are multiples of retained earnings.

$$1X + 4X + 3X + 2X = \$800,000$$

$$
\begin{array}{rll}
1X = & 80,000: & \text{Retained earnings} \\
4X = & \$320,000: & \text{Common stock} \\
3X = & 240,000: & \text{Preferred stock} \\
2X = & 160,000: & \text{Capital debt}
\end{array}
$$

Total new financing　　　$800,000

A more typical case may be one in which new financing is planned to readjust the present capital structure to different proportions. Suppose that the capital structure to begin with is $1 million made up of 10 percent or $100,000 preferred stock, 80 percent common stock, 10 percent or retained earnings, and no debts and that the goal is to ration a new $800,000 issue so that the new $1.8 million capital structure will be in model proportions. First, the dollar values that are needed to meet the model requirements after the new financing are determined; second, the values in the capital structure are subtracted from the plan for the expanded capital structure; and, third, the necessary adjustments are made through the plan for new financing. These steps are illustrated in Table 18.2. The table indicates that the equity structure is actually top-heavy and that extra low solvency risks have been emphasized in the past.

An expansion in the capital structure was assumed in the case above, but the same method can be used to change the quality composition of the present struc-

TABLE 18.2
ADJUSTING TO MODEL DIMENSIONS
IN CAPITAL STRUCTURE EXPANSION

	Structure After New Financing		Present Structure		Plan for New Financing	
$1X + 4X + 3X + 2X =$	$1,800,000					
$1X =$	180,000	$-$	$ 100,000	$=$	$+$$ 80,000	Retained earnings
$4X =$	720,000	$-$	800,000	$= -$	80,000	Common stock
$3X =$	540,000	$-$	100,000	$= +$	440,000	Preferred stock
$2X =$	360,000	$-$	0	$= +$	360,000	Capital debt
	$1,800,000	$-$	$1,000,000	$=$	$800,000	

ture without changing its total size. Adjustments are made in this case by a plan of *refinancing* in the manner illustrated in Table 18.3. The first column shows how the $1 million of financing would be rationed using the 10-40-30-20 relationship for retained earnings, common stock, preferred stock, and capital debt. The second column subtracts the present balances, and the third column shows how the structure needs to be refinanced to reach model dimensions. The zero (0) at the bottom of the last column indicates that there will be no net addition to the structure as a whole.

TABLE 18.3
ADJUSTING TO MODEL DIMENSIONS BY REFINANCING

Financial Form	Planned Structure		Present Structure		Plan for Refinancing
Retained earnings	$ 100,000	—	$ 100,000	=	+ 0
Common stock	400,000	—	800,000	=	− $400,000
Preferred stock	300,000	—	100,000	=	+ 200,000
Capital debt	200,000	—	0	=	+ 200,000
	$1,000,000	—	$1,000,000	=	0

The main criticism of this method of planning is that, even though taken from actual experiences, the question to decide is just how accurately a ratio of debts to total capital structure measures the riskiness of the structure. In essence, a ratio basis alone is not sufficient for planning the structure.

INCOME TURNOVER RATIOS

This method of planning establishes a capital structure based on model turnover relationships between expected net income and capital financing forms. In this method every planned structure is tuned to eventual retirement or liquidation, even common stock and retained earnings. This is a more dynamic approach to planning than the ratio method discussed above. Retained earnings may be included with common stock for this purpose since the model solvency goal is to be able eventually to return the total equity capital to the common stockholders. The following working rules are suggested. After-tax net profits should turn over into capital debts three times: debt/net profit $= 3$; into preferred stock six times: preferred stock/net profit $= 6$; and into common equity twenty times: common equity/net profits $= 20$. If there are to be no debts in the capital structure, preferred stock may be equivalent to six years of average earnings; but, if debts are outstanding, the debts will be subtracted and only the difference alotted to preferred stock. The twenty-year turnover for common equity may represent something like the expected life span of the business; but, if debts or preferred stock or both are planned for the capital structure, their combined amount will be subtracted from the twenty-year value and only the difference allotted to common equity; the size is such that it can be retired in total with 20 years net profit.

Putting these rules into use, we assume first that the present structure conforms to the 3/1, 6/1, 20/1 model turnover relationships suggested above between debt, preferred stock, common equity, and expected annual income. We assume further that a $2 million capital investment is planned that is expected to return on the average $100,000 annually over its life. Now that we have the key income figure for the pattern of financing, it is a simple matter to ration the $2 million of new financing as indicated in Table 18.4.

TABLE 18.4
RATIONING NEW FINANCING
THE INCOME TURNOVER METHOD

Financial Form	Expected Profits		Turnover Ratio		Senior Claims		Plan for New Financing
Capital debt:	$100,000	×	3	—	0	=	$ 300,000
Preferred stock:	100,000	×	6	—	$300,000	=	300,000
Common equity:	100,000	×	20	—	600,000	=	1,400,000
						Total	$2,000,000

A more typical problem would be to readjust the present capital structure to the turnover ratios indicated above to compare the resulting structure with the results using the ratio method. This is done in four steps as follows. Add the expected profits to the level of present profits. Second, multiply this by the model ratios scheduled for each of the three segments of the capital structure, subtracting senior claims where they exist. This will give the capital-structure plan in dollar amounts including the new financing. Third, the present values in the structure are subtracted from the expanded capital structure; and, fourth, the necessary adjustments are made through the plan for new financing. To illustrate, assume that the present capital structure is based on an average annual profit flow of $200,000 and that the following turnover ratios are prevelant: debt/net profits = 5; preferred stock/net profits = 8; and common equity/net profits = 20. Debts are then $1 million; preferred stock is $600,000 ($1,600,000 — $1,000,000); and common equity is $2.4 million ($4,000,000 — $1,600,000). The new project is expected to return a $100,000 addition to annual net profits. With this information, the last three steps in reshaping the capital structure are illustrated in Table 18.5. In the adjusted present plan there will be a cutback on some debts and both forms

TABLE 18.5
ADJUSTING TO MODEL DIMENSION BY NEW FINANCING

Financial Form	Total Expected Profits	Model Turnover Ratio	Senior Claims	Structure After Financing	Present Capital Structure	Plan for Financing
Capital debt:	$300,000 ×	3	— $ 0	= $ 900,000 —	$1,000,000 =	$ — 100,000
Preferred stock:	300,000 ×	6	— 900,000 =	900,000 —	600,000 =	300,000
Common equity:	300,000 ×	20	— 1,800,000 =	4,200,000 —	2,400,000 =	1,800,000
		29		$6,000,000 —	$4,000,000 =	$2,000,000

of equity financing will be expanded to improve the solvency status of the business for future short- and long-term borrowing.

PROFIT CONSIDERATIONS

Profit from capital budgeting, as we have seen, is determined primarily by how effectively capital is invested to affect the profit function. The rate of contribution to profit is determined by $b - c$ and the total operating profit by $X(b - c)$. We identify this as the contribution to fixed costs and expenses and finally to profits after interest and taxes: $[X(b - c) - a](1 - tr)$. The capital structure cannot be discussed without referring frequently to the elements in this equation.

COST OF CAPITAL

The capital structure may contain fixed charges which increase the size of a in the profit function. This is an obstruction just like salaries, property taxes and insurance; they are fixed charges to overcome with the contribution from $X(b - c)$ which can be overcome only by making the correct investment decisions. The investor allows for effects of a capital structure's interest charge in estimating expected profits, so that it is only by indirection that debt charges affect a company's cost of capital. There are some who are not satisfied with the share-value approach to the cost of capital developed in Chapter 17, who try to compromise this issue by turning to a weighted average cost of capital. If it is a definite figure that we want, simple to calculate but difficult to apply to practical capital budgeting problems, then the company's capital structure may be planned in the way illustrated below.

TABLE 18.6
PRESENT CAPITAL STRUCTURE
WEIGHTED AVERAGE COST

Capital Structure	Amount	+	Relative Weights		Capital Costs (%)		Weighted Average Costs
Capital debts	$ 20,000		.2	×	3.5	=	0.7
Preferred stock	30,000		.3	×	5.5	=	1.7
Common stock	40,000		.4	×	8.0	=	3.2
Retained earnings	10,000		.1	×	7.0	=	0.7
	$100,000		1.0		24.0		6.3

Suppose that a new capital expansion of $100,000 is planned and that we are looking for an overall plan that will lower the average costs while still giving consideration to solvency. Since management is not bound to the margins suggested above for controlling solvency, they can consider shifting more of the weight in the capital structure to borrowing forms. Interest is 3.5 percent on an after-tax basis: $0.7(1 - 0.5) = 3.5$. There is some room in the structure for capital borrowing and also for preferred stock financing at this time, but the tax shield makes debts more appealing than preferred stock. We will assume that after sampling the debt and equity markets, financial managers decide to raise the total debt to $80,000. Table 18.7 shows how debt financing has lowered the average cost of capital.

TABLE 18.7
PLANNING THE STRUCTURE FOR LOWER AVERAGE COSTS

Capital Structure	Amount		Relative Weights		Average Costs (%)		Weighted Average Costs
Capital debts	$ 80,000	=	0.48	×	3.5	=	1.68
Preferred stock	30,000	=	.18	×	5.5	=	0.99
Common stock	40,000	=	.23	×	8.0	=	1.84
Retained earnings	20,000	=	.11	×	7.0	=	0.77
	$170,000		1.00		24.0		5.28

For the following reasons an average value of this kind is of little use to financial managers seeking to maximize share values. First, a contract cost, like an interest cost, and preferred dividends are combined in the structure with implied costs for common shares and retained earnings. Contract and implied costs are of two different qualities; items of unlike quality like apples and oranges cannot be combined and averaged. Second, we will recall that one of the main functions of the cost of capital is to serve as a cutoff rate for capital investment. It is rather meaningless to expect an average value of unlike items to serve as a cutoff rate for new investment. Even if the items were the same quality, an average rate runs contrary to the underlying principle that any project earning above the cutoff rate is a profitable project. It is contrary to this principle because, with an average, half of the costs are above that point and half are below. Any investment project that just meets the average has a fifty-fifty chance, therefore, that it is operating below actual cost of capital. It follows from this that those projects producing in the bracket above the average cost of capital cause share values to decrease. Finally, as pointed out in Chapter 17, borrowing costs and preferred dividend charges affect the cost of capital indirectly through the investment market as opportunity costs to the financing concern. But the important thing is that it is not the individual firm's capital structure alone that determines this opportunity cost r_2 that sets E_e. It is the availability of alternative investments in the total risk class rather than in any one firm's capital structure alone that determines opportunity risk costs r_2 and indirectly E_e and a company's cost of capital E_e/P_m.

LEVERAGE EFFECT

Leverage effect is the effect of capital financing with fixed charges, like debts and preferred stock, upon after tax net profits of common stock.

The capital structure can be planned so that given a certain debt structure earnings per share (*EPS*) of common stock will benefit linearly with the increase in earnings before interest and taxes (*EBIT*). This is best understood by a system of model building. Three models are constructed below to illustrate this principle, starting with the structure containing common stock only numbered I; followed by the structure with a combination of common stock and debt financing II; and, finally, the structure with common, debt, and preferred stock financing III. With the first equation *EPS* can be determined very simply for any quantity of *EBIT*. The coefficient $(I - tr)/S$ is the key value because it sets the after-tax unit profit margin; it is a contribution coefficient resembling $(b - c)$ in the profit equation and is the slope of the linear function.

(I)

$$EPS_1 = X\frac{(1 - tr)}{S_1}$$ 18.1

Where: EPS_1 = After-tax earning per share
$X = EBIT$
$(I - tr)$ = After-tax income adjustment
S_1 = Shares of common stock

Equation II performs the same function subject to a fixed interest charge before taxes. In this model $X - I$ is the operation of subtracting a fixed interest charge from a variable *EBIT*. It is assumed that the total capital structure is the same size as in I except that debt now replaces some of the equity; in this case the coefficient marking the slope of the linear function is $(1 - tr)/S_2$.

(II)

$$EPS_2 = (X - I)\frac{(1 - tr)}{S_2}$$ 18.2

Finally, model III assumes that preferred, as well as debt, replaces some of the initial common stock in the structure. This extends the equation somewhat; while interest is deductible before taxes, preferred dividends are paid without benefit of tax deduction. The first part of the equation determines after-tax net profits as in II, and the latter D is preferred dividends subtracted from net profits after interest and taxes. The remainder is divided by the outstanding shares to determine *EPS*; the coefficient and the slope of the linear function is $[(1 - tr) - D]/S_3$.

(III)

$$EPS_3 = (X - I)\frac{(1 - tr)}{S_3} - \frac{D}{S_3}$$ 18.3

Now we can substitute hypothetical values in each of the equations to show

how they are solved. In I, assume that the business has a common stock structure with 10,000 shares outstanding and that the tax rate is 40 percent.

(I)

$$EPS_1 = X\frac{(1 - 0.4)}{10,000}$$

For any value of X, that is for any variable quantity of *EBIT*, this little "program" will tell management what his shareholders will earn on each share of stock. In structure II there are 8,000 shares of common stock, and a $50,000 debt bearing 6 percent ($3,000) interest is added. The tax rate is unchanged at 40 percent. Substituting:

(II)

$$EPS_2 = (X - \$3,000)\frac{(1 - 0.4)}{8,000}$$

For any value of X, managers again can tell what their shareholders will earn with this revised structure. In structure III, there are 6,000 shares of common stock and $50,000 in preferred stock bearing an 8 percent dividend causing another fixed charge of $4,000. The tax rate is still 40 percent.

(III)

$$EPS_3 = (X - \$3,000)\frac{(1 - 0.4)}{6,000} - \frac{\$4,000}{6,000}$$

Now we have three different kinds of capital structures with different degrees of leverage. The best way to illustrate the effect of a changing *EBIT* on *EPS* in all cases simultaneously is to graph them as in Figure 18.1. Before constructing the graph, attention is called to the break-even concept as it would apply to these equations. By solving any pair of these equations simultaneously, a value is obtained for *EBIT* in which it is a matter of indifference from the viewpoint of *EPS* which capital structure is used. To illustrate suppose that management is considering structures I and II and wants to know what amount of *EBIT* would produce the same *EPS* for each structure. We simply solve the following equations simultaneously:

(IV)

$$\frac{X(1 - tr)}{S_1} = \frac{(X - I)(1 - tr)}{S_2}$$

$$\frac{X(1 - 0.4)}{10,000} = \frac{(X - \$3,000)(1 - 0.4)}{8,000}$$

$$\frac{X - 0.4X}{10,000} = \frac{0.6X - \$1,800}{8,000}$$

$$X = \$15,000$$

E.P.S.

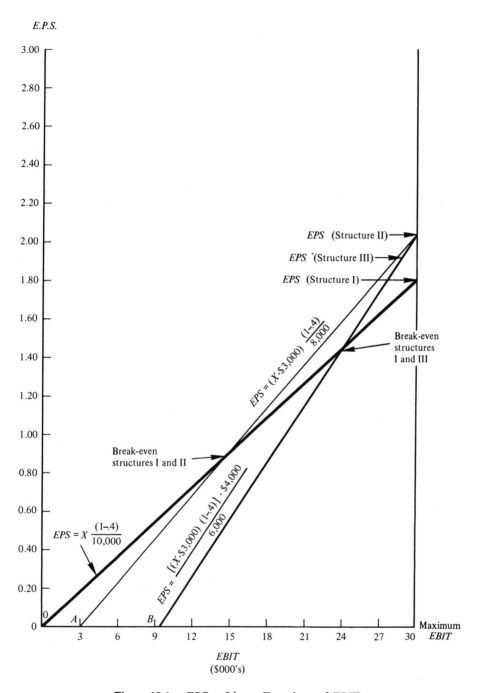

Figure 18.1. *EPS* as Linear Functions of *EBIT*.

429

Substituting $15,000 in each of the equations, it is proven that when *EBIT* is $15,000 both of the structures will produce the same return ($0.90) per share.

(I)

$$\frac{\$15,000(1 - 0.4)}{10,000} = \$0.90$$

$$\frac{(\$15,000 - \$3,000)(1 - 0.4)}{8,000} = \$0.90$$

The analysis here is not designed to emphasize the advantage of one form of financing over another but to provide a tool that combines the effect of certain constants and variables on the return per share of stock. The value of the models lies primarily in helping financial managers identify major control areas in capital financing. First, the quantity of *EBIT* is directly related to the first part of the profit function: $EBIT = X(b - c)$. To the extent that financial managers can control the elements X, b, and c, they can control *EBIT*. The control exercised over *EBIT* in turn affects pb and the company's present share value pb/d. Second, the quantity of shares sold and the price at which they are sold affects the return per share. A high price for the shares reduces the number that needs to be sold. But the success of an issue of common shares depends on E_e which is the future net profits per share that the market requires of the firm. Third, the models should emphasize the advantage to *EPS* of being able to borrow at a low $r_1 + r_2$. Since no control exists over r_1, emphasis needs to be placed on r_2, which again is related to the elements in the profit function. A very important fact is evident in the graph, namely, that what appears to be beneficial leverage can easily turn out to be detrimental. The intersection points on the graph illustrate this, and it is even more evident below the origin of the axis where returns per share of stock would become negative.

Figure 18.1 contains important information about the effect of increases in *EBIT* on *EPS*, given different degrees of leverage in the capital structure. The graph of the equation $EPS = X[(1 - 0.4)/10,000]$ is the *EPS* function of *EBIT* when no leverage is contained in the capital structure. The line of the equation $EPS = (X - \$3,000)[(1 - 0.4)/8,000]$ is the *EPS* function of *EBIT* when debt leverage is contained in the structure; and the graph of equation $EPS = [(X - \$3,000)(1 - 0.4)]/6,000 - \$4,000/6,000$ is the *EPS* function of *EBIT* when both debt and preferred stock leverage are contained in the structure. In each equation *EPS* is a linear function of earnings before interest and taxes X; all other elements in the equations are constants. The coefficients signify the constant rates of change in *EPS* given the change in *EBIT*. In terms of the basic linear equation, this means that the coefficient determines the constant rate of change in Y given the change in X and, as pointed out earlier, the slope of the function.

Points O, A and B on the X axis need additional consideration. These points indicate the quantity of *EBIT* required to just break even; that is, to produce (0) *EPS* with each of three capital structures. Let us identify these points in terms of the familiar $X(b - c) - a$; using this approach we will see that the financial charges are actually no different than any other fixed charges in planning current profits. At point O of structure I, $P = X(b - c) - a = 0$, at which point there are no fixed financial charges in a. This means that *EPS* will begin as soon as $X(b - c) - a > 0$, when a includes no interest. At point A of structure II, $P = X(b - c) - a = 0$; and *EPS* will begin as soon as $X(b - c) - a > 0$, allowing for $3,000 of interest charges in a. At point B of structure III, $P = X(b - c) - a - [D/(1 - tr)] = 0$; and *EPS* will begin after a and $6,667 of before-tax dividends: $4,000/(1 - 0.4) = 6,667$ or after $9,667.

Let us solve for the starting *EBIT* or X values on the graph by setting each of the *EPS* values equal to zero.

(I)

$$X\frac{(1 - 0.4)}{10,000} = EPS_1 = 0$$

$$\frac{0.6x}{10,000} = 0$$

$$0.6X = 0$$

$$X = 0$$

(II)

$$X - \$3,000\frac{(1 - 0.4)}{8,000} = EPS_2 = 0$$

$$\frac{(X - 3,000)(.6)}{8,000} = 0$$

$$0.6x - 1,800 = 0$$

$$0.6X = 1,800$$

$$X = \$3,000$$

(III)

$$(X - \$3,000)\frac{(1 - 0.4)}{6,000} - \frac{\$4,000}{6,000} = EPS_3 = 0$$

$$\frac{(X - \$3,000)(0.6)}{6,000} - \frac{\$4,000}{6,000} = 0$$

$$0.6X - 1,800 = 4,000$$

$$0.6X = 5,800$$

$$X = \$9,667$$

SUMMARY

Closely aligned with the subject of the cost of capital and of the structure of financial institutions supplying capital funds is the subject of planning the capital structure. Of primary concern to financial managers is establishing a distribution of financing that will secure for the business the benefits of solvency and profitability. It was shown that, by establishing models of debts and equity, a systematic plan could be followed that would allow the capital structure to maintain efficient capital financing ratios. Considered also was the weighted average cost of capital based on the distribution within the capital structure of debts and common stock obligations. The weighted average cost of the factors in the capital structures provides a model for planning, but should not be confused with the cost of capital and its applications as developed in the preceding chapter to the net capital portion only of the capital structure.

An important consideration is the leverage effect resulting from the use of fixed payment forms of capital financing. It was shown using equations and also graphic illustrations, just where the break-even point occurs for different compositions of debt and equity in the capital structures. The point of indifference between whether to use one kind of capital structure as against using another kind was solved with simultaneous equations and also by locating the break-even point on the graph.

PROBLEMS

1. Compare the following financial structures by answering the questions below.

Company A		Company B	
Current assets	$100,000	Current assets	$375,000
Fixed assets	200,000	Fixed assets	525,000
Total	$300,000	Total	900,000
Current liabilities	$40,000	Current liabilities	150,000
Note payable (5 years from date)	20,000	Bonds	250,000
Bonds	30,000	Preferred stock	100,000
Preferred stock	10,000	Common stock (100,000 shares	
Common stock (10,000 shares		@ $40 each)	300,000
@ $15 each)			
Retained earnings	150,000	Retained earnings	100,000
Total	$300,000	Total	$900,000

    a. Identify the gross capital and the capital structures of each company. Explain the difference.

    b. Compare the solvency risks of the two companies.

    c. Assume net profit of Company A averages $30,000 annually and that net profit of company B averages $60,000 annually. How solvent is each firm in terms of liquid debt-paying capacity? Which of the firms is more solvent?

2. You set up the following model composition of the capital structure as a guide line for changing the present structure of Company B letting X equal retained earnings, $4X$ equal common stock, $3X$ equal preferred stock, and $2X$ equal capital debt. Show how the present structure would be changed to meet the model. What is accomplished for the business by making this kind of a change?

3. Using the model X equal capital debt, $2X$ equal preferred stock, $4X$ equal common stock, and $3X$ equal retained earning, assume that you will expand the capital structure by $500,000. What will the new capital structure be? How will it affect the risk condition of the structure?

4. You consider using a capital structure standard based on the following relationship between expected net profits and the respective financing balance: Capital debts should be 2 times expected net profits, preferred stock 3 times, and common equity 10 times. Assuming profits will average $50,000, how will the following capital structure be affected by these standards?

   Capital debt $= \$100,000$
   Preferred stock $= 50,000$
   Common stock $= 100,000$

5. Given below is Company A's capital structure with assigned costs.

COMPANY A
CAPITAL STRUCTURE

	Cost (%)	Cost ($)
Capital debts:		
Long-term note	6	$ 80,000
Mortgage bonds due in 1990	6	190,000
Stockholders' Equity:		
Preferred stock	7	200,000
Common stock	12	3,000,000
Retained earnings	12	500,000
Total capital structure		$3,970,000

   a. Determine the weighted average *cost* of capital.
   b. Show how you would change the structure to lower average costs.
   c. What are the advantages of this method and its theoretical and practical limitations?

6. The following equations are given:

$$EPS_1 = \frac{X(1 - tr)}{S_1}$$

$$ESP_2 = \frac{(X - 1)(1 - tr)}{S_2}$$

$$EPS_3 = \frac{[(X - I)(1 - tr)]}{S_3} - \frac{D}{S_3}$$

   a. Identify each.

b. Assuming that the company has $100,000 of 6 percent debt, $50,000 of 7 percent preferred, and 10,000 shares of common stock, set up the proper functional relationship between *EPS* and *EBIT*. What purpose will this model serve?

c. Assume that the following information is available: $I = \$4,000$, $tr = 0.4$, and $S_2 = 15,000$. Set up simultaneous equations for determining the quantity of *EBIT* that will result in the same *EPS* for this case where no preferred stock is used and in the case above where it is used. Prove your answer.

d. Graph the following two functions:

$$EPS_1 = \frac{X(1 - 0.4)}{4,000}$$

$$EPS_2 = \frac{(X - \$2,000)(1 - 0.4)}{2,000}$$

e. What value if any are tools such as these for financial managers?

19

Shareholder
Relationships

Attention has been given throughout the book to share values in the securities market. Control exercised over these values was indirect and impersonal, by making current and capital management decisions through the business entity. This chapter will consider financial management and shareholder relationships as they are affected by numerous situations including the form of the stock contract, changing shareholders' capital interests, and changing control media, and as they are affected by a company's dividend policies.

THE STOCK CONTRACT

Financial managers are bound to honor capital stock contracts and to respect the rights of the present shareholders spelled out in those contracts, although they may have been contracted by earlier generations of financial managers.

Stated simply, common shares are registered units of ownership. Legally, the term is associated with the rights, and limitations on the rights, of the owners which have evolved out of the common law. As financial managers, we are concerned primarily with the human element and with these rights and limitations as they affect the persons who hold the shares and as they affect obligations of financial managers to those persons.

The Right to Vote One of the cardinal rights of the common shareholder is his right to elect the board of directors of a corporation at the annual stockholders' meeting. Common law has defined this right more specifically to mean that each share of common stock has one vote for each position on the board of directors, which votes may be cast in person or by proxy. Thus, if 1,000 shares of common stock are newly issued by a business with a five-member board of directors, that business is authorizing in effect 5,000 new votes to be cast at future elections, 1,000 for each of the five positions. The rule that the votes must be cast in this matter—1,000 votes for each director—has earned the title of *noncumulative* voting. In their relationships with common stockholders, financial managers are concerned with the results of such voting rights in the hands of one or more persons and their control possibly over financial policy matters. Right or wrong in the eyes of financial managers, these policies have to be adhered to. Financial managers must also be concerned with the effects on these stockholders of an issue of still more shares of stock with these same voting rights. Any one or more stockholders owning or representing owners with more than 50 percent of the outstanding shares can always be sure of electing a complete board of directors for dominating financial policy. No other person or group of persons with a minority interest has any representation. Besides the annual election of directors, common stockholders are allowed to vote on special issues that would affect their position in the business, for example, (1) increasing the authorized capital stock, (2) changing the par value of present shares, (3) changing the purpose of the business operations, (4) selling the company's assets, and (5) merging or consolidating with one or more other businesses. The student should consider possible conflicts in financial policy as developed in this book and policy as it might develop from these legal rights of common shareholders.

Some states allow the issuance of shares with *cumulative* voting. Cumulative voting gives the stockholders the right to cumulate their votes and cast them for one, two, or more positions on the board as they desire. One or more strong minority members on a board of directors can do much to educate the others on technical financial matters and help to convey to the majority members the company's financial management goals.

The Right to Share in Profits   We should not confuse the right of common stockholders to share in net book profits with the right to share in dividends. Common stockholders are the beneficiaries of whatever benefits accrue to them as residual claimants to net profits. These benefits may take several tangible forms, but increased dividends is not necessarily one of them.

Right to Dividends   The only basic right that common stockholders have to dividends is the right to receive them after they are declared. When the decision is made by management to pay a dividend, the dividends payable account is credited. This is an unsecured short-term debt of the business that gives the stockholders the same claims to funds in the going concern and in liquidation as other unsecured creditors, and financial managers cannot deny them this claim to cash even though the company's financial position may be weakened by the payment. But unless dividends are declared, management is not obligated to pay dividends to common stock even though profits are earned.

The Preemptive Right In common law, present shares have a right to *preempt* a new issue of common shares before they are offered for sale to the public. This does not mean that the shares have to be sold at a lower price to the present stockholders than they would be to the public, although as a general rule they are. Nor does it prevent the business from selling the shares in an outside market if the present stockholders do not subscribe. Common stockholders are further accommodated by the receipt from the issuing company of tangible negotiable *stock purchase rights*, which may be exercised by subscribing to new shares or which may be sold in the securities markets. Legal controversies have arisen in the past between stockholder and corporation in defining a new issue for subscription rights. The courts now rule generally that a new issue exists for exercising preemptive rights anytime that the interval between two security distributions marks a distinct break in the outflow of the securities into the market. The right to preempt new issues is significant to cost of capital analysis; any decrease in share value has the effect of raising the discounting rate in the securities market which is the cost of capital of the individual firm.

The Right to Assets in Liquidation As the ultimate owners of the business, common stockholders have the right to share, on a pro rata basis, in the assets that are distributed in a voluntary or forced liquidation. But in these instances common shareholders are the residual owners and all other security forms are senior claimants. With a possible array of such senior securities as mortgage bonds, debenture bonds, short-term credit instruments, and preferred stock, it is difficult to measure the value of this right-to-share assets in liquidation, and this does create a problem in financial management.

PREFERRED SHARES

Preferred share legal rights are more clearly spelled out by statute and on the stock certificate itself than are the legal rights of common shareholders.

The Pennsylvania General Incorporation Statutes were the first in 1872 to make a blanket provision allowing any corporation organized in the state to issue preferred stock. Every general incorporation statute now allows businesses to issue preferred or preference shares with privileges and limitations stated in their charters and on their stock certificates. The statutes do not stipulate the preferences or restrictions specifically but merely open the door for boards of directors, advised hopefully by financial managers, to make such stipulations.

The Right to Vote Unless the right to vote is taken away or modified, preferred stock has the same voting rights as common stock. But this right is frequently taken away from preferred shares and replaced by special voting privileges in case the business fails to pay preferred dividends at regular quarterly intervals. Until those delinquencies are corrected, the preferred shares may be allowed to (1) elect all of the board members, (2) elect a majority or minority on the board, (3) cast two or three votes for each share of preferred stock. Unless financial managers are aware of the important financial obligation in preferred dividends, serious policy changes may take place that would preclude executing sound financial practices as developed in earlier chapters.

Sharing Profits and Dividends   Preferred stockholders do not share the benefits of net profits as residual owners. Capital investments of preferred shareholders are not affected by profit growth as the capital is of common-stock shareholders. The general legal rule of importance to financial managers is that dividends do not have to be declared on preferred shares any more than on common if the best interests of the owners are served by withholding the dividends. A compelling factor in decision making, however, is that as long as preferred dividends are unpaid, dividends cannot be paid on common stock which could then affect common share values.

Shares with Noncumulative Dividends   Shares bearing noncumulative dividend obligations block the payment of common-stock dividends on a year-to-year basis only. Thus, failure to have paid dividends on the noncumulative preferred in the past does not deter paying dividends on common shares today, so long as the current year's dividends are paid first to the preferred. Preferred shares bearing cumulative dividends have been a more serious concern for financial managers. Shares with cumulative dividends block the payment of common-stock dividends until accrued preferred dividends are paid. This has a cash significance but is not profit related. The blockage to common dividends continues to grow whether the business operates profitably or unprofitably as long as the dividends on the preferred are not fully paid. Thus, "... the term *cumulative* in connection with preferred dividends is practically always defined in terms of dividend payment and not of earnings; that is, dividends *not paid* accumulate whether earned or not."[1]

Participating in Extra Dividends   Financial managers may wonder about their obligations to preferred shares beyond the dividends stated in the contract. The prevailing legal rule is that when nothing is said in the contract, preferred stock does not have a right to share in extra dividends like common stock does. To avoid the risk of future legal disputes though, it is best to state clearly in these instruments that the shares are not entitled to dividends above the fixed amount. In some cases financial management may recommend participation as a matter of expediency in marketing the shares. One way of doing this is to pay dividends after the fixed contract amount at the same rate per share as is paid to common. Another method is to share the total sum of dividends after the stated rate at a fixed ratio, for example, 20 percent to preferred and 80 percent to common. Still another way allows equal participation with common up to a given sum, after which preferred will no longer share. When the participating feature is included, therefore, the line may get pretty thin between a preferred and common share, which may complicate decision making for financial managers.

Preemption of New Issues   In a dispute over the right to preempt a new issue of common shares, the courts will treat preferred shares the same as common if

---

[1] W. H. S. Stevens, "Rights of Non-Cumulative Preferred Stockholders," *Columbia Law Review*, XXXIV, p. 1439.

they are fully voting and if they are fully participating in extra dividends. If they are not fully voting and participating, however, they cannot have the common-law right of preemption. But even if they would qualify in the common law, this right may be denied them in the preferred stock certificate. By the same token if the shares have less than full voting and participating rights and we want the shares to have the right of preemption, it may be given to them. We have to decide in granting or denying this right whether it would interfere with our common goal of maximizing common share values.

Redeemable Shares Redemption makes preferred shares callable at the option of management to clear the equity structure of senior securities. The call price will be a flat rate usually such as 105 percent or 110 percent of the par value of the stock regardless of when or how many of the shares are called. Since the stock has no maturity, it is not given a schedule of redemption rates. In addition to the redemption price the business is obligated on the redemption date to pay in the case of cumulative preferred stock all dividend arrears. The redemption provision must be included in the financing contracts because in the common law no stock, common or preferred, is redeemable. We may provide also for calling all or part of the stock. When only part of the shares are called, they will be chosen by lot. Since all the shareholders are registered with the business or its registrar, notices of redemption can be sent directly to the owners.

Convertible Shares In convertible shares the holders are allowed at their option to convert the preferred shares into common. This is not a common-law right of the shareholders and, therefore, has to be conveyed in writing *via* the stock certificates. This is another means of clearing the equity structure of senior securities, but unlike redemption it does not cause a loss in cash. The provision can be expected to strengthen the sale of the shares because of its speculative opportunities. Also in periods when the company's cost of capital is high, it may offer a favorable, indirect approach to common stock sales. The preferred form supplies the capital for investment; then, as the investment becomes profitable and the discount rate (cost of capital) for the company's common shares decreases, preferred stockholders are motivated to exchange their securities for common. Financial managers should also consider the depressing effect on common shares and the consequent increase in the cost of capital that may result from a mass conversion of preferred into common shares. If convertible preferred is issued, enough common stock has to be held in reserve during the contract period to make the exchange when the shareholders demand it. The preferred shares on receipt are cancelled, so that they cannot be reissued; and the charter is amended to reduce the amount of authorized preferred. As a precautionary measure, financial managers should make the shares redeemable when they are convertible; so that, when the atmosphere is right for conversion, the action may be stimulated by calling the stock for redemption and allowing the shareholders twenty or thirty days in which to exercise their conversion prior to redemption. Any shares not converted by that time can then be called in.

Shares with Sinking Funds A conservative practice gaining favor with financial managers is the inclusion of sinking-fund provisions in preferred stock with a view to eventually clearing preferred stock out of the equity structure. Stock sinking funds are likely to assess profits a fixed percentage, such as 5 percent or 10 percent annually, for this purpose. This makes for flexibility and does not expose the common stockholders' capital to undue risk. If net profits (after preferred dividends) are earned, sinking-fund payments will be made; if they are not earned, the payments do not need to be made. The funds are invested in relatively liquid securities during the interim; and when they reach a certain amount, say $5,000, these securities are cashed to call in the shares. Repurchased shares are usually cancelled rather than being held in the treasury for resale: as stated in the charter, "thereupon the authorized preferred stock shall be deemed to be, and shall be reduced to the extent of the aggregate par value of the shares thereof so redeemed or purchased for the sinking fund."

Liquidation Provisions   In liquidating the business, either voluntarily or involuntarily, preferred shares are usually given a prior claim to the assets over the common stockholders. The common-law right to share on a pro rata basis in the remaining assets applies to all shares alike. Therefore, the right to a prior claim must be written into the contract.

SHAREHOLDERS' CAPITAL INTERESTS

Decisions to conserve shareholders' capital interests follow the dictates of good judgment rather than the "letter of the law" in seeking to develop good shareholder relations. But to maintain favorable shareholder relations it is necessary sometimes to take action for the preservation of the present shareholders' capital that would not necessarily have favorable effects on share values. This is where certain action can be taken by financial managers to affect share values without going through the communication mediums of the securities market.

VALUE TYPES

Book values and stock market values are both evidences of capital interests to shareholders. The former is a *fundamental* security value that the shareholder looks on as a measure of the value of his capital in case of a general company liquidation. Book value of a share of common stock is the quotient of the company's common equity and total outstanding shares.

$$\text{Book value} = \frac{\text{Common equity}}{\text{Outstanding common shares}}$$

Common equity is the net worth of a business minus the redemption or liquidation value, whichever is higher, of outstanding preferred stock. It is also the sum of capital stock, capital surplus, and retained earnings. In the long run, either or both the numerator and denominator of the ratio may change and thus change book value. A more conservative view of book value results when intangible assets are removed, thus producing a tangible book value figure.

$$\text{Tangible book value} = \frac{\text{Common equity} - \text{Intangible assets}}{\text{Outstanding common shares}}$$

Book value also has a going concern significance because of retained earnings. An increasing book value is a symbol of efficiency and conservatism in financial management, and the stockholder sees in growing retained earnings the possibility of someday receiving a large cash or stock dividend. Considered below are some of the financial decisions that can directly affect the shareholders' capital interests by changing book values.

Issuing Shares Below Their Value   The effect on shareholders' book values is the same whether shares are sold to present shareholders or to new shareholders through the capital market. Table 19.1 shows why this is true.

TABLE 19.1
SELLING STOCK BELOW BOOK VALUE

	125,000 Shares	*25,000 New Shares to Present Shareholders @ $32 Per Share*	*25,000 New Shares through Capital Market @ $32 Per Share*
Capital stock	$3,750,000	$4,500,000	$4,500,000
Capital surplus	750,000	800,000	800,000
Retained earnings	1,000,000	1,000,000	1,000,000
Common equity	$5,500,000	$6,300,000	$6,300,000
Book value	5,500,000 = $44	6,300,000 = $42	6,300,000 = $42
	125,000	150,000	150,000

Starting with book value of $44 per share when the business has 125,000 shares outstanding, it is decided now to sell 25,000 more shares at $32 per share to raise $800,000 in working capital. Of special note is that the present shareholders' capital interests are reduced by the same amount of $2 per share regardless of whether the shares are sold to the present owners themselves or to an outside investor. A given stockholder with 100 shares of stock valued at $4,400 (100 × $44) now has a value of only $4,200 (100 × $42), for those same shares have lost $200 in capital value.

If present stockholders are permitted to buy the shares ahead of outside stockholders, such permission is granted in writing by the issuance of negotiable-stock-purchase rights at the rate of one for each of the old shares. With 25,000 new shares and with 125,000 shares outstanding, five rights are authorized for purchasing one new share: 125,000/25,000 = 5. Let us consider the shareholder with 100 shares now holding 100 rights to subscribe to 20 (100/5) new shares at $32 each. If he exercises those rights to purchase the shares, his losses in book value of $2 on each of the old shares are regained by the $10 gain in book value on the new; and he has suffered no net capital loss.

$$\text{Loss on old shares:} \qquad 100 \times \$2 = \$200$$
$$\text{Gain on new purchases:} \quad 20 \times \$10 = \$200$$

But this is not so if the shares are sold to outside investors because then this is a one-way road with the present stockholders losing $2 in book value on every old share and gaining nothing from the new.

Although the effect on market value may not respond in exactly this amount, there will be a decline in market value from the time that the stock purchase rights are traded in the market; but the shareholder can recover this loss by selling his rights, or exercising them, by buying the lower priced shares. The closer we get to the present market price, the less reduction there will be; and this is one of the most important problems in a new common stock issue, to know how much to lower the price on the new issue to assure its sale and at the same time to preserve as much as possible of the present shareholders' capital values. To show how this will preserve their capital, assume that our company has outstanding 75,000 shares of stock selling at $50 each and that it plans to issue 25,000 new shares at a subscription price to the present shareholders of $42 each. This means that three subscription rights from the old shares authorize the holder to buy one new share for $42. The market price after the new issue can be expected to decline to an amount equal roughly to the weighted average of the two quantities of stock:

	Quantity Weights		Sale Price		Total Value
Old stock	75,000	×	$50	=	$3,750,000
New stock	25,000	×	42	=	1,050,000
Total	100,000				$4,800,000

Weighted average market value $\dfrac{4,800,000}{100,000} = \$48$

An investor now with 60 shares loses $120 (60 × $2) on old shares but by subscribing to 20 new shares (60/3) is able to regain his total loss at the rate of $6 on each share (20 × $6 = $120).

Splitting Shares Splitting shares directly reduces the shareholders' capital interest in the individual share but not in his total shareholdings. By reducing the book value of outstanding shares financial managers are able to broaden the market for the stock at the same time conserving the shareholders' total capital interest in the business. If this fact is understood by the shareholder, favorable relations will be maintained; but, if it is not understood, relations may become strained between financial managers and the present shareholders.

The split in book value is inversely proportional to the split in shares. If a share with $40 of book value is split into four new shares, each resulting share must have a book value of $10, regardless of whether they were par or no-par.

The shareholder, who had one share worth $40 formerly, now has four shares worth $10 each; but cutting the pie in more pieces does not change the size of the pie. Sometimes it is felt that there are too many shares outstanding for the size of the market and a *reverse* split is recommended in which case the shares are joined in larger units, but still the total size of the pie is the same. A one-for-four reverse split where the present par value is $25, will result in one new share with a par value of $100. The capital interests of the shareholder measured in book value are the same, however, after the reverse split as before regardless of whether the stock was par or no-par.

Splitting shares affects market values in the same way that it does book values. By splitting shares, management can expect the decline in their market values to be just about proportional to their decline in book values. A split-up of stock increases the supply of shares so drastically usually that the market values drop precipitously, and the new price tends to drop in inverse proportion to the size of the split. Thus, if a share is split 5/1, new market price to the old will be in the ratio of 1/5. Furthermore, if the market is on an upward trend, the split shares may rise more rapidly than if the old shares had been retained, resulting in an actual addition to the market value of the stockholders' capital. If the market is in a weak state, however, it would be a dangerous policy on the part of management to split stock in the expectation of producing capital gains for the stockholders. Suppose that market price before a 5/1 split was $100; the split will drive price down to 1/5 = $20. But the shareholder's capital interests are not impaired because he will now have 5 of the $20 shares.

Declaring Stock Dividends   Stock dividends are distributions of dividends in shares of stock. An important decision affecting the form of the distribution was made when the United States Supreme Court stated in 1920 that stock dividends received in the same form as the stock on which it is paid are not income for tax purposes. Since that time, common stock dividends have been distributed extensively on outstanding common shares. Dividends are usually declared on a percentage basis of outstanding shares, but they are limited in value to the quantity of retained earnings. A 10 percent stock dividend when there are 100,000 outstanding shares means that 10,000 shares will be distributed with one going to every 10 of the old shares. Any stock dividend can be restated as a stock split using the following formula:

$$X = (1 + r)$$

Where: X = Stock split equivalent of any given stock dividend
r = Stock dividend stated as a portion of the outstanding shares

Suppose that a 50 percent stock dividend is declared; this is the same as saying that each of the old shares is split $1\frac{1}{2}$ for 1. It is the same in a stock split as the holder exchanges his old share for $1\frac{1}{2}$ new shares.

$$X = (1 + 0.5)$$
$$= 1.5$$

The effect of a 50 percent stock dividend on book value is the same, therefore, as a 1½ for 1 stock split. This is proven arithmetically in Table 19.2 where 10,000 shares of stock with a $30 par value are outstanding originally. A 1½ for 1 stock split is illustrated in the second column and a 50 percent stock dividend is illustrated in the third.

TABLE 19.2

STOCK SPLIT AND STOCK DIVIDEND EFFECTS ON BOOK VALUES

	Before Stock Split or Stock Dividend	*After 1.5 for 1 Stock Split*	*After 50 Percent Stock Dividend*
Capital stock (10,000 shares)	$300,000	$300,000 (15,000 shares)	$450,000 (15,000 shares)
Retained earnings	200,000	200,000	50,000
Common equity	500,000	500,000	500,000
Book value	$500,000 = $50 / 10,000	$500,000 = $33.33 / 15,000	$500,000 = $33.33 / 15,000

A small stock dividend may not have a noticeable effect on the market value of shares; but, as they increase in size, they may cause market prices to fall in the same manner as stock splits. A 20 percent stock dividend, which would be considered reasonable, would be equivalent to a stock split of only 1.2 for 1 share. Stock dividends are capitalizations of retained earnings and, therefore, do not reduce the shareholders total capital interest in the business.

CHANGING CONTROL MEDIA

Control over the board of directors, and indirectly over financial management policy, can be tightened or relaxed by the type of shares that are issued.

FORMS THAT STRENGTHEN PRESENT CONTROL

Nonvoting common and preferred shares are the most effective instruments for perpetuating present shareholder control. A relatively small investment in voting stock can give control over capital many times the size of the shareholders' investment, to say nothing of the debt capital that it may control. Table 19.3 is an equity structure composed of three forms of stock and two kinds of surplus. Class A common and preferred stock are nonvoting. To be completely secure in control, shareholders would need just over 5,000 shares of Class B common stock. We cannot tell what the market price of the shares would be from the equity structure, but their book value is $200,000 compared with the total structure that they control which is almost fifteen times as large.

Another stock form that helps to accomplish the same purpose less directly is *treasury stock*. To illustrate, we will suppose that the shareholders supporting

TABLE 19.3
CLASSIFIED EQUITY STRUCTURE

Preferred stock (10,000 shares $100 par)	$1,000,000
Common stock Class A (100,000 shares $10 par)	1,000,000
Common stock Class B (10,000 shares $20 par)	200,000
Capital surplus	200,000
Retained earnings	500,000
Total	$2,900,000

the present management hold 4,500 shares out of 10,000 shares, which has been a plurality of the shares actually voted at meetings but not a majority. The shareholders and present management still run a risk of losing control to some outside group with 4,501 shares. To eliminate this risk altogether for the present shareholders and their management representatives, 1,001 shares can be bought by the business for its own treasury with no money out of the shareholders' pockets. Although treasury shares are nonvoting, the control effect is the same as though they were. The 4,500 votes now are an absolute majority because only 4,499 are left outside this group. After the meeting the shares may be reissued, held in the treasury, or as a final resort canceled by amending the charter.

Sale of new shares by the use of rights may also be the deciding factor of whether or not a present controlling group will be able to hold onto its control. Distributing rights on a pro rata basis eliminates the risk of losing control. For instance, if the present control group holds 5,200 or 52 percent of 10,000 outstanding shares, a new issue of 2,000 shares will give them rights to purchase 1,040 shares (52 percent of the new issue), which will maintain their 52 percent ownership of the total 12,000 shares. If this right were not extended to the shares or if the present group decided to sell the rights instead of exercising them, control might easily pass to a new group.

While the technique is neither directly related to the stock forms nor a permanent solution to the problem, a *classified board of directors* can be a temporary means of maintaining present control. A classified board provides for the election of a portion of the membership each year, so that in no one year will the present control be completely changed. This control tool is reserved usually for boards large enough to be divided into several groups of three or more.

FORMS THAT LESSEN PRESENT CONTROL

Cumulative voting, which in some states is given to the shareholders by law and in other states by charter provision, can be a serious threat to present shareholders if their votes are spread too thinly, the fact that cumulative voting is used more often to gain only minority representation on the board of directors notwithstanding. The minority as well as the majority stockholding group can use the following formula to tell exactly how many shares are needed to gain a desired representation on the board. Suppose that an outside group wants four representatives to control a five-man board in a company with 10,000 shares outstanding. Using this formula the number required is determined as follows:

$$X = \frac{s \times d}{D + 1} + 1$$

Where: X = The number of shares required to elect the desired number of directors
s = Total shares outstanding
d = Number of directors desired
D = Total directors on the board

Substituting:

$$X = \frac{10,000 \times 4}{5 + 1} + 1$$
$$= 6,667 \text{ shares}$$

Multiple voting stock is used infrequently to gain representation on the board of directors. This may be a special form of common or preferred stock issued temporarily and granting two, three, or more votes to each share. It is usually reserved for preferred stock and is often dormant until the business defaults on its regular preferred-dividend payments. *Convertible* preferred stock is always a threat to present shareholders' control. Even where the common-law principle of preemption prevails, the present shareholders have no preemptive rights to new shares issued for preferred-stock conversion.

DIVIDEND POLICIES

Policy considerations are concerned with decisions for distributing cash dividends. Although financial managers are under no obligation to pay dividends, they usually feel an obligation to follow some kind of regular plan of dividend payment that will benefit their shareholders in the long run. Opinions differ widely as to what are the best policies to follow, and we will consider briefly the most popular policies now followed.

DISTRIBUTE AS LONG AS THE STOCKHOLDERS CAN EARN MORE THAN THE BUSINESS

This policy is the inverse of the relative cost of retaining earnings. Following this policy dividends would be distributed as long as the shareholders have a chance of earning more on the funds than could be earned for the stockholders by the business. As a decision-making tool, this is stated as a ratio of the dollar profits that the business expects to earn, to the dollar profits that the stockholders can expect to earn.

$$\text{Relative cost of distributing dividend} = \frac{\text{Dollar return from retained earnings}}{\text{Dollar return from stockholders' investment}}$$

The signal is given to distribute dividends when this ratio is less than 1. Substituting the values $3,000/2,498, we get a ratio of 1.21, which indicates that the loss in distributing the dividend is too high to be justified. *As a general policy dividends will be distributed as long as this ratio is 1.0 or less but will be discontinued when it rises above 1.* The prospect for distributing dividends would be improved by any item that would decrease the return that the business can earn on retained earnings or that would increase the return that shareholders could earn on their personal investments.

Several doubts are expressed by financial managers in considering this as their guiding tool for decision making. First it assumes that small increments of additional net profits are the only concern of the shareholders when actually growth of their capital is often more important. Second, it assumes that financial managers know what their stockholders' investment opportunities are. Third, it disregards stockholders' problems and costs of reinvesting small increments of dividends. Fourth, it makes a questionable distinction between retained earnings and paid-in capital for distribution purposes. If shareholders can earn more than management can on retained earnings, what is to stop them from earning more on their paid-in capital, and, if this is the case, why not distribute the total capital and dissolve the business? Considered below are somewhat more arbitrary, but simpler policies to administer than the one discussed above.

DISTRIBUTE A FIXED DOLLAR AMOUNT OF DIVIDENDS

This policy weights the importance of regularity in dividends of a given dollar size above everything else. The size of the dividends is often large, so that not much of the profit is left to retained earnings. Following this policy, it is not necessary to earn currently the designated dollar amount of the dividend so long as the funds are available in working capital for making the payment. Theoretically, there is no connection in this policy between dividends paid and current profits earned; but, actually, only the companies with stable incomes seem to use this policy, and they may even put ceilings on the amount that can be paid in nonprofitable years to prevent a depletion of their retained earnings and working capital.

This policy tends to treat common shareholders somewhat like preferred shareholders and gives no particular consideration to the important role played by the investment of retained earnings or dividend receipts by the stockholders. Demand for stock of this kind, where the company continues to meet the dividend, will usually find favorable reception from persons and institutions that depend on the cash to meet living and operating expenses. Increases and decreases in market values may even be of little concern to these investors, and this condition tends to produce a steady long-run demand that automatically stabilizes the market value for the stock. One danger in using this policy is that if the distributions are too large and the dividend takes a large portion of accumulated working capital, the company may not be able to withstand the shock of possible operating losses.

Minimum dollar amount with a step-up feature

This policy modifies the former and is based on the proposition that present shareholders want a dividend income of a regular dollar amount, however small it may be. Profits are given more consideration in determining dividends than they are in the policy above, but they are just one of the factors that are considered in making a step-up to a higher dividend. This policy has enabled many businesses to point with pride at long records of twenty-five years or more of dividend payments of some kinds. We should note at the outset that the small amount of the fixed dividend is set not to assure the accumulation of earnings but to reduce the chances of ever missing a dividend, for whatever that is worth in the market. Such records may place the stocks on the *legal lists*, which qualifies them for the investment portfolios of state-regulated institutions such as life insurance companies, mutual savings banks, and certain kinds of pension funds and investment trusts. This policy sets the dividend low enough so that there is little chance of a default, but at the same time it allows a great deal of flexibility for paying higher dividends and does not commit the business to adopt the larger payments as part of the future fixed dividend. If profits are large, a larger dividend may be distributed, but there is no compulsion to do so. This is a popular policy for firms with fluctuating incomes because it provides managers with a policy guide without restricting seriously their freedom of funds use. Certain shareholders also like it because it allows them to plan on set amounts of cash and at the same time to be pleasantly surprised when "extra" dividends are paid.

Fixed percentage of net profits

One of the most mechanical and theoretically the most flexible dividend policy is the one that attaches payments directly to net profits. This is called the *payout ratio*, and will consequently fluctuate at the same rate as profits. Our first impulse is to support a policy of this kind because it is related to the ability to pay measured by profits. If the business loses its ability to pay by experiencing operating losses, there will be no dividends regardless of the stockholders' need or desire or opportunity to invest the funds. If a 30 percent payout ratio is adopted, then 30 percent of every dollar of after-tax profit will be distributed. We should note, however, that this policy leaves management less freedom for decision making than the policy just discussed. Internal financing with retained earnings is automatic and inversely related to the payout ratio; a 30-percent payout is a 70-percent pay-in ratio, and a 70-percent payout is a 30-percent pay-in. But at any given payout ratio, the dollar amount of dividends and the dollar additions to retained earnings will both increase with increasing dollar profits and decrease with decreasing dollar profits. One of the most appealing features of the policy to some is its conservatism and its guarantee against over or under payment, since it does not allow management to pay a dividend if profits are not earned in the current period, and it does not allow management to forego a dividend if profits are earned.

FIXED PERCENTAGE OF MARKET VALUE

Since shareholders sometimes translate their dollar dividend returns into percentage returns of the market price of their stock, financial managers may tie dividends to the value of the company's shares rather than to profits. This requires first setting up a representative dividend return as a target rate. The target may be the average dividend for the industry, or it may be the rate paid by a closely competitive firm. The reciprocal of the ratio will give us a turnover of the dividends in the market price called the *times dividend earned* ratio. If 5 percent of market price is considered a desirable dividend rate, then at a market price of $50.00, $2.50 will be paid; and if it increases to $60.00, $3.00 will be paid. The times dividend earned ratio though will always be 20 regardless of how the market price fluctuates: $50.00/$2.50 = 20 times and $60.00/$3.00 = 20 times. To turn the dividend over more times would indicate under payment, and to turn it over less times would indicate overpayment. This has all of the simple mechanical features of the fixed percentage of net profits method, but it singles out the market as the ideal valuation base. Underlying this policy is a general belief that management owes an obligation to the shareholders to align dividend payments with the rates paid by competitors and by the industry as a whole on their market investment values.

SOME GENERAL QUESTIONS AND OBSERVATIONS

The scope of dividend management is somewhat broader than just the issues that have been emphasized in these policies. Some of the additional questions and the observations that may typically confront financial managers are considered here.

DO WE NEED A DIVIDEND POLICY?

Our policy may be not to have a policy but instead to raise the dividend distribution issue anew each time the financial statements are prepared. This might be called an *eclectic policy* since financial managers and other board members will consider all and any factors including working capital, net profits, book values, market values, future financing, and shareholders' investment opportunities. This approach has the advantage of maximum flexibility and rationality, but it is premised on the assumption that the present management group is qualified and properly equipped with tools and skills for evaluating and translating all kinds of data into a dollar dividend. Few businesses are qualified to do this, and usually the ones that are qualified are the ones most likely to have well-established dividend policies of the kinds discussed earlier. In general, it can be said that shareholders prefer to own stock in companies with some kind of *regular* dividend payment plan even though the businesses may be forced at times to depart from their policies, because knowing what management plans to do with profits gives the stockholders a positive basis for judging the proficiency of financial managers.

THE EXTRA DIVIDEND

Any one of the policies discussed earlier may become more flexible without impairing its basic purpose and objective by keeping the door open, so to speak, for paying extra year-end dividends or even a series of extra dividends on a shorter basis when it appears to be in the best interests of the shareholders. The extra dividend approach is especially effective when it is combined with paying a small fixed-dollar amount. It may also be used as an interim dividend while management is considering the feasibility of stepping up to permanent, higher level *regular* dividends. Extra dividends, regardless of how many consecutive years they are paid, are understood by the shareholders to be temporary and are relatively easy to back away from if profits decline for several quarters. This policy generally brings favorable reactions from the shareholders.

SHOULD WE BORROW TO PAY DIVIDENDS?

To some financial managers, it is little short of criminal to borrow cash to pay dividends. In some cases, the objection is well founded; but borrowing for this purpose should not be rejected unequivocally. Those who would do so are likely to be looking to the business as an entity rather than as a medium for serving its shareholders. Their concern is primarily for the solvency risk that is created by the borrowing, but by now we should be aware that management skill in ascertaining how to maintain favorable shareholder relations is a part of the calculable risk of doing business. It might even indicate poor management for a profitable business not to borrow on some occasions to pay dividends, even if it means pledging assets as security. A profitable business may find itself in need of cash for dividends as the result of seasonal surges in operations or long-run readjustments to permanent higher levels of operations. The exception to this would be the business going through a general contraction in long-run operations; paying dividends under these conditions would not be opposed, but generally borrowing for this purpose would not be recommended.

SHOULD WE CONSIDER SHAREHOLDER COMPOSITION?

The question of whether shareholder composition should be studied by financial managers to help shape their dividend policies is frequently considered. But the question of how much study to give to this factor is still an unsettled one among financial managers. Having access to the roster of common stockholders enables financial managers to answer the following questions: What percentage of the total shares does each stockholder own? What percentage of the total shares are owned by the largest shareholder and by the largest shareholding group? Listing the shareholders in the order of size, how many of the shareholders account for 20 percent, 40 percent, 50 percent, and so forth of total shareholdings? What portion of the shareholders are institutions and what portion individual investors? If they are institutional investors, what is their income tax status; and how many are dominated in their stockholdings by the legal lists of investment securities? These and other questions may be asked by financial managers to help shape dividend policies. But there is another side to this coin as well; many corporations are too large or their ownership changes hands too often to justify spending time tracking down the owners and making dividend decisions to meet their personal requirements. Another argument often heard is that dividend decisions should be made entirely independently of the stockholders, letting them indicate by their demand for the shares whether the company's policies meet their special needs.

SHOULD DIVIDENDS BE USED TO EXACT COOPERATION FROM THE SHAREHOLDERS?

Special dividends are sometimes offered as inducements to shareholders to go along with certain long-run financial plans that are important to the welfare of the business and its owners. Obviously, security holders are able to appreciate these benefits more easily with a cash-dividend inducement than without. Suppose that management wants to split the company's stock to bring it down to a broader trading base in preparation for a new financing but that the present shareholders have long been accustomed to a high priced stock and a high dividend and are not prone to vote for a stock split. To assure their support a new dividend policy may be announced that would yield the stockholders more dividend dollars each year then on their old investment. To illustrate, assume that an $8.00 regular dividend is paid on a $100 share of stock which we want to split 4 for 1. Now a new dividend policy is announced paying $2.20 on the new shares. For the equivalent of 1 old share, the stockholders will receive annually $8.80 in place of $8.00; and, at the same time, there may be a chance of capital gains because of the broader trading base. Sometimes the higher dividend is announced for the old shares and then just carried on to the new shares after the split. In this case, the present $100 would have declared an $8.80 year-end dividend announcing it as a general policy goal, at the same meeting where the directors decide on the stock split. When the first quarter dividend is declared, it will be $2.20 instead of $2.00. Other similar dividend inducements may be made to interest shareholders in exercising stock purchase warrants and to interest preferred shareholders and creditors in converting their securities to common stocks.

SUMMARY

This chapter considers the problem of maintaining favorable stockholder relations. The chapter seeks to review the basic rights of both the common shareholders and the preferred shareholders as suppliers of permanent capital to the business organization. The common goal in financial management we will recall is to maximize the value of the company's common shares. This is not designed necessarily to increase the wealth of the present stockholders, although this is an inevitable result of such a policy. The goal of share value maximization is designed primarily as a goal to more efficient management of the many facets of financial analysis for decision making. The shareholder has certain legal rights as a holder of stock certificates, but he has the right also to expect from financial managers the kind of treatment that will assure him that his capital interest in the business will be protected and increased in every manner possible and by any means lying within the scope of the financial managers decision-making authority. Special areas of decision making that can adversely affect the wealth and the control of the present shareholder group include issuing shares at prices below the present market, granting options to present officers to buy the company's shares below the market price, and depriving present shareholders of their common-law rights to buy their pro rata share of a new stock issue.

PROBLEMS

1. Company A is planning a $10 million capital expenditure for increasing net working capital and fixed capital and will use common stock financing to raise the funds.

   a. What effect will this decision have on the company's gross capital, equity capital?

   b. What primary marketing facilities would be available to the business? What benefits and limitations exist in each?

   c. Suppose that the issue causes the company's share values to decrease with E_e remaining the same. What does this tell us about the change in the company's cost of capital? Was the change in the cost of capital independent of the new issue of stock or was it caused by the new issue?

2. Financial managers have to respect the contractual rights of common shareholders in their financial relations.

   a. What are three basic rights of the shareholders? Indicate how they might affect financial managers' capital financing decisions.

   b. Suppose that financial managers wish to convey an idea to the board of directors respecting qualitative techniques of analysis that the board heretofore had been prone to shun. How can cumulative voting help to resolve this, and what can financial managers do, if anything, to obtain cumulative voting in the company?

   c. Does management have to respect any specific right of common shareholders regarding rights to dividends?

3. Suppose that a preferred issue can be sold bearing a 6 percent dividend. E_e/P_m for the firm is 12 percent.

a. Would issuing large quantities of preferred stock lower the company's cost of capital? Explain.

b. What is the single most important right of the preferred shareholder that financial managers have to respect? How could it impair financial management of the firm?

c. What is a preferred-stock sinking fund? How is it managed and what is its financial significance to management?

4. New common stock is issued at a price below its present book value.

	Before Sale	After Sales of 50,000 New Shares at $10 Each
	100,000 Shares	150,000 Shares
Capital stock (100,000 shares @ $10 each)	$1,000,000	$1,500,000
Retained earnings	500,000	500,000
Total	$1,500,000	$2,000,000

a. Determine book value before and after the stock sale. What effect does this have on the book value of a share?

b. A given shareholder has 1,000 shares. If the preemptive right is asserted, how many new shares can he buy; and what is the effect on his capital interest in the business? If the shares had been sold to "outsiders," what would the effect have been on his capital status?

c. Market price of the shares was $20 before the new issue. If market value drops exactly inversely to the rise in the number of shares, what will the resulting share price be? Why is it important from the viewpoint of maintaining good stockholder relations to offer these shares to present shareholders?

5. Company X has 100,000 shares outstanding which are selling at $20 per share. The company has retained earnings of $400,000.

a. The company decides to issue a 20 percent stock dividend. Where will the shares come from for issuance?

b. Does Company X have enough retained earnings to issue a 20 percent stock dividend using the market basis of valuation? If so, what will happen to retained earnings? What will happen to share values? What will happen to the shareholders' capital interests in the business? What, if anything, will happen to the company's cost of capital?

c. Express the stock dividend in terms of a stock split. Would this be considered a large stock dividend? What does action like this do to shareholder relations? Explain.

6. Company D has outstanding 100,000 shares of cumulative voting stock selling at $20 each. The board of directors has 6 members. Financial managers feel that, if they could get a representative on the board who could explain the concept and purpose behind the net-cash-flow concept of capital investing, the company would grow; and its share values would increase noticeably. How much would have to be invested to accomplish this?

20

Capital
Borrowing

Capital borrowing adds debt to a company's capital structure. This adds to the risk factor r_2 for future borrowing. It raises the cost of capital (E_e/P) of the borrowing firm only if the investors in the common stock market look on the debt securities as a new investment opportunity bearing a higher return than former debt offerings, proportionate to the risk that they take. In this chapter, we will consider quantitative and qualitative factors that affect the balance of debts in the capital structure and the way that the debts affect the long-run stability of the business.

QUANTITATIVE FACTORS

Quantitative factors in capital borrowing are the factors that determine the amount of indebtedness that a company can incur, given certain capital variables. The quantity of borrowing that a company can do results in effect from matching the lender's standards against the borrower's net capital reserves and cash flows. Four variables will be considered for their quantitative effects on borrowing. One variable is equity capital, a second is gross capital, a third net earning after taxes but before interest (EBI), and a fourth net cash flow (NCF).

CAPITAL BORROWING: A FUNCTION OF EQUITY CAPITAL

In Chapter 11, dealing with current unsecured borrowing, it was shown how borrowing is limited, with the quantity of equity capital given. In budgeting capital, however, equity capital is variable; that is, investment projects can be financed with capital stock and with retained earnings as well as with capital debt. More important, the quantity of capital borrowing available to a business is a function of the quantity of equity capital. The model below establishes the dependent relationship of capital borrowing D to equity capital E, where the coefficient r is the standard set by the lending community or, mathematically, the rate of borrowing allowed per dollar of equity capital:

$$D = r(E) \qquad\qquad 20.1$$

If Y is substituted for D and X for E, the student will immediately recognize this as a simple linear function. To give this tool meaning for planning borrowing potential, a quantitative value has to be given to r. Let the coefficient r set by the lending community be 0.75 meaning that for every \$1.00 of equity capital produced by the business either by common stock financing or by retained earnings \$0.75 will be loaned. This is the constant change in D produced by a given change in E. The function may be stated now as:

$$D = 0.75E$$

The capital borrowing function above will convert any proposed amount of equity financing into potential borrowing. The limit on D is determined by E. Although management is not likely to issue large quantities of common stock just so large sums of money can be borrowed, if profitable investment projects are being considered, it may be beneficial to build a sound foundation of equity capital so that a superstructure of capital debt can be added for further expansion. The only limiting factor in E is the cost of capital E_e/P_m. That is, if E_e is increased because of the added risk from overexpansion, with P_m increasing at a slower rate, this is the same as saying that the market's discounting rate for the firm (the firm's cost of capital) has increased. This makes E more costly to attain and will restrict correspondingly the quantity of D.

CAPITAL BORROWING: A FUNCTION OF GROSS CAPITAL

Gross capital is the sum of net working capital and fixed capital. It is distinguished from equity capital because it is not identified with any certain form of financing, gaining its resources from the total capital structure. What we are concerned with here is the asset side of the picture though as a potential for capital borrowing. When capital borrowing is done, it increases gross capital at a coefficient of 1; that is, a change in capital borrowing of \$1.00 increases gross capital by \$1.00. Let G equal gross capital and D equal capital debt, then:

$$\Delta D = \Delta G \qquad\qquad 20.2$$

Assume that the lending community sets a 0.5 borrowing rate (r) permitting

$0.50 to be borrowed on each $1.00 of gross capital; then the equation $D = r(G)$ becomes the function:

$$D = 0.5(G)$$

But if capital borrowing is based on gross capital which the borrowing creates at the rate of 1, then the amount of allowable borrowing based on gross capital is represented by a geometric series $P + rP + rP_2 + rP_3 \ldots n$, and the limit of the borrowing is an infinite geometric series:

$$D = \frac{G}{(1 - r)} \qquad \text{20.3}$$

Where: D = Limit of borrowing based on gross capital
G = Initial gross capital base
r = Rate of borrowing on gross capital

Now the borrowing function may be restated as follows:

$$D = 0.5(G + \sum_{1}^{n} \Delta G) \leq \frac{G}{(1 - 0.5)}$$

To illustrate, let gross capital (fixed and net working capital) equal $1 million and let the borrowing coefficient be 0.5; then the theoretical limit on borrowing, assuming no other constraint, is:

$$D = \frac{\$1,000,000}{(1 - 0.5)}$$
$$= \$2,000,000$$

This figure is too large for two reasons. For one it represents an infinite series of borrowings, and management cannot borrow an infinite number of times. Second, and more important from the applied viewpoint, the lending community will probably place a fixed dollar limit on the borrowing equal to the quantity of equity in the gross capital. With an equity constraint replacing the theoretical geometric limit, the tool for measuring unused borrowing power is greatly simplified as:

$$D = E - r(G) \qquad \text{20.4}$$

Where: D = Unused borrowing
E = Equity capital
r = Borrowing rate
G = Gross capital

Given $E = \$1$ million and $r = 0.5$, the quantity of allowable borrowing is a function of gross capital. Let $E = \$1,000,000 = G$:

$$D = \$1,000,000 - 0.5(\$1,000,000)$$
$$= \$500,000$$

But let the other extreme be considered where the company's gross capital is $1 million of equity capital and $1 million debt capital, then:

$$D = \$1,000,000 - 0.5(\$2,000,000)$$
$$= 0$$

With $1 million of debt capital added, the gross capital of the business increases to $2 million, $1 million of equity and $1 million of debt capital. How much is required of total gross capital to support $1 million of capital borrowing? The solution to this is determined by setting $D = 0$ and solving for G.

$$0 = \$1,000,000 - 0.5(G)$$
$$0.5G = \$1,000,000$$
$$G = \$2,000,000$$

Since equity capital is contained in gross capital, G can never be less than $1 million; and, since the limit on borrowing is $1 million, gross capital cannot exceed $2 million, that is as long as equity capital remains unchanged. With this model, assuming that equity capital remains at $1 million, financial managers can determine at any hypothetical gross capital condition between 0 and $2 million how much borrowing power the company has.

One of the important factors affecting the demand for, and supply of, a company's common shares, and consequently its share values, is the quality of the capital structure that accomodates the quantitative growth in gross capital. The student will recall from Chapter 2 that

Gross capital = Capital structure

But that:

Gross capital ≠ Capital structure

The lack of identity (≠) between gross capital and the capital structure requires financial managers to make qualitative studies of the capital structure, as well as of gross capital, in planning to maximize share values.

Table 20.1 will illustrate qualitative changes in the capital structure from continuing debt financing, that have significant effects upon solvency risks and consequently upon the valuation of shares. Assume that the business starts with $1,000,000 of gross capital, all supplied by the common shareholders and, there-

TABLE 20.1
QUALITATIVE EFFECTS OF A .6 (ΔG)
EXPANSION FUNCTION

Period	Quantity of Equity E	ΔG	D = .6(ΔG)	Total Debt D	Capital Structure G	Ratio D/G	Ratio D/E
1	1,000,000	1,000,000	600,000	600,000	1,600,000	.375	.600
2	1,000,000	600,000	360,000	960,000	1,960,000	.489	.960
3	1,000,000	360,000	216,000	1,176,000	2,176,000	.540	1.176
4	1,000,000	216,000	129,600	1,305,600	2,305,600	.566	1.305

fore, representing equity financing altogether. Then suppose that the business can borrow such that $\Delta D = .6(\Delta G)$; that is any addition to gross capital will support 60 percent more borrowing, and assume that management borrows four times on a total equity of $1,000,000.

Examining Table 20.1 reveals several important facts about the effect of increased borrowing upon the quality of the capital structure, as well as about the quantity of gross capital. Quantitatively gross capital and the capital structure are the same so that G serves as the value in the denominator of the capital struc- ture ratio. First, it should be noted that although indebtedness has increased from $600,000 at the end of the first period to $1,305,600 at the end of period 4, equity has not increased during the four periods. This is not to imply that equity could not have increased during the periods, but merely that it would not necessarily increase just because gross capital and the capital structure are increasing. Second, it should be noted in the ratio D/G that debt is becoming an increasing portion of the capital structure, thus adding to the solvency risk of the business as a whole. Checking the rate of change will show that the ratio is increasing at a decreasing rate. The stock market has its own definition of what constitutes a risky level for this ratio, and discounts accordingly budgeted profits from the expansion of gross capital in valuing outstanding shares. Third, it should be noted in the D/E ratio that debt is not only increasing, but that it exceeds the quantity of equity after the second borrowing; this ratio, it will be noted, also is increasing at a decreasing rate. This ratio is a clear-cut measure of solvency risk that the stock market under- stands for discounting budgeted profits resulting from the expansion of gross capital.

CAPITAL BORROWING: A FUNCTION OF EARNINGS BEFORE INTEREST

The capital lending fraternity also relates a company's borrowing potential to its capacity for generating earnings before interest (*EBI*). This is a special adapta- tion of cash coverage. To acknowledge the priority of the income tax claim over the interest claims of the creditors, the following method is used to compute the *EBI*.

$$EBI = (EBIT - I)(1 - tr) + I \qquad 20.5$$

Where: EBI = Earnings before interest
$EBIT$ = Earnings before interest and taxes
I = Dollars of interest

Substitute assuming that $EBIT = \$50,000$, $I = \$4,800$ and that the tax rate is 40 percent. Interest charges are used just to determine the tax base and, therefore, are added back to after-tax profits for this concept of interest-paying capability. With interest a constant value, financial managers can use this model to convert any *EBIT* value into *EBI*. With a slight modification of the equation in one opera- tion, we can determine the *coverage* of interest by *EBI*. The equation for determining the coverage of interest by *EBI* is as follows: let EBI_c represent EBI/I. The independent variable is still *EBIT* and EBI_c is a function of *EBIT*. With this tool, financial managers can convert any expected *EBIT* figure into interest coverage.

$$EBI = (\$50,000 - \$4,800)(1 - 0.4) + \$4,800$$
$$= \$31,920$$

$$EBI_c = \frac{(EBIT - I)(1 - tr) + I}{I} \qquad\qquad 20.6$$

$$= \frac{\$31,920}{4,800}$$

$$= 6.65$$

To quantify borrowing potential precisely, we have to know what the coverage standards are of the lenders. Knowing what these are enables us to evaluate the condition (6.65) as above or below the standard and then to plan borrowing accordingly. If the EBI_c requirement is 4/1, then we more than meet the borrowing standard. How much interest will $31,920 (*EBI*) support if as stated above it is required to be 4 times as large as interest (*I*)? The answer to this is the solution of the equation:

$$4I = EBI \qquad\qquad 20.7$$

$$I = \frac{31,920}{4}$$

$$= \$7,980$$

The expected *EBIT* will support much more debt than is presently in the capital structure with interest of only $4,800. To find out how much more debt the income can support, subtract present interest from the maximum interest and capitalize the difference by the expected borrowing rate. Assume that the borrowing rate is 8 percent, then:

$$\text{Additional borrowing} = \frac{\$7,980 - \$4,800}{0.08}$$

$$= \$39,750$$

Simply because creditors would allow a debt expansion to $39,750 is no assurance that the stock market will look favorably upon the debt for share valuation. If the increase in debt causes the securities market to demand a higher (E_e) per share of stock, it will drive up the cost of equity capital (*d*) for discounting purposes, and the present value V_p of budgeted net profits (*pb*) will decrease causing a decrease in demand for and in the market price of the shares. In terms of opportunity costs, this is the same as saying that the larger quantity and higher returns to buyers of the company's debts will cause investors to prefer debt contracts to its common stock contracts causing the latter to decline in price.

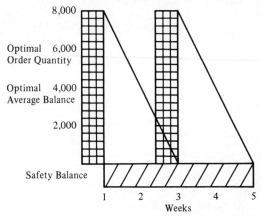

Figure 20.1. Borrowing Potential—Functions of Gross Capital (Equity Capital = $1 million).

CAPITAL BORROWING: A FUNCTION OF NET CASH FLOW

The lending community may look at NCF_e as a source of funds for paying off the principal sum of the debt. First, financial managers want to convert NCF_e into a debt-paying force. After providing for preferred dividends, and perhaps for diverting a certain amount of NCF_e to investment purposes, assume that management can see $0.20 out of every dollar of NCF_e as cash for retiring debt. This makes annual funds available for debt retirement (NCF_d) a function of the expression:

$$NCF_d = 0.20(NCF_e)\qquad\qquad 20.8$$

Where: NCF_d = Annual funds expected to be available for debt retirement

0.20 = Portion of each dollar of NCF_e available for debt retirement

NCF_e = Expected net cash flow

This tool will convert any NCF_e into annual debt-paying potential; but, to change it into borrowing potential, debt repayment standards of the lending community need to be known. Assume that, for businesses of a given risk class, the capital debt market sets a ten-year debt limit. The quantity of allowable borrowing is determined then by solving the equation:

$$D = 10(NCF_d)\qquad\qquad 20.9$$

Where: D = Allowable borrowing

10 = Maximum lending period in years

NCF_d = Annual cash available for debt retirement

QUALITATIVE FACTORS

After determining the quantitative limits to borrowing, financial managers should take a careful look at the alternative forms of debt to reduce borrowing costs even by a small amount if it is possible and to reduce the risk of default wherever this is possible. This is the technical side of capital borrowing where financial managers may have to call for assistance from debt analysts outside the business. Discussed briefly here are the generally distinguishable qualities of the debt contract that affect borrowing costs and solvency risks.

DEBT FORMS AND COSTS OF BORROWING

Compared with equity financing, the cost of borrowing capital is usually relatively low. This may be attributed partly to the lower risks of marketing the securities which reduces the underwriters' spread and increases net proceeds to the business. Another more important reason is their lower risk to the investors. But even among the different debt forms there are also built-in features that cause some borrowing forms to cost the borrower more than others. Financial managers should find out what these factors are and then take action to control them.

SECURED BONDS

Although this is not true in short-term borrowing, in capital borrowing a given business can usually borrow at a lower cost on secured debts than on unsecured. The lower cost of the capital on secured borrowing is compensation for the lower risk of capital loss to the lender when debts are secured by capital assets compared with debts that are unsecured. Even special clauses in secured debts may lower their costs slightly. One in particular is the *after-acquired property* clause found in some mortgage bonds. This clause causes all future properties acquired by the business to be automatically added to the mortgage for the security of the present bondholders. All property, whether real, personal, or mixed, whether now owned or hereafter acquired by the Company, and wheresoever situated, "including all lands, rights of way, and roads," is covered by the mortgage. This has the effect of increasing the security margin for the present creditors when new properties are purchased, regardless of where the funds came from for making the purchase.

If the secured bond with an after-acquired-property clause is a *closed-end* bond, it has a chance of bearing a slightly lower interest charge than one that is left open. A bond issue that allows the business to issue $10 million, for example, and no more at a later date is a closed-bond issue. This prevents diluting the creditors' capital and interest claims. For the assurance that the closed-end provision offers, the creditor is willing usually to make some small concession in the return he receives on his capital.

Convertible bonds which are convertible into the company's common stock at the bondholders' option are certain to exert some pressure on pushing down the cost of borrowing. Investors who buy these securities have some speculative interests, and this kind of investor tends to discount the importance of interest income compared with prospects for capital gains in the stock market. In exchange for a good chance of a capital gain in the common stock market through conversion, investors may be willing to accept a lower interest rate on the bonds.

Warrants are written promises of the business to sell stock, usually common, to the bondholders at a fixed price or schedule of prices over a stated time during the life of the bond. The warrants are attached to the bonds; some are *detachable*; others are *nondetachable*. Detachable warrants are negotiable instruments that may be traded in the securities market separately from the bonds, while nondetachable warrants have to be traded as part of the bond itself and are void if detached. The cost-reducing feature of the bond with warrants attached results because the investor is willing to speculate on the chance that a capital gain can be made by exercising the warrant in the stock market. Some resemblance exists between the convertible bond and the bond with warrants in their cost-reducing effects. But, there are differences that should be noted by financial managers. First, exercising warrants increases the capital-stock structure of the business without decreasing the outstanding debts, while conversion decreases capital debts at the same time that it increases capital stock. Although the effect in both cases is to increase the equity/debt ratio, the coverage will increase at a faster rate when convertible bonds are converted than when warrants are exercised because in the former the denominator of the ratio decreases at the same time as the numerator increases. Second, converting bonds does not usually increase the company's cash, but using the warrants always increases cash and working capital for the business. Converting bonds and exercising warrants both tend to decrease share prices by increasing the quantity of shares.

SUBORDINATED DEBENTURES

Subordinated debentures are junior to all present and future forms of short- and long-term debts in their claims to interest and to the principal sums of their debts. To induce investors to buy bonds of this kind usually requires a sharp increase in the borrowing costs for the business. Below is a typical statement found in this kind of contract which makes it easier to understand why higher interest rates have to be paid.

> The payment of the principal of and interest on each and all of the debentures and of sinking-fund payments . . . shall be expressly subordinated in the extent of any receivership, insolvency, bankruptcy . . . liquidation or any other marshalling of the assets and liabilities of the company, to the payment of all other indebtedness of the company that may at any time and from time to time be outstanding.

SOLVENCY RISK

Borrowing is a risky way of raising funds. In general this results from the legal obligation to pay interest in fixed amounts and on fixed dates and to return the principal sum of the borrowing to the investor when the debts mature. Failure to perform these responsibilities are acts of insolvency that may have serious effects on the stockholders' capital interests and the company's cost of capital (d). But bond forms have different degrees of built-in riskiness for the issuing business and its stockholders. Although management cannot avoid these basic risks altogether, through negotiations with investment bankers and other institutional sources of capital, he can bargain for the forms that hold these risks to a minimum.

Debenture bonds are less risky for the business than secured bonds. This is an unsecured bond which means that in case of default the creditors have to follow certain lengthy procedures before operations of the business can be halted. The first step is to *accelerate* the maturity of the debt; and then, if the debt is not paid within the stated time, a *judgment* may be directed against the business. But if the business corrects the default before the judgment becomes effective, the legal action stops. A secured debt, on the other hand, gives the creditor or his agent the right to enter the mortgaged premises which may disrupt the going concern status of the business and cause a permanent loss in share values. What may be more damaging in the case of secured bonds is the right of the mortgage trustee to sell the property and at his discretion to set an "upset price" on the properties. Foreclosure proceedings are instituted and properties may be withheld from normal business use before the sale, which causes the discount rate (d) on shares to go extremely high and share prices to go extremely low.

Income bonds are special instruments that make the payment of interest contingent on earnings, but they have a fixed maturity date. The business is protected against becoming insolvent in lean years when the income is inadequate to meet interest. Income bonds are sometimes used to reorganize or adjust the capital structures of faltering and failed businesses, to lessen the risk of insolvency and repeated failure. For this reason they are often called adjustment bonds. But this debt form should be considered by profitable businesses as well as a vehicle for reducing solvency risks and forestalling financial failures. The income bond may be secured or unsecured, and the interest may be cumulative or noncumulative. Income bonds with cumulative interest are more risky to the business than those with noncumulative interest because interest not paid in the present year is added to the company's debts. To compensate for low risk to the business, interest rates are high causing (d) also to increase and V_p of common shares to decrease.

Bonds issued to refund or pay off a maturing capital debt preserve the solvency of the business by delaying the final maturity date. This is particularly important when debts can be delayed for twenty or thirty years, thus preserving the solvency of the business and stabilizing the value of its shares. Refunding is easier to do in companies with stable income, like public utilities, than commercial and industrial companies and more feasible with mortgage bonds than with debentures. Often the new issue serves a double purpose of refunding an old issue and also supplying funds to improve the value of the capital properties. But continuous, heavy debt may raise (d) and cause V_p to decline.

Most capital debts are redeemable, which means that the business has the option to call at a stated price, or schedule of prices, part or all of its debts at any time before they mature. The risk reducing effect of the bonds operates indirectly in the following way: the redemption clause allows the business to use funds to repay part of its debts whenever management recommends it. This has a solvency advantage because it removes funds from working capital that might have been used for dividends or for fixed capital investments. It also reduces solvency risk by disposing of a debt which in the future could be very difficult to repay. The indenture states that (1) the company will announce the redemption dates and prices in a metropolitan newspaper in the city where the trustee is located and (2) that bonds will be selected by *lot* when less than all of the bonds are called. The effect of redemption upon (d) is hardly discernible.

Bonds that are convertible at the option of the bondholder into other securities, usually common stock, potentially reduce a company's solvency risks as they do its borrowing costs. The conversion procedure, indicates: (1) the type of securities into which the bonds are convertible, usually common stock; (2) the rate of conversion; (3) the time and method of issuing the capital stock, including a statement of the moment when the bondholders' status ends and the stockholders' status begins; (4) the procedure for authorizing enough shares to complete the conversion; and (5) the method of compensating bondholders with claims to fractional shares of stock. If the bonds are converted, the solvency risks of the business and the present shareholders are immediately reduced; but, until that time, they potentially reduce solvency risk. But there are certain controls over this action. As a general rule, the lower the conversion price of the common stock is set in relation to the market price of the stock the more likely the bondholder is to convert. If the conversion price is set below the current market price, some bondholders will convert right away; and, if the market rises, even gradually, more and more conversion will occur until it is completed. Suppose that the market price of the outstanding stock is $28 per share, and the conversion price is $25. A $1,000 bond will then return the investor 40 shares of stock worth $1,120 (40 × $28). A conversion price of $20 would have returned $1,400 in the exchange (50 × $28) and normally would have accelerated the conversion. The conversion price may be set above the market also, so that present shareholders' interests will not be diluted by a sudden increase in outstanding common shares. If the conversion price is too low, the stock market may anticipate this by raising (d) and thus lowering V_p and market prices of common shares.

SERIAL AND SINKING-FUND DEBTS

Capital debts may come due all at one time, ten, fifteen, or more years from the date of the borrowing, or they may come due in serial installments or in some more indirect way by investing first in sinking-fund securities. The single-payment form, regardless of whether it is secured or unsecured, is less risky than the multiple-payment form of debt. The reason for this is that with more time to employ the funds, the business has a better chance of generating working capital to meet its debts when they finally mature. To get the quantity of capital that is needed, management may have to make concessions of this nature and agree to return capital in regular installments or to make payments into a sinking fund before the debt matures. The specific bond forms are called serial bonds when the principal is returned directly to the creditors and sinking-fund bonds when payments are first made into a sinking fund. Sinking-fund bonds are used more often than serial bonds for business borrowing, but the solvency risk is basically the same for the two forms. Higher solvency risks and lower borrowing costs $(r_1 + r_2)$ cause less favorable investment opportunities, lower E_e demands, and lower cost of capital (d).

SUMMARY

First, it is necessary to establish that the quantity of capital borrowing that a business is qualified to do is a function of the quantity of net capital owned by that business. Thus, the quantity of equity capital in the capital structure plays a major part in determining the amount of leverage that the capital structure is able to add under favorable borrowing terms. Another important factor affecting the quantity of capital borrowing that a company can obtain is the size of its flow of funds. In addition to these quantitative factors there are qualitative aspects of borrowing which are affected by the following items:

1. The quantity and quality of security behind a long-term debt financing determine the quantity of such financing that can be done.
2. The matter of convertibility of a borrowing contract into an equity security is an important factor affecting the quantity of future borrowing.

Other factors for consideration include specific contact forms like subordinated debentures, income bonds, refunding bonds, redeemable bonds, and convertible bonds. Special consideration is given to the effect of the different quality forms of debt on the solvency condition of the business on its costs of equity capital, and on the present value of its shares.

PROBLEMS

1. Company B has the following capital structure:

Capital debt	$1,000,000
Capital stock	4,000,000
Retained earnings	1,000,000
Total	$6,000,000

The lending community makes the basic requirement that capital debt not exceed 80 percent of a company's equity capital.

 a. Set up the equation showing the functional relationship of borrowing to equity.
 b. Does management need to count the assets to know how much equity capital his company has? If not, how much equity capital does Company B have?
 c. How much debt would be allowed with the present capital? How much more could be borrowed without violating the constraint?
 d. But in capital investment (fixed or net working capital) the quantity of equity capital may change. Suppose that $1 million of equity capital is budgeted to a new plant addition and that 25 percent of this would be financed internally with retained earnings. How much capital stock would have to be issued? Set up the equation and solve, indicating the total allowable borrowing for the business and the allowable borrowing above its present capital structure.
 e. If the only constraint placed on a business is its equity capital, how much borrowing could be done given the function: $D = 0.8(E)$? How would a net working capital constraint affect the limit of borrowing?
 f. Referring to question d again, suppose that there were no other constraint on the quantity of borrowing other than $0.8(E)$. What are the practical limitations from the viewpoint of cost of capital and internal rate of return?
 g. What, if anything, can be done to change the coefficient in $D = 0.8(E?)$

2. Company C has the following capital structure.

Capital debt	$2,500,000
Capital stock	5,000,000
Retained earnings	1,500,000
Total	$9,000,000

The lending community makes the basic requirement that capital debt not exceed 60 percent of the company's gross capital.

    a. What is Company C's gross capital, or do we need the asset structure to determine this?

    b. Has Company B used fully its borrowing potential? If not, how much remains?

    c. A constraint of this kind based on gross capital has an element of self-perpetuation built into it; that is, the more borrowing the company does the more it can continue to do. Explain.

3. Our Company X has the following *average* operating statement for the past three years.

Net sales	$400,000
Cost of goods sold	300,000
Gross profit	100,000
Operating expenses	50,000
Operating profit	50,000
Interest charges	10,000
Profits before taxes	40,000
Taxes	16,000
After-tax profit	$ 24,000

What is the solution to the following using data from the statement above?

$$EBI_c = \frac{(EBIT - I)(1 - tr) + I}{I}$$

4. Financial managers of Company Y want to portray graphically for the board of directors the effect of equity capital on the quantity of allowable borrowing where capital lenders relate their lending to a company's gross capital. For this purpose, the managers used the example in which a 0.6 lending coefficient was used and in which borrowing concern would have two hypothetical equity structures, one of $1 million and the other of $1.5 million.

    a. Place the linear functions of the two alternative equity situations on the same graph.

    b. What significant differences would you point out in interpreting the two functions to the board?

    c. How would you relate the capital structure differences to capital investment and to the cost of capital?

    d. Because of the self-perpetuation feature, a dollar limit in terms of equity capital is usually included in the borrowing model. Set up the equation with borrowing as a function of gross capital, when $r = 0.6$, $E = 6.5 million, and $G = 9 million. Has Company C used up its borrowing potential? If not, how much more can be borrowed? How can this tool be used for simulating borrowing? Is there any way of raising the limit above $6.5 million?

e. Suppose that the equity constraint of $6.5 million were not placed on the business, what would the theoretical limit of its borrowing be? Why is this not a realistic figure?

f. The capital lending market requires a turnover ratio of interest into *EBI* of 2. The interest rate on borrowing is 8 percent. What is the limit of capital borrowing? Suppose that the borrowing limit is greater in this case than it is using some other constraint like equity capital. Which of the limits will the company use?

5. Referring to the average income statement in problem 4, what is missing to make that an average net-cash-flow statement?

a. Supply the figure necessary to convert the present statement into an *NCF* value of $32,000.

b. Assume that the company has free $0.15 out of each dollar of NCF_e for NCF_d and that it expects an average net cash flow for the next five years of $40,000. Set up the equation for determining NCF_d, substituting the expected average net-cash-flow figure mentioned above.

c. The capital debt market from which funds are obtained limits its loans to fifteen-year maturities. How much, based on NCF_d in your answer to b can the business borrow?

6. Company A has the following debt structure.

1st mortgage bonds	$4,000,000
2nd mortgage bonds	1,000,000
Debenture bonds	1,500,000
Subordinated debentures	500,000
Total	$7,000,000

a. Evaluate the individual debts above for their effect on cost of borrowing and their effect on solvency risk and cost of capital (d).

b. Debenture bonds are made convertible. What does this do to the cost of borrowing and to solvency risk and cost of capital (d)?

c. What effect, if any, would a sinking-fund clause in the subordinated debenture have on its interest rate and cost of capital (d)?

d. What effect on solvency risk would there be in replacing the straight debenture bonds with serial bonds? Are serial bonds any more risky for the business than sinking fund bonds?

e. What effect would an after-acquired-property clause with a closed-end provision have on the cost of the first mortgage bond issue?

f. Should preferred stock have been included in the above list of securities?

21

Leasing and Fixed-Asset Purchasing

In Chapter 20, general conditions of borrowing and significant decision-making aspects of bond forms were considered, without relating the financing to any specific capital use. This chapter will consider the important issues of financing to bring fixed capital directly into the business. Our purpose here is to examine the competing methods of doing this with the view to establishing the best long-run operating climate for the company's shares.

THE LEASE PLAN OF FINANCING

The lease plan of financing is a service in which the property user, called the *lessee*, is obligated to make a fixed number of rental payments to the owner, called the *lessor*, after which possession of the property is returned to the owner. It is technically correct to call these properties fixed capital but not fixed assets because fixed assets represent only that portion of fixed capital that is owned by the company.

GENERAL FACTORS

Since the physical properties in leasing are emphasized at the expense of the financial factors, the financial factors will be emphasized here. The tangible lease agreement is called the *leasehold*. While the practice of capitalizing leaseholds and putting them in the capital structure has not found general acceptance as yet, it is universally agreed that leasehold obligations should be acknowledged somewhere in the balance sheet to give the shareholders and creditors a picture of the total cash burdens on future income. Lease rentals on business properties are usually paid in cash at the end of each period of use. This means that no cash advance occurs when the lease agreement is drawn, although the lessee at that time is given possession of the properties. The contract stipulates that rental will be paid at a given time and place over the whole life of the lease.

Of no small concern to financial managers is the tax deductible feature of lease rentals. The lease has been said to offer the only means of depreciating land for tax purposes. The explanation for this is as follows: businesses may deduct for tax purposes the rental that they pay for combined land and building; if the properties are owned by the business, only depreciation on buildings is deductible for tax purposes. But there is another way of looking at this that comes closer to the subject of this chapter. The rental payments on a lease are calculated to return to the lessor his capital investment plus what he calls a given interest return. While the payments on a capital loan are calculated to do the same for the investor, the business is allowed to deduct only the interest portion of these payments for tax purposes. This may have some effect, as will be seen later, on the decision to finance with one form as against another.

INSTITUTIONAL SERVICES

The role of certain financial institutions and special leasing agencies has been noteworthy in the development of capital-leasing services. These institutions put up their own working capital to buy the properties, which are released for business use. Commercial banks, as will be seen later, are more active in financing purchases than rentals of fixed assets. But large commercial finance companies are particularly interested in the shorter lease contracts maturing in three to five years. Flexibility is provided by allowing the business to select capital for the finance company to purchase, and by the finance company offering to buy from the business capital already in use for leaseback to the business.

Life insurance companies are active lessors of railroad equipment and real estate, preferring longer contracts that mature after five years. The Equitable Life Insurance Company was the forerunner in the field of railroad equipment leasing by leasing cars to an Eastern railroad on a basic fifteen-year plan at $1.55 per car per day for the first five years and $1.10 per day thereafter for the next ten years. Under this plan, after the fifteen years were up, the railroad could renew its lease at a basic rate of 0.20 per car per day. In commercial property leasing, life insurance companies have no peer. A common practice is to finance a large retail store construction and then to buy the total properties for leaseback as soon as it is completed. Not only insurance companies but trust funds, investment companies, and pension funds may invest in real estate, including factory facilities on leaseback arrangements.

Besides financial institutions that supplement their regular lending and securities investing with leasing services, leasing companies have been organized independently for this purpose; and manufacturers in some industries offer their products for lease as well as for sale. The scope of their activities varies: some will custom-purchase for the lessee almost any kind of machinery or equipment, while others limit their activities to certain products.

Leasing forms are either straight leases in which the business is obligated to pay rental over the full service life of the capital, or they may be modified leases giving the business an option to terminate the lease before its regular expiration date or to buy the properties before or at the expiration date of the lease.

The Basic Financial Form   The financial form of the lease is constructed so that the leasing agency can return a reasonable profit over the life of the investment at a *cost of capital* low enough to induce businesses to use this service instead of capital borrowing. *Covenants* of the lease are designed to protect the lessor's interests. They require the lessee to (1) pay rentals on given dates and in stated amounts over the full life of the lease, (2) not remove the properties from the premises or to sublet them without consent from the lessor, and (3) take ordinary care in maintaining and preserving the properties. The most important of these provisions financially is the first because it determines the solvency risk and cost of the capital to the business.

The *level rental plan* is the basic financing form. Payments are determined in the following way. Suppose that the lessor agrees to buy a machine or group of machines for the business costing a total of $50,000 and that he expects a 10 percent return on the outstanding balance of his investment. Ten percent is selected for convenience rather than as a representative rate of return charged by lessors. This amounts to a *simple average rate of return* on his investment of 10 percent. We should note that no allowance is made when setting the rate for compound interest that the lessor can earn from reinvesting the rental incomes. Rental incomes are taxable to the lessor, but the rental payments are tax deductible for the lessee business. Table 21.1 is an illustration of how this agreement is translated into a

TABLE 21.1
DETERMINING LEVEL RENTALS

Year	Interest @ 10%		Principal @ $5,000 Per Year		Level Rental Paid by Lessee
1	$ 5,000		$ 5,000		$ 7,750
2	4,500		5,000		7,750
3	4,000		5,000		7,750
4	3,500		5,000		7,750
5	3,000		5,000		7,750
6	2,500		5,000		7,750
7	2,000		5,000		7,750
8	1,500		5,000		7,750
9	1,000		5,000		7,750
10	500		5,000		7,750
Total	$27,500	+	$50,000	=	$77,500

schedule of level rental payments assuming a ten-year service life on the lease. The lessee returns over the life of the project $27,500 or a 55 percent simple interest on his initial investment.

Form with the Option to Terminate   In some cases, in machinery and equipment leasing in particular, the lessee is given the option to terminate the lease before its expiration date. As a "cost" for this service, the total rental payments may be increased, or the rate of rental payments may simply be accelerated and larger payments will be necessary in the early years of the lease. The larger early receipts help to compensate the investor for the rapid loss of market value if he should have to reclaim the properties during the first few years of use. At the same time, the larger sums provide extra income for reinvestment. From the lessee's viewpoint, of course, larger payments in early years incur (1) extra solvency risks and (2) reduced net cash flow because he is deprived of the chance to reinvest the funds in his own business. In some cases, the lessee may have several options to terminate, with the shorter termination dates requiring still larger rental payments in early years. Table 21.2 reallocates the payments at an accelerated rate, granting

TABLE 21.2
OPTION TO TERMINATE AFTER THIRD YEAR

Year	Annual Rentals	Cumulative Rentals
1	$20,000	$20,000
2	20,000	40,000
3	20,000	60,000
4	2,500	62,500
5	2,500	65,000
6	2,500	67,500
7	2,500	70,000
8	2,500	72,500
9	2,500	75,000
10	2,500	77,500

the business one option to terminate any time after the first three years. Notice that the total payments are the same as in Table 21.1 without the termination option, but more than 77 percent of the rentals will have been paid before the option can be exercised at the end of the third year. After that date, the accumulation rate is curbed sharply. To terminate at this date would be a costly experience; but not to terminate would be even more costly if the capital itself is not returning income enough to meet the rentals, or if continuing with this lease is depriving the business of using other lower-cost forms of financing. A modified lease of this kind may cause tax problems.

Form with the Option to Purchase   The option to purchase may be offered jointly with the option to terminate, or with the straight level-rental payments. Usually no extra rental is charged, nor are rental payments accelerated for this option. Not until the option is exercised is the cost felt. And then the longer we wait to exercise it, the more it will cost in total cash outlays; although the purchase price of the capital facilities decreases with time, it does not decrease as fast as the rentals accumulate. Table 21.3 shows the effect on annual cash outlays of exercising the option to purchase. The first column is taken from Table 21.2. The second column states the percentage that the purchase price is of the original $50,000 price of the capital, and the third column states the prices in dollars. The last column tells us how much total capital would be expended exercising the option at any one of the alternative purchase prices. Again, a controversy may arise in this case over deductibility of rentals for taxes.

TABLE 21.3
LEASE FORM WITH OPTION TO PURCHASE

Year	(1) Cumulative Rentals (3-Year Termination Option)	(2) Percentage Purchase Price of Original Price of Capital	(3) Purchase Price	(4) (1) + (3) Total Capital Expended
1	$20,000	70	$35,000	$55,000
2	40,000	40	20,000	60,000
3	60,000	30	15,000	75,000
4	62,500	28	14,000	76,500
5	65,000	25	12,500	77,500
6	67,500	24	12,000	79,500
7	70,000	22	11,000	81,000
8	72,500	20	10,000	82,500
9	75,000	18	9,000	84,000
10	77,500	16	8,000	85,500

DECISION-MAKING FACTORS

As financial managers, we are concerned primarily with the facts about leasing that will help us to make better decisions, even if it means rejecting this form of capital financing for some other. In order to weight the decisive factors that influence a leasing decision, we will examine the effect on solvency risks, capital costs, quantity of financing, and external controls.

Solvency Risks What is there about leasing that affects solvency risks to the owners of a business? The first impression is that leasing is exceptionally risky because: (1) payments are high compared with interest on borrowed capital, and (2) payments are fixed without regard to the level of operations or profitability of the capital. But these observations are too general for decision making. Exact measurements can be made of the present value of lease payments, and they can be effectively compared with funds available from operations for making the payments to give us a more exact indication of their burden and risk to the business. Because lease payments are a nontaxable payment, net profits before taxes are available for meeting these payments. It should also be mentioned that the equity measurements that are meaningful in qualifying for capital borrowing are relatively meaningless for leasing.

The most important question of solvency risk is related to the quantity of debt payable in case of default. The lease is an agreement to make continuing payments until the expiration date, but this is not usually interpreted by the courts to mean a *prima facie* obligation to make all of the payments. In a default on a lease, the lessor does better to sue for damages rather than for the unpaid portion of the lease. Courts have held in this respect that to demand more than damages would be an "unenforceable penalty" on the lessee. In the case of a bankrupt business, the courts tend to allow the lessor one or at the most two years of rental on an annual lease commitment.

Comparative Cash Flows   Cash flows are important decision-making factors in leasing as they are in other forms of capital financing. Later we can compare leasing with borrowing, but first let us consider the simpler task of comparing and evaluating alternative lease plans of financing. The simplest tool for comparing the competing lease offerings is *present value*. The procedure is as follows. First, funds are budgeted to an individual capital project on the basis of its superior income producing potential, assuming a given discounting rate. Then the present values of competing streams of rental payment will point out the most efficient lease contract for executing the financing. We will find that the lowest present value is not necessarily the one with the smallest number of dollars paid out. Lease contracts calling for small payments in early years and large payments in later years may cost less in present values than a smaller total stream of payments that reverses this order. The present-value method can also be used to measure the termination option. The 10 percent discount column in Table II in the Appendix indicates a present value of 6.145 for an annual $1 flow for ten years. This multiplied by $7,750 in annual rentals produces a present value of $47,624 for Table 21.1. The flow of rental payments for the termination option, however, is accelerated; and, therefore, two different discounting values are required: one for the payments of $20,000 during the first three years and another for the payments during the last seven years. Using a 10 percent discounting factor these values are summarized as follows:

Cash Payments		Table Factor		
$20,000	×	2.487	=	$49,740
2,500	×	3.658	=	9,145
		Present value with option		$58,885
Present value with no option				47,624
Difference				$11,261

The cash flow cost of the termination option is the difference between the present value of the level flow and the present value of the accelerated flow, or $11,261. On the surface, this looks like a high price to pay for the option; but whether this is too high or not depends on whether (1) continued operation of an unsuccessful project is justified considering the risk of (2) legal suits resulting from breaking the lease contract.

The present-value analysis will suffice for decision making as long as the capital services offered by alternative deals are the same, and it is reasonable to assume that this will be the case. In some situations, comparisons have to be made on a relative basis to help decide between projects of different size; and this requires choosing the lease with the lower *relative cash frow*. This means carrying our measurement one step further and stating the present value of future rentals in relation to the value of the capital investment:

$$\text{Relative present values} = \frac{\text{Present value of future rentals}}{\text{Value of capital investment}}$$

The lower ratio indicates the lower relative present value of the expenditures. Suppose that two leasing projects represent investments of $50,000 and $70,000 respectively and that the present values of the respective rental flows are $47,000 and $58,000. It would be relatively cheaper to lease the larger $70,000 project in this case, assuming that the larger volume of services rendered by the first project is commensurate to its higher investment value.

$$\frac{58,000}{70,000} = 0.83$$

$$\frac{47,000}{50,000} = 0.94$$

Qualifying for Financing   How do the built-in characteristics of the lease affect leasing and additional capital borrowing? This question may be answered by asking another more direct one: To what extent, if at all, is our credit in the capital-debt market affected by the quantity of leasing that is noted in our balance sheet? Some uncertainty still exists about how to classify leasehold obligations for future credit. But piecing together fragments from the actions of lessor and capital creditors, we may throw some light at least on this important subject. The fact that leasing limits are sometimes established by lessors for individual businesses is evidence that leasing does have an effect on capital credit. While lease obliga tions are not found in the capital structure, the debt and equity composition of the capital structure does affect the size of the lease line, a large equity structure being favored more than a large debt structure for this purpose. The lease line may even be geared directly to the capital structure; thus, the leasing ceiling may be set at 20 percent of the equity structure or 50 percent of the capital structure.

A rule of this kind is more effective in checking future leasing than it is in checking capital borrowing. To illustrate, suppose that the capital structure is $400,000 and that capital debts and leasehold obligations are each $100,000, or 25 percent of the capital structure. Doubling each of these dollar figures would increase the capital debt ratio to 40 percent ($200,000/$500,000) and the leasehold ratio to 50 percent ($200,000/$400,000). In periods of high cash flows, rental burdens are likely to be disregarded, but overlooked is the fact that one or two years of low incomes could have serious consequences. It should be recognized also that defaulting on lease rental may result in immediate losses of vital producing properties that could freeze future income. On the other side and acting to soften the effects of leasing on capital credit are the limited claims to funds, in damage suits brought by the lessors.

Finally, we cannot disregard the effect of leaseholds upon the cost of capital (d) and resulting equity financing. The beneficial efiects that the stock market sees in the leasehold upon net cash flow and the profit budget (pb) for increasing present value (V_p) of the company's shares may be partially, if not wholly, offset by a higher discounting rate (d) from a rising (r_2) and (E_e) caused by the added risks of excessive lease contracts, although reference to these contracts appears only in the footnotes of the balance sheets. Whether or not present value (V_p) and market price of the shares will drop depends upon whether the relative rate of increase in the size of the profit budget ($\Delta pb/pb$), resulting from planned asset use and appearing in the numerator of the capitalization ratio, exceeds the relative rate of increase in the size of the discounting factor ($\Delta d/d$), appearing in the denominator of the ratio.

External Controls   The lessor's controls are confined entirely to his properties that are on the premises of the business. The lessor has no control over the size of the debt structure, equity structure, or working capital as the creditor does in unsecured and in secured capital lending. But lessors' controls over the properties are somewhat tighter than in most forms of borrowing; and these rights to control are upheld in the courts because there is no question about where the title to the property rests. There is no question of the lessor's right to enter the premises, to inspect his properties, or even to take them back at any time that the lease covenants are violated. Lessors have the right to sue the business for damages in case of nonpayment of rentals and to force it into bankruptcy if the damages are not paid.

THE PURCHASE PLAN OF FINANCING

Like leasing, financing to purchase fixed assets is available in forms that differ in degree if not in kind. Each method has the following characteristics in common: (1) some portion of the purchase price of the asset has to be paid for in advance by the business; (2) the new capital is security on the debt; (3) the debt is repaid in installments; (4) the total cost of the assets is included in the capital accounts; (5) the debt created by the borrowing is added to the capital structure; and (6) the business retains and owns the properties when they are fully paid for. We will review the market for this kind of financing, the forms, and then the general decision-making factors that are most likely to influence financial managers in choosing between different purchasing forms and between different forms of leasing and purchasing.

INSTITUTIONAL SERVICES

Commercial banks, which are relatively inactive in capital leasing, offer valuable financial services in making possible fixed-asset purchases, particularly of chattels like machinery, equipment, and fixtures. While commercial banks also make substantial advances for real estate purchases, national banks are not allowed to finance more than 60 percent of the purchase price or construction cost of buildings unless the loans are guaranteed by the Federal Housing Administration. Unless real estate purchases and construction costs are FHA-guaranteed, they are also limited in length of maturity. The total amount of real estate loans by national banks may not exceed 100 percent of their capital and surplus or 60 percent of their savings and time deposits whichever is greater. They are also restricted by the 10 percent rule (maximum of 10 percent of capital and surplus) on individual loans to any one customer.

Commercial finance companies do not make real estate loans, but they have been the most aggressive force in lending to buy machinery and equipment. They finance the purchases of laundry and cleaning equipment, stationary gasoline and diesel engines, bottling and printing equipment, bowling equipment, business and commercial trucks, and road construction machinery and equipment. Several large manufacturing corporations in the machine tool, electrical machinery and equipment, and construction goods industries have formed their own sales finance companies to speed up the financing and sales of their products. Commercial finance companies prefer the shorter financings with maturities between three and five years as do commercial banks. Life insurance companies are the main suppliers of funds for costly long-term capital purchases of railroad and other transportation equipment and certain commercial and factory properties. Investment banks are also active in this market, supplying cash for large purchases of equipment and commercial and industrial real estate. Investment banks, as we know, are first and foremost securities middlemen and, therefore, are interested primarily in financing purchases that will supply large quantities of marketable bonds.

PURCHASE FINANCING

Borrowing for fixed-asset purchasing is unique in that the debts that are created are secured by liens on the properties that they help to buy. Cash advances made by financial institutions will vary between 60 percent and 80 percent of the purchase price of the assets, depending on the types of assets. Several forms of purchase financing will be considered here.

Commercial Machinery and Equipment Purchases The most common financing used for making purchases of this kind are the conditional sales contract and the chattel mortgage. Maturity of the contract can be set to meet the needs of the parties but is usually attuned to the depreciable life of the asset. Most commercial and industrial facilities are depreciable for this purpose within ten years. Usually up to 80 percent of the purchase price of the asset can be financed; 100 percent of the purchase price is entered in the fixed assets section of the balance sheet, and the unpaid portion of the purchase price becomes a capital liability. Instructions for repaying the debt and for possessing and using the properties are clearly noted in the sales contract. The debt is evidenced by an ordinary collateral installment

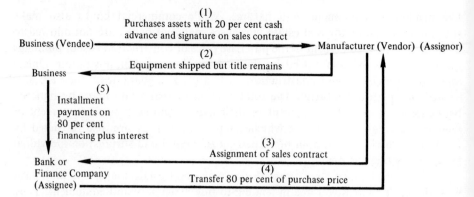

Figure 21.1.   Purchase with Conditional Sales Contract.

note. Important to financing this purchase is assigning the sales contract to the financial institution. Figure 21.1 sketches for us the steps in the financing numbered in order.

Using the chattel mortgage, the manufacturer is saved the risk of credit extension even on a temporary basis as he is paid in full in cash before the goods are shipped. The chattel mortgage is a contract between the business purchaser (mortgagor) and the bank or finance company (mortgagee). Underlying title to the properties in this contract is in the purchaser, unlike the conditional sale in which title is received only after the last installment payment. Figure 21.2 illustrates the transaction in which a chattel mortgage is used to finance the asset purchase.

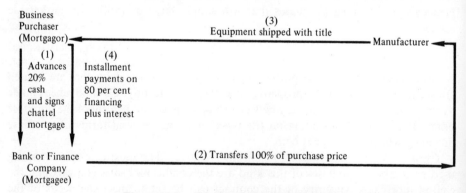

Figure 21.2.   Purchase with Chattel Mortgage.

Railroad Equipment Purchases   The equipment trust has been the mainstay in making railroad equipment purchases since before the turn of the century. This is called an equipment trust because the title to the equipment is held in trust for the investors by a trustee. The trust method of financing equipment purchases is a means of bypassing the after-acquired property clause in the old railroad mortgages. By conveying title from the manufacturer directly to a trustee on an equipment trust agreement, the after-acquired-property clause in the real property mortgage is bypassed. By means of a specially constructed lease, the possession and use of the equipment is transferred to the railroads as soon as it is manufactured with title passing when the last lease rental is paid.

Equipment trust certificates are in effect serial bonds. Equipment trust certificates are issued in amounts usually of more than $1 million and are sold in the capital market to investment banks for public sale and distribution. By rule of the Interstate Commerce Commission railroads have to extend a published invitation to investment banks to bid competitively on these offerings.

Attached to each certificate are *dividend warrants* rather than interest coupons, but for all intents and purposes these are interest obligations. The trustee promises on the warrant to pay the dividend, "but only out of rentals or other money received by the undersigned [trustee] pursuant to the agreement and lease." This statement frees the trustee from personal liability in case the railroad fails to pay the rental when it comes due. The certificates are issued in denominations of $1,000 and are payable at maturity to the bearer. Rather than trying to diagram equipment trust financing, steps in the procedure are listed below:

1. The invitation to bid is published in metropolitan newspapers. In this invitation, the company tells what it will buy and what percentage of the cost of the equipment it wishes to have financed: 70 percent, 80 percent, and the like.

2. The company may reject all bids; but, if not, the bid offering the lowest *cost of capital* must be accepted. Costs are usually computed for this purpose on a yield basis to the investor bank. Thus the bank offering to buy the issue of certificates at the lowest yield to the investor is the one that the railroad must accept.

3. The railroad places the order for the equipment with the manufacturer and pays 20 percent of the purchase price in advance. Or if the funds are on deposit with the trustee, the latter may make the 20 percent advance.

4. The company prepares and conveys serial equipment trust certificates, which usually start maturing the year after their issue, to the trustee who promises on the certificates to pay the dividend warrants and the principal sum of the debt when they mature *but only out of lease rentals* received from the railroad. To make doubly sure of the railroad's liability on the debts, a company *guaranty* is contained on the back of each certificate.

5. The certificates are then transferred to the winning investment banker. If he is the manager of an underwriting syndicate, the certificates are distributed to the members for advertising and sale with the yield prices to the investors for each serial published in the advertisement.

6. The trustee pays the manufacturer the balance due on the equipment

when it is completed for delivery. A bill of sale is given to the trustee confirming ownership of the equipment.

7. The railroad leases the equipment from the trustee on special lease terms requiring that the rentals that are paid to the trustee be used to pay the dividend warrants, retire the principal sum of the certificates, and compensate the trustee for his services.

8. As the certificates are paid at maturity, they are cancelled; and, when all certificates are cancelled, the trust agreement and the lease are terminated. The trustee gives the railroad a bill of sale indicating the new owner of the equipment.

The equipment trust is a relatively low-cost form of financing but is still limited pretty much to financing transportation equipment. Two reasons at least for this are: first, unless a large quantity of financing is done at one time, the cost of the borrowing could be high. Second, the high investment quality of transportation equipment certificates is traceable to the long service life and marketability of used transportation equipment.

Real Estate Purchases   When a first mortgage is placed on newly purchased real estate, the mortgage is called a *purchase-money mortgage*. The mortgage in other words secures the purchase money that is advanced to the mortgagor to help him complete a construction project or to buy a project already completed. The debt is paid off with interest on an installment basis. Funds are supplied by private placement institutions and investment banks. If the financing is underwritten by investment banks, mortgage bonds will be issued for trading in the capital debt markets. If the financing is a public sale, an indenture trustee will be appointed to hold the investors' purchase-money lien and to serve as a liaison between the business and its bondholders. If an after-acquired-property clause is contained in the mortgage, all newly acquired properties are added to the lien. Possession and use of the properties are guaranteed to the business as long as it does not default on any provision of the mortgage. The business may even sell the properties as long as they are sold "at a price equal at least to its fair value as stated by an independent engineer." In case the business is in default on any provision, the final action against the business short of bankruptcy is the *foreclosure sale*.

DECISION-MAKING FACTORS

In some cases the different purchase forms are competitive, for example, purchasing with a conditional sale or a chattel mortgage. But they do not have the wide differences that so clearly marked other forms of capital borrowing; in fact, the similarities of the purchase forms are more apparent than their differences. We will reexamine these forms for important decision-making characteristics and then compare them with their closest competitor—the lease form of financing. The financing forms will compete on common grounds of solvency and liquidity risks, present values, future financing, and creditors' controls.

Solvency and Liquidity Risks Purchase contracts of all kinds are capitalized, which places them in the debt structure. This is not just an accounting coincidence, but it is representative of the underlying solvency risk in the financing. Any law court will uphold the creditor's claim to the full unpaid portion of the debt as long as the business is a going concern and to a proportionate amount of the capital of a bankrupt organization without the creditor having to sue for damages. The amount of the risk is closely identified with the amount of debts in the total capital structure. Other quantitative measures of the risk are the fund-flow relationships between annual incomes and annual expenditures for interest and principal. Cash flow analysis is particularly important in this kind of borrowing because of the installment method of repayment.

One of the disadvantages often cited of purchasing instead of leasing capital is the down payment, the advance rental, the owner's equity in the assets, or whatever we want to call it. The important effect of this on working capital is apparent; for example, on a $100,000 purchase at a 20-percent down payment, the business has to part with $20,000 in net working capital before securing the property. The risk is quite different—having to pay this today rather than being able to spread it over ten years as may be done in a lease. In the lease, not only are these payments delayed; but, in a sale and lease-back, the business receives the cash advance itself with 100-percent present value in exchange for a contract to pay rentals in the future with declining present values. But if the business can withstand the liquidity shock of the initial payment of a purchase contract, the business will be compensated by paying smaller installments than on a lease. The solvency risks in individual purchasing plans are affected decisively by the installment schedule. The balance of the debt can be paid in equal amounts, in smaller annual amounts in early years and large payments near the end or in larger annual payments at the start with small payments in the later years. "Balloon" payment schedules would seem to be beneficial because they give the business a longer time to secure the funds, while telescoped payments would seem to have the opposite effect of exposing the business to greater risks by having a shorter time to secure the funds.

A good basis for comparing the riskiness of competing debt forms is to consider the causes of default as they are stated in the securing contract itself. The mortgages (chattel and purchase-money) and the trust agreements are likely to summarize the major causes of default in the *covenants* of their debt agreements. The more promises that have to be made to the creditors in the covenants the greater chance there is of defaulting. Usually promises are concentrated on paying the debt and on protecting and caring for the securing property. In long-term indebtedness, particularly in the purchase money mortgage form, however, certain restrictions may be placed on future borrowing and on managing working capital; all adding to the risks of default and insolvency. Using the covenants of the debt contract as a basis for comparison, we can safely say that the scope of the risk exposure is broader for borrowing than for renting the capital facilities.

The procedure of the creditor in enforcing demands on the insolvent business is another matter for financial managers to consider in comparing solvency risks of different forms of purchases and comparing purchasing with leasing. The two competing forms for commercial machinery and equipment purchases are the conditional sale and the chattel mortgage with the solvency risk probably greater in the former than in the latter. In a chattel as well as a real estate mortgage, the purchaser owns the properties from the time of the purchase; and they cannot be taken from him except at a foreclosure sale. In financing transportation equipment purchases, conditional sale and chattel mortgage forms compete with the equipment trust plan. Here the formality of the debtor-creditor relations in a public distribution of equipment trust certificates may be more risky in case of a default than is a private placement of the conditional sale or chattel mortgage.

Present Value In extending our measuring tools to capital borrowing, we are guided by the purpose of selecting from competing outflows of funds the one with the lowest present value. Our problem is complicated somewhat as outflows for lease payments are compared with outflows of interest and principal to creditors because of the income-tax factor. Assume that we are confronted with several alternatives from leasing to borrowing, each one qualified to supply the asset needs. The choice for financing can turn on the comparison of the relative costs of competing forms of financing measured by their relative present values. To illustrate the procedure, we will assume three alternative methods are available for financing a $50,000 investment. The cash outflows are summarized in Table 21.4. First is a level rental lease plan with the same flow of payments at the end of

TABLE 21.4
REPAYMENT SCHEDULE FOR $50,000 FINANCING

Year	Level Rental	Conditional Sale Principal	Interest	Total	Chattel Mortgage Principal	Interest	Total
		$10,000		$10,000	$15,000		$15,000
1	$ 7,750	4,000 +	$ 3,200 =	7,200	3,000 +	$ 2,800	5,800
2	7,750	4,000 +	2,880 =	6,880	3,000 +	2,560	5,560
3	7,750	4,000 +	2,560 =	6,560	3,000 +	2,370	5,370
4	7,750	4,000 +	2,240 =	6,240	3,000 +	2,080	5,080
5	7,750	4,000 +	1,920 =	5,920	3,000 +	1,840	4,840
6	7,750	4,000 +	1,600 =	5,600	3,000 +	1,600	4,600
7	7,750	4,000 +	1,280 =	5,280	3,000 +	1,360	4,360
8	7,750	4,000 +	960 =	4,960	14,000 +	1,120	15,120
9	7,750	4,000 +	640 =	4,640			
10	7,750	4,000 +	320 =	4,320			
	$77,750	$50,000 +	$17,600	$67,600	$50,000 +	$15,730	$65,730

each year for ten years, based on a 10 percent return on the lessor's investment. Second is a conditional sales plan in which 20 percent of the purchase price of the asset has to be paid in advance and the remainder in ten equal installments of $4,000 each starting at the end of the first year. Interest on the unpaid balance is to be at the rate of 8 percent. Third is a chattel mortgage plan in which a 30 percent cash advance is required, the remainder to be paid in seven equal installments of $3,000 each, starting at the end of the first year, and a final payment of $14,000 at the end of the eighth year. Interest is also computed at 8 percent on the unpaid balance. The reader should understand that these are arbitrary rates used merely to illustrate a certain skill for decision making rather than to establish that one method of financing is superior to another.

Why would capital creditors be willing to finance the loans at 8 percent while the lessor expects 10 percent on his investment? Consider the following: (1) the creditor has the general credit strength of the business as well as the securing assets to depend on for ultimate payment in case of a forced liquidation; and (2) lending institutions usually have diversified investments so that losses on one investment may be offset by gains on others.

At what rate of discount should the payments be brought back to present values? We will be arbitrary in this case and select a 10 percent discounting rate. The present value of the $77,750 flow of rental payments becomes $47,624. This is the product of $7,750 annual rental and the ten-year discounting factor 6.145 from Table II in the Appendix. The tax factor has to be considered if we are to make a realistic comparison of the alternative forms. Lease rentals are deductible for taxes as interest is, but the principal payments on the debts are not deductible. So, to make a valid comparison of the flows, we can either put rental payments on an after-tax basis by multiplying by $1 - tr$, or we can put the principal payments on a before-tax basis by dividing by $1 - tr$; we will use the latter. We will assume that the business has a 40-percent tax rate. In dividing principal payments by $1 - tr$, the $10,000 advance payment on the conditional sale is raised to $16,667 determined as follows: $10,000/(1 - .40) = $16,667$. Then the ten $4,000 payments by the same method are each raised to $6,667. The $15,000 advance principal payment on the chattel mortgage is raised to $25,000 determined as follows: $15,000/(1 - .40) = $25,000$. In the same manner, the next seven payments of $3,000 are raised to $5,000 each; and the final payment of $14,000 is raised to $23,333. Table 21.5 offers a tax-adjusted comparison of the present values. Part I adjusts each of the interest payments for the two borrowing contracts to a present value basis. Part II compares the present values of the three forms. On the basis of Part II, leasing proves to be the most economical method and the chattel mortgage the most costly. The writer would emphasize, however, that this represents the order of preferences only under the assumptions that were made in this situation and is not a general statement of relative costs. The decisions in actual cases will be affected by the following variables: (1) rate of interest used by the lessor to determine level rentals, (2) interest rate charged on the individual loan contracts, (3) pattern of installment payments on the debt forms and the lease, and (4) by the selected rate of discount. Businesses falling in the higher income brackets tend to benefit from leasing rather than buying their capital assets, and any time federal income taxes increase, there should be a tendency for leasing activities to increase.

Suppose we wish to compare the costs of leasing and borrowing projects of unequal size. Then some relative measure has to be used in place of the simple dollar comparison used here for ranking the projects on a present value basis.

TABLE 21.5
PRESENT CASH VALUES COMPARED
PART I
INTEREST PAYMENTS
PRESENT VALUES

Year	Table Factor 10%		Conditional Sale Interest		Present Value	Table Factor 10%		Chattel Mortgage Interest		Present Value
1	0.909	×	3,200	=	$ 2,909	0.909	×	2,800	=	$ 2,545
2	.826	×	2,880	=	2,379	.826	×	2,560	=	2,115
3	.751	×	2,560	=	1,923	.751	×	2,370	=	1,180
4	.683	×	2,240	=	1,530	.683	×	2,080	=	1,421
5	.621	×	1,920	=	1,192	.621	×	1,840	=	1,143
6	.564	×	1,600	=	902	.564	×	1,600	=	902
7	.513	×	1,280	=	657	.513	×	1,360	=	698
8	.467	×	960	=	448	.467	×	1,120	=	523
9	.424	×	640	=	271	.424	×			
10	.386	×	320	=	123	.386	×			
			$17,600		$12,334			$15,730		$10,527

PART II
PRESENT VALUE SUMMARY

Lease rentals $7,750 × 6.145		$47,624
Conditional sale:		
Interest (Part I above)		$12,334
Advance payment	$16,667 × 1	16,667
Ten principal payments	$ 6,667 × 6.145	40,969
		69,970
Chattel mortgage:		
Interest (Part I above)		$10,527
Advance payment	$25,000	25,000
Seven payments	$ 5,000 × 4.868	24,340
Final payment	$23,333 × .467	10,897
		$70,764

One method is to compare the present values of alternative outflows of funds with the values of their respective financing projects. In Table 21.5, this was not necessary because the principal sum was a constant $50,000. But suppose that we are considering one of three alternative financing projects requiring $40,000, $60,000, and $70,000 respectively. Assume that these are labelled lease, conditional sale, and mortgage plans. According to this ranking, we are getting *most for our money* in the mortgage plan because the relative value of the outflows is less than for either one of the other two plans.

$$\text{Efficiency ratio} = \frac{\text{Present value of future outflow}}{\text{Present value of investment}}$$

$$\text{Lease plan} \qquad \frac{\$47,624}{40,000} = 1.19$$

$$\text{Conditional sale plan} \qquad \frac{69,970}{60,000} = 1.17$$

$$\text{Chattel mortgage plan} \qquad \frac{70,764}{70,000} = 1.01$$

The relative cash rankings are as follows: the lease plan is least desirable, the conditional sale is next, and the chattel mortgage plan is the most desirable; hence, the chattel mortgage plan is the investment project that will be executed from the cash flow viewpoint.

Additional Financing In considering future financing, the four borrowing forms offer interesting comparisons. The conditional sale permits no further borrowing on the security of these assets until the contract is concluded and the assets belong to the business. Until such time, the assets are owned by the financial institution; and the business is prohibited from using them to secure further borrowing. The same is true of the equipment trust since those properties belong to the trustee. Mortgages, on the other hand, in acknowledging the debtor's title to the property, usually cannot prevent him from using the same property for a second mortgage loan.

The general credit effect of the four forms on future financing is the same. They are all capitalized debt forms that increase the debt portion of the capital structure, and reduce the equity/debt relationship. Furthermore, the drains on current income are increased whenever new assets are bought with any one of these forms, and future creditors respond adversely to this in making their lending decisions. In comparing debts with the lease form, three factors should be considered. First, leases tend to be more beneficial to future financing than capital borrowing because they are not capitalized. Second, their somewhat larger cash drains on income may be discouraging to future creditors. Third, their properties are never available to secure future borrowing, even after the lease is terminated, unless the properties are purchased by the business.

External control in the four borrowing forms is directed primarily at protecting the creditors' interests in the properties. This includes allowing the creditors, or the trustee in case of public sales, to enter the premises of the business to examine the properties. The conditional sale and the equipment trust also allow the owners to take direct possession of the properties in case of a default. The two mortgage forms do not give control over the properties to the mortgagee except indirectly as the result of a foreclosure. The securing forms seldom extend their controls beyond the immediate securing properties, except that purchase money mortgages may put restrictions on future borrowing, on dividend payments, and on indiscriminate uses of net working capital.

SUMMARY

The lease plan of financing in contrast to the outright borrowing of capital for fixed asset purchases offers financial managers an opportunity to obtain the use of a maximum quantity of fixed assets with a minimum initial capital investment.

From the analysis of the discounting process on several occasions, it was seen that capital expenditures made at the beginning of the income stream and in early years of the stream have high present values. A lease contract in effect *defers* that capital expenditures to later dates. Considered from the net-cash-flow point of view the lease contract needs to be evaluated in terms of the present value of the lease payments. Making a decision to purchase or lease capital assets with the use of long-term debt contracts must be determined by making a comparison of the present values of the competing flows of cash expenditures. In deciding between competing outflows of funds, the lease plan or purchase plan will be selected which is discounted back to the lowest present value.

PROBLEMS

1. The following figures are given for three alternative methods of repaying debts created to purchase fixed assets worth $50,000. Adjust the principal payments to a before-tax basis first, assuming a 50 percent tax, and then bring the outflows of cash back to present values with the 12 percent table values given in the table below. Which of the three forms of debt contracts is the lowest cost in terms of the conservation of cash?

COMPARING THREE DEBT REPAYMENT METHODS

Year	Interest	Unadjusted Principal	12% Factor	Interest	Unadjusted Principal	12% Factor	Interest	Unadjusted Principal	12% Factor
1	$2,500		0.893	$2,500	$5,000	0.893	$2,500		0.893
2	2,500		.797	2,200	5,000	.797	2,500		.797
3	2,500		.712	2,050	5,000	.712	2,500		.712
4	2,500		.636	1,750	5,000	.636	2,500		.636
5	2,500		.567	1,500	5,000	.567	2,500	$ 5,625	.567
6	2,500		.507	1,250	5,000	.507	2,219	5,625	.507
7	2,500		.453	1,000	5,000	.453	1,937	5,625	.453
8	2,500		.404	750	5,000	.404	1,656	5,625	.404
9	2,500		.361	500	5,000	.361	1,375	5,625	.361
10	2,500	$50,000	.322	250	5,000	.322	1,000	21,875	.322

2. The Ace Construction Company owns and operates road construction equipment such as bulldozers, graders, concrete mixers, and concrete ready-mix trucks. One of the graders is ready for replacement. While the company has enough working capital on hand to buy the grader outright, the president and his chief engineer are bidding on a dam construction which, if won, will mean adding to the labor force and adding supplies, tools, and certain small equipment. Management is considering five prospects for financing the present equipment replacement: (1) an outright cash purchase, (2) a purchase on some kind of equipment contract, (3) a straight lease, (4) a lease with an option to buy, and (5) a sale and leaseback arrangement. What factors should be considered

in each in view of the company's working capital position and its desire and need for future borrowing?

3. The president of the Ace Construction Company finally decided to lease the grader instead of buying it. But he was confused by the different offers of the manufacturing company itself, of a machinery and equipment leasing company, and of a large commercial finance company. Each one argued that its method of financing was superior: the manufacturer because it offered the company a chance to get rid of the large payments by making them during the first two years, the machinery and equipment leasing company because its payments would be the same every year for five years, and the finance company because it claimed the advantage of balloon payments in which smaller payments would be made during the first three years than during the latter two. The president laid out the three plans appearing below and looked for a valuation tool that would help him choose the lowest cost plan of financing. See Appendix for discounting tables. Interest on each plan is 8 percent of the unpaid balance. Using an 8-percent discount rate, which plan actually offered the most advantageous financing for the Ace Construction Company?

	Manufacturer's Plan	*Machinery and Equipment Dealer's Plan*	*Finance Company's Plan*
1st year	$ 5,000	$ 3,000	
2nd year	5,000	3,000	$ 1,000
3rd year	2,000	3,000	1,000
4th year	2,000	3,000	2,000
5th year	2,000	3,000	13,000
Total	$16,000	$15,000	$17,000

4. The Watson Company manufactures steel wire, cables, and steel bands used for supporting heavy packing crates. The business has a profit-planning committee made up of three management officials who have been using only the time-adjustment principle in making capital investment and capital financing decisions. Recently they were confronted with an unusual problem that involved both financing and capital investment factors. They were considering adding a cold steel extruding machine to the present operating line on a lease arrangement. They found that two different machines were offered for lease. The sale price of one was $90,000 and the other $60,000, with the sum of the rental payments and the operating efficiency proportionately higher for the first. It was apparent to the committee that the decision to invest would have to turn on a comparison of the relative present values of the two outflows of rental payments expressed in the ratio:

$$\text{Payment ratio} = \frac{\text{Present value of future rentals}}{\text{Sale price of the capital investment}}$$

The following sale prices and rental payments were under consideration:

	First Machine	Second Machine
Sale price	$ 90,000	$60,000
Rentals:		
1st year	10,000	20,000
2nd year	10,000	20,000
3rd year	10,000	20,000
4th year	10,000	8,000
5th year	20,000	—
6th year	20,000	—
7th year	22,000	—
Total rentals	$102,000	$68,000

Which machine should they lease?

5. The profit committee of the Phillips Company learned that the City Bank of Cashville was interested in making loans to finance purchases of commercial and industrial machines and equipment on conditional sales contracts. Before going to the bank to inquire about the cost of the financing, the committee reviewed the general features of conditional sales financing and compared it with leasing from the viewpoints of (1) effect on working capital, (2) effect on solvency risks, (3) effect on future financing, and (4) effect on internal control. What did they discover? Explain.

6. The Samson Variety Stores, Inc. had decided to add a new unit to its present chain. The financial manager of the chain had discussed the financing of such an addition at quite some length with a life insurance company that was interested in expanding its commercial real estate investments of this nature. He discovered that the insurance company would be willing to make a mortgage loan to finance about 80 percent of the store's cost, or it would enter into a lease arrangement with the store. Since the store was to cost $40,000, this would mean that a cash investment of $8,000 (0.20 × $40,000) would be required if the mortgage were used. Deciding to let his decision rest on a comparison of the present values of the two streams of payments, the financial manager sought out the financing details of the two plans. Interest would be computed at 7 percent of the unpaid balance, and the interest and principal would be combined in annual level payments over sixteen years. The rental contract would call for annual level payments over sixteen years with interest at 8 percent on the unpaid balance. At the end of the sixteen years the insurance company would own the building.

The financial manager set up two schedules of payments for the two forms of financing, comparing the two streams of payments in actual dollars. After doing this, he noted that the interest and the rental payments were both before-tax payments but that the principal payments on the debt were after-tax payments. He adjusted the interest payments to an after-tax basis. The remainder plus average interest were discounted to the present at 8 percent. The present value of $16,000 scrap value was subtracted to get a net present value. Which financial procedure should the manager follow?

PART VIII

SPECIAL MANAGEMENT PROBLEMS

22

Changing
Ownership

In the ordinary course of business, common stock changes hands without affecting the capital structure or the purpose and operating status of the business. In special situations, however, changes in ownership are extreme; for example, the total assets of a business may be sold, holding companies may seek controlling interests in the outstanding stock, and companies may merge and consolidate their resources. This chapter will examine briefly these special ownership problems from the financial manager's viewpoint of making decisions that will have favorable effects on share values.

SALE OF TOTAL ASSETS

An interesting change takes place in ownership on the sale of total assets. The business entity exchanges the specific producing assets for cash and financial instruments like promissory notes, bonds, and stocks. The owners, on the other hand, hold the same shares of stock after the sale as before. The financial status of the owners will be affected according to the sale price of the assets; a profitable sale will add to their capital, and an unprofitable sale will subtract from their capital. Business managers may legally sell and replace some of the assets in the ordinary course of business, but selling all of the assets so alters the fundamental operations that it requires consent from common and preferred owners. Creditors cannot prevent the sale of the assets, but the loan agreement may require that the business retire its debts immediately from the proceeds of the sale. Several courses of action are open to management after the sale. One is to reinvest the proceeds in other forms of productive assets and to continue operating under an amended

493

charter. The other is to cancel the charter ribute the proceeds to the present stockholders, and dissolve the business a' her.

Theoretically, decisions to sell the s should be motivated by the same principles that motivate ordinary capi vestment decisions; that is, if financial managers have a chance to employ present capital more profitably in other lines of business or if they feel that t present shareholders could invest the funds themselves more profitably, the c al should be liquidated and the proceeds reinvested or distributed to the ers. But, unfortunately for the shareholders, this theory is seldom put into r ce. Managers are sometimes guilty of holding onto the assets too long, unti' lly they are forced to sell them at a loss. Instead of waiting to consider a sale operations are losing money, the most opportune time to sell them is when s and share values are at their peak.

CHAN TO THE HOLDING COMPANY FORM OF OWNERSHIP

We think of the ners of a business usually as natural persons instead of business entities, a business entity may hold controlling interest in another business. Control' g interest is evidenced in voting stock, usually common, and is exercised by el ing directly, or with the support of other stockholders, a majority of the boar of directors in the subsidiary company. Such *holding company* ownership may :cur practically unnoticed by management, or it may occur openly and publicly. ometimes a company desiring to secure controlling interest in another may e n advertise to purchase a certain quantity of the shares at a slight premium in c er to gain control. In some cases, the present financial managers may publicly ppose the holding company's efforts to buy the stock at bargain prices; but. course, they have no direct control over the shareholders' decisions to sell old onto their shares.

However sudden and complete the changeover in ownership may be, it does not affect the going-concern status of the business, nor does it create a different set of current and capital financial management goals and objectives from those developed in earlier chapters. But the points of emphasis and the methods and skills of financial management may be changed when controlling ownership passes from individuals to another business entity.

After the ownership change, capital expenditures and the methods of capital financing may be substantially changed. The reason for this is that a new package of capital is brought into the business. A decision may be to expand or contract greatly the capital facilities of the subsidiary. Suddenly the leverage factor may loom up in the capital structure as the holding company lends cash to its subsidiary or as it guarantees the principal and interest payments on its public bond issues. If the subsidiary issues more common stock, it will probably sell it directly to the holding company to strengthen its control over the subsidiary. The current finances of the subsidiary may not command the same amount of attention; in some cases, the new owner makes all of the current loans to its subsidiary instead of letting the subsidiary go outside the holding company system. In some cases, the present management of the subsidiary will not be changed; but, in others, it may be changed to conform to broader objectives of the holding company system as a whole.

The legality of holding company forms of ownership is often misunderstood. It is not illegal per se for a business to hold the stock or even to hold a controlling interest in other businesses; instead, it is the manner in which the control is exercised that determines legality. The Clayton Act of 1914 that restricts holding companies from acting to lessen competition does not prevent the organization of holding companies. Section 7 of the Act states:

> No corporation shall acquire, directly, or indirectly, the whole or any part of the stock or other share capital of two or more corporations engaged in commerce where the effect of such acquisition, or the use of such stock by the voting or granting of proxies or otherwise, may be to substantially lessen competition between such corporations, or any of them whose stock or other share capital is so acquired, or to restrain such commerce in any section or community, or to tend to create a monopoly of any line of commerce.

The death sentence clause of the Holding Company Act of 1935 forced many nonoperating public utility holding companies to dispose of their common stock holdings. The Act also grants the SEC (Securities and Exchange Commission) authority to help shape the capital structures of public utilities affected by the SEC's enforcement of the Act. But neither is designed to prevent legal holding company relations among public utilities.

CHANGING OWNERSHIP BY MERGING

One of the most important methods of changing the ownership status of a business that financial managers should consider at all times is outright combination of the assets, debts, and equity of two or more businesses. The typical transaction is one in which a small firm is merged into a larger firm by an exchange of the two companies' common stock. The stock of the smaller firm is cancelled, and the shareholders shift their ownership to the larger business. Owners of the businesses now have a broader capital base for more profitable long-run operations. The financial motivations for merging are the same for both businesses, namely to increase profits and/or to decrease liquidity and solvency risks. In most cases, the merger will put the merging business in a stronger position for future capital investment and financing. Theoretically, it is the responsibility of financial management to constantly seek mergers that will benefit their shareholders.

THE PARTICIPATING PARTIES

Who are the decision makers in a merger? This question is best answered by going through the merging procedure. First, the executive offices—the presidents, board chairmen, and other top-level financial managers—of the merging companies have to be in general agreement with the goals and advantages of the merger. The merger may be doomed at the start if certain officers foresee a loss of authority and prestige. But financial managers may be able to override this opposition by taking the proposal directly to the board of directors. Second, the boards of directors of both companies have to agree and accept the detailed plans for the securities exchange. Third, if the businesses are in such regulated industries as transportation, power transmission, and communication, they have another obstacle to overcome in gaining consent from the proper government regulatory commissions. Manufacturing, mining, and merchandising companies may submit their proposals to the United States Justice Department or the Federal Trade Commission for an opinion as to the legality of the proposed merger, but they are not compelled to do so. In 1950, Congress amended the Clayton Act of 1914 making it illegal to merge when the *effect of the merger is to lessen competition*; but this does not make mergers illegal nor does it require governmental approval. The fourth and final decision has to come from the shares themselves. In some cases, this is routine; but, in others, it may be the most serious stumbling block of all. Usually a two-thirds majority vote of both companies' outstanding shares is enough to consummate the merger, but an opposing minority may complain in a *court of equity* that the plan is prejudicial to their interests. As a result of the complaint, the merger may be prevented; or the firms may have to pay off the dissenting shareholders with an amount of cash representing the fair value of their shares. If the proposed merger is accepted by the necessary majority, the merged business dissolves giving up its charter of incorporation. The existence of the merging business is unaffected, and the only charter amendment that may be needed is authorization to issue new shares of stock for executing the exchange.

ROLE OF THE SENIOR SECURITY HOLDERS

Preferred stock is included in the two-thirds majority vote required to authorize a merger unless it is specifically disallowed in the charter. But even if it is disallowed, preferred shareholders as a group may complain in a court of equity that the merger would result in needless expense for the business and that it would place the preferred stock in a junior security position. If the preferred stock is redeemable and the company has cash on hand, it may just call in the preferred stock before the merger to prevent complaints and unfavorable publicity from preferred shareholder dissent. If cash is not available, it may be justifiable in some cases for a business to borrow money to retire the shares. Holders of unsecured bonds cannot prevent mergers but they may require the business to pay off its debts in cash before consummating the merger, or they may prevent the merging business from relegating the securities to a junior position in the expanded capital structure. Real estate liens follow the properties to the remaining business. *But neither secured or unsecured bondholders have the right to vote with common and preferred shareholders to approve or disapprove a merger plan.*

THE EXCHANGE OF SHARES

More than anything else financial managers are preoccupied with constructing tenable plans for securities exchange that will be acceptable to the board of directors and shareholders of both companies. Managers of the two companies are pitted against each other in negotiating for favorable terms for their respective shareholders. Three basic valuation methods are used for negotiation—the book value, the capitalized earnings value, the price-earnings value, and stock market values of the shares.

The Book Value Basis of Exchange If the book-value method is used for setting the exchange ratio, shares will be exchanged in the ratio of their book values. Some of the points of disagreement that are likely to arise in negotiation are whether or not to include intangible assets in the book values of the stock and whether or not to value fixed operating assets at their original cost less depreciation or at their reproduction value. While these issues are important, they are too controversial for our consideration here. The effect of the book-value method of exchange on the shareholders' capital interests may be clarified with an illustration. Assume that Company A is the smaller business and that Company B is the larger merging concern. The common equity structures and their respective values are illustrated in Table 22.1 below. If shares are exchanged strictly on a book-value

TABLE 22.1
COMPARATIVE BOOK VALUES OF COMPANIES A AND B

	Company A	*Company B*
Allowances for plant expansion	$125,000	$ 200,000
Common stock	300,000	1,200,000
	(30,000 shares)	(300,000 shares)
Premium from the sale of shares	100,000	300,000
Retained earnings	75,000	700,000
	$600,000	$2,400,000
Book value	$20	$8
Exchange ratio:	$20/$8	
	2.5 shares of B for 1 share of A	

basis, shares in Company A should exchange for shares in Company B in the ratio of their book values *before* the merger. In the illustration, the exchange ratio is 2.5 shares of Company B for 1 share of Company A. For each unit of capital value worth $20 in Company A, the stockholders will receive $2\frac{1}{2}$ units of ownership worth $8 each in Company B.

This is a relatively simple and a direct method of valuation; but, as financial managers, we are obligated to consider other methods that may benefit our shareholders. Book values do not reflect relative earning capacities of the two businesses. If shares have earning capacity greater than $2\frac{1}{2}$ times the shares of Company B, the book-value method leaves something to be desired for shareholders in A.

Another factor is that the book value is an accumulation of past rather than planned financial experiences. It falls down as a statement of the present value V_p of budgeted net profit pb, and the capitalized earnings method of valuation may be what is needed to show up our shares in a better light.

The Capitalized-Earnings Basis of Exchange Considering the capitalized-earnings method of valuation, the future stream of profits or cash flow that A is expected to generate becomes an important bargaining factor. The discounting mechanics are contained in the ratio: pb/d where pb is the average annual net profits that Company A expects to contribute, and d is the discounting rate. pb is the crucial variable when the firms are in the same risk class because the discounting rate d in that case would be basically the same for both businesses. But if the merging concerns are different, d as well as pb will differ for the two businesses. Let us say that A is expected to contribute \$75,000 in annual net profits and that the share earnings are expected to be \$2.50 (\$75,000/30,000). If 10 percent is a reasonable cost of capital rate, the present value of A's shares is \$25 (\$2.50/0.10) compared with \$20 in book value. Shares of A would receive a \$5 bonus above the book value by using this method of valuation. The relative and not the absolute value is the important item, of course, and this depends on what values are assessed on B. If Company B's capitalized-earnings value is no higher than \$8, the exchange ratio for A is increased from 2.5 shares to 3.5 (\$25/\$8) shares. But if Company B's capitalized-earnings values are increased as well, the advantage to A may be reduced or even be eliminated altogether.

Some concern may be expressed by the financial representatives of B at the chance that this more generous exchange of shares will *overcapitalize* their company in the postmerging period. There is no way of ascertaining this until after the merger is completed and the operation is tested except with a simulation run before the merger is completed. If they wait until the profits are earned after the merger, it may be too late to correct the condition. If profits average less than \$2.50 each for all of Company B's shares after the exchange, it may be said that the shareholders of A were too high and that B is overcapitalized; but, if earnings are more than \$2.50, it may be said that the shareholders of A were underpaid and that the merger was undercapitalized. The capitalization method is not a foolproof substitute as we can see for the book value, but there is still another approach that financial managers can make to this problem of trying to get the best exchange possible for their shareholders.

Price-earnings Basis of Exchange. The student will recognize in the capitalization rate for valuation the cost of capital d, which is the discounting rate for determining present value of a company's common shares: $V_p = pb/d$. He will also recall that the reciprocal of the cost of capital $1/d$ is the turnover ratio or the price-earnings ratio for the share. As a valuation formula, we have then $V_p = 1\, pb/d$. The same result is obtained as in capitalizing by d, except that the operation in this case is multiplication instead of division. To illustrate, we convert the capitalization rate into a price-earnings ratio as follows: P/E ratio $= 1/0.10 = 10$. Now the present value of A's common shares budgeted to earn $2.50 is:

$$V_p = \frac{1}{d} pb$$
$$= 10\ (\$2.50)$$
$$= \$25.$$

The Market Price Basis of Exchange   How effective are the investors' and speculators' valuations of the respective stocks for working out an equitable securities exchange? To many this is the most realistic approach to the problem because it is simple, direct, and objective. This method of valuation is premised on an active and accurate market valuation system for the securities of both companies. If one of the securities is actively traded and the other is not, the market method of valuation tends to lose its effectiveness; or, if communications between financial management and the securities market are more effective for one company than the other, the market will not be an accurate valuation medium.

The market valuation method is premised on the investors and speculators being accurate and objective calculators of *true* values. Throughout this book we have emphasized the importance of this assumption for attaining the common goal in financial management of share value maximization.

Let us see how it would be under marketing conditions in which expected net profits of the two companies' shares are discounted to the present, and both securities are actively traded with no inclination to manipulate the market. Historical values are of little use for this purpose. Often the negotiating parties use comparative market values of the two securities just one day prior to the exchange. If these conditions are maintained, the closing prices of the respective stocks on the day before the exchange may be the basis for exchange. And computing the exchange ratio is just as simple as dividing one stock market price into another. Assume that Company A's stock on this date was selling for $27 and Company B's for $16; the ratio of exchange then would be only 1.69 ($27/$16).

In the negotiations between financial managers, all three of the methods discussed here will probably be brought into play as representatives of the companies assert their strongest point. In most cases, the parties are willing to compromise the issues; but, in some cases, because of the failure to agree on values, the merger does not get beyond the talking stage. Mergers are usually relatively simple financial exchanges in which some kind of acceptable exchange arrangement is worked out following one or more of the patterns discussed.

CHANGING OWNERSHIP BY CONSOLIDATION

Two or more businesses may consolidate by combining their assets and capital structures in the formation of a new company. The value of the resulting business is equal to the sum of the tangible and intangible assets of the consolidating businesses. New shares are offered for the consolidation. The same general purpose motivates consolidation as motivates merging; that of maximizing the present value of remaining shares. Greater solvency for all of the stockholders may also be a factor as may be the improved prospects for future financing and control. The challenge to financial management of Company A is basically the same as in the merger—to get as generous an allocation as possible of the new shares in exchange for their old. The technicalities of negotiation differ somewhat, however, because financial managers of both companies have to dip into the same pool of shares for their stockholders. Theoretically, financial managers should aggressively seek consolidations that are favorable to their shareholders even though they may reduce the financial managers' status in the new organization, but this practice is not always followed.

THE PARTICIPATING PARTIES

The participating parties are the same as in a merger. The procedure for consolidation is as follows. First, financial representatives of the companies consider the advantages and disadvantages of consolidating and work out through negotiation what seems to be a suitable capital structure for the new company. This is an important step and may determine the long-run success or failure of the combination. Most important is the opportunity that it offers financial managers to apply the principles of capital investment and capital-structure planning that will most benefit the shares. This is a more clearly defined problem in consolidating than it is in merging because the latter is just an expansion of the common stock structure. Second, and probably a more controversial issue than the former, is rationing or allocating the new authorized shares to the shareholders of the combining businesses. This is the crucial problem of deciding what portion of the pool of shares in the new company should go to each group. When the financial managers have worked out their plans for the new capital structure and for distributing the shares among the participating stockholders, the plans have to be approved by the boards of directors of both businesses. Here they are likely to be debated at some length and sent back to the financial managers for reconsideration and possibly revision. Third, when the plan of consolidation passes the boards, it is submitted to the shareholders of both companies for approval. Letters from the presidents of the companies will be sent to the shareholders explaining the purpose and the terms and conditions of the consolidation and asking them to support it.

Minority stockholders may object to the consolidation on grounds that it is inexpedient or unfair. If the court refuses to grant an injunction against consolidation on these grounds, the objecting minority may nevertheless demand a fair cash settlement in place of taking stock in the new company. Market value is a strong criteria for deciding fair cash value, but book values and capitalized-earnings values may also play a part in settling minority shareholders' claims. Creditors are not allowed to prevent a consolidation, but they have the right to be paid in cash or to have their debts *assumed* by the new business. Secured creditors may actually be in a stronger position after consolidation than before because in addition to this security they have the general credit backing of the larger and more powerful business. If the creditors were unsecured, they remain unsecured after consolidation except that the bonds that are now assumed by the consolidated company may be less risky than they were prior to consolidation.

PLANNING THE CAPITAL STRUCTURE

The main considerations in this joint planning project are for increasing profits, decreasing wherever possible the solvency risks, and improving the chances for future financing. In planning a more profitable capital structure, financial managers have several courses of action open to them. First, the quality of the debt structure may be changed to lower the borrowing costs. Experiences in planning the capital structures of their own going concerns should qualify financial managers for planning a low-cost capital structure for the consolidation. The consolidation should be especially suited to increasing leverage on favorable cost terms. For one thing, new assets brought into a combination are available for secured borrowing on a first mortgage. If one of the businesses already has a second-mortgage bond outstanding, they may be replaced by a larger issue of *consolidated first-mortgage bonds* on favorable borrowing terms. Introducing serial bonds and adding sinking-fund and conversion provisions to the debentures are other refinements of the debt forms that may reduce borrowing costs. The risks of fluctuating incomes are apparent, although consolidation itself may help stabilize long-run incomes through price and market control in the operating equation $P = X(b - c) - a$. Maybe the consolidating businesses are already overleveraged; then the number one problem is to plan a higher cost structure with less built-in risk by the issuance of common and preferred stock. Since the creditors cannot be expected to exchange their debt securities voluntarily for equities, the proceeds from a public marketing of the latter may be used to retire the indebtedness until the planned balance is attained.

Special attention should also be given to the needs for new financing after consolidation. Decisions made today to consummate the consolidation will influence capital and short-term financing in the future, which may spell the success or failure of the whole project. For future borrowing, particularly unsecured, relatively large equity structures are best. Secured borrowing is benefited somewhat by the large equity structure but not as much as unsecured. Secured borrowing is affected mainly by the quality of the fixed assets. Sometimes consolidating the retained earnings alone of two companies provides a favorable basis for future external financing of all kinds. If common stock financing is planned, we need to consider again the benefits of debt leverage in the present consolidated structure. An overcapitalized equity structure may be more detrimental to common stock financing in the future than an overcapitalized debt structure because of its effect on the cost of capital. But because of the added risk of loss, the heavily leveraged debt structure may itself cause E_e and the resulting cost of capital d to rise sharply.

THE EXCHANGE OF SHARES

The proportion of the total capital value contributed by each company to the consolidation determines the share rationing. To illustrate the effect of valuation methods, we will assume that the shares are rationed by the book-value, capitalized-earnings-value, and market-value methods. It is agreed that the new consolidated Company C should authorize 400,000 common shares. Company A is expected to contribute $75,000 annually and Company B $300,000 annually to the consolidated company's earnings. The capitalization rate for the industry is 10 percent resulting in capital contributions of $750,000 and $3 million respectively. The market price of the stock of Company A with 30,000 shares is $27 and of Company B with 300,000 shares is $16, which results in capital values of $810,000 and $4.8 million respectively. A summary of the methods and their effect on share rationing is illustrated in Table 22.2. These shares will be distributed to shareholders on a pro rata basis.

TABLE 22.2
EXCHANGE OF SHARES COMPARATIVE VALUATION METHODS

		% of Total		Total Shares		Shares Distributed
Book values:						
Company A	$ 600,000	20	×	400,000	=	80,000
Company B	$2,400,000	80	×	400,000	=	320,000
Company C	$3,000,000	100				400,000
Capitalized earnings:						
Company A	$ 750,000	20	×	400,000	=	80,000
Company B	3,000,000	80	×	400,000	=	320,000
Company C	$3,750,000	100				400,000
Market values:						
Company A	$ 810,000	14.44	×	400,000	=	57,760
Company B	4,800,000	85.56	×	400,000	=	342,240
Company C	$5,610,000	100.00				400,000

SUMMARY

This chapter considers issues of changing ownership as a form of special financial management problem. Considered here are the financial effects of offering for sale all of a company's assets. This brings into the company a fund of cash which must either be reinvested if the firm would stay in business or be used to liquidate the business and to distribute to the present shareholder the cash resources. A second form of changing ownership is establishing the holding company as a means of control. Third, ownership in a business may be changed by merging with some other corporation. Mergers result in the dissolution of one of the merging companies and continuing the other, with a resulting larger quantity of assets and a larger capital structure. The main problems confronted in merging are related to the valuation of the respective companies and their shares for working out a fair and equitable exchange. Finally, a change in ownership may occur through a consolidation of two or more firms. Consolidation means eliminating the identity of all of the original firms and forming a new corporate identity. The corporate problems involved are very similar to those of a merger, consisting primarily of working out a reasonable exchange of shares for old shares of the companies joining in the consolidation.

PROBLEMS

1. The Vandrew Corporation advertised in several metropolitan newspapers that it would buy all shares tendered by the common stockholders of Drawvan Corporation for $15 per share and pay 20 cents per share for brokerage services. The buyer also offered to pay the sellers' federal and state transfer taxes. There were 20,000 shares outstanding.

    a. How would you classify this kind of change in ownership?

    b. How much would the transaction cost Vandrew if all outstanding shares were purchased?

    c. Suppose less than 100 percent of the shares are tendered for sale. Would the purpose of the financing have failed? Explain.

    d. Show how this kind of financing might be used as an intermediary step to a merger.

2. Companies X and Y having the following capital structures are considering a merger.

	X	Y
Capital debt	$1,000,000	
Preferred stock (20,000 shares @ $100 each)	2,000,000	$ 1,000,000 (10,000 shs @ $100 each)
Common stock (100,000 shares @ $50 each)	5,000,000	8,000,000 (200,000 shs @ $40 each)
Retained earnings	1,000,000	2,000,000
Total	$9,000,000	$11,000,000

    a. Suppose that Y takes the initiative for merging. Does the company have enough common shares to implement a merger?

    b. Explain how capital budgeting tools and skills developed in earlier chapters can be used to plan a merger such as this.

    c. If book value is used as the exchange basis, what would the shareholders in X receive for each share given up? Would shareholders in X be penalized for having capital debt in the structure? What happens to the capital debt if the merger is consummated?

    d. What will happen to the two preferred stocks if the companies merge?

    e. Annual E_e per share for X is $5 and for Y it is $4 before the merger.

Using a 12 percent discounting rate, what would the exchange ratio be for the shares?

   f. Compute an average exchange ratio for the shares using the three methods discussed in the chapter assuming that X's shares sell for $45 and Y's for $65 in the market.

   g. Could a merger like this affect Company Y's cost of capital? Explain.

   h. Could more than two companies be merged simultaneously?

3. Companies A and B below decide to consolidate their resources.

A		B	
Current assets	$400,000	Current assets	$ 100,000
Fixed assets	100,000	Fixed assets	1,000,000
Total	$500,000	Total	$1,100,000
Current liabilities	$100,000	Current liabilities	100,000
Capital stock	200,000	Capital debt	300,000
Retained earnings	200,000	Capital stock	500,000
		Retained earnings	200,000
Total	$500,000	Total	$1,100,000

   a. What justification is there for a consolidation in this case, considering liquidity and solvency?

   b. Could the consolidation be treated as a capital budgeting problem? Explain. Suppose that expansion is considered simultaneously with the consolidation. How would you use capital budgeting techniques in this case?

   c. If you were in the financial management organization of X, what aspect of your financial condition would you emphasize to benefit your shareholders in a merger or a consolidation?

   d. What additional information is needed to bring about an equitable exchange of shares in a consolidation of the two businesses?

   e. Could more than two companies organize simultaneously to form a consolidation?

   f. Comment on the difference between the purposes of capital planning and capital structure planning in a consolidation.

23

Modifying and Reorganizing the Capital Structure

In this chapter we will consider remedies for two types of financial mismanagement. In one, the capital structure is out of tune with operations and causes serious threats to solvency and profitability. When this develops, modifying the capital structure may save the business from failure. In the other, the business has failed already, and modifying the capital structure is not enough; a complete reorganization of the structure may preserve the going concern and prevent a forced liquidation.

NEGOTIATING MODIFICATIONS

To avoid insolvency and complete business failure, financial managers may negotiate with their creditors and preferred and common stockholders for modifications in their contracts that will decrease risk and increase the chances of future profits and firmer share values.

A TOP-HEAVY DEBT STRUCTURE

A debt structure is top-heavy when the flow of funds from operations is not enough to service and maintain it. When this happens, some kind of action has to be taken to change the debt portion of the structure. In privately placed debts, the first thought is to take our problem to the creditor; but if the debt is publicly held, the indenture trustee has to be contacted. The business is further handicapped in a public holding by the high cost of negotiating concessions from what may amount to hundreds or even thousands of bondholders. As a practical matter, therefore, modifications of debt structure may be limited to privately placed debts. Some of the *refinancing* granted by the creditors in this case may be lower interest rates, income bond, or notes in exchange for regular interest-bearing bonds, extended maturity dates on the debts, readjusted installment payments on inter-mediate and long-term debts, and removal or postponement of sinking-fund pay-ments. Getting the creditors to agree to these concessions may require giving them stock purchase options, debts with conversion privileges, or stock with multiple voting rights. If the debts are single-payment contracts, the creditor may extend their maturities but put them on an installment basis to keep closer control over the funds.

A TOP-HEAVY PREFERRED STOCK STRUCTURE

Mismanagement of capital finances may be evidenced by a disproportionate amount of preferred stock as well as debts, compared with the income flow required to service their cumulative dividends. Negotiations with preferred shareholders may result in noncumulative in place of cumulative dividends. If a fixed sinking-fund clause should be the cause of cash shortage, changing this to sinking-fund payments that fluctuate with profits may be the solution. In extreme cases, preferred shareholders may be asked to accept common in place of preferred shares, thus making them junior security holders and possibly weakening the present common stockholders' control over the business; in exchange for these modifications, man-agement can expect the preferred shares to request warrants to purchase common stock, options to convert their stock to common, and special voting rights. If management is allowed to substitute noncumulative for cumulative preferred in refinancing, the dividend rate on the noncumulative shares may have to be raised slightly.

MODIFYING TO REMOVE DIVIDEND ARREARAGE

The prospect of dividend arrearages is always a threat to the business with cumulative preferred stock; and, until the condition is corrected, the cost of both common and preferred stock capital is bound to increase to the disadvantage of the present share values. Dividend delinquencies usually also give the preferred share increased voting power that may transfer control of the business from com-mon stockholders' shares and even unseat the present management. Arrearages are footnoted in the balance sheet instead of being included in the dividends payable of the current liabilities because they are not debts of the business. Some of the most extreme cases of dividend arrears occurred in the railroad industry. The only chance of removing the delinquency is by appealing to the stockholders to accept some kind of settlement of cash, securities, special controls over management, or a combination of these.

The challenge is to get the preferred shareholders to accept a settlement that will remove the arrears causing a minimum loss in present common share values. From the long-run viewpoint, modifications should give special consideration to preventing a recurrence of the arrearages. If a cash settlement is offered, the preferred shareholders may agree to cancel a certain percentage of their claims altogether. Borrowing to pay arrears may even be justifiable if paying them off clears the slate for future equity financing at lower capital costs. Whether or not a business can afford to take the risk of borrowing to retire preferred obligations depends on the prospects for future income to repay the debt. A good policy may be to clear the capital structure of the source of the trouble at the same time that the arrears are removed, by redeeming the preferred stock itself or by offering to exchange common stock, or even by extending capital debts if the cost of borrowed capital is low enough to compensate for taking the added risk. Since redemption of preferred stock requires first that all accumulated dividends be paid, this may be the time to offer the shareholders a package deal composed of cash to redeem the preferred stock, and new security forms to remove the dividend arrears all at the same time.

Attention is called briefly to the balance sheet effects of correcting arrearages. Several adjustments may have to be made on the books to keep them in balance. For example, when cash is used to retire the arrears, an asset is lost without reducing debts correspondingly. The loss in cash has to be offset then by reducing retained earnings or even the common stock itself. The advantage of using retained earnings is that the adjustments can be made without shareholder consent, while reducing the value of the common stock shares requires consent from the shareholders. In either case, the net effect is the same; the size of business assets and the size of the capital structure are reduced. The effect of changing the par value of preferred stock for the settlement of preferred dividend arrears with a new issue of common stock is illustrated in Table 23.1; $100,000 in preferred divi-

TABLE 23.1
RETIRING PREFERRED STOCK ARREARS WITH A NEW CLASS OF COMMON

	Capital Structure with Arrears*	Capital Structure without Arrears
Common stock (30,000 shares)	$3,000,000	$3,000,000
Common stock (Class B)	—	100,000
Preferred stock (10,000 shares)	1,000,000	900,000
	(Par $100)	(Par $90)
Capital debt	500,000	500,000
Total	$4,500,000	$4,500,000

*$100,000 cumulative dividend arrears

dend arrears are retired by giving the shareholders an equivalent quantity of newly authorized Class B common stock and by reissuing with the stockholders consent a $90 par value preferred stock in place of the present $100 par. To do this consent is required from preferred and common shareholders.

OVERCOMING A PAR VALUE HANDICAP

If stock sales are handicapped by high par values, the solution lies in lowering their values or in removing par values altogether. This requires shareholders' consent and charter amendment, but it should not be difficult to obtain if it is understood that reducing the values has no effect essentially on the shareholders' capital interests. The effect on the equity structure is to reduce common stock and to increase stock premium as illustrated in Table 23.2. The capital structure

TABLE 23.2
REDUCING PAR VALUES AND CREATING A STOCK PREMIUM

	Capital Structure Before Reducing Par Value	Capital Structure After Reducing Par Value
Common stock (30,000 shares)	$3,000,000	$ 750,000
	($100 par)	($25 par)
Stock premium	—	2,250,000
Preferred stock (10,000 shares)	1,000,000	1,000,000
Capital debt	500,000	500,000
	$4,500,000	$4,500,000

is modified by reducing the par value of common stock from $100 to $25, thereby creating a stock premium for the 30,000 shares of $2.24 million. By removing par value entirely, the capital stock account would simply be whatever value is arbitrarily stated; and the balance would all go into stock premium. Nothing is accomplished by this transaction except to remove the legal obstruction to selling shares at a price below $100.

REDUCING BOOK AND MARKET VALUES

The most direct way to reduce book and market values of individual shares is to split the shares. This may set the stage for a new common stock issue by generating activity in the market for the lower priced shares. Whether this effort will succeed depends on stockholders' willingness to accept new lower security values in place of the old. The effect of the stock split on the capital structure is to increase the total number of shares without affecting the equity structure as a whole or the capital interests of individual shareholders as a whole.

LEGAL REGULATION

In 1948, the Mahaffie Act [Section 20(b) of the Interstate Commerce Act] was passed by Congress to allow the Interstate Commerce Commission to assist in railroad recapitalizations with the hope of avoiding bankruptcy and complete reorganization for some companies. The Commission may accept or reject a recapitalization plan submitted by the company, or the Commission may accept it subject to certain adjustments. After it is accepted by the Commission, it is offered to the security holders for their approval. Acceptance by 75 percent of the affected securities makes the plan binding on the minority group. Security holders whose interests are not affected by the plan do not vote on its proposals. Any group contending that their property rights would be impaired may ask the court to review the plan, but there are no provisions for cash settlements or privileged treatment of insurgent security holders. Of some historical interest may be the fact that shortly after passage of the Act, the Commission allowed the Boston and Maine Railroad to issue 811,268 shares of common stock to retire eight classes of preferred stock and the old common by offering 2.75 shares of common for 1 share of Prior Preferred; 1.37 share of common for 1 share of 5 percent Series A preferred; 0.47 share of common for 1 of 8 percent Series B preferred; 0.44 share of common for 1 share of 7 percent Series C preferred; 0.54 share of common for 1 share of 10 percent Series D preferred; 0.35 share of common for 1 share of $5\frac{1}{2}$ percent Series E preferred; 0.07 share of common for 1 share of unserialed 6 percent preferred; and 0.05 share of new common for 1 share of unserialed 6 percent preferred; and 0.05 share of new common for 1 share of the old.

BUSINESS FAILURE AND REORGANIZING THE CAPITAL STRUCTURE

According to one definition of failure, a business has failed unless it continues to generate profits. But this kind of failure does not necessarily lead to bankruptcy and reorganization of the capital structure. A more common meaning of failure is insolvency, or inability of a business to meet its debts when they come due. This definition ties business failure to the flow of funds. Another meaning of business failure puts the accent on balance sheet values; according to this meaning, a business fails when it is *legally insolvent*, meaning that its equity structure (including the preferred stock section) is a negative value. Stated in terms of total assets and total liabilities, a business fails when its total liabilities (long-term and short-term) exceed its total assets. When this stage is reached, the equity structure of the business must be a negative value. Looking at it from the fund-management viewpoint, the *legal* meaning of insolvency may not actually be very different from the financial. The terms *bankruptcy* and *remedies in bankruptcy* are found in federal and state bankruptcy statutes. Grounds for bankruptcy exist whenever it is established that the business would be unable now or later to pay its debts fully. Financial managers of business are concerned primarily with the *remedies* for bankruptcy, particularly as they apply to reorganizing the capital structures of incorporated businesses and getting them back into operation.

Despite evidence of business failures on all sides, much disagreement still exists as to what causes them. Local surveys and national surveys have been made on the causes of business failure, and newspaper surveys and professional studies by the United States Department of Commerce and by private credit-rating agencies such as Dun and Bradstreet have been conducted to look for some common controllable cause or causes of failure. An important discovery brought out in the statistics of business failure is that the causes change over time. In the first few years after World War II, for example, business failures were attributed primarily to scarcity of inventories, scarcity of skilled labor, and scarcity of capital equipment. By the 1950's the brunt of responsibility was placed squarely on management, and it rests there still. Incompetence and inexperience are given as the two major causes of business failure. This plus the fact that a large percentage of business failures are among relatively new businesses should serve as a warning to those planning to organize new businesses.

The capital structures of failed businesses were reorganized under common-law procedures long before the present bankruptcy laws were written, and common-law *extensions* and *compositions* of capital and current debts are still recognizable forms of financial reorganization. Extensions are agreements by creditors to extend the maturity date on defaulted debts. The creditors mutually agree not to sue the business for default until it has had a certain time extension in which to pay its debts. All creditors are not forced to cooperate, however, and those that do not may sue the business while the creditors making the extension stand aside in hopes that the business will be able to survive the suits and maintain its operations. The theory behind the extension is that, if the main creditors agree to withhold legal action until the business overcomes its crisis, it may recover and become stronger in the future. This is a simple and temporary form of reorganization that may be successful in some cases where there are a small number of large creditors who are able to influence others to fall into line with the plan. But this form of reorganization has a serious shortcoming; this simple reorganization plan makes no attempt to get to the bottom of the problem.

Compositions are agreements in which the creditors decide to readjust their claims and to take less than their face amount in full settlement of the debts. This reduces the size of the debt structure and gives the business a new start without going through bankruptcy proceedings. But it is also more successful generally when the debts are held by a few large creditors. All creditors are not forced to go along on the agreement, and those that do not may sue the business for their defaulted debts. Compositions fall short of the main purpose in reorganization, which is to correct the errors in the capital structure that caused the present defaults. Reducing the balance of the defaulted debt may be a temporary solution, but what solution does it offer for the debt not yet matured and those not yet incurred?

Equity reorganizations had been the typical method of solving bankruptcy problems of incorporated businesses short of complete liquidation; but since the 1933 and 1938 amendments to the bankruptcy laws, corporate bankruptcy proceedings are taken to Federal District Courts. The court had dominated the equity reorganization proceedings that had been forced on the business by the creditors. In fulfilling the purpose of his office, the judge was concerned with equitable distributions of securities or assets to the creditors and not primarily with preservation of the going concern. A legal representative received and managed the corporate properties during reorganization to preserve the creditors' interests. The receiver was given wide jurisdiction in recommending to the court certain operating and financing policies for the bankrupt business. An important factor was that during its receivership the business could not be sued nor would it be allowed to pay its debts except with consent of the court. In the meantime, creditors were organizing in separate camps to plan reorganization strategy.

Protective committees with their self-appointed leaders sprang up to represent and to write the plan for a totally reorganized capital structure. The leader of the committee was usually a large creditor or an investment banker who had underwritten the debt issue and who felt a responsibility for protecting his clients holding the debts. This meant that reorganization settled down to a struggle between different protective committees, each one with its own reorganization plan to submit. Clients deposited their securities and agreed that they would take no independent action against the business and that they would follow the procedure set down by the protective committee. Although the committee agreed to report its actions to the creditors, it reserved the right to make and enforce its own rules of conduct. The court would accept what it deemed the most equitable plan for all of the security holders, but it reserved the right to adjust the plans, to reject them all, or to appoint a reorganization committee with representatives from the various creditor classes. It is easy to see why months and sometimes even years passed before a final plan was accepted. In the meantime, the business often exhausted its resources to the point of no return.

<h2 style="text-align:center">SPECIAL CORPORATE REORGANIZATION</h2>

During the years of the Great Depression the instrumentalities for equity reorganizations fell far short of meeting the needs of the period. Congress realized that new reorganization machinery was needed to service large incorporated forms of business. The philosophy behind the legislation was to maintain the going concern as a productive unit that would take up the slack of unemployed human and natural resources.

Railroad Reorganization The overleveraged capital structures of the railroads made them the first casualties of the economic crisis and depression. And it was this industry that most needed public assistance in reorganizing its mismanaged capital structures. In 1933, Section 77 of the Federal Bankruptcy Act permitted railroads to petition the Federal District Court in a *voluntary* bankruptcy proceeding. The law allows any railroad that is insolvent in the financial or legal sense to declare itself a voluntary bankrupt and to submit to the court a proposed plan of reorganization. It also allows creditors holding 5 percent or more of the company's defaulting debts to declare the company a bankrupt. An important step was taken when this legislation gave the leading role in the reorganization to a disinterested third party, the *trustee in bankruptcy*, instead of to the creditors themselves. The trustee is appointed for the specific purpose of constructing with the aid of the Interstate Commerce Commission and creditor representatives a fair and feasible capital structure reorganization. Protective committees may be formed but only after the completed plan has been submitted and accepted by the court. Then if creditors feel that they are being treated unjustly, they may form what amounts to grievance committees. When, after this, the plan is finally accepted it shall:

> ... be binding upon the debtor, all stockholders thereof, including those who have not, as well as those who have, accepted it, and those adversely affected by the plan, and whether or not their claim shall have been filed, and, if filed, whether or not approved, including creditors who have not, as well as those who have, accepted it.

The property is returned to the original company or to a newly chartered company, and that company has another chance now to operate profitably outside the shadows of its past failures as ". . . the debtor shall be discharged from its debts and liabilities, except such as may consistently with the provisions of the plan be reserved in the order confirming the plan. . . ."

Reorganization Under Chapters X and XI All corporations except railroads may now be reorganized voluntarily or involuntarily under Chapter X of the Bankruptcy Laws, the Chandler Act, passed by Congress in 1938. The first action of the bankruptcy court is to prevent management from paying business debts, and creditors are prevented from bringing suit against the business. The actual work of planning the reorganization is delegated by the court to the trustee in bankruptcy. The SEC (Securities and Exchange Commission), the creditors, and even the stockholders may be requested by the trustee to express opinions, but they are not given decision-making authority. From the procedural viewpoint, this is the major difference between a reorganization in a special bankruptcy court and a reorganization in equity.

The plan of reorganization, of course, determines the quantity and quality of debts and equity in the capital structure. The final plan must contain provisions that change the original status of one or more classes of creditors, and it must state which creditors' claims, if any, are to be paid in cash in full and which are not to be affected at all by the plan. The most important part of the plan deals with lowering the solvency risk in the capital structure and building a sound foundation for future operations. In general, any exchange of securities that lowers the risk makes it easier to do short- and long-term financing after the reorganization. The plan may provide for cancellation or modification of bond indentures and loan agreements, extending the maturity dates on existing debts, changing interest rates, and issuance of new securities. Unsecured debts may be offered in exchange for secured; and, to give them special appeal, they may be made convertible into common stock; or they may contain warrants to purchase stock at a low price. If income bonds exist at the time of failure, preferred stock may replace them. Preferred and common shares may be offered in place of secured and unsecured debts in some cases if the future income flow seems too uncertain to support fixed liabilities. Preferred shares may receive common shares in exchange; but, if the whole equity structure is a negative value at the time of bankruptcy as it often is, the old owners are automatically eliminated. This raises the important question of who shall be the new owners of the reorganized business. The creditors may be if they received common stock in place of their debts and depending on whether or not they keep the stock or sell it.

Separate procedure may take place under Chapter XI of the Federal Bankruptcy Act instead of Chapter X. This is less formal than reorganization under Chapter X; it has been described as not so harsh partly for the reason that the SEC does not automatically participate in the reorganization plan. It is felt by some that the SEC's treatment adds severity to the procedure of reorganization under Chapter X that is not present in dealing with the bankruptcy under Chapter XI. Reorganization under this chapter must be requested by the failed business and results usually in arrangements through extensions and compositions similar to those worked out in the common law.

By way of general observation, it should be pointed out that bankruptcy proceedings do not follow closely the analysis that have been developed throughout this book. That is, share values are disregarded altogether in decision making for reorganization; the primary concern of the bankruptcy court is to treat creditors fairly and keep the business solvent temporarily at least. Neither is the cost of capital given serious consideration in recommending the makeup of the capital structure. One reason that reorganized businesses have difficulty regaining financial stability and growth is that the new capital structure is not planned carefully from the financial manager's point of view, considering costs of borrowing and their effect on cost of capital and common share values.

SUMMARY

Modifying and reorganizing the capital structure is quite different from changing ownership through the sale of assets or the merger or consolidation of two or more companies. This latter situation is concerned with maintaining the same business entity and leaving basically undisturbed its total assets and the balance of assets and concentrating altogether on improving the solvency condition of the company's capital structure by reducing long-term debts. In some cases the market price of common shares may be aided by also removing preferred shares from the capital structure or modifying their dividend terms. These debts, while effective during periods of high profits, may burden the business with fixed obligations that could cause insolvency and lead to bankruptcy as well. In case of bankruptcy, a corporation may appeal to the bankruptcy courts for assistance in reorganizing their capital structures to lighten their debt burden in the hopes of continuing in business with fewer debts and a greater ratio of net capital than in the past. Services of efficient and knowledgeable financial managers are important even at this late stage of corporation existence, although the goals of the financial managers at this stage are oriented to salvaging the resources in a desperate effort to retain the going-concern status of the firm.

PROBLEMS

1. The following capital structure represents the condition of your business at the present time. You decide to clear the preferred-dividend arrears off your records by issuing a new class of nonvoting common stock and to redeem the preferred stock.

PRESENT CAPITAL STRUCTURE

Capital debt	$ 60,000
Preferred (6% cumulative)	400,000*
Common (100,000 shares) ($10 par)	1,000,000
Capital surplus	500,000
Retained earnings	100,000
Total	$2,060,000

*$96,000 in arrears

    a. Is your company insolvent in either the financial or legal sense?

    b. Does the $100,000 of retained earnings indicate funds available for dividends?

    c. How could you be delinquent on dividends and still have retained earnings?

    d. Trace the procedure required to accomplish the plan of removing arrears and retiring preferred stock. Would it be feasible and justifiable to borrow to retire preferred stock in this case?

    e. Reconstruct the capital structure showing the results of your plan. What do you expect the new plan to do, if anything, for (1) profits, (2) liquidity, (3) solvency, (4) cost of capital, and (5) present share values?.

2. At $130, the price of your stock had risen above the popular stock price bracket for the companies of your type. You had noticed a low turnover of your shares, and you feel that the stock is not reflecting the full impact of supply and demand. You decide to recommend a four-for-one stock split to remedy this. The condition of your capital structure before the split is illustrated below.

PRESENT CAPITAL STRUCTURE

Capital debt	$ 100,000
Preferred (5% cumulative)	300,000
Common (500,000 shares) ($80 par)	4,000,000
Capital surplus	2,000,000
Retained earnings	1,000,000
Total	$7,400,000

    a. What procedure would be followed to accomplish the stock split?

    b. Reconstruct the capital structure showing the modifying effect.

    c. Why should you care whether or not the full impact of the market is felt by your stock since your business does not receive cash from the securities market?

d. How would this refinancing affect, if at all, future (1) profits, (2) liquidity, (3) solvency, (4) cost of capital, (5) share values?

3. The new management of Company Y inherited the following capital structure:

PRESENT CAPITAL STRUCTURE

First and refunding mortgage bonds due 1990	$ 22,500,000
General consolidating mortgage bonds due 2000	120,000,000
First cumulative adjustment bonds due 1980	40,000,000*
Equipment obligations	60,000,000
Prior preferred stock (8% cumulative)	100,000,000
Cumulative preferred stock (7½% cumulative)	50,000,000†
Common stock (1,000,000 shares @ $100 par)	100,000,000
Retained earnings	10,000,000‡
Total	$502,000,000

*$10,000,000 interest arrears
†$60,000,000 interest arrears
‡$20,000,000 interest arrears

a. What kind of a company is this most likely to be?
b. What is the book value of its common stock, and how close do you expect the market and book values of the stock to be to each other?
c. Reconstruct this capital structure incorporating modifications that you deem feasible under the present laws for refinancing and recapitalization. Be sure that you give the long-run interests of the present stockholders primary consideration.

4. The following capital structure is in default and has been proclaimed a bankrupt under Chapter X of the Federal Bankruptcy Laws by action of the first mortgage bondholders who had not been receiving their interest payments. Assume that you are hired by the trustee in bankruptcy to assist in writing a reorganization plan. List and justify the proposals that you would offer considering the dual purpose of treating the present creditors fairly and at the same time exercising the utmost consideration for continuing an organization wherein the business can look forward to profits and rising share values.

INSOLVENT CAPITAL STRUCTURE

First mortgage bonds	$20,000,000
Second mortgage bonds	10,000,000
Debenture bonds	10,000,000
Income bonds	5,000,000
Preferred stock	40,000,000
Common stock	90,000,000
Retained earnings	(140,000,000)
Total	$35,000,000*

*Gross capital consists of $15 million fixed assets, $10 million inventories, $5 million receivables, and $5 million cash.

24

Planning
a
New
Business

The purpose of organizing a new business is the same as that of operating a going concern, namely to generate profit and to increase share values. In this chapter, we will review first the general policy considerations in financial management as they apply to organizing a new business. Second, we will analyze the specific legal forms of business and determine how each choice affects the general problem areas in financial management.

GENERAL POLICY CONSIDERATIONS

Whatever form the new business takes, the actual organization should always be preceded by financial planning, which means in this case projecting different aspects of short- and long-run operations and fund management for some time in the future. We reverse the order of planning, however, from that of the going concern. First, the capital plan has to be established for the new concern, and then the short-run operation and its supporting fund management issues are fitted into the capital plan.

ESTABLISHING THE CAPITAL PLAN

The capital plan establishes the limits, as we have learned, for decision making in current operations; and, unless these limits are established in a sound way before the first day of operations, the new business may be destined for an early failure. We have learned also that the basic limiting factors in the long-run operation are the plans for budgeting capital uses of funds and budgeting capital sources of funds.

Budgeting Capital Expenditures The quantity and quality of capital expenditures in the early years of operation are affected primarily by the type of business and the size of its initial operations. For example, to organize a public utility or communication business would require large quantities of tangible and intangible fixed capital such as franchises, rights-of-way, land, buildings, pipelines, wire lines, cables, and machinery and equipment. The individual items of capital will differ as will the methods of financing them; but, in both of these industries, fund uses will be directed primarily to fixed-capital investment rather than to net working capital. The scale of operations has to be large right at the start because of the large quantity of fixed capital, the high level of fixed costs, and the resulting high-level break-even point.

The capital expenditure problems of manufacturing and merchandising businesses run a wider gamut, with some requiring much more fixed capital than others. But in new manufacturing businesses, working capital always raises a major planning problem. The starting scale of operations also has a wider range than public service businesses. Thus, a steel or automobile manufacturing company would have to start at higher percentage of its operating capacity to break even than almost any kind of a wholesale or retail merchandising business.

One of the most challenging problems for the financial organizer is knowing how much investment is needed to meet the minimum long-run operating needs of the business and how much is needed to meet certain efficiency standards and profit goals for those first crucial years. Aside from having to decide on the size of the capital budget, the financial organizer is confronted with making decisions between competing capital assets. This is where internal rate of return and present dollar value analysis can be applied for ranking competing capital proposals. The fact that the business is new does not prevent the organizer from judging investment proposals by using a cost of capital cutoff at the start that is representative of the risk class that the new company is entering. In fact one business proposal can be weighed against another proposal in terms of their comparative internal rates of return. For example, the internal rate of return on a combined net-working-capital and fixed-capital investment in a proposed men's clothing store may be compared with the internal rate of return from a women's specialty shop and with the internal rate of return from a children's store.

The Capital Financing Plan The capital financing plan is the problem basically of planning the sources of capital funds for the new business. If there still is a doubt about the relationship between capital fund sources and uses in the going concern, that doubt should be erased now as sources and uses of funds are considered for the new concern. We can see clearly that the capital sources in the new business are the limiting factors to capital investment because the organizers depend on external sources of funds for their initial capital; and, if investors withhold their funds, they can prevent the business from organizing right at the start.

The capital structure of the new business is as important to its welfare as in the going concern. But the high risk of failure in the new business tends to limit the scope of planning to a simple capital structure with a minimum of solvency risk and profit leverage. In the new business, the risk of loss turns on mismanagement of the assets because capital debts seldom appear in the capital structure. The cost of capital in the new business for this reason is high; to sell shares of stock in a new business, the organizers have to promise a higher rate of return E_e/P_m than is required in the going concern.

The future financing potential and, therefore, the expansion prospects for the business are affected by the quantity of equity that the organizers themselves supply and by the quantity of supporting equity capital that they can interest others in supplying. The larger this initial amount of equity funds the better chance the new business has of borrowing on an unsecured as well as on a secured basis in the near future. We are all familiar with the important part played by the equity structure in short- as well as long-term borrowing. But borrowing potential of the new business is affected by how the funds are invested in the business as well as by whether they are equity or debt funds. Thus, funds invested in fixed capital usually have less short-term borrowing potential than the same amount of equity invested initially in net working capital. And there are different degrees of borrowing value within each of the two general classes of working and fixed capital. The borrowing value of working capital, for example, is affected by whether the funds are invested in marketable securities, receivables, or investories; and the borrowing value of fixed assets is affected by whether the funds are invested in machinery and equipment or land and buildings. A 20 percent or smaller equity investment will usually meet the down payment on new machinery and equipment on a conditional sale or chattel mortgage, where a larger percentage may be needed for a purchase money mortgage on land and buildings. And the same fixed-capital facilities that can be bought with 20 percent equity would yield only a fraction of their cost on a cash loan after the assets are used. Short-term credit may be obtained for the first sixty days, but after that cash generating potential has to be proven to obtain credit.

An important question before the organizer is how much to borrow to supplement the initial equity. In some cases, this question is answered for him by the creditors but, in others, the equity margin may be large enough to create considerable flexibility. Where the flexibility exists, the decision should turn on the issues of risk, profitability, and control. Even if it means expanding the equity of the business again soon after organization at a relatively high cost of capital which will be apparent in the low P_m and high E_e, this may be a sounder policy than to shoulder the new business with the risks particularly of capital debts. While retained earnings would be ideal for their low risk, this is not a feasible source of funds in the first years of operation. One other important source of capital to the new business, however, that the organizer should not fail to consider is the capital lease. This may have a great impact on the amount of borrowing that is needed and may even reduce substantially the need for equity. Some equity is needed in the capital structure for leasing but usually not as much as would be needed for borrowing to gain possession and use of fixed capital.

It was seen in an earlier chapter that the risks and costs of the lease relative to capital borrowing vary according to the terms of the agreements and the preference for termination and renewal options. But in a new organization when cash funds are scarce, this may be a less risky alternative than putting a long-term debt in the capital structure. In making cost comparisons between leasing and purchasing fixed capital, allowance should be made for the comparative present values of the two flows as was done in Chapter 21. Differences in the extent of the control exercised by creditors and lessors over the assets at this stage are inconsequential by comparison with the risk and profitability considerations of the alternative methods of financing.

One other important factor to consider in planning capital finances is the establishment of contacts with financial institutions. It is one thing to decide on what forms of financing should be used to supplement the equity capital but still another to locate the sources that are willing to supply the funds on favorable terms. What services can the organizers expect from the securities exchanges and over-the-counter markets? There is little chance that an untested issue could be listed on a securities exchange. The exchange can be of some general help, however, in the initial stock pricing while the organizers study day-to-day market prices of competitive businesses in the industry. This is not precise information for price setting, but it will give the organizers a range of prices for setting limits on the new issue. In the primary market, underwriting may prove difficult and expensive for the new business because investment bankers shy away from new companies. Some investment banks may take the securities on a *best effort* basis, but this puts the risk of marketing the securities right back on the business. One way of overcoming this handicap is for the organizers to sell the initial stock by personal solicitation, and this is frequently done. Still another method of some significance is to place a large part of the issue privately with a SBIC (Small Business Investment Corporation), many of which have been organized under the Small Business Administration precisely for this purpose of supplying equity and debt capital to new but promising small businesses. A common practice is for the SBIC to buy a certain amount of stock directly from the business and to lend an additional amount. To qualify for this service, the business must have assets of less than $5 million and annual after-tax net profits of less than $25,000. Most new businesses meet these qualifications.

THE SHORT-RUN OPERATIONS

Setting the capital plan for the new business automatically sets the constraints for current operations and for the current internal and external sources and uses of funds. The substance of these problems were discussed in Parts III to V.

Profit Planning and Control With the capital constraints on output and sales set by the level of investment and the initial capital structure, profit planning reverts back primarily to the day-to-day problems of planning and controlling short-run sales, costs, and expenses. But the planning decisions are more uncertain than in the going concern because of the lack of markets for the goods and services and the lack of a labor and management force, raw materials supply sources, and short-term borrowing services. The operating budget that is used by the going concern can be used to overcome some of the problems during the first few years. The tools and skills are the same, but the figures are different. And, without past experiences, the figures will be more difficult to estimate. Business organizers necessarily will turn for help to the experiences of other businesses and to persons and public and private research agencies with special planning skills and experiences. Key figures are the monthly sales estimates and cost of sales and operating expenses. If financial management can determine the functional relationship that exists, published figures of going concerns are helpful as are industry figures supplied by trade associations and research agencies.

Planning Current Asset Requirements   The operating profit goals are often at odds with the liquidity goals in managing the individual current assets. This is particularly important in organizing new businesses in which organizers will notice that building up liquid assets tends to restrict profits at the same time that it reduces risk of loss in assets. The issue is primarily one of planning the proper balance between the short-run profit goals of the business and the necessary liquidity and flexibility in the current assets. To accomplish this goal each current asset has to be budgeted through the operating process. We are governed by the general rule that, as more funds are diverted to the less liquid assets like inventories and receivables, the chances of making larger profits increase; but, at the same time, the chances of loss also increase. As the investments lose their liquid quality by moving farther away from cash, they are a greater risk and responsibility to management and, therefore, have to be more closely planned and controlled. The practical problem of deciding what quantity of funds to hold in each asset is the main decision-making issue. The organizer would do well to consider the quantitative models considered in Part IV of the text as the first step to decision making. This may then be supplemented by drawing on the experience of businesses in the same general risk class for actual values.

Planning Short-Term Financing   A plan for the short-term financial structure will go hand-in-hand with planning current asset uses; this is the plan to finance current asset needs. We should recall that the quantity and the quality of current financing is limited at first by the quantity and quality of the capital assets, which are supplied by items in the capital structure. In turn, current liabilities will supply additional current assets and set outer limits on current trade credit and cash borrowing the moment the size and composition of capital assets is established. The larger the capital the more generously management can plan its current finances and seasonal additions to current assets. A gross capital of $200,000 will support more, although not necessarily twice as much, short-term credit as $100,000 of capital. The quality of the structure has an important conditioning effect being acceptable for supporting short-term financing as we have learned with fixed capital and net working capital. Working capital is highly acceptable for both secured and unsecured borrowing. Perhaps we are able to see more clearly now the cause and effect relationships between what has been called throughout the book the current operating decision and the capital management decision applied to the new firm.

Finally, the organizers are faced with the question of how much short-term financing to qualify for from each source of trade credit and cash borrowing. This means planning trade credit lines with suppliers, borrowing lines with commercial banks, and receivables sales agreements with commercial finance companies and factors. Again the organizers need to understand the basic elements in the quantitative models discussed in earlier chapters before going to actual supply sources for the credits.

SELECTING THE FORM OF ORGANIZATION

There are numerous forms of business organization operative in our business community each with distinctive characteristics that affects its financial status. The three forms that financial managers should examine closely before choosing a form are the corporation, the proprietorship, and the partnership. In addition to these important forms there are certain miscellaneous organizations that will be discussed briefly.

THE CORPORATION

Without stopping to consider the organization procedure or the advantages and disadvantages of the form, the incorporated business has been used throughout the book for analysis and for illustrative purposes. The reason for using the corporation is that it is a complete entity through which all degrees of financial management skills are applicable. Now we put ourselves in the position of having to decide whether this is the right form of organization for our special purpose.

The corporation is a *legal entity*. This characteristic of the corporation was first explicitly formulated in the Dartmouth College case of 1891 in which Chief Justice John Marshall wrote:

> A corporation is an artificial being, invisible, intangible, and existing only in contemplation of law. Being the mere creature of law, it possesses only those properties which the charter of its creation confers upon it, either expressly or as incidental to its very existence. . . . Among the most important are immortality, and if the expression may be allowed, individuality; properties by which a perpetual succession of many persons are considered as the same and may act as a single individual.[1]

A large body of court and statutory law has been developed since this case to give the legal entity status of the corporation practical meaning for financing and operating a business. The legal entity status enables the corporation to use state and federal courts, to sue and be sued by other natural and corporate persons, to free its stockholders of personal liability on corporate debts, to assure trans-

---

[1] *Trustees of Dartmouth v. Woodward*, 4 Wheat (U.S.), 518.

ferability of shares, and to assure continuity of the business despite death, mental incompetency, or bankruptcy of its owners personally.

The corporation is a statutory business. A statutory business comes into existence only when the organizers conform strictly to the incorporation procedure outlined in the state laws. Incorporation statutes are codified by the states which greatly simplifies and speeds up incorporation proceedings. The right to incorporate is extended to all natural and corporate persons for any purpose or purposes that are not in violation of the constitution or laws of the state. The Delaware law, a favorite state for incorporation, permits:

> Any number of persons, not less than three, . . . to establish a corporation for the transaction of any lawful business, or to promote or conduct any legitimate objects or purposes . . . excepting for any purposes as are excluded by the Constitution of this State, upon making and filing a certificate of Incorporation in writing.

Religious, charitable, and fraternal groups may incorporate without capital shares, and financial institutions such as commercial banks and trust companies, mutual savings banks, insurance companies, and savings and loan associations that are vested with strong public interests are forced to incorporate.

The *charter of incorporation* is the corporation's license to exercise the rights and obligations of legal entity, but it is a relatively simple instrument containing just enough specific information to allow the state incorporation officers and future shareholders to distinguish the concern from others, to identify its organizers, and to provide a measurable capital stock basis for assessing organization fees and taxes. The typical charter will contain the:

1. Name of the company.
2. Nature and purpose for which the business is organized.
3. Aggregate number of authorized shares divided into par and no-par values, with a statement of the par, and stated values of each class of stock.
4. Classes of capital shares, with a complete statement of all preferences, restrictions, and qualifications of each class, together with the total quantity of each class.
5. Names and residences of the organizers and the number of shares subscribed by each.
6. Life span of the corporation.

Here is a summary list of the advantages of the corporate form as a vehicle for accomplishing the financial management goals. First, it protects the shareholders' personal estates. While common shareholders stand to lose their total business investment in a corporation's shares, their personal estates are untouchable by the creditors even though the business fails and goes into complete liquidation. Protection of the shareholder's personal capital is one of the main reasons for the popularity of this form wherever large sums of money have to be borrowed. Second, management of the corporation is taken out of the hands of the owners directly, which may be an unwieldy number of persons, and put into the hands of a small representative body of experts including financial managers. Third, separating the corporate person from the natural persons who own and manage the business gives stability, continuity, and perpetuity to the corporation in its own right no matter what happens to the shareholders or the managers. Fourth, corporate entity facilitates short- and long-term borrowing. With its own operating statements, balance sheets, and supplementary financial reports and statements, creditors can easily analyze, evaluate, and forecast financial conditions of the business. Fifth, as an entity the corporation serves a useful purpose in reducing the tax burden in some cases on the owners. Corporate tax rates being less than personal rates in some cases, shareholders may benefit from organizing this form of business rather than one in which the owners are taxed individually. Sixth, transferability of ownership through share exchange is a privilege that adds liquidity to the shareholders' investment. This works two ways: to improve the investment position of the present owners and to make it easier for the business to issue new shares of stock.

Some drawbacks to organizing as a corporation also exist, but they do not seem to be weighted heavily enough to offset its important advantages. First, the organizers have to follow strict statutory procedures. Second, organization fees and taxes have to be paid. Then there are also annual franchise taxes paid in the states where business is transacted. Third, there is a good chance that the organizers will lose their control over the incorporated business as outstanding shares are increased. Fourth, corporations are required to reveal to the public and to regulatory agencies more about their financial transactions in operating statements, balance sheets, and special financial reports than other business forms are required to reveal.

THE SINGLE PROPRIETORSHIP

The majority of all business enterprises are single proprietorships, operating most frequently in retail merchandising, personal service, and construction industries and less often in manufacturing, processing mining, public utility, and transportation businesses. Proprietorships are easy to organize and equally easy to terminate. They are *common-law* businesses, which means that they can be brought into existence without conforming to any special statutory procedure. Funds to start the business come usually from personal savings and from family borrowings, borrowings from friends, and from short-term inventory credit. Inventory, comprising the major portion of the assets usually are supplied on short-term credit by manufacturers and distributors. There are no public issues of securities by proprietorships, and neither do they place bonds and stocks privately with financial agencies. The quantity of capital is obviously small.

Income earned by the business is not taxed separately as income is to the corporate person. If profits are retained in the business, the owner, unlike the owners of an incorporated business, pays the same personal taxes as he would if the funds were withdrawn. But taxes are paid only once; they are not paid again when the profits are taken out. Using the corporate form, we have the alternative of leaving all of the after-tax profit in the business, withdrawing part of it, or withdrawing all of it. The corporation pays taxes as a business entity, and shareholders pay taxes only on dividends received.

Solvency risk is one of the other important factors to consider before forming the proprietorship. At common law, the proprietor is liable for business debts just as he is for debts incurred for his own person and family. Creditors can liquidate the proprietor's personal assets as well as his business assets in satisfaction of their business claims, with the exception of statutes in some cases exempting the proprietor's homestead, his personal effects, and tools that he uses to earn a living. Another factor of importance is future financing. It might seem that personal liability of the proprietor would facilitate future borrowing for the business; but this does not necessarily follow for the reasons that: (1) the proprietor tends to have all of his wealth invested in the business; (2) death, mental incompetency, or personal bankruptcy terminates the business and may require a forced sale of the assets at a loss to the creditors; and (3) creditors may be wary of the proprietor's methods of financial record keeping especially as he is tempted to overstate the value of his assets and of his income for borrowing.

THE GENERAL PARTNERSHIP

The general partnership is a voluntary organization of two or more persons who combine their personal assets and skills in management for their mutual benefit in business. Like the proprietorship, this form belongs to the group of small businesses that operate mainly in merchandising, personal servicing, and construction businesses. In addition, the partnership is used by financial and professional groups such as brokers, securities underwriters, attorneys, accountants, engineers, and physicians primarily to combine the specialized skills of the individuals. The organization procedure is informal, requiring merely an oral or written agreement outlining the rights and responsibilities of the individual partners in their business relations with each other. Initial funds for financing come from the owners' savings, family loans, trade credit, loans from commercial banks and finance companies, and isolated loans from public lending agencies. But with operations on a somewhat larger scale, with more capital, and with more persons to share the repayment of debts, partnerships may have better opportunities than proprietorships to expand at least their short-term borrowing.

Profits are shared equally under the common law regardless of their individual investment in the business, unless otherwise provided by partnership agreement. Equal shares in profit is still the predominant method of the general partnership except when the investments of the owners differ greatly or when the quantity of capital fluctuates widely; then special care is taken to share on a pro rata basis as in the corporation. Suppose that A and B have investments in their partnership of $6,000 and $12,000 respectively and that profits are to be shared proportionately. A will receive two thirds of the profits and B one third. If the partnership has fluctuating amounts of capital, provisions may be made for averaging the partners' investments on a monthly basis for profit sharing. In Table 24.1, a $10,000 profit is shared by the two partners on a weighted average monthly investment basis. Note that *sharing* profits does not mean *distributing* profits since the owners have the option of leaving their profits in the business or of taking them out. Funds are not left in the business unless the partners are following on expansion program.

TABLE 24.1
STATEMENT OF PARTNERS' CAPITAL ACCOUNTS
(YEAR ENDING DECEMBER 31)

Partner A		Dollars Per Month
From January 1 to June 30	$6,000 × 6 =	$ 36,000
(on July 1, added $1,000)		
From July 1 to September 31	7,000 × 3 =	21,000
(on October 1, added $1,500)		
From October 1 to December 31	8,500 × 3 =	25,500
		$ 82,500
Partner B		
From January 1 to May 31	$12,000 × 5 =	$ 60,000
(on June 1, withdrew $2,500)		
From June 1 to September 30	9,500 × 4 =	38,000
(on October 1, withdrew $1,000)		
From October 1 to December 31	8,500 × 3 =	25,500
		$123,500
Total weighted investment	$206,000	
A's share	82,500/$206,000 × $10,000 =	$ 4,005
B's share	123,500/$206,000 × $10,000 =	5,995
Total		$10,000

Risks of failure and bankruptcy should perhaps be given more careful attention in organizing a general partnership than in organizing a single proprietorship because of the law of *general agency*, which gives each partner the right to bind the others on a business contract, provisions in the partnership agreement to the contrary notwithstanding. Every partner then is exposed to the risks of loss resulting from the poor business judgment of every other partner. Any partner paying more than his share of the business debts, however, has the right to be reimbursed by the others to the extent of his overpayment, but this is little consolation unless the other partners have personal wealth outside their business investment.

To some extent, however, personal liability of each partner makes it easier to obtain short-term financing. But it is still not easy for partners to get capital for their business except on a secured credit basis because: (1) partners tend to have most of their wealth tied up already in the business and (2) death, incompetency, and bankruptcy of any one of the partners automatically terminates the partnership. Solvency risks can be reduced by bringing new partners with more capital into the organization, which is fundamentally the same as the corporation issuing more common stock. This reduces the risk of capital loss for each of the old partners and also broadens the capital base for future borrowing; but, by the same token, it reduces each partner's share of the profit. Finally, the control of this business has to be shared by the partners. Decisions are made only by unanimous consent of the partners. Failure to secure unanimous consent on any basic policy issue may result in dissolving the partnership. Bringing new partners into the organization reduces the control of the present owners unless the new members are specifically "silent" partners. Bringing new partners into the organization also introduces instability due to mismanagement.

THE LIMITED PARTNERSHIP

The limited partnership overcomes some of the risks of the general partnership. This organization requires one or more general partners with unlimited personal liability and one or more special or *limited* partners who run no risk beyond losing their paid-in investment in the business. It is more stable than the general partnership because death, incompetency, and bankruptcy of the limited partners does not bring the business to a close. Like corporations, limited partnerships are statutory organizations; but they do not have the legal entity status that separates the business from its owners and that gives the corporation financial stability.

Limited partners usually are given a noncumulative *preferred* interest in profits before general partners with their *common* interests are allowed to share in the profits. The limited partners also have the right in some cases to participate in profits after the fixed sum on a pro rata basis with general partners. Limited partners that do not participate with general partners give *leverage* to the capital structure of the organization for borrowing like preferred shares do to the corporation. Limited partners are taxed on their share of the profits, whether this share is withdrawn or left in the business.

The solvency effect of the two classes of owners is noteworthy. General partners (common owners) can be sued personally by creditors for the debts of the business. Limited partners (preferred owners) are exempt from the suit if they can establish their limited partnership status. Theoretically, the limited partnership offers a better borrowing base than the general partnership, the reason being that the low risk to limited partners stimulates them to invest; and this broadens the borrowing base. Whether this works out in practice depends on the actual size of the limited partner's investment. Limited partnerships with large ownership interest are actually quite rare except brokerage firms and investment banking concerns. In these instances, large short- and long-term borrowings may be possible; but small limited partnerships with two or three members may be less qualified, because of the partners' limited personal liability, than a general partnership of the same size for securing short-term credit. Factors restricting capital borrowing by these organizations are: (1) limited partners who possess most of the wealth cannot be sued while the general partners who can be sued often have little wealth outside of what they have invested in the business, and (2) death or bankruptcy of the general partner automatically dissolves the limited partnership. In preparing the *articles of limited partnership*, it is important to designate that decision making rests exclusively in the general partners, since failure to do so could make the limited partners personally liable, like general partners, for the debts of the business. Limited partners may demand an accounting of the financial operations and conditions from time to time from the general partners, but they are not allowed to make decisions affecting business operations or to participate in any way that might lead outsiders to believe that they are general partners.

MISCELLANEOUS BUSINESS FORMS

Two other legal forms may be considered by business organizers in special situations. One is the *business trust* or what may be better known as the *Massachusetts trust*. This is an accepted common law form except that in some states it has been treated as a general partnership. Its purpose, basically, is to give the owners, called the *beneficiaries*, limited liability like the stockholders in a corporation without going through the more formal and costly procedure of statutory organization. *Declaration of trust* conveys to the certificate holders limited liability and to the trustee absolute authority to manage and control the operations and finances of the business. For tax purposes, it is treated the same as a corporation, but the owners are taxed only on the earnings that the trustee distributes to them. From the viewpoint of risk, we are cautioned to check into the legal rulings of the state courts where such organization is planned because, if the beneficiaries are treated as general partners, the beneficiaries may suffer greatly in case of business failure.

The trust certificates, which are comparable to common shares in the corporation, are transferable in the open market and may even be listed on the stock exchange. Capital financing is feasible because the credit of the business is established by the amount of its equity capital rather than the uncertain, and difficult to locate, personal wealth of its certificate holders. But if the beneficiaries (certificate holders) of the trust participate in any way in managing the affairs of the business, a good chance exists that they may be held personally liable for business debts like general partners.

The *joint stock company* is another common law business. Shareholders personally bear the risks of the company's debts like general partners, but the organization is more stable than the partnership as its continuity is not affected by the physical or financial condition of its owners. The shares of stock are transferable, as they are in the corporation, without affecting the continuity of the business; and, in some cases, they are listed on national stock exchanges. The joint stock company is taxed with corporations. The great risk to the owners is that they may be named jointly in a suit for the payment of business debts. Except for avoiding statutory incorporation procedures, the joint stock company has no advantages to offer over the corporation and is, therefore, seldom used.

SUMMARY

The concluding chapter of the text considers problems connected with planning the finances for a new business. The reader has reasoned through phases of financial management as they related specifically to the going concern. Most businesses are formed or organized by inexperienced persons who have not had the benefit of working through the many problems of financial management that the student has experienced in going through this text. Forming a new business requires the utmost skill and knowledge because of the many problems that may lie ahead.

After setting up the form of capital assets and the type of capital structure that will be used to raise the funds for these assets, a short-run plan may employ optimizing techniques such as were discussed in the chapters on income and profits, inventory, receivables, and cash management. Further, in connection with the current operation, a plan for obtaining short-term credit must be established, allowing for the limitations placed on the organization because of the initial quantity of capital. Finally, after establishing certain definite plans for goal attainment, the organizers need to give some consideration to alternative forms of businesses such as the corporate entity, the proprietorship, the general partnership and the limited partnership.

PROBLEMS

1. You are thinking of organizing a business for selling women's and children's wearing apparel. You have had several years of experience as a clerk and floor manager in a department store and have saved about $12,000. You also have another $10,000 equity in your home which could be tapped for $5,000 if it were needed. After inquiring about sales volume of similar businesses in about the same population setting you estimate first-year sales for your business of about $45,000. You learn that about 80 percent of sales will probably be on credit and that the customers will pay their bills on the average of about forty days after the purchase.

    You discover also that a business in this locality selling men's and boys' wearing apparel and another specializing in millinery turn over their inventories in sales annually about four and five times respectively. You also learn from the local bank that the typical retail business in the community keeps a cash balance of about $2,000 in its account. The investment in store fixtures would cost about $2,500. To these capital needs you feel should be added current operating expenses for the first three months, which would include $350 for monthly wages, $600 for your own monthly withdrawals, $300 monthly for rental, $60 monthly for heat and utilities, and $30 each month for advertising.

    a. What are your total initial cash needs?
    b. What would your initial balance sheet be?

   c. Is there any room in this analysis for making a capital budgeting decision?

   d. What is your cost of capital?

   e. What form of business would you organize?

2. As the next step, you decide to project your profits for the first year in a one-year pro forma income statement. For this purpose, you use a set of average operating margins prepared by a private research agency for your particular kind of business. You make some adjustments to these average ratios, and you come up with the following model operations.

MODEL OPERATING RATIOS

	%
Gross sales	105.0
Net sales	100.0
Cost of goods sold	70.6
Gross margin	29.4
Operating expenses:	
Owner's withdrawals	12.0
Wages	.5
Rental	6.0
Advertising	1.2
Bad debt losses	.2
Utilities	1.0
Buying expenses	.4
Depreciation of fixtures	.4
Total costs and expenses	21.7
Net profit before taxes	7.7

   a. Convert this to an expected net cash flow NCF_e for a ten-year period.

   b. Determine the internal rate of return on the investment.

   c. Using a cost of capital figure that you think is reasonable for the business, what is the present value of the NCF_e; and how does it compare with your investment?

   d. What would you gain and lose by incorporating a business of this kind?

3. Now your wearing apparels store has done well for the first five years and you see an opportunity for a similar store in the neighboring city about 60 miles away. You have been able to save a little money in those years but not enough to finance more than half the capital needs of a business this size. You are thinking about taking in a partner who lives in that city and who can manage the store. You would help get it started and then maybe drop in every week or so. But before making a definite decision in the matter, you stop to evaluate the profit prospects and the risks that would have to be undertaken. You consider the possibility of incorporating and letting the new store be a branch of the

present one, and you are wondering whether any other legal form of organization would better meet your needs.

   a. Can capital budgeting be applied in this case?
   b. Does a nonincorporated business have a capital structure? Is there any
      need for planning a capital structure in this case? If so, what would
      it contain?
   c. Would this expansion make you reconsider your form of business organ-
      ization? Comment.

4. The Ranking Motorcycle Company manufactures frames, handlebars, fenders,
   seats, and ignition systems but buys its engines, transmissions, and clutches
   from the Metropolitan Machinery Company, which also produces for sale to
   competitors. The Ranking Company had experienced some difficulty recently
   getting machinery on time and getting it to conform to changing specifications.
   The present management of Ranking who owned all of the shares in the company felt that they had the know-how and that they could recruit enough skilled
   labor and capital to organize a machinery manufacturing company as a subsidiary of the Ranking Company. The plan was to buy a building that would
   cost $100,000 and to lease the machines. A $20,000 investment would be needed
   to equip the building for handling the power requirements, and it was felt that
   $9,000 would be invested on the average in raw materials, $6,000 in partly
   finished goods, and $16,000 in finished goods. A cash balance of $3,000 would
   have to be kept on hand by the new business. The company would sell to the
   Ranking Company exclusively and on a sixty-day credit. The company expected
   to buy about $10,000 worth of machinery monthly from the new business.

   a. Capital facilities would last for ten years as the initial planning period.
      At the end of this time, the building is expected to bring $10,000 if
      sold. Net working capital on hand at the end of the tenth year is expect-
      ed to be worth $5,000. Annual NCF_e is $15,000. Management estimates
      its cost of capital (cutoff rate for investment) to be 12 percent. Should
      capital be budgeted to this enterprise?
   b. If Ranking has no debt in its present capital structure, how would you
      propose that the capital structure be planned to meet the expansion
      needs?

Appendix

TABLE I ANNUITY TABLE
PRESENT VALUE OF $1 EXPECTED AT THE END OF YEAR N

Years Hence	1%	2%	4%	6%	8%	10%	12%	14%	15%	16%	18%	20%	22%	24%	25%	26%	28%	30%	35%	40%	45%	50%
1	0.990	0.980	0.962	0.943	0.926	0.909	0.893	0.877	0.870	0.862	0.847	0.833	0.820	0.806	0.800	0.794	0.781	0.769	0.741	0.714	0.690	0.667
2	0.980	0.961	0.925	0.890	0.857	0.826	0.797	0.769	0.756	0.743	0.718	0.694	0.672	0.650	0.640	0.630	0.610	0.592	0.549	0.510	0.476	0.444
3	0.971	0.942	0.889	0.840	0.794	0.751	0.712	0.675	0.658	0.641	0.609	0.579	0.551	0.524	0.512	0.500	0.477	0.455	0.406	0.364	0.328	0.296
4	0.961	0.924	0.855	0.792	0.735	0.683	0.636	0.592	0.572	0.552	0.516	0.482	0.451	0.423	0.410	0.397	0.373	0.350	0.301	0.260	0.226	0.198
5	0.951	0.906	0.822	0.747	0.681	0.621	0.567	0.519	0.497	0.476	0.437	0.402	0.370	0.341	0.328	0.315	0.291	0.269	0.223	0.186	0.156	0.132
6	0.942	0.888	0.790	0.705	0.630	0.564	0.507	0.456	0.432	0.410	0.370	0.335	0.303	0.275	0.262	0.250	0.227	0.207	0.165	0.133	0.108	0.088
7	0.933	0.871	0.760	0.665	0.583	0.513	0.452	0.400	0.376	0.354	0.314	0.279	0.249	0.222	0.210	0.198	0.178	0.159	0.122	0.095	0.074	0.059
8	0.923	0.853	0.731	0.627	0.540	0.467	0.404	0.351	0.327	0.305	0.266	0.233	0.204	0.179	0.168	0.157	0.139	0.123	0.091	0.068	0.051	0.039
9	0.914	0.837	0.703	0.592	0.500	0.424	0.361	0.308	0.284	0.263	0.225	0.194	0.167	0.144	0.134	0.125	0.108	0.094	0.067	0.048	0.035	0.026
10	0.905	0.820	0.676	0.558	0.463	0.386	0.322	0.270	0.247	0.227	0.191	0.162	0.137	0.116	0.107	0.099	0.085	0.073	0.050	0.035	0.024	0.017
11	0.896	0.804	0.650	0.527	0.429	0.350	0.287	0.237	0.215	0.195	0.162	0.135	0.112	0.094	0.086	0.079	0.066	0.056	0.037	0.025	0.017	0.012
12	0.887	0.788	0.625	0.497	0.397	0.319	0.257	0.208	0.187	0.168	0.137	0.112	0.092	0.076	0.069	0.062	0.052	0.043	0.027	0.018	0.012	0.008
13	0.879	0.773	0.601	0.469	0.368	0.290	0.229	0.182	0.163	0.145	0.116	0.093	0.075	0.061	0.055	0.050	0.040	0.033	0.020	0.013	0.008	0.005
14	0.870	0.758	0.577	0.442	0.340	0.263	0.205	0.160	0.141	0.125	0.099	0.078	0.062	0.049	0.044	0.039	0.032	0.025	0.015	0.009	0.006	0.003
15	0.861	0.743	0.555	0.417	0.315	0.239	0.183	0.140	0.123	0.108	0.084	0.065	0.051	0.040	0.035	0.031	0.025	0.020	0.011	0.006	0.004	0.002
16	0.853	0.728	0.534	0.394	0.292	0.218	0.163	0.123	0.107	0.093	0.071	0.054	0.042	0.032	0.028	0.025	0.019	0.015	0.008	0.005	0.003	0.002
17	0.844	0.714	0.513	0.371	0.270	0.198	0.146	0.108	0.093	0.080	0.060	0.045	0.034	0.026	0.023	0.020	0.015	0.012	0.006	0.003	0.002	0.001
18	0.836	0.700	0.494	0.350	0.250	0.180	0.130	0.095	0.081	0.069	0.051	0.038	0.028	0.021	0.018	0.016	0.012	0.009	0.005	0.002	0.001	0.001
19	0.828	0.686	0.475	0.331	0.232	0.164	0.116	0.083	0.070	0.060	0.043	0.031	0.023	0.017	0.014	0.012	0.009	0.007	0.003	0.002	0.001	
20	0.820	0.673	0.456	0.312	0.215	0.149	0.104	0.073	0.061	0.051	0.037	0.026	0.019	0.014	0.012	0.010	0.007	0.005	0.002	0.001	0.001	
21	0.811	0.660	0.439	0.294	0.199	0.135	0.093	0.064	0.053	0.044	0.031	0.022	0.015	0.011	0.009	0.008	0.006	0.004	0.002	0.001		
22	0.803	0.647	0.422	0.278	0.184	0.123	0.083	0.056	0.046	0.038	0.026	0.018	0.013	0.009	0.007	0.006	0.004	0.003	0.001	0.001		
23	0.795	0.634	0.406	0.262	0.170	0.112	0.074	0.049	0.040	0.033	0.022	0.015	0.010	0.007	0.006	0.005	0.003	0.002	0.001			
24	0.788	0.622	0.390	0.247	0.158	0.102	0.066	0.043	0.035	0.028	0.019	0.013	0.008	0.006	0.005	0.004	0.003	0.002	0.001			
25	0.780	0.610	0.375	0.233	0.146	0.092	0.059	0.038	0.030	0.024	0.016	0.010	0.007	0.005	0.004	0.003	0.002	0.001				
26	0.772	0.598	0.361	0.220	0.135	0.084	0.053	0.033	0.026	0.021	0.014	0.009	0.006	0.004	0.003	0.002	0.002	0.001				
27	0.764	0.586	0.347	0.207	0.125	0.076	0.047	0.029	0.023	0.018	0.011	0.007	0.005	0.003	0.002	0.002	0.001	0.001				
28	0.757	0.574	0.333	0.196	0.116	0.069	0.042	0.026	0.020	0.016	0.010	0.006	0.004	0.002	0.002	0.002	0.001	0.001				
29	0.749	0.563	0.321	0.185	0.107	0.063	0.037	0.022	0.017	0.014	0.008	0.005	0.003	0.002	0.002	0.001	0.001	0.001				
30	0.742	0.552	0.308	0.174	0.099	0.057	0.033	0.020	0.015	0.012	0.007	0.004	0.003	0.002	0.001	0.001	0.001					
40	0.672	0.453	0.208	0.097	0.046	0.022	0.011	0.005	0.004	0.003	0.001	0.001										
50	0.608	0.372	0.141	0.054	0.021	0.009	0.003	0.001	0.001	0.001												

TABLE II ANNUITY TABLE
PRESENT VALUE OF $1 RECEIVED ANNUALLY FOR N YEARS

Years (N)	1%	2%	4%	6%	8%	10%	12%	14%	15%	16%	18%	20%	22%	24%	25%	26%	28%	30%	35%	40%	45%	50%
1	0.990	0.980	0.962	0.943	0.926	0.909	0.893	0.877	0.870	0.862	0.847	0.833	0.820	0.806	0.800	0.794	0.781	0.769	0.741	0.714	0.690	0.667
2	1.970	1.942	1.886	1.833	1.783	1.736	1.690	1.647	1.626	1.605	1.566	1.528	1.492	1.457	1.440	1.424	1.392	1.361	1.289	1.224	1.165	1.111
3	2.941	2.884	2.775	2.673	2.577	2.487	2.402	2.322	2.283	2.246	2.174	2.106	2.042	1.981	1.952	1.923	1.868	1.816	1.696	1.589	1.493	1.407
4	3.902	3.808	3.630	3.465	3.312	3.170	3.037	2.914	2.855	2.798	2.690	2.589	2.494	2.404	2.362	2.320	2.241	2.166	1.997	1.849	1.720	1.605
5	4.853	4.713	4.452	4.212	3.993	3.791	3.605	3.433	3.352	3.274	3.127	2.991	2.864	2.745	2.689	2.635	2.532	2.436	2.220	2.035	1.876	1.737
6	5.795	5.601	5.242	4.917	4.623	4.355	4.111	3.889	3.784	3.685	3.498	3.326	3.167	3.020	2.951	2.885	2.759	2.643	2.385	2.168	1.983	1.824
7	6.728	6.472	6.002	5.582	5.206	4.868	4.564	4.288	4.160	4.039	3.812	3.605	3.416	3.242	3.161	3.083	2.937	2.802	2.508	2.263	2.057	1.883
8	7.652	7.325	6.733	6.210	5.747	5.335	4.968	4.639	4.487	4.344	4.078	3.837	3.619	3.421	3.329	3.241	3.076	2.925	2.598	2.331	2.108	1.922
9	8.566	8.162	7.435	6.802	6.247	5.759	5.328	4.946	4.772	4.607	4.303	4.031	3.786	3.566	3.463	3.366	3.184	3.019	2.665	2.379	2.144	1.948
10	9.471	8.983	8.111	7.360	6.710	6.145	5.650	5.216	5.019	4.833	4.494	4.192	3.923	3.682	3.571	3.465	3.269	3.092	2.715	2.414	2.168	1.965
11	10.368	9.787	8.760	7.887	7.139	6.495	5.937	5.453	5.234	5.029	4.656	4.327	4.035	3.776	3.656	3.544	3.335	3.147	2.752	2.438	2.185	1.977
12	11.255	10.575	9.385	8.384	7.536	6.814	6.194	5.660	5.421	5.197	4.793	4.439	4.127	3.851	3.725	3.606	3.387	3.190	2.779	2.456	2.196	1.985
13	12.134	11.343	9.986	8.853	7.904	7.103	6.424	5.842	5.583	5.342	4.910	4.533	4.203	3.912	3.780	3.656	3.427	3.223	2.799	2.468	2.204	1.990
14	13.004	12.106	10.563	9.295	8.244	7.367	6.628	6.002	5.724	5.468	5.008	4.611	4.265	3.962	3.824	3.695	3.459	3.249	2.814	2.477	2.210	1.993
15	13.865	12.849	11.118	9.712	8.559	7.606	6.811	6.142	5.847	5.575	5.092	4.675	4.315	4.001	3.859	3.726	3.483	3.268	2.825	2.484	2.214	1.995
16	14.718	13.578	11.652	10.106	8.851	7.824	6.974	6.265	5.954	5.669	5.162	4.730	4.357	4.033	3.887	3.751	3.503	3.283	2.834	2.489	2.216	1.997
17	15.562	14.292	12.166	10.477	9.122	8.022	7.120	6.373	6.047	5.749	5.222	4.775	4.391	4.059	3.910	3.771	3.518	3.295	2.840	2.492	2.218	1.998
18	16.398	14.992	12.659	10.828	9.372	8.201	7.250	6.467	6.128	5.818	5.273	4.812	4.419	4.080	3.928	3.786	3.529	3.304	2.844	2.494	2.219	1.999
19	17.226	15.678	13.134	11.158	9.604	8.365	7.366	6.550	6.198	5.877	5.316	4.844	4.442	4.097	3.942	3.799	3.539	3.311	2.848	2.496	2.220	1.999
20	18.046	16.351	13.590	11.470	9.818	8.514	7.469	6.623	6.259	5.929	5.353	4.870	4.460	4.110	3.954	3.808	3.546	3.316	2.850	2.497	2.221	1.999
21	18.857	17.011	14.029	11.764	10.017	8.649	7.562	6.687	6.312	5.973	5.384	4.891	4.476	4.121	3.963	3.816	3.551	3.320	2.852	2.498	2.221	2.000
22	19.660	17.658	14.451	12.042	10.201	8.772	7.645	6.743	6.359	6.011	5.410	4.909	4.488	4.130	3.970	3.822	3.556	3.323	2.853	2.498	2.222	2.000
23	20.456	18.292	14.857	12.303	10.371	8.883	7.718	6.792	6.399	6.044	5.432	4.925	4.499	4.137	3.976	3.827	3.559	3.325	2.854	2.499	2.222	2.000
24	21.243	18.914	15.247	12.550	10.529	8.985	7.784	6.835	6.434	6.073	5.451	4.937	4.507	4.143	3.981	3.831	3.562	3.327	2.855	2.499	2.222	2.000
25	22.023	19.523	15.622	12.783	10.675	9.077	7.843	6.873	6.464	6.097	5.467	4.948	4.514	4.147	3.985	3.834	3.564	3.329	2.856	2.499	2.222	2.000
26	22.795	20.121	15.983	13.003	10.810	9.161	7.896	6.906	6.491	6.118	5.480	4.956	4.520	4.151	3.988	3.837	3.566	3.330	2.856	2.500	2.222	2.000
27	23.560	20.707	16.330	13.211	10.935	9.237	7.943	6.935	6.514	6.136	5.492	4.964	4.524	4.154	3.990	3.839	3.567	3.331	2.856	2.500	2.222	2.000
28	24.316	21.281	16.663	13.406	11.051	9.307	7.984	6.961	6.534	6.152	5.502	4.970	4.528	4.157	3.992	3.840	3.568	3.331	2.857	2.500	2.222	2.000
29	25.066	21.844	16.984	13.591	11.158	9.370	8.022	6.983	6.551	6.166	5.510	4.975	4.531	4.159	3.994	3.841	3.569	3.332	2.857	2.500	2.222	2.000
30	25.808	22.396	17.292	13.765	11.258	9.427	8.055	7.003	6.566	6.177	5.517	4.979	4.534	4.160	3.995	3.842	3.569	3.332	2.857	2.500	2.222	2.000
40	32.835	27.355	19.793	15.046	11.925	9.779	8.244	7.105	6.642	6.234	5.548	4.997	4.544	4.166	3.999	3.846	3.571	3.333	2.857	2.500	2.222	2.000
50	39.196	31.424	21.482	15.762	12.234	9.915	8.304	7.133	6.661	6.246	5.554	4.999	4.545	4.167	4.000	3.846	3.571	3.333	2.857	2.500	2.222	2.000

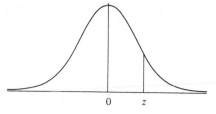

AREAS
UNDER THE
STANDARD
NORMAL CURVE
FROM 0 TO z

z	0	1	2	3	4	5	6	7	8	9
0.0	.0000	.0040	.0080	.0120	.0160	.0199	.0239	.0279	.0319	.0359
0.1	.0398	.0438	.0478	.0517	.0557	.0596	.0636	.0675	.0714	.0754
0.2	.0793	.0832	.0871	.0910	.0948	.0987	.1026	.1064	.1103	.1141
0.3	.1179	.1217	.1255	.1293	.1331	.1368	.1406	.1443	.1480	.1517
0.4	.1554	.1591	.1628	.1664	.1700	.1736	.1772	.1808	.1844	.1879
0.5	.1915	.1950	.1985	.2019	.2054	.2088	.2123	.2157	.2190	.2224
0.6	.2258	.2291	.2324	.2357	.2389	.2422	.2454	.2486	.2518	.2549
0.7	.2580	.2612	.2642	.2673	.2704	.2734	.2764	.2794	.2823	.2852
0.8	.2881	.2910	.2939	.2967	.2996	.3023	.3051	.3078	.3106	.3133
0.9	.3159	.3186	.3212	.3238	.3264	.3289	.3315	.3340	.3365	.3389
1.0	.3413	.3438	.3461	.3485	.3508	.3531	.3554	.3577	.3599	.3621
1.1	.3643	.3665	.3686	.3708	.3729	.3749	.3770	.3790	.3810	.3830
1.2	.3849	.3869	.3888	.3907	.3925	.3944	.3962	.3980	.3997	.4015
1.3	.4032	.4049	.4066	.4082	.4099	.4115	.4131	.4147	.4162	.4177
1.4	.4192	.4207	.4222	.4236	.4251	.4265	.4279	.4292	.4306	.4319
1.5	.4332	.4345	.4357	.4370	.4382	.4394	.4406	.4418	.4429	.4441
1.6	.4452	.4463	.4474	.4484	.4495	.4505	.4515	.4525	.4535	.4545
1.7	.4554	.4564	.4573	.4582	.4591	.4599	.4608	.4616	.4625	.4633
1.8	.4641	.4649	.4656	.4664	.4671	.4678	.4686	.4693	.4699	.4706
1.9	.4713	.4719	.4726	.4732	.4738	.4744	.4750	.4756	.4761	.4767
2.0	.4772	.4778	.4783	.4788	.4793	.4798	.4803	.4808	.4812	.4817
2.1	.4821	.4826	.4830	.4834	.4838	.4842	.4846	.4850	.4854	.4857
2.2	.4861	.4864	.4868	.4871	.4875	.4878	.4881	.4884	.4887	.4890
2.3	.4893	.4896	.4898	.4901	.4904	.4906	.4909	.4911	.4913	.4916
2.4	.4918	.4920	.4922	.4925	.4927	.4929	.4931	.4932	.4934	.4936
2.5	.4938	.4940	.4941	.4943	.4945	.4946	.4948	.4949	.4951	.4952
2.6	.4953	.4955	.4956	.4957	.4959	.4960	.4961	.4962	.4963	.4964
2.7	.4965	.4966	.4967	.4968	.4969	.4970	.4971	.4972	.4973	.4974
2.8	.4974	.4975	.4976	.4977	.4977	.4978	.4979	.4979	.4980	.4981
2.9	.4981	.4982	.4982	.4983	.4984	.4984	.4985	.4985	.4986	.4986
3.0	.4987	.4987	.4987	.4988	.4988	.4989	.4989	.4989	.4990	.4990
3.1	.4990	.4991	.4991	.4991	.4992	.4992	.4992	.4992	.4993	.4993
3.2	.4993	.4993	.4994	.4994	.4994	.4994	.4994	.4995	.4995	.4995
3.3	.4995	.4995	.4995	.4996	.4996	.4996	.4996	.4996	.4996	.4997
3.4	.4997	.4997	.4997	.4997	.4997	.4997	.4997	.4997	.4997	.4998
3.5	.4998	.4998	.4998	.4998	.4998	.4998	.4998	.4998	.4998	.4998
3.6	.4998	.4998	.4999	.4999	.4999	.4999	.4999	.4999	.4999	.4999
3.7	.4999	.4999	.4999	.4999	.4999	.4999	.4999	.4999	.4999	.4999
3.8	.4999	.4999	.4999	.4999	.4999	.4999	.4999	.4999	.4999	.4999
3.9	.5000	.5000	.5000	.5000	.5000	.5000	.5000	.5000	.5000	.5000

Index